SOCIAL FORCES and the LAW

A Guide for the Businessman and the Citizen

EXAMINATION COPY

RONALD A. ANDERSON

Professor of Law and Government,
Drexel Institute of Technology

Member of the Pennsylvania and Philadelphia Bars

Coauthor of *Business Law Principles and Cases*, Fourth Edition
and *Business Law*, Eighth Edition

Author of *Anderson's Uniform Commercial Code;*
Anderson's Uniform Commercial Code Legal Forms;
Government and Business, Third Edition;
Anderson's Pennsylvania Civil Practice;
Couch's Cyclopedia of Insurance Law (Second Edition);
Wharton's Criminal Law, Procedure, and Evidence

Consulting Editor of the *Pennsylvania Law Encyclopedia*

SOUTH-WESTERN
PUBLISHING CO.
CINCINNATI
CHICAGO
DALLAS
BURLINGAME, CALIF.
NEW ROCHELLE, N. Y.

L20

Library of Congress Catalog Card Number: 69-20122

1 2 3 4 5 6 H 4 3 2 1 0 9

Printed in the United States of America

PREFACE

Less than a hundred years ago Holmes jarred the legal philosophers by declaring that law is not logic but life. He further declared that there is no rule of law which, if traced back to its source, would not be found to be based upon a decision of public policy. Today these views of Holmes are generally accepted as true.

Today, for example, we are all familiar with the typical "nonlegal" approach to the legal question of the requirement of privity in product liability cases, as may be illustrated by the recent case of *Dippel* v. *Sciano,* 37 Wis.2d 443, 155 N.W.2d 55 (1967) where the court stated: "The rule that there could be no liability upon warranty, express or implied, without privity of contract came into being in England in *Winterbottom* v. *Wright* (1842), 10 M & W 109, 152 Eng. Rep. 402. It was an outgrowth of the beginning of the Industrial Revolution when it was thought necessary to protect struggling and unstable industry against an onslaught of disastrous claims. Typical of the disregard of the claims of persons injured by products is a quotation from Winterbottom, 'It is, no doubt, a hardship upon the plaintiff to be without a remedy, but by that consideration we ought not to be influenced.' We have long since passed from the unsure days of Industrial Revolution to a settled and affluent society where we must be concerned about the just claims of the injured and hapless user or consumer of industrial products. The doctrine of laissez faire and caveat emptor have given way to more humane considerations.

"Without belaboring its development, it can now be said that the majority of the jurisdictions of the United States no longer adhere to the concept of no liability without privity of contract. The reason, which has been reiterated most often, is that the seller is in the paramount position to distribute the costs of the risks created by the defective product he is selling. He may pass the cost on to the consumer via increased prices. He may protect himself either by purchasing insurance or by a form of self-insurance. In justification of making the seller pay for the risk, it is argued that the consumer or user has the right to rely on the apparent safety of the product and that it is the seller in the first instances who creates the risk by placing the defective product on the market. A correlative consideration, where the manufacturer is concerned, is that the manufacturer has the greatest ability to control the risk created by his product since he may initiate or adopt inspection and quality control measures thereby preventing defective products from reaching the consumer.

"A different consideration which has often been expressed is that the abolition of privity in implied warranty or the imposition of strict liability avoids the circuity of action. In a single suit the plaintiff may proceed against all or the most affluent member in the distributive chain. . . ."

But while it is one thing to say that this is not "law" but social engineering or to say that the quest for justice has given the courts vision beyond mere rules of law, can we not formulate some standards so that the judge, the lawyer, the businessman, and the citizen have some sense of direction and see more clearly the issues to be determined? On the basis of an examination of every case reported in the United States since 1950 and of long experience with judicial and legislative processes, it is concluded that there are certain social forces which influence the making of a judicial decision. These social forces are examined in this book so that the person responsible for management decisions, the citizen having the right to vote, and the person interested in the direction in which society is moving will have a better appreciation of what law is, the uncertainties involved, and the future of our way of life.

In terms of organization, this book is divided into three parts:

    I. A Governed Society

   II. The Social Forces That Make the Law

  III. The Law in Operation

It is believed that this is the preferable sequence in which this material should be studied by the student-reader because each part in a general sense lays the groundwork for the subsequent part or parts. Depending upon the preferences and the experiences of the teacher and the background and the capacities of the students, however, a different sequence may be found to be desirable.

The book is written for use in a one-term course. In the interest of providing the instructor ample material from which he can select the material best suited to his needs, the book is longer than can be covered in one term. In the instructor's manual, detailed plans will suggest the selection and omission of materials in order to permit the coverage of the material within one term, whether that be a semester-term or a quarter-term. Part II of the book represents the largest part of the book. It consists of 21 chapters, each of which, after an introductory survey chapter, is devoted to the study of a particular social force that makes the law. Each of these chapters is divided into sections, with each section typically consisting of a text statement and a court opinion. Condensation of the material for the purpose of classroom consumption can be effected by omitting some of the opinions in these chapters. More drastic condensation may be effected by omitting both opinions and some of the text of these chapters.

At the end of each chapter in the book there are questions for review. These pass through the range of questions that merely test the ability of the student to recall the material in the chapter to actual cases which the student is called upon to decide on the basis of the social forces which will confront a court. Other questions provide the student with the answer made by the court and call upon the student to analyze the reason for the court having reached the conclusion that it did.

This book is written so that it can be used for the student who will have only one term of law or one term of law or political science, or who is interested in law only in the liberal arts sense of informing him about the world in which he lives. When so employed, it is contemplated that the teacher will omit many of the end-of-chapter questions, as discussed more specifically in the teacher's manual. The book is likewise written so that it can be used at the upper-class or graduate level as a terminal study in a sequence of courses on management, law, or political science. When used as a terminal or higher level course, it is contemplated that more complete coverage of the book will be made by the teacher and that greater time will be devoted to the analysis of the opinions and to the solution of the end-of-chapter problems. It is, of course, obvious that the more advanced student will find more meaning in the book than the beginning student; but, by avoiding unnecessary and distracting technicalities, the beginning student, as well as the advanced student, will find much in this book to advance his understanding and appreciation of both the law and the American way of life.

R.A.A.

CONTENTS

PART I. A GOVERNED SOCIETY

PART II. THE SOCIAL FORCES THAT MAKE THE LAW

TABLE OF CASES

PART I. A GOVERNED SOCIETY

Chapter 1

THE PROBLEM

§ 1:1. Why Management Should Understand the Law

(a) Generally. There is a belief that management does not need to understand the law because management has a legal staff. This belief is absurd. From the short-term point of view, management must understand the law so that it can discuss matters intelligently with its own attorney. Unless management is willing to follow blindly the advice of its attorney, it must prepare itself to discuss matters with him and to determine how far to go in the many areas in which the law is not clear. From a long-term point of view, management must understand the law, as distinct from particular rules of law, in the same way that management must understand people, markets, and problems of production.

1

The most significant reason why management must understand law is that management alone understands the business it is managing. Law is merely a device. The lawyer knows rules, but he does not know any particular business unless he has been associated with the business for a very long time. Your lawyer cannot give you practical advice until he knows your business position. Will he ever know it as thoroughly as you? Therefore, you must bridge the gap between knowledge of your business and the rules of law. As a businessman, you must be sensitive to the direction in which the law is moving. This is not the direct concern of the lawyer who is primarily concerned with what the law is.

Moreover, as a practical matter, things often happen too quickly so that you cannot consult your attorney for his advice. Likewise, you must understand the law so that you know what to do until your lawyer comes.

(b) Litigation is a nuisance. When you pass the matter over to your lawyer or your insurer, you are still involved for you must cooperate with your attorney and your insurer. You must provide information, you must attend meetings and trials, and you and your employees are subject to discovery proceedings. None of this is so burdensome that it will impair your operations over the years, but these events are an annoyance and a nuisance. Is it not good management to avoid subjecting yourself to such nuisances by running your business in a litigation-proof manner? In order to do so, you must have some understanding of what the law requires of you.

(c) Uncertainty of litigation. The only certain way of not losing a lawsuit against you is by never being sued. There is great uncertainty in the law because much of your case will hang upon what the jury believes to have happened. If they do not believe you and your witnesses, there is the danger that you will lose the case. Moreover, there is the possibility that because of a change in the law the insurance policy that you have does not cover the liability which tomorrow's court decides exists.

(d) Cooperation with your attorney and insurer. When you turn the case over to your attorney or to your insurer, you are under a duty to cooperate and be as helpful in the defense of the case as possible. Actually the need for cooperation begins before then. As discussed in Chapter 32, from the very beginning of the occurrence or transaction from which the claim arises, there should be a careful recording of what was done and a preservation of any evidence that is involved. This enables you, when you see your attorney or your insurer, to turn over the best case possible rather than one which is difficult, if not impossible, to defend. Moreover, an appreciation of the law will make you more sensitive as to when you are involved in a matter which calls for consultation with your lawyer or your insurer.

The more you know about the law, the more you will be able to act like a good client and be of help to your lawyer and your insurer. Remember that the lawyer is not a magician and cannot save you when you have let a hopeless case build itself around you. While the insurer would still be bound by its contract, remember that the insurer may cancel most of its contracts with you or increase the rates, so that there may be harmful side effects of your not having acted in such a way as to assist your attorney and insurer. Moreover, the liability might be so great that it is in excess of the insurance coverage.

As management, you are concerned not only with the litigation of today but also the world of tomorrow. Great concern is felt in many circles over the future of free enterprise. Much of the answer can be found in understanding the law. Much depends upon your understanding the pattern of law by which society is governed. The businessman must think not only in terms of today's transactions but must, with longer vision, look to the future years. The problems of social responsibility demand that he look beyond the immediate answer to specific questions to his attorney of "Can I do this?"

(e) Objectives of this book. It is not the object of this book to set forth the specific rules of law that will govern the relations and the liabilities of management and other persons. In contrast, the purpose is to examine the values or social forces which cause law to change and to adopt the particular conclusions that it follows. Just as the businessman studies patterns of economic behavior, human behavior, individual behavior, this book is a study of law as a behavior pattern—not law as a science predicated upon exact rules of demonstrable validity, but rather law as a sociopolitical outgrowth of the needs and desires of the people.

§ 1:2.   The Businessman as a Citizen

The man in business is becoming increasingly aware of the fact that he is a member of society and, as a citizen, has social responsibilities over and beyond the mere meeting of his payroll and the paying of his creditors. The businessman, with long experience in dealing with people and problems, can rightfully be expected by society to lead the way in seeking solutions to its problems. In spite of the great strides in science and technology, relatively little progress has been made in solving man's basic problems. Man's great problems are still his relationship to God and his relationship to other men, individually as persons, and collectively as groups and nations. The problems have remained the same and, if anything, their solution has become the more difficult because there are now more material things to desire, the economic interdependence of the individual has intensified his problems, and modern science has removed the protective buffers of space between nations.

That more progress has not been made in the problems of relationships is not surprising when we recognize the distinctive character of learning in those areas. In the field of science, mathematics, and all the areas of learning based upon the compilation of data, each generation can stand upon the shoulders of the past. The medical student does not have to rediscover the circulation of the blood; he can accept it as a fact. The astronaut does not have to rediscover the course of the planets; he can accept it as a fact. Our young engineer does not have to stay under an apple tree in the hope that the force of gravity will be manifested unto him.

Contrast all this with the field of spiritual and human relationships. Can you hand a book to a child and impart to him the depth of understanding and appreciation which years of experience have built in your mind? Of course, you can do much toward directing him to think of such things and to lay the groundwork for his thinking, but can you give him your understanding and beliefs? Did your parents and your teachers succeed in giving to you their understanding and their beliefs? They gave you a most valued direction, but beyond that it was the passing years and all that those years brought with them that has given you your present-day maturity.

If you give school children a vocabulary test, you will undoubtedly find that many children can give you a satisfactory definition of God, of truth, of friendship, of honor, of tears, of sorrow, of death, of work, of happiness, of success. But how many slings and arrows of outrageous fortune must be borne—how many tides in the course of human events must ebb and flow—how much of life must be lived—before the full meaning, the real significance of those words will come home to them? It might not be far from the truth to say that maturity is really understanding what the definitions in the dictionary mean.

The sorry fact is that just about the time a given generation has reached the maturity which would enable it to progress in the solution of the basic social problems, its allotted years expire. The new generation that follows is not able to start where the preceding generation stopped. While it is true that one generation overlaps another, the general characteristic is that the new generation is still years behind the former generation at the time when it should be alongside of it to take over and continue the work. By the time it is qualified for that task, another new, relatively immature, generation is taking over—a generation which has not lived enough of life to have learned as fully and with as much conviction the lessons that the parting generation has learned. Thus, by the time each new generation has become an old and wiser generation, it finds that it must surrender the reins of leadership to a new generation.

This is not defeatism. Progress is being made in the field of human affairs. But recognize how slow that progress has been. When it is realized that six long centuries had to drag past King John and Magna Carta before the great idea of democracy would be dreamed and would become a reality, one recognizes the slowness of the process of improvement. That is, society, and in an industrialized economy, management in particular, must recognize and appreciate the true nature of the formal system of governing relationships that we call law.

Law must be recognized as rules created by society by which society at the time wishes itself to be governed—rules which society adopts because those rules advance or further or protect certain interests which society at the time holds dear—rules which society can modify, change, and even throw away when they no longer serve the purpose of society. Management must recognize that there is no such thing as total or permanent security for the individual, or management, in our sociolegal system. Management cannot place a blind trust in the "legal system" and just go on year after year assuming that the law will always be right and will always do the right thing. Management must know that law is a variable and that it does not provide total and unchanging security.

As a businessman, management should, of course, appreciate the hazards and the uncertainties of litigation and the legal system. But most of all, as a citizen, the manager must grow to accept responsibility to see that the legal system, including governmental law as well as private citizen law, shall not change in a way harmful to the basic American principles. As a voter, the manager must accept his responsibility for the quality of our laws and his duty in the selection of the men who interpret and enforce them.

§ 1:3. A Problem of Democracy

If we lived in a monarchy ruled over by a king, management would not find it necessary to understand the forces that make the law. This is because the law would be largely the whim or judgment of the ruler. The present ruler and the young prince, who would some day ascend the throne, should be "groomed" in the principles of governing. But since the ruler, whether the old king or the young prince, would rule by his personal opinion, it mattered little for management to understand the basis for the law.

In America, both courts and legislatures are attuned to the stirring principles of the Declaration of Independence and the Constitution of the United States. Law in America is what the will of the people desire. There is, of course, a time lag and obviously every law does not at every minute express the desire of all of the people. Sometimes laws exist not because they are desired but rather because they are not sufficiently disliked to be changed. Nevertheless, the fact remains that over a period of time the law in a democratic society changes to advance the social values which the society holds dear. Statutes may expressly break with the past, judges may reverse prior decisions. In one way or another, social forces change the rules governing society when sufficient of the people so desire.

There is thus another dimension to governing and to law when we are thinking of a democracy, which dimension we did not find in a monarchy. If we wish our American society to achieve the goals of which a democracy is capable, we must all understand the nature of the law and the forces that make it change. Particularly management, which because of its economic importance in the modern society occupies a position of leadership, which because of its experience with facing and meeting problems may very well have a better appreciation of the problems and the merits of proposed solutions, has a prime responsibility in understanding the forces which make the law.

Questions for Review

1. Why should management understand the nature of the law?

2. Is the interest of the ordinary voter in understanding the law the same as the interest of management?

3. Can management protect itself adequately by having a competent legal staff and liability insurance?

4. What major problem is encountered in the solution of problems in governing?

5. Is there any difference in the problems of good governing in a democratic society and in a nondemocratic society?

6. Make a list of the rights or interests that you feel are basic to the kind of world in which you want to live.

Chapter 2

THE MAKERS OF THE LAW

§ 2:1. Generally

The law that governs you in your daily life is made by a variety of institutions or organizations. These are most commonly a legislative body, a court, an administrative agency, and a chief executive. Because of its rising importance in the American way of life, particular attention will be given to the administrative agency.

§ 2:2. The Legislative Body

(a) National. The official legislative body of the United States is the Congress, consisting of two houses or chambers composed of delegates elected by the respective states. To the lower house each state sends a number of delegates, the number being such percentage of the total number of delegates as the population of the sending state bears to the national

population. That is, the total national population of the United States is divided by the total number of delegates in the lower house or House of Representatives. This produces a ratio figure which is then divided into the population of the state, yielding the number of representatives that the state is entitled to elect to the House of Representatives. Thus, the number of delegates that a state sends to the lower house rises or falls depending upon whether the population of the state represents a greater or smaller percentage of the national population. To avoid confusion, however, this readjustment is not automatic but is made periodically and then continues until the next readjustment is made.

In the upper house of the Congress of the United States, called the Senate, each state has two senators. This means that the voting power of every state is the same in the Senate, in contrast with the House of Representatives in which it varies with the population of the state.

In the history of a typical federal law, that is, a law adopted by this Congress, a proposal is presented to one of the two houses. After being approved by that house, the proposal, called a bill, is sent to the other house where it is then approved or rejected, and if approved, is then sent to the President of the United States for his signature. In most instances the President signs the bill and it becomes the law. In some instances the President refuses to sign the bill, and it is then sometimes repassed by the Congress over his veto and becomes law.

(b) State. Every state has a law-making body, which, with one exception, is also a bicameral or two-chambered body, as in the case of the national Congress.

Originally, the state legislatures made the same distinction as is found in the Congress between a lower house based on population and an upper house organized on equal voting for each unit of government. As the result of the adoption of the "one-man, one-vote" rule by the Supreme Court, it is now necessary that in each house there be representation directly according to population. This will be considered in greater length in § 10:4.

(c) Municipal. In every city there is a city council or similar body, which has the power to make certain kinds of laws for the protection and governing of the city and its peoples. Similar bodies are found in "smaller cities," which may have the name of township, borough, and so on.

The city council is ordinarily a single body consisting of members elected directly according to the population. The authority of a municipal council is very limited, and it has only such powers as the state in which it is located has chosen to give it.

(d) Authorities. During the last thirty years, the pattern has developed of creating separate, independent bodies to handle particular matters.

For example, irrigation and drainage may be a problem facing a particular geographic area. Instead of providing that each local municipal government shall take a part in solving the problem, the state legislature may create an independent body or commission to handle the drainage and irrigation problems within a given geographic area, without regard to what local governments are embraced within that territory. Such authorities are to a large degree separate little governments, that is, they generally have the power to issue bonds to raise money to finance the plans which they adopt. They fall short of being truly independent governments in that they do not have courts and cannot arrest or send persons to jail. When the question of law enforcement arises, they must make use of the existing government organizations.

These authorities have the advantage that they operate in an area as broad as the problem without regard to local boundary lines. Thus the power of a given irrigation authority will ordinarily extend over the entire water drainage area, which may embrace a number of counties and many municipalities, such as cities, townships, boroughs, and so on. Such authorities are also commonly created in connection with urban renewal and with the construction and operation of parking facilities in cities.

The authority, however it is organized, has some central body or group which makes rules as to what should be done and what should not be done by the authority. These are rules of law, for they establish a standard to govern conduct and can be enforced in some way. The fact that the law-making body of the authority is not elected does not mean that their rules are any the less law. In America we are accustomed to thinking of law-makers as being elected. While that is characteristic of the American way of life as established in our Constitution of 1790, it is not an essential element in the definition of a lawmaker. That concept merely relates to who put the lawmaker in charge. It is the nature of the work that he does when in charge which determines whether he is a lawmaker.

§ 2:3.　The Court

According to what might be called the dictionary definition, the courts apply the law and do not make the law. In actual operation, the distinction between making the law, as being the job or function of the legislature, and the interpreting or applying the law, as being the function of the courts, becomes a little blurred; and the courts in fact make the law. It is true that, in a great many cases, judges merely apply a recognized or accepted rule of law to a set of facts. In such a case, the judge is merely declaring the law. When, however, the court is faced with a set of facts that do not come within the scope of any previously recognized or established rule of law, there is no law for him to declare.

To illustrate, consider the problem presented when the first suit was brought to recover damages against an air transport company for the death of a passenger in an airplane crash. The court was faced with the problem of deciding how the liability of an air carrier should be determined. Since this was, by hypothesis, the first case of its kind, there would be nothing in the law books or decisions determining or stating what the rule of law was. The judge was nevertheless required to decide the case, and in so doing he made new law because before that time there was no law applicable to those facts. If it is contended that he did not make the law, but merely declared preexisting law, difficult questions arise. How did he find out the preexisting law, if such a case had never been decided before? If he was merely declaring the law, when did it come into existence? Did it spring into being the minute the Wright Brothers defied the law of gravity for twelve fateful seconds in 1903, or did the principle of the liability of air carriers come down to the courts before the air carrier was invented? If so, how long before? The concept of principles of law floating about for thousands of years in some rarefied atmosphere until, at some later date, a judge, faced with a new fact situation, draws the principle from the clouds in the manner of a judicial Franklin is not one that appeals to common sense.

The fact must be accepted that a judge, when faced with a new situation, makes new law, just as though the legislature or the Congress had adopted a new statute. To be sure, the new law may draw on past law for support or analogy, and the court will desire to make it conform to the prior law or the policy of the prior law as far as is practical and reasonable. Nevertheless, when a rule of law results from a decision where there was no rule of law before, it is obvious that the court has made law.

The manner in which judges make the law will be considered further in Part II.

§ 2:4.   The Administrative Agency

(a) Origin. Historically, government meant the crown or king of England, ignoring earlier forms of government that existed both in ancient and intermediate periods of history. Whatever was done by the royal British officers was done by the authority of the crown. Such local city governments as existed in the early days of England may be said to have existed by the will or pleasure of the king in the sense that, if he chose, he could send in his royal officers to take charge.

In the course of time, both in England, the English colonies, and then in the American states and under the United States Constitution, "government" becomes divided into the three branches of legislative, executive, and judicial. Such a division could be explained in terms of workload division; that is, there came to be too much work for one man or one group to do it all, and it was practical to break up the work according to its nature. In theory, the division was sought by many as a means of protection from royal tyranny. If the king is all powerful, there is a greater danger that he may be a tyrant or, to paraphrase the epigram, nothing corrupts so absolutely as absolute power. Conversely, if power is divided into three branches, each branch would find itself checked on the road to becoming a tyrant because it lacked the power possessed by the other two branches and the probabilities would be that the other branches would not wish to join in the same plan of tyranny. It is true that if all three branches conspired together, there could be tyranny, but the mathematical odds would be against all three branches agreeing on any one course of action and of agreeing to use their combined purpose for an evil power.

This philosophy may be illustrated by the family car. You can keep your brother from taking the family car by removing the spark plugs. He, in turn, can prevent you from taking the car by keeping the keys. The net result is that no one drives the car and the car will not become involved in a collision. As long as you and your brother are content with the car's not being used, the above procedure keeps everyone happy; but if it is desired to drive to the store, something must be done to reassemble the car by bringing the spark plugs and the keys and the car together. Otherwise stated, as long as nothing is to be done with the car, the theory of division is satisfactory, that is, the theory of division is based upon a negative or do-nothing attitude. A positive or do-something attitude requires a different form of government.

As the American society began moving into the Twentieth Century, problems arose that society wished to control or regulate. In terms of the above analysis, society was moving from a negative attitude of "government do nothing" to a positive attitude of "government do something." For example, a new food packing industry was rising, but the packed foods were not always pure and safe to eat. The public demanded control of the problem, a demand which ultimately culminated in the adoption of the Federal Pure Food and Drug Act of 1907. In order to handle the problems, these new regulatory statutes generally created separate agencies. Much like the local authorities above noted, these administrative agencies existed independently of the established branches of government. They might be regarded as satellite bodies or governments. As will be further discussed in Chapter 31, these new agencies were given power to make the "law" within their sphere of authority.

(i) *Theoretical objections.* There is some theoretical difficulty in conferring upon an administrative agency or government commission the power to make laws. Centuries of democratic struggle have firmly imbedded in our cultural pattern the concept that "law" may only be made by the popularly-elected representatives of the people. Revolution and gradual evolution have combined to eliminate the concept of rule-making by kings, of a divine right of kings, or of rule by a leader class, so that the democratic way of life is identified as that in which the governed make the laws by which they govern themselves through electing the person to make those laws.

It is apparent that if an administrative agency has power to make law, a departure is being made from the basic theory of American democratic government because the administrative agency is composed of one or more persons all of whom are typically appointed, as opposed to elected, and there is no direct accounting to the public for what they do. If we wish to make a parallel, we can observe that the American Revolution was directed against a monarch who was not elected by the governed and who could make the laws. Like George III, the administrative agency is not elected by the governed nor responsible to them.

How can we explain or justify the rise of such an independent administrative agency in our American way of life? In simple terms, the necessity of getting the job done has caused a shift from the fear of unified power to a willingness of taking a chance with unified power. Today, probably the major part of the business life of the country is governed by "laws" made by administrative agencies. There are over 250 major federal agencies regulating the field of business and commercial enterprise.

The fact that these agencies make "law" is not to be obscured by the fact that they may be called "rules" or "regulations." We must regard as law anything that establishes a governmental standard, violation of which standard will subject the violator to some punishment or discipline. Thus an Act of Congress establishing a minimum wage of $1.60 an hour is a law not because of the formal reason that it was created by Congress but because it establishes a standard wage scale that employers must observe, and any employer failing to do so is subject to certain penalties. Assume that Congress instead of specifying the exact wage to be paid created a "wage commission" and authorized it to set the wage and that, acting under such authorization, the wage commission adopted a regulation that the minimum wage should be $1.60 an hour. Would the requirement that the employer pay $1.60 an hour be any less "law" because it had been imposed by the commission rather than by the Congress?

It is apparent that it serves no useful purpose to attempt to say that the commission regulation is not a law. Rather, it is better that we consider why our society has been willing to depart from so hard-won a concept of legislation by popularly-elected representatives as to permit law-making by "decree" by "unknown" appointees. As above stated, the answer in simple terms is "necessity." Society desired that a certain job be done, and the better way of getting it done or perhaps the only way of getting it done was to depart from the pattern of governmental machinery that worked satisfactorily in the days of a negative attitude toward government, and to devise new machinery to work when the attitude to the government had become positive. Let us consider further this aspect of necessity because necessity, as distinguished from abstract theory, has been by far the greater element in the growth of American law.

(ii) *Necessity for delegation of rule-making authority.* In a relatively simple or primitive community, society can content itself with the adoption of rules or law decrees prohibiting certain lines of conduct and specifying the penalty to be imposed for the violation of those standards. In such a state, the conduct that is permitted and the conduct that is prohibited are relatively clearly divided. It is not necessary to correlate the economic conditions or other circumstances to determine whether a practice is condemned. The classification or division between that which is lawful and that which is unlawful is both universal and static.

To illustrate, larceny has for centuries been set apart as being unlawful conduct. While technicalities arise as to the precise definition of larceny, for practical purposes it is a course of conduct that may be readily separated or isolated from other forms of conduct. A prohibition against larceny is likewise a universal concept within the particular community or state; that is, the conduct is condemned to the same extent regardless of the geographic place of its commission. Larceny is also larceny independently of the conduct of any other party or of the community in which it is committed. Moreover, there is virtually no need to change the standard of larceny at any particular moment. It is true that the course of law has been to widen the definition of larceny beyond that of the common law so as to include takings that were not condemned at the common law. This has been done by expanding the category of the places from which a taking of property is larceny, the nature of property that may be the subject of larceny, and the persons who may commit it. This growth has been the work of several centuries and from the standpoint of any one year presents a static rather than a dynamic picture.

(iii) *Details of administration.* As we move into the more modern era of regulation, particularly the regulation of business, the picture changes. The lawmaker widens his horizon, not merely to attempt prohibition of specific types of conduct, but to regulate enterprises or activities generally in the interest of achieving a social betterment. It is no longer possible or desirable for the lawmaker to prescribe every detail. When he passes a statute based on the policy that prices should be "reasonable" or that licenses should be granted where required by the "public interest," it becomes impossible for the lawmaker to give a precise definition of "reasonable" or "public interest." The practice has therefore developed of appointing or selecting an administrator who is charged with the duty of making regulations to carry out the legislative purpose of maintaining reasonable prices or of granting licenses in the public interest.

Had the lawmaker not been willing to entrust this authority to the administrator, it would have been necessary for the statute to specify in detail every fact situation in which the price would be reasonable or the issuance of a license would be in the public interest. The inability of the lawmaker, however far-sighted, to foresee every possible contingency is obvious. Even assuming such an ability, the statute would be so long and detailed that few persons would be able to know its full meaning. By delegating authority to the administrator, the legislative body is free to confine its attention to the basic or underlying principles of policy, leaving to the administrator the task of filling out the details.

(iv) *Flexibility of administration.* This entrusting or delegation of authority to the administrator is further necessitated by the fact that what is "reasonable" or in the "public interest" depends upon a correlation of facts to arise in the future. A sudden shortage or an unexpected surplus may throw out of line any prior rigid fixing of a "reasonable price." The regulation must therefore be dynamic rather than static, and it would be unsatisfactory and productive of great injustice for the lawmaker to fix a rigid price. The necessity for correlation of the regulation to changing factors demands a flexibility of regulation that cannot be possessed by a lawmaking body meeting only at intervals.

The flexibility of administration made possible by regulation by an administrator is also desirable from the standpoint of the mechanics of regulation. The period of the regulation of modern business has been comparatively short. While we have obtained considerable experience in certain lines of regulation, there are many fields recently embarked on in which regulation of necessity has been made on the basis of trial and error. In the absence of prior experience, no other course is available than to adopt the regulation that appears the best and then to modify or change it from time to time as experience dictates. To do this requires both a day-to-day surveillance of the workings of the regulation and the ability to change the regulation quickly as wisdom dictates. A statute cannot provide this flexibility. All lawmaking bodies in the United States meet at intervals. In many of the states, the legislature meets only every other year. Under such a system, regulation by the lawmaker necessarily assumes a spasmodic, intermittent character and cannot be currently adjusted to change with the times.

(v) *Expert administration.* In addition to the necessity of the situation, which requires the delegation of regulation or rule-making authority to the administrator, there is also the advantage to be gained of administration by an expert. If the administrator is properly qualified for his position, he will have a far greater knowledge of his subject than could be expected of the lawmaker. The regulation by the administrator should therefore be better than the amateur regulation by the lawmaker. This is not intended to belittle the lawmaker, but is merely a recognition of the fact that each member of a lawmaking body cannot have the experience and the knowledge of a specialist in every field of business that the government may wish to regulate. It is also a recognition of the fact that, if a business is to be regulated, the person making the regulation cannot know too much about that business.

Of course, if the administrator is not competent, these benefits will not be obtained by delegating to him the authority to regulate. If he is not expert in the field, if he is not alert to change, if he is not quick to realize the good or the bad effects of a particular regulation, there may result confusion, hardship, and partisanship as great as though the matter was not in the hands of an administrator. This obviously is not an argument against delegating legislative authority, but is merely an argument to exert all the power of a democracy to make certain that those authorized to administer are competent to do so.

(vi) *Localized administration.* The administrative regulation is not required to have the universality of a traditional statute. It may be necessary to divide the country into areas or zones to regulate price within the separate units. A "reasonable" price for one area of supply or competition may be unreasonable for another. It would be extremely difficult, if not impossible, for a lawmaking body to devise a law with such variations.

§ 2:5.   The Executive

This term refers to action taken by the President of the United States, the governor of a state, or the mayor or commissioner of a city. In the case of smaller governmental units, such as townships, there may be a person in the executive position or the lawmaking body of the unit may also serve as the executive. Historically, the function of the executive, as is seen from the very name itself, was to execute or carry out the enforcement of the laws. Today, at least at the state and national level, the executive performs more the function of making or sharing in the making of laws than that of overseeing the enforcement of the laws.

In the case of the President, we tend to think of his lawmaking role as being a sharing in the legislative process with the Congress; the Congress adopting the law and the President participating in such adoption by signing the law. With the rise of the American party system, the President has become the leader of his party and thus becomes the legislative leader of the nation in the official sense that it is "his" program which is presented to the Congress. The President has thus unofficially come to perform part of the function officially performed by the Prime Minister of England.

In many areas the President may also function to establish the rule of conduct that governs us. Sometimes this is seen as action taken in cooperation with Congress. For example, tariff laws may authorize the President to raise or increase the tariff on imports when in his discretion he finds certain facts to exist. Thus tariff laws have authorized such an increase when the President found that the country where the imports originated discriminated against American-made goods entering the country, or when there was a certain disparity between the labor cost of production of the goods in the foreign country and the production of like goods in the United States. The President has the authority to make treaties with the advice and consent of two thirds of the Senate, as distinguished from both the houses of Congress, which treaties can in some cases have the effect of law without any further legislative action being taken.

Acting by himself, the President may make executive agreements with foreign countries. The President has also an indirect lawmaking power in the sense that as Commander in Chief of the Armed Forces he can take action which, as a practical matter, puts Congress in a position where it must adopt certain kinds of laws in order to protect the national interests thereafter.

Questions for Review

1. What is the advantage of a local governmental authority dealing with matters, such as irrigation, drainage, and water supply?

2. What effect does the existence of such local authorities have on the future existence or value of the state-national federal system?

3. What are the functions of courts?

4. How can you reconcile the conclusion that judges make the law with the principle that lawmakers must be elected by the people?

5. If judges make the law, what training should a person have before being made a judge?

6. What practical and theoretical basis is there for a division of government into three branches?

7. Is the three-branch or tripartite division of governmental bodies suited for a society based upon the principle of (a) laissez-faire or (b) regulation?

8. By what authority can an administrative agency make rules which have the effect of laws?

9. Why are they given this power?

10. What are the advantages of lawmaking by administrative agencies?

11. Has the lawmaking function of the President changed?

Chapter 3

THE NATURE OF LAW

§ 3:1. What Is Law?

Laws are the rules that society adopts to govern itself. For the moment we are ignoring the detail of which element or branch of government makes the law. The recognition that rules of law are made by man for man is significant in what is excluded thereby. If we accept the fact that law is made by man, we eliminate the concept that law is in any sense divine. This statement does not deny nor minimize the importance of religious beliefs and values in motivating society to adopt particular rules of law. Since law is made by man in the way in which man wants to be governed, it is apparent that everything which contributes to the moral and ethical "man" is going to have some bearing on the selection of the laws by which he wishes to be governed.

To return to the main theme, it is apparent that the laws by which our conduct is governed cannot be regarded as God-given in the sense of the

Ten Commandments. To believe otherwise leads us to absurdities when we consider the fact that the maximum speed at which an automobile can be driven in Pennsylvania is 50 miles per hour whereas in Maryland, which is just below the southern border of Pennsylvania, the maximum speed is 55 miles per hour. It must be apparent that the choice of any speed limit and the choice of 50 miles per hour in one state and 55 miles per hour in the other state is merely a matter of man's choice, specifically the men in the Pennsylvania state legislature and the men in the Maryland state legislature speaking on behalf of the people who elected them to their respective offices. It is an absurdity bordering on the blasphemous to contend that at that remote date when the world began, it was predestined that there would be a western hemisphere and that during the years 1763 to 1767 a Mason-Dixon boundary line would separate the colonies of Pennsylvania and Maryland and that later, after they had become states and the internal combustion engine had been invented, the legislators of those two states would meet and those to the north would be moved to set 50 miles per hour as the maximum speed limit while those to the south would be moved to adopt 55.

The above illustration also serves to point out another negation contained in the definition of law. It is not a mandate of nature or physical science. There is nothing in the speed laws of the two named states nor in the geographic terrain of those two states which in any way would indicate that the laws adopted "existed" in the sense that the law of gravity existed before it was recognized. If you are building a bridge or an airplane, you must recognize the law of gravity. It is there not because society deemed it preferable to have such a law to keep everything firmly planted on the ground, rather than floating or flying into space, but just because the law of gravity does exist. In the case of speed laws, it is apparent that there was the freedom of choice on the part of the two state legislatures to have no law, to have a law which would merely impose an obligation to avoid reckless driving, or to have a law specifying a maximum number of miles, and in the latter case to designate any number of miles that the legislature chose.

It is important that the citizen come face to face with the nature of law because he will then see the responsibility that he bears as a voting citizen. If law were a matter of inevitable science, neither you nor I would have any concern about what it was or what it becomes. Likewise, if the law were divinely-mandated, it is obvious that we feeble mortals would play no part in the growth of the law. But when we recognize that law is what we make it, the responsibility for the future of the American way of life is placed directly upon our shoulders. If the laws of the country do not meet the needs of the country, it will be your fault and my fault. No one would be so optimistic as to say that we will be able to solve all our problems by trying, but it is apparent that no progress will be made if we do not try. The rights for which millions of Americans have toiled and fought and died are ours, but with those rights is the responsibility for their preservation. Let us consider further the nature of law so that we can understand how it grows and thus understand the part that we play in its growth and preservation.

§ 3:2. Understanding the Law

Much of the difficuly in seeking to understand the law is the result of regarding it as an absolute and exact science. The ideal of a definite body of law is not only attractive to the student but is dear to the heart of everyone. Long-revered is the maxim that "in the known certainty of the law lies the safety of all." The purpose of establishing our Constitution is to the end that we may have a government of laws and not of men.

The truth of the matter is that the certainty, the precision, and the logic of the law are very relative matters. In truth the law is an arbitrary set of rules that we have agreed upon to govern ourselves. And our reason for so doing is the quest for justice and the advancement of the various social objectives that we hold dear.

§ 3:3. The Absolutes and the Arbitraries

(a) The absolutes. Law is not absolute, for anything which is absolute is the same at all times and all places. For example, the gravitational pull of the earth, that is, the law of gravity already noted, is the same in every state of the United States. It is also the same in every other country. Thus, it is geographically constant. The law of gravity is also the same at all times. Go back to the remote day when the prehistoric cave man threw a spear. It fell to the ground because of the same force that centuries later would make an apple fall on Newton's head, that today makes an airplane crash to the earth, and that centuries hence will continue to bring you down.

The law of gravity is also inevitable. It operates at the same point with the same power regardless of what you do. It is true that you can fly, but that does not mean that you have repealed or destroyed the law of gravity. It only means that you have overcome it with a superior force—and remember that the moment you stop working with the superior force, down you come. The law of gravity is therefore an absolute; for it is universal, timeless, and inevitable.

(b) The arbitraries. In contrast with those things which are absolute, as the law of gravity, are those things which are the way they are merely because we want them that way. For example, we outlawed the flying wedge in football, just because we decided that it should be outlawed. Similarly, we have changed the rules for basketball. We change women's hair styles. We change the size and length of automobiles. And so on, whenever it suits us, meaning society, to do so, we change.

Our action in making such decisions is arbitrary. This word often has a bad sound because we generally think of a person who is arbitrary as being capricious, corrupt, or tyrannical. Let me use arbitrary in the simple sense of a standard which is the opposite of an absolute; one which is dependent upon will or discretion. That is to say, it is just what it is because someone in charge wants it that way, not because it must inevitably and at all times and at all places be that way.

(c) *What does a straight line mean?* Look at this and state what it means:

—

Depending upon your experience and training, you may say it is a dash, a hyphen, an underscore, a minus sign, the indication of a negative charge, or even the letter "n" in Gregg shorthand. Now rotate or turn the line 45 degrees, thus:

/

Now you may think of a fraction, divided by, or you may associate it with the address form of "c/o," or if you are familiar with the Fortran language of computers, you will recognize that the slant line may be used to indicate the beginning of a new record. Let us rotate the line 45 more degrees, and we have:

|

Now of course we see that it is a "one." Is it not peculiar that this little line changes its meaning in terms of its position? It is still the same line. It has just as much lead or ink in it regardless of its position, but you and I choose to give it a particular meaning in terms of its position. Of course, it is a little discouraging to think that if you stand up, or sit down, or lie down, or even stand on your head, you are always the same old you. This little line has us stopped.

But to return to the main theme, suppose that we place two little straight lines parallel to each other. If horizontal, as:

=

we will probably all agree that it means "equals." But let us rotate it 90 degrees, as:

||

Now we say that it is eleven, but if we were ancient Romans, we would recognize it as meaning two; and if we are binary computers, we recognize it as three.

The practical explanation for the foregoing is that there are only so many kinds of lines that can be drawn on paper and that if we all agree that with reference to a particular subject a particular line shall have a particular meaning, no one is harmed. Just the opposite, we are able to have effective and exact communication between us. But note that we are "arbitrary" in agreeing upon any meaning, for there is no "absolute" which makes any particular meaning universal, timeless, and inevitable.

(d) What does "one" mean? Suppose we agree that

|

stands for "one." Do you know what "one" means? Does it have an absolute value? Or an arbitrary value which can mean anything you want it to mean? Let us turn to the law for our answers of what "one" means and consider various situations which raise the question of what is "one."

Assume that a thief steals your suitcase. We say that he has committed larceny. How many larcenies? Why, one, of course. Suppose, however, that your suitcase contains a pair of your shoes. How many larcenies now? Is it one larceny for the aggregate of everything taken, or are there three larcenies: one for the suitcase, one for the left, and one for the right shoe? And if the shoes have laces, are there two additional larcenies for the two laces? I am sure that most of us would regard the one act of taking your property from you as merely one larceny, and also regard my question as somewhat silly.

Suppose, however, that the suitcase belongs to one person and the shoes to another person. Now we have two persons wronged by the one act of taking the suitcase. Is it still one larceny because there was one "taking" or are there two larcenies because there are two victims?

Assume that the suitcase was owned by one person and various objects contained in the suitcase were owned by three different persons. If we say that four persons are wronged by the defendant, which is the fact, and that therefore there are four larcenies, we have the possibility that the defendant by one stroke has committed four crimes and made himself a habitual criminal upon whom a life sentence could be imposed.

Let us take a variation of this theme. This time, in the night our hero drives up to a warehouse with a truck. He enters and steals a bag of flour. He takes only one bag because that is all he can carry at one time. He puts the bag into the truck and then goes back for another bag. Bag after bag he steals. Forty-eight bags in all. Is he now guilty of 48 larcenies and subject to the punishment of one larceny times 48? We might even have him steal 48 bags of coffee and then have the interesting question of whether the taking of each bag of coffee constitutes one larceny for the bag, one larceny for the binding twine, and one larceny for each coffee bean.

Take the offense of maliciously destroying property. Now our defendant enters a hothouse and one by one breaks 517 potted geraniums, he himself being in a similar condition. The penalty for maliciously destroying property is a $50 fine. Is he liable for $50 or 517 times $50?

And again, our hero, whether sober or not, speeds cross country driving at an illegal rate of speed. During the course of his wild drive, he passes through five boroughs, two townships, and four cities—always at the continuously illegal rate of speed. Is he guilty of one offense of illegally speeding or of 11 offenses?

I suspect you have the feeling that in all these cases there is merely one act by the defendant, even though it may be an act which continues over time, or through a geographic distance, or which affects a number of items, or a number of items owned by different persons; and that since the defendant did one act, he should only be punished for one crime. In general, the law agrees with you, and most courts will say in the cases above given that there is only one offense because there is only one act.

What's hard about all this? After all, it's just plain common sense that if a person does only one act he commits only one crime. Well, let's just apply this common sense principle logically. "Logic" means that from now on we will say that it is the number of acts rather than the number of things or persons affected which determines the number of crimes which are committed: one act, one crime.

Let's see how logical we really want to be. Let's apply the rule of "one act" to the case of a bus which runs off the road into a ditch with a driver and 48 passengers. The bus is damaged and each person in the bus is injured. How many accidents are there? The newspaper headline says: "Bus Accident." But if there is only one accident, what happened to each of the persons in the bus? Does each of the persons go home and say, "I just had *one-fiftieth* of an accident"—or does he say that he had *"an"* accident? Actually there was only one act, that of the bus going off the road, or the negligence or fault of some person which caused it to do so. The fact that the bus was damaged and each of the 49 persons in the bus was injured does not alter the fact that there was only one "act." If, however, we say that each person who is injured in the bus has had his own private "accident," then we find ourselves engaged in the curious double-talk that for one purpose there is one accident and for another purpose there are 50 accidents. Now you see that logic has created a real dilemma. If we say that the act determines the number, we must say one act means one accident. This, of course, comes home to insurers where the automobile liability policy sets a maximum limitation on liability "per accident." In contrast, if we look not at the number of acts but at the number of interests or persons harmed, we would say that there were 50 accidents and the liability of the insurer would accordingly be enhanced. There is a conflict of authority as to the number of "accidents" in the above case.

If we are still sure that one act means one legal consequence, assume that the defendant recklessly runs over and kills two pedestrians at the same moment. Is it one manslaughter or two manslaughters by automobile? Suppose he kills a person with a high-powered rifle bullet which passes through the first person, killing both that victim and another person. Again, the problem, is it one or two homicides? Suppose the defendant throws a bomb into a crowded hall and kills 100 people. Has he committed one murder or 100 murders?

Let us carry the matter a step further and put the question in its possible procedural setting. The defendant who has killed 100 people with one bomb is prosecuted for the murder of one of the victims. For some reason, he is acquitted on that charge. He is then prosecuted for the murder of the second victim. He then raises the defense that as he did only one act he committed only one murder, for which he has already been put in jeopardy and therefore he cannot be tried again for the same act. If we sustain this defense, we say that the defendant cannot be held liable for the remaining 99 killings.

Obviously, when it comes to taking a human life, we are just not going to say that one act is only one crime. Instead, "common sense" tells us that every person killed represents a separate crime, and that is what most courts do say. But what about logic? If I take the lives of four different people by one act, I am guilty of four homicides, but if I steal the property of four persons by one act, I commit only one larceny. Why should the test for the number of crimes be the number of the acts done when it is larceny but the number of the victims when it is a question of human lives?

The only answer is the obvious one that society just doesn't want to be too tough when merely property is concerned, but when life is involved it will be as tough as possible. This distinction, you recognize, is arbitrary in that it is not inevitable, it is not universal, it is not timeless, and it is not even consistent. But you and I like the distinction. It sits well with us emotionally, because it fits in with our feelings deeply rooted in our socio-theological mores and our democratic concepts of the dignity of the human life. We, and the law with us, therefore reject the cold and logical consistency and make the rule of law vary to suit our feelings of what is just. We make "one" mean one thing in some cases and something else in others.

§ 3:4. The Quest for Justice

(a) Generally. In the last two sections we have come face to face with the heart of the problem. Law seeks justice, which is exactly what we want it to do but, in seeking justice, it must often sacrifice logic and precision. This is where the difficulty comes in, for if we do not recognize law as a quest for justice, we cannot understand why it is that law grows and changes as man's concept of justice changes and as the socioeconomic world in which he lives changes.

Of course we add to our difficulties when we speak of "justice" as changing, but it would be a mistake to assume that justice is a universal value which means the same to all people in all ages. Many factors and institutions have made their contribution in the molding and change of the concepts of justice. Home and school training, religion, enlightened self-interest, social and business groups, and the various media of modern communication and entertainment all have played and continue to play a part. Furthermore, each individual's concept of justice varies in terms of his personality, his training, and his social and economic position. Obviously, justice has different meanings to the employer and to the employee, to the millionaire and the pauper, to the industrial worker and the farmer, and above all, to the plaintiff and the defendant.

(b) Conflicting aims. The problem is made further complicated by the fact that you cannot devise rules of law to keep everyone happy. Somebody wins, and somebody must lose. You cannot have both sides win. This means that quite frequently you will have conflicting social objectives and then society, through the law, must make a choice as to which objective is to prevail.

For example, we all believe in preserving the United States and we all believe in preserving freedom of speech and freedom of action. Yet if the defendant makes treasonable statements and seeks to protect them under the garb of free speech, we do not hesitate to suppress free speech in the interest of the greater social objective of preserving the government. Likewise, although we exalt freedom of the individual, we recognize that a military draft is necessary for the protection of the state.

Within a strictly economic field, we favor the determination of prices, such as rents, by the unrestricted operation of the laws of supply and demand. Yet in time of war we recognize a greater social necessity to provide adequate housing at reasonable prices and therefore establish rent ceilings.

In the tort field, consider the dilemma of the law when faced with the situation of harm caused without physical impact: society hesitating between remedying the injury of the genuine claimant on the one hand and on the other protecting the defendant from bogus claims of perjured plaintiffs— seeking to lay down a general rule that will do justice in all cases, or at least in most cases.

If you examine any rule of law or statute, you will find that it has one or more underlying objectives, and that frequently in advancing certain objectives it defeats other equally praiseworthy objectives. But remember all this conflict is for the sake of justice.

(c) The variables. The problems suggested by the above are made all the more difficult of solution because of the variables.

First of all, it is important to recognize that while as of any moment the law appears to stand still, it is constantly moving or changing. By way of analogy, consider a coastline or river bed. Ordinarily, at any one moment when you look at it, you see no change. But if you would study the maps for the last century, you would see change. Consider the camera picture sequences you have seen of the opening of a flower. When you use your own eyes to look at the flower, it is at any one moment of time motionless and no change is apparent. But when seen through the camera study, it grows rapidly.

There is a great tendency in our analysis of human problems to lose the sense of time, motion, direction, or change. We tend to identify the present tense with timelessness and assume that it has always been this way and always will be this way. Even though you know that there was once a day when there were no automobiles or airplanes, you are so accustomed to them that for practical purposes you cannot imagine a world without them. Just as you cannot create in your imagination what the world was like 50 years ago, you cannot imagine what it will be like 50 years from now. We readily accept the conclusion that many laws of 50 years ago are out of date. But what should we be doing to today's laws to keep them up to date so that they will serve the needs of society 50 years from now? Is it possible to have laws prepared in advance or must we wait until something goes wrong and then breathlessly rush in and strive to avert further disaster?

We accept without dispute the need for plans, whether it be what you are going to do when you finish school or whether it is General Motors planning its production for the next year. It would certainly seem that our nation and the laws which run our nation are deserving of equally thoughtful planning. This we will not fully appreciate until we recognize the fact that the significant aspect of life is change and that law itself is life and therefore it changes.

Secondly, it is important to recognize that there are factors changing our society in what might be called a geometric progression. That is to say, our problems are not increasing in number or complexity in terms of 2, 4, 6, 8, 10; but increasing rather more like 2, 4, 8, 16, 32. This is explained in terms of the rising population, the rising number of inventions, and the rising standards of living. For example, in 1900, the United States had a smaller population. Of that population, the percentage of people who owned carriages was smaller than the percentage of today's population which owns automobiles. When two automobiles collide today, the probability of damage is far greater than when two carriages collided in 1900, not only in terms of damage to vehicles but also to others in chain collisions. Contemplate the highway injury problems in the year 2000 A.D. when it is estimated that the national population will have risen from the present 200 million to 331 million. I leave it to you to imagine the harm-causing potential that the automobile of that year will have. Are we as a nation doing what has to be done to safeguard against that greater potential for greater damage?

Translating the lesson to be drawn from this illustration to the field of law generally, we have the greater question whether society is training itself to make the changes to the law which society will deem necessary. As man can only think of the future in terms of the past, the next group of chapters will be devoted to considering those forces which in the past have affected or influenced the course of the law. An appreciation of them will perhaps give us some guidance in knowing where we and the law should go in the future or at least giving us a sense of flexibility so that we can be more alert to the need for change when it arises and more adroit in making the desired changes.

Questions for Review

1. What is law?

2. What is the social significance of your answer?

3. What is meant by saying that an absolute value is inevitable, universal, and constant?

4. Is a rule of law an absolute?

5. When a defendant does one act which affects several individuals, has he committed one wrong for his one act, or has he committed as many wrongs as there are victims harmed by his act?

6. Analyze the reason for your difficulty in giving an answer to Question 5.

7. Is your answer to Question 5 the same without regard to whether the actual problem before the court is (a) a crime against property, (b) a crime against the person, or (c) a crime affecting life?

8. Are your answers to Questions 5 and 7 based upon logic?

9. Is justice an absolute value?

10. What factors complicate the orderly growth of law?

11. What can be learned from the past which will assist us in making the laws for the future?

Chapter 4

UNLIMITED POWER OF GOVERNMENT REGULATION

§ 4:1.   Importance to Management

Government regulation of business is of extreme importance to the businessman because of the fact that much of the "law" with which the businessman comes into contact is a government regulation, or the result of a government regulation, rather than a traditional rule of law made by the legislature or interpreted by the courts. This becomes doubly important when it is recognized that the power to regulate business is today virtually without limit. The only way in which the businessman can protect himself from government regulation is through appeal to the voter and the lawmaker. Neither the Constitution nor the economic theories of freedom of contract and laissez-faire any longer bar regulating business.

Of equal importance to the businessman is the recognition and realization of the importance of administrative agencies in carrying out the regulation of business. To the extent that the lawmaker has created such agencies, they are the "government" so far as the regulated business is concerned. For practical purposes, the agency having jurisdiction as to a particular matter may in effect be the lawmaker, the judge, and the policing authority all in one. The administrative agency is often for the businessman the "law of the land." For the most part, the contact of the businessman with government will be dealing with an agency or operating under the regulations of an agency. For the businessman, "government" in the next quarter of the Twentieth Century is not the government described in the written constitutions but by the system of administrative agencies.

§ 4:2.   The Role of Government

Without considering the merits or demerits, the fact cannot be disputed that from a negative "do-nothing" concept of government, the American society has swung over to a positive "do-something" or "do-everything" attitude. Critics of the new social philosophy point out that just as a backseat driver would be a better passenger if he said nothing and allowed the driver to drive unimpeded, a society is better off if its government does not attempt to get into the act and that the natural forces of supply and demand can drive society much better than can a government.

It is impossible to establish scientifically which view is correct or wrong because socioeconomic life and theories cannot be tested by the same techniques as are available to a scientist. The latter has the happy ability to repeat the same experiment as many times as his heart desires, making such modifications as he chooses until he is able to finally demonstrate that the absence or presence of a particular factor produces a particular result. In the case of human life, both individual and national, we cannot play the record over again at all, let alone play it over with controlled variation. We therefore can never really be certain as to the effect that would have been produced had certain action been taken or not been taken.

Many people feel that the negative or laissez-faire role of government is suited only to a society with a small population, a simple economy, and a low technological development. As long as the local bread you buy, made by Joe the baker on the street corner, is not wrapped, and had been made by his father and grandfather before him, it is practical or at least reasonably practical for society to let you protect yourself by your own judgment and experience when you buy a loaf of bread. Today, when you buy a wrapped or canned bread product made possibly miles away by a total stranger, you are trusting more to luck or relying on your past experience. At this point, you and society want someone to step in and protect you where your judgment is not sufficient. Once you admit this need for some control or protective element you have opened the door to government regulation of business.

Add to the socioeconomic scene the great increase in our population with some 10 major cities each having a greater population than existed in all of the 13 states combined when our nation was born, the increase in our geographic expanse from 13 to 50 states, the change of our country from a predominantly rural to an urban society with its modern factory system and with its myriad products that if defective can injure or kill, it can be seen why the individual has been willing to let government step in and protect him, or why we have in fact demanded that government do something to protect us from the various evils against which we cannot protect ourselves.

Today no one fully believes in free enterprise. If you believed in free enterprise, you would immediately write your Congressman demanding that every federal law controlling industry be repealed, starting with the Pure Food and Drug Act. If you really believed in free enterprise, you would not have federal meat inspectors at packing houses. How would society then be protected? Merely by the operation of the laws of supply and demand. If Company X put out in cans the meat of cows that had died from various bovine diseases, instead of only the meat of good healthy animals which were killed intentionally, a number of persons would probably become sick and die. If this occurred with sufficient frequency, the public would stop buying the X brand products until either Company X went out of business or improved its standard in order to stay in business. The only difficulty with this theory of self-regulation is the length of time that it would take and the number of innocent deaths that might first occur. Are you willing to be a martyr in the name of free enterprise to die from bad meat so that society is warned not to make any further purchases of X brand meats? I suspect that you would prefer that government should inspect the meat so that you can be assured that the meat from Company X and from any other company is fit to eat. If that is your preference, you have just lost your standing in the Adam Smith Club. If that is your preference, you do not actually believe in free enterprise and it is merely a question in your mind of how much free enterprise and how much government regulation there should be. Thus, the problem before us becomes purely quantitative (how much regulation) rather than qualitative—free enterprise or regulated society.

§ 4:3.   The Constitutionality of Government Regulation

The citizen must recognize that within the area of regulation of business (and that comprises government ownership as well as control), there is virtually no limitation on the power of either state or federal government. It can safely be said that any law which relates to business or the economy will be sustained as constitutional. By the very token that it was enacted as a statute, it is apparent that there is a significant group of society which believes in such a law; and when this is true the Supreme Court will not interpose its personal opinion as to whether the law is good or bad.

The objection of the man on the street that "it's un-American," "it's unconstitutional," or "they can't do this to me," carries no weight with the court. The man on the street—the businessman, the citizen—must realize that there is no guardian angel in the form of a judicial system to protect America from stupid laws. This is illustrated by such cases as *Secretary of Agriculture* v. *Central Roig Refining Co.*, 338 U.S. 604 (1950), in which, acting under the Sugar Act of 1948, the Secretary of Agriculture made quota allowances to sugar refineries in the Puerto Rico area. The effect of these allowances was to restrict the available quota to those who were in business during the base or reference period, thereby excluding any newcomers into the business; and to limit each of the old producers to a fixed percentage regardless of whether improved methods in his plant or other changes would have resulted in a greater control of the market by a more efficient producer.

The Court sustained the law, declaring, "The problem which confronted Congress was not the setting of quotas abstractly considered but so to fix their amount as to achieve approximate justice in the shares allotted to each area and the persons within it. To recognize the problem is to acknowledge its perplexities.

"Congress was thus confronted with the formulation of policy peculiarly within its wide swath of discretion. It would be a singular intrusion of the judiciary into the legislative process to extrapolate restrictions upon the formulation of such an economic policy from those deeply rooted notions of justice which the Due Process Clause expresses. The final judgment (in adopting the law) is too apt to be a hodgepodge of considerations, including considerations that may well weigh with legislators but which this Court can hardly disentangle.

"Suffice it to say that since Congress fixed the quotas on a historical basis it is not for this Court to reweigh the relevant factors, and perchance, substitute its notion of expediency and fairness for that of Congress. This is so even though the quotas thus fixed may demonstrably be disadvantageous to certain areas or persons. This Court is not a tribunal for relief from the crudities and inequities of complicated experimental economic legislation. . . ."

The same attitude of the Court is more concisely stated in *Williamson* v. *Lee Optical of Oklahoma*, 348 U.S. 483 (1955), in which the Court declared: "The day is gone when this Court uses the Due Process Clause of the Fourteenth Amendment to strike down state laws, regulatory of business and industrial conditions, because they may be unwise, improvident, or out of harmony with a particular school of thought. 'For protection against abuses by legislatures the people must resort to the polls, not to the court.' "

The businessman and the citizen must learn this lesson—there is no court, no constitution, no wall, between our dear America and anything else. It is the lawmaker who determines how our land shall be run, how business shall be regulated, whether we shall have free enterprise and free ownership. And if any law be evil, the remedy is only in the vote. If more businessmen, if more citizens, knew this, we would have more voting, more intelligent voting, and a greater public-spirited participation in government affairs.

§ 4:4.   Basis for the Attitude of the Supreme Court

The position of the court described above is not based on any foreign ideology nor any domestic political platform. Some may challenge this statement and claim that the Roosevelt New Deal changed the prior constitutional law. But going back to 1920, we find the Supreme Court in *Green* v. *Frazier,* 253 U.S. 233, sustaining the right of North Dakota to set up a state-owned banking, housing, grain warehousing, and flour mill system, the Court refusing to interfere in the name of the due process clause after the lawmaker of North Dakota adopted such laws and they were sustained by the Supreme Court in North Dakota. In simple terms, this means that in 1920 when the world was still ringing with the expropriations following the Russian Revolution, the Supreme Court held that no provision of the federal Constitution was violated by state ownership of basic industries.

Next consider three decisions of the Supreme Court in 1934. Now do not think that because Roosevelt had by this time been elected President the Supreme Court was in sympathy with his views. To avoid any mistake on that score, consider for the moment that prior to 1937, the only New Deal laws that the Supreme Court held constitutional were those relating to money and banking. All the enterprise-regulating laws were held unconstitutional. The Court in 1934 was clearly not a Roosevelt Court; it was the Court of nine old men at whom Democratic fists were shaken in anger for binding the economy to a horse-and-buggy era. What did these nine old men do in 1934?

In *Home Building & Loan Ass'n.* v. *Blaisdell,* 290 U.S. 398 (1934), the Court sustained state mortgage moratorium laws even though by postponing the enforcement of mortgages such laws altered the mortgage contract. The Court, in reaching this result, had to evade the express provision of the Constitution that "No state shall . . . pass . . . any law impairing the obligation of contracts." (Art. I, Sec. 10, Cl. 1) And further, the Court had to ignore the history of the period of the framing of the Constitution which makes it unavoidably clear that the framers intended to prohibit the adoption of any stay or moratorium law.

Next in 1934, the Supreme Court in *Nebbia* v. *New York,* 291 U.S. 502, sustained the New York state law establishing a minimum price for the resale of milk. In that case the Court recognized "the admitted power to correct existing economic ills by appropriate regulation of business, even though an indirect result may be a restriction of the freedom of contract or a modification of charges for services or the price of commodities." The Court declared that "a state is free to adopt whatever economic policy may reasonably be deemed to promote the public welfare, and to enforce that policy by legislation adapted to its purpose." The Court rejected the concept that a business could be regulated only if it were a monopoly or a public utility or held a grant or franchise.

And again in 1934, the Supreme Court in *Puget Sound Power & Light Co.* v. *Seattle*, 291 U.S. 619, sustained the right of a city to own and operate a municipal power plant in competition with a private plant, even though the private plant was required to pay taxes which supported the city plant. The Court did not consider the case difficult to determine, for it stated that "the decisions of this Court leave no doubt that a state may, in the public interest, constitutionally engage in a business commonly carried on by private enterprise, levy a tax to support it . . . and compete with private interests engaged in a like activity." The Court held that the private enterprise faced with government competition cannot claim exemption from such taxation for it cannot be claimed that the public body "upon entering the business forfeited its power to tax any competitor."

What do these four cases establish? They hold that a state may own a business, regulate a business, regulate prices, and regulate the enforcement of contracts whenever the state considers that the state economic conditions require such regulation. In reaching these conclusions, the Supreme Court was not influenced or motivated by any foreign ideology of state ownership or control. The opinions of the Court make it clear that no abstract philosophy or theory was here involved, only the Court recognizing the economic realities and permitting the lawmaker to exercise his power to legislate as he saw fit to remedy the evils of the time. It is significant that the first Roosevelt appointee did not reach the Supreme Court until the fall of 1937.

What then was the great strife between the New Deal and the Old Deal? To the minds of many the New Deal stands for government regulation and ownership, while the Old Deal stands for absence of regulation and free enterprise. The four cases cited above show without question that the Old Deal court found nothing unconstitutional in government regulation and ownership at the state level. The line of conflict was at the national level— the Old Deal denying the power of the federal government to regulate or own business for economic control purposes while the New Deal advocated such power. It is therefore erroneous and misleading to think of one party as standing for free enterprise and the other party as the foe of free enterprise. The only quarrel between the two parties was over which government was to do the regulating.

§ 4:5.   Absence of a Free Enterprise Party

Today the advocates of free enterprise cannot find protection at the state or national level in any political party. One might have suspected that the Republicans were merely biding their time until they were again in power in the federal government and that as soon as that day arrived they would abolish all the New Deal laws which finally the Supreme Court came to sustain beginning in 1937. Had they done so, the voter could then make a choice between the two major political parties on the basis that one stood for federal regulation of the economy and the other was opposed to it.

The Congressional record under the subsequent Republican administration speaks for itself. There was no open repeal of all the New Deal laws. There was no repudiation of the principle of federal regulation of the economy. This is strikingly demonstrated by the history of the labor-management regulation. The New Deal National Recovery Act, as an incident to creating codes by which the various industries were to govern themselves, provided for compulsory collective bargaining and union recognition. This Act was held unconstitutional in 1935. A new statute, the Wagner Labor Relations Act of 1935, was then adopted, based to a large extent on this same concept of collective bargaining and union recognition. In 1937, this statute was held constitutional by the United States Supreme Court, that Court thereby reversing the line of its prior New Deal decisions and embarking upon a new era in constitutional interpretation.

The opposition of the Republicans to this decision was unbounded. Both the man in the street and the lawyer would have expected that when the Republicans were again in office, the repeal of this Labor-Management Act would be number one on their legislative agenda. The Republicans came into power and 10 years later in 1947, by the Taft-Hartley Act, the Labor-Management Act of 1935 was amended and expanded. Instead of repudiating the doctrine that the federal government could regulate labor-management relations, the Republicans exercised that very doctrine they had reviled one decade before. And again in 1959, the Republican administration adopted the Labor-Management Reporting and Disclosure Act, extending further the exercise of control by the federal government over labor-management relations.

This is pointed out in no way to belittle any party or persons, but only to reemphasize that in spite of the slogans, political platforms, and phrases to which we periodically render lip service, it is the economy which dictates the course of events. It is the economy and the needs of the time, and the demands of the people engendered by those needs, which have made both major political parties and the Supreme Court all agree that the lawmaker, state or national, may regulate the economy in any way that he sees fit.

§ 4:6.   A Flexible Approach to the Role of Government

The businessman must maintain a flexible and open-minded approach to the subject of government regulation and ownership. Some people blindly believe that free enterprise is the only solution and salvation for the economic world, while others just as blindly believe that government regulation and ownership is the only cure.

Free enterprise should be preserved not because of any imbedded economic belief or party affiliation, but because in the trials and tribulations of free enterprise men and industries become mature and capable. Let us consider by analogy the child who is tied to his mother's apron strings, or subject to parental control, or who is able to fall back upon parental resources. We do not consider such a child grown up and mature, even though he has attained man's age. We can all look back in our own lives and recognize the wondrous alchemy that changed us from boys into men when we found ourselves financially dependent upon ourselves and ourselves alone. It is not until the individual knows that if he doesn't get a job, if he doesn't make a sale, if he doesn't make good, that he will go hungry, that he really grows up. It is not until you have had the dread choice of "sink or swim" and met the challenge and rode above the waters, that you were fully a man. As long as you were able to fall back on Dad, or run to Mother, you were not self-reliant, independent, or a man.

Free enterprise gives our economy the self-reliance, the independence, and the maturity that each one of us acquired when we learned to stand up on our own and face life and to meet its problems. There is the grave danger that industries will not improve and will not reach their peak if there is not the necessity of free competition driving them on. There is the grave danger that all activity will be run by a common pattern and society will lose the great experimental value of individual variations. There will not be the same care to avoid mistake and waste if loss can be added to and written off by the next budget allotment to the government-subsidized or government-owned industry.

Above all, free enterprise provides the training ground from which the leaders of government itself may be drawn. If government is to regulate the economy (and it will do so increasingly in the future), government needs leaders who are experienced in business and in meeting the problems of business. If there is no free enterprise area from which such leaders are to be taken, where does government obtain the leaders it will need?

At the same time, one must appreciate the relationship between free enterprise and government regulation and recognize the need for a flexible approach as to when one is to gain and the other yield. When Jackson marched to New Orleans to fight the British, the needs of national defense were amply met by each woodsman bringing his own rifle, his own powder, and his own shot. Today, when the call to battle is sounded, who can bring his own aircraft carrier? A century ago it was reasonable and feasible to require that each householder maintain the stretch of highway fronting his land. Such a system would be absurd today, and of course we must have government highways. In the rural areas we still have volunteer firemen. In the more thickly populated areas such a system is intolerable.

Questions for Review

1. How can theories of governmental control of business be tested?

2. Is this a scientific technique?

3. Do you believe 100 percent in free enterprise?

4. If your answer for Question 3 is "no," then state where and how you draw the line between the extent to which free enterprise should exist and the extent to which government should regulate.

5. What boundary does the Constitution set to the extent to which government can regulate "free" enterprise?

6. "The Constitution is the bedrock that protects you from unreasonable government regulation of business." Appraise this statement.

7. The power of government to regulate business has been sustained by the Supreme Court on the basis of what philosophical writing?

8. What was the conflict between the Old Deal under Hoover and the New Deal under Roosevelt?

9. Which political party in the United States is the champion of free enterprise?

10. What socioeconomic forces have led to the answer that you have given to Question 9?

11. What should be your attitude toward government regulation of business?

PART II. THE SOCIAL FORCES THAT MAKE THE LAW

Chapter **5**

A SURVEY

§ 5:1.   Introduction to the Social Forces

In the chapters in this part are considered the various social forces that underlie the law. The enumeration or listing of these forces is not "official" in any sense but is merely the author's personal opinion based upon a study of many cases. The numerical arrangement of the objectives or social forces has no significance, that is, the points are not arranged in any order of importance. As will be seen in the course of the chapters which follow, the social forces meet with varying fortunes. In some cases, a given objective is advanced. In others, the same objective is defeated.

Likewise care should be taken to avoid making an arithmetic balance between objectives. Hence, the fact that three objectives favor the plaintiff and two objectives favor the defendant does not mean that the plaintiff will win. As will be seen, social forces can have varying value so that one

37

strong force may outweigh two forces which, at the time and in the facts of the particular case, are deemed of lesser importance.

§ 5:2. What Are Rights?

In the everyday world we hear people protest that this or that cannot be done to them because they have rights. What are rights? And who has them?

In answering these questions everyone tends to make the mistake of thinking of the present as being a characteristic of what always was and always will be. Consider for a moment the right of privacy. Today the "right of privacy" is recognized as an essential element of American law and everyone concedes that there is such a right. Before 1890 the right of privacy did not exist in American law. Is it not strange that with all the generations of loyal Americans before 1890 the right of privacy was not recognized? Certainly the men who wrote the Declaration of Independence were conscious of "rights." Surely the men who insisted that the Bill of Rights Amendments be added to the new Constitution in 1790 were conscious of rights. How can we explain that those men and the law did not come around to recognizing a right of privacy until a full century later?

The answer in very simple terms is that people worry about the problems which face them. Back in the days of the Declaration of Independence and the framing of the Constitution, no one was concerned about the right of privacy. Notice the extent of the fears and concern of the framers of the Bill of Rights Amendments to the Constitution. The Fifth Amendment to the Constitution, added in 1790, states, "the right of the people to be secure in their persons, house, papers, and effects, against unreasonable searches and seizures, shall not be violated, and no warrants shall issue, but upon probable cause, supported by oath and affirmation, and particularly describing the place to be searched, and the person or things to be seized." The man of 1790 was afraid of a recurrence of the days of George III. In a voice reminiscent of James Otis decrying against the writs of assistance, the framers of the Fifth Amendment declared what we today would have regarded as a segment of privacy—protection from police invasion of privacy. The man of 1790 was just not concerned with invasion of privacy by a private person. While a snooping person could be prosecuted to some extent under a Peeping Tom Statute, this was limited to some area or conduct relating to peeping into a house or similar place and was only a criminal liability. The victim could not sue for damages for the invasion of privacy.

What should we say of the right of privacy? If we are honest with history, all that we can say is that modern man thinks highly of his privacy and wants it to be protected. Knowing that the law is responsive to the wishes of society we can go one step further and say that the right is protected. But note that we should go no further than to say that it is a right which society wishes to protect at the present time. If circumstances arise in our national life, which are such that privacy will hamper or endanger national defense, it is clear that the "right" of privacy will be ignored. We should therefore approach problems relating to rights with an open mind, realizing that there are only such rights as we the people, through our legal system, choose to recognize. It is unrealistic to believe that there are basic rights which must exist.

Various proposals have been made for the formation of national or central data banks which, is effect, would keep detailed records of each person, enterprise, and region. It is readily apparent that for the purpose of determining the needs and resources of the nation, such detailed information would be of great value. For example, what are the true facts about the teacher shortage, the patterns of crime, the problems of automobile insurance? Everyone agrees that before anything can be done about our great national problem, we must have the facts. The initial problem is what is the best way to obtain those facts and to be sure that the facts are today's facts and not facts compiled years ago. It is these considerations which in time may lead to the curtailment of the right of privacy and force us to turn our backs on our fears of improper use or even oppression by those in control of the computerized data banks.

From one standpoint, requiring the disclosure of endless information to the government is a destruction of the concept of privacy. From another point of view, it is merely the recognition that privacy, like all rights, is limited. At present the right of privacy is recognized as a "between persons" right. It does not exist as between the government and the individual, except to the extent that the protection from search and seizure and self-incrimination may be regarded as protecting privacy. The national data bank problem is therefore basically that of whether the concept of privacy should be expanded to apply to a situation to which it never applied before, nor could apply until the national population became large, the computer came into existence, and government abandoned the laissez-faire policy of former years. It is believed that social pressures of getting the national jobs done will, in time, lead to the confinement or restriction of the concept of privacy to private persons so that government will not be restricted in its acquisition and use of information.

I believe most wholeheartedly in the American way of life and the concepts on which our society of government is based, but that does not obscure the fact that once upon a time there was no American way of life and that the concept of man possessing rights recognized by government was the fruit of more than a mere revolution. It was a product of creation. While many religious leaders, philosophers, and poets spoke of the rights of man and of the dignity of man, governments laughed at such pretensions and held man tight in a society based on status. A man had rights, not as a man but because he held a given status. If he were a nobleman, he had the rights of a nobleman of his degree. If he were a warrior, he had the rights of a warrior. If a slave, he had very little rights at all. In each case, the law saw only status; it was not the man who had rights but the status of nobleman, the status of warrior, the status of slave.

In the course of time, serfdom displaced slavery in much of the western world. Eventually feudalism disappeared and with the Treaty of Westphalia of 1644, putting an end to the Thirty Years War, the modern society of nations was deemed to appear. Surely one might say that in such a "new world order" man had rights. No, not as a man but only as a subject. Even when the English colonies settled in America, they brought with them not the rights of men but the rights of British subjects. Even when the colonies were within one year of war, their Second Continental Congress presented to King George III the Olive Branch Petition in which they beseeched him to recognize their rights as Englishmen. For almost a year the destiny of the colonies hung in the balance as to whether they should stay within the empire seeking to obtain recognition of their rights as Englishmen, a "status" recognition, or whether they should do something more.

Finally, the ill-advised policies of George III and the eloquence of Thomas Paine's Common Sense tipped the scales and the colonies spoke on July 4, 1776, not in the terms of the rights of English subjects but in terms of the rights of man existing independently of any government. Had the American Revolution been lost, the Declaration of Independence would have gone rattling down the corridors of time with many another failure. More fortunately for us, the American Revolution was won, and the new government that was established was based upon "man" as the building block rather than upon "subjects." Rights of man replaced the concept of rights of subjects. With this transition, society comes from status to freedom. The obligations of a king to his faithful subjects were replaced by the rights of man existing without regard to the will or authority of any king. America is now going through the growing stages of determining what is embraced by the concept of "rights of man." To cite one growing problem, note the right of privacy. Other rights will be observed growing up and are still growing.

Some may criticize the above analysis on the theory that rights existed before they were recognized. This raises the obvious question of when did they begin to exist. Let us take the rights of free speech, freedom of the press, and free assembly. If these rights existed in law before our Constitution declared them to exist, when did they come into existence? Did they exist in ancient Egypt under the Pharoahs, in ancient Rome under the Caesars, in the Holy Roman Empire under Charlemagne, in feudal England under the early Edwards? Did freedom of the press exist before there was printing? Before there was writing? The concept of legal rights floating in the air, unrecognized by any government, is absurd enough but to have them floating in the air only over that portion of the British Empire, which becomes the United States, is doubly absurd.

The only analysis that avoids such absurdities is to recognize that men possess legal rights only when the government, which has authority over them, is required to or chooses to recognize such rights. This is an important conclusion because it gives us a proper attitude toward change. Since there is no once-and-for-all definitive statement of legal rights, it follows that legal rights change as times change and that in a democratic society the extent to which rights are recognized and respected depends upon the will of the people.

Notice also the changing evaluation made with the passage of time. The student of American colonization will recall the praise bestowed by his history books upon the tolerant-minded Lord Baltimore who, in establishing the colony of Maryland, spurned the British pattern of requiring officials to swear to belief in the established church. Thanks to his liberality, test oaths were not required in Maryland, and the Maryland state constitution ultimately built upon the foundation of his philosophy when it declared that "no religious test ought ever to be required as a qualification for any office of profit or trust in this State, other than a declaration of belief in the existence of God. . . ." In 1961, the requirement that a notary public swear to a belief in God in order to qualify him for his office was challenged on the ground that it established a religion or regulated the free exercise of religion. The United States Supreme Court did not regard the provision of the Maryland Constitution as outstanding liberalism, but held the provision of the Maryland Constitution was unconstitutional because "the power and authority of the State of Maryland thus is put on the side of one particular set of believers—those who are willing to say they believe in 'the existence of God.' . . . This Maryland religious test for public office is unconstitutionally invading . . . freedom of belief and religion and therefore cannot be enforced. . . ."[1]

§ 5:3. Operation of the Social Forces

From the fact that rights are rights only to the extent that they are recognized by society, it follows that it is not useful to speak in terms of what abstract rights do or do not exist. Whether a right exists will be determined by the operation of the social forces that make the law. For example, I have the right of free speech. From this it follows that I can say anything about you I wish and you cannot sue me for my statements. Yet we know that this is not so, and we know it is the law that you can sue me for damages for saying certain untrue things about you. Therefore such free speech right as I possess is subject to some limitation, a limitation which exists in terms of protection of your personality from injury by words.

---

[1] *Torcaso* v. *Watkins,* 367 U.S. 488 (1961).

Notice that you cannot simplify the matter by saying, "Oh well! Free speech means only freedom to speak the truth." Suppose that 10 years ago you served a jail sentence for embezzlement and since that time have lived a model life. Suppose that I am a newspaper reporter and publish an article called "Prison Reform Works" in which I describe many persons who had gone to prison but had reformed and became model citizens. In this article I describe and name you as an outstanding example of reform. Everything in the article is true and everything is said in a way seeking to praise you. But the fact remains that I am raking up the past and saying that you are a jailbird. Which should prevail—my right of free speech or your right of privacy?

As an example of the interplay and conflict of objectives, let us consider rent control. If we wish to protect the freedom of the use of property, we will allow the landlord to rent his property in any condition he chooses and at any price he chooses. Underlying this decision will be our belief that if his property is not in good condition, the competition of other landlords will force him to improve his property or to reduce his rent. An examination of the facts, however, may show such a serious housing shortage that property in poor condition can be rented at a high price. Under such circumstances we cannot depend upon the forces of supply and demand to make the landlord improve his property or reduce his rent. Society therefore adopts a law regulating the condition of leased property or specifying the maximum rents which landlords may charge. That is, society seeks to protect the tenant from exploitation by the landlord. By adopting such a control law, society is sacrificing the objective of protecting the freedom of the use of property by the landlord to the objective of protecting the tenant from the landlord's exploitation.

As another example, the objective of protecting title may conflict with the objective of furthering trade. Consider again the example of the stolen property that was sold by the thief to one who purchased it for value and in good faith, without reason to know that the goods had been stolen. If we are to further the objective of protecting the title to the property, we will conclude that the owner can recover the property from the innocent purchaser. This rule, however, will discourage trade, for people will be less willing to buy goods if they run the risk that the goods were stolen and may have to be surrendered. If we instead think only of taking steps to encourage buying and selling, we will hold that the buyer takes a good title because he acted in good faith and paid value. If we do this, we then destroy the title of the original owner and obviously abandon our objective of protecting title to property. As a general rule, society has followed the objective of protecting title. In some instances, however, the objective of furthering trade is adopted by statute, and the buyer is given good title as in certain cases of the purchaser of commercial paper (notes, drafts, and checks) or to the purchaser from a regular dealer in other people's goods.

§ 5:4. Law as an Evolutionary Process

As of any one minute, or even over a number of years, law appears to be static and, in fact, a number of legal principles have remained the same over the centuries. But many rules of law have changed and are changing.

In the first place, the law changes as society seeks to improve its existing rules in order to attain more closely the standards of justice and morality. This change in the law, in turn, may be a reflection of a social and economic change. For example, the law governing relations between landlord and tenant originated in the era of feudalism in which the owner of the land was economically, socially, and politically dominant. The law at that time, therefore, reflected his desires and was designed primarily to protect his interests. In modern society the owner of the land no longer holds that position of dominance; and the law has changed to conform to new concepts of justice and fairness, and greater recognition and protection are given to the rights and interests of the tenant.

Let us consider another example of this type of change. When the economy was patterned on a local community unit in which everyone knew each other and each other's product, the concept of "let the buyer beware" expressed a proper basis on which to conduct business. Much of the early law of the sales of goods was predicated on this philosophy. In today's economy, however, with its emphasis on interstate, national, and even international activities, the buyer has little or no direct contact with the manufacturer or seller, and the packaging of articles makes their presale examination impossible. Under the circumstances the consumer must rely on the integrity of others to an increasing degree. Gradually practices that were tolerated and even approved in an earlier era have been condemned, and the law has changed to protect the buyer by new warranty and tort theories when his own caution can no longer protect him.

Moreover, new principles of law are being developed to meet the new situations that have arisen. Every new invention and every new business practice introduces a number of situations for which there is no satisfactory rule of law. For example, how could there have been a law governing the liability of a food canner to the consumer before canning was invented? How could there have been a law relating to stocks and bonds before those instruments came into existence? How could there have been law with respect to the liability of radio and television broadcasters before such methods of communication were developed? This pattern of change will continue as long as man strives for better ways to achieve his desires.

NEW JERSEY v. CULVER

23 N.J. 495, 129 A.2d 715 (1957)

Culver was given a life sentence under a habitual criminal statute on the basis that he was a fourth offender. After he had been in prison seven years, it was determined that there were only two prior offenses and that the life sentence was therefore illegal. The court then entered the correct sentence. Culver appealed on the ground that the court had no authority to correct the illegal sentence and therefore he must be allowed to go free.

OPINION BY VANDERBILT, C.J. . . .

No one can question that the release of the defendant, a properly convicted criminal offender, . . . is an undesirable result. . . . One of the great virtues of the common law is its dynamic nature that makes it adaptable to the requirements of society at the time of its application in court. . . . The nature of the common law requires that each time a rule of law is applied it be carefully scrutinized to make sure that the conditions and needs of the times have not so changed as to make further application of it the instrument of injustice. Dean Pound posed the problem admirably in his Interpretations of Legal History (1922) when he stated, "Law must be stable, and yet it cannot stand still." . . .

The factors to be weighed in the balance in determining the present course of the law include the reasons for the rule, the present requirements of the environment in which the rule is to be applied, the dangers incident to any change, and the evils resulting from its continuance. The power of growth is inherent in the common law. . . .

In *State* v. *Gray*, 37 N.J.L. 368 (Sup.Ct., 1875), the court set aside the defendant's sentence to a term in prison at hard labor as illegal because the specific offense for which he had been convicted was not punishable at hard labor. In discharging him from custody, the court held that at common law it had no power to impose the proper sentence or to remand for that purpose; and in the absence of statute granting such power, the only course open to it was to set the prisoner free. The court relied for its authority on an ancient rule dating back to the time of Lord Coke and on decisions in other states which in turn had relied on the English precedents. . . .

The greater number of American cases have adopted the rule that . . . an invalid or illegal sentence, which is beyond the power of the trial court to impose, may be corrected after the execution of the sentence has begun and without regard to the term of court at which it is done. . . .

It is easy to see from our own cases the sound basis for the ancient English rule. In *Patterson* v. *State*, 48 N.J.L. 381, 383, 4 A. 449, 450 (Sup.Ct., 1886), we are told that:

"In the early days of English criminal jurisprudence, when even a trifling larceny was punishable with death, there was reason why the judicial mind should exhaust its ingenuity in aid of the defense, and seize upon every technicality to avert from the prisoner a punishment so disproportionate to his crime. In our time a more humane system of criminal law has been adopted, which graduates the punishment according to the magnitude of the offense, and in which there is nothing to shock our sense of justice. The reason for resorting to mere technicality to enable the criminal to evade the sanctions of the law no longer exists, and the practice to which that reason led should therefore cease. Men who make their lives a scourge to society must answer its violated laws, and can justly demand in a judicial tribunal nothing except a fair trial according to the laws of the land, in which no substantial right is denied them. . . . It is of the utmost importance to society that its criminal classes shall understand that the penalty surely follows the crime."

. . . The reason for construing the law in favor of a dangerous criminal had long since disappeared. . . .

"It is revolting to have no better reason for a rule of law than that so it was laid down in the time of Henry IV. It is still more revolting if the grounds upon which it was laid down have vanished long since, and the rule simply persists from blind imitation of the past." [Holmes] Collected Legal Papers 187 (1920).

Blind imitation of the past is what we find as the basis for holding in *State* v. *Gray, supra.* . . .

We believe that the sentences originally imposed on this defendant were in fact improper and that the court's jurisdiction to impose a correct sentence had not expired until a valid sentence was imposed. "To hold otherwise would allow the guilty to escape punishment through a legal accident." . . .

[Judgment affirmed.]

§ 5:5. The Social Forces

The social forces which will be considered in the following chapters are

    (1) Protection of the Government
    (2) Protection of Public Welfare, Safety, and Morals
    (3) Protection from Fraud
    (4) Furtherance of Good Faith and Business Ethics
    (5) Protection of the Person
    (6) Protection of Property
    (7) Protection of Title
    (8) Protection of Freedom of Personal Action
    (9) Protection of Freedom of Use of Property
   (10) Enforcement of Intent
   (11) Protection from Exploitation
   (12) Protection from Hardship Situations
   (13) Protection from Government Action
   (14) Protection from Group Oppression
   (15) Furtherance of Trade
   (16) Creditor Protection
   (17) Debtor Protection
   (18) Stability
   (19) Flexibility
   (20) Practical Expediency

Questions for Review

1. What rights have always been recognized?

2. Make a list of the rights which you consider essential.

3. Which of the rights you have listed are protected by the United States Constitution?

4. If you were living in 1750, which of these rights would have been important to you?

5. If you answer Questions 2 and 4 differently, explain the reason for your difference.

6. What significance did the American Revolution have in the classification of rights?

7. Are rights universal values that have existed for all time?

8. What does the Torcaso case discussed in § 5:2 prove to you?

9. At any one time, is each right of constant importance or value?

10. What relationship is there between technological change and change in the law?

11. Analyze the Culver case in § 5:4 in terms of the social forces involved in the decision. Explain why the prevailing social forces prevailed and why those rejected did not.

Chapter 6

PROTECTION OF THE GOVERNMENT

§ 6:1. Generally

A number of laws are designed to protect the existing governments, both state and national. Laws condemning treason, sedition, and subversive practices are examples of society taking measures to preserve governmental systems. Less dramatic are the laws that impose taxes to provide for the support of those governments and that provide for compulsory military service to protect them from enemy aliens.

Although the state in a democratic society exists for the welfare and advancement of the individual, the objective of protecting the state comes into conflict with other social objectives that favor the advancement of the individual. Thus the necessity of maintaining the state by a draft army runs counter to the objective of protecting the freedom of personal action. The same is true of laws aimed at subversive activities. Tax laws may be regarded as opposed to the objective of permitting the owner to make free use of his property.

In some instances, the relation of protection of the state to other objectives is not clear. For example, when government imposes higher taxes to carry out governmental programs is it furthering trade or hindering it? To the extent that the higher tax rate diverts dollars from the market place to the government treasury or frightens people from expanding economic activity, the higher taxes may be regarded as retarding trade. To the extent that the higher taxes may reduce the amount of public purchasing and thus check inflation, the higher taxes may be regarded as preserving a sounder economic balance between supply and demand and thus furthering trade over the long term. It can also be argued that there is a short-term further-ing of trade in that the more government spends, the more somebody is selling to the government, and, in turn, the more such persons have to buy materials and pay for services.

These are matters that can neither be answered dogmatically nor tested scientifically. It is impossible to make a tax change and then, after a given time period, restore the tax law to its original form, turn back the economic clock, and let the economy take its course, thereafter making a comparison of the end results of the two methods. The laboratory-controlled repeated-experiment technique of science does not work in the field of human and economic relations. That is why we can only appreciate the social forces that make the law, but we cannot accurately evaluate them.

§ 6:2. Physical Existence of Government

The protection of the state can override what the individual would regard as basic freedom. Thus compulsory military service has been held valid as against the contention that it imposed involuntary servitude. In times of great emergency, the law approves the ignoring of safeguards that would otherwise be deemed essential.

UNITED STATES v. CALTEX

344 U.S. 149 (1952)

Caltex and other oil companies had terminal facilities in Manila harbor in the Philippine Islands at the outbreak of World War II. In order to prevent these facilities from falling into the control of the advancing enemy, the United States Army notified the oil companies that the facilities were requisitioned by the army and then demolished them. After the war, Caltex and the other companies sued the United States in the Court of Claims for compensation. From a decision in their favor, the United States appealed.

OPINION BY VINSON, C.J. . . .

United States v. *Pacific R. Co.,* 120 U.S. 227 (1887), . . . involved bridges which had been destroyed during the War Between the States by a retreating Northern Army to impede the advance of the Confederate Army. Though the point was not directly involved, the Court raised the question of whether this act constituted a compensable taking by the United States and answered it in the negative:

> The destruction or injury of private property in battle, or in the bombardment of cities and towns, and in many other ways in the war, had to be borne by the sufferers alone as one of its con-sequences. Whatever would embarrass or impede the advance of the

enemy, as the breaking up of roads, or the burning of bridges, or would cripple and defeat him, as destroying his means of subsistence, were lawfully ordered by the commanding general. Indeed, it was his imperative duty to direct their destruction. The necessities of the war called for and justified this. The safety of the state in such cases overrides all considerations of private loss.

. . . The common law had long recognized that in times of imminent peril—such as when fire threatened a whole community—the sovereign could, with immunity, destroy the property of a few that the property of many and the lives of many more could be saved. And what was said in the Pacific Railroad case was later made the basis for the holding in *Juraqua Iron Co.* v. *United States,* 212 U.S. 297 (1909), where recovery was denied to the owners of a factory which had been destroyed by American soldiers in the field in Cuba because it was thought that the structure housed the germs of a contagious disease.

Had the army hesitated, had the facilities only been destroyed after retreat, respondents would certainly have no claims to compensation. The Army did not hesitate. It is doubtful that any concern over the legal niceties of the situation entered into the decision to destroy the plants promptly while there was yet time to destroy them thoroughly. Nor do we think it legally significant that the destruction was effected prior to withdrawal. The short of the matter is that this property, due to the fortunes of war, had become a potential weapon of great significance to the invader. It was destroyed, not appropriated for subsequent use. It was destroyed that the United States might better and sooner destroy the enemy.

The terse language of the Fifth Amendment is no comprehensive promise that the United States will make whole all who suffer from every ravage and burden of war. This Court has long recognized that in wartime many losses must be attributed solely to the fortunes of war, and not to the sovereign. No rigid rules can be laid down to distinguish compensable losses from noncompensable losses. Each case must be judged on its own facts. But the general principles laid down in the Pacific Railroad case seem especially applicable here. Viewed realistically, then, the destruction of respondents' terminals by a trained team of engineers in the face of their impending seizure by the enemy was no different than the destruction of the bridges in the Pacific Railroad case. Adhering to the principles of that case, we conclude that the court below erred in holding that respondents have a constitutional right to compensation on the claims presented to this Court.

DISSENTING OPINION BY DOUGLAS, J., in which BLACK, J., concurs.

I have no doubt that the military had authority to select this particular property for destruction. But whatever the weight of authority may be, I believe that the Fifth Amendment requires compensation for the taking. The property was destroyed, not because it was in the nature of a public nuisance, but because its destruction was deemed necessary to help win the war. It was as clearly appropriated to that end as animals, food, and supplies requisitioned for the defense effort. As the Court says, the destruction of this property deprived the enemy of a valuable logistic weapon.

It seems to me that the guiding principle should be this: Whenever the Government determines that one person's property—whatever it may be—is essential to the war effort and appropriates it for the common good, the public purse, rather than the individual, should bear the loss. . . .

§ 6:3. Supremacy of Federal Laws

In the United States, in which there is both the national government and the government of the individual states, the social force of protecting government takes on the refinement of maintaining the supremacy of the federal law as against any contrary state law.

FREE v. BLAND

369 U.S. 663 (1962)

J. W. Free purchased several United States saving bonds, Series E and F, in the names of "Mr. or Mrs. Free." They were husband and wife and lived in Texas in which community property is recognized. Upon the death of Mrs. Free, the bonds were claimed by Mr. Free and by a son of Mrs. Free by a former marriage whose claim was based on the theory that since the bonds were purchased with community money, an interest in them passed upon the death of Mrs. Free to her estate and then to him as her son. From a judgment awarding the son the money value of a half interest in the bonds, Mr. Free appealed.

OPINION BY WARREN, C.J. . . .

Article 1, § 8, Clause 2 of the Constitution delegates to the Federal Government the power "to borrow money on the credit of the United States." Pursuant to this grant of power, the Congress authorized the Secretary of the Treasury, with the approval of the President, to issue savings bonds in such form and under such conditions as he may from time to time prescribe, subject to certain limitations not here material. . . . Exercising that authority, the Secretary of the Treasury issued savings bonds under regulations which provided . . . that the co-owner of a savings bond issued in the "or" form who survives the other co-owner "will be recognized as the sole and absolute owner" of the bond, . . . and that "no judicial determination will be recognized which would defeat or impair the rights of survivorship conferred by these regulations." . . . The Treasury has consistently maintained that the purpose of these regulations is to establish the right of survivorship regardless of local state law. . . .

The respondent, however, contends that the purpose of the regulations is simply to provide a convenient method of payment. This argument depends primarily on the distinction between stating that the surviving co-owner will "be recognized as" the sole owner and stating that the surviving co-owner will "be" the sole owner. This distinction is insubstantial. The clear purpose of the regulations is to confer the right of survivorship on the surviving co-owner. Thus, the survivorship provision is a federal law which must prevail if it conflicts with state law. . . .

The success of the management of the national debt depends to a significant measure upon the success of the sales of the savings bonds. The Treasury is authorized to make the bonds attractive to savers and investors. One of the inducements selected by the Treasury is the survivorship provision, a convenient method of avoiding complicated probate proceedings. Notwithstanding this provision, the State awarded full title to the co-owner but required him to account for half of the value of the bonds to the decedent's estate. Viewed realistically, the State has rendered the award of title meaningless. . . . If the State can frustrate the parties' attempt to use the bonds' survivorship provision through the simple expedient of requiring the survivor to reimburse the estate of the deceased co-owner as a matter of law, the State has interfered directly with a legitimate exercise of the power of the Federal Government to borrow money. . . .

We hold, therefore, that the state law which prohibits a married couple from taking advantage of the survivorship provisions of United States savings bonds merely because the purchase price is paid out of community property must fall under the Supremacy Clause. . . .

[Judgment reversed.]

§ 6:4.   Exclusion of State Action

The supremacy of federal law in some instances has the effect of excluding state action, that is, the federal government and it alone is the government which may regulate a given matter. In such situations, it is said that the federal power preempts the field in question.

LOCAL 24 v. OLIVER

358 U.S. 283 (1959)

Members of Local 24 owned their own trucks. They would hire out to drive their trucks as employees of various carriers. Through collective bargaining under the National Labor Management Relations Act, the union and the employing carriers had made an agreement, Article XXXII of which specified the "rental" to be paid by the employing carriers to each truck owner for his services in driving his truck for the carriers. Oliver, one of the truck-owning employees, sued in an Ohio state court to invalidate the rental provision of the agreement on the ground that the Ohio antitrust law made it illegal.

OPINION BY BRENNAN, J. . . .

The point of the Article is obviously not price-fixing but wages. The regulations embody . . . a direct frontal attack upon a problem thought to threaten the maintenance of the basic wage structure established by the collective bargaining contract. The inadequacy of a rental which means that the owner makes up his excess costs from his driver's wages not only clearly bears a close relation to labor's efforts to improve working conditions but is in fact of vital concern to the carrier's employed drivers; an inadequate rental might mean the progressive curtailment of jobs through withdrawal of more and more carrier-owned vehicles from service.

. . . We must decide whether Ohio's antitrust law may be applied to prevent the contracting parties from carrying out their agreement upon a subject matter as to which federal law directs them to bargain. Little extended discussion is necessary to show that Ohio law cannot be so applied. . . . The carriers as employers were under a duty to bargain collectively with the union as to the subject matter of the Article. . . .

The goal of federal labor policy, as expressed in the Wagner and Taft-Hartley Acts, is the promotion of collective bargaining; to encourage the employer and the representative of the employees to establish, through collective negotiation, their own charter for the ordering of industrial relations, and thereby to minimize industrial strife. . . . Within the area in which collective bargaining was required, Congress was not concerned with the substantive terms upon which the parties agreed. . . .

The purposes of the Acts are served by bringing the parties together and establishing conditions under which they are to work out their agreement themselves. To allow the application of the Ohio antitrust law here would wholly defeat the full realization of the congressional purpose. The application would frustrate the parties' solution of a problem which Congress has required them to negotiate in good faith toward solving, and in the solution of which it imposed no limitations relevant here. . . . We believe that there is no room in this scheme for the application here of this state policy limiting the solutions that the parties' agreement can provide to the problems of wages and working conditions. . . . Since the federal law operates here, in an area where its authority is paramount, to leave the parties free, the inconsistent application of state law is necessarily outside the power of the State. . . . Of course, the paramount force of the federal law remains even though it is expressed in the details of a contract federal law empowers the parties to make, rather than in terms of an enactment of Congress. . . . Clearly it is immaterial that the conflict is between federal labor law and the application of what the State characterizes as an antitrust law. ". . . Congress has sufficiently expressed its purpose to . . . exclude state prohibition, even though that with which the federal law is concerned as a matter of labor relations be related by the State to the more inclusive area of restraint of trade." . . .

We have not here a case of a collective bargaining agreement in conflict with a local health or safety regulation; the conflict here is between the federally sanctioned agreement and state policy which seeks specifically to adjust relationships in the world of commerce. If there is to be this sort of limitation on the arrangements that unions and employers may make with regard to these subjects, pursuant to the collective bargaining provisions of the Wagner and Taft-Hartley Acts, it is for Congress, not the States, to provide it.

Questions for Review

1. Define the social force of protection of the government.

2. Give illustrations of its application.

3. Analyze each opinion in this chapter in terms of the social forces involved in the decision. See § 5:5 for a list of the social forces. With respect to each opinion, explain why the prevailing social forces prevailed and why those rejected did not. In each case in which there is a dissenting opinion, also make this analysis for the dissenting opinion.

4-8. On the basis of the social forces involved, what decision should be made in each of the following cases?

4. *Self-incrimination. Public officer.* Perla, a city official, was questioned before a grand jury as to misconduct in office. He refused to answer certain questions on the ground that his answers might incriminate him. He was removed from his office for refusing to waive his immunity against self-incrimination, by virtue of a statute providing that any public officer refusing to waive immunity in such case should be removed from office. He claimed that the statute violated his constitutional rights. Was he correct? *New York* v. *Perla,* 21 N.Y.2d 608, 237 N.E.2d 215.

5. *Traffic control. Reviewability of city determination.* Drivers involved in an intersection collision sued the city on the theory that the city traffic lights had caused the collision because there was only a 4-second interval between the change of traffic flow, which it was claimed did not permit the "off" traffic to clear the intersection in time. The city showed that it had adopted the 4-second interval after extensive studies had been made. The drivers claimed that the court should direct the jury to consider whether the 4-second interval was reasonable or whether the city had been negligent. Were the drivers correct? *Weiss* v. *Fote,* 7 N.Y.2d 579, 200 N.Y.S.2d 409.

6. *False imprisonment. Police officers.* The defendant was arrested for maintaining over three dogs in her home without a kennel license. Upon her repeated failure to reduce the number of dogs or to obtain a kennel license, she was arrested. She later sued the police officers for false imprisonment on the ground that the kennel licensing ordinance was invalid. Was she entitled to recover damages? *Rosvall* v. *Provost,* Minn., 155 N.W.2d 900.

7. *War. Exclusion.* During World War II, United States citizens of Japanese extraction were excluded from the Pacific coast states even though their loyalty to the United States was beyond question. Was this military measure valid? *Korematsu* v. *United States,* 323 U.S. 214.

8. *Draft. Burning of card.* When O'Brien was prosecuted for burning his draft card, he raised the defense that the right to free speech gave him the privilege to express his disapproval of the draft and of the war in this manner. Was he correct? *United States* v. *O'Brien,* 391 U.S. 367.

9-13. What social forces were involved, which prevailed, and which were defeated in the following decisions?

9. **Limitation of liability. Adequate fire protection.** A clause limiting liability of city for failure to furnish "adequate" fire protection does not apply where city failed to provide any fire protection. *Shelby Mutual Insurance Co.* v. *Grand Rapids*, 6 Mich.App. 95, 148 N.W.2d 260.

10. **Highways. Underbrush.** Underbrush by side of road that obscured view did not constitute "defect in highway" within statutes permitting recovery of damages for such. *Stanley* v. *South Carolina State Highway Dept.*, 249 S.C. 230, 153 S.E.2d 687.

11. **Unclaimed property. What law governs?** The California Uniform Disposition of Unclaimed Property Act provided that where wages were unclaimed, the employer could pay the money into a state fund. The state of California brought an action against the Pacific Far East Line to compel it to pay unclaimed wages into the state fund. The steamship line raised the defense that as these were the wages of seamen and as the federal government had jurisdiction over the high seas, any state law was displaced and could not be applied. It was held the state law was not displaced. *California* v. *Pacific Far East Line*, Cal.App.2d, 68 Cal.Rptr. 67.

12. **Presumption. Validity.** A federal statute is constitutional which declares that where a person is found in the presence of an illegal still and has no reasonable explanation for his presence, the jury may conclude that he was guilty of the crime of illegally operating the still. *United States* v. *Gainey*, 380 U.S. 63.

13. **Contracts. Restitution.** A contract to restore what has been embezzled contains an implied contract to refrain from prosecuting for crime and is therefore invalid. *Gallaher Drug Co.* v. *Robinson*, 42 Ohio Ops.2d 347, 13 Ohio Misc. 216, 232 N.E.2d 668.

Chapter 7

PROTECTION OF PUBLIC WELFARE, SAFETY, AND MORALS

§ 7:1. Generally

The law seeks to protect the public welfare, safety, and morals in many ways. Laws relating to quarantine, food inspection, and compulsory vaccination are designed to protect the public health. Laws regulating the speed on the highway and those requiring fire escapes or guard devices around moving parts of factory machinery protect safety. Laws prohibiting the sale of liquor to minors and those prohibiting obscenity protect the morals of the public.

The objective here under consideration frequently is in harmony with other social objectives. Thus, the law against murder may be regarded as not only advancing public safety but also as preserving the state and protecting the person of those who without such law might be the victims. Laws aimed at public health may serve to protect you in the use of your property and protect you from oppression. Accordingly, the prohibition of your neighbor from opening a slaughterhouse on his land benefits you as an individual and as the owner of your house. There are, of course, negative aspects to the limitation on your neighbor; he is restricted in the free use of his property.

Furtherance of trade occupies a mixed position. Your land has greater market value and can be more readily sold because it has the protection against the neighboring slaughterhouse. To that extent, persons will be more willing to buy your land and trade is thereby furthered. But to the contrary, your neighbor's land is less attractive to a prospective buyer because he cannot make free use of it; and, to that extent, trade in your neighbor's land is hampered. The deciding factor in this situation is the *n* factor—the number of times that the situation is likely to occur. It is probable that more people will be seeking to buy your land for nonslaughterhouse purposes than will be seeking to buy your neighbor's land for slaughterhouse purposes. Therefore since everyone cannot win, less harm will be done by disappointing the seekers of slaughterhouses than the greater number of nonseekers of slaughterhouses.

The *n* factor is also important in determining whether your neighbor's free use of his property should prevail over your right to protection. While it is true that as stated it is merely one neighbor against another, it is clear that for every slaughterhouse there will be a larger number of neighbors affected. Thus the balance is seen to be the desire of one man to run his slaughterhouse as against the desires of a large number of neighbors who will be harmed if he does. Here the law follows the numbers and decides in favor of giving protection to the greater number rather than to permit free use by the one.

It is not to be thought from the foregoing that the courts base their conclusions on statistical data. Nevertheless, there are sufficient indications that frequency and probabilities are important factors in determining which of two equally logical choices should be made by the court. For the most part, the court's information as to frequencies and probabilities is not based on what would be regarded as accurate statistical data but is largely the judge's belief, right or wrong, as to what conditions exist. More frequently it will be the dissenting opinion that will use statistical data to prove that the rule of the majority of the court is not fitted to reality. This is seen frequently in cases involving criminal procedure where the majority opinion speaks in terms of abstract principles of protecting the accused from government oppression, while the dissenting opinion points out the impracticality of such abstractions when viewed in the light of statistical data showing the rate of crime increase, the percentage of repeating criminals and so on.

§ 7:2. Criminal Law

The social force here considered manifests itself in the field of criminal law, where particular conduct is punished because it is believed harmful to society to permit such conduct to exist or continue. Not only is the force seen in the fact that certain conduct is made criminal, but also the desire to obtain a conviction is frequently held to justify departures from basic procedures and attitudes. For example, if you were found in possession of counterfeit money or a narcotic, it is presumed that you know of its unlawful nature and had an unlawful intent. If you write out a bad check and do not make it good within 10 days, it is presumed that you intended to defraud.

It is true that you can disprove these presumptions and show that you are in fact innocent; but you, the defendant, will have the job of proving your innocence, just the reverse of the traditional approach that the prosecution has the burden of proving that you are guilty.

In some instances, the criminal law punishes even though the defendant did not know nor intend to commit any wrong. Thus the proprietor of a store or a barroom that makes an illegal sale to a minor is generally held criminally liable for the sale even though made by an employee, although the proprietor had acted in good faith and had no reason to believe that a sale was made to a minor, the employee had no reason to believe that the minor was under age, and the employer had in good faith given instructions that no sales be made to minors.

The desire of society to protect its members is further seen in laws making the use of the highways of the state an implied consent or agreement by the driver that he may be sued in the courts of that state. Such use may also be made an "implied consent" that a sample of the motorist's blood be taken from him to establish that he was intoxicated and introduced in evidence against him, even though he in fact objected thereto.

SCHMERBER v. CALIFORNIA

384 U.S. 757 (1966)

The defendant Schmerber was involved in a collision and was accused of driving while under the influence of intoxicating liquor. While in the hospital, a sample of his blood was taken by a physician under the direction of a police officer. This sample was taken without any search warrant and over the protest of the defendant and his attorney. He was later convicted of driving while intoxicated after a trial at which the result of the blood test was admitted in evidence over his objection. He appealed on the ground that his constitutional rights had been violated by taking such blood sample without his permission and then admitting it as evidence at his trial without his consent.

OPINION BY BRENNAN, J. . . .

[The defendant] contended that . . . the withdrawal of the blood and the admission of the analysis in evidence denied him due process of law under the Fourteenth Amendment, as well as specific guarantees of the Bill of Rights secured against the States by that Amendment; his privilege against self-incrimination under the Fifth Amendment; his right to counsel under the Sixth Amendment; and his right not to be subjected to unreasonable searches and seizures in violation of the Fourth Amendment. The Appellate Department of the California Superior Court rejected these contentions and affirmed the conviction. . . .

We hold that the privilege [against self-incrimination] protects an accused only from being compelled to testify against himself, or otherwise provide the State with evidence of a testimonial or communicative nature, and that the withdrawal of blood and use of the analysis in question in this case did not involve compulsion to these ends. . . .

The critical question, then, is whether petitioner was thus compelled "to be a witness against himself." . . .

In *Miranda* v. *Arizona,* 384 U.S. 436, 16 L.Ed. 694, 715, 86 S.Ct. 1602, 10 A.L.R.3d 974, the Court said of the interests protected by the privilege: "All these policies point to one overriding thought: the constitutional foundation underlying the privilege is the respect a government—state or federal—must accord to the dignity and integrity of its citizens. To maintain a 'fair state-individual balance,' to require the government 'to shoulder the entire load' . . . to respect the inviolability of the human personality, our accusatory system of criminal justice demands that the government seeking to punish an individual produce the evidence against him by its own independent labors, rather than by the cruel, simple expedient of compelling it from his own mouth." The withdrawal of blood necessarily involves puncturing the skin for extraction, and the percent by weight of alcohol in that blood, as established by chemical analysis, is evidence of criminal guilt. Compelled submission fails on one view to respect the "inviolability of the human personality." Moreover, since it enables the State to rely on evidence forced from the accused, the compulsion violates at least one meaning of the requirement that the State procure the evidence against an accused "by its own independent labors."

As the passage in Miranda implicitly recognizes, however, the privilege has never been given the full scope which the values it helps to protect suggest. History and a long line of authorities in lower courts have consistently limited its protection to situations in which the State seeks to submerge those values by obtaining the evidence against an accused through "the cruel, simple expedient of compelling it from his own mouth. . . . In sum, the privilege is fulfilled only when the person is guaranteed the right 'to remain silent unless he chooses to speak in the unfettered exercise of his own will.'" Ibid. The leading case in this Court is *Holt* v. *United States,* 218 U.S. 245, 54 L.Ed. 1021, 31 S.Ct. 2. There the question was whether evidence was admissible that the accused, prior to trial and over his protest, put on a blouse that fitted him. It was contended that compelling the accused to submit to the demand that he model the blouse violated the privilege. Mr. Justice Holmes, speaking for the Court, rejected the argument as "based upon an extravagant extension of the Fifth Amendment," and went on to say: "[T]he prohibition of compelling a man in a criminal court to be witness against himself is a prohibition of the use of physical or moral compulsion to extort communications from him, not an exclusion of his body as evidence when it may be material. The objection in principle would forbid a jury to look at a prisoner and compare his features with a photograph in proof." . . .

It is clear that the protection of the privilege reaches an accused's communications, whatever form they might take, and the compulsion of responses which are also communications, for example, compliance with a subpoena to produce one's papers. . . . On the other hand, both federal and state courts have usually held that it offers no protection against compulsion to submit to fingerprinting, photographing, or measurements, to write or speak for identification, to appear in court, to stand, to assume a stance, to walk, or to make a particular gesture. The distinction which has emerged, often expressed in different ways, is that the privilege is a bar against compelling "communications" or "testimony," but that compulsion which makes a suspect or accused the source of "real or physical evidence" does not violate it. . . .

In the present case, however, no . . . shadow of testimonial compulsion upon or enforced communication by the accused was involved either in the extraction or in the chemical analysis. Petitioner's testimonial capacities were in no way implicated; indeed, his participation, except as a donor, was irrelevant to the results of the test, which depend on chemical analysis and on that alone. Since the blood test evidence, although an incriminating product of compulsion, was neither petitioner's testimony nor evidence relating to some communicative act or writing by the petitioner, it was not inadmissible on privilege grounds. . . .

This conclusion also answers petitioner's claim that in compelling him to submit to the test in face of the fact that his objection was made on the advice of counsel, he was denied his Sixth Amendment right to the assistance of counsel. Since petitioner was not entitled to assert the privilege, he has no greater right because counsel erroneously advised him that he could assert it. His claim is strictly limited to the failure of the police to respect his wish, reinforced by counsel's advice, to be left inviolate. No issue of counsel's ability to assist petitioner in respect of any rights he did possess is presented. The limited claim thus made must be rejected. . . .

It was also contended that the chemical analysis should be excluded from evidence as the product of an unlawful search and seizure in violation of the Fourth and Fourteenth Amendments. . . .

The overriding function of the Fourth Amendment is to protect personal privacy and dignity against unwarranted intrusion by the State. . . . "[T]he security of one's privacy against arbitrary intrusion by the police" [is] "at the core of the Fourth Amendment" and "basic to a free society." . . .

The values protected by the Fourth Amendment thus substantially overlap those the Fifth Amendment helps to protect. History and precedent have required that we today reject the claim that the Self-Incrimination Clause of the Fifth Amendment requires the human body in all circumstances to be held inviolate against state expeditions seeking evidence of crime. But if compulsory administration of a blood test does not implicate the Fifth Amendment, it plainly involves the broadly conceived reach of a search and seizure under the Fourth Amendment. That Amendment expressly provides that "[t]he right of the people to be secure in their *persons,* houses, papers, and effects, against unreasonable searches and seizures, shall not be violated. . . ." (Emphasis added.) It could not reasonably be argued, and indeed respondent does not argue, that the administration of the blood test in this case was free of the constraints of the Fourth Amendment. Such testing procedures plainly constitute searches of "persons," and depend antecedently upon seizures of "persons," within the meaning of that Amendment. . . .

We begin with the assumption that once the privilege against self-incrimination has been found not to bar compelled intrusions into the body for blood to be analyzed for alcohol content, the Fourth Amendment's proper function is to constrain, not against all intrusions as such, but against intrusions which are not justified in the circumstances, or which are made in an improper manner. In other words, the questions we must decide in this case are whether the police were justified in requiring petitioner to submit to the blood test, and whether the means and procedures employed in taking his blood respected relevant Fourth Amendment standards of reasonableness.

In this case, as will often be true when charges of driving under the influence of alcohol are pressed, these questions arise in the context of an arrest made by an officer without a warrant. Here, there was plainly probable cause for the officer to arrest petitioner and charge him with driving an automobile while under the influence of intoxicating liquor. The police officer who arrived at the scene shortly after the accident smelled liquor on petitioner's breath, and testified that petitioner's eyes were "bloodshot, watery, sort of a glassy appearance." The officer saw petitioner again at the hospital, within two hours of the accident. There he noticed similar symptoms of drunkenness. He thereupon informed petitioner "that he was under arrest and that he was entitled to the services of an attorney, and that he could remain silent, and that anything that he told me would be used against him in evidence." . . .

Although the facts which established probable cause to arrest in this case also suggested the required relevance and likely success of a test of petitioner's blood for alcohol, the question remains whether the arresting officer was permitted to draw these inferences himself, or was required instead to procure a warrant before proceeding with the test. Search warrants are ordinarily required for searches of dwellings, and, absent an emergency, no less could be required where intrusions into the human body are concerned. The requirement that a warrant be obtained is a requirement that the inferences to support the search "be drawn by a neutral and detached magistrate instead of being judged by the officer engaged in the often competitive enterprise of ferreting out crime." . . . The importance of informed, detached and deliberate determinations of the issue whether or not to invade another's body in search of evidence of guilt is indisputable and great.

The officer in the present case, however, might reasonably have believed that he was confronted with an emergency, in which the delay necessary to obtain a warrant, under the circumstances, threatened "the destruction of evidence." . . . We are told that the percentage of alcohol in the blood begins to diminish shortly after drinking stops, as the body functions to eliminate it from the system. Particularly in a case such as this, where time had to be taken to bring the accused to a hospital and to investigate the scene of the accident, there was no time to seek out a magistrate and secure a warrant. Given these special facts, we conclude that the attempt to secure evidence of blood-alcohol content in this case was an appropriate incident to petitioner's arrest.

Similarly, we are satisfied that the test chosen to measure petitioner's blood-alcohol level was a reasonable one. Extraction of blood samples for testing is a highly effective means of determining the degree to which a person is under the influence of alcohol. . . . Such tests are a commonplace in these days of periodic physical examinations and experience with them teaches that the quantity of blood extracted is minimal, and that for most people the procedure involves virtually no risk, trauma, or pain. Petitioner is not one of the few who on grounds of fear, concern for health, or religious scruple might prefer some other means of testing, such as the "breathalyzer" test petitioner refused. . . . We need not decide whether such wishes would have to be respected.

Finally, the record shows that the test was performed in a reasonable manner. Petitioner's blood was taken by a physician in a hospital environment according to accepted medical practices. We are thus not presented with the serious questions which would arise if a search involving use of medical technique, even of the most rudimentary sort, were made by other than a medical environment—for example, if it were administered by police in the privacy of the stationhouse. To tolerate searches under these conditions might be to invite an unjustified element of personal risk of infection and pain.

We thus conclude that the present record shows no violation of petitioner's right under the Fourth and Fourteenth Amendments to be free of unreasonable searches and seizures. It bears repeating, however, that we reach this judgment only on the facts of the present record. The integrity of an individual's person is a cherished value of our society. That we today hold that the Constitution does not forbid the State's minor intrusions into an individual's body under stringently limited conditions in no way indicates that it permits more substantial intrusions, or intrusions under other conditions.

DISSENTING OPINION BY BLACK, J., in which DOUGLAS, J., concurs. . . .

To reach the conclusion that compelling a person to give his blood to help the State convict him is not equivalent to compelling him to be a witness against himself strikes me as quite an extraordinary feat. The Court, however, overcomes what had seemed to me to be an insuperable obstacle to its conclusion by holding that ". . . the privilege protects an accused only from being compelled to testify against himself, or otherwise provide the State with evidence of a testimonial or communicative nature, and that the withdrawal of blood and use of the analysis in question in this case did not involve compulsion to these ends." . . .

I cannot agree that this distinction and reasoning of the Court justify denying petitioner his Bill of Rights' guarantee that he must not be compelled to be a witness against himself.

In the first place it seems to me that the compulsory extraction of petitioner's blood for analysis so that the person who analyzed it could give evidence to convict him had both a "testimonial" and a "communicative nature." The sole purpose of this project, which proved to be successful, was to obtain "testimony" from some person to prove that petitioner had alcohol in his blood at the time he was arrested. And the purpose of the project was certainly "communicative" in that the analysis of the blood was to supply information to enable a witness to communicate to the court and jury that petitioner was more or less drunk. . . .

It is a strange hierarchy of values that allows the State to extract a human being's blood to convict him of a crime because of the blood's content but proscribes compelled production of his lifeless papers. Certainly there could be few papers that would have any more "testimonial" value to convict a man of drunken driving than would an analysis of the alcoholic content of a human being's blood introduced in evidence at a trial for driving while under the influence of alcohol. In such a situation blood, of course, is not oral testimony given by an accused but it can certainly "communicate" to a court and jury the fact of guilt. . . .

How can it reasonably be doubted that the blood test evidence was not in all respects the actual equivalent of "testimony" taken from petitioner when the result of the test was offered as testimony, was considered by the jury as testimony, and the jury's verdict of guilt rests in part on that testimony? The refined, subtle reasoning and balancing process used here to narrow the scope of the Bill of Rights' safeguard against self-incrimination provides a handy instrument for further narrowing of that constitutional protection, as well as others, in the future. Believing with the Framers that these constitutional safeguards broadly construed by independent tribunals of justice provide our best hope for keeping our people free from governmental oppression, I deeply regret the Court's holding. . . .

DISSENTING OPINION BY DOUGLAS, J. . . .

We are dealing with the right of privacy which, . . . we have held to be within the penumbra of some specific guarantees of the Bill of Rights. . . . Thus, the Fifth Amendment marks "a zone of privacy" which the Government may not force a person to surrender. . . . Likewise the Fourth Amendment recognizes that right when it guarantees the right of the people to be secure "in their persons." No clearer invasion of this right of privacy can be imagined than forcible blood-letting of the kind involved here.

DISSENTING OPINION BY FORTAS, J. . . .

I would reverse. In my view, petitioner's privilege against self-incrimination applies. I would add that, under the Due Process Clause, the State, in its role as prosecutor, has no right to extract blood from an accused or anyone else, over his protest. As prosecutor, the State has no right to commit any kind of violence upon the person, or to utilize the results of such a tort, and the extraction of blood, over protest, is an act of violence. . . .

§ 7:3. Economic Planning and Development

Although the law respects private property, your property may be taken from you for the public good. It is true that the government must compensate you when it takes your property. However, in many instances the sum of money awarded the property owner is in fact not equivalent to what he has lost because the owner has the problem of reinvesting his money or relocating his home or business.

This taking of land for a public purpose is called eminent domain. It may exist for a wide range of taking of property, as for highways, low cost housing projects, and government buildings. The governmental authorities earlier discussed, § 2:2, generally have the power to take land by eminent domain. In some instances, the criticism has been made that the authorities have unnecessarily taken more land than they needed so that they could sell off the surplus to business and political friends.

RABINOFF v. DISTRICT COURT

145 Colo. 225, 360 P.2d 114 (1961)

Rabinoff and others filed a petition to stop a proceeding in the district court under the Colorado Urban Renewal Act. This statute authorized a local agency or Authority to condemn large areas of land as slum or blighted, to demolish the buildings thereon, and then to resell the land to private persons, who could utilize the property as their own, subject to certain building and improvement restrictions. The petitioners, who owned homes and businesses in the area affected, claimed that the Act was unconstitutional on the ground that their property was being taken for a private and not a public purpose.

OPINION BY DOYLE, J. . . .

The parties agree that the properties in question are not slums in the sense that the entire area is in disrepair or deterioration. On the other hand, it would appear . . . that the area poses a future hazard to the health and welfare of the community. Some allegedly do not comply with the Denver Health and Safety Ordinances, while others are conceded to be in full compliance with these ordinances. . . .

The petitioners argue that the act in question is devoid of public purpose and public use; that by authorizing the taking of private property, the demolishing of buildings thereon, the reselling to private persons with restrictions, it is not a public use as contemplated by the Colorado Constitution. It is said that this is a giant private real estate development designed to take private property from one group of individuals for the purpose only of vesting it in a different group. The present efforts are compared to the sequestration of property by Henry VIII. On this it is said:

"It is strange to find abhorred historic parallels reenacted in our own polity, without even being recognized. No difference obtains at all between the policy whereby in Medieval and Renaissance periods lands were redistributed or sequestered for the benefit of those who enjoyed state favor at the moment, and this procedure, whereby the lands of the many are taken deliberately to be redistributed to and agglomerated in the hands of the few, because the uses as so agglomerated concur more completely with the notions of the supra-governmental 'planners' as to what is good for the community." . . .

The narrow inquiry . . . is whether the power of eminent domain can be exercised in circumstances such as the present, wherein the public authority does not intend to permanently retain the property which it proposes to condemn. We do not consider the actual use by the public after the taking to be the appropriate test as to whether or not the use is a public one. The main object of this legislation is to eliminate slum and blighted areas. . . .

The acquisition and transfer to private parties is a mere incident of the chief purpose of the act which is rehabilitation of the area. . . .

The fact that when the redevelopment is achieved, the properties are sold to private individuals for the purpose of development does not rob the taking of its public purpose. . . .

The high courts of 26 states have upheld such statutes. On the other hand, a decision of unconstitutionality has been reached in only two states, Florida and South Carolina. . . .

Does the fact that the buildings here in question are not in an extremely dilapidated condition render the statute inapplicable or its application invalid?

The definitions of slum and blighted areas contained in . . . the act are sufficiently broad to include the Avondale area. A slum area is one which by reason of dilapidation, deterioration, age, obsolescence, insufficient light, air, sanitation, or overcrowding [creates] a fire hazard or [constitutes] a menace to the health, safety, morals or welfare of the community. A blighted area is somewhat more broadly defined as one which by reason of a substantial number of slum *deteriorated* or *deteriorating* structures or by reason of inadequate street layout endangers life or property, retards the growth of the community, constitutes a social or economic liability, etc.

In view of the scope of these definitions, it is not essential that the properties affected shall be in a state of disrepair calling for condemnation as nuisances. The cases which have considered the present issue point out that the approach to urban redevelopment cannot be on a structure to structure basis, inconsistent with its basic objectives. . . . There is a strict viewpoint in some of the cases that the area must be one which has deteriorated rather than one which is in the process of deteriorating. Most of the decisions, however, take a more liberal view and hold that the authority is not powerless to prevent deterioration. . . .

[Petition dismissed.]

CONCURRING OPINION OF McWILLIAMS, J. . . .

DISSENTING OPINION BY HALL, C.J. . . . and MOORE and FRANTZ, JJ. . . .

DISSENTING OPINION BY MOORE, J. . . .

I am primarily interested in the protection of constitutional limitations upon the power of any man, or group of men, to govern the people. This involves the preservation of individual freedom of action, and individual liberty, of which we talk so much and concerning which we do so little. With every passing year, by judicial opinions of the kind to which I now dissent, we nibble upon and whittle away the freedoms of the people; subjecting them more and more to unreasonable restraints, compelling compliance with governmental commands which are far in excess of any powers constitutionally authorized.

On March 4, 1939 . . . the then Chief Justice of the Supreme Court, Charles Evans Hughes, said, concerning the purpose of the constitution: "We protect the fundamental rights of minorities, in order to save democratic government from destroying itself by the excesses of its own power. The firmest ground for confidence in the future is that more than ever we realize that, while democracy must have its organization and controls, *its vital breath is individual liberty."*

Under the act being considered the Urban Renewal Authority is given discretionary power of the most fantastic nature which could be exercised in a most arbitrary manner—to acquire *without the consent of the owner* the private property of untold thousands of citizens. And this may be accomplished notwithstanding that the "contemplated use" to be made of the property completely excludes the public, and on the contrary involves a private use and development of a kind to be bargained for, said *use* to be carried on for private profit! Vast amounts of public funds are to be expended in forcing unwilling owners of real estate to convey their property even though such property in no way whatever threatens the public health, safety, or morals. The Urban Renewal Authority then conveys the property to private interests who undertake to create an atmosphere in the area purchased which is more to the liking of those who occupy the seats of power in the new dictator agency. These private interests, introducing new, or continuing the old private uses, anticipate a profit. Thus the state plunges into the business of underwriting and financing private transactions in real estate and land development as a partner of those who speculate in real estate ventures, and in land development for profit.

If the . . . provisions of the constitution are impotent to prevent this socialistic plunge by the state into financial partnership with specially selected real estate promoters and developers of subdivisions who thereby acquire privately owned property without the consent of the owners, with the avowed purpose of putting to private uses for profit, then the constitution is dead insofar as it purports to assure the citizens that they have the "inalienable" right "of acquiring, possessing and protecting property." If countless thousands of property owners in practically any section of the city which happened to be conveniently "old" can thus be compelled to surrender their property to new purchasers for uses strictly private, we should discontinue the pretense that individual freedom of choice in matters pertaining to property has any constitutional protection against a tyrannical exercise of governmental power. If, as the majority opinion holds, the constitution is impotent in the instant situation, then there is no point at which extreme encroachments upon rights guaranteed by the constitution can be stopped, since no grandiose multimillion dollar project can be conceived which would not carry with it some incidental or colorable public purpose. . . .

FRANTZ, J. concurs in the views hereinabove expressed.

HALL, C.J. . . . joins in the dissent of MOORE, J.

DISSENTING OPINION BY FRANTZ, J. . . .

Those in this court who deem the law consonant with the Constitution of this state and those who believe it sets the authority of this fundamental document at naught are equally in favor of progress and advancement. Our differences arise from considerations of the general good as opposed to those of the individual as they are expounded and made the subjects of rights and duties in the Constitution. The collision of doctrinal thought involves the primacy of the majority and the subordination of the individual, and, as in this case in some of its phases, a minority. . . .

Vindication for the Urban Renewal Law is expressly found in the police power. But police power cannot be exercised in respect to unoffending property. . . .

Lawful, harmless properties may not be destroyed under a police power measure because located in an area containing properties which may be so treated, or nestled between such properties as are or may be proper subjects for exerting the police power. What becomes of the natural, essential, and inalienable right to acquire, possess, and protect property if lawful, harmless buildings and improvements can be razed because so located? Lawful, harmless structures are the proper subjects of acquisition, possession, and protection. To hold otherwise would render empty and meaningless declarations of rights in the Constitution which have been considered precious to and inherent in man.

There are other disturbing elements in this case which provoke comment in view of the right of persons, regardless of their station in life, to acquire, possess, and protect property inoffensive from the standpoint of health, safety, morals, and welfare of the public. How are the great masses of the people to realize their aspirations of acquiring and possessing property, pursuing happiness, and enjoying life and liberty unless they are permitted to acquire and hold property, however humble in character? Are persons in extremely humble circumstances to be denied the opportunity to acquire and possess a home? . . .

And where do the persons of meager means in the area involved go if this project becomes reality? Probably they can do no better than seek the equivalent of that which they presently have. In all probability that means the removal to an area having the same characteristics as the one from which they are evicted. Continuing with probabilities, they would eventually face the same fate that will befall them in this case. An alternative would be to become renters, for it is not likely that they can afford homes of better quality. Thus, their constitutional right to acquire and possess property becomes a mirage—expressed in ghostly words with only a semblance of substance. . . .

"There is a proneness to regard constitutions as instruments of boundless accommodation, taking on so many shapes as in truth to be shapeless . . . That their generalities make for living documents covering changes in a developing society, no one will deny; but there are 'no trespass' signs in these constitutions effective against encroachment by the executive, legislative and judicial departments in certain areas, and among these areas are the natural rights of man enumerated in the Bill of Rights." . . .

§ 7:4. Highway Safety

The state has a substantial interest in the protection of safety on the highway. Here the power of the state rests on two foundations: (a) the state's ownership of the highway, and (b) the state's interest in protecting its citizenry. In cases involving safety, the first ground is generally ignored by the courts; that ground having prominence only when the question raised is whether the state can impose licensing requirements and taxes, make the user of the highways the equivalent of appointing an agent to accept service of process in a lawsuit, or as constituting consent to submit to tests for intoxication. When the question is safety, it is the latter ground which is emphasized.

PEOPLE v. CARMICHAEL

56 Misc.2d 289, 288 N.Y.S.2d 931 (1968)

Carmichael was prosecuted for riding a motorcycle without wearing a protective helmet as required by statute. He claimed that the statute was unconstitutional.

OPINION BY MORTON, J. . . .

A determination of the validity of the instant statute depends largely on the ability of the state to regulate the proscribed conduct under its so-called police power. The police power of the state is a basic right inherent in all civilized government . . . and is loosely defined as the means by which the legislature exercises a supervision over matters involving the common welfare, and enforces the observance, by each individual member of society, of the duties which he owes to others and to the community at large. . . .

The instant subdivision (together with four others also relating to motorcycles) was enacted at the request of the Department of Motor Vehicles following an extensive study by a special committee appointed by the Commissioner. . . . The Departmental Memorandum to the Legislature . . . citing the results of this study, stated that "The number of accidents involving motorcycles is increasing rapidly. In fact, motorcycle accidents increased by 105 percent in 1965 as compared to 1964, while the total registration of these vehicles increased by 83 percent. Fatalities increased by 63.6 percent and personal injury accidents by 100 percent. A summary of the Department statistics indicates that 89.2 percent of the motorcycle accidents result in injury or death and that almost all fatalities occurring as a result of such accidents involve head injuries. Most of these fatalities could have been avoided, or the severity lessened, by the use of a proper helmet." In recommending the proposed legislation, the department further related that such ". . . should go far in protecting the drivers and passengers on motorcycles."

The purposes for which the police power may be validly exercised are varied and include matters which affect the general welfare of the people . . . together with areas covering public health and safety. . . . The extent of this concern is substantial, and in construing Sunday Labor Laws, it has been held that ". . . it is to the interest of the state to have strong, robust, healthy citizens, capable of self-support, of bearing arms, and of adding to the resources of the country." . . .

It is apparent that the challenged legislation requiring the wearing of a protective helmet for self-protection is a valid purpose of legislative action under the police power of the state. Indeed, the inherent danger of operating a motorcycle, not only to the driver but to other users of the highway, has likewise been considered in upholding the validity of this statute as a valid objective of the state's police power. . . .

The legislature may enact laws prohibiting that which is harmful to the welfare of the people, even though such interferes with the liberty of the individual, so long as it is reasonable. . . . While concededly the instant legislation may infringe on the rights of the individual, it is equally apparent that such is incidental to a valid exercise of the police power and is not unreasonable. When the sole object and general tendency of legislation is to promote public welfare, there is no invasion of the Constitution even if enforcement of the law interferes to some extent with liberty or property. . . .

A Michigan statute requiring the wearing of crash helmets by motorcyclists and their passengers was held unconstitutional in *American Motorcycle Association* v. *Davids,* Mich.App., 158 N.W.2d 72 (1968), the court stating: . . .

It is contended by the plaintiffs that the legislative concern is solely related to the safety of the motorcyclist and passenger and can have no possible relationship to the safety and well-being of other persons, much less the public at large. Based on the premise that the individual in our society is still master of his fate and captain of his soul, plaintiffs cite the following maxim:

"The maxims are, first, that the individual is not accountable to society for his actions, insofar as these concern the interests of no person but himself." John Stuart Mill, Utilitarianism, Liberty and Representative Government, E. P. Dutton & Co. Inc. (1950 ed., p. 201). . . .

Does a direct relationship to the public, health, safety and welfare exist in the present case? . . .

The Attorney General . . . contends that the State has an interest in the "viability" of its citizens and can legislate to keep them healthy and self-supporting. This logic could lead to unlimited paternalism. A further contention pertains to the doctrine of *parens patriae,* the special relationship of the State to youth, but this has little merit since the statute is not so limited.

There can be no doubt that the State has a substantial interest in highway safety, . . . but the difficulty with adopting this as a basis for decision is that it would also justify a requirement that automobile drivers wear helmets or buckle their seat belts for their own protection!

These arguments all prove too much. . . .

This statute has a relationship to the protection of the individual motorcyclist from himself but not to the public health, safety and welfare. . . .

Questions for Review

1. Define the social force of protection of public welfare, safety, and morals.

2. Give illustrations of its application.

3. Analyze each opinion in this chapter in terms of the social forces involved in the decision. See § 5:5 for a list of the social forces. With respect to each opinion, explain why the prevailing social forces prevailed and why those rejected did not. In each case in which there is a dissenting opinion, also make this analysis for the dissenting opinion.

4-8. On the basis of the social forces involved, what decision should be made in each of the following cases?

4. *Fluoridation of water. Validity.* The City of Columbia provided for the fluoridation of the city water supply. Hall claimed that this deprived him of his constitutional right to drink unfluoridated water since there was no other water supply, and further attacked the validity of the plan on the ground that dental cavities are not contagious and therefore a public health problem did not exist. Was he correct? *Hall* v. *Bates, Mayor of Columbia,* S.C., 148 S.E.2d 345.

5. *Automobiles. Parking.* Does a statute imposing liability for "negligent operation" of motor vehicles apply to negligent parking on highway? *Hakes* v. *Paul,* 34 Wis.2d 209, 148 N.W.2d 699.

6. *Bicycles. Vehicle.* Is a bicycle a "vehicle" within the meaning of statutes governing the use of the highways? *Sacca* v. *Marshall,* 180 Neb. 855, 146 N.W.2d 375.

7. *Schools. Discipline.* May a state university require adult behavior of students on and off campus and suspend students repeatedly speeding? *Cornette* v. *Aldridge,* Tex.Civ.App., 408 S.W.2d 935.

8. *Swimming pool. Government regulation.* Is a country club swimming pool restricted to members and their families a "public swimming pool" within the meaning of government regulations fixing the standards for such pools? *Lucas* v. *Hesperia Golf & Country Club,* Cal.App.2d, 63 Cal.Rptr. 189.

9-13. What social forces were involved, which prevailed, and which were defeated in the following decisions?

9. *Lottery. Giveaway program.* Promotion drawing for prizes by store was not a lottery, although to participate it was necessary to obtain a free card and to be in the store at the time of the drawing; since the procurement of such card or being in the store was not consideration and therefore there was not consideration essential to a lottery. *People* v. *Brundage,* 7 Mich.App. 364, 150 N.W.2d 825.

10. *Automobiles. Excessive speed.* Speed may be excessive although under the speed limit. *Gustin* v. *Johannes,* 36 Wis.2d 195, 153 N.W.2d 70.

11. *Negligence. Insanity.* The fact that a motorist is mentally ill, deficient, or insane, does not excuse him from civil liability for failing to comply with the assured-clear-distance-ahead provision of the motor vehicle code. *Kuhn* v. *Zabotsky*, 9 Ohio2d 129, 224 N.E.2d 137.

12. *Malicious prosecution. Wrong identification.* A bank teller and his bank are not liable for malicious prosecution when the teller in response to police inquiry mistakenly but innocently identifies the plaintiff as the person passing bad checks, and the teller thereafter testifies thereto under subpoena. *Yianitsas* v. *Mercantile National Bank*, Tex.Civ.App., 410 S.W.2d 848.

13. *What law governs. Statute "in this state."* New York statute imputing a bailee's negligence to the bailor of the automobile may apply to a foreign death where the most significant contacts were with New York, on theory that statute establishing rule of imputation, in speaking of "in this state," was merely broadening terms of former statute which referred to "upon a public highway" and not as intentionally excluding application of statute from a foreign death claim. *Farber* v. *Smolack*, 20 N.Y.2d 198, 282 N.Y.S.2d 248.

Chapter 8

FURTHERANCE OF GOOD FAITH AND BUSINESS ETHICS

§ 8:1. Generally

It is apparent that any legal society will provide for liability for disloyalty, such as treason in the case of disloyalty to the government, or breach of duty by an agent or trustee, as when he makes a secret profit for himself at the expense of the principal or employer. In the complexity of modern life, there are situations where the agent or trustee can obtain personal advantage without actually harming the principal or employer. The tendency of the law is to condemn such conduct, partly to discourage conduct that could easily slide over into situations which would cause harm, and partly out of practical expediency to avoid long litigation over whether certain acts of the agent did or did not cause harm to the principal or employer.

§ 8:2. Agents

An agent must be loyal or faithful to his principal. He must not obtain any secret profit or advantage from his relationship. To illustrate, if an agent knows that his employer is negotiating for a lease and secretly obtains the lease for himself, the court will compel the agent to surrender the lease to the principal. Likewise, an agent cannot purchase property of the principal which the agent was employed to sell, without the principal's express consent. Similarly, an agent's wife cannot purchase in her own name property of the principal which the agent was hired to sell.

If the agent owns property, he cannot purchase it from himself on behalf of his principal without disclosing to the principal his interest in the transaction. If he fails to disclose his interest, the principal may avoid the transaction even if he was not financially harmed by the agent's conduct. Or the principal can approve the transaction and sue the agent for any profit realized by the agent.

An agent cannot act as agent for both parties to a transaction unless both know of the dual capacity and agree to it. If he does so act without the consent of both parties, the transaction is voidable at the election of any principal who did not know of the agent's status.

An agent must not accept secret gifts or commissions from third persons in connection with his activities as agent. If he does, the principal may sue him for those gifts or commissions. It is immaterial whether the principal can show that he was harmed. Such practices are condemned because the judgment of the agent may be influenced by the receipt of gifts or commissions. A principal may also recover from his agent any secret profit that he has made in violation of his duty of loyalty to his principal.

An agent is, of course, prohibited from aiding the competitors of his principal or disclosing to them information relating to the business of the principal. It is also a breach of duty for the agent to deceive the principal with false information.

The social forces underlying the above rules are readily recognizable. An agent should not be permitted to exploit his position at the expense of his principal. The device of employing agents is an essential part of a modern economy and therefore it would hinder trade if the device were not made as "fraud proof" as possible. To the extent that the misconduct of an agent would deprive the principal of property, the concept of loyalty protects property of the principal. Practical expediency is involved in the rule that the principal is not required to prove that a disloyal practice of an agent caused harm. In many instances, it would be difficult or impossible to prove that the practice of the agent was harmful to the employer. If the agent were permitted to raise the defense that the principal was not harmed, the dishonest agent would be encouraged to take the risk of being disloyal because he might be able to convince the jury that no harm was actually caused by his misconduct. Practical expediency is also seen in the procedural sense that virtually every lawsuit of a principal against an agent would be prolonged by the agent's making the contention that what he had done had not actually harmed the principal. In the interest of getting through with a trial as swiftly as possible, to avoid delaying the trial docket, expediency urges that the number of open issues be reduced to a minimum.

SAMS v. RIGG

339 Ill.App. 25, 88 N.E.2d 673 (1949)

Sams employed Rigg, a broker, to sell real estate owned by him. Rigg sold the property, but he told Sams that it was sold for a smaller amount than was actually paid. When Sams learned that he had not been paid the full purchase price, he sued Rigg to recover (1) the difference between the actual price and the amount paid him and (2) the commissions which the broker had deducted as his compensation. From a judgment for the plaintiff, the defendant appealed.

OPINION BY O'CONNOR, J. . . .

"The relation of principal and agent is one of trust and confidence; and where such confidence is reposed and such relation exists, it must be faithfully acted upon and preserved from any intermixture of imposition. The rule is the same no matter how large or how small the commission paid may be or whether the agent is a mere volunteer at a nominal consideration. . . . An agent acting for the purchaser of land, whether by appointment or as a volunteer, must see that he meets fairly and squarely the responsibility of his position and does not take any advantage, either for his own gain or to the injury of the person whom he represents. . . . The rule is well established in equity that the relation existing between principal and agent for the purchase or sale of property is a fiduciary one; and the agent, in the exercise of good faith, is bound to keep his principal informed on all matters that may come to his knowledge pertaining to the subject matter of the agency. . . . An agent must not put himself, during the continuance of his agency, in a position adverse to that of his principal. To the latter belongs the exercise of all the skill, ability, and industry of the agent." . . .

Applying the foregoing rules to the facts in this case, we must necessarily say that this case presents a state of facts clearly showing that the appellant [Rigg] here did not act in good faith. He did not disclose to his principal all matters coming to his attention or knowledge during the course of the transaction which pertained to the subject matter of the agency. He did not disclose the price the ultimate purchaser paid for the property. On the contrary, he furnished to the appellee [Sams] a statement showing that the purchase price was $1,500, which was less by $300 than the price actually received. He charged $1.65 for revenue stamps, which indicated and represented that the purchase price was $1,500 and not the real purchase price. We can conceive of no more flagrant violation of a duty to disclose all facts and circumstances which falls upon an agent in dealing with his principal. . . .

An agent cannot take any advantage of his position to speculate to the injury of his principal, and all profits and advantages gained in the transaction of the agent belong to the principal. . . . Under the relation of the parties, here appellee had a right to all the benefits and advantages of the transaction, being the sum of $300 not accounted for. . . .

Appellant further contends that he is entitled to the sum of $75 commission, which he claims to have earned as a 5 percent commission on a sale price of $1,500. . . .

"An agent is entitled to compensation only on a due and faithful performance of all his duties to his principal. . . . In the application of this rule, it makes no difference whether the result of the agent's conduct is injurious to the principal or not, as the misconduct of the agent affects the contract from considerations of public policy rather than of injury to the principal." . . .

The conduct of the appellant was of such a character as to deprive him of the $300 profit made by him at the expense of his principal and the claim for $75 as compensation for services rendered by him to the appellee. . . .

[Judgment for plaintiff affirmed.]

§ 8:3.   Corporate Officers and Directors

The officers and directors of a corporation are in a sense the agents of the corporation and are subject to many of the duties of agents, including that of loyalty. In the case of such officers and directors, the concept of loyalty is carried beyond prohibiting actual disloyalty, to the point of prohibiting them from taking advantage of a corporate opportunity. Thus if there is an opportunity to acquire property or some interest, which they should realize the corporation would want to acquire for itself, it is improper for the directors or officers to step in and acquire that interest for themselves unless it is clear that the corporation is financially unable or is unwilling to acquire the interest for itself.

DIAMOND v. OREAMUNO

29 App.Div.2d 285, 287 N.Y.S.2d 300 (1968)

Diamond was a shareholder of Management Assistants Inc. (MAI), a New York corporation. Diamond sued Oreamuno and another director of the corporation, Gonzalez, on behalf of all shareholders to recover from them an alleged secret profit, which they had made. It was shown that the defendant directors had sold their stock in the corporation before the report of the lower earnings of the corporation was made public. They thus sold their stock at $23.75 a share. After the earnings report was released the stock fell to $11 a share. It was claimed by the plaintiff that this difference between the two prices should be paid by the directors to the corporation. The corporation had not lost any money in consequence of the transactions.

OPINION BY BOTEIN, P.J. . . .

According to the complaint, Oreamuno and Gonzalez are respectively the chairman of the board of directors and the president of MAI, and with their wives own almost 14 percent of MAI's common stock. By the end of August, 1966, it became apparent to Oreamuno and Gonzalez, "solely by virtue of their position as MAI's chief executive and operating officers," that the corporate earnings would be sharply reduced from both the July, 1966, and the August, 1965, figures. This information did not become known to the shareholders of MAI or the investing public until October 18, 1966, when MAI published its August, 1966, operating results. They showed that MAI earned $66,233 in August, 1966, as compared with $262,253 in July, 1966, and $114,048 in August, 1965. Before such publication, and in September, 1966, Oreamuno sold 28,500 shares of MAI's common stock, and Gonzalez 28,000 shares. The complaint does not state who bought the shares. Plaintiff concededly bought none and does not charge that MAI bought any. Whether the purchasers were or were not existing stockholders we regard as irrelevant to the controlling issue. . . .

Defendants . . . take the following flat position: "A corporation does not have a cause of action against a director who sells his own stock in the corporation to a third person relying upon information known by him by virtue of his office but not disclosed publicly. Whether or not the insider is liable to the purchaser of such stock, there is no liability to the corporation which sustained no loss." They add: "There was no diversion of any corporate or business opportunity; the corporation was not planning to sell any stock; there was no waste or diversion of a corporate asset; and there was no damage to the corporation's business, credit or reputation. The sale did not affect the control of the corporation."

We think defendants' position neglects an established principle of agency. "A corporation aggregate can only act by agents. Its trustees or directors are its agents for managing its affairs." . . . The information Oreamuno and Gonzalez acquired pertained to, and they obtained it in the course of managing, the affairs of MAI, their principal. To it their relation was "essentially that of trustee and *cestui que trust*" . . . and "the responsibility of the fiduciary is not limited to a proper regard for the tangible balance sheet assets of the corporation." . . . What they acquired, and its avails if they exploited it, they were bound to hold for the benefit of MAI. . . . This would hardly be questioned if for a consideration they had disclosed such confidential information to a trader in securities, nor would it be suggested that their principal, though deprived of the benefit of the consideration, had suffered no loss. . . .

Had MAI itself been planning to market stock, the possibility of harm to it, resulting from competing sales by the two directors, might furnish an added element of liability. . . . Not only would the avails of the inside information be withheld from the corporation, but the method of realizing them might possibly damage it. Indeed there may be other damaging factors which cannot be found literally within the boundaries of the offending transactions. The prestige and goodwill of a corporation, so vital to its prosperity, may be undermined by the revelation that its chief officers had been making personal profits out of corporate events which they had not disclosed to the community of shareholders. . . . "If insiders are free to trade on undisclosed material information, they are subject to a conflict of interest that may affect their judgment not only in the timing of disclosure, but also in the timing of the underlying events themselves. Still worse, the insiders' interest in personal trading profits not only may affect their judgment in the timing of disclosure, but also may cause such events to be created—for example, a dividend might be declared when sound business judgment would have omitted it. That is garden-variety mismanagement, and the only effective way to prevent it is to bar the conflict of interest in the first place. Nor are these conflicts of interest the only danger to the corporation's welfare. The pursuit of personal trading profits is likely to distract the insider from the pursuit of corporate tasks, for which the corporation presumably is paying full, adequate compensation already and expects full, singleminded dedication in return."

We need not in this case concern ourselves with these added elements. These fiduciaries are not being charged because they sold stock, or because transactions in securities might subvert their proper functioning as executives of MAI or blemish its reputation. They are being charged because they converted into money to their own use something belonging not to them but to their corporation—inside information. That the method of conversion consisted of transactions in securities is not the legally significant factor.

This conclusion is not inconsistent with New York law regarding purchases and sales of stock by directors. "Ordinarily," it was said in *Hauben* v. *Morris,* 255 App.Div. 35, 46, 5 N.Y.S.2d 721, 730, aff'd. 281 N.Y. 652, 22 N.E.2d 482, "a director may deal in securities of his corporation without subjecting himself to any liability to account for profits, for the corporation as such has no interest in its outstanding stock or in dealings in its shares among its shareholders." A like thought was expressed in *Securities Comm'n* v. *Chenery Corp.,* 318 U.S. 80, 88, 63 S.Ct. 454, 459, 87 L.Ed. 626: "As the Commission concedes here, the courts do not impose upon officers and directors of a corporation any fiduciary duty to its shareholders which precludes them, merely because they are officers and directors, from buying and selling the corporation's stock." But in neither case was the use of inside information the issue. Indeed in Chenery the court, in exonerating the officers and directors, was careful to mention the absence of any finding that they "acted covertly or traded on inside knowledge" (p. 86, 63 S.Ct. p. 458). Whatever the authority of these cases for the proposition that a director owes no fiduciary duty to the corporation in his capacity as a holder of stock, they hardly support a thesis that he owes no such duty as a possessor of corporate inside information. The Restatement of Agency 2d (§ 388, Comment [c]), puts the matter compactly:

"c. *Use of confidential information.* An agent who acquires confidential information in the course of his employment or in violation of his duties has a duty not to use it to the disadvantage of the principal, see § 395. He also has a duty to account for any profits made by the use of such information, although this does not harm the principal. Thus, where a corporation has decided to operate an enterprise at a place where land values will be increased because of such operation, a corporate officer who takes advantage of his special knowledge to buy land in the vicinity is accountable for the profits he makes, even though such purchases have no adverse effect upon the enterprise. So, if he has 'inside' information that the corporation is about to purchase or sell securities, or to declare or to pass a dividend, profits made by him in stock transactions undertaken because of his knowledge are held in constructive trust for the principal. He is also liable for profits made by selling confidential information to third persons, even though the principal is not adversely affected." [1]

Oreamuno and Gonzalez may conceivably be sued by the purchasers of their stock for culpable failure to disclose material information, and some argument is made that they may incur double liability if the suits should be brought and prove successful. . . . We see no need to reach the point on the present record.

It is not charged that directors other than Oreamuno and Gonzalez participated in the sales by those two, and we regard the allegations against the others as insufficient to warrant keeping them in the action.

The order entered on March 1, 1967 should be modified, on the law, to deny the motion of defendants Oreamuno and Gonzalez to dismiss the complaint as to them. . . .

§ 8:4.   Financial Advisors

The necessity of having specialized knowledge and the difficulty of acquiring such knowledge in today's complex world has led to the development of various services, consultants, and advisory services. In the case of

---

[1] A statutory adaptation of the principle is found in section 16(b) of the Securities Exchange Act of 1934 [15 U.S.C. § 78p(b)], dealing with "short-swing" trading by insiders in certain classes of the securities to which the Act applies. The section requires an insider to turn over to his corporation any profit realized by him from any purchase and sale, or any sale and purchase, within any period of less than six months. Designed as a " 'crude rule of thumb' " to curb the abuse of inside information (*Blau* v. *Lamb*, 2 Cir., 363 F.2d 507, 515), the section is applicable even though the insider "did not utilize, or even possess, confidential corporate information" (*Blau* v. *Max Factor & Company*, 9 Cir., 342 F.2d 304, 307, n. 6, cert. den. 382 U.S. 892, 86 S.Ct. 180, 15 L.Ed.2d 150). This legislation is not involved in the instant suit but it is of interest here because of its provision that the profit "shall inure to and be recoverable by the issuer." For this provision, it was explained on behalf of the draftsmen to the House Committee on Interstate and Foreign Commerce, " 'is simply an application of an old principle of the law that if you are an agent and you profit by inside information concerning the affairs of your principal, your profits go to your principal.' " (2 Loss, Securities Legislation, 1123). Some years later, successfully opposing before the Committee a proposal to repeal the provision, the Chairman of the Securities and Exchange Commission explained its basis as follows: "The Exchange Act proceeds on the theory that the confidential information which a corporate insider cannot help but have is information which in a real sense belongs to the corporation, since he acquired it confidentially and in his representative capacity as an official or principal shareholder of the corporation. Thus, this information is regarded by the act as the corporation's property, not the personal property of the insider to do with as he chooses. Since such corporate knowledge is the property of the beneficiary corporation, any profits resulting from its use belong to the insiders no more than does the inside information itself." (Hearings before House Committee on Interstate and Foreign Commerce on Proposed Amendments to Securities Act of 1933 and to Securities Exchange Act of 1934, 77th Cong. 1st Sess. (1942), p. 1257). . . .

many of them, there is no personal relationship between the services and the customer of the service. The relationship is just as impersonal and distant as the relationship with your magazine publisher when you subscribe to his magazine. In other instances, the service is personal and is tailored to your personal needs. In such case, the "custom-tailoring" of the service to meet your needs is one of the big selling points in persuading you to subscribe or patronize. The social force seeking to protect you from disloyalty is therefore on the alert that the advisor does not misuse his position to make a profit for himself.

SECURITIES & EXCHANGE COMMISSION v. CAPTIAL GAINS RESEARCH BUREAU

375 U.S. 180 (1963)

The Capital Gains Research Bureau furnished advice on purchasing securities and was registered under the Federal Investment Advisers Act. The Bureau would purchase shares for itself, and then recommend them to clients as a long-term investment, and would sell its shares at a profit when the market price rose in response to purchases thereafter made. The Securities & Exchange Commission sought an injunction to require the Bureau to inform its clients as to whether it had any of the stock that it was recommending to them. The Commission based its action on the provision of the Act that prohibited any conduct of an investment adviser which "operated as a fraud or deceit upon any client or prospective client." The Bureau raised the defense that it did not intend to cause any loss to its clients, and that they, in fact, sustained no loss; and that, therefore, there was no fraud on its part. From decisions in favor of the Bureau, the Commission appealed.

OPINION BY GOLDBERG, J. . . .

We are called upon in this case to decide whether under the Investment Advisers Act of 1940 the Securities and Exchange Commission may obtain an injunction compelling a registered investment adviser to disclose to his clients a practice of purchasing shares of a security for his own account shortly before recommending that security for long-term investment and then immediately selling the shares at a profit upon the rise in the market price following the recommendation. The answer to this question turns on whether the practice—known in the trade as "scalping"—"operates as a fraud or deceit upon any client or prospective client" within the meaning of the Act. We hold that it does and that the Commission may "enforce compliance" with the Act by obtaining an injunction requiring the adviser to make full disclosure of the practice to his clients. . . .

The decision in this case turns on whether Congress, in empowering the courts to enjoin any practice which operates "as a fraud or deceit upon any client or prospective client," intended to require the Commission to establish fraud and deceit "in their technical sense," including intent to injure and actual injury to clients, or whether Congress intended a broad remedial construction of the Act which would encompass nondisclosure of material facts. . . .

Congress intended the Investment Advisers Act of 1940 to be construed like other securities legislation "enacted for the purpose of avoiding frauds," not technically and restrictively, but flexibly to effectuate its remedial purposes. . . . Accordingly, we hold that the Investment Advisers Act of 1940 empowers the courts, upon a showing such as that made here, to require an adviser to make full and frank disclosure of his practice of trading on the effect of his recommendations.

. . . The high standards of business morality exacted by our laws regulating the securities industry do not permit an investment adviser to trade on the market effect of his own recommendations without fully and fairly revealing his personal interests in these recommendations to his clients.

Experience has shown that disclosure in such situations, while not onerous to the adviser, is needed to preserve the climate of fair dealing which is so essential to maintain public confidence in the securities industry and to preserve the economic health of the country.

§ 8:5.   Commercial Bribery

Assume that the purchasing agent of a department store accepts a payment from a manufacturer in return for buying the manufacturer's goods for the department store. Here there has been a breach of the loyalty owed by the agent as discussed in § 8:2. In a growing number of states, the making of such a payment is punishable as the crime of commercial bribery. Is the department store bound by the contract with the manufacturer, or may it use the misconduct of its agent to set aside the contract? To take matters one step further, assume that the purchasing agent deals with an agent of the manufacturer so that the manufacturer has no actual knowledge of the misconduct. In such case can either the department store or the manufacturer avoid the contract?

Note that this is not the traditional case of fraud as described in Chapter 27 in which one party makes a misrepresentation of fact. In the situation above described, there is no misrepresentation but merely a bribing of the purchasing agent to exercise his judgment or discretion in a particular way.

McCONNELL v. COMMONWEALTH PICTURES CORP.

7 N.Y.2d 465, 199 N.Y.S.2d 483 (1960)

Commonwealth Pictures Corp. agreed to pay McConnell $10,000 and a specified commission if he could persuade Universal Pictures Company to give Commonwealth the distribution rights on its pictures. Without the knowledge of either Universal or Commonwealth, McConnell obtained the distribution rights by paying an agent of Universal the $10,000 Commonwealth paid McConnell. McConnell thereafter sued Commonwealth for the agreed commission. From a judgment in favor of McConnell, Commonwealth appealed.

OPINION BY DESMOND, C.J. . . .

[The lower court] said that, since the agreement sued upon—between plaintiff and defendant—was not in itself illegal, plaintiff's right to be paid for performing it could not be defeated by a showing that he had misconducted himself in carrying it out. The court found a substantial difference between this and the performance of an illegal contract. We take a different view. Proper and consistent application of a prime and long-settled public policy closes the doors of our courts to those who sue to collect the rewards of corruption.

New York's policy has been frequently and emphatically announced in the decisions. "It is the settled law of this State (and probably of every other State) that a party to an illegal contract cannot ask a court of law to help him carry out his illegal object, nor can such a person plead or prove in any court a case in which he, as a basis for his claim, must show forth his illegal purpose. . . . The money plaintiff sues for was the fruit of an admitted crime and 'no court should be required to serve as paymaster of the wages of crime.' "

. . . It is true that some of the leading decisions . . . were in suits on intrinsically illegal contracts, but the rule fails of its purpose unless it covers a case like the one at bar. . . .

We are not working here with narrow questions of technical law. We are applying fundamental concepts of morality and fair dealing not to be weakened by exceptions. So far as precedent is necessary, we can rely on *Sirkin* v. *Fourteenth Street Store,* 124 App.Div. 384, 108 N.Y.S. 830 . . . and *Reiner* v. *North American Newspaper Alliance,* 259 N.Y. 250, 181 N.E. 564, 83 A.L.R. 23. . . . Sirkin is the case closest to ours and shows that, whatever be the law in other jurisdictions, we in New York deny awards for the corrupt performance of contracts even though in essence the contracts are not illegal. Sirkin had sued for the price of goods sold and delivered to defendant. Held to be good was a defense which charged that plaintiff seller had paid a secret commission to an agent of defendant purchaser. There cannot be any difference in principle between that situation and the present one where plaintiff (it is alleged) contracted to buy motion-picture rights for defendant but performed his covenant only by bribing the seller's agent. In the Reiner case (supra), likewise, the plaintiff had fully performed the services required by his agreement with the defendant but was denied a recovery because his performance had involved and included "fraud and deception" practiced not on defendant but on a third party. . . .

Perhaps this application of the principle represents a distinct step beyond Sirkin and Reiner . . . in the sense that we are here barring recovery under a contract which in itself is entirely legal. But if this be an extension, public policy supports it. We point out that our holding is limited to cases in which the illegal performance of a contract originally valid takes the form of commercial bribery or similar conduct and in which the illegality is central to or a dominant part of the plaintiff's whole course of conduct in performance of the contract. . . .

[Judgment reversed.]

DISSENTING OPINION BY FROESSEL, J. . . .

This is not a case where the contract *sued upon* is intrinsically illegal . . . or was *procured* by the commission of a crime. . . .

In the instant case, the contract which plaintiff is seeking to enforce is perfectly valid, and it was not intended or even contemplated that plaintiff would perform the contract by illegal or corrupt means. Having received and retained the full benefits of plaintiff's performance, defendant now seeks to "inject into" its contract with plaintiff, "which was fair and legal in itself, the illegal feature of the other independent transaction." . . . This court is now adopting a rule that a party may retain the benefits of, but escape his obligations under, a wholly lawful contract if the other party commits some illegal act not contemplated nor necessary under the contract. By way of a single illustration, an owner may thus avoid paying his contractor for the cost of erecting a building because the contractor gave an inspector a sum of money to expedite an inspection.

The majority opinion seeks to distinguish between "major" and "minor" illegality and "direct" and "peripheral" corruption. It decides this case on the ground that the manner in which plaintiff performed his admittedly valid contract with defendant was "gravely immoral and illegal." Such distinctions are neither workable nor sanctioned by authority. If a contract was lawfully made, and did not contemplate wrongdoing, it is enforceable; if, on the other hand, it was *procured* by the commission of a crime, or was in fact for the performance of illegal services, it is not enforceable. These are the criteria distinguishing enforceable from unenforceable contracts—not "nice" distinctions between degrees of illegality and immorality in the performance of lawful contracts, or whether the illegal act of performance was "directly" or "peripherally" related to the main contract. . . .

Here, the contract between plaintiff and defendant was perfectly legal, and defendant is seeking to avoid its obligations under the contract—of which it has reaped the benefits for some 12 years—by asserting the illegality of a *different* and subsequent agreement between plaintiff and a third party. This it should not be permitted to do. . . .

DISSENTING OPINION BY VAN VOORHIS, J. . . .

Public morals and fair dealing are likely to be advanced by limiting rather than by enlarging the rule that is being extended to the facts of this case. This rule is grounded on considerations of public policy. Courts will not intervene between thieves to compel them to divide the spoils. But in a situation like the present, it seems to me that the effect of this decision will not be to restrain the corrupt influencing of agents, employees or servants but to encourage misappropriation of funds and breaches of faith between persons who do not stand in corrupt relationships with one another. The public interest is not served best by decisions which put a premium on taking unconscionable advantage of such situations, or which drive the enforcement of obligations of this kind underground. . . .

§ 8:6. Employee Pirating

The extent to which the law protects an employer from employee-pirating depends upon the position of the defendant. If the one who lures the employees away is a stranger, he may be sued for malicious interference with contracts to the extent described in Chapter 27. If he is an officer of the employer, who leaving the employer takes with him other employees, his conduct may also constitute a breach of his duty to exercise good faith as an officer of the employer.

BANCROFT-WHITNEY CO. v. GLEN

64 Cal.2d 327, 49 Cal.Rptr. 825, 411 P.2d 921 (1966)

Glen was the president of Bancroft-Whitney, a California publisher. Matthew Bender Co., a New York publisher, desired to form a western division. Glen and Bender Co. discussed plans by which key employees of Bancroft-Whitney could be induced to leave Bancroft-Whitney and work for the new enterprise. Glen gave Bender Co. and its president, Bender, information as to names, qualities, and salaries of Bancroft-Whitney personnel so that Bender Co. would know which persons to solicit and what to pay them. With the aid of this information, Bender Co. was able to persuade a substantial number of employees of Bancroft-Whitney to leave it and work for the new Bender Co. division. Bancroft-Whitney then sued Glen, Matthew Bender Co., and Bender, the latter's president, for the damages which Bancroft-Whitney had sustained.

OPINION BY MOSK, J. . . .

We are not concerned with the simple right of one competitor to offer the employees of another a job at more favorable terms than they presently enjoy or the right of an employee (or an officer of a corporation) to seek a better job. The question here is whether the president of a corporation is liable for the breach of his fiduciary duty because of the conduct described above . . . and whether, under these facts, those who hire the employees are guilty of unfair competition for acting in concert with the president.

The general rules applicable to the duties of a corporate officer have been frequently stated. . . . These obligations were cogently described as follows: "Corporate officers and directors are not permitted to use their position of trust and confidence to further their private interests. While technically not trustees, they stand in a fiduciary relation to the corporation and its shareholders. A public policy, existing through the years, derived from a profound knowledge of human characteristics and motives, has established a rule that demands of a corporate officer or director, peremptorily and inexorably, the most scrupulous observance of his duty, not only affirmatively to protect the interests of the corporation committed to his charge, but also to refrain from doing anything that would work injury to the corporation, or to deprive it of profit or advantage which his skill and ability might properly bring to it, or to enable it to make in the reasonable and lawful exercise of its powers." Section 820 of the Corporations Code provides that an officer must exercise his powers in good faith, with a view to the interests of the corporation.

There are only a few cases cited by the parties which involve the specific question whether an officer may offer employees of his corporation jobs with a competing enterprise he is preparing to join. These cases are not consistent in their results and appear to rest on general principles relating to the obligations of a fiduciary. . . . The mere fact that the officer makes preparations to compete before he resigns his office is not sufficient to constitute a breach of duty. It is the nature of his preparations which is significant. No ironclad rules as to the type of conduct which is permissible can be stated, since the spectrum of activities in this regard is as broad as the ingenuity of man itself.

The parties hereto have emphasized the issue whether an officer must disclose to the corporation his acts preparatory to entering into competition with it. This question is not identical with the issue whether the officer must reveal that he is negotiating for his own employment with a prospective employer, although, obviously, the two problems overlap since it is impossible for the officer to disclose his activities relating to the formation of a competing enterprise without also disclosing his own plans to join the competitor.

There is broad language in some cases to the effect that protection of the corporation's interest requires full disclosure of acts undertaken in preparation for entering into competition. . . . An analysis of these cases indicates, however, that the liability for breach of fiduciary duty was not predicated on the officer's mere failure to disclose such acts, but upon some *particular circumstance* which rendered nondisclosure harmful to the corporation or upon the officer's wrongful conduct apart from the omission.

There is no requirement that an officer disclose his preparations to compete with the corporation in every case, and failure to disclose such acts will render the officer liable for a breach of his fiduciary duties only where particular circumstances render nondisclosure harmful to the corporation. . . . Conversely, the mere act of disclosing his activities cannot immunize the officer from liability where his conduct in other respects amounts to a breach of duty. The significant inquiry in each situation is whether the officer's acts or omissions constitute a breach under the general principles applicable to the performance of his trust.

In our view, the conduct of Glen in the present case, when assessed by the standards set forth above, amounts to a breach of his fiduciary duties to plaintiff as a matter of law. The undisputed evidence shows a consistent course of conduct by him designed to obtain for a competitor those of plaintiff's employees whom the competitor could afford to employ and would find useful. If Glen while still president of plaintiff had performed these acts on behalf of Bender Co. without also obligating himself to join the company, there could be no doubt that he would have violated his duties to plaintiff. Surely his position in this regard cannot be improved by the fact that he was also to be employed by Bender Co. and was to share in the profits of the new western division. . . .

Another significant aspect of Glen's activities on behalf of Bender relates to the list of employees and their salaries. . . . It is beyond question that a corporate officer breaches his fiduciary duties when, with the purpose of facilitating the recruiting of the corporation's employees by a competitor, he supplies the competitor with a selective list of the corporation's employees who are, in his judgment, possessed of both ability and the personal characteristics desirable in an employee, together with the salary the corporation is paying the employee and a suggestion as to the salary the competitor should offer in order to be successful in recruitment. This conclusion is inescapable even if the information regarding salaries is not deemed to be confidential. No case has been cited or found considering the question whether a list of salaries paid by a corporation to its employees is confidential. We are of the view, however, that such an unpublished list does constitute confidential information and that an officer of a corporation violates his trust if he reveals it to a competitor for the purpose of enabling the solicitation of the corporation's employees by the competitor.

The Restatement of Agency provides that the rule prohibiting the disclosure of confidential information by an agent applies "not only to those communications which are stated to be confidential, but also to information which the agent should know his principal would not care to have revealed to others or used in competition with him. It applies to unique business methods of the employer, trade secrets, *lists of names,* and all other matters which are peculiarly known in the employer's business. It does not apply to matters of common knowledge in the community nor to special skill which the employee has acquired because of his employment." (Rest.2d Agency, § 395, com. b.) (Italics added.) The salaries paid by a corporation to its employees are not matters of common knowledge and, even among corporation employees, they are divulged only to those persons or organizations directly concerned with personnel matters or to responsible fiduciaries.

Defendants argue that the salary information is not confidential because the employees could have revealed their own salaries to Bender Co. or anyone else. It requires little talent to distinguish between a situation in which an individual voluntarily discloses his own salary to another and one in which the unpublished salary list of a group of prospective employees is revealed to a competitor for the purpose of facilitating the recruitment of the corporation's personnel.

The assistance given by Glen to the solicitation of the editors on the list is also to be condemned as a breach of his fiduciary duty. . . .

It is clear from the evidence set forth above that Bender was aware of or ratified Glen's breach of his fiduciary duties in all but a few respects, that he cooperated with Glen in the breach, and that he received the benefits of Glen's infidelity. It cannot be said here, as was stated in another context by Justice Pitney in *International News Service* v. *Associated Press* (1918) 248 U.S. 215, 239, 39 S.Ct. 68, 72, 63 L.Ed. 211, that Bender Co. did not "reap where it has not sown." Under all the circumstances, Bender and Bender Co. must be held liable for their part in Glen's breach of his fiduciary duties. . . .

They encouraged the sowing and reaped the benefit. They cannot now disclaim the burden.

None of the authorities relied upon by defendants is inconsistent with the conclusion we reach herein. . . . They either involve situations in which an officer or employee resigned from the corporation *before* offering employment to the corporation's personnel . . . or in which the only issue was whether one corporation individual could properly offer another corporation's employees better terms of employment. . . .

Defendants argue that even if we conclude that Glen breached his fiduciary duty and that the other defendants are guilty of unfair competition, we cannot award any damages for this wrongdoing because plaintiff has failed to show that the departure of the employees was proximately caused by defendants' actions. They admit that the primary reason the employees left was that they were offered higher salaries by Bender Co. As recounted above, it was Glen's breach that enabled Bender to determine the amount of salary which would induce these persons to leave plaintiff's employ. Under these circumstances there is no merit in defendants' contention. The causal relationship between Glen's violation of duty and Bender's persuasive inducement to the plaintiff's personnel is crystal clear.

Defendants urge that plaintiff itself bears responsibility for the ultimate departure of its employees because it failed to offer higher salaries in order to induce them to return after they had reached agreement with Bender Co. We cannot indulge in an assumption that such offers would have been accepted under the circumstances. In any event, the question of plaintiff's conduct subsequent to the successful recruitment campaign of defendants relates to the question of damages rather than to proximate cause. To hold otherwise would suggest that a corporation could not protect itself against an officer's breach of fiduciary duties in this regard, no matter how flagrant his conduct, since it could always be said that the corporation which lost its employees might have offered them additional salary to return and that the departing employees might have accepted these offers. . . .

Questions for Review

1. Define the social force of furthering good faith and business ethics.

2. Give illustrations of its application.

3. Analyze each opinion in this chapter in terms of the social forces involved in the decision. See § 5:5 for a list of the social forces. With respect to each opinion, explain why the prevailing social forces prevailed and why those rejected did not. In each case in which there is a dissenting opinion, also make this analysis for the dissenting opinion.

4-7. *On the basis of the social forces involved, what decision should be made in each of the following cases?*

4. *Legitimation. Subsequent invalid marriage.* A statute providing for the legitimation of an illegitimate child by the marriage of his parents provided that "when parents of an illegitimate child shall marry subsequent to his birth and recognize him and treat him as their child, such child shall be deemed

to have been the legitimate child of both of his parents. . . .” The natural parents of an illegitimate child married after his birth. The marriage was not valid, however, because the mother was still lawfully married to a first husband. Did this subsequent bigamous marriage make the child legitimate? *Calogero's Estate,* 51 N.J. 345, 240 A.2d 429.

5. *Teacher tenure. Out of school conduct.* The state statute declared that a teacher could be discharged only for “gross inefficiency or immorality; for willful and persistent violations of reasonable regulations of the board of education; or for other good and just cause.” Hale was employed as a teacher and was discharged because he had failed to report a minor collision of his car with a parked car and had denied that there was a collision when questioned by a witness and a police officer, which in itself was a violation of a state statute that made it a misdemeanor to leave the scene of an accident without stopping or making a report. He was discharged as a teacher because of such conduct. Was the discharge proper? *Hale* v. *Board of Education,* 13 Ohio 92, 234 N.E.2d 583.

6. *Corporate opportunity. Recovery of assets.* Brooks, Kinsel, and Remo were officers and directors of the Missouri Valley Limestone Co. In their corporate capacities they were sent out to locate new quarry lands so that the company could keep in business. They took a lease on land owned by Claar, but took it in their own name. Thereafter Snater, who owned 92 percent of the stock of the corporation, sold his stock to Schildberg Rock Products Co. Schildberg then sued Brooks, Kinsel, and Remo to require them to assign their lease of the Claar land to Schildberg. Decide. *Schildberg Rock Products Co.* v. *Brooks,* 258 Iowa 759, 140 N.W.2d 132.

7. *Including payment by bank. Broken promise to accept draft.* Schenk's Motor Sales had a checking account in the Home Savings Bank. Schenk drew a check on the bank payable to the General Finance Corp. in excess of the amount in its account. The bank certified and paid the check in reliance on the telephoned statement of General Finance Corp. that it would pay a draft which Schenk had deposited in its account. General Finance Corp. thereafter refused to pay the draft, correctly citing the rule of law that an acceptance to pay a draft is not binding unless it is written. Was the bank entitled to recover from General Finance? *Home Savings Bank* v. *General Finance Corp.,* 10 Wis.2d 417, 103 N.W.2d 117.

8-12. *What social forces were involved, which prevailed, and which were defeated in the following decisions?*

8. *Contract. Promissory estoppel.* Where telecasting station promised advertiser to make certain time spots available for commercials and on the basis thereof the advertiser made a contract with his client for advertising by telecasting, the telecasting station was bound by its promise by promissory estoppel. *Dunnan & Jeffrey* v. *Gross Telecasting,* 7 Mich.App. 113, 151 N.W.2d 194.

9. *Agency. Net sale.* The rule that an agent selling to a third person under a net sale contract by which the agent may retain all in excess of a specified

sales price is not required to disclose the identity of the purchaser, does not apply where the net sale price is arrived at after the principal agreed to accept a stated offer from an unidentified third person. Where the net sale amount is computed by deducting the agent's commission, and then agreeing to sell for the balance "nct cash to me"; and consequently the agent must disclose that the contemplated buyer was related to him, as his mother-in-law. *Loughlin* v. *Idora Realty Co.,* Cal.App.2d, 66 Cal.Rptr. 747.

10. *Agency. Implied authority.* An insurer's agent has implied authority to make an oral binder for insurance and to backdate the policy where he had continually followed the practice of making contracts in such manner and of backdating them to the application date, with the result that the insurer could not claim that it was wrong for him to issue policies in such manner and the insurer therefore could not recover from the agent for the loss which had occurred between the date of such an oral binder and the sub-sequent rejection of the application by the insurer. *Lewis* v. *Travelers Insurance Co.,* 51 N.J. 244, 239 A.2d 4.

11. *Insurance. Liability of broker.* An insurance broker acts as the agent of the insured and is therefore liable to the insured where the broker fails to notify the insured of the cancellation of a policy, and no substitute was procured. *Foster* v. *Nunmaker Discount Co.,* La., 201 So.2d 215 (Broker sent one notice that was returned for incorrect address and did nothing more to communicate with the insured.)

12. *Insurance. Nominal owner.* Where, with the knowledge of the insurer's agent, title to an automobile is taken in name of nominal buyer because buyer was bad credit risk, the agent's knowledge was imputed to the insurer, and the insurer was estopped from avoiding liability on the ground that the nominal buyer was not the true owner. *Thibeau* v. *Feenstra,* La., 198 So.2d 707.

Chapter 9

PROTECTION FROM FRAUD

§ 9:1. Generally

Protection from fraud is found in a variety of forms. In its most direct form of protection, the law imposes liability upon a person guilty of fraud for the damages caused thereby, as discussed in Chapter 27, and permits the victim to set aside any contract which he was induced to make. Apart from such obvious antifraud measures, there are many situations in which the law reaches a particular decision because it is fearful that if it decides differently, it will be encouraging fraudulent claims. In some instances, the law will regard as "fraud" conduct that is merely unfair.

§ 9:2. Tort Claims

The law is much concerned in some situations with whether a claim which is made in court is fraudulent. Thus the law has been reluctant to allow recovery for shock and fright because it is obviously difficult to determine whether a person did sustain shock and fright or if he sustained as much shock and fright as he claims. Thus it was held by many courts that there could not be any recovery for shock or fright unless it was intentionally caused. That is, if someone negligently drove their car near you and almost hit you, he would not be liable for the shock which was caused you; whereas if he had intentionally done this to scare you, he would be liable for the shock and fright. Notice that where the conduct of the other party is intentionally designed to scare you, the law is more concerned about the evil character of his conduct than the danger that you might be making a false claim as to the fact of being frightened or the extent of your fright.

Where fright was negligently caused but in addition the plaintiff was touched by the defendant, many courts allowed recovery. That is, if you were touched by the negligently-driven car, even though the touching was just a slight brushing of your coat which in itself caused you no harm, recovery was allowed because the fact that you had been touched by the defendant's car was a reasonable guarantee that you spoke the truth when you said that you had been frightened and sustained a shock. Otherwise stated, the fact that there was an impact, however slight, was a guarantee against the existence of fraud about which the court was so concerned. Most courts today have gone beyond the "impact" rule and hold that there is liability for negligently-caused shock or fright which leads to actual illness of the victim as long as the jury believes that the negligence in fact caused the shock or fright and that the illness of the victim in fact resulted from the shock or fright.

BOSLEY v. ANDREWS
393 Pa. 161, 142 A.2d 263 (1958)

Cattle owned by Andrews strayed onto the farm of the Bosleys and began to damage the crops. Mrs. Bosley attempted to drive the cattle off of the farm when suddenly a bull in the group of cattle charged at her. When it was within about 25 feet of her she collapsed, and the bull was apparently driven off by a dog. Mrs. Bosley was not touched by the bull, but the shock aggravated a heart condition which she did not know that she had. She sued Andrews for the damages for the heart disability that resulted from the fright and shock.

OPINION BY BELL, J. . . .

The rule is long and well established in Pennsylvania that there can be no recovery of damages for injuries resulting from fright or nervous shock or mental or emotional disturbances or distress, unless they are accompanied by physical injury or physical impact. . . .

What plaintiff is really asking us to do is to review and change the rule which has been so long and clearly established by our cases, because the courts of many other States and the Restatement allow recovery for shock and emotional disturbances where there has been no physical injury or physical impact. . . .

To allow recovery for fright, fear, nervous shock, humiliation, mental or emotional distress—with all the disturbances and illnesses which accompany or result therefrom—where there has been no physical injury or impact, would open a Pandora's box. A plaintiff might be driving her car alertly or with her mind preoccupied, when a sudden or unexpected or exceptionally loud noise of an automobile horn behind or parallel with her car, or a sudden loud and unexpected fire engine bell or siren, or a sudden unexpected frightening buzz-sawing noise, or an unexpected explosion from blasting or dynamiting, or an unexpected nerve-wracking noise produced by riveting on a street, or the shrill and unexpected blast of a train at a spot far from a crossing, or the witnessing of a horrifying accident, or the approach of a car near or over the middle line, even though it is withdrawn to its own side in ample time to avoid an accident, or any one of a dozen other everyday events, can cause or aggravate fright or nervous shock or emotional distress or nervous tension or mental disturbance. Such an event, if compensable, may cause normal people, as well as nervous persons and persons who are mentally disturbed or mentally ill, to honestly believe that the sudden and unexpected event caused them fright or nervous shock or nervous tension with subsequent emotional distress or suffering or pain or miscarriage or heart attack, or some kind of disease. In most cases, it would be impossible for medical science to prove that these subjective symptoms could not possibly have resulted from or been aggravated or precipitated by fright or nervous shock or nervous tension or emotional disturbance or distress, each of which can in turn produce an ulcer or headaches or fainting spells or, under some circumstances, a heart attack, or a serious disease. For every wholly genuine and deserving claim, there would likely be a tremendous number of illusory or imaginative or "faked" ones. Medical science, we repeat, could not prove that these could not have been caused or precipitated or aggravated by defendant's alleged negligent act.

We have considered all of the contentions of the plaintiffs but find no merit in them. . . .

DISSENTING OPINION BY MUSMANNO, J. . . .

Following ten days' confinement to bed [Mary Bosley] was taken to the Greenville Hospital where she remained 17 days. Since then her health has never been good. She suffers sinking spells and blackouts, she is weak and exhausted, she has become a periodical guest of clinics and hospitals. It is the medical opinion of Dr. G. H. Diehl, who treated her from the day of the bull episode, that the angina pectoris, with which she is at present afflicted, was precipitated by "the running, the chasing and the fear that was caused when the bull chased her." It is his opinion further that Mrs. Bosley "will probably always have angina pectoris and cardiac insufficiency in the future." . . .

The Majority Opinion of this Court states at the outset that Mrs. Bosley "sought to recover damages for a heart disability which resulted from her

fright and shock upon being chased by a Hereford bull owned by defendant."
The Majority thus admits that Mrs. Bosley's heart disability is a result of the
fright and shock caused by the aggressiveness of the defendant's bull. . . .

But this Court says that even if we conclude that Mrs. Bosley's present
physical disablement is the result of the fright, shock, and strain she experienced when the defendant's bull chased her, she is not entitled to a
verdict because it would be bad policy to allow her to recover. The Majority
says: "To allow recovery for fright, fear, nervous shock, humiliation, mental
or emotional distress—with all the disturbances and illnesses which accompany or result therefrom—where there has been no physical injury or impact,
would open a Pandora's box." . . .

The great fear of the Majority seems to be that if we should allow the
plaintiff in this case to submit her case to a jury, and, incidentally, *that is
all she is seeking,* the courts would be besieged with "faked" cases. The
Majority prophesies with alarm: "For every wholly genuine and deserving
claim, there would likely be a tremendous number of illusory or imaginative
or 'faked' ones."

But are our courts so naive, are they so gullible, are they so devoid of
worldly knowledge, are they so childlike in their approach to realities that
they can be deceived and hoodwinked by claims that have no factual, medical,
or legalistic basis? If they are, then all our proud boasts of the worthiness
of our judicial system are empty and vapid indeed.

The Majority's apprehension that if we should allow the instant case to
go to a jury for factual determination, the courts would be engulfed in a
tidal wave of lawsuits, is to look upon a raindrop and visualize an inundation.
Many jurisdictions now permit recovery where physical disablement tortiously
caused is not made manifest through visible trauma, and I have seen no
report that in those States the courts are awash in trumped-up cases. Many
States at one time followed the nonliability doctrine but later abandoned
it. . . .

The Majority Opinion says that: "The rule is long and well established
in Pennsylvania that there can be no recovery of damages for injuries resulting from fright or nervous shock or mental or emotional disturbances or
distress, unless they are accompanied by physical injury or physical impact."

It is true that this Court has consistently denied recovery in the type
of cases described in this quotation, but that does not mean that, consonant
with law, reason, and justice, it should continue to do so. *Stare decisis* is
the viaduct over which the law travels in transporting the precious cargo of
justice. Prudence and a sense of safety dictate that the piers of that viaduct
should be examined and tested from time to time to make certain that they
are sound, strong and capable of supporting the weight above. One of the
piers supposedly upholding the span of nonliability is the case of *Huston* v.
Freemansburg, 212 Pa. 548, cited in the Majority Opinion. A review of that
alleged authority will reveal it to be made up of something less than the
durable masonry which should be the foundation of any jurisprudential structure in America. Chief Justice Mitchell, who wrote the opinion in that
case, said: "In the last half century the ingenuity of counsel, stimulated by
the cupidity of clients and encouraged by the prejudices of juries, has

expanded the action for negligence until it overtops all others in frequency and importance, but it is only in the very end of that period that it has been stretched to the effort to cover so intangible, so untrustworthy, so illusory and so speculative a cause of action as mere mental disturbance. It requires but a brief judicial experience to be convinced of the large proportion of exaggeration and even of actual fraud in the ordinary action for physical injuries from negligence, and if we opened the door to this new invention, the result would be great danger, if not disaster to the cause of practical justice."

With all the respect that one naturally holds for the jurists of the past, I cannot generate any veneration for this intemperate outburst. On the contrary, I believe that it should be repudiated and condemned. It amounts to an unjust attack on our whole judicial system. It lays under suspicion every attorney at the bar, casts a shadow on every plaintiff litigant, and shamelessly condemns juries as being motivated by unworthy intentions. Fifty-three years have passed since Mitchell's philippic, but, despite his dire prophecies, there is no report of disaster in those States which allow recovery for mental and nervous disorders caused by tort, even though unaccompanied by physical injury.

A brief recital of the facts in some of the cases decided by this Court on the subject under discussion will demonstrate that not all the decisions commend themselves to the goddess of Justice.

I quote verbatim the Majority's reference to one of the cases: "In *Fox* v. *Borkey,* 126 Pa., supra, plaintiff was husking with her husband. An explosion occurred which was caused by defendant's blasting; the earth trembled and dirt blew over them as if it were hail. Plaintiff fell to the ground, trembling all over with shock; she became very nervous and had heart trouble and 'was reduced to a physical wreck by the grossly negligent, if not intentional, misconduct of the defendant.'" In that case the jury returned a verdict for the plaintiff but this Court reversed. Under the Majority's own summation it can scarcely be said that the reversal was just.

In *Morris* v. *L. & Wyo. Val. R. R. Co.,* 228 Pa. 198, the plaintiff suffered a miscarriage as the result of the derailment of the railway car in which she was riding, the derailment being caused by defendant's negligence. It was admitted that the miscarriage resulted from the nervous shock occasioned by the car bumping over the track at an open switch. Nevertheless this Court affirmed a judgment of nonsuit.

Another case cited by the Majority Opinion is equally insupportable in justice. In *Ewing* v. *P. C. & St. L. Ry. Co.,* 147 Pa. 40, the plaintiff averred in her statement of claim that the defendant railroad company, through negligence, ran a train of cars into another car and, in the resulting collision, one of the cars was catapulted to and on her house. Although she sustained no bone fractures or bleeding wounds, the plaintiff, because of the fear of imminent death, suffered nervous shock, she "became sick and disabled," and "continues to suffer great mental and physical pain." The lower court [dismissed the complaint. This was affirmed on appeal.] In its . . . opinion this Court asked the rhetorical question: "What duty did the company owe this plaintiff?" The answer is a simple one. It owed the plaintiff the duty of keeping its cars on the railroad track and not hurling them on to her house.

Raising the same irrelevant and exaggerated alarm in the Ewing case which the Majority is raising here, the Court said there: "If mere fright, unaccompanied with bodily injury, is a cause of action, the scope of what are known as accident cases will be very greatly enlarged; for, in every case of a collision on a railroad, the passengers, although they may have sustained no bodily harm, will have a cause of action against the company for the 'fright' to which they have been subjected." But Mrs. Ewing was not a passenger. She was in her own house when the sky began to rain railroad cars. . . .

But even if we were to assume the absolute correctness in law and justice of this Court's decisions which in the past have denied liability for mental and nervous conditions not connected with physical fracture and laceration, this would not be to say that such liability cannot be proclaimed today. It could well be that conditions have changed and, therefore, the whole problem should be reevaluated, especially in view of the tremendous progress which has been made in the fields of mental, cardiac, and neurological research. With highly sensitive equipment and with accurately developed laboratory formulae, plus a profounder knowledge in the whole cyclopedia of health versus disease, doctors and scientists no longer stand helpless before the problem of determining the causation of abnormal behavior in man. And if that increased knowledge decreases the possibility of fraudulent claims evading the argus-eyed vigilance of court and jury, there should be a change in the judicial attitude toward the type of claim under consideration.

The Supreme Court of Maryland, addressing itself to this very subject, well said: ". . . It is objected that the effect of fright is subjective, imaginative, conjectural, and speculative, and therefore easily simulated and feigned, so that its actual existence is difficult to ascertain, and, if found to exist, is inherently insusceptible of compensation by any precise pecuniary standard. These considerations undeniably tend to multiply fictitious or speculative claims, and to open to unscrupulous litigants a wide field for exploitation, but these difficulties are common, are surmountable, and *so should not prevent the operation of the general and fundamental theory of the common law that there is a remedy for every substantial wrong . . ."* (*Bowman* v. *Williams,* 164 Md. 397, 403). . . .

It seems to me that it is a violation of the living spirit of the law to adhere to an ancient rule which has no pragmatic application to realities of today. A precedent, in law, in order to be binding, should appeal to logic and a genuine sense of justice. What lends dignity to the law founded on precedent is that, if analyzed, the particularly cited case wields authority by the sheer force of its self-integrated honesty, integrity, and rationale. A precedent cannot, and should not, control, if its strength depends alone on the fact that it is old, but may crumble at the slightest probing touch of instinctive reason and natural justice. With such criteria in mind, it is difficult to understand how this Court can allow damages for mental and nervous disability if incurred at the same time that a finger is bruised, but will deny compensation of any kind to the victim who sustains no outer mutilation but will be invalided for life because his inner mechanism has been shattered beyond repair. . . .

To determine liability by what follows rather than by what precedes and accompanies a catastrophe is like concluding that no earthquake has occurred because no one was killed. . . .

One can think of many situations where a person could be gravely injured by a trespassing force which in no way physically touched him. For instance, the violent displacement of air caused by an explosion negligently performed could deafen a passerby who would most assuredly be entitled to recover from the trespasser even though he could show no outer lesion on his person. Instruments and expert examination would attest to ruptured eardrums. How would such evidence differ from the evidence presented by the doctors in this case, which was medical proof that the plaintiff had suffered organic damage to the heart? . . .

The nervous system is peculiarly susceptible to nontangible excitation, and it is not to be denied that the wrecking of nerve ganglia can often be more disabling than the breaking of bones or the tearing of flesh. And where it is definitely established that such injury and suffering were proximately caused by an act of negligence, why should the tortfeasor not be liable in damages? . . .

In conclusion I would say that the Majority Opinion has concentrated its argument principally on the proposition that it would be unwise to allow recoveries for mental and nervous disorders following fear, fright, and shock. However, the plaintiff is not claiming damages because of any mental or nervous ailment. At the risk of tiresome repetition I must repeat that she is asking for a verdict as the result of *physical damage* done to her heart. . . . Thus, in considering the nature and the extent of the plaintiff's disability we are dealing with something very tangible and very concrete. . . .

As soon as the bull crossed the frontiers of the Bosley farm, its owner, Dale Andrews, was guilty of a trespass. Whatever damage succeeded that invasion, and because of that invasion, was Dale Andrews' responsibility. Under the law of [trespass], Andrew's liability was almost automatic. . . .

§ 9:3.   Contract Claims

(a) *Generally.* The law is fearful that false claims may be made as to the terms or existence of contracts. Because of this, certain kinds of contracts must be in writing or they cannot be shown to exist. For example, a contract for the sale of an interest in land must ordinarily be in writing to be enforced. Claims cannot be asserted against the estate of a dead man unless in writing or proven to exist by the testimony of third persons. In both situations, the law is afraid to permit the alleged buyer or the alleged creditor of the estate to prove his case solely on his own oral statements.

Thus, a barrier is set up against fraud. The rule of law here noted may also be regarded as furthering the objective of practical expediency because a trial is quickly cut short if no writing is produced or the testimony of third persons cannot be presented. In contrast, the trial could be very long and drawn out if the law would permit the claim to be established by oral testimony because it then would be necessary to determine whether the claimant and any other witnesses were telling the truth as to what they say was said, as well as to determine the legal significance of what was said.

(b) Protection of written agreements from fraud. Once there is a written agreement, the law is then concerned with protecting the written agreement from false claims that the agreement between the parties is not exactly as stated. This is true without regard to whether the writing was in the first instance executed because a statute so required or because the parties voluntarily or out of caution made the writing.

Once the writing exists, it cannot be shown that there was a prior inconsistent oral agreement. Likewise, it cannot be shown that at the time the writing was executed, it was agreed that any of its provisions should not be binding or that there should be any other terms to the agreement. There are certain qualifications to the above statements, but it is a safe-working rule to treat a written document as being the full and final statement of the parties as of the time that it was executed.

The reason for the refusal of the law to go behind the written agreement is that the law is afraid that the claim of an inconsistent oral agreement is fraudulently made, or, as an alternative, that the oral agreement though once existing had been abandoned in the course of negotiations and that it would be a "fraud" on the other contracting party to revive the terms which had been abandoned when it came time to execute the final written contract.

PARADISE BEACH HOMES, INC. v. SOUTH ATLANTIC LUMBER CO.

118 So.2d 825 (Fla., 1960)

At the time a mortgage was executed, the parties did not know the exact debt that was owed. Instead of waiting until this was determined, the parties inserted an estimated sum in the mortgage and orally agreed that the mortgage would not become effective until the true amount owed was determined. Later the mortgagee sought to enforce the original amount of the mortgage. When the mortgagor sought to prove the oral agreement as to adjusting the amount of the debt, the mortgagee objected that this proof was barred by the parol evidence rule as it was oral evidence that would contradict the amount shown by the written mortgage.

OPINION BY CARROLL, J. . . .

Simply stated, the parol evidence rule is a rule declaring that parol evidence is inadmissible to vary the terms of a valid written instrument. . . . It is not a rule of evidence but a rule of substantive law. . . . The rule rests upon a rational foundation of experience and policy and is essential to the certainty and stability of written obligations. . . .

The simple statement of the parol evidence rule as set forth in the preceding paragraph may be misleading, however, unless one comprehends the numerous clarifications of and exceptions to this rule that have been recognized by the courts.

Among the clarifications recognized by the courts in Florida are these: when the statement of a term, such as the consideration, in a written agreement is not a complete statement, parol evidence may be admissible as to that term . . . the parties to a written contract may prove by parol evidence facts consistent with the agreement, although not expressed in it . . . where a particular element of an alleged extrinsic negotiation is not dealt with in the writing, it is presumed that the writing does not represent the entire transaction, and parol evidence in proof thereof is admissible, . . . parol evidence may be introduced to explain ambiguities or uncertainties in a written contract. . . .

One of the most important exceptions to the parol evidence rule, an exception which we think is applicable to the facts in the present appeal, is that parol evidence is admissible to prove a condition precedent to the written contract for the purpose of showing that there existed no binding contract. . . .

" ' . . . A conditional delivery or execution of a writing may be shown by parol. . . . Parol evidence is admissible to show that a written contract, although manually delivered to the obligee therein named, was not to become a binding obligation except upon the happening of a certain event, such as an inspection and approval by the buyer of goods which are the subject matter of the sale.' " . . .

"Also, in Corbin on Contracts, volume 3, section 589, pp. 318-320, it is said:

" 'Everyone agrees that the mere existence of a written document does not prove that a contract has been made. This is true, even though the document has all the appearance of a contract complete in every detail, with signatures, witnessing clause, and other legal symbols. Everyone agrees, also, that if no contract has been made, the 'parol evidence rule' has no application. This has supplied one of the frequently used methods by which courts have explained their admission of oral testimony in conflict with a document. A written document, unconditional on its face and fully executed, can be shown by oral testimony to have been delivered subject to a condition precedent. As long as the condition has not occurred, so they say, no contract has been made. Therefore, oral proof of the conditional delivery is admissible in spite of the face of the document to the contrary. . . .

The chancellor erred in excluding the evidence relating to the oral understanding of the plaintiff and the defendant at the time of the execution of the note and mortgage, on the ground that such evidence was admissible to show a condition precedent to the existence of the note and mortgage as valid instruments, under the thoroughly-recognized exception to the parol evidence rule, as discussed above.

Examining in the light of the foregoing cases the defendant's evidence excluded by the chancellor here, we find that the essential purpose of such evidence was to prove that, since the parties did not know the amount of the indebtedness of the defendant to the plaintiff at the time the note and mortgage were executed, the president of the defendant, because of the importunations of the plaintiff, nevertheless executed these instruments and delivered them to the plaintiff with the understanding and on the condition that they were not to become effective until they were adjusted so that the amount of the note would reflect the true indebtedness owed by the defendant to the plaintiff, later to be ascertained. Such evidence showed a conditional delivery of the instruments, and parol evidence of that understanding was admissible. Excluding that evidence was inevitably harmful, reversible error. . . .

§ 9:4.   Fine Print

Fraud may be present where there is a printed contract or document that contains certain clauses in such fine print that it is reasonable to believe the other contracting party will never take the time to or be able to read such fine print.

It is difficult to classify the fine print situation today. Originally it was probably likely that such fine print was purposely used to conceal from the reader what was in the fine print. Today it is more likely the result of the desire to save paper costs. There is also an element of avoiding "customer shock." If you wish to rent a house and would be asked to sign a 10-page printed lease, you might hesitate to rent from that particular landlord. When, however, he hands to you one large folded sheet printed in small type you do not have the same "customer shock" and do not realize that all of the 10 pages of material have been squeezed onto the one large folded sheet. Also the enterprise may wish to avoid the asking of many questions by its customers, and does so by putting the question-provoking provisions in such small print that the customer overlooks them.

In some instances, the legislature has outlawed certain fine print. It is common to find statutes declaring that insurance policies may not be printed in type of smaller size than designated in the statute. Consumer protection statutes designed to protect the credit buyer frequently require that particular clauses be set in large type. When a merchant selling goods under a written contract disclaims the obligation that the goods be fit for their normal use, the Uniform Commercial Code requires that such waiver be set forth "conspicuously," which it defines as requiring "a term or clause . . . [to be] so written that a reasonable person against whom it is to operate ought to have noticed it. A printed heading in capitals . . . is conspicuous. Language in the body of a form is 'conspicuous' if it is in larger or other contrasting type or color. . . ." [UCC § 2-316(2), § 1-201(10)]

While the fine print case has been historically regarded as a "fraud" situation, there are indications that the concept of unconscionability will be extended to this situation; thus shifting the emphasis to a consideration of the effect upon the victim rather than the nature of the conduct of the actor. Thus the concept of unconscionability of the Uniform Commercial Code has been cited as authority for reaching the conclusion that a provision on a bank signature card waiving trial by jury was void as unconscionable because there was no reason for the depositor to know that he was making any contractual agreement when he signed the card, and the waiver was in such fine type that "considerable effort" was required to decipher it.

ROGERS v. U.S.F. & G. CO.

67 Cal.Rptr. 251 (Cal.App.2d, 1968)

Rogers insured his coin and stamp collection with the U.S.F. & G. Co., through its agent, Demers. After a loss was sustained and he demanded payment from the insurer, it raised the defense that it was not liable because Rogers had failed to keep a separate inventory of the coins and stamps as was specified in a rider to the policy. Rogers claimed that he was not bound by the rider.

OPINION BY HUFSTEDLER, A.J. . . .

The premise of Fidelity's argument is that paragraph 8 of a rider to the policy required Rogers to keep an inventory of all of his stamps and coins which were insured and that the uncontradicted evidence establishes that Rogers failed to do so. For reasons hereinafter discussed we hold that paragraph 8 did not become a part of the insurance contract. . . .

It is unnecessary to discuss the evidence except as it relates to the question whether or not paragraph 8 of the rider was a part of the insurance contract. Paragraph 8 is found on the second page of a two-page rider entitled, "Coin & Stamp Dealers Floater." The physical condition of the rider almost has to be seen to be believed. The first page of the rider has an allonge affixed to the bottom of the page by Scotch tape and two staples. The staples not only clip the allonge to the first page, but also fasten together the first and second pages of the rider. Two more staples driven through the upper left- and right-hand corners of the rider further clamp the two pages of the rider to one another. Without removing the staples it is possible to read the second page of the rider if one presses the two pages apart, forming a cylinder, and reads the text of the second page sideways. The first page of the rider appears to be complete on its face; the language of the allonge completes the text of the last-numbered clause on the page.

Rogers testified that at the time the policy was delivered to him, it was in substantially the same condition as it was when it was introduced into evidence, "expect it came unstapled in one section." Demers handed Rogers the policy and told him to read it. Rogers testified, "I noted that it was stapled together and I asked, 'Why is this piece stapled together?" and he said something about, 'That covers the rider,' whatever that meant, so I disregarded what was underneath at the time and just glanced at the back, and I folded it up and then put it away." He assumed that the second page of the rider did not pertain to him. It was not called to Roger's attention and he never read it until after the theft occurred and Fidelity asserted paragraph 8 to avoid liability.

Fidelity could not rely upon the condition found on the second page of the rider. Contractual terms in minute type have sometimes been enforced. But the ophthalmological talents courts have sometimes ascribed to a contracting party do not include periscopic vision.

The trial court could properly conclude from the evidence that the second page of the rider never became an effective part of Fidelity's contract of insurance with Rogers. With the deletion of the second page of the rider, there is no foundation for Fidelity's argument that the failure of Rogers to perform the terms of paragraph 8 foreclosed his recovery. . . .

§ 9:5. Innocent Misrepresentation

Historically, the concept of fraud did not include an innocent misrepresentation, that is, a false statement made in good faith, as an essential element of fraud was that the actor had made his statements with knowledge that they were false or with reckless indifference as to whether they were true or not. Traditionally, courts of equity began to grant relief by permitting a party to avoid a contract entered into on the basis of an innocent misrepresentation made by the other contracting party. This was a recognition of the oppressive character of the situation—the transaction was cancelled or rescinded, but no liability was imposed on the person misleading the other since he was innocent of conscious wrongdoing. With the fusion of law and equity as an incident of modern judicial reform, there has been an absorption into the traditional law case of some of the equity concepts so that in certain instances a person sued on a contract may avoid liability on the ground that he had been induced to enter into it by a misrepresentation innocently made by the plaintiff.

What if the misrepresentation occurs in the stage of negotiations before any contract has been made? Is there any liability for a party's innocent misrepresentation in negotiations or is the possibility of such a misrepresentation one of the risks that the other contracting party takes when he enters into the contract without making further investigation on his own behalf? In the case which follows, the concept is discussed in terms of negligence. This tends to confuse the problem involved, which is whether there is a duty that requires a negotiating party to act in such a way that the other party is not misled. Stated in terms of social forces, it is whether there is a duty to prevent the creation of a hardship situation.

WOMACK v. UNITED STATES

389 F.2d 793 (Ct.Claims, 1968)

Womack bid to supply the United States Bureau of Land Management with cards, which the latter would use for record keeping. It was recognized that the quantity needed could not be predetermined and the advertising for bids for the cards stated that the quantities to be contracted for were estimates and were subject to 25 percent variance. Womack was the successful bidder and contracted to supply the cards required at a fixed price. It was later discovered that the number of cards needed in fact exceeded the advertised number by more than 25 percent. Womack made a claim against the

United States for compensation for the cards in excess of the estimated quantity.

PER CURIAM. . . .

In the early 1950's the Department of the Interior, through its Bureau of Land Management (BLM), initiated a study directed to a program for the comprehensive revision and modernization of the record system covering title and usage of federal lands in 17 Western States, including Utah.

Plaintiffs, whose regular business was the preparation and sale of oil and gas maps for the petroleum industry, were generally aware of BLM's planned undertaking and were interested in participating in it as a private contractor. Accordingly, they maintained contact with BLM's Washington personnel throughout the preliminary study phase of the program. Their views and recommendations were solicited by and were furnished to BLM.

By 1955 the methods and procedures for this large and unique undertaking were settled upon.

It was decided that all phases of the project, except the initial one, would be performed by private concerns under contracts awarded and administered by BLM. A special staff was established by BLM to administer and coordinate the entire project. Mr. Earl Thomas, Associate Director of BLM, was the responsible head of the overall program. Mr. Everett Eynon, now deceased, as Manager of the so-called Records Improvement Project, supervised day-to-day operations and performance by private contractors. Mr. Harold K. Johnson served as Mr. Eynon's general assistant and performed inspection functions at contractors' premises as well. Mr. Fred W. Heine, an attorney versed in land law, had basic responsibility for drafting the supply contracts, including the contract in suit, let by BLM under the program.

During a period of approximately one year, from August, 1955, BLM itself microfilmed all previously unfilmed title and usage source documents in its files and in the files of various other Government agencies. In all, some four million documents were microfilmed. Each roll of film negative contained approximately 1,600 document images. For control purposes BLM assigned a number to each film roll and prepared an index showing the subject matter to which each roll related.

When the microfilming was finished, BLM awarded Recordak Corp. a contract to make 35 mm. positive celluloid prints of the negative rolls.

Next, a contract was let to the Filmsort Division of the Dexter Folder Company for cutting the positive print rolls into individual images and mounting them in the window area of aperture-type tabulating cards.

The next step in the project was the preparation of a so-called Control Document Index for each of the 17 States involved. This operation, performed by the York Tabulating Service under a unit-price BLM contract awarded October 13, 1955, consisted essentially of identification and sorting of the aperture cards. Specifically, York viewed each aperture card and key-punched into it the subject matter depicted in its film image. When that subject matter related to more than one township of the State to which the card pertained, a cross-reference-type tabulating card was prepared for each additional township involved. After these operations were completed, all cards were segregated by State and the cards for each State arranged according to meridian, township and range.

Because of York Tabulating's limited financial resources, BLM agreed to a partial-payment arrangement under which York was permitted to bill for cards in lots of approximately 100,000 after they had gone through the initial, or State sort. Each York billing gave a breakdown showing the number of cards that were involved for each State. BLM maintained a current record showing, by State, the cumulative total of cards for which it had been billed.

The final phase in the BLM project, and the one with which the contract in suit is concerned, involved basically a transposition of the information contained in the Control Document Index onto title and use status plats, with an accompanying historical index, that were to be prepared for each township of the State to which the Control Document Index pertained. In such an operation the amount of work involved in annotating the plats and compiling the historical indices varied directly with the number of cards in the Control Document Index for the State in question.

In May 1956, BLM advised the plaintiffs that the Records Improvement Project was progressing satisfactorily and that an invitation for bid on a contract to prepare the annotated plats and historical indices for either Utah or New Mexico, as the lead State in the program, would be issued within the following several weeks.

On August 14, 1956, John Vorhies telephoned BLM's Earl Thomas to inquire as to when the invitation for the Utah contract would be issued. After Mr. Thomas stated that the Utah invitation would be issued shortly, Vorhies asked how many cards there would be in the Utah Control Document Index. He explained that this information would be important for bidding purposes. After consulting briefly with his associates, Mr. Thomas stated that an approximation of the card quantity would be put in the invitation so that it would be made known to all interested bidders. Prior to this request from Mr. Vorhies, BLM had not intended to include any reference in its invitation to the size of the Control Document Index.

On August 17, 1956, at which time it had been billed for 58,691 Utah cards by York Tabulating, BLM issued the invitation for bids on the contract in suit.

The invitation, specifying an opening date of September 18, 1956, called for a fixed-price bid for the preparation of a master title plat, a use status plat and a historical index for each township in Utah, Oregon or both. The specifications, referring to the Control Document Index, stated: "There are an estimated sixty-five thousand (65,000) mounted aperture and cross-reference cards for the State of Utah. . . ." Additionally, the specifications provided that: "A standard diagram shall be used for the basic master title plat as is set forth in the detail information for an estimated eighty-five per centum (85 percent) of the townships for which the plats are prepared under this contract." Finally, the specifications included the following general provision: "All estimated quantities in this contract are subject to a twenty-five per centum (25 percent) increase or decrease."

The estimate as to card quantity represented the best collective judgment of the members of BLM's Record Improvement Project staff. They based their judgment on the number of Utah cards for which York had billed (58,691) by the time that the invitation was issued and their impressions as to York's percentage of completion on Utah, gained from the bi-weekly inspection visits of BLM personnel to the York premises.

The estimate as to percentage of Utah townships that could be platted on standard diagrams was based on the judgment of Mr. Earl Harrington, Chief of BLM's Division of Cadastral Engineering. Mr. Harrington was a man of 50 years' professional experience and unquestioned competence. In arriving at his standard diagram estimate for Utah, he reviewed 800 plats from locations throughout the State.

The invitation advised interested bidders that a BLM representative would be in Salt Lake City during the week of August 27 to discuss the proposed contract and answer questions. The representative was Mr. Fred Heine, and Travis Womack met with him at the appointed time and place. At their meeting Womack asked why BLM could not be specific as to the number of Utah cards. Mr. Heine explained that use of an estimate was unavoidable because York Tabulating had not completed the Control Document Index for Utah. He added that BLM felt that its estimate was entirely sound and that, while not completely through, York was very close to being finished with Utah. During his stay in Salt Lake City, Womack examined a sufficient number of plats at the Land Office to satisfy himself that BLM was correct in estimating that 85 percent of the Utah townships could be platted on standard diagrams.

Following the Salt Lake City meeting with Mr. Heine, plaintiffs went to work on the formulation of their bid. Among the things that they did to arrive at a bid price for Utah was a time study on the preparation of a historical index and plat annotations for what they deemed a representative 35-section township. The historical index and the plats for such an average township, plaintiffs assumed, would each have 25 information entries; one entry for each of 25 cards from the Control Document Index. This assumption of card quantity per township was derived by dividing the estimated total quantity of 65,000 index cards by the total number of townships in Utah— approximately 2,550 according to the invitation for bid.

Plaintiffs submitted their bid to BLM on September 15, 1956, with the express stipulation that it was subject to acceptance by the Government within seven days of bid-opening, September 18, 1956. As previously noted, the bid contained separate fixed-price proposals for both Utah and Oregon.

At the opening, it developed that plaintiffs' bid for the State of Utah was second-low. The low bidder was the firm of Bush and Fogel of Salt Lake City. Within a day or two of being notified of the results of the bidding, that firm asked to be relieved of its bid.

Almost immediately after the opening, plaintiffs learned that they had been slightly underbid for the Utah job. They did not know of the low bidder's desire to be relieved, but they felt that they should be awarded the Utah work in any event because the total of their bid prices for both Utah and Oregon was low. On September 21, 1956, John Vorhies came to Washington to persuade BLM that plaintiffs should be awarded the entire contract. On that day and the day following he conferred with Messrs. Thomas, Eynon, Johnson and Heine.

In the course of the conferences, Mr. Thomas advised Vorhies of the low bidder's request to be relieved of its bid and asked whether plaintiffs would be willing to grant the Government an additional 10 days within which it could accept their bid for Utah. Because of appropriations and other considerations of timing, BLM was anxious to avoid setting aside all bids and readvertising the contract for Utah. During the discussions relating to BLM's requested time extension, Mr. Vorhies asked precisely how many cards were involved in the Control Document Index for Utah. The BLM representatives advised him that as of that time York had billed for 64,604 Utah cards. They stated that although a few more cards might be forthcoming, York had finished with its work on Utah for all practical purposes. This expression, which Mr. Vorhies had no reason to question, represented the honest judgment and belief of the BLM representatives at the time, and Mr. Vorhies relied on its accuracy in giving BLM a written agreement to the requested extension of time. In fact, the BLM personnel expressed gratification that their earlier estimate of 65,000 Utah cards had proved so accurate.

On September 25, 1956, BLM's Harold Johnson made one of his periodic inspection visits to York Tabulating. On this particular occasion he went for the primary purpose of determining when York would be finally finished with the Utah Control Document Index. He, of course, knew that BLM had already been billed for 64,604 Utah cards. He also knew that, under York's procedures, billings were submitted on the basis of card count after the initial sort of aperture cards by State and prior to the subsequent sorts that were done to arrange the cards in required sequence by meridian, township and range. Mr. Johnson asked York's president about the status of the Utah cards and was advised by him that all such cards had been through the initial sort by State and that approximately 13 working hours of sorting would be required to place the cards in final sequence. Johnson accepted this representation without further questioning and without consulting any of York's various production records with which he was familiar and which were readily available to him for inspection. He let the matter rest even though he could not understand why, if only 13 hours of sorting work remained, York could not specify a firm date for completion and shipment of the index, and even though this information was the prime objective of his visit.

On September 28, 1956, BLM awarded the contract for Utah to plaintiffs. On that same date, York billed BLM for an additional 16,244 Utah cards. When BLM received this billing in the ordinary course of the mails, all members of the Records Improvement Project were completely surprised because they had all felt certain that York's September 13 billing, bringing the total of Utah cards to 64,604, was its final billing of any consequences so far as card quantity was concerned. In fact, York billed BLM for significant quantities of Utah cards in both October and December, 1956. Ultimately, the Utah Control Document Index numbered 105,000 cards.

In addition to the substantial overrun of Control Document Index cards encountered by plaintiffs in the course of performance of their contract, it developed that instead of having to draw special plats for only 15 percent of the Utah townships, as estimated in the invitation for bid, it was necessary to do this special work for approximately 45 percent of the townships in order to meet contract requirements respecting diagramming. Thus, instead of the projected 383 irregular townships, there were actually 1,148 requiring special diagramming.

On March 5, 1957, Change Order No. 2 to the subject contract was executed by the parties. It allowed plaintiffs additional compensation on account of both the excessive size of the Control Document Index and the inordinate number of irregular townships. In each instance plaintiffs were compensated at an agreed rate for the excess over the estimated quantities plus 25 percent. Respecting the cards, they were paid for the excess over 81,250 (65,000 plus 25 percent of 65,000). As to the irregular townships, they were paid for the excess over 479 (383 plus 25 percent of 383).

The parties have agreed that for purposes of this suit, by which plaintiffs seek compensation for the extra work represented by the first 25 percent of excess over the contract estimates, if plaintiffs are entitled to recover on the additional card issue, the amount of that recovery should be $19,440.17. Similarly, should they be found entitled to recover on the irregular township issue, it is agreed that the recovery should be $2,391.86.

Plaintiffs seasonably filed a claim with the Contracting Officer for the amounts sought in the present suit. After he denied the claim, they appealed to the Interior Board of Contract Appeals. Plaintiffs' principal position before the Board was essentially as it is here; that prior to award of the contract the Government possessed sufficient information to put it on notice that the estimates set forth in the invitation for bid were erroneous. The Board denied the appeal, holding that even if plaintiffs' factual contentions were accepted they made out no more than a basis for relief by way of rescission or damages for breach—relief beyond the Board's jurisdiction. . . .

Although the defendant denies liability on both claims in suit, it does not deny that the amount of plaintiffs' work was directly affected by the quantities of both index cards and irregular townships. In awarding additional compensation under Change Order No. 2, defendant recognized this fact. Accordingly, the materiality of the quantities estimated in the invitation for bid is not disputed.

Plaintiffs contend that they should recover on the card issue because, on the basis of information in its possession or readily and singularly available to it when it awarded the contract in suit, the Government knew or reasonably should have known that its estimate of 65,000 index cards was so seriously in error as to constitute a misrepresentation amounting to a breach of contract.

Defendant's position is that it should not be held liable because it seasonably disclosed to the plaintiffs everything that it actually knew about the quantities of Utah cards, and because it was not until after the award that it knew as a matter of fact that its estimate was significantly wrong. In these circumstances, defendant says, the 25 percent variance in quantity clause contained in the contract operates to place the risk of the first 25 percent of card overrun on the plaintiffs as a matter of law. Because of the general variance in quantity clause there can be no recovery, according to defendant, unless it is found that at the time of the award it actually knew that there would be more than 81,250 Utah cards (65,000 plus 25 percent thereof) and deliberately withheld that information from the plaintiffs. In essence, defendant is saying that the variance in quantity clause has the effect of converting the 65,000 estimate to an estimate of 81,250.

Defendant's position is incorrect both as to the requirement of scienter in establishing an actionable misrepresentation for breach of contract purposes and as to the legal impact on an estimate of a general variance in quantity clause.

While the evidence supports the defendant's claim as to the extent of its actual knowledge and its timely disclosure of that knowledge to the plaintiffs, it also shows that an exercise of reasonable care would have alerted it, at least by the time of award of the contract, to the substantial incorrectness of its unquestionably honest but equally erroneous impressions concerning the highly relevant matter of card quantity.

The evidence as to additional relevant information reasonably available to the Government is substantial.

Mr. Harold Johnson, Assistant Manager of BLM's Records Improvement Project, acknowledged at the trial that an analysis of the film roll index established and maintained by BLM in Washington would have enabled it to project at least the minimum number of index cards that would be required for the State of Utah. This was never done even though BLM was genuinely interested in ascertaining the number of cards that would likely be involved.

More significant was Mr. Johnson's visit to the York premises on September 25, 1956. His primary purpose in making the trip was to expedite completion and shipment of the Utah index. He went with the knowledge that as of September 13, 1956, BLM had been billed for 64,604 Utah cards and with the impression that this figure represented substantially all of such cards. He also knew that the bids for the final phase of the Utah work had been opened on September 18, 1956; that the low bidder had sought leave to withdraw; and that in the course of Washington meetings on September 21 and 22, 1956, BLM had requested John Vorhies to extend the acceptance time for plaintiffs' bid. Finally, he knew from personal observation that during those meetings Vorhies inquired as to the total number of Utah cards and was told by members of the Records Improvement Project that the final number would closely approximate the previously estimated figure of 65,000.

Thus, informed, Mr. Johnson asked York's president, Milan Bump, about a firm completion date for the Utah index. Although Bump told him that all Utah cards had been sorted by State, meridian and quadrant and that only 13 hours would be required to complete the final sorting, he would not specify a date for completion prior to October 5, 1956. Even though Johnson was at a loss to understand why it would take from September 25 to October 5 to perform 13 hours of sorting work, he made no effort to verify Bump's statement as to the current condition of the Utah cards by consulting any of the several York production records with which he was familiar and which were freely available to him. Had he examined these records, it would have been apparent to him that all Utah cards had not, in fact, been sorted by State, meridian and quadrant. Furthermore, at no time during this visit did Johnson ask Bump about the total number of Utah cards that might be anticipated or whether the bills already received by BLM, through September 13, covered substantially all of such cards. . . . It must be said that Mr. Johnson's total failure to consult York's production records or to even inquire of Mr. Bump as to total card quantity constituted negligence on BLM's part. Thus, the information that was there for the asking but not sought is to be imputed to BLM in determining whether, at the subsequent time of the award to plaintiffs, the 65,000 card estimate constituted a material misrepresentation. Considering all of the circumstances, it constituted such a misrepresentation and not the less so because it was attributable to defendant's negligence rather than to any conscious attempt to deceive the plaintiffs. Whatever the case in tort or other areas, intent to mislead is not an essential element of actionable misrepresentation in the breach of contract context. . . . An inadvertent misrepresentation stemming from negligence is fully as damaging as a deliberate one to the party who relies on it to his detriment. Notably, the victim of a misrepresentation amounting to a breach of contract is made whole by compensatory, not punitive damages.

The unqualified and mechanical application of the 25 percent variance in quantity clause to the card estimate clause, as urged by defendant, fails to accord the two provisions meanings which permit them to function in a complementary manner. Under defendant's view, the general clause serves to make all deviations from the estimate, however occasioned, and however foreseeable, noncompensable so long as the deviation does not exceed 25 percent on either side of the estimate. . . .

An estimate as to a material matter in a bidding invitation is an expedient. Ordinarily it is only used where there is a recognized need for guidance to bidders on a particular point but specific information is not reasonably available. . . . Intrinsically, the estimate that is made in such circumstances must be the product of such relevant underlying information as is available to the author of the invitation. If the bidder were not entitled to so regard it, its inclusion in the invitation would be surplusage at best or deception at worst. Assuming that the bidder acts reasonably, he is entitled to rely on Government estimates as representing honest and informed conclusions. . . . In short, in promulgating an estimate for bidding-invitation purposes, the Government is not required to be clairvoyant but it is obliged to base that estimate on all relevant information that is reasonably available to it.

By adding a general variance in quantity provision to a bidding invitation for a fixed-price contract, the Government does not dilute the standard to which it is held with respect to particular estimates that it includes elsewhere in the invitation. In conjunction with an estimate, the proper office of such a general clause is to afford a flexibility sufficient to accommodate actual deviations from the estimate that are not reasonably predictable at the time that the estimate is made and during the time that it remains subject to reliance by the bidder. It embraces variations that are attributable to facts that are not among those reasonably available to the estimator. The latitude that it affords may not properly be used to excuse the estimator from using and disclosing relevant information that is reasonably available to him. Thus, it may be said that its role is to preserve the stability of a fixed-price contract despite fortuitous departures, up or down, from the estimated amount of work to be done.

In summary, the defendant overreaches when it says that the variance in quantity clause, within its percentage limits, put the risk of an index card overrun, whatever its cause and foreseeability, on the plaintiffs. Specifically, the clause apportions only a particular type of risk to the parties, the risk of an excess or shortage resulting from factors not reasonably apparent to them at the time that they entered into their contract. The clause does not require one party to bear the first 25 percent of the burden of the other party's negligence.

The irregular township issue well illustrates a proper application of the general variance in quantity clause.

The Government estimated in its invitation that 85 percent of the Utah townships could be platted on a standard diagram. The estimate was made by a respected and experienced cadastral engineer after reviewing 800 plats from locations throughout the State of Utah.

Prior to bidding, Travis Womack went to the Salt Lake City Land Office and reviewed a sufficient number of Utah plats to convince him that the Government's estimate respecting standard diagramming was accurate.

When plaintiffs performed their contract, they found that by applying criteria that were agreeable to both themselves and BLM, only 55 percent of the Utah townships could be platted on the less costly standard diagrams.

In support of their claim, plaintiffs argue only that the Government's estimate should be deemed a misrepresentation because it ultimately proved to be so wide of the mark. The contention is without merit because error *per se* is not misrepresentation.

The evidence shows that both parties exercised reasonable care and diligence in arriving at and testing the accuracy of the 85 percent estimate. It was only the actual experience of performing the contract that demonstrated that they were both badly mistaken in their forecasts. When they entered into their contract, both parties knew that the actual total number of regular townships could not feasibly be determined in advance of performance. In these circumstances, the variance in quantity clause put the risk of the first 25 percent of low-side forecasting error on the plaintiffs. The Government had informed them as best it reasonably could for bidding purposes, and they had confirmed its estimation by their own investigation. Though both parties were substantially mistaken as a matter of fact, the plaintiffs are not entitled to the equitable relief of reformation because their contract cast on them the risk of just such a contingency. . . . Plaintiffs have failed to show any change in the requirements, in this respect, during performance of the contract.

Questions for Review

1. Define the social force of protection from fraud.

2. Give illustrations of its application.

3. Analyze each opinion in this chapter in terms of the social forces involved in the decision. See § 5:5 for a list of the social forces. With respect to each opinion, explain why the prevailing social forces prevailed and why those rejected did not. In each case in which there is a dissenting opinion, also make this analysis for the dissenting opinion.

4-6. On the basis of the social forces involved, what decision should be made in each of the following cases?

4. *Fraud. Liability for opinion.* Where the owner knows that the roof of a building is leaking, is he liable for fraud when he expresses the opinion that the roof was in "good" condition and was "like new?" *Lackey* v. *Ellingsen,* Ore., 432 P.2d 307.

5. *Fraud. Misrepresentation as to signatures.* When a husband returns loan application papers to the bank, is he guilty of fraud where the signatures of his wife on the forms had not been made by her? *Universal C.I.T. Credit Corp.* v. *Tatro,* Mo., 416 S.W.2d 696.

6. *Premises liability. Water on kitchen floor.* Is a host liable when a Christmas dinner guest falls on water near refrigerator? *Ralls* v. *Baliendo,* 198 Kan. 84, 422 P.2d 862.

7-10. What social forces were involved, which prevailed, and which were defeated in the following decisions?

7. *Limitation of liability. Fine print and obscure.* Air carrier's limitation of liability not binding where unreadable because fine print and not understandable. *Lisi* v. *Alitalia-Linee Aeree Italiane,* [C.A.2d] 370 F.2d 508.

8. *Sales. Examination of goods.* The sale of an automobile cannot be avoided on the ground that the head room in the rear seat was too low for comfort, as such condition was apparent upon inspection of the automobile and could have been easily ascertained by the simple test of sitting in the back seat. *Hendricks* v. *Colonial Buick,* La., 204 So.2d 55.

9. *Product liability. Fraud.* A seller is liable for knowingly making false representations that a car was reconditioned, in good condition, and just like a new car, even though the buyer could have discovered the falsity of these statements had he exercised due care. The buyer's son had in fact driven the car several times, and the written contract stated that the transaction was "not guaranteed-sold as is," which contract the buyer had not read fully because of faulty knowledge of English. *Corona* v. *Esposito,* 4 Conn.Cir. 296, 230 A.2d 624.

10. *Insurance. Binder.* Where a statute limits the duration of both oral and written binders of insurance, there cannot be an oral extension of a written binder beyond the maximum period permitted initially by the statute. *Restaurant Enterprises* v. *Sussex Mutual Insurance Co.,* 96 N.J.S. 26, 232 A.2d 434.

PROTECTION OF THE PERSON

§ 10:1. Generally

At an early date laws developed to protect the individual from being injured or killed. The field of criminal law is devoted to a large extent to the protection of the person. In addition, under civil law a suit can often be brought to recover damages for the harm done by such acts. For example, a reckless driver of an automobile who injures a pedestrian is subject to a criminal penalty. He is also liable to the injured person for the payment of damages, which may include not only medical and hospital cost but also loss of time from work and pain and suffering. In time, the protection of personal rights has broadened to protect reputation and privacy and to protect contracts from malicious interference by outsiders.

The outstanding legal phenomenon of the last 300 years has been the remarkable driving force of the objective of protecting the person. That objective has made great progress in two directions: (a) expansion beyond protection of the mere physical man; and (b) expansion beyond the mere protection in the sense of shielding from harm to that of providing for the individual, and in so doing to provide or assist without discrimination because of religion, sex, previous condition of servitude, or race.

§ 10:2. Protection of the Personality

The law has gone beyond protecting the mere physical person to protecting the vague concept of the dignity of the individual. We all accept without question the validity of a law imposing liability for slander and libel. Yet, if society believed 100 percent in the freedom of personal action, I should be able to say anything I chose about you, and you would not be able to sue me whether what I said was true or false. That is, society would take the position that my right of free speech was so important that it would be better for me to speak without fear and leave you to hope that my listeners would be able to distinguish between what was true and what was false. The fact that the law limits my right to speak shows a desire to protect you from more than physical injury.

The right of privacy is another illustration of protecting from a harm that is not a physical harm. If man were living in primitive conditions with many persons crowded in the same room or barracks, the idea of privacy would be a physical impossibility. In a sense, a concept of privacy is a symbol of a highly-developed economic system in which the individual has the protection of four walls and a roof.

Once the spark of the concept of privacy catches flame, it is fanned by other forces, such as protecting the individual from oppression by the government, or protecting the individual from exploitation by others making profit out of the invasion of his privacy, and protection from oppression by those who would invade his privacy merely for the sake of curiosity or of doing harm.

KORN v. RENNISON

21 Conn.Sup. 400, 156 A.2d 476 (1959)

The substance of this complaint of the plaintiff was that, through an arrangement between Rennison and other defendants, a photograph of Korn, the plaintiff, was published for advertising purposes in the defendant newspaper without the knowledge, consent, or permission of the plaintiff and in violation of her personal liberties and private rights. As a result, the defendants received monetary benefits and advantages while the plaintiff received none and was subjected to ridicule, embarrassment, vexation, and humiliation. The plaintiff, a minor, brought this action by her mother to recover damages.

OPINION BY ALCORN, J. . . .

The defendants argue that . . . a right [of privacy] was not recognized at common law and therefore, in the absence of statute, it cannot exist in Connecticut today. When Samuel D. Warren and Louis D. Brandeis first gave form and substance to the right of privacy in 1890, it was one objective of their discussion in 4 Harvard Law Review 193 to demonstrate that the right found support in comon-law principles. Underlying their reasoning is the premise that the common law is not static and its protecting arm does not become immobilized from lack of precedent.

In the years intervening since the right was thus defined, a constantly increasing number of jurisdictions have recognized its independent existence. Press, photography, radio, and television represent elements in constantly changing conditions which impinge upon individual privacy. With the environmental changes of modern living has grown the need that man's inner nature and feelings as well as his body and possessions receive the protection of the law. Hence, the right of privacy has become established in nearly half the states. . . .

The line to be drawn between reasonable demands of individual privacy and public interest in legitimate news is not always easy to define, but the boundary is more readily perceived in the case of commercial advertising. . . . No case decided within the last fifteen years has been found in which the existence of a right of privacy has been denied. Decisions which originally denied the right have, with apparently a single exception, since been overruled, modified, or altered by statute. Rhode Island appears to stand alone as an unqualified precedent for denying a recovery in damages for an invasion of the right of privacy. . . .

The right of privacy, as developed, finds expression in the Restatement, 4 Torts § 867, as follows: "A person who unreasonably and seriously interferes with another's interest in not having his affairs known to others or his likeness exhibited to the public is liable to the other."

The statement of the rule emphasizes the importance of the facts of the individual case presented. The recognition of the right as a basis for . . . [an] action in jurisdictions faced with the question unaided by statute, and the practical unanimity of recent opinion, place the right within the purview of the common law. . . .

[Objection of defendants dismissed.]

§ 10:3.   Protection of the Mind

It is agreed by everyone that freedom of religion is an essential element of the American way of life. Yet interestingly enough, the federal Constitution protects freedom of religion only as against invasion by federal action. That is, there is no provision of the United States Constitution which guarantees to the individual that he shall have freedom from the control of religion by governmental action generally. The Supreme Court, however, has interpreted the Fourteenth Amendment of the Constitution to guarantee to the individual, as against invasion by the states, religious freedom guaranteed by the First Amendment as against Congressional invasion.

ENGEL v. VITALE

370 U.S. 421 (1962)

The New York State education program provided for a voluntary non-denominational prayer in public schools. This was attacked as a violation of the freedom of religion guaranteed by the First Amendment.

OPINION BY BLACK, J. . . .

[The Board of Regents directed] the following prayer to be said aloud by each class in the presence of a teacher at the beginning of each school day:

"Almighty God, we acknowledge our dependence upon Thee, and we beg Thy blessings upon us, our parents, our teachers and our Country."

This daily procedure was adopted on the recommendation of the State Board of Regents, a governmental agency created by the State Constitution to which the New York Legislature has granted broad supervisory, executive, and legislative powers over the State's public school system. These state officials composed the prayer which they recommended and published as a part of their "Statement on Moral and Spiritual Training in the Schools," saying: "We believe that this Statement will be subscribed to by all men and women of good will, and we call upon all of them to aid in giving life to our program."

Shortly after the practice of reciting the Regents' prayer was adopted by the School District, the parents of ten pupils brought this action in a New York State Court insisting that use of this official prayer in the public schools was contrary to the beliefs, religions, or religious practices of both themselves and their children. Among other things, these parents challenged the constitutionality of both the state law authorizing the School District to direct the use of prayer in public schools and the School District's regulation ordering the recitation of this particular prayer on the ground that these actions of official governmental agencies violate that part of the First Amendment of the Federal Constitution which commands that "Congress shall make no law respecting an establishment of religion"—a command which was "made applicable to the State of New York by the Fourteenth Amendment of the said Constitution." . . .

We think that by using its public school system to encourage recitation of the Regents' prayer, the State of New York has adopted a practice wholly inconsistent with the Establishment Clause. . . .

We think that the constitutional prohibition against laws respecting an establishment of religion must at least mean that in this country it is no part of the business of government to compose official prayers for any group of the American people to recite as a part of a religious program carried on by government.

It is a matter of history that this very practice of establishing governmentally composed prayers for religious services was one of the reasons which caused many of our early colonists to leave England and seek religious freedom in America. The Book of Common Prayer, which was created under governmental direction and which was approved by Acts of Parliament in 1548 and 1549, set out in minute detail the accepted form and content of prayer and other religious ceremonies to be used in the established, tax-supported Church of England. . . .

It is an unfortunate fact of history that when some of the very groups which had most strenuously opposed the established Church of England found themselves sufficiently in control of colonial governments in this country to write their own prayers into law, they passed laws making their own religion the official religion of their respective colonies. . . .

By the time of the adoption of the Constitution, our history shows that there was a widespread awareness among many Americans of the dangers of a union of Church and State. These people knew, some of them from bitter personal experience, that one of the greatest dangers to the freedom of the individual to worship in his own way lay in the government's placing its official stamp of approval upon one particular kind of prayer or one particular form of religious services. They knew the anguish, hardship and bitter strife that could come when zealous religious groups struggled with one another to obtain the government's stamp of approval from each King, Queen, or Protector that came to temporary power. The Constitution was intended to avert a part of this danger by leaving the government of this country in the hands of the people rather than in the hands of any monarch. But this safeguard was not enough. Our Founders were no more willing to let the content of their prayers and their privilege of praying whenever they pleased be influenced by the ballot box than they were to let these vital matters of personal conscience depend upon the succession of monarchs. The First Amendment was added to the Constitution to stand as a guarantee that neither the power nor the prestige of the Federal Government would be used to control, support or influence the kinds of prayer the American people can say—that the people's religions must not be subjected to the pressures of government for change each time a new political administration is elected to office. Under that Amendment's prohibition against governmental establishment of religion, as reinforced by the provisions of the Fourteenth Amendment, government in this country, be it state or federal, is without power to prescribe by law any particular form of prayer which is to be used as an official prayer in carrying on any program of governmentally sponsored religious activity.

There can be no doubt that New York's state prayer program officially establishes the religious beliefs embodied in the Regents' prayer. The respondents' argument to the contrary, which is largely based upon the contention that the Regents' prayer is "nondenominational" and the fact that the program, as modified and approved by state courts, does not require all pupils to recite the prayer but permits those who wish to do so to remain silent or be excused from the room, ignores the essential nature of the program's constitutional defects. Neither the fact that the prayer may be denominationally neutral nor the fact that its observance on the part of the students is voluntary can serve to free it from the limitations of the Establishment Clause, as it might from the Free Exercise Clause, of the First Amendment, both of which are operative against the States by virtue of the Fourteenth Amendment. Although these two clauses may in certain instances overlap, they forbid two quite different kinds of governmental encroachment upon religious freedom. The Establishment Clause, unlike the Free Exercise Clause, does not depend upon any showing of direct governmental compulsion and is violated by the enactment of laws which establish an official religion whether those laws operate directly to coerce nonobserving individuals or not. This is not to say, of course, that laws officially prescribing a particular form of religious worship do not involve coercion of such individuals. When the power, prestige, and financial support of government is placed behind a particular religious belief, the indirect coercive pressure upon religious minorities to conform to the prevailing officially approved religion is plain. But the purposes underlying the Establishment Clause go much further than that. Its first and most immediate purpose rested on the belief that a union of government and religion tends to destroy government and to degrade religion. The history of governmentally established religion, both in England and in this country, showed that whenever government had allied itself with one particular form of religion, the inevitable result had been that it had incurred the hatred, disrespect and even contempt of those who held contrary beliefs. That same history showed that many people had lost their respect for any religion that had relied upon the support of government to spread its faith. The Establishment Clause thus stands as an expression of principle on the part of the Founders of our Constitution that religion is too personal, too sacred, too holy, to permit its "unhallowed perversion" by a civil magistrate. Another purpose of the Establishment Clause rested upon an awareness of the historical fact that governmentally established religions and religious persecutions go hand in hand. . . .

It is true that New York's establishment of its Regents' prayer as an officially approved religious doctrine of that State does not amount to a total establishment of one particular religious sect to the exclusion of all others—that, indeed, the governmental endorsement of that prayer seems relatively insignificant when compared to the governmental encroachments upon religion which were commonplace 200 years ago. To those who may subscribe to the view that because the Regents' official prayer is so brief and general there can be no danger to religious freedom in its governmental establishment, however, it may be appropriate to say in the words of James Madison, the author of the First Amendment:

"[I]t is proper to take alarm at the first experiment on our liberties. . . . Who does not see that the same authority which can establish Christianity, in exclusion of all other Religions, may establish with the same ease any particular sect of Christians, in exclusion of all other Sects? That the same authority which can force a citizen to contribute three pence only of his property for the support of any one establishment, may force him to conform to any other establishment in all cases whatsoever?" . . .

DISSENTING OPINION BY STEWART, J. . . .

With all respect, I think the Court has misapplied a great constitutional principle. I cannot see how an "official religion" is established by letting those who want to say a prayer say it. On the contrary, I think that to deny the wish of these school children to join in reciting this prayer is to deny them the opportunity of sharing in the spiritual heritage of our Nation.

The Court's historical review of the quarrels over the Book of Common Prayer in England throws no light for me on the issue before us in this case. England had then and has now an established church. Equally unenlightening, I think, is the history of the early establishment and later rejection of an official church in our own States. For we deal here not with the establishment of a state church, which would, of course, be constitutionally impermissible, but with whether school children who want to begin their day by joining in prayer must be prohibited from doing so. Moreover, I think that the Court's task, in this as in all areas of constitutional adjudication, is not responsibly aided by the uncritical invocation of metaphors like the "wall of separation," a phrase nowhere to be found in the Constitution. What is relevant to the issue here is not the history of an established church in sixteenth century England or in eighteenth century America, but the history of the religious traditions of our people, reflected in countless practices of the institutions and officials of our government.

At the opening of each day's Session of this Court we stand, while one of our officials invokes the protection of God. Since the days of John Marshall our Crier has said, "God save the United States and this Honorable Court." Both the Senate and the House of Representatives open their daily Sessions with prayer. Each of our Presidents, . . . has upon assuming his office asked for the protection and help of God. . . .

One of the stanzas of "The Star-Spangled Banner," made our National Anthem by Act of Congress in 1931, contains the verse: ". . . And this be our motto 'In God is our Trust.' "

In 1954 Congress added a phrase to the Pledge of Allegiance to the Flag so that it now contains the words "one Nation *under* God indivisible, with liberty and justice for all." In 1952 Congress enacted legislation calling upon the President each year to proclaim a National Day of Prayer. Since 1865 the words "IN GOD WE TRUST" have been impressed on our coins.

Countless similar examples could be listed, but there is no need to belabor the obvious. It was all summed up by this Court just ten years ago in a single sentence: "We are a religious people whose institutions presuppose a Supreme Being." *Zorach* v. *Clauson,* 343 U.S. 306, 313, 96 L.Ed. 954, 962, 72 S.Ct. 679.

I do not believe that this Court, or the Congress, or the President has by the actions and practices I have mentioned established an "official religion" in violation of the Constitution. And I do not believe the State of New York has done so in this case. What each has done has been to recognize and to follow the deeply entrenched and highly cherished spiritual traditions of our Nation—traditions which come down to us from those who almost two hundred years ago avowed their "firm Reliance on the Protection of divine Providence" when they proclaimed the freedom and independence of this brave new world.

[I dissent.]

This case is unusual in that before 1937 the Supreme Court refused to recognize that the First Amendment applied to the states. The decision is also unusual in condemning so innocent a matter as a voluntary, school prayer to a nondenominational God, which was certainly a long distance away from being an official compulsory prayer to a sectarian God, which all members of the community were required to observe. It is likewise interesting to note the higher sensitivity of the Supreme Court in the area of individual freedoms—the Court being alarmed at such a minor danger as that contained in the school prayer; whereas if the question were whether a state or federal law regulating business were constitutional, the Court would take the approach that the law was valid as long as it was not arbitrary or capricious, and the mere fact that the Court disagreed with the law would not make it unconstitutional.

It is believed that no sound answer can be found to meet the dissenting opinion. But the fact remains that the majority of the Court was willing, rightly or wrongly, to find in the Constitution a guarantee of protection from a state prayer of a nondenominational character. The fact remains that somehow out of nothing there arose a "right" that the Court would protect. This in itself is evidence that the social force of protecting the mind of the person made a great advance.

Note, however, that we cannot say that wherever men's minds are concerned, there can be no control. Consider, for example, that it is illegal to practice bigamy even though it is proper under one's religious belief. A parent omitting to provide medical treatment for a sick child because such treatment is counter to the parent's religious belief is guilty of manslaughter when the child dies from such neglect, and the parent's religious belief is no defense. Also religious belief is no excuse for failing to comply with a state compulsory vaccination law. Likewise, a court can order that a child be given a blood transfusion, although the parent refuses to permit it on religious grounds.

Thus, it would appear that while freedom of mind, as expressed in religious belief, is a right of prime importance when the issue is between the individual and the government in the abstract, the right of belief is subordinated when physical harm is threatened to others if the belief is put into actual practice, or when observance of the belief would be deemed inconsistent with the prevailing concepts of morality.

§ 10:4. Protection of the Political Person

It will be recalled that in § 2:2 it was stated that in every state legislature, with one exception, there was a lower house and an upper house. Typically until 1954, the lower house was selected according to population, whereas the upper house was selected on the basis of some district representation the effect of which was generally to give rural communities a greater proportion of state senators than the urban communities. That is, the same unbalance existed in the state legislature as exists today in the United States Congress in which the lower house is elected on the basis of population, while the upper house is selected on the basis of equal representation to each state—each state having two senators and no more than two senators, regardless of how small or how large its population.

In 1954, the United States Supreme Court in *Baker* v. *Carr,* 369 U.S. 186, held that under the equal protection clause of the United States Constitution, it was necessary for both houses of a state legislature to be selected on the basis of population. Underlying the decision was the concept of the court of "one man, one vote," by which every man could cast a vote that had just as much strength or weight in electing a state senator as every other voter in the state, without regard to whether the voter be from a rural or from an urban community.

It is not our present purpose to consider whether this is a sound way to run a state government nor whether it is the function of the United States Supreme Court to determine a question so fundamental to the political structure of the individual states. The fact remains that prior to the declaration by the Supreme Court of the "one man, one vote" rule, there was no such doctrine recognized in the law. This does not mean that there should not be such a doctrine. We are only concerned with what social force caused the law to come to recognize such a doctrine, thereby ignoring the objective of stability. The force prevailing was protection of the person, using that term in the sense of protecting the political person.

First, let us examine the past to see whether there was a "one man, one vote" concept in earlier times. Prior to the American Revolution, when the American forefathers were still colonials, they were familiar with and apparently accepted the system of organization of a legislature that permitted an unequal representation through being based on districts not defined in terms of population. When the colonies insisted that England could not impose taxes on the colonies, it was on the theory that the colonies were not represented in the British Parliament and not that the Parliament was itself improperly organized because there was a selection by geographic districts unrelated to population.

In the Declaration of Independence, which carefully catalogs the complaints of the colonials against George III, there is no reference made to any concept of "one man, one vote." It is a bit difficult to believe that the revolutionary fathers believed in "one man, one vote" when in most colonies, and later in most states, a man could not vote unless he possessed a specified amount of property nor in most of the New England states unless he belonged to the official church. It was to take the Fifteenth Amendment, adopted in 1870, the Nineteenth Amendment, adopted in 1920, and the Twenty-Fourth Amendment, adopted in 1964, and the Harper case decided in 1966, to insure that all adult persons in the United States could vote, without regard to race, color, or previous condition of servitude, sex, or the nonpayment of a poll tax.

Massachusetts, so outstanding a leader in the revolutionary fight for the rights of man, established a state legislature by its Constitution of 1780, which ignores any "one man, one vote" concept. By that Constitution, 40 senators were to be selected from districts determined "by the proportion of the public taxes paid by the said districts." In the lower House of Representatives, representation was stated to be "founded upon the principle of equality," although the Constitution then proceeded to give each corporate town the right to elect a designated number of representatives depending upon the number of taxpayers living within the town. Property qualifications existed, both for voting and office holding, in the upper and the lower houses.

The men who drew our present Constitution of 1790 were not aware of any principle of "one man, one vote" as is seen from the fact that the United States Senate is organized on the basis of an equal number of senators from each state, the very principle which the Supreme Court has outlawed for state legislatures. And to avoid any suggestion that this form of representation was accidental or that its significance was not perceived, note that the Fifth Article of the Constitution in defining the amending process expressly declares, "that no state, without its consent, shall be deprived of its equal suffrage in the Senate." The plain and obvious answer of the history of the time was that society was more concerned with the bringing of the large states and the small states together in a union than it was in determining the weight or significance of the vote of each individual.

That the equality of the individual's voting power was ignored is further seen from the fact that in electing members to the United States House of Representatives, the vote of a voter of a slave-owning state weighed more heavily than one in a nonslave owning state. This for the reason that the latter was allowed only that percentage of the total membership of the lower house which the population of the state bore to the national population. In contrast, the slave-holding state, by virtue of Article I, Section 2, Clause 3, of the Constitution could add three-fifths of the slave population to the total of its free population in determining what percentage its population represented of the total population of the United States.

The method of selecting senators also involved a disparity or inequality of the voting power of the ordinary individual. By Article I, Section 3, Clause 1, of the United States Constitution, United States Senators were "chosen" by the legislatures of the respective states. In a sense, this was compounding inequality because it meant that within a state there was inequality as to the ability of a voter to elect a United States Senator as well as inequality between the voters in one state and the voters in another state in the election of their respective senators. It was not until the adoption of the Seventeenth Amendment in 1913 that the selection of United States Senators was removed from the state legislatures, and the senators were then chosen by popular election.

The acceptance by the framers of the Constitution of the concept of unequal voting rights is further seen in the provision of the United States Constitution for the electoral college by which the President and the Vice-President of the United States are elected. Under the electoral college system, the voters vote for electors who, in turn, select the President and the Vice-President. The framers of the Constitution contemplated that the electors would exercise an independent choice and select the men they deemed best fitted for the jobs. With the rise of the American party system, the existence of which was not contemplated by the framers of the Constitution, the electors traditionally select as their choice for President and Vice-President the persons who have been nominated as the candidates by their respective parties. That is, the Democratic electors choose the Democratic candidate for President and the Democratic candidate for Vice-President. Similarly, the Republican electors vote for the Republican candidates for those offices. The inequality in this system arises from the fact that the organization of the electoral college is a hybrid of state representation and of popular representation. Each state has as many electors as it has representatives in the lower houses of Congress, plus two additional electors. This brings into the electoral college part of the disparity that has been noted already in connection with the selection of two senators from each state. The disparity is further enhanced by the fact that the votes of each state are cast in the electoral college on the basis of "winner take all" with the result that if the electors of party *A* are elected in a given state by a very narrow margin, all of the electoral votes of that state are cast for the candidate of their party. Thus the electoral college vote can often appear to be a landslide for one party or candidate when in fact the margin of victory was very narrow.

It is not without significance that inhabitants of the District of Columbia have no voice in the election of members of Congress nor any voice in the adoption by the Congress of the laws that govern the district. This question has been decided several times by the United States Supreme Court, the conclusion being reached that the Revolutionary battle cry of "no taxation without representation" has no application to the District of Columbia. Accordingly, the inhabitants of the district not only do not have an equal vote but also do not have a vote at all. The Twenty-Third Amendment to the United States Constitution, adopted in 1961, gave the right to the District of Columbia to elect electors to serve as part of the electoral college system in the selection of a President and a Vice-President. No change was made in the direction of giving each man in the District of Columbia an equal vote, nor any vote at all.

Against this historical background, the concept of "one man, one vote" is clearly a new step in the defining of the rights of man.

GRAY v. SANDERS

372 U.S. 368 (1963)

Under the Georgia county unit system, each county was given a particular weight in elections depending upon the bracket in which its population placed it. In order to win a state election, it was necessary for a candidate to win a majority of the county units. Sanders brought an action against the Secretary of the State of Georgia and the Georgia State Democratic Executive Committee to enjoin them from using this system in a Democratic state primary.

OPINION BY DOUGLAS, J. . . .

The District Court held that . . . "the vote of each citizen counts for less and less as the population of the county of his residence increases," 203 F.Supp. 158, 170, note 10. It went on to say:

"There are 97 two-unit counties, totaling 194 unit votes, and 22 counties totaling 66 unit votes, altogether 260 unit votes, within 14 of a majority; but no county in the above has as much as 20,000 population. The remaining 40 counties range in population from 20,481 to 556,326, but they control altogether only 287 county unit votes. Combination of the units from the counties having the smallest population gives counties having population of one-third of the total in the state a clear majority of county units." Ibid. . . .

It held that the county unit system as applied violates the Equal Protection Clause, and it issued an injunction, not against conducting any party primary election under the county unit system, but against conducting such an election under a county unit system that does not meet the requirements specified by the court. 203 F.Supp. 158. In other words, the District Court did not proceed on the basis that in a statewide election every qualified person was entitled to one vote and that all weighted voting was outlawed. Rather, it allowed a county unit system to be used in weighting the votes if the system showed no greater disparity against a county than exists against any State in the conduct of national elections. . . .

This case, unlike *Baker* v. *Carr,* 369 U.S. 186, 7 L.Ed.2d 663, 82 S.Ct. 691, supra, does not involve a question of the degree to which the Equal Protection Clause of the Fourteenth Amendment limits the authority of a State Legislature in designing the geographical districts from which representatives are chosen either for the State Legislature or for the Federal House of Representatives. . . . The District Court, however, analogized Georgia's use of the county unit system in determining the results of a statewide election to phases of our federal system. It pointed out that under the electoral college, required by Art. 2, § 1, of the Constitution and the Twelfth Amendment in the election of the President, voting strength "is not in exact proportion to population. . . . Recognizing that the electoral college was set up as a compromise to enable the formation of the Union among the several sovereign states, it still could hardly be said that such a system used in a state among its counties, assuming rationality and absence of arbitrariness in end result, could be termed invidious." 203 F.Supp., at 169.

Accordingly the District Court as already noted held that use of the county unit system in counting the votes in a statewide elections was permissible "if the disparity against any county is not in excess of the disparity that exists against any state in the most recent electoral college allocation." 203 F.Supp., at 170. Moreover the District Court held that use of the county unit system in counting the votes in a statewide election was permissible "if the disparity against any county is not in excess of the disparity that exists . . . under the equal proportions formula for representation of the several states in the Congress." Ibid. The assumption implicit in these conclusions is that since equality is not inherent in the electoral college and since precise equality among blocs of votes in one State or in the several States when it comes to the election of members of the House of Representatives is never possible, precise equality is not necessary in statewide elections.

We think the analogies to the electoral college, to districting and redistricting, and to other phases of the problems of representation in state or federal legislatures or conventions are inapposite. The inclusion of the electoral college in the Constitution, as the result of specific historical concerns, validated the collegiate principle despite its inherent numerical inequality, but implied nothing about the use of an analogous system by a State in a statewide election. No such specific accommodation of the latter was ever undertaken, and therefore no validation of its numerical inequality ensued. . . . Georgia gives every qualified voter one vote in a statewide election; but in counting those votes she employs the county unit system which in end result weights the rural vote more heavily than the urban vote and weights some small rural counties heavier than other larger rural counties. . . .

The Fifteenth Amendment prohibits a State from denying or abridging a Negro's right to vote. The Nineteenth Amendment does the same for women. If a State in a statewide election weighted the male vote more heavily than the female vote or the white vote more heavily than the Negro vote, none could successfully contend that that discrimination was allowable. . . . How then can one person be given twice or 10 times the voting power of another person in a statewide election merely because he lives in a rural area or because he lives in the smallest rural county? Once the geographical unit for which a representative is to be chosen is designated, all who participate in the election are to have an equal vote—whatever their race, whatever their sex, whatever their occupation, whatever their income, and wherever their home may be in that geographical unit. This is required by the Equal Protection Clause of the Fourteenth Amendment. The concept of "we the people" under the Constitution visualizes no preferred class of voters but equality among those who meet the basic qualifications. The idea that every voter is equal to every other voter in his State, when he casts his ballot in favor of one of several competing candidates, underlies many of our decisions.

The Court has consistently recognized that all qualified voters have a constitutionally protected right "to cast their ballots and have them counted at Congressional elections." . . . Every voter's vote is entitled to be counted once, . . . and, as previously noted, there is no indication in the Constitution that homesite or occupation affords a permissible basis for distinguishing between qualified voters within the State.

The only weighting of votes sanctioned by the Constitution concerns matters of representation, such as the allocation of Senators irrespective of population and the use of the electoral college in the choice of a President. Yet when Senators are chosen, the Seventeenth Amendment states the choice must be made "by the people." Minors, felons, and other classes may be excluded. See *Lassiter* v. *Northampton County Election Board,* supra., 360 U.S. p. 51. But once the class of voters is chosen and their qualifications specified, we see no constitutional way by which equality of voting power may be evaded. . . .

The conception of political equality from the Declaration of Independence, to Lincoln's Gettysburg Address, to the Fifteenth, Seventeenth, and Nineteenth Amendments can mean only one thing—"one person, one vote."

While we agree with the District Court on most phases of the case and think it was right in enjoining the use of the county unit system in tabulating the votes, we vacate its judgment and remand the case so that a decree in conformity with our opinion may be entered.

[It is so ordered.]

DISSENTING OPINION BY HARLAN, J. . . .

When *Baker* v. *Carr,* 369 U.S. 186, 7 L.Ed.2d 663, 82 S.Ct. 691, was argued at the last Term, we were assured that if this Court would only remove the roadblocks . . . to judicial review in "electoral" cases, this Court in all likelihood would never have to get deeper into such matters. State legislatures, it was predicted, would be prodded into taking satisfactory action by the mere prospect of legal proceedings.

These predictions have not proved true. As of November 1, 1962, the apportionment of seats in at least 30 state legislatures had been challenged in state and federal courts, and, besides this one, 10 electoral cases of one kind or another are already on this Court's docket. The present case is the first of these to reach plenary consideration.

Preliminary, it is symptomatic of the swift pace of current constitutional adjudication that the majority opinion should have failed to mention any of the four occasions on which Georgia's County Unit System has previously been unsuccessfully challenged in this Court. . . .

The Court's holding surely flies in the face of history. For, as impressively shown by the opinion of Frankfurter, J., in *Baker* v. *Carr,* 369 U.S., at 301-324, "one person, one vote" has never been the universally accepted political philosophy in England, the American Colonies, or in the United States. The significance of this historical fact seems indeed to be recognized by the Court, for it implies that its new-found formula might not obtain in a case involving the apportionment of seats in the "State Legislature or for the Federal House of Representatives." Ante, pp. 827, 828.

But, independently of other reasons that will be discussed in a moment, any such distinction finds persuasive refutation in the Federal Electoral College whereby the President of the United States is chosen on principles wholly opposed to those now held constitutionally required in the electoral process for statewide office. One need not close his eyes to the circumstance that the Electoral College was born in compromise, nor take sides in the various attempts that have been made to change the system, in order to agree with the court below that it "could hardly be said that such a system used in a state among its counties, assuming rationality and absence of arbitrariness in end result, could be termed invidious." 203 F.Supp., at 169.

Indeed this Court itself some 15 years ago rejected, in a comparable situation, the notion of political equality now pronounced. In *MacDougall* v. *Green,* 335 U.S. 281, 93 L.Ed. 3, 69 S.Ct. 1, challenge was made to an Illinois law requiring that nominating petitions of a new political party be signed by at least 25,000 voters, including a minimum of 200 voters from each of at least 50 of the 102 counties in the State. The claim was that the "200 requirement" made it possible for "the voters of the less populous counties . . . to block the nomination of candidates whose support is confined to geographically limited areas." Id. 335 U.S. at 283. In disallowing this claim, the Court said (id. 335 U.S. at 283, 284):

"To assume that political power is a function exclusively of numbers is to disregard the practicalities of government. Thus, the Constitution protects the interests of the smaller against the greater by giving in the Senate entirely unequal representation to populations. It would be strange indeed, and doctrinaire, for this Court, applying such broad constitutional concepts as due process and equal protection of the laws, to deny a State the power to assure a proper diffusion of political initiative as between its thinly populated counties and those having concentrated masses, in view of the fact that the latter have practical opportunities for exerting their political weight at the polls not available to the former. The Constitution—a practical instrument of government—makes no such demands on the States."

Certainly no support for this equal protection doctrine can be drawn from the Fifteenth, Seventeenth, or Nineteenth Amendment. The Fifteenth Amendment simply assures that the right to vote shall not be impaired "on account of race, color, or previous condition of servitude." The Seventeenth Amendment provides that Senators shall be "elected by the people," with no indication that all people must be accorded a vote of equal weight. The Nineteenth Amendment merely gives the vote to women. And it is hard to take seriously the argument that "dilution" of a vote in consequence of a legislatively sanctioned electoral system can, without more, be analogized to an impairment of the political franchise by ballot box stuffing or other criminal activity, . . . or to the disenfranchisement of qualified voters on purely racial grounds. . . .

A violation of the Equal Protection Clause thus cannot be found in the *mere* circumstance that the Georgia County Unit System results in disproportionate vote weighting. It "is important for this court to avoid extracting from the very general language of the Fourteenth Amendment a system of delusive exactness. . . ." *Louisville & N. R. Co.* v. *Barber Asphalt Paving Co.* 197 U.S. 430, 434, 49 L.Ed. 819, 821, 25 S.Ct. 466 (Holmes, J.). What then remains of the equal protection claim in this case?

At the core of Georgia's diffusion of voting strength which favors the small as against the large counties is the urban-rural problem, so familiar in the American political scene. In my dissent in *Baker* v. *Carr,* 369 U.S., at 336, I expressed the view that a State might rationally conclude that its general welfare was best served by apportioning more seats in the legislature to agricultural communities than to urban centers, lest the legitimate interests of the former be submerged in the stronger electoral voice of the latter. In my opinion, recognition of the same factor cannot be deemed irrational in the present situation, even though all of the considerations supporting its use in a legislative apportionment case are not present here.

Given the undeniably powerful influence of a state governor on law and policy making, I do not see how it can be deemed irrational for a State to conclude that a candidate for such office should not be one whose choice lies with the numerically superior electoral strength of urban voters. By like token, I cannot consider it irrational for Georgia to apply its County Unit System to the selection of candidates for other statewide offices in order to assure against a predominantly "city point of view" in the administration of the State affairs. . . .

The disproportions in the Georgia County Unit System are indeed not greatly out of line with those existing under the Electoral College count for the Presidency. The disparity in population per Electoral College vote between New York (the largest State in the 1960 census) and Alaska (the smallest) was about 5 to 1. There are only 15 Georgia counties, out of a total of 159, which have a greater disparity per unit vote, and of these 15 counties 4 have disparity of less than 6 to 1. It is thus apparent that a slight modification of the Georgia plan could bring it within the tolerance permitted in the federal scheme.

It was of course imponderables like these that lay at the root of the Court's steadfast pre-*Baker* v. *Carr* refusal "to enter [the] political thicket." . . . Having turned its back on this wise chapter in its history, the Court, in my view, can no longer escape the necessity of coming to grips with the thorny problems it so studiously strove to avoid in *Baker* v. *Carr*. . . .

What then should be the test of "rationality" in this judicially unfamiliar field? My Brother Clark has perhaps given us a clue in the legislative inactivity—absence of any other remedy—crazy quilt approach contained in his concurring opinion in *Baker* v. *Carr*, supra., 369 U.S. at 253-262. But I think a formulation of the basic ground rules in this untrod area of judicial competence should await a fully developed record. This case is here at an interlocutory stage. The temporary injunction before us issued upon a record consisting only of the pleadings, answers to interrogatories, affidavits, statistical material, and what the lower court described as a "liberal use of our right to take judicial notice of matters of common knowledge and public concern." 203 F.Supp., at 160, note 1. No full-dress exploration of any of the many intricate questions involved in establishing criteria for judging "rationality" took place, the opinion and decree below issued the day following the hearing, and the District Court observed that, while its standards of equal protection (which this Court now puts aside) "may appear doctrinaire to some extent," it was constrained to act as it did because of the then (but no longer existing) urgency of the situation. 203 F.Supp., at 170.

Surely, if the Court's "one person, one vote" ideology is constitutionally untenable, as I think it clearly is, the basic ground rules implementing *Baker* v. *Carr* should await the trial of this or some other case in which we have before us a full developed record. Only then can we know what we are doing. . . . A matter which so profoundly touches the barriers between federal judicial and state legislative authority demands nothing less.

I would vacate the judgment of the District Court and remand the case for trial.

Questions for Review

1. Define the social force of protection of the person.

2. Give illustrations of its application.

3. Analyze each opinion in this chapter in terms of the social forces involved in the decision. See § 5:5 for a list of the social forces. With respect to each opinion, explain why the prevailing social forces prevailed and why those rejected did not. In each case in which there is a dissenting opinion, also make this analysis for the dissenting opinion.

4-8. On the basis of the social forces involved, what decision should be made in each of the following cases?

4. **Enterprise liability. Identity of payor.** May a wife recover damages from a service station where the negligent installation work of the latter prevented the automobile from decelerating which resulted in injury, where the service work was ordered by the husband, and paid for by the husband's employer? *Woodrick v. Smith Gas Service*, 87 Ill.App.2d 88, 230 N.E.2d 508.

5. **Schools. Guidance procedure.** Does a suspended student have constitutional right to counsel in a guidance conference? *Madera v. Board of Education*, [C.A.2d] 386 F.2d 778.

6. **Illegitimate child. Tort liability of father.** May an illegitimate child recover damages from its natural father for the harm of causing it to be born illegitimate? *Pinkney v. Pinkney*, Fla., 198 So.2d 52.

7. **Elections. Poll tax.** Although the Twenty-Fourth Amendment to the United States Constitution prohibits making the payment of a poll tax a condition to vote in a federal election, there is no provision in the Constitution which contains a similar prohibition with respect to state elections. May a state prohibit voting at state elections by persons who have not paid a state poll tax? *Harper v. Virginia State Board of Elections*, U.S., 86 S.Ct. 1079.

8. **Dead bodies. Autopsy.** May damages be recovered by a widow for an unauthorized autopsy performed on her deceased husband where she did not learn thereof until 10 days later and autopsy incisions were not visible at the time of the funeral? *Eastin v. Ochsner Clinic*, La., 200 So.2d 371.

9-12. What social forces were involved, which prevailed, and which were defeated in the following decisions?

9. **Privacy. Athlete.** Nationally-known professional golfer can enjoin game manufacturer from using his name in connection with a golf game even though the advertising and package referred only to "23 famous golfers" and the inclusion of plaintiff could only be determined after purchasing the game and opening the box. *Palmer v. Schonhorn Enterprises, Inc.*, 96 N.J.S. 72, 232 A.2d 458.

10. **Insurance. Use.** Where security guard at request of automobilist used his gun to break car window when keys were locked inside, harm "arises out of the use" of the car within policy coverage when one of the passengers standing near the car is injured when the guard's gun is accidently discharged. *Cagle v. Playland Amusement, Inc.*, La., 202 So.2d 396.

11. **Premises liability. Trespassing children.** Owner of private residential swimming pool is liable for drowning of 5-year-old child who was visiting neighbor where the owner did not maintain adequate fencing around the pool, since the placing of such fencing would not have imposed a great burden upon him. *Giacona v. Tapley*, 5 Ariz. 494, 428 P.2d 439.

12. **Rescue. Not admission of liability.** The fact that other driver takes the injured driver to hospital and later inquires as to his condition is not an admission of liability. *Lyons v. Levine*, 352 Mass. 769, 225 N.E.2d 593.

PROTECTION OF PROPERTY

§ 11:1. Generally

Just as both criminal and civil laws have developed to protect the individual's physical well-being, such laws also have developed to protect one's property from damage, destruction, and other harmful acts. Property may be taken by the government for payment of taxes. In time of war property may be taken as a matter of military necessity even though the property is not used by the armed forces but is destroyed to prevent its falling into enemy hands.

§ 11:2. Governmental Taking

Apart from the taking of property as above described, the owner of property is protected by constitutional guarantees that his property may only be taken for a public purpose and that when so taken, just compensation must be made to him for the value of the property. Since the Constitution provides for compensation only when there has been a "taking," it becomes essential to determine what is a "taking." Assume that the government acquires a tract of land and puts a courthouse thereon, it is apparent that there has been a taking of the owner's land. Assume that the government built a dam which caused the river water to back up for miles and create an artificial lake that floods the land of the plaintiff. Has his land been taken? Assume that the activity of the government in the neighborhood causes damage to the plaintiff's land but does not prevent the plaintiff from continuing to use the land. Has there been a taking? In the latter two cases, the flooding by the dam, and the impairment of the value, both caused an economic loss rather than a physical taking of the property.

If I put a large padlock on the front door of your home and thereby prevent you from getting into your house, no one would say that I have "taken" your home from you. It is true that I have excluded you from entering it or enjoying it. But that is not a "taking" and as the Constitution only provides for compensation when there is a "taking," it should not include mere exclusion. Consider the case of your house again. Suppose that I open up a slaughterhouse next to your house. You thereafter would not enjoy your house as much as before and because of this its value to you, as well as to a possible buyer, is lower than before. Yet when you sue me to stop my slaughterhouse, you would not claim that I took your house but merely that I have unreasonably interfered with its use by you. Surely this is not a "taking."

If the social objective of stability is alone considered in eminent domain, there would be no recovery for "taking" in either the flooding water case or the governmental interference case. But this would strip the plaintiff's property of protection, as well as be oppressive to the plaintiff, and therefore the law holds that there is such a taking in the two cases above considered that the government must pay compensation to the extent that there has been a reduction in or impairment of the value of the property to the owner.

UNITED STATES v. CAUSBY

328 U.S. 256 (1946)

OPINION BY DOUGLAS, J. . . .

The problem presented is whether respondents' property was taken within the meaning of the Fifth Amendment, by frequent and regular flights of army and navy aircraft over respondents' land at low altitudes. . . .

Respondents own 2.8 acres near an airport outside of Greensboro, North Carolina. . . . The 30 to 1 safe glide angle approved by the Civil Aeronautics Authority passes over this property at 83 feet, which is 67 feet above the house, 63 feet above the barn and 18 feet above the highest tree.

. . . Since the United States began operations in May, 1942, its four-motored heavy bombers, other planes of the heavier type, and its fighter planes have frequently passed over respondents' land and buildings in considerable number and rather close together. They come close enough at times to appear barely to miss the tops of the trees and at times so close to the tops of the trees as to blow the old leaves off. The noise is startling. And at night the glare from the planes brightly lights up the place. As a result of the noise, respondents had to give up their chicken business. . . . The result was the destruction of the use of the property as a commercial chicken farm. Respondents are frequently deprived of their sleep and the family has become nervous and frightened. Although there have been no airplane accidents on respondents' property, there have been several accidents near the airport and close to respondents' place. These are the essential facts found by the Court of Claims. On the basis of these facts, it found that respondents' property had depreciated in value. It held that the United States had taken an easement over the property on June 1, 1942, . . .

It is ancient doctrine that a common-law ownership of the land extended to the periphery of the universe—*Cujus est solum ejus est usque ad coelum*. But that doctrine has no place in the modern world. The air is a public highway, as Congress has declared. Were that not true, every transcontinental flight would subject the operator to countless trespass suits. Common sense revolts at the idea. To recognize such private claims to the airspace would clog these highways, seriously interfere with their control and development in the public interest, and transfer into private ownership that to which only the public has a just claim.

. . . If, by reason of the frequency and altitude of the flights, respondents could not use this land for any purpose, their loss would be complete. It would be as complete as if the United States had entered upon the surface of the land and taken exclusive possession of it.

We agree that in those circumstances there would be a taking. Though it would be only an easement of flight which was taken, that easement, if permanent and not merely temporary, normally would be the equivalent of a fee interest. It would be a definite exercise of complete dominion and control over the surface of the land. . . . The owner's right to possess and exploit the land—that is to say, his beneficial ownership of it—would be destroyed.

. . . The path of glide for airplanes might reduce a valuable factory site to grazing land, an orchard to a vegetable patch, a residential section to a wheat field. Some value would remain. But the use of airspace immediately above the land would limit the utility of the land and cause a diminution in its value. . . .

We have said that the airspace is a public highway. Yet it is obvious that if the landowner is to have full enjoyment of the land, he must have exclusive control of the immediate reaches of the enveloping atmosphere. Otherwise buildings could not be erected, trees could not be planted, and even fences could not be run. The principle is recognized when the law gives a remedy in case overhanging structures are erected on adjoining land. The landower owns at least as much of the space above the ground as he can occupy or use in connection with the land. . . . The fact that he does not occupy it in a physical sense—by the erection of buildings and the like— is not material. As we have said, the flight of airplanes, which skim the surface but do not touch it, is as much an appropriation of the use of the land as a more conventional entry upon it. We would not doubt that if the United States erected an elevated railway over respondents' land at the precise altitude where its planes now fly, there would be a partial taking, even though none of the supports of the structure rested on the land. The reason is that there would be an intrusion so immediate and direct as to subtract from the owner's full enjoyment of the property and to limit his exploitation of it. While the owner does not in any physical manner occupy the stratum of airspace or make use of it in the conventional sense, he does use it in somewhat the same sense that space left between buildings for the purpose of light and air is used. The superadjacent airspace at this low altitude is so close to the land that continuous invasions of it affect the use of the surface of the land itself. We think that the landowner, as an incident to his ownership, has a claim to it and that invasions of it are in the same category as invasions of the surface.

§ 11:3. Governmental Restrictions

Does every loss in value constitute a taking? Zoning laws commonly place limitations on land that may lessen the value of the land. For example, the owner of a given piece of land could make more money if he were allowed to build a high-rise apartment on the land than if he is limited to a one-family residential building. If the zoning laws limit him to the latter type of building, he has lost some of the value of his land. It is held, however, that he has no claim against the government for compensation, even though he had purchased the land before the zoning law was adopted. Thus the owner finds himself deprived of the value or of some of the value of his property without any compensation being given him.

Is there a "taking" if the government restriction is so all-inclusive that it prevents the owner from making any use of his property? The Eureka case which follows is significant as supporting the proposition that the loss a business sustains when government regulations cut it off from labor and supplies is not compensable. While the case was decided against the background of the war power, there is nothing that prevents its extension to any pattern of regulation, whether in war or peace, once the validity of the regulation is conceded. Furthermore, if it be thought that the war power is essential to the Eureka doctrine, it must be remembered that the war power is not limited to the power to wage war but embraces preparation for war and the healing of the wounds of war. In a century of constant international tension, which has known two major wars, two major police actions, and endless minor conflicts, there are few measures, if any, that could not be justified on the premise of making the nation prepared and industrially sound for a possible future war.

In sustaining the validity of restrictions on the use of property, it is seen that the social force in favor of protecting property is outweighed by the forces favoring the protection of the government or the general welfare, safety, or morals.

UNITED STATES v. CENTRAL EUREKA MINING CO.

357 U.S. 155 (1958)

In order to divert miners and mining equipment from gold mining to other more essential forms of mining, the War Production Board issued an order L-208 in 1942, classifying gold mining as nonessential and ordering all gold mines to shut down. After World War II, Central Eureka Mining Company, which was one of the gold mines closed down by the government order, brought suit in the Court of Claims against the United States to recover compensation for the loss sustained by the closing of the mine.

OPINION BY BURTON, J. . . .

It is clear from the record that the Government did not occupy, use, or in any manner, take physical possession of the gold mines or of the equipment connected with them. Cf. *United States* v. *Pewee Coal Co.,* 341 U.S. 114, 95 L.Ed. 809, 71 S.Ct. 670. All that the Government sought was the cessation of the consumption of mining equipment and manpower in the gold mines and the conservation of such equipment and manpower for more essential war uses. The Government had no need for the gold or the gold mines.

. . . Traditionally, we have treated the issue as to whether a particular governmental restriction amounted to a constitutional taking as being a question properly turning upon the particular circumstances of each case. . . . The mere fact that the regulation deprives the property owner of the most profitable use of his property is not necessarily enough to establish the owners right to compensation. . . . In the context of war, we have been reluctant to find that degree of regulation which, without saying so, requires compensation to be paid for resulting losses of income. . . . The reasons are plain. War, particularly in modern times, demands the strict regulation of nearly all resources. It makes demands which otherwise would be insufferable. But wartime economic restrictions, temporary in character, are insignificant when compared to the widespread uncompensated loss of life and freedom of action which war traditionally demands.

We do not find in the temporary restrictions here placed on the operation of gold mines a taking of private property that would justify a departure from the trend of the above decisions. The WPB here sought, by reasonable regulation, to conserve the limited supply of equipment used by the mines and it hoped that its order would divert available miners to more essential work. Both purposes were proper objectives; both matters were subject to regulation to the extent of the order. L-208 did not order any disposal of property or transfer of men. . . . The damage to the mine owners was incidental to the Government's lawful regulation of matters reasonably deemed essential to the war effort. . . .

DISSENTING OPINION BY HARLAN, J. . . .

I dissent because I believe that the Fifth Amendment to the Constitution requires the government to pay just compensation to the respondents for the temporary "taking" of their property accomplished by WPB Order L-208. . . .

L-208 was the only order promulgated during World War II which by its terms required a lawful and productive industry to shut down at a severe economic cost. . . . As a result of the Order the respondents were totally deprived of the beneficial use of their property. Any suggestion that the mines could have been used in such a way (that is, other than to mine gold) so as to remove them from the scope of the Order would be chimerical. Not only were the respondents completely prevented from making profitable use of their property, but the Government acquired all that it wanted from the mines—their complete immobilization and the resulting discharge of the hardrock miners. It is plain that as a practical matter the Order led to consequences no different from those that would have followed the temporary acquisition of physical possession of these mines by the United States.

In these circumstances making the respondents' right to compensation turn on whether the Government took the ceremonial step of planting the American Flag on the mining premises, cf. *United States* v. *Pewee Coal Co.,* 341 U.S. 114, 116, 95 L.Ed. 809, 813, 71 S.Ct. 670, is surely to permit technicalities of form to dictate consequences of substance. In my judgment the present case should be viewed precisely as if the United States, in order to accomplish its purpose of freeing gold miners for essential work, had taken possession of the gold mines and allowed them to lie fallow for the duration of the war. Had the Government adopted the latter course it is hardly debatable that respondents would have been entitled to compensation. See *United States* v. *Pewee Coal Co.,* (U.S.) supra. . . .

§ 11:4.   Patents and Copyrights

(a) Generally. Apart from the protection afforded to property from theft, fire, and other hazards, an owner's property rights may in some instances have a greater protection by virtue of his having a patent or a copyright. Ordinarily property protection is concerned with someone taking or damaging your property, as your automobile, whereas patents and copyrights protect the manufacturer's design of the automobile to prevent someone else from copying it.

(b) Nature. A patent is a federal grant that gives the inventor of a machine or device a monopoly. The grant terminates after 17 years and cannot be renewed; but within that time, the owner of the patent has the exclusive right to make, use, and sell the device or permit others to do so, for which a payment is ordinarily made. After the 17 years have expired, anyone may use the invention. A copyright is a similar exclusive grant given by the federal government with respect to artistic creations. The copyright lasts for 28 years and may be renewed for another 28 years. When an article is not patented or a work is not copyrighted, anyone may duplicate and market it, without regard to the fact that he may be moving into a market already built up by another.

SEARS, ROEBUCK & CO. v. STIFFEL CO.
376 U.S. 225 (1964)

Stiffel manufactured a floor lamp which it patented. After this lamp became popular, Sears, Roebuck & Co. made an identical lamp, which they then sold successfully at a lower price. Stiffel sued Sears for an injunction claiming that his patent had been infringed and that Sears was guilty of unfair competition. The injunction was granted, and Sears appealed.

OPINION BY BLACK, J. . . .

The District Court, after holding the patents invalid for want of invention, went on to find as a fact that Sears' lamp was "a substantially exact copy" of Stiffel's and that the two lamps were so much alike, both in appearance and in functional details, "that confusion between them is likely, and some confusion has already occurred." On these findings the court held Sears guilty of unfair competition, enjoined Sears "from unfairly competing with [Stiffel] by selling or attempting to sell pole lamps identical to or confusingly similar to" Stiffel's lamp, and ordered an accounting to fix profits and damages resulting from Sears' "unfair competition."

The Court of Appeals affirmed. 313 F.2d 115. That court held that, to make out a case of unfair competition under Illinois law, there was no need to show that Sears had been "palming off" its lamps as Stiffel lamps; Stiffel had only to prove that there was a "likelihood of confusion as to the source of the products"—that the two articles were sufficiently identical that customers could not tell who had made a particular one. . . .

The grant of a patent is the grant of a statutory monopoly. . . .

When the patent expires, the monopoly created by it expires, too, and the right to make the article—including the right to make it in precisely the shape it carried when patented—passes to the public. . . .

Obviously a State could not, consistently with the Supremacy Clause of the Constitution, extend the life of a patent beyond its expiration date or give a patent on an article which lacked the level of invention required for federal patents. To do either would run counter to the policy of Congress of granting patents only to true inventions, and then only for a limited time. Just as a State cannot encroach upon the federal patent laws directly, it cannot, under some other law, such as that forbidding unfair competition, give protection of a kind that clashes with the objectives of the federal patent laws.

In the present case the "pole lamp" sold by Stiffel has been held not to be entitled to the protection of either a mechanical or a design patent. An unpatentable article, like an article on which the patent has expired, is in the public domain and may be made and sold by whoever chooses to do so. What Sears did was to copy Stiffel's design and to sell lamps almost identical to those sold by Stiffel. This it had every right to do under the federal patent laws. That Stiffel originated the pole lamp and made it popular is immaterial. "Sharing in the goodwill of an article unprotected by patent or trademark is the exercise of a right possessed by all—and in the free exercise of which the consuming public is deeply interested." . . . To allow a State by use of its law of unfair competition to prevent the copying of an article which represents too slight an advance to be patented would be to permit the State to block off from the public something which federal law has said belongs to the public. The result would be that while federal law grants only 14 or 17 years' protection to genuine inventions, . . . States could allow perpetual protection to articles too lacking in novelty to merit any patent at all under federal consitutional standards. This would be too great an encroachment on the federal patent system to be tolerated.

Sears has been held liable here for unfair competition because of a finding of likelihood of confusion based only on the fact that Sears' lamp was copied from Stiffel's unpatented lamp and that consequently the two looked exactly alike. Of course there could be "confusion" as to who had manufactured these nearly identical articles. But mere inability of the public to tell two identical articles apart is not enough to support an injunction against copying or an award of damages for copying that which the federal patent laws permit to be copied. Doubtless a State may, in appropriate circumstances, require that goods, whether patented or unpatented, be labeled or that other pre-cautionary steps be taken to prevent customers from being misled as to the source, just as it may protect businesses in the use of their trademarks, labels, or distinctive dress in the packaging of goods so as to prevent others, by imitating such markings, from misleading purchasers as to the source of the goods. But because of the federal patent laws a State may not, when the article is unpatented and uncopyrighted, prohibit the copying of the article itself or award damages for such copying. . . . The judgment did both and in so doing gave Stiffel the equivalent of a patent monopoly on its unpatented lamp. That was error, and Sears is entitled to a judgment in its favor. . . .

§ 11:5. Procedural Protection

The social force of protecting property has led to the creation of pro-cedures and remedies for enforcing claims of an owner so that he can get his property back or its money equivalent. Various rules of evidence have sprung up as a means of assisting the owner in the protection of his property. In some instances, established rules of evidence have been modified where they would bar the owner from proving his claim.

Questions for Review

1. Define the social force of protection of property.

2. Give illustrations of its application.

3. Analyze each opinion in this chapter in terms of the social forces involved in the decision. See § 5:5 for a list of the social forces. With respect to each opinion, explain why the prevailing social forces prevailed and why those rejected did not. In each case in which there is a dissenting opinion, also make this analysis for the dissenting opinion.

4-7. On the basis of the social forces involved, what decision should be made in each of the following cases?

4. Product liability. Inadequate warning. Is a manufacturer of weed killer liable to a remote farmer-user when canned weed killer bore a warning against planting corn after using killer but did not warn against planting any other crop, the farmer planting a different crop which was shown to be damaged by the weed killer? *Corprew* v. *Geigy Chem. Corp.*, 271 N.C. 485, 157 S.E.2d 98.

5. Insurance. Physical loss. Does an insurance covering "physical loss" of oil in tank cover loss from shortage in quantity? *Murray Oil Products Inc.* v. *Royal Exchange Assurance Co.*, 21 N.Y.2d 440, 288 N.Y.S.2d 618.

6. Product liability. Label. When there is no antidote for a poisonous product, is the manufacturer protected by labeling the product as a poison and by stating on the label the first aid measures which should be taken? *Rumsey* v. *Freeway Manor Minimax*, Tex.Civ.App., 423 S.W.2d 387.

7. Bailment. Holdover bailee. When a bailee retains possession of a rented car beyond the rental period, does he thereby become a converter so that a liability policy applicable while the car was being used by a "renter" was not applicable because of an exclusion clause in the policy which excluded liability if the automobile had been stolen or converted? *Guaranty National Insurance Co.* v. *Mihalovich*, Wash.2d, 435 P.2d 648.

8-10. What social forces were involved, which prevailed, and which were defeated in the following decisions?

8. Parking lot. Proof of innocence. When it is shown that the plaintiff left his car in the possession and control of a parking lot and the lot thereafter failed to produce the car on demand, the parking lot has the burden of proving that it was innocent of any fault causing the loss. *Continental Insurance Co.* v. *Myers Bros. Operations,* 56 Misc.2d 435, 288 N.Y.S.2d 756.

9. Limitation of liability. What constitutes. The requirement in the lease that the landlord rebuild the premises in case of destruction "by fire, or the elements, or other cause" does not free the tenant from liability when the premises are destroyed because of the tenant's negligence. *National Motels Inc.* v. *Howard Johnson,* [C.A.4th] 373 F.2d 375.

10. Conversion. Automobile keys. Where an automobile salesman refuses to return to a customer the keys to the customer's automobile on pretext that he cannot find them and finally surrenders keys after a policeman is called, a verdict for conversion of the automobile, and not just the keys, is proper; and it was immaterial that the customer could have obtained another set of keys from home. *Russell-Vaughn Ford, Inc.* v. *Rouse,* 281 Ala. 567, 206 So.2d 371.

Chapter 12

PROTECTION OF TITLE

§ 12:1.   Generally

Because of the importance of ownership of property, one of the objectives of the law has been to protect the title of an owner to his property so that he remains the owner until it is clearly proved that he has transferred the title to someone else. Thus, if property is stolen, the true owner may recover it from the thief. He may even recover his property from a person who purchased it in good faith from the thief without any knowledge that the goods had been stolen. Likewise, it is immaterial whether the owner was negligent in caring for his property; that is, neither the thief nor the third party buying from the thief can raise the objection or the defense that the owner should be barred from claiming his property or its money value because his negligence made the theft possbile.

FARM BUREAU MUTUAL AUTOMOBILE INSURANCE CO. v. MOSELEY

47 Del. 256, 90 A.2d 485 (1952)

Grunwell's automobile, which he insured with the Farm Bureau Mutual Auto Insurance Co., was stolen. The insurance company paid Grunwell under the policy. The car was thereafter found in the possession of Moseley who had purchased it from a used car dealer. The identity of the thief was never established, but both Moseley and the used car dealer had acted in good faith. A new engine had apparently been placed in the car by the thief. Moseley had also made additions to the car. The insurance company sued Moseley to recover the automobile. From a judgment in favor of the insurance company. Moseley appealed.

OPINION BY RICHARDS, P.J. . . .

The owner of goods or chattels which have been stolen is not divested of his ownership of the property by the larcenous taking. He may follow and reclaim the stolen property wherever he finds it.

A sale by the thief, or by any person claiming under the thief, does not vest title to the property in the purchaser as against the legal owner. The fact that the sale was made in the ordinary course of business and the purchaser acted in good faith makes no difference.

The subsequent possession by the thief is a continuing wrong; and if the wrongdoer increases the value of the property by his labor upon it, or by substituting parts for those which were on it when he acquired it, or by adding new parts to it, the property in its enhanced value or changed condition, still belongs to the original owner and he may retake it with the accessions thereto. . . .

The automobile in question having been identified as stolen property, the defendant Moseley has no title to it as against the claim of the plaintiff, who acquired title from Mr. Grunwell, the owner from whom it was stolen.

The property right to the automobile being in the plaintiff, I render judgment in its favor for the automobile.

The engine which was in the automobile at the time it was stolen from Mr. Grunwell, having been removed by the thief or someone who claimed under the thief and another engine put in its place, the new engine became a part of the automobile and the plaintiff is entitled to retain it as his property.

It does not appear that the defendant Moseley knew that the automobile had been stolen when he purchased it, consequently there was no willful wrongdoing by him. This being true, he is entitled to the sun visor, seat covers, and gasoline tank which he attached to the automobile while it was in his possession. The distinction between a willful and involuntary wrongdoer is recognized by the authorities.

[Judgment affirmed with modification.]

§ 12:2. Proof of Transfer of Ownership

As an aspect of protecting the title of the owner, the law is reluctant to conclude that someone else has become the owner. Therefore the law will regard the owner as remaining the owner until it is clearly proven that someone else is the owner.

RUST v. PHILLIPS

208 Va. 629, 159 S.E.2d 623 (1968)

After the death of Rust, the question was raised whether certain commercial paper had been given by him by inter vivos or lifetime gifts to his children. These were found after his death in his safe deposit box in unsigned envelopes bearing each child's name.

OPINION BY SNEAD, J. . . .

David N. Rust, Jr. died on October 14, 1963, at the age of 82. At the time of his death he was mentally alert and in full possession of his faculties. . . . Until his death, decedent was engaged in the business of making and buying real estate loans.

For approximately twenty years, decedent employed his daughter, Elizabeth R. Phillips, as a part-time secretary to assist him with his affairs. Mrs. Phillips was given a "power of attorney . . . so that . . . [she] could do certain things for him." In addition, decedent appointed her a deputy to enter his safe deposit box at the Leesburg office of the Loudoun National Bank (now First and Merchants National Bank) where he kept his investments. Sometimes decedent would enter the box, and on occasions Mrs. Phillips would enter it "whenever he told me to."

Mrs. Phillips testified that on June 14, 1963 ". . . my father asked me to get certain notes from his safe deposit box for him, which I did." He then dictated letters to his six children. Each letter was dated June 14, 1963, and reads as follows:

"The enclosed notes of $——— are a gift for Christmas. The interest is to start December 29, 1963."

The decedent signed the letters typed by Mrs. Phillips, placed them in separate envelopes along with the real estate notes in the amounts heretofore stated, and sealed the envelopes. He then handed all the envelopes to Mrs. Phillips, and, after being thanked by her for his gift, expressed hope that "the money would do some good." Mrs. Phillips stated that at her father's instruction she returned the six sealed envelopes on the same day to decedent's safe deposit box. All of the notes involved were either payable to bearer or indorsed in blank. The envelopes remained in the safe deposit box, sealed, until decedent's death on October 14, 1963.

Subsequent to decedent's death, the executors of his estate opened the box for inventory purposes and the six sealed, unstamped envelopes were found among the contents of the box. The executors delivered the envelopes to the respective addressees, each of whom signed a receipt for the envelope and its contents.

Mrs. Phillips testified that she did not inform any of the children of the alleged gifts prior to her father's death, and that if he had requested a return of the envelopes "I suppose an employee would do what the boss says." . . . [There was some indefinite evidence which indicated that Rust may have intended to mail the envelopes to the named beneficiaries, but in fact they were not to mailed.]

Mary R. Clarke stated she also had a conversation with her father "in the summer of 1963," at which time "he said he was going to . . . 'Split another melon,' and that he was going to give us the money." She testified that she did not "know the amount he was going to give," and that decedent did not indicate when he contemplated making the gifts.

The decedent wrote a letter to his daughter, Caroline Williams, on October 9, 1963, five days before his death occurred, in which he stated "I have had a very prosperous year and I am going to let you and Elizabeth participate in it for Christmas."

The record shows that decedent was aware of the impact of estate taxes. In 1957 he wrote letters to his children advising that he was making a distribution of notes valued at $250,000, and that "an equal division will be made" among the six children when he returned from a trip. He enclosed a receipt to be signed and returned as "evidence that the notes are yours." He expressed the hope that "the money will do some good." However, after consultation with a certified public accountant he changed his mind and the gifts were not made. In 1959 decedent did execute a gift program whereby each child received a substantial sum of money.

The record further shows that investments made by decedent for some of the children were retained in his lock box; that Mrs. Phillips had secured a lock box of her own prior to 1962 in which she kept her valuables, and that according to the bank's records no entry was made by anyone in decedent's lock box between June 5 and 19 in 1963.

"It is well settled that the law does not presume a gift and where a donee claims title personal property by virtue of a gift *inter vivos,* the burden of proof rests upon him to show every fact and circumstance necessary to constitute a valid gift by clear and convincing evidence. . . .

"The common elements necessary to establish a gift *inter vivos* . . . are: '(1) The gift must be of personal property; (2) possession of the property must be delivered at the time of the gift to the donee, or some other for him and the gift must be accepted by the donee; and (3) the title of the property must vest in the donee at the time of the gift.' . . .

"In order for a gift *inter vivos* to be effective there must be an intention *in praesenti* on the part of the donor to make the gift and there must be such actual or constructive delivery as divests the donor of all dominion and control over the property and invests it in donee. . . .

Tested by the foregoing principles, we find, as a matter of law, that the evidence adduced falls short of being sufficient to establish that the decedent made valid *inter vivos* gifts of the negotiable notes in question. The essential element of delivery is lacking. The decedent instructed Mrs. Phillips, his paid secretary, to return the six unstamped envelopes containing the notes in question to his lock box to be mailed at a later date, and in so doing she acted as her father's agent. No time for the mailing or delivery was fixed by decedent. Mrs. Phillips was never told to mail or deliver the envelopes to the children. All she was told was to return the envelopes to decedent's lock box. At one time decedent said to Mrs. Phillips "maybe he'd mail them . . .

but then he said no, maybe not today." This clearly indicated that he was not ready to relinquish all dominion and control over the property and invest it in his children. In addition, Mrs. Phillips, who was the only person present with decedent when the transaction took place, testified that she considered the negotiable notes involved "under the control of my father. I wasn't giving it."

The testimony . . . concerning conversations had with the decedent in the summer of 1963, after the envelopes had been placed in the lock box, does not show that a delivery of the notes had been made. Their testimony indicates the donor intended to make delivery at some future time. . . . No hard and fast rule can be laid down as to what will constitute a sufficient delivery to support a gift *inter vivos* for all cases. . . . A determination of whether such a gift was validly made depends upon the particular facts and circumstances of the case. . . .

[Reversed and remanded.]

§ 12:3. Adverse Possession

(a) Generally. Title to land may be acquired by holding it adversely to the true owner for a certain period of time. In such case, the possessor acquires title, even though admittedly he had no lawful claim to the land before that time. In order to acquire title in this manner, possession must be (1) actual; (2) visible and notorious so that the owner, upon making reasonable inspection of the land, could discover the presence of someone thereon making an adverse claim; (3) exclusive as to third persons as well as the owner; (4) hostile in the sense that the holding is under a claim inconsistent with the rights of the owner; and (5) continuous for a required number of years. In many states, this period is 20 years or 21 years, although statutes in some states provide a lesser period. If a lawsuit is brought by the ousted owner before the expiration of this period, the time stops running and the adverse possessor does not acquire title.

(b) Protection of title. At first glance, the concept of adverse possession would appear to destroy title since the possessor acquires the title. In terms of practical operation, the rule serves to protect title. For example, your title to your land may be perfect except that it cannot be determined whether a John Jones who acquired the land in 1860 was the same person who in 1865 sold the land to a former owner through whom you claim the title. If in 1969 you had to prove that the 1860-1865 transactions were valid, you would have a difficult and ordinarily impossible task before you so that if your title depended upon your ability to show what happened, you would lose your land, even though by hypothesis there was nothing wrong with your title.

The rule of adverse possession operates as a compromise. You do not have to go back a century to prove everything that happened, all that you need do is go back 21 years and show that you or those from whom you claim were in adverse possession of the land. Once that is shown, no further questions can be asked to challenge your title.

Moreover, the rule of adverse possession serves to protect from fraudulent claims as to what happened a long number of years ago. Assume that your title depends upon the fact that A and B who owned your land in 1860 were married and that when A died, B acquired the land by survivorship. No question is raised that if B then owned the land, you finally became the owner of whatever B owned and are therefore the present owner. A false claim could be raised that A and B were not married. For example, it could be asserted that the deed, substituting real names for A and B, read "Henry and Mary Brown." You claim that they were husband and wife, but as far as the deed goes, they could have been brother and sister, father and daughter, mother and son, as well as persons purporting to be, but in fact not married. Let us assume that the claim made that they were not husband and wife is false. How can you disprove that assertion? In many instances, the jury will be suspicious of the claimant who has waited all these years before doing anything so that you would probably win the lawsuit. In many instances, it would be difficult to prove what happened. In many cases, you would be unwilling to take a chance on the outcome of a lawsuit and would probably pay the fraudulent claimant a sum of money to buy him off. By virtue of the concept of adverse possession, such false claims are automatically barred by proving your possession for the required number of years.

Although there is no statistical data to support the conclusion, it would appear reasonable to suppose that the number of persons making false claims after 21 years is likely to be much greater than the number of persons who, having honest claims, will wait for more than 21 years before bringing a lawsuit. The legal system is therefore willing to be influenced by the greater likelihood that title would be protected against false or nonmeritorious claims and therefore throws out of court all old claims.

It is to be noted that with the modern era of easy transportation and communication, the likelihood that the true owner would be unaware of the presence of the unlawful possessor becomes increasingly less. To this extent the social force of protecting title against false claims becomes increasingly greater.

(c) Easements by prescription. The concept of owning land by virtue of continued possession is extended to owning the right to cross another's land. The right to cross another's land is called an easement, and the method of acquiring an easement by hostile conduct is described as prescription, rather than adverse possession. Since it would be absurd to require that you be crossing the other land every minute of the day, and night as well, the requirements of adverse possession are modified in the interest of practical expediency when we are dealing with the protection of title to or a right in an easement arising from the lapse of time.

As in the case of adverse possession, the social force underlying the principle is the ownership of the easement holder in the right in the land of another, rather than the protection of a wrongdoer, who, by illegally crossing another's land continuously, at last acquires a lawful right to do so.

CRAMER v. JENKINS

339 S.W.2d 15 (Mo., 1966)

Cramer had used a path across certain land for a number of years. This land was later purchased by Jenkins. Some time thereafter, Jenkins started to farm the land and attempted to prevent its use by Cramer. Cramer brought an action to establish his right to cross the land. From a judgment in favor of Cramer, Jenkins appealed.

OPINION BY HYDE, P.J. . . .

Defendant's brief admits that plaintiff "has used this way for the statutory period and if he satisfies this court as to the other elements of prescription, he has acquired the way he claims." However, defendant claims plaintiff's possession was not hostile. Defendant cites *Gates* v. *Roberts,* Mo.Sup. 350 S.W.2d 729, 732, saying: " 'Hostile possession' means possession opposed and antagonistic to the claims of all others . . . and imports the occupation of land by the possessor with the intent to possess the land as his own." However, the Gates case was not an easement case; but involved a claim of title to an entire city lot. . . . It is said: "[T]he principal difference being in the character of the claim and use" in easement cases. . . . The claimant of an easement only claims a right to make a certain use of land and does not claim to possess the whole title and exclude the owner from it for all purposes.

The American Law Institute Restatement of the Law of Property, . . . "The satisfaction of the above stated prerequisites for 'adversity,' namely, that the use has not been made in subordination to the rights of the claimed servient owner, but, rather, has been made under claim of right is commonly inferred, rather than directly proved. Thus proof that a particular use of another's land has in fact occurred normally justifies, in most states, a finding that the use has been adverse until this presumption is challenged by rebutting evidence." . . . Defendant's own testimony . . . would warrant a finding that plaintiff's use of this roadway was not in subordination to defendant because plaintiff's use began long before defendant became the owner of the land and, although such use was known to defendant when he bought the land, he neither said anything about it nor made any objection to it until 1954, when he decided it would be more convenient to him to plow over it. We consider that plaintiff's evidence made a prima facie case which the court properly could decide was not overcome by defendant's evidence.

Defendant, arguing the use was permissive and not under a claim of right, says that when plaintiff's use began in 1919, the land now owned by defendant was in prairie grass, unenclosed, not farmed by the owner, and that anyone could cross it at any point. Defendant says the land was not plowed to the drainage ditch until 1937 or 1938 and that all of it was not plowed until defendant became the owner. Defendant's position seems to be that plaintiff's use of the way could not have been adverse when part of the land was swampy, in prairie grass, and not farmed or plowed by the owner and that, when defendant began to farm it, plaintiff had to do something more than continue the use he had been making to give defendant knowledge that his use was adverse to defendant's title. . . . Even though some of this land was swampy, nevertheless the ground along the drainage ditch appears to have always been a good place for a road and that was its location throughout the entire period. There were visible markings of the roadway and plaintiff worked it "with the blade on the back of a Ford tractor." Moreover, plaintiff used this way for the statutory period after the land owned by defendant was being cultivated. Furthermore, defendant's land was not unsettled territory. . . .

Defendant further argues that plaintiff's possession of the way was not exclusive, pointing out that defendant himself used it and that the evidence showed others owning or farming land beyond plaintiff's land used it. We know of no case holding that to obtain an easement of right of way the user must prevent the owner of the land from using it. . . . On the contrary, it is said: "The adverse user must be exclusive in the sense that the right does not depend for its enjoyment on similar rights in others. . . . The use may be exclusive in the required sense even though it is participated in by the owner of the servient tenement, or by owners of adjoining land." . . . "The requirement of 'exclusive,' as regards acquirement of an easement of way by prescription, does not mean that the claimant shall have been the sole user, or the only one who could or might enjoy the same or a similar right over the same land, but simply that the individual right shall not depend for its enjoyment upon a similar right in others, being, by virtue of some distinction of its own, independent of all others."

Although this way was not fenced, it was in a well defined location, continuously used by plaintiff as his means of ingress and egress from 1919 to 1954 "without a word said or a finger lifted in antagonism to it" until defendant after having seen plaintiff use it over this period (and from 1941 to 1954 while defendant was farming the land) asserted a hostile right to plow this roadway and prevent plaintiff from using it. Our conclusion is that the evidence warranted a finding of an easement by prescription in plaintiff to this roadway and that the court reached the correct result in ruling plaintiff had an easement for ingress and egress to his land over this roadway. . . .

[Judgment affirmed.]

Questions for Review

1. Define the social force of protecting title.

2. Give illustrations of its application.

3. Analyze each opinion in this chapter in terms of the social forces involved in the decision. See § 5:5 for a list of the social forces. With respect to each

opinion, explain why the prevailing social forces prevailed and why those rejected did not. In each case in which there is a dissenting opinion, also make this analysis for the dissenting opinion.

On the basis of the social forces involved, what decision should be made in the following case?

4. *Stock transfer. Absence of delivery.* Archie owned 300 shares of stock in the Puget Sound Power & Light Co. With the intention to make a gift of the stock to Helen, he delivered the stock certificate to the corporation together with a separate assignment of the stock to Helen, and a check to the corporation for the amount required to pay the state stock transfer tax. Archie then died, and it was claimed that the gift did not take effect because there had not been any delivery to Helen. The Uniform Stock Transfer Act, then in effect, specified that shares of stock can only be transferred by delivery of the indorsed certificate or by the delivery of the certificate and a separate assignment. Was this contention correct? *Henderson v. Tagg,* Wash. 2d, 412 P.2d 112.

5-7. *What social forces were involved, which prevailed, and which were defeated in the following decisions?*

5. *Wills. Revocation by divorce settlement.* Where husband and wife obtain a divorce and make a property settlement, such settlement agreement revokes the prior will of the husband although the husband fails to revoke the will in any of the ways that the statute declares may be employed to revoke a will, even though such implied revocation was not known under the common law. *Luff v. Luff,* [C.A.Dist.Col.] 359 F.2d 235.

6. *Banks. Forged indorsement by joint payee.* Where a check is made payable to joint payees and one indorses his own name and forges the name of the other, such other joint payee may sue the collecting bank that made payment on the strength of such indorsements. UCC § 3-116. *White v. Crocker-Citizens National Bank,* Cal.App.2d, 61 Cal.Rptr. 481.

7. *Trust. Absence of acceptance by trustee.* A father purchased an annuity, naming his daughter as beneficiary. He wrote her that it was his intention that the amount payable under the annuity would go to the daughter and her two brothers, to be divided among them by her judgment as to "when and how." She did not make any reply to this letter, although after his death she testified in the lawsuit over the disposition of the proceeds of the annuity that she regarded the statement of the father as constituting a command. It was held that although she did not communicate her assent to her father during his lifetime, her silent acquiescence and her continued willingness to be bound by her father's directive was a sufficient agreement to create a trust. *Land's Estate,* 99 N.J.S. 500, 240 A.2d 453.

Chapter 13

PROTECTION OF FREEDOM OF PERSONAL ACTION

§ 13:1. Generally

In the course of the passing centuries, man became concerned with what he himself could do as well as with protection against what others might do to him or his property. At one time he was primarily concerned with the restrictions that the monarchs were placing upon his freedom to act. This became particularly pronounced in the era before the American Revolution when the rulers of Europe, acting under the mercantilist theory, regulated the economy to benefit themselves. In the Anglo-American stream of history, man's desire for freedom from political domination gave rise to the American Revolution, and the desire for freedom from economic domination gave rise to the free enterprise philosophy. Today we find freedom as the dominant element in the constitutional provisions for the protection of freedom of religion, press, and speech and also in such laws as those against trusts or business combinations in restraint of trade by others.

This right of freedom of personal action, however, cannot be exercised by one person in such a way that it interferes to an unreasonable extent with the rights of others. Freedom of speech, for example, does not mean freedom to speak or write a malicious, false statement about another person's character. In effect, this means that one person's freedom of speech must be balanced with another person's right to be free from defamation of character or reputation.

§ 13:2. Freedom of Expression and Demonstration

There is, of course, no law which prohibits any one from thinking a particular way. Thus the question of freedom of thought does not arise in the abstract but only in connection with conduct which demonstrates or expresses the particular thought.

The social force favoring freedom of demonstration and expression of thought is not limited to adult persons or voters but is given protection with respect to all persons.

BURNSIDE v. BYARS

363 F.2d 744 (C.A.5th, 1966)

Burnside was a high school student. He and a number of other students came to class wearing "freedom buttons," which bore the words "one man, one vote" and the initials SNCC. The school principal adopted a regulation prohibiting the wearing of such buttons. Burnside and several other students were expelled for wearing such buttons. There was no evidence of any disturbance or commotion caused by them or resulting from their wearing such buttons.

OPINION BY GEWIN, C. J. . . .

Appellants [the parents of several of the expelled students] contend that the school regulation forbidding "freedom buttons" on school property is an unreasonable rule which abridges their children's First and Fourteenth Amendment freedom of speech. It is the contention of the appellees that the regulation imposed by the principal is reasonable in maintaining proper discipline in the school and the District Court did not abuse its discretion in declining to issue a preliminary injunction. . . .

The right to communicate a matter of vital public concern is embraced in the First Amendment right to freedom of speech and therefore is clearly protected against infringement by state officials. . . . Particularly, the Fourteenth Amendment protects the First Amendment rights of school children against unreasonable rules and regulations imposed by school authorities.

"The Fourteenth Amendment, as now applied to the States, protects the citizen against the State itself and all of its creatures—Boards of Education not excepted." . . .

But the liberty of expression guaranteed by the First Amendment can be abridged by state officials if their protection of legitimate state interests necessitates an invasion of free speech. . . . The interest of the state in maintaining an educational system is a compelling one, giving rise to a balancing of First Amendment rights with the duty of the state to further and protect the public school system. The establishment of an educational program requires the formulation of rules and regulations necessary for the maintenance of an orderly program of classroom learning. In formulating regulations, including those pertaining to the discipline of school children, school officials have a wide latitude of discretion. But the school is always bound by the requirement that the rules and regulations must be reasonable. It is not for us to consider whether such rules are wise or expedient but merely whether they are a reasonable exercise of the power and discretion of the school authorities.

Regulations which are essential in maintaining order and discipline on school property are reasonable. Thus school rules which assign students to a particular class, forbid unnecessary discussion in the classroom and prohibit the exchange of conversation between students are reasonable even though these regulations infringe on such basic rights as freedom of speech and association, because they are necessary for the orderly presentation of classroom activities. Therefore, a reasonable regulation is one which measurably contributes to the maintenance of order and decorum within the educational system.

The regulation which is before us now prohibits the wearing of "freedom buttons" on school property. The record indicates only a showing of mild curiosity on the part of the other school children over the presence of some 30 or 40 children wearing such insignia. Even the principal testified that the children were expelled not for causing a commotion or disrupting classes but for violating the school regulation. Thus it appears that the presence of "freedom buttons" did not hamper the school in carrying on its regular schedule of activities; nor would it seem likely that the simple wearing of buttons unaccompanied by improper conduct would ever do so. Wearing buttons on collars or shirt fronts is certainly not in the class of those activities which inherently distract students and break down the regimentation of the classroom, such as carrying banners, scattering leaflets, and speechmaking, all of which are protected methods of expressions, but all of which have no place in an orderly classroom. If the decorum had been so disturbed by the presence of the "freedom buttons," the principal would have been acting within his authority and the regulation forbidding the presence of buttons on school grounds would have been reasonable. But the affidavits and testimony before the District Court reveal no interference with educational activity and do *not* support a conclusion that there was a commotion or that the buttons tended to distract the minds of the students away from their teachers. Nor do we think that the mere presence of "freedom buttons" is calculated to cause a disturbance sufficient to warrant their exclusion from school premises unless there is some student misconduct involved. Therefore, we conclude after carefully examining all the evidence presented that the regulation forbidding the wearing of "freedom buttons" on school grounds is arbitrary and unreasonable, and an unnecessary infringement on the students' protected right of free expression in the circumstances revealed by the record. . . .

We wish to make it quite clear that we do not applaud any attempt to undermine the authority of the school. We support all efforts made by the school to fashion reasonable regulations for the conduct of their students and enforcement of the punishment incurred when such regulations are violated. Obedience to duly constituted authority is a valuable tool, and respect for those in authority must be instilled in our young people.

But, with all of this in mind, we must also emphasize that school officials cannot ignore expressions of feelings with which they do not wish to contend. They cannot infringe on their students' right to free and unrestricted expression as guaranteed to them under the First Amendment to the Constitution, where the exercise of such rights in the school buildings and schoolrooms do not materially and substantially interfere with the requirements of appropriate discipline in the operation of the school. . . .

§ 13:3.   Freedom of Economic Action

(a) Generally. As an element of freedom of personal action, a person ordinarily has the freedom to make any contract that he chooses. Except as will be noticed in subdivision (b) of this section, this means that he can make any contract, sell at any price, buy or sell where or when he wants to, and refuse to make a contract if he does not wish to.

JAMUR PRODUCTIONS CORP. v. QUILL

273 N.Y.S.2d 348, 51 Misc.2d 501 (1966)

In 1966 the employees of the New York City Transit Authority, who were public employees by virtue of such employment, went on strike in violation of a New York statute prohibiting striking by public employees and in violation of an injunction issued by a New York court. The resulting strike caused financial loss to members of the public generally. Some of these, including Jamur Productions Corp., brought an action against the unions involved to recover damages for loss caused them by the strike. It was conceded that the strike was contrary to the statute and the court order.

OPINION BY MURPHY, J. . . .

The plaintiffs assert virtually identical causes of action. All arise out of the transit strike, which commenced on January 1, 1966. Undoubtedly, the work stoppage left an indelible imprint upon the minds of everyone affected. Without question, the strike had an awesome impact upon the citizenry of this City, and indeed, the country. Yet, for the purposes of this discussion, it is necessary to set forth the purely legal consequences of the strike. . . .

Prior to January 1, 1966, the members of the Unions were employed by the New York City Transit Authority in the operation of rapid transit subways and buses in this City. Clearly, they were "public employees" for the purpose and within the confines of the Condon-Wadlin Act. . . . It is uncontested that the strike called by the Unions was totally effective. It is asserted that the strike was violative of the Condon-Wadlin Act, and was continued in defiance of an injunction issued by this court. . . . It must also be assumed, for the limited purpose of this motion, that the plaintiffs' allegations are correct and unassailable insofar as it is claimed that they sustained economic damage by virtue of the paralysis imposed upon the City as a result of the transit stoppage.

The causes of action asserted in the various complaints may be classified as follows:

1. Causes based upon assertions that the Unions' actions constituted an intentional violation of a statute (Condon-Wadlin Act), thus causing damage to the plaintiffs. Concomitantly, causes are asserted based upon the claim that the strike was in violation of an injunction, and that the resultant damages to plaintiffs are compensable. . . .

2. Causes based upon the claim that the strike was violative of the Universal Declaration of Human Rights of the United Nations, as stated in the declaration of the United Nations on December 10, 1948, Article 29. . . .

Widespread dislocation of economy, universal inconvenience, and even damage to the plaintiffs are not questioned.

At the outset, it is alleged that the activities of the Unions were undertaken in contravention of the Condon-Wadlin Act, and that the intentional violation thereof gives rise to a claim for damages. It is further alleged that the defendants were aware of the paralysis of public and private activities which would result, and of the irreparable damage, injury and economic loss which would be inflicted upon all of the residents of the City and all persons engaged in gainful employment here. It is charged that there was an intent not only to dishonor the statute but to disobey decrees of the court enjoining strike action. Parenthetically, it is claimed that the plaintiffs are within the class of those intended to be protected by the statute.

The consideration of these causes of action involves a determination of whether the plaintiffs, as individuals or individual business entities, may assert these causes where the statute relied upon does not specifically so provide and as a corollary thereto, whether the actions of the offending Unions in fact constituted a violation of the statute as of the date on which plaintiffs claim to have been injured.

It is clear that not every violation of a statute gives rise to civil liability on the part of the violator.

". . . [T]here are statutes which are construed as creating no duty of conduct toward the plaintiff. The courts have been careful not to exceed the purpose which they attribute to the legislature. This judicial self-restraint has served as an argument for those who contend that an action cannot be founded upon a duty to another; but there is of course a special reason, in the theory of the separation of powers, for such reluctance to go beyond the Legislative policy" (Prosser, Law of Torts, 2d ed., p. 154).

No solution to the problem embodied in the above quotation is afforded by the argument advanced by the plaintiffs that the Condon-Wadlin Act was intended to protect "the people," for without a prior determination that the "people" are so referred to in an individual, rather than a collective sense, the contention is of no significant value. Plaintiffs' argument that the alleged wrongful acts were obviously aimed at the individuals who constitute the body politic of this City, overlooks that it was the Union members' employer, namely, the New York City Transit Authority, which was the professed and most direct target of these actions. This is true even though the officials of the Transit Authority and the Transit Authority itself, could be most directly affected only by pressure brought through inconvenience foisted upon the public.

It is inherent, in its defined role, that a labor union must affect third parties in the course of the bargaining process with its "adversary," the employer.

> "The principal weapons which the unions have developed are the strike, the boycott, and the practice of picketing. These devices are used to force the employer to shut down his plant or business either by depriving him of labor or of customers until compliance with the demands of the union is made. Contractual relations are, of course, interfered with, deliberately and intentionally by the defendant unions" (1 Harper and James, The Law of Torts, p. 523).

The Unions' primary weapon, exclusive of public opinion, is a strike, which action effectively affects the employer's ability to deal with third parties. Thus, it may be correct for the plaintiffs to argue that the Unions voluntarily chose to disregard the statute, and the injunction too. But at the same time, the Unions may not have been presented with a choice, for the alternative was to abjure in the use of its most substantial, and perhaps only effective weapon. To have adopted the latter scheme would have severely jeopardized the Unions' ability to bargain effectively.

Language in some cases explicitly supports the view that "[a] wilful interference with [the employer's] . . . business without the justification normally flowing from a lawful strike is actionable and warrants a judgment for damages. . . . Unions would be liable in damages unless a "legal privilege affords them immunity" (1 Harper and James, Law of Torts, p. 523). In the Restatement of Torts, Volume 4, Section 775, it is stated:

> "Workers are privileged intentionally to cause harm to another by concerted action if the object and the means of their concerted action are proper; they are subject to liability to the other for harm so caused if either the object or the means of their concerted action is improper." (Accord, Dangel & Shriver Labor Unions, § 289).

Here, the objectives of the strike—to obtain higher wages, better working conditions, etc.—may not be deemed improper. The means used—a strike—may not be classified as improper per se, but only improper by virtue of the statute and the court ordered injunction.

The plaintiffs' causes of action based upon the alleged violations of the Condon-Wadlin Act by the Unions, are not tenable. Even a cursory examination of the statute would reveal that a cause of action is not granted to the plaintiffs under the Condon-Wadlin Act, because of an illegal strike. The statute does not afford a right of action to a specified class.

Section 108 of the Civil Service Law [Condon-Wadlin Act] provides, in part:

> "2. Prohibition against strikes. No person holding . . . , employment in the . . . service of any authority, commission or board . . . shall strike. . . .
> "4. Termination of employment. Notwithstanding any other provision of law, any public employee who violates the provisions of this section shall thereby abandon and terminate his appointment or employment and shall no longer hold such position, or be entitled to any of the rights or emoluments thereof, except if appointed or reappointed as hereinafter provided."

No duty is created thereby save to honor the command. While penal consequence is included, it does not provide for any private remedial or damage action for injuries resulting from violation. "A statute 'creates' no liability unless it discloses an intention express or implied that from disregard of a statutory command a liability for resultant damages shall arise 'which would not exist but for the statute.' " . . . With respect to whether a cause of action is created by implication, . . . :

> "That depends, at least in great measure, upon whether the duty is imposed for the special benefit of a particular group or class of persons. Only in such case can it be said that the statute creates a liability per se. When the statute merely defines, in the interest of the general public, the degree of care which shall be exercised under specified circumstances, it does not 'create' a new liability."

It is needless to repeat what was the known and perhaps intended result of the strike action, but to halt it was the function of the New York City Transit Authority, possessing the right correlative to the defendants' duty by seeking and securing injunctive relief, which it did.

It is clear that there is an absence, within the statute, of the existence of any remedial actions enuring to plaintiffs.

The New York State Legislature, by special act, immunized the strikers against the enforcement of the penalties. If there was any determination to accomplish beyond what the special act provides, it cannot be doubted that the Legislature would have done so. The Legislature did not act although the occasion was ripe. The failure to act must be regarded as an expression of public policy. The absence of remedial action in favor of the general public before Condon-Wadlin, the failure of Condon-Wadlin to so provide expressly or by implication, and the failure to so provide by the act lead inexorably to the conclusion that the plaintiffs are without any cognizable action at law. . . .

It is urged that the Unions' actions, effected in disregard of the probable consequences of such acts and the likelihood of injury to others, constituted a breach of a duty resulting in harm to plaintiffs. The consideration thereof necessarily depends upon whether a duty exists, and if so, to whom that duty is owed.

To be sure, the plaintiffs were not in a direct contractual relationship with defendants. At most, they were third party beneficiaries of the contract that existed between defendants and the Transit Authority as employer.

> "Rights are not abstractions but exist only correlatively with duties. Everyone who has been damaged by an interruption in the expected tenor of his life does not have a cause of action. The law demands that . . . the damaged plaintiff be able to point the finger of responsibility at a defendant owing, not a general duty to society, but a specific duty to him." . . .

In an action similar to the case at bar involving a strike illegal under the Labor Management Relations Act of 1947, Section 303 (29 U.S.C. Sec. 187), *United Mine Workers of America* v. *Osborne Mining Co., Inc.,* 279 F.2d 716 (6th Cir., 1960), cert., den. 364 U.S. 881, 81 S.Ct. 169, 5 L.Ed.2d 103, a claim of damage was asserted in favor of the plaintiff's sales agency, Love & Amos. The agency sought recovery based upon the business lost as a result of the defendant Union's illegal strike. While the agency was denied recovery, the plaintiff-employer's suit for damages was sustained. It should be noted, moreover, that in the Osborne case, specific statutory authority for suits was provided within the Labor Management Relations Act (§ 303, right of action "[w]hoever shall be injured in his business or property"). The court stated. . . .

> "In the present case, . . . Osborne was not a party to any conspiracy nor is there any claim that Osborne committed any wrong of any kind against Love & Amos. The theory of the complaint of Love & Amos against U.M.W. is that U.M.W. by its secondary boycotts destroyed Osborne's business and in consequence thereof Love & Amos were deprived of commissions which it otherwise would have earned under its contract with Osborne. In other words, U.M.W.'s violation of the federal law destroyed Osborne and Love & Amos were injured because of its contractual relations with Osborne. . . .
>
> ". . . This damage is incidental and too remote for recovery under federal law. . . .
>
> "The failure of Love & Amos to recover here is not attributable to lack of supporting evidence. It was because it never had and could not assert any federally recognized cause of action or ground for recovery. . . ."

The plaintiffs argue that Osborne, and other similar cases upon which defendants rely, involved actions instituted against private employers and private employees, while here, the strikers were public employees and the employer an agency of government performing a governmental function. In addition, plaintiffs assert that the damage claimed in Osborne was incidental and direct, while in the instant matter, the damage was intended and direct. These finely drawn distinctions are without legal basis. Whether or not a cause of action arises out of unlawful strike action does not rest upon the nomenclature attached to the parties, to wit, public or private. . . .

In an analogous case (*Isbrandtsen Co., Inc.* v. *Local 1291, International Longshoremen's Association,* 204 F.2d 495 [3 Cir., 1953]), one of plaintiff's vessels was chartered to another, when the Union struck the ship against Lavine Shipping Co., hired by the charterer to unload. The strike was in violation of the Lavine-union collective bargaining agreement, and plaintiff sustained damage. The court (p. 498) rejected the contention that intent

". . . to benefit all the world who might be helped by the faithful perform-ance of the contract would give these remote parties rights against one who broke it. It may well be that Isbrandtsen suffered a loss of use of its boat because a strike stopped the unloading of [the vessel]. . . . It also may be that the people who had cargo to ship on the next voyage lost a market by the delay. And it may be that the people who did not get the goods on the next voyage, on time, lost a profitable bargain on that account. *But neither in contract nor in tort have duties been extended very far beyond the immediate parties to the facts out of which a cause of action is said to arise. . . .*"

In substance, recovery is restricted to those to whom a duty was owed and who were within the foreseeable zone of risk or injury. Plaintiffs must be denied recovery on this theory because it is evident that the strike was not aimed at each as apart from the public generally.

At the same time the damages sued for are too remote and too indirect. In a proceeding arising out of alleged wrongful acts by public employers or employees (absent specific statutory authority empowering such an action), the plaintiff must show damages incurred by himself different in character from those sustained by the public generally. . . . The injuries sustained by plaintiffs are no different in kind or quality from those sustained by everyone affected by the strike. The intentional nature of the tort herein, it may be argued, was directed against everyone. But in actuality, it was directed against no one in particular, except the employer, who does not sue herein.

The extension of liability urged by the plaintiffs is dramatic and drastic, and without a readily ascertainable or definable limit. Under the circum-stances, this court, sitting at *nisi prius,* will not effectuate the choices espoused by plaintiffs without more specific and compelling authority than presented hereon. To include within the realm of recovery those to whom injury was unforeseeable and amount of damages unpredictable at the time of the act complained of, is not mandated by the cases . . . , nor by traditionally ac-cepted theories of contract or tort law. . . .

The claims based upon the alleged violation of plaintiffs' human rights, under the United Nations Declaration, are insufficient and dismissed. It need not be questioned but that what occurred here in the wake of the strike and the consequent assault upon the people of this city, and elsewhere, would be considered a serious deviation from the pattern of human rights and behavior envisaged by the principles espoused in the United Nations Universal Declaration of Human Rights. Like the doctrinal codes and commands of religious bodies and orders, their precepts of ethical behavior do not yet entail judicial authority and condemnation for failure of faith. While natural right and doctrinal teachings doubtlessly guide the courts of this land, they are not in the texture of known categories of actions available here, despite the growth of regard and concern for redress of tortious wrongs. In short, no claim of the type asserted by plaintiffs can be founded thereon. . . .

Finally, reference is made to the public pronouncements of union officials, who, it is asserted, maliciously inflicted extreme injury and suffering upon a helpless public. Plaintiffs . . . invoke the sovereign and constitutional source of power of "We the People" and Article X of the Bill of Rights. These arguments may appeal to one's emotions in recalling the first two weeks of 1966. However, this court must base its determination upon and be necessarily responsive to only legal principles. It is not for this court to determine whether a particular disposition may be more socially desirable, nor is it the function of this court to set forth its personal philosophy of the merits of the Condon-Wadlin Act.

The unlawful strike is now history, and the hardships suffered by the general public need not be repeated. However, no legal theory has been advanced which may reasonably and judicially be extended to afford the plaintiffs the relief requested. As a result, the consequences and damages which evolved from the action of the Unions are not compensable. . . . Thus, while there may have been damage and loss, there has been no violation of any recognized legal right of the plaintiffs and no remedy is afforded them by any act of the legislature or any common-law doctrine. In a final analysis, it appears that in the case of strike action by employees in the public service, any remedy in favor of the general public must emanate from explicit legislative action, rather than court adjudication.

The motions of the Unions to dismiss the complaints are granted. . . .

(b) Limitations on the freedom of contract. A number of limitations have been imposed on the freedom of economic action. The courts and the lawmakers have combined to make invalid certain provisions which they feel so harmful to other social values that the freedom of action of one party should be modified or sacrificed in order to protect the interests of other persons. The big question is to what extent will society monitor or control a contract? Historically, a contract was valid unless it called for the commission of a crime. This prohibited zone was later broadened to condemn any contract that was contrary to public policy. This is a vague standard because an act is a crime because public policy has so declared it. Public policy as used to condemn a contract would seem to refer to something which had not yet been declared a crime but which the court thinks should be. In the present decade, the courts are going a step further declaring contracts and provisions invalid when they are unconscionable. This aspect will be considered further in § 26:8(b). Limitations are commonly placed upon selling and agreements relating to marketing in order to protect either person from oppression or as part of a general economic development program.

BULOVA WATCH CO. v. ZALE JEWELRY CO.
371 P.2d 409 (Wyo., 1962)

Three actions were brought to have the Wyoming Fair Trade Act declared unconstitutional.

OPINION BY HARNSBERGER, J. . . .

The Act appears as Chapter 2, Title 40, §§ 40-8 to 40-17 inclusive, W.S.1957, and those of its provisions deemed important to this decision are as follows:

"§ 40-10. *Contracts fixing minimum sale or resale price authorized for commodities sold under trademark, brand name, etc.*—No contract relating to the sale or resale of a commodity which bears, or the label or container of which bears the trademark, brand, or name of the producer or distributor of such commodity and which commodity is in free and open competition with commodities of the same general class produced or distributed by others shall be deemed in violation of any law of the State of Wyoming by reason of any of the following provisions which may be contained in such contract:

"(A) That the buyer will not resell such commodity at less than the minimum price stipulated by the seller.

"(B) That the buyer will require of any dealer to whom he may resell such commodity an agreement that he will not, in turn, resell at less than the minimum price stipulated by the seller.

"(C) That the seller will not sell such commodity:

"(1) to any wholesaler, unless such wholesaler will agree not to resell the same to any retailer unless the retailer will in turn agree not to resell the same except to consumers for use and at not less than the stipulated minimum price, and such wholesaler will likewise agree not to resell the same to any other wholesaler unless such other wholesaler will make the same agreement with any wholesaler or retailer to whom he may resell; or

"(2) to any retailer, unless the retailer will agree not to resell the same except to consumers for use and at not less than the stipulated minimum price. . . .

"§ 40-11. *Acts deemed to be violations of contracts fixing minimum prices.*—For the purpose of preventing evasion of the resale price restrictions imposed in respect of any commodity by any contract entered into pursuant to the provisions of this act . . . (except to the extent authorized by the said contract):

"(A) The offering or giving of any article of value in connection with the sale of such commodity;

"(B) The offering or the making of any concession of any kind whatsoever (whether by the giving of coupons or otherwise) in connection with any such sale; or

"(C) The sale or offering for sale of such commodity in combination with any other commodity, shall be deemed a violation of such resale price restriction, for which the remedies prescribed by section 6 of this act . . . shall be available. . . ."

"§ 40-12. *Who may establish minimum price.*—No minimum resale price shall be established for any commodity, under any contract entered into pursuant to the provisions of this act . . . , by any person other than the owner of the trademark, brand or name used in connection with such commodity or a distributor specifically authorized to establish said price by the owner of such trademark, brand or name. . . ."

"§ 40-14. *Wilful violation of minimum price contract as unfair competition.*—Willfully and knowingly advertising, offering for sale or selling any commodity at less than the price stipulated in any contract entered into pursuant to the provisions of this act . . . , *whether the person so advertising, offering for sale or selling is or is not a party to such contract,* is unfair competition and is actionable at the suit of any person damaged thereby. . . ." (Emphasis supplied.)

This last section is generally referred to as the "nonsigner" provision.

In the interest of brevity, where reference is made to trademark, brand, name, et cetera, the single word trademark will be used and the single word producer will be used to include manufacturer or distributor where proper, and reference to the Fair Trade Act may be made by use of the single word Act. . . .

On July 2, 1890, the Congress enacted a law to protect trade and commerce against unlawful restraints and monopolies. This law is known as the Sherman Antitrust Act. . . . In 1911, the Federal court in *Dr. Miles Medical Co.* v. *John D. Park & Sons Co.,* 220 U.S. 373, 31 S.Ct. 376, 55 L.Ed. 502, held that price-fixing contracts between manufacturers and dealers were in restraint of trade. By further enactment of September 26, 1914 . . . Congress created a Federal Trade Commission, declaring in its section 5 . . . that unfair methods of competition were unlawful. Thereafter on August 17, 1937, Congress, by what has become known as the Miller-Tydings Amendment, . . . legalized

". . . contracts or agreements prescribing minimum prices for the resale of a commodity which bears, or the label or container of which bears, the trademark, brand, or name of the producer or distributor of such commodity and which is in free and open competition with commodities of the same general class produced or distributed by others, when contracts or agreements of that description are lawful as applied to intrastate transactions, under any statute, law, or public policy now or hereafter in effect in any State, Territory, or the District of Columbia in which such resale is to be made, or to which the commodity is to be transported for such resale. . . ."

and declared

". . . the making of such contracts or agreements shall not be an unfair method of competition under section 5, as amended and supplemented, of the Act entitled 'An Act to create a Federal Trade Commission. . . .' "

Antecedent to this permissive legislation, California, in 1931, had adopted a "Fair Trade Law," . . . which, however, did not contain any nonsigner provision, but in 1933, California added the nonsigner clause. . . . This California law, as amended in 1933, became a pattern for Fair Trade Acts, although it was enacted before the Miller-Tydings Amendment, and it has been substantially followed in the forty-six states which at one time or another adopted Fair Trade laws.

After *Schwegmann Bros.* v. *Calvert Distillers Corp.,* . . . 341 U.S. 384, 71 S.Ct. 745, 95 L.Ed. 1035, 19 A.L.R.2d 1119, . . . declared a Fair Trade law containing a nonsigner clause was in violation of the Sherman Antitrust Act, Congress, on July 14, 1952, amended the Sherman Antitrust Act so as to overcome the criticisms of the Schwegmann case and expressly permitted states to authorize contracts between parties which would be binding upon nonsigners. This amendment is usually referred to as the McGuire Act. . . .

The Wyoming Fair Trade Act is similar to or identical with provisions appearing in Fair Trade Acts adopted by forty-six states of the Union.

Seventeen of these states hold the Acts constitutional. . . .
Cases from twenty states hold . . . the Acts unconstitutional. . . .

The pendulum of state decision has now definitely swung from the constitutional to the unconstitutional side. This numerical majority is not in itself conclusive of the matter, but it does seem to portend a change in judicial thinking and is justified by better reasoning and logic.

The focal point of the constitutional attack in the cases before us is § 40-14, . . . containing what is frequently referred to as a "nonsigner clause." The correct answer to its constitutionality is beclouded by the irreconcilable conflict of decisions rendered. . . .

In giving our views respecting the nonsigner clause of Wyoming's Fair Trade Act, . . . we find it unnecessary to discuss the question of the Act's being violative of the Federal Constitution, or of our agreement or disagreement with the varying opinions expressed by either the majority or the dissenting members of the United States Supreme Court on this subject. It is sufficient to consider only the validity of the Act under the Wyoming Constitution, a question of which this court has complete jurisdiction and final authority. This is not intended to suggest that we be unmindful of the views of other courts, especially those grounded in sound reason and logic and based upon principles of law which have so borne the test of time and trial as to be firmly implanted in our system of jurisprudence. But we recognize that in the determination of that which is considered due process, proper exercise of police power and permissible delegation of legislative authority, "personal preference, not reason, seems, however, to be controlling" in many cases, and in many instances due process "is what the judges say it is; and it differs from judge to judge, from court to court." . . . This is evidenced, not only by the disparity between the decisions of the various courts of our country regarding these questions, but more especially by the changing positions courts of the same jurisdiction have taken from time to time.

Many of the enunciations of our learned Chief Justice, in his masterful opinion in *State* v. *Langley,* 53 Wyo. 332, 84 P.2d 767, are apropos of some of the questions to be decided here, and are precepts which we are unwilling to disturb.

The question before the court in the Langley case was the constitutionality of . . . and is a part of our antidiscrimination laws.

Among these pronouncements the court held: That police power is an attribute of sovereignty inherent in the State's legislative body unless expressly limited by Constitution; that the due process clause of our Constitution has a substantive aspect which definitely limits police power; that a law will not be declared unconstitutional unless clearly so; that even though police power is an attribute of sovereignty essential to civilized government and inherent in the legislative body, the means adopted for its exercise must be reasonable and designed to accomplish the end in view; that the purposes for which the police power is invoked must have relation to the public weal, must be within the scope and in furtherance of that power, and the means adopted must be reasonable and appropriate for the accomplishment of and have a substantial connection with the end in view; that under its police power the legislature may provide for the general economic welfare of the people and decide whether free and unlimited competition shall prevail; that courts, employing a standard of reasonableness as applied to the facts, are the final arbiters as to whether the law is an unwarranted invasion of rights guaranteed by the Constitution; and that generally the use of property and the making of contracts shall be free of governmental interference, but neither property rights nor contract rights are absolute.

The opinion also points out at 84 P.2d 770 that Art. 1, § 6, Wyoming Constitution, "does not state that 'no person shall be deprived of life, liberty or property,' but states that no person shall be deprived thereof 'without due process of law.' "

However, at 84 P.2d 771, the opinion takes issue with the philosophy that the legislature may forbid or restrict any business if it has a sufficient force of public opinion behind it, calling attention to Art. 1, § 7, Wyoming Constitution, which says:

> "Absolute, arbitrary power over the lives, liberty and property of freemen exists nowhere in a republic, not even in the largest majority."

Article 1, § 6, Wyoming Constitution, requires that lawful process be employed before a person is deprived of life, liberty or property. The liberty envisioned is not alone a liberty of person such as is offended by enslavement, imprisonment or other restraint. It contemplates a person's liberty to do all that is not made unlawful. Hence, persons are at liberty to make lawful contracts. Equally, persons are at liberty to refrain from making contracts. And a prime requisite of contract obligation is that the undertaking is voluntarily assumed and not occasioned by fraud, duress or any form of compulsion, governmental as well as private. Voluntary engagement by contract entails the contractual assumption of a binding obligation as opposed to an obligation imposed by law.

Furthermore, we cannot unqualifiedly accept the . . . theory that an implied offer of contract is made by the producer when he affixes on or to a commodity a notice that it is to be resold at a price certain, or that the purchase of such a marked item is an implied acceptance of that offer which completes or gives rise to an implied contract between the producer and all subsequent buyers. Even if the producer may expressly or by such implication, make a price-fixing contract with the purchaser to whom the producer sells the article, in order to imply there is a continuing offer of contract by the producer to other buyers down through all intermediate channels of trade until the commodity reaches the ultimate consumer, it must be assumed the producer has retained the title to the commodity itself, as well as title to its trademark. Otherwise the producer would be without any right to cumber such future transfers of the article.

A legislative act which purports to burden a person with a contractual covenant agreed to by private parties or private interests, but not agreed to by the nonsigning retailer, violates that person's liberty not to so contract if he elects and robs that person of his liberty without due process. The legislature may not impress contractual duties which have been voluntarily assumed by others as the contractual duty of a person not a party to such contracts. This is more especially true where the terms of the contracts are ordained and dictated by the selfish interests of private persons, primarily for their benefit, and are adverse and antagonistic to the interest and desire of the nonsigner who is here sought to be controlled against his will.

Article 1, § 37, Wyoming Constitution, recognizes the Federal Constitution as the supreme law of the land. Its cogency in this case is found in the due process provisions of the Fourteenth Amendment which it will not be necessary to separately discuss.

Article 2, § 1, Wyoming Constitution, vests the State's government in three distinct departments—the legislative, executive and judicial. This needs no present comment, as the legislative function will be dealt with in the following.

Article 3, § 1, Wyoming Constitution, vests legislative power in the State's legislature. This provision is invoked under the claim that the Act is an unlawful delegation to private parties of that legislative power and without any safeguards for the protection of the public. Even though the legislature be empowered to impress merchandising with a limitation intended to prevent discrimination and tortious competition, such a power can only be exercised by the legislature itself. . . .

The criticized Act only permits the making of certain price-fixing contracts which were formerly considered to be in violation of the Sherman Antitrust Act. This legislation does not establish prices at which products may be lawfully retailed, nor does it prescribe a formula by which such prices may be determined, as do our antidiscrimination laws. . . . The Act leaves to the uncontrolled and uncertain discretion, option and whim of private parties that determination of a retail price suitable to their own interests and for their private benefit, without any regard for the welfare of the public and in derogation of the public's right to a voice in the matter or even to be represented by any public authority interested in the people's behalf. By the passage and approval of the Fair Trade Act, no sale price of any commodity was made unlawful or restrainable. When the legislature had completed its law-making effort, no one could have been prosecuted or restrained because of this new enactment. It is only after the legislative power of this State had been fully exercised and exhausted that it is left to private interests, at their choice, to step in and by their unsupervised, independent, supplemental and selfish action make unlawful and restrainable that which was until then entirely lawful and not subject to judicial restraint. If such legislative delegation of law-making power is permitted, that body may at will abdicate all its law-making prerogatives and pass on the entire law-making power of our State to special private interests. We have found no better way to condemn such legislation than the words of the court in *Yick Wo* v. *Hopkins,* 118 U.S. 356, 370, 6 S.Ct. 1064, 1071, 30 L.Ed. 220:

> ". . . the very idea that one man may be compelled to hold his life, or the means of living, or any material right essential to the enjoyment of life, at the mere will of another, seems to be intolerable in any country where freedom prevails, as being the essence of slavery itself." . . .

The disposition of the judicial branch of government has always been to scrupulously refrain from encroaching in the slightest way into the legislative field of policy making where factual or economic factors require latitude of discretion. We will not and we do not substitute our opinions in such matters for the considered judgment of our lawmakers. Yet, we ourselves have a function to perform, a constitutional right, and the paramount duty to insist that the legislature not renounce its legislative power by any such attempt to delegate it away. We approached the limit of judicial tolerance in upholding legislative fiat in the so-called trading stamp matter, *Steffey* v. *City of Casper,* Wyo., 357 P.2d 456 (1960), rehearing 358 P.2d 951 (1961). We conceded the legislative right to directly prohibit a sales practice which that body evidently deemed was inimical to public welfare. What we cannot approve of here is the attempt to delegate to others the legislative right to prohibit.

Aside from the improper delegation of legislative power are the further questions of the reasonableness of the law and whether it is an unwarranted invasion of the rights guaranteed by our Constitution. We have heretofore acknowledged that, notwithstanding, property rights and the right to make contracts should be free from governmental interference, still these rights are not absolute. This, of course, means the sovereign may, in proper circumstance, limit the exercise of these rights. When, however, governmental limitation is attempted by giving unto private interests the right to prescribe conditions of use, sale, and contract respecting a person's property, such legislation is so grossly unconscionable that courts, as the final arbiters of its reasonableness, must hold the law an unwarranted invasion of the private liberty and property guaranteed by the Constitution of this State.

The police power of the legislature is great indeed. Its exercise in the protection and preservation of the public safety, its health, its morals, and in behalf of its general welfare is not merely laudable, it is essential. But however great its power, it is nonetheless not beyond limitation. Even if it be agreed that the philosophy behind the enactment of this law brings it within the long-range welfare of the public by assisting in the preservation of certain businesses which can no longer continue to exist without governmental subsidy and the supposed protection accorded by the Act, still the means adopted to accomplish the purpose must provide a legal process by which to infringe the liberty or the property of persons affected. What day in court is given them? To what authority, board, officer, tribunal or court may such persons make representations in their own interest or behalf before the sale price is fixed? It would be bad enough if such a price-fixing formula were accomplished through some public official acting without hearings, but the price-fixing method prescribed by the Act is without even that vestige of due process.

Article 10, § 8, Wyoming Constitution, expressly prohibits the *consolidation* or *combination* of corporations to prevent competition, *to control or influence productions or prices,* or to in any manner interfere with the public good or general welfare.

The language of this constitutional prohibition leaves in doubt the meaning which our constitutional framers intended should be given the emphasized words. Notwithstanding, it seems plain they sought some restriction on corporations controlling or influencing prices. The Fair Trade Act is so designed as to permit a single corporation, as well as a single individual, acting with either another corporation or another individual, to control and influence prices. Even though the control and influence are limited to the producer's own product, these nevertheless go beyond the manufacturer's right to sell or not to sell at a price of its own choosing, and admit of a corporate producer combining with a corporate retailer to control and influence the price of a trademarked article through all channels of intermediate trade, clear down to the ultimate consumer. It puzzles to understand how this should be interpreted as being other than a prohibited control or influence of prices and a limitation of free, open and competitive marketing in derogation of the right and welfare of the public to enjoy the fruits of such free enterprise. Although we will not at this time hold the Act is violative of the express prohibition of this constitutional provision, it is certainly out of harmony with its spirit, and, in its application to corporate bodies, its so-called "horizontal" price fixing brings it close to contravening Art. 10, § 8, of our Constitution. Whether actually unconstitutional or not, the Act unquestionably furnishes a device by which retailers may combine with producers to fix prices, using the producer as an intermediary and thus by indirection accomplish that which is undesirable. However, because the wording of the constitutional provision is uncertain, we cannot say that the Act is clearly violative of its provision.

Many courts, both state and federal, some of which have been cited herein, holding Fair Trade Acts constitutional, do so on the theory that when the producer sells a trademarked commodity it does not sell its trademark but retains under separate title the ownership of the trademark.

It would seem to be an unjustifiable, untenable and somewhat absurd legal fiction to say that by simply inscribing his trademark upon, attaching it to, or accompanying it with an article a producer obtains or retains a divisible and separate title to the trademark which does not pass with the marketing and delivery of the commodity itself to the buyer. When a producer elects to identify his product with a trademark and launches it into the marts of trade, he has created and sold an entity—a unit—an integrated article—which its purchaser is not required to destroy or deface in order to lawfully market it at a price suitable to him, provided only that he has not offended antidiscrimination laws. If the producer does not want to sell the product bearing his trademark, it is his privilege to refrain from so doing. And when he does so identify his product, he is privileged to determine the price which he is willing to accept for it as a trademark commodity. He may fix one price for the article with his trademark and accept a different price for an identical article not bearing his trademark. In either case he sells that which he wants to sell and obtains the price he asks for what he sells. However, the commodity he sells embodies the entire article, including whatever he has added to it, or placed upon it, or which accompanies it. He has been paid the full price demanded by him. When such a sale is made, the seller gives into the buyer's possession everything which he has placed upon or with the object of sale. He retains no part of it. If there is any merit at all in the theory of continuing separate identity and ownership of the trademark as distinguished from the article itself, a simple answer is that by affixing to or accompanying with the object of sale the owner's trademark, and placing the commodity thus identified upon the market, the producer or distributor has offered and sold all his interest in that portion of his trademark which he placed in use upon or with the article sold, and in so doing has consented to its continued use by all purchasers.

From what has been said, it should be clear that the Wyoming Fair Trade Act is unconstitutional as an improper delegation of legislative power, as offending the required due process protection, and as being beyond the police power of the State. . . .

§ 13:4.   Labor Picketing

The changing fortunes in the status of labor picketing disclose a conflict between the interests of management, labor, and third persons. In terms of social forces, the question involved is whether labor has the freedom to act in a particular way in opposition to the freedom of management to act as it chose. To the extent that management is or represents the owner of the plant, the right of management to act freely as it chooses also involves the right to use property free of restraint. The extent to which the law permits or approves picketing or other labor conduct, the law is in effect deciding that the freedom of labor is to be given superior weight or value over that given management or ownership.

At the turn of the century, labor picketing, regardless of its purpose or how peaceful, was regarded as illegal. Gradually the concept developed that working men had the right to picket their employer's place of business as long as they did not trespass on his private property, did not obstruct the right of the public to pass on the highway, and did not use force or intimidation. Thus "peaceful picketing" came to be recognized as lawful in the twenties, meaning that in the absence of any contrary statute, working men could picket as long as no force or intimidation were employed. In 1940 this recognition of the right to picket was carried a step further to hold that a state legislature could not make all picketing illegal. Otherwise stated, from the ordinary level of merely being a right which existed as long as the state legislature permitted it to exist, picketing was elevated to the position of being a constitutionally-protected right which not even a state legislature could prohibit.

Apart from the economic or sociological aspects of this conclusion, this was remarkable as a matter of legal principle for to sustain this conclusion the Supreme Court held that picketing was a form of free speech and that the Constitution's First Amendment's guarantee of free speech was binding upon the states. Historically it was surprising to find that "free speech," which refers to criticism of the government, that is, speech of a political nature against the background of conflict between the citizen and government, should be extended to embrace criticism of one person against another in the area of economic controversy. Whether this expansion is proper as a matter of good government need not be considered here. The fact is that when the framers drafted the First Amendment, it was clear from the history of the times and the other words of the First Amendment that they were concerned only with the right of the citizen to criticize the government, that is, with "political free speech." Note the association of terms and ideas of the First Amendment, which guarantees free speech: "Congress shall make no law respecting an establishment of religion, or prohibiting the free exercise thereof; or abridging the freedom of speech, or of the press; or the right of the people peaceably to assemble, and to petition the government for a redress of grievances."

Accepting the Supreme Court's interpretation that the free-speech guarantee of the First Amendment does extend to labor picketing, the reader of the Constitution would conclude that this protection was only afforded as against hostile federal action. As above noted, the language of the First Amendment says: "Congress shall make no law. . . ." Nothing is stated that the states "shall not." The conclusion of the Supreme Court that the protection of picketing afforded by the First Amendment extended not only as against Congressional action but also as against state action is part of the remarkable conversion of the concept of protection from the federal government to protection from all governments, which has already been noted in § 10:3.

Shortly after adopting the concept that labor picketing was constitutionally-protected free speech, the Supreme Court began to recede from that extreme position by permitting certain limitations to be imposed by state action, such as by requiring that the picketing occur in the physical area of the dispute (the place of employment in which the labor dispute existed) rather than at the site of another enterprise that happened to be owned by the same employer. For example, it was held that union construction workers picketing an owner having a house built with nonunion labor could not picket a restaurant which that owner happened to own in the nearby city. Here the court was influenced by the fact that third persons having nothing to do with the construction dispute, that is, patrons of the restaurant, were being brought into the strife between the union and the building owner. The Supreme Court felt that it was unfair to permit "the conscription of neutrals" in this manner and therefore limited the right to picket to the area of the construction site. Additional limitations were imposed upon picketing until in 1957 the Supreme Court had for practical purposes abandoned the concept of labor picketing as constitutionally-protected free speech. In *International Brotherhood of Teamsters* v. *Vogt,* 354 U.S. 283, the dissenting opinion recognized that by the opinion of the majority "the Court signs the formal surrender [of the doctrine of constitutional protection of picketing]. . . . State courts and state legislatures are [now] free to decide whether to permit or suppress any particular picket line for any reason other than a blanket policy against all picketing. . . ."

AMALGAMATED FOOD EMPLOYEES v. LOGAN VALLEY PLAZA

391 U.S. 308 (1968)

Logan Valley Plaza owned a shopping center. It leased one of its store buildings to Weis Markets. Amalgamated Food Employees, a labor union, peacefully picketed Weis because it employed nonunion men. The Pennsylvania court enjoined the picketing because it was on the shopping center's parking lot, which was private property. The labor union claimed that it had the constitutional right to picket in the shopping center lot.

OPINION BY MARSHALL, J. . . .

Logan Valley Plaza, Inc. (Logan), . . . owns a large, newly developed shopping center complex, known as the Logan Valley Mall, located near the City of Altoona, Pennsylvania. The shopping center is situated at the intersection of Plank Road, which is on the east of the center, and Good's Lane, which is to the south. Plank Road, also known as U.S. Route 220, is a heavily traveled highway along which traffic moves at a fairly high rate of speed. There are five entrance roads into the center, three from Plank Road and two from Good's Lane. Aside from these five entrances, the shopping center is totally separated from the adjoining roads by earthen berms. The berms are 15 feet wide along Good's Lane and 12 feet wide along Plank Road.

At the time of the events in this case, Logan Valley Mall was occupied by two businesses, Weis Markets, Inc. (Weis), the other respondent herein, and Sears, Roebuck and Co. (Sears), although other enterprises were then expected and have since moved into the center. Weis operates a supermarket and Sears operates both a department store and an automobile service center. The Weis property consists of the enclosed supermarket building, an open but covered porch along the front of the building, and an approximately five-foot wide parcel pickup zone that runs 30 to 40 feet along the porch. The porch functions as a sidewalk in front of the building and the pickup zone is used as a temporary parking place for the loading of purchases into customers' cars by Weis employees.

Between the Weis building and the highway berms are extensive macadam parking lots with parking spaces and driveways lined off thereon. These areas, to which Logan retains title, provide common parking facilities for all the businesses in the shopping center. The distance across the parking lots to the Weis store from the entrances on Good's Lane is approximately 350 feet and from the entrances on Plank Road approximately 400 to 500 feet. The entrance on Plank Road furthest from the Weis property is the main entrance to the shopping center as a whole and is regularly used by customers of Weis. The entrance on Plank Road nearest to Weis is almost exclusively used by patrons of the Sears automobile service station into which it leads directly.

On December 8, 1965, Weis opened for business, employing a wholly nonunion staff of employees. A few days after it opened for business, Weis posted a sign on the exterior of its building prohibiting trespassing or soliciting by anyone other than its employees on its porch or parking lot. On December 17, 1965, members of Amalgamated Food Employees Union, Local 590 began picketing Weis. They carried signs stating that the Weis market was nonunion and that its employees were not "receiving union wages or other benefits." The pickets did not include any employees of Weis, but rather were all employees of competitors of Weis. The picketing continued until December 27, during which time the number of picketers varied between 4 and 13 and averaged around 6. The picketing was carried out almost entirely in the parcel pickup area and that portion of the parking lot immediately adjacent thereto. Although some congestion of the parcel pickup area occurred, such congestion was sporadic and infrequent. The picketing was peaceful at all times and unaccompanied by either threats or violence.

On December 27, Weis and Logan instituted an action in equity in the Court of Common Pleas of Blair County, and that court [enjoined] petitioners from, . . . "picketing and trespassing upon . . . the [Weis] storeroom, porch and parcel pickup area . . . [and] the [Logan] parking area and entrances and exits leading to said parking area." The effect of this order was to require that all picketing be carried on along the berms beside the public roads outside the shopping center. Picketing continued along the berms and, in addition, handbills asking the public not to patronize Weis because it was nonunion were distributed. . . .

That court explicitly rejected petitioners' claim under the First Amendment that they were entitled to picket within the confines of the shopping center. . . . On appeal the Pennsylvania Supreme Court, with three Justices dissenting, affirmed the issuance of the injunction on the sole ground that petitioners' conduct constituted a trespass on respondents' property.

We start from the premise that peaceful picketing carried on in a location open generally to the public is, absent other factors involving the purpose or manner of the picketing, protected by the First Amendment. . . . To be sure, this Court has noted that picketing involves elements of both speech and conduct, *i.e.*, patrolling, and has indicated that because of this intermingling of protected and unprotected elements, picketing can be subjected to controls that would not be constitutionally permissible in the case of pure speech. . . .

The case squarely presents, . . . the question whether Pennsylvania's generally valid rules against trespass to private property can be applied in these circumstances to bar petitioners from the Weis and Logan premises. It is clear that if the shopping center premises were not privately owned but instead constituted the business area of a municipality, which they to a large extent resemble, petitioners could not be barred from exercising their First Amendment rights there on the sole ground that title to the property was in the municipality. *Lovell* v. *Griffin,* 303 U.S. 444 (1938); *Hague* v. *CIO,* 307 U.S. 496 (1939); *Schneider* v. *State,* 308 U.S. 147 (1939); *Jamison* v. *Texas,* 318 U.S. 412 (1943). The essence of those opinions is that streets, sidewalks, parks, and other similar public places are so historically associated with the exercise of First Amendment rights that access to them for the purpose of exercising such rights cannot constitutionally be denied broadly and absolutely.

The fact that Lovell, Schneider, and Jamison were concerned with hand-billing rather than picketing is immaterial so far as the question is solely one of right of access for the purpose of expression of views. Handbilling, like picketing, involves conduct other than speech, namely, the physical presence of the person distributing leaflets on municipal property. If title to municipal property is, standing alone, an insufficient basis for prohibiting all entry onto such property for the purpose of distributing printed matter, it is likewise an insufficient basis for prohibiting all entry for the purpose of carrying an informational placard. While the patrolling involved in picketing may in some cases constitute an interference with the use of public property greater than that produced by handbilling, it is clear that in other cases the converse may be true. Obviously, a few persons walking slowly back and forth holding placards can be less obstructive of, for example, a public sidewalk than numerous persons milling around handing out leaflets. That the manner in which handbilling, or picketing, is carried out may be regulated does not mean that either can be barred under all circumstances on publicly owned property simply by recourse to traditional concepts of property law concerning the incidents of ownership of real property.

This Court has also held, in *Marsh* v. *Alabama,* 326 U.S. 501 (1946), that under some circumstances property that is privately owned may, at least for First Amendment purposes, be treated as though it were publicly held. In Marsh, the appellant, a Jehovah's Witness, had undertaken to distribute religious literature on a sidewalk in the business district of Chickasaw, Alabama. Chickasaw, a so-called company town, was wholly owned by the Gulf Shipbuilding Corporation. "The property consists of residential buildings, streets, a system of sewers, a sewage disposal plant and a 'business block' on which business places are situated. . . . [T]he residents use the business block as their regular shopping center. To do so, they now, as they have for many years, make use of a company-owned paved street and sidewalk located alongside the store fronts in order to enter and leave the stores and the post office. Intersecting company-owned roads at each end of the business block lead into a four-lane public highway which runs parallel

to the business block at a distance of 30 feet. There is nothing to stop highway traffic from coming onto the business block and upon arrival a traveler
may make free use of the facilities available there. In short the town and
its shopping district are accessible to and freely used by the public in general
and there is nothing to distinguish them from any other town and shopping
center except the fact that the title to the property belongs to a private
corporation." 326 U.S., at 502-503.

The corporation had posted notices in the stores stating that the premises
were private property and that no solicitation of any kind without written
permission would be permitted. Appellant Marsh was told that she must
have a permit to distribute her literature and that a permit would not be
granted to her. When she declared that the company rule could not be utilized
to prevent her from exercising her constitutional rights under the First Amendment, she was ordered to leave Chickasaw. She refused to do so and was
arrested for violating Alabama's criminal trespass statute. In reversing her
conviction under the statute, this Court held that the fact that the property
from which appellant was sought to be ejected for exercising her First Amendment rights was owned by a private corporation rather than the State was an
insufficient basis to justify the infringement on appellant's right to free expression occasioned thereby. Likewise the fact that appellant Marsh was herself not a resident of the town was not considered material.

The similarities between the business block in Marsh and the shopping
center in the present case are striking. The perimeter of Logan Valley Mall
is a little less than 1.1 miles. Inside the mall were situated, at the time of
trial, two substantial commercial enterprises with numerous others soon to
follow. Immediately adjacent to the mall are two roads, one of which is a
heavily traveled state highway and from both of which lead entrances directly
into the mall. Adjoining the buildings in the middle of the mall are sidewalks
for the use of pedestrians going to and from their cars and from building
to building. In the parking areas, roadways for the use of vehicular traffic
entering and leaving the mall are clearly marked out. The general public has
unrestricted access to the mall property. The shopping center here is clearly
the functional equivalent to the business district of Chickasaw involved in
Marsh.

It is true that, unlike the corporation in Marsh, the respondents here do
not own the surrounding residential property and do not provide municipal
services therefor. Presumably, petitioners are free to canvass the neighborhood with their message about the nonunion status of Weis Market, just as
they have been permitted by the state courts to picket on the berms outside
the mall. Thus, unlike the situation in Marsh, there is no power on respondents' part to have petitioners totally denied access to the community
for which the mall serves as a business district. This fact, however, is not
determinative. In Marsh itself the precise issue presented was whether the
appellant therein had the right, under the First Amendment, to pass out
leaflets in the business district, since there was no showing made there that
the corporate owner would have sought to prevent the distribution of leaflets
in the residential areas of the town. While it is probable that the power to
prevent trespass broadly claimed in Marsh would have encompassed such

an incursion into the residential areas, the specific facts in the case involved access to property used for commercial purposes.

We see no reason why access to a business district in a company town for the purpose of exercising First Amendment rights should be constitutionally required, while access for the same purpose to property functioning as a business district should be limited simply because the property surrounding the "business district" is not under the same ownership. Here the roadways provided for vehicular movement within the mall and the sidewalks leading from building to building are the functional equivalents of the streets and sidewalks of a normal municipal business district. The shopping center premises are open to the public to the same extent as the commercial center of a normal town. So far as can be determined, the main distinction in practice between use by the public of the Logan Valley Mall and of any other business district, were the decisions of the state courts to stand, would be that those members of the general public who sought to use the mall premises in a manner contrary to the wishes of the respondents could be prevented from so doing.

Such a power on the part of respondents would be, of course, part and parcel of the rights traditionally associated with ownership of private property. And it may well be that respondents' ownership of the property here in question gives them various rights, under the laws of Pennsylvania, to limit the use of that property by members of the public in a manner that would not be permissible were the property owned by a municipality. All we decide here is that because the shopping center serves as the community business block "and is freely accessible and open to the people in the area and those passing through," *Marsh* v. *Alabama,* 346 U.S., at 508, the State may not delegate the power, through the use of its trespass laws, wholly to exclude those members of the public wishing to exercise their First Amendment rights on the premises in a manner and for a purpose generally consonant with the use to which the property is actually put.

We do not hold that respondents, and at their behest the State, are without power to make reasonable regulations governing the exercise of First Amendment rights on their property. Certainly their rights to make such regulations are at the very least coextensive with the powers possessed by States and municipalities, and recognized in many opinions of this Court, to control the use of public property. Thus where property is not ordinarily open to the public, this Court has held that access to it for the purpose of exercising First Amendment rights may be denied altogether. See *Adderley* v. *Florida,* 385 U.S. 39 (1966). Even where municipal or state property is open to the public generally, the exercise of First Amendment rights may be regulated so as to prevent interference with the use to which the property is ordinarily put by the State. Thus we have upheld a statute prohibiting picketing "in such a manner as to obstruct or unreasonably to interfere with the free ingress or egress to and from any . . . county . . . courthouses." . . . Likewise it has been indicated that persons could be constitutionally prohibited from picketing "in or near" a court "with the intent of interfering with, obstructing, or impeding the administration of justice." . . .

In addition, the exercise of First Amendment rights may be regulated where such exercise will unduly interfere with the normal use of the public property by other members of the public with an equal right of access to it. Thus it has been held that persons desiring to parade along city streets may be required to secure a permit in order that municipal authorities be able to limit the amount of interference with use of the sidewalks . . . by regulating the time, place, and manner of the parade. . . .

Petitioners' picketing was directed solely at one establishment within the shopping center. The berms surrounding the center are from 350 to 500 feet away from the Weis store. All entry onto the mall premises by customers of Weis, so far as appears, is by vehicle from the roads along which the berms run. Thus the placards bearing the message which petitioners seek to communicate to patrons of Weis must be read by those to whom they are directed either at a distance so great as to render them virtually indecipherable—where the Weis customers are already within the mall—or while the prospective reader is moving by car from the roads onto the mall parking areas via the entrance ways cut through the berms. In addition, the pickets are placed in some danger by being forced to walk along heavily traveled roads along which traffic moves constantly at rates of speed varying from moderate to high. Likewise, the task of distributing handbills to persons in moving automobiles is vastly greater (and more hazardous) than it would be were petitioners permitted to pass them out within the mall to pedestrians. Finally, the requirement that the picketing take place outside the shopping center renders it very difficult for petitioners to limit its effect to Weis only.

It is therefore clear that the restraints on picketing and trespassing approved by the Pennsylvania courts here substantially hinder the communication of the ideas which petitioners seek to express to the patrons of Weis. The fact that the nonspeech aspects of petitioners' activity are also rendered less effective is not particularly compelling in light of the absence of any showing, or reliance by the state courts thereon, that the patrolling accompanying the picketing sought to be carried on was significantly interfering with the use to which the mall property was being put by both respondents and the general public. As we observed earlier, the mere fact that speech is accompanied by conduct does not mean that the speech can be suppressed under the guise of prohibiting the conduct. Here it is perfectly clear that a prohibition against trespass on the mall operates to bar all speech within the shopping center to which respondents object. Yet this Court stated many years ago. "[O]ne is not to have the exercise of his liberty of expression in appropriate places abridged on the plea that it may be exercised in some other place." . . .

The sole justification offered for the substantial interference with the effectiveness of petitioners' exercise of their First Amendment rights to promulgate their views through handbilling and picketing is respondents' claimed absolute right under state law to prohibit any use of their property by others without their consent. However, unlike a situation involving a person's home, no meaningful claim to protection of a right of privacy can be advanced by respondents here. Nor on the facts of the case can any significant claim to protection of the normal business operation of the property be raised. Naked title is essentially all that is at issue.

The economic development of the United States in the last 20 years reinforces our opinion of the correctness of the approach taken in Marsh.

The large-scale movement of this country's population from the cities to the suburbs has been accompanied by the advent of the suburban shopping center, typically a cluster of individual retail units on a single large privately owned tract. It has been estimated that by the end of 1966 there were between 10,000 and 11,000 shopping centers in the United States and Canada, accounting for approximately 37 percent of the total retail sales in those two countries.

These figures illustrate the substantial consequences for workers seeking to challenge substandard working conditions, consumers protesting shoddy or overpriced merchandise, and minority groups seeking nondiscriminatory hiring policies that a contrary decision here would have. Business enterprises located in downtown areas would be subject to on-the-spot public criticism for their practices, but businesses situated in the suburbs could largely immunize themselves from similar criticism by creating a *cordon sanitaire* of parking lots around their stores. Neither precedent nor policy compels a result so at variance with the goal of free expression and communication that is the heart of the First Amendment. . . .

"Ownership does not always mean absolute dominion. The more an owner, for his advantage, opens up his property for use by the public in general, the more do his rights become circumscribed by the statutory and constitutional rights of those who use it." Logan Valley Mall is the functional equivalent of a "business block" and for First Amendment purposes must be treated in substantially the same manner.

The judgment of the Supreme Court of Pennsylvania is reversed. . . .

CONCURRING OPINION BY DOUGLAS, J. . . .

Picketing on the public walkways and parking area in respondents' shopping center presents a totally different question from an invasion of one's home or place of business. While Logan Valley Mall is not dedicated to public use to the degree of the "company town" in *Marsh* v. *Alabama,* 326 U.S. 501, it is clear that respondents have opened the shopping center to public uses. They hold out the mall as "public" for purposes of attracting customers and facilitating delivery of merchandise. Picketing in regard to labor conditions at the Weis Supermarket is directly related to that shopping center business. Why should respondents be permitted to avoid this incidence of carrying on a public business in the name of "private property"? It is clear to me that they may not, when the public activity sought to be prohibited involves constitutionally protected expression respecting their business. . . .

It is said that the picketers may be banished to the publicly owned berms, several hundred feet from the target of their criticism. But that is to make "private property" a sanctuary from which some members of the public may be excluded merely because of the ideas they espouse. Logan Valley Mall covers several acres and the number of picketers at any time has been small. The courts of Pennsylvania are surely capable of fashioning a decree that will ensure noninterference with customers and employees, while enabling the union members to assemble sufficiently close to Weis' market to make effective the exercise of their First Amendment rights.

DISSENTING OPINION BY BLACK, J. . . .

Anyone familiar with the operations of a modern-day supermarket knows the importance of the so-called "pickup zone"— an area where the frequently numerous bags of groceries bought in the store can be loaded conveniently into the customers' cars. The phenomenon of the supermarket combined with widespread ownership of automobiles and refrigeration facilities has made the purchase of large quantities of groceries on a single shopping trip a common occurrence in this country. And in line with this trend the stores have had to furnish adequate loading areas and facilities including in many instances, such as here for example, extra employees to assist in loading customers' cars. Respondent Weis' parcel pickup zone is fairly typical of the type of loading area that has been provided: it is located alongside the front of the store and is 4 to 5 feet wide, 30 to 40 feet in length, and is marked off with bold double yellow lines; the words "Parcel Pickup" are printed in large letters in the zone. Testimony at trial showed that this pickup area was used "strictly for customers to come and enter to pick up their parcels which they had purchased. . . . They drive into this particular area, and there the groceries are loaded into the cars by [Weis employees] on . . . pickup duty."

It seems clear to me, in light of the customary way that supermarkets now must operate, that pickup zones are as much a part of these stores as the inside counters where customers select their goods or the check-out and bagging sections where the goods are paid for. I cannot conceive how such a pickup zone, even by the wildest stretching of *Marsh* v. *Alabama,* 326 U.S. 501, could ever be considered dedicated to the public or to pickets. The very first section of the injunction issued by the trial court in this case recognizes this fact and is aimed only at protecting this clearly private property from trespass by the pickets. Thus the order of the court separately enjoins petitioners from:

"(a) Picketing and trespassing upon the private property of the plaintiff Weis Markets, Inc., Store No. 40, located at Logan Valley Mall, Altoona, Pennsylvania, including as such private property the storeroom, porch and parcel pickup area." . . .

I think that this Court should declare unequivocally that Section (a) of the lower court's injunction is valid under the First Amendment and that petitioners cannot, under the guise of exercising First Amendment rights, trespass on respondent Weis' private property for the purpose of picketing. It would be just as sensible for this Court to allow the pickets to stand on the checkout counters, thus interfering with customers who wish to pay for their goods, as it is to approve picketing in the pickup zone which interferes with customers' loading of their cars. . . .

I would go further, however, and hold that the entire injunction is valid. With the exception of the Weis property mentioned above, the land on which this shopping center (composed of only two stores at the time of trial and approximately 17 now) is located is owned by respondent Logan Valley Plaza, Inc. . . . Now petitioners contend that they can come onto Logan's property for the purpose of picketing and refuse to leave when asked, and that Logan cannot use state trespass laws to keep them out. The majority of this Court affirms petitioners' contentions. But I cannot accept them, for I believe that whether this Court likes it or not the Constitution recognizes and supports the concept of private ownership of property. The Fifth Amendment provides that "no person shall . . . be deprived of life, liberty, or property, without due process of law; nor shall private property be taken for public use without just compensation." This means to me that there is no right to picket on the private premises of another to try to convert the owner or others to the views of the pickets. It also means, I think, that if this Court is going to arrogate to itself the power to act as the government's agent to take a part of Weis' property to give to the pickets for their use, the Court should also award Weis just compensation for the property taken.

In affirming petitioners' contentions the majority opinion relies on *Marsh v. Alabama, supra,* and holds that respondents' property has been transformed to some type of public property. But Marsh was never intended to apply to this kind of situation. Marsh dealt with the very special situation of a company-owned town, complete with streets, alleys, sewers, stores, residences, and everything else that goes to make a town. The particular company town involved was Chickasaw, Alabama, which, as we stated in the opinion, except for the fact that it "is owned by the Gulf Shipbuilding Corporation . . . has all the characteristics of any other American town. The property consists of residential buildings, streets, a system of sewers, a sewage disposal plant and a 'business block' on which business places are situated." 326 U.S., at 502. Again toward the end of the opinion we emphasized that "the town of Chickasaw does not function differently from any other town." 326 U.S., at 508. I think it is fair to say that the basis on which the Marsh decision rested was that the property involved encompassed an area that for all practical purposes had been turned into a town; the area had all the attributes of a town and was indistinguishable from any other town in Alabama. I can find very little resemblance between the shopping center involved in this case and Chickasaw, Alabama. There are no homes, there is no sewage disposal plant, there is not even a post office on this private property which the Court now considers the equivalent of a "town." Indeed, at the time this injunction was issued, there were only two stores on the property. Now there are supposed to be about 17, but they are all conceded to be "commercial establishments." The remainder of the property in the center has been laid out as a large parking lot with individually marked parking spaces provided for business customers. All I can say is that this sounds like a very strange "town" to me.

The majority opinion recognizes the problem with trying to draw too close an analogy with Marsh, but faces a dilemma in that Marsh is the only possible authority for treating admittedly privately owned property the way the majority does. Thus the majority opinion concedes that "the respondents here do not own the surrounding residential property and do not provide municipal services therefor." But that is not crucial, according to the majority, since the petitioner in Marsh was arrested in the business district of Chickasaw. The majority opinion then concludes that since the petitioner in Marsh was given access to the business district of a company town, the petitioners in this case should be given access to the shopping center which was functioning as a business district. But I respectfully suggest that this reasoning completely misreads Marsh and begs the question. The question is under what circumstances can private property be treated as though it were public? The answer that Marsh gives is when that property has taken on *all* the attributes of a town, *i.e.,* "residential buildings, streets, a system of sewers, a sewage disposal plant and a 'business block' on which business places are situated." 326 U.S., at 502. I can find nothing in Marsh which indicates that if one of these features is present, *e.g.,* a business district, this is sufficient for the Court to confiscate a part of an owner's private property and give its use to people who want to picket on it.

In allowing the trespass here, the majority opinion indicates that Weis and Logan invited the public to the shopping center's parking lot. This statement is contrary to common sense. Of course there was an implicit invitation for customers of the adjacent stores to come and use the marked off places for cars. But the whole public was no more wanted there than they would be invited to park free at a pay parking lot. Is a store owner or several of them together less entitled to have a parking lot set aside for customers than other property owners? To hold that store owners are compelled by law to supply picketing areas for pickets to drive store customers away is to create a court-made law wholly disregarding the constitutional basis on which private ownership of property rests in this country. . . . These pickets do have a constitutional right to speak about Weis' refusal to hire union labor, but they do not have a constitutional right to compel Weis to furnish them a place to do so on his property. . . .

DISSENTING OPINION BY HARLAN, J. . . .

The petitioner argues for reversal of the decision below on two separate grounds: first, that petitioner's picketing was protected by the First Amendment from state injunctive interference of this kind; second, that the Pennsylvania courts have strayed into a sphere where the power of initial decision is reserved by federal labor laws to the National Labor Relations Board. I think that, if available, the second or "preemption" ground would plainly be a preferable basis for decision. Because reliance on preemption would invoke the authority of a federal statute through the Constitution's Supremacy Clause, it would avoid interpretation of the Constitution itself, which would be necessary if the case were treated under the First Amendment. . . . Dependence on preemption would also assure that the Court does not itself disrupt the statutory scheme of labor law established by the Congress, a point to which I shall return. . . .

Turning to the First Amendment question, I believe that in the circumstances it is not an appropriate one for this Court to decide. This controversy arose in the course of a labor union's efforts to achieve labor goals by informational picketing. Although no preemption question is properly before us, I do think that we can take notice that this is an area in which Congress has enacted detailed legislation . . . and has set up an administrative agency to resolve such disputes in the first instance. The reason why it was deemed necessary to fashion the doctrine of preemption under the federal labor laws was that it would be intolerably disruptive if this statutory scheme were interpreted differently by state and federal courts. . . . It seems to me that a similar objection applies to this Court's resolution of such disputes by resort to the Constitution. For the establishment by this Court of a rigid constitutional rule in a field where Congress has attempted to strike a delicate balance between competing economic forces, and in circumstances where we cannot know how the controversy would be settled by Congress' chosen instrument, may also have a considerable disruptive effect. I therefore believe that we should exercise our discretion not to reach the First Amendment issue, and that we should dismiss the writ as improvidently granted. Such a disposition would not be unfair to the petitioner, since the failure to bring the preemption question properly before us was its own.

DISSENTING OPINION BY WHITE, J. . . .

The reason why labor unions may normally picket a place of business is that the picketing occurs on public streets which are available to all members of the public for a variety of purposes that include communication with other members of the public. The employer businessman cannot interfere with the pickets' communication because they have as much right to the sidewalk and street as he does and because the labor laws prevent such interference under various circumstances; the government may not interfere on his behalf, absent obstruction, violence, or other valid statutory justification, because the First Amendment forbids official abridgment of the right of free speech.

In *Marsh* v. *Alabama,* 326 U.S. 501 (1946), the company town was found to have all of the attributes of a state-created municipality and the company was found effectively to be exercising official power as a delegate of the State. In the context of that case, the streets of the company town were as available and as dedicated to public purposes as the streets of an ordinary town. The company owner stood in the shoes of the State in attempting to prevent the streets from being used as public streets are normally used.

The situation here is starkly different. As Mr. Justice Black so clearly shows, Logan Valley Plaza is not a town but only a collection of stores. In no sense are any parts of the shopping center dedicated to the public for general purposes or the occupants of the Plaza exercising official powers. The public is invited to the premises but only in order to do business with those who maintain establishments there. The invitation is to shop for the products which are sold. There is no general invitation to use the parking lot, the pickup zone, or the sidewalk except as an adjunct to shopping. No one is invited to use the parking lot as a place to park his car while he goes elsewhere to work. The driveways and lanes for auto traffic are not offered for use as general thoroughfares leading from one public street to another. Those driveways and parking spaces are not public streets and thus available for parades, public meetings, or other activities for which public streets are used. It may be more convenient for cars and trucks to cut through the shopping center to get from one place to another, but surely the Court does not mean to say that the public may use the shopping center property for this purpose. . . .

The most that can be said is that here the public was invited to shop, that except for their location in the shopping center development the stores would have fronted on public streets and sidewalks, and that the shopping center occupied a large area. But on this premise the parking lot, sidewalks, and driveways would be available for all those activities which are usually permitted on public streets. It is said that Logan Valley Plaza is substantially equivalent to a business block and must be treated as though each store was bounded by a public street and a public sidewalk. This rationale, which would immunize nonobstructive labor union picketing, would also compel the shopping center to permit picketing on its property for other communicative purposes, whether the subject matter concerned a particular business establishment or not. Nonobstructive handbilling for religious purposes, political campaigning, protests against government policies—the Court would apparently place all of these activities carried out on Logan Valley's property within the protection of the First Amendment, although the activities may have no connection whatsoever with the views of the Plaza's occupants or with the conduct of their businesses.

Furthermore, my Brother Black is surely correct in saying that if the invitation to the public is sufficient to permit nonobstructive picketing on the sidewalks, in the pickup zone, or in the parking area, only actual interference with customers or employees should bar pickets from quietly entering the store and marching around with their message on front and back.

It is not clear how the Court might draw a line between "shopping centers" and other business establishments which have sidewalks or parking on their own property. Any store invites the patronage of members of the public interested in its products. I am fearful that the Court's decision today will be a license for pickets to leave the public streets and carry out their activities on private property, as long as they are not obstructive. I do not agree that when the owner of private property invites the public to do business with him he impliedly dedicates his property for other uses as well. I do not think the First Amendment, which bars only official interferences with speech, has this reach. In Marsh, the company ran an entire town and the State was deemed to have devolved upon the company the task of carrying out municipal functions. But here the "streets" of Logan Valley Plaza are not like public streets; they are not used as thoroughfares for general travel from point to point, for general parking, for meetings, or for Easter parades.

If it were shown that Congress has thought it necessary to permit picketing on private property, either to further the national labor policy under the Commerce Clause or to implement and enforce the First Amendment, we would have quite a different case. But that is not the basis on which the Court proceeds, and I therefore dissent.

§ 13:5.   Freedom of Management Decision

(a) Generally. Under the present legal system, management is free to make decisions relating to management policies. There are limitations in the sense that when management makes contracts with third persons and groups, management may be restricted to observe certain standards. Thus

management must agree to pay a wage which is not less than that established by the applicable, ordinarily the federal, minimum wage law. Management in most areas must bargain collectively with the representative, ordinarily the union, chosen by its employees. When the enterprise is a corporation, management may be subject to the further limitation of answering to its shareholders for a financially unwise decision. For example, in one instance where the directors directed that a branch plant be closed and the building torn down in order to flee from the local union, it was held that the directors had acted capriciously and were liable in a shareholders' action to indemnify the corporation for the loss which they had caused it.

(b) Procedure for decision. In the case of corporate enterprises, the field of corporation law will specify the mechanics for formalizing a decision, as by a resolution by the board of directors. Third persons dealing with the corporation may require certain formal proof of management decision. For example, when a corporation opens a bank account, it is generally necessary to furnish the bank with a resolution of the board of directors authorizing the opening of the bank account.

When management decision involves a particular employee, must any formal requirements be observed? It could be argued that since the right to work for the corporation is a property right, that any "unfair" decision made by management with respect to employment deprives the employee of his property rights without due process of law. At present there is no requirement that any particular procedure be followed. It is desirable, however, that whenever management decision is made in an area in which there is a potential of a charge of discrimination whether racial, union, or otherwise, management should make a careful record of the action taken in order to have evidence at a later date as well as to have a permanent record of what had occurred.

NELSON v. BOARD OF EXAMINERS

21 N.Y.2d 408, 235 N.E.2d 433 (1968)

Nelson and others were interviewed by the Board of Examiners of the New York Board of Education for the position of elementary school principal. They were rejected and then claimed that the interview testing made of the respective applicants was procedurally inadequate and that they should be given another interview test.

OPINION BY SCILEPPI, J. . . .

The 17 petitioners in this proceeding were candidates in an examination conducted by the respondent Board of Examiners for licenses as principals of day elementary schools. The examination consisted of three parts: a written test, a supervision test, and an interview test. The petitioners passed the first two tests but failed the third and, consequently, were denied licenses.

According to section 24 of the Board's General Regulations Governing Examinations, the purpose of an interview test was as follows: *"An interview test* to evaluate any or all of the following: the applicant's ability to discuss problems relating to his subject or to the teaching of his subject or to the position sought; those aspects of personality as to which an interview affords a basis of judgment; the applicant's oral reading ability; and his use of English in discussion. Other aspects of the applicant's fitness may also be evaluated, such as his experiential background, his command of a foreign language (in the case of foreign language licenses), etc." Each interview test was conducted by a panel of four assistant examiners. The panels consisted of two elementary school principals, a college professor, and a speech expert. The assistant examiners were selected by the Board of Examiners under the supervision and direction of Dr. Isidore Bogen, the member of the Board of Examiners who was in charge of administration of the examination. At the beginning of each examination day, Dr. Bogen delivered a one-hour briefing to all persons who were to act as assistant examiners on that day. All examiners were required to attend the briefing even though they may have attended other briefings on other examination days. Written instructions concerning examination procedures and a statement of the problem on which the candidates were to be examined were given to the examiners during these briefings. Each interview test was 45 minutes in duration. On the day of the interview test, each applicant was given a written problem which dealt with a specific aspect of elementary education. The problem was designed to measure the candidate's awareness of what was taking place in the academic world and his ability to express himself and respond to challenges in a face-to-face encounter with an examining panel. The applicant was given one hour to examine the question and to make notes in preparation for his answer to or discussion of the problem. The applicant was allowed to bring these notes into the examination room and to refer to them while discussing the problem, but he was not allowed to read his answer to the panel. During the first 15 minutes of the interview test, the applicant gave his answer to the problem without interruption. During the remaining 30 minutes of the interview, the examiners asked the candidate questions. There was no requirement that the panel restrict its questions to the specific problem presented to the candidate. Questions relevant to any aspect of elementary school administration were permissible.

During the course of the examination, the examiners, other than the speech expert, had before them rating sheets which contained 21 items of performance under the four major categories of "speech," "oral discussion," "interpersonal relationships" and "other traits of personality." "Speech" was broken down into the items of "language usage and diction," "clearness and fluency of expression," "enunciation and pronunciation," and "voice quality and inflection." "Oral discussion" was broken down into the items of "comprehension of problems," "comprehensiveness of treatment of problems," "definiteness and practicality of proposals," "soundness of judgment (e.g., in making decisions)," "presentation of ideas in organized sequence," "clarity of explanation," "appropriateness and adequacy of illustrations," and "ability to meet challenges effectively." "Interpersonal relationships" was broken down into the items of "understanding interpersonal aspects of problems and proposals," "tact: sensitivity of feelings of other people," "ability to establish rapport with other people," and "resourcefulness in leading other people." "Other traits of personality" was broken down into the items of "appearance," "courtesy," "poise," "frankness," and "vitality." Next to each item of performance on the rating sheet there was room for comments of the assistant examiners. The examiners had to mark the candidate's performance in each category according to the following system: if the performance was unsatisfactory, he received a grade of very poor or inadequate; if his performance was satisfactory, he received a grade of passable, good or superior. These ratings had numerical equivalents ranging from 1 to 10 with 6 being the passing mark.

The examiners, other than the speech expert, were also required to keep "running notes" on the candidate's performance. Dr. Bogen instructed the examiners to make these running notes as complete as possible. Since the examiners were not trained stenographers and since the examiners were required to make these running notes while questioning an applicant, the notes were not intended to serve as a verbatim transcript of the candidate's answers and performance. They were intended, however, to capture the gist of the candidate's answers to the questions asked of him and to capture the examiners' impressions of the candidate's personality and ability.

The speech expert had before him an "oral English work sheet" containing various categories of speech performance. This sheet provided spaces for rating the candidate in "conversational speech," "voice," and "enunciation and pronunciation" and it contained spaces for "additional comments."

After the examination was over and the candidate had left the room, the members of the examining panel individually gave the candidate a tentative rating on the interview test rating sheets or in the case of the speech expert on the oral English work sheet. The panel members then entered into a discussion of the candidate's performance, with the speech expert participating only with respect to the candidate's performance in the category of speech and other personality traits. After the discussion had been completed, each panel member made his final ratings on the individual items of performance and arrived at a final overall rating. Although the overall rating was to be based on the total pattern of the candidate's performance, it was not necessarily an arithmetic average of the ratings on the individual items of performance. Since the speech expert had only an advisory role, his rating did not enter into the final overall rating of the examining panel. The panel's final rating was arrived at by taking the rating which was between the highest and lowest of the individual ratings.

If the panel decided to fail a candidate, they were required to write out a statement entitled "Reasons for Failure." This statement was a succinct presentation of the candidate's shortcomings with illustrations of the same. A panel member who disagreed with the majority of the panel could write a minority report expressing his reasons for the disagreement.

The panel's recommendation, together with the prepared question presented to the candidate, the candidate's notes, the examiners' running notes, the rating sheets and the statements of reasons for failure, was submitted to

Dr. Bogen for a review. Upon reviewing this information, Dr. Bogen recommended that the rating be accepted by the school board of examiners if he was convinced that there was a substantial basis for the panel's rating.

Special Term vacated the results of the petitioners' tests for three reasons:

(1) Respondent did not employ sufficiently objective standards in rating petitioners' performance;

(2) the "running notes" made by the assistant examiners were insufficient to enable review by examiners of equal ability and experience. . . .

The Appellate Division, while affirming Special Term's judgment, disagreed with its reasoning in part. The court held that the "21 items delineating the four major categories of the test were sufficiently objective." It agreed, however, that the panel's running notes did not provide an adequate record for review. The Appellate Division made no mention of the necessity for approval of the assistant examiners by the Civil Service Commission.

Section 6 of article V of the Constitution of the State of New York provides: "Appointments and promotions in the civil service of the state and all of the civil divisions thereof . . . shall be made according to merit and fitness to be ascertained, as far as practicable, by examination which, as far as practicable, shall be competitive."

. . . In Matter of *Fink* v. *Finegan,* 270 N.Y. 356, 1 N.E.2d 462, the petitioner was a candidate for police surgeon, medical officer in the Fire Department, or medical examiner in the Department of Sanitation. He had passed the written tests and thereafter he took an oral examination consisting of technical questions of a medical nature, which he answered correctly. Nevertheless, he failed the oral examination because in the opinion of the examiners he was lacking in executive ability. This court vacated the results of the test. We held that there was no showing that executive ability was a quality necessary for the position sought nor did the notice of examination inform the petitioner that this quality would be tested. Furthermore, there were no objective standards set for measuring the petitioner's executive ability nor was there any showing that such standards could not be set. We went on to hold that "An examination cannot be classed as competitive unless it conforms to measures or standards which are sufficiently objective to be capable of being challenged and reviewed, when necessary, by other examiners of equal ability and experience." . . . The court noted, however, that some civil service positions require qualities which cannot be measured objectively and in those cases subjective standards would be permitted.

In Matter of *Sloat* v. *Board of Examiners,* 274 N.Y. 367, 9 N.E.2d 12, 112 A.L.R. 660, the petitioner applied for a teaching license in fine arts. She was subjected to a number of tests including an interview test and a teaching test. The petitioner failed both of these tests and was denied a license. She attempted to have the results of the test set aside on the ground that the test was not objective as was required by our holding in *Matter of Fink* (supra). This court concluded that petitioner's reliance on *Matter of Fink* was misplaced and refused to set aside the results of the test: "The mandate of the Constitution for the ascertainment of merit and fitness, so far as practicable, by competitive examination, may not be transformed into an interdict against the examinations which are best adapted for the demonstration of fitness. It would be impossible to formulate a standard by which such qualities may be defined or measured with entire objectivity. The law does not require the impossible or forbid the reasonable. The record discloses that here the examiners have based determination upon their estimates of qualities which, it is reasonably clear, affect the merit and fitness of a teacher and that this estimate is derived from tests calculated reasonably to show those qualities. Evidently it is not practicable to apply such tests in exactly the same form to each competitor or to make exact comparisons between them. That is true in some degree of every examination, especially of examinations calculated to show intellectual ability and broad cultural learning. Exact definition of the qualities which are essential or desirable may be impossible; exact formula or standard by which such qualities may be measured has never been achieved; mechanical application of any standard is certainly not practicable. Much must be left here to the judgment of the examiners. The test cannot be wholly objective and to the extent that it is subjective the result may depend as much upon the fitness of the examiners as upon the fitness of the candidate. That is a risk inherent in all systems of examination." . . .

In the case at bar, the petitioners were candidates for the position of day elementary school principal. The qualities one must possess to adequately fulfill the duties of such a position are many and varied. He must have a capacity for leadership. He must be capable of establishing rapport with teachers, students and parents. He must be imaginative and capable of expressing his ideas to others, either individually or in groups. These qualities cannot be measured with any degree of precision. In such cases "Much must be left . . . to the judgment of the examiners" . . . and the "examinations may be subjective insofar as objectivity is impracticable or impossible." . . .

The petitioners contend, and the courts below agreed, that since the interview tests were not stenographically or electronically recorded, they were not susceptible of objective review by other examiners. The petitioners specifically point to the "running notes" made by the examiners during the course of the interview which were in some instances fragmentary and illegible. In response to the petitioners' contention, the Board of Education argues that many of the traits and qualities which are tested by the interview tests do not lend themselves to stenographic or electronic recording. In addition, argues the board, review of the results of the interview test is not limited to the examiner's running notes. The reviewer of the test results has before him the test question, the applicant's preparatory notes, the interview test rating sheets, the oral English work sheet, the statement of reasons for failure, as well as the running notes.

While much might be said in favor of stenographic or electronic recording of the interview tests, it cannot be said that they are required as a matter of law. . . . All that the law requires is that the results of the examination be so stated so that they are capable of being reviewed. . . . The records of the interview tests submitted to the Board of Examiners were sufficient to meet this requirement. . . .

To conclude, the interview test was sufficiently objective under the circumstances, the record was adequate for review. . . .

Accordingly, the order appealed from should be reversed, without costs, and the petition herein dismissed.

Questions for Review

1. Define the social force of protection of freedom of personal action.

2. Give illustrations of its application.

3. Analyze each opinion in this chapter in terms of the social forces involved in the decision. See § 5:5 for a list of the social forces. With respect to each opinion, explain why the prevailing social forces prevailed and why those rejected did not. In each case in which there is a dissenting opinion, also make this analysis for the dissenting opinion.

4-6. On the basis of the social forces involved, what decision should be made in each of the following cases?

4. *Insurance. National service life.* Is a change of insurance beneficiary from the first to the second wife of the insured binding when divorce decree prohibits change of beneficiary? *Thoen* v. *Thoen,* Cal.App.2d, 56 Cal.Rptr. 614.

5. *Restrictive covenant. Employment.* Pierce worked for the Mutual Loan Company in Sioux City, Iowa. His job was to call delinquent customers to obtain payment. By the written contract of employment, he had agreed not to enter the employ of any competing small loan business in the same town while employed or for one year thereafter. Upon the termination of his employment with Mutual Loan Co., he went to work for a competing personal loan company. Mutual sought an injunction to prevent him from working for the competitor. Decide. *Mutual Loan Co.* v. *Pierce,* 245 Iowa 1051, 65 N.W.2d 405.

6. *Schools. Beards.* The school district required that all students be clean shaven. Akin, aged 15, claimed that this violated his right of free speech and expression and deprived him of liberty and invaded his private life because it affected his appearance after school hours as well as while in school. Was the school regulation valid? *Akin* v. *Board of Education,* Cal.App.2d, 68 Cal.Rptr. 557.

What social forces were involved, which prevailed, and which were defeated in the following decision?

7. *Free speech. Teacher.* Pickering was a public school teacher. A proposal to increase school taxes was defeated by the voters. He then wrote a letter to the editor of the local newspaper criticizing the way in which the Board of Education was meeting the problem of raising new funds. He was fired because of this letter, but it was held that the discharge was improper since the right of free speech entitled him to speak upon matters of public interest, even though he stood in the position of an employee of the public school system. *Pickering* v. *Board of Education,* 391 U.S. 563.

Chapter 14

PROTECTION OF FREE USE OF PROPERTY

§ 14:1. Generally

Closely related to the objective of protection of freedom of personal action is that of protecting the freedom of the use of property. This freedom is achieved by prohibiting, restraining, or penalizing the acts of others that would hamper the reasonable use of property by its owner.

Absolute freedom of this kind would permit its owner to make any use he chose of his property—even in a way that would harm others, to sell it at any price he desired, or to make any disposition of it that he wished. Such freedom is not recognized today, for everywhere we find some limitation of the right of the owner of property to do as he pleases with it.

The law prohibits an owner from using his property in such a way as to injure another or another's property. Further, zoning laws may limit the use of his land. Building restrictions in a deed may restrict the type of building that the owner may construct on his land. Fire laws and building codes may specify details of construction of his building. Labor laws may require that he equip a business building with safety devices.

§ 14:2. Construction Use

In the absence of zoning or building codes, or particular provisions in the deed by which the owner acquired his property, the owner may build on his land as he chooses. Sometimes he is limited in so doing when he acts maliciously as by building a spite fence merely to harm his neighbor. Where, however, the construction is made in good faith, the social value in favor of the free use by the owner of the property is deemed to outweigh the harm that the neighbor sustains as the result of the construction.

FONTAINEBLEAU HOTEL CORP. v. FORTY-FIVE TWENTY-FIVE, INC.

114 So.2d 357 (Fla., 1959)

The Eden Roc and the Fontainebleau are neighboring hotels in Miami Beach, Florida. Fontainebleau proposed to construct a 14-story annex to its building on its land. This construction would block the view of the Atlantic Ocean for persons in the Eden Roc Hotel. The Forty-Five Twenty-Five, Inc., which was the owner of Eden Roc, brought an action against the Fontainebleau Hotel Corp. to prevent the construction of the annex. From a decision against the construction, Fontainebleau appealed.

PER CURIAM. . . .

This is indeed a novel application of the maxim *sic utere tuo ut alienum non laedas.* This maxim does not mean that one must never use his own property in such a way as to do any injury to his neighbor. . . . It means only that one must never use his property so as not to injure the lawful *rights* of another. . . . "It is well settled that a property owner may put his own property to any reasonable and lawful use, so long as he does not thereby deprive the adjoining landowner of any right of enjoyment of his property *which is recognized and protected by law, and so long as his use is not such a one as the law will pronounce a nuisance.*" [Emphasis supplied.]

No American decision has been cited . . . in which it has been held that —in the absence of some contractual or statutory obligation—a landowner has a legal right to the free flow of light and air across the adjoining land of his neighbor. Even at common law, the landowner has no legal right, in the absence of an easement or uninterrupted use and enjoyment for a period of 20 years, to unobstructed light and air from the adjoining land. . . .

There being, then, no legal right to the free flow of light and air from the adjoining land, it is universally held that where a structure serves a useful and beneficial purpose, it does not give rise to a cause of action, either for damages or for an injunction under the maxim *sic utere tuo ut alienum non laedas,* even though it causes injury to another by cutting off the light and air and interfering with the view that would otherwise be available over adjoining land in its natural state, regardless of the fact that the structure may have been erected partly for spite. . . .

We see no reason for departing from this universal rule. If, as contended on behalf of plaintiff, public policy demands that a landowner in the Miami Beach area refrain from constructing buildings on his premises that will cast a shadow on the adjoining premises, an amendment of its comprehensive planning and zoning ordinance, applicable to the public as a whole, is the means by which such purpose should be achieved. (No opinion is expressed here as to the validity of such an ordinance, if one should be enacted

pursuant to the requirements of law.) . . . But to change the universal rule—
and the custom followed in this state since its inception—that adjoining
landowners have an equal right under the law to build to the line of their
respective tracts and to such a height as is desired to them (in the absence,
of course, of building restrictions or regulations) amounts, in our opinion,
to judicial legislation. . . .

[Judgment reversed.]

§ 14:3.   Production Use

If the owner of property has the free use of his property, he can, in the
case of land, generally grow anything and as much as he chooses thereon.
In the case of other kinds of property, such as sheet metal, he can make anything which he chooses, without regard to whether it has any social value
or is just a waste of good metal. That is, society does not set up any official
judge or censor to determine what is good and what is bad for the economy.
The American system ordinarily leaves to the consumers of the country to
determine whether a product is to be purchased and thus further production
of the product inspired. If they purchase, a given use will thrive and continue;
if they do not, it will dwindle and cease.

Sometimes production is regulated by the government in the interest of
protecting the general welfare and economy by the avoidance of economic
unbalances through overproduction. Sometimes, as in the case of safety
devices, regulation is imposed to protect the public from physical harm. Here
the social values of protecting the public safety, protecting the person of the
consumer, and thereby furthering trade, serve to outweigh the social value
of a free use of a seller's property. In wartime, the protection of the government may by itself outweigh all other considerations and justify restrictions
on the use, manufacture, or priority of use, of property, where government
and essential war industries have first call on materials needed for the war
effort.

WICKARD v. FILBURN

317 U.S. 111 (1942)

OPINION BY JACKSON, J. . . .

The appellee filed his complaint against the Secretary of Agriculture of
the United States, three members of the County Agricultural Conservation
Committee for Montgomery County, Ohio, and a member of the State
Agricultural Conservation Committee for Ohio . . . to enjoin enforcement
against himself of the marketing penalty imposed by the amendment of May
26, 1941, to the Agricultural Adjustment Act of 1938, upon that part of his
1941 wheat crop which was available for marketing in excess of the marketing quota established for his farm. He also sought a declaratory judgment that
the wheat marketing quota provisions of the Act as amended and applicable

to him were unconstitutional because not sustainable under the Commerce Clause or consistent with the Due Process Clause of the Fifth Amendment. . . .

In July of 1940, pursuant to the Agricultural Adjustment Act of 1938, as then amended, there were established for the appellee's 1941 crop a wheat acreage allotment of 11.1 acres and a normal yield of 20.1 bushels of wheat an acre. . . . He sowed, however, 23 acres, and harvested from his 11.9 acres of excess acreage 239 bushels, which under the terms of the Act as amended on May 26, 1941, constituted farm marketing excess, subject to a penalty of 49 cents a bushel, or $117.11 in all. The appellee has not paid the penalty and he has not postponed or avoided it by storing the excess under regulations of the Secretary of Agriculture, or by delivering it up to the Secretary. The Committee, therefore, refused him a marketing card, which was, under the terms of Regulations promulgated by the Secretary, necessary to protect a buyer from liability to the penalty and upon its protecting lien.

The general scheme of the Agricultural Adjustment Act of 1938 as related to wheat is to control the volume moving in interstate and foreign commerce in order to avoid surpluses and shortages and the consequent abnormally low or high wheat prices and obstructions to commerce. Within prescribed limits and by prescribed standards the Secretary of Agriculture is directed to ascertain and proclaim each year a national acreage allotment for the next crop of wheat, which is then apportioned to the states and their counties, and is eventually broken up into allotments for individual farms. Loans and payments to wheat farmers are authorized in stated circumstances.

The Act provides further that whenever it appears that the total supply of wheat as of the beginning of any marketing year, beginning July 1, will exceed a normal year's domestic consumption and export by more than 35 percent, the Secretary shall so proclaim not later than May 15 prior to the beginning of such marketing year; and that during the marketing year a compulsory national marketing quota shall be in effect with respect to the marketing of wheat. Between the issuance of the proclamation and June 10, the Secretary must, however, conduct a referendum of farmers who will be subject to the quota to determine whether they favor or oppose it; and if more than one third of the farmers voting in the referendum do oppose, the Secretary must prior to the effective date of the quota by proclamation suspend its operation. . . .

It is urged that under the Commerce Clause . . . Congress does not possess the power it has in this instance sought to exercise. . . . The sum of this is that the federal government fixes a quota including all that the farmer may harvest for sale or for his own farm needs, and declares that wheat produced on excess acreage may neither be disposed of nor used except upon payment of the penalty or except it is stored as required by the Act or delivered to the Secretary of Agriculture.

Appellee says that this is a regulation of production and consumption of wheat. . . . In answer the government argues that the statute regulates neither production nor consumption, but only marketing; . . .

In the Shreveport Rate cases . . . the Court held that railroad rates of an admittedly intrastate character and fixed by authority of the state might, nevertheless, be revised by the federal government because of the economic effects which they had upon interstate commerce. The opinion of Mr. Justice Hughes found federal intervention constitutionally authorized because of "matters having such a close and substantial relation to interstate traffic that the control is essential or appropriate to the security of that traffic, to the efficiency of the interstate service, and to the maintenance of the conditions under which interstate commerce may be conducted upon fair terms and without molestation or hindrance." . . .

Questions of federal power cannot be decided simply by finding the activity in question to be "production" nor can consideration of its economic effects be foreclosed by calling them "indirect." . . . "The commerce power is not confined in its exercise to the regulation of commerce among the states. It extends to those activities intrastate which so affect interstate commerce, or the exertion of the power of Congress over it, as to make regulation of them appropriate means to the attainment of a legitimate end, the effective execution of the granted power to regulate interstate commerce. . . . The power of Congress over interstate commerce is plenary and complete in itself, may be exercised to its utmost extent, and acknowledges no limitations other than are prescribed in the Constitution. . . . It follows that no form of state activity can constitutionally thwart the regulatory power granted by the commerce clause to Congress. Hence the reach of that power extends to those intrastate activities which in a substantial way interfere with or obstruct the exercise of the granted power." . . .

Whether the subject of the regulation in question was "production," "consumption," or "marketing" is, therefore, not material for purposes of deciding the question of federal power before us. . . . Even if appellee's activity be local and though it may not be regarded as commerce, it may still, whatever its nature, be reached by Congress if it exerts a substantial economic effect on interstate commerce and this irrespective of whether such effect is what might at some earlier time have been defined as "direct" or "indirect."

[The Court summarized] the economics of the wheat industry.

In the absence of regulation the price of wheat in the United States would be much affected by world conditions. During 1941 producers who cooperated with the Agricultural Adjustment program received an average price on the farm of about $1.16 a bushel as compared with the world market price of 40 cents a bushel. . . .

The effect of consumption of homegrown wheat on interstate commerce is due to the fact that it constitutes the most variable factor in the disappearance of the wheat crop. Consumption on the farm where grown appears to vary in an amount greater than 20 percent of average production. The total amount of wheat consumed as food varies but relatively little, and use as seed is relatively constant.

. . . The effect of the statute before us is to restrict the amount which may be produced for market and the extent as well to which one may forestall resort to the market by producing to meet his own needs. That appellee's own contribution to the demand for wheat may be trivial by itself is not enough to remove him from the scope of federal regulation where, as here, his contribution, taken together with that of many others similarly situated, is far from trivial. . . .

It is well established by decisions of this Court that the power to regulate commerce includes the power to regulate the prices at which commodities in that commerce are dealt in and practices affecting such prices. One of the primary purposes of the Act in question was to increase the market price of wheat and to that end to limit the volume thereof that could affect the market. It can hardly be denied that a factor of such volume and variability as home-consumed wheat would have a substantial influence on price and market conditions. This may arise because being in marketable condition such wheat overhangs the market and if induced by rising prices tends to flow into the market and check price increases. But if we assume that it is never marketed, it supplies a need of the man who grew it which would otherwise be reflected by purchases in the open market. Homegrown wheat in this sense competes with wheat in commerce. The stimulation of commerce is a use of the regulatory function quite as definitely as prohibitions or restrictions thereon. This record leaves us in no doubt that Congress may properly have considered that wheat consumed on the farm where grown if wholly outside the scheme of regulation would have a substantial effect in defeating and obstructing its purpose to stimulate trade therein at increased prices.

It is said, however, that this Act, forcing some farmers into the market to buy what they could provide for themselves, is an unfair promotion of the markets and prices of specializing wheat growers. It is of the essence of regulation that it lays a restraining hand on the self-interest of the regulated and that advantages from the regulation commonly fall to others. The conflicts of economic interest between the regulated and those who advantage by it are wisely left under our system to resolution by the Congress under its more flexible and responsible legislative process. Such conflicts rarely lend themselves to judicial determination. And with the wisdom, workability, or fairness of the plan we have nothing to do. . . .

§ 14:4.   Competitive Use

Where the owner in good faith uses his property in competition with others, such other persons cannot complain that they are harmed by the competition. If the owner does not compete fairly, however, as when he attempts to deceive the public into believing that his product was made by the complaining manufacturer, other social values involved outweigh the desire to permit the competition. That is, the social values of protecting the public generally and of protecting other sellers from the oppression of unfair competition outweigh the social value in favor of a free unrestrained competition.

Questions for Review

1. Define the social force of protection of free use of property.

2. Give illustrations of its application.

3. Analyze each opinion in this chapter in terms of the social forces involved in the decision. See § 5:5 for a list of the social forces. With respect to each opinion, explain why the prevailing social forces prevailed and why those rejected did not. In each case in which there is a dissenting opinion, also make this analysis for the dissenting opinion.

4-7. *On the basis of the social forces involved, what decision should be made in each of the following cases?*

4. **Premises liability. Trespasser.** A 9-year old boy running from a dog, ran onto the land of the defendant and was killed by striking a cable which the defendant had stretched between two trees several feet from the ground. Was the defendant liable? *Johnson* v. *Williams,* Fla., 192 So.2d 339.

5. **Release from liability. Lease of commercial warehouse.** A lease of a commercial warehouse declared that the landlord was not liable for damage caused by water from any source. The landlord also owned and had control of a vacant warehouse adjoining the one that was rented. Because of his negligence with respect to the vacant warehouse, a waterpipe therein froze, broke, and caused water to flow into the rented warehouse where it damaged property of a customer of the tenant. The customer claimed that the landlord was liable for the damage thus caused. The landlord claimed that it was not liable because of the clause releasing it from water damage liability. Was this a valid defense? *Commercial Warehouse Co.* v. *Hyder Brothers,* 75 N.Mex. 792, 411 P.2d 978.

6. **Zoning restriction. Gas station.** A tract of land was owned by the bank. The area was zoned residential. The bank claimed the right to use its land as a gasoline station and showed that although the value of the land was $9,000, it could sell the land to an oil company for a gas station for $35,000. In deeds dated 1928 and 1931, it was specified that the "above described lots shall be known as business lots." Was the bank entitled to use the land as a gasoline station? *LaSalle National Bank* v. *Palatine Village,* 92 Ill.App.2d 327, 236 N.E.2d 1.

7. **Civil rights. Motel.** A motel catering to interstate travelers claimed that the Civil Rights Act of 1964 could not be applied to it as this would, in effect, tell it how to use its property and thus take its property without due process of law and constitute a taking without just compensation. Decide. *Heart of Atlanta Motel* v. *United States,* 379 U.S. 241.

8-12. *What social forces were involved, which prevailed, and which were defeated in the following decisions?*

8. **Premises liability. Falling fan.** Where patron was injured when counter-weight of a ceiling fan fell because of defective welding, the proprietor could not be held liable on the theory of a nondelegable duty to maintain premises in a safe condition, the circumstances being such that the defect was not apparent on inspection and that collapse would not have occurred if welding had been properly made. *Mai Kai* v. *Colucci,* Fla., 205 So.2d 291.

9. **Leases. Motive of termination.** When the landlord lawfully terminates a lease in accordance with its notice provision, it is immaterial that he may

have been motivated by the desire to retaliate against the tenant for having made complaint as to condition of the premises to the appropriate housing authority. *Edwards* v. *Habib*, [C.A.Dist.Col.] 227 A.2d 388.

10. *Insurance. Noncooperation.* Insurer cannot claim noncooperation of insured for not living at address given his employer or moving without giving a new address where insured had no knowledge of the policy or any obligation to furnish information and the insurer was not diligent in attempting to locate insured. *Carpenter* v. *Superior Court*, 101 Ariz. 565, 422 P.2d 129.

11. *Lease. Use of premises.* A recital in a lease that the tenant will use the premises for a stated purpose is permissive and is not a restrictive covenant that he will only use it for that purpose. Consequently, where it was stated that the tenant bank would use the premises for banking purposes, there was no breach of the lease when the bank thereafter sublet the premises to a school district, which used the premises for an adult education program. *Baron Bros.* v. *National Bank of South Dakota*, S.D., 155 N.W.2d 300.

12. *Premises liability. Landlord.* Landlord not liable for leakage from air-conditioning unit where lease expressly exonerated him from liability, even though he had been negligent in keeping the unit in repair. *Home Indemnity Co.* v. *Basiliko*, 245 Md. 412, 226 A.2d 258.

Chapter 15

ENFORCEMENT OF INTENT

§ 15:1. Generally

The law usually seeks to enforce the expressed intention of a party to a contract. This objective is closely related to the concept that the law seeks to protect the individual's freedom of action. For example, if a person provides by his will for the distribution of his property when he dies, the law will generally allow the property to pass to the persons intended by the deceased owner. The law will likewise seek to carry out the intention of the parties to a business transaction. To illustrate, if you and an electrician agree that he shall rewire your house for $200, the law will ordinarily enforce that contract because that is what was intended by both parties.

The extent to which the intent of one person or of several persons will be carried out has certain limitations. Sometimes the intent is not effective unless it is manifested by a particular formality. For example, a deceased person may have intended that his friend should receive his house, but in most states that intent must be shown by a written will signed by the deceased owner. Likewise, in some cases the intent of the parties may not be carried out because the law regards the purpose of the intent as illegal or otherwise improper.

The question of intent may arise in connection with the question of what was the intent of (a) the lawmaker who adopted the law, (b) the individual who established the transaction or relationship, or (c) the two or more individuals who made the contract or other agreement. In many instances, the courts will find an implied intent where this is deemed desirable in order to avoid a result which the court regards as oppressive.

§ 15:2.   Intent of the Lawmaker

Not infrequently when a lawmaker adopts a statute he fails to cover the situation which thereafter arises. This is the result of either carelessness on the part of the lawmaker or the development of a factual situation which could not have been foreseen. This question also arises in connection with the interpretation of constitutions as will be discussed in § 23:2.

RADCLIFFE COLLEGE v. CAMBRIDGE

350 Mass. 613, 215 N.E.2d 892 (1966)

Radcliffe College planned to build a library. The appropriate officials of the City of Cambridge required that the college provide off-street parking, allowing one car space for every 1,000 feet of gross floor area. The college claimed that this ordinance was void because of a Massachusetts statute which declared that "no ordinance . . . which . . . limits the use of land . . . for any educational purpose . . . shall be valid," the theory of the college being that the land which the city required to be used for parking lots could not be used by the college for educational purposes.

OPINION BY WHITTEMORE, J. . . .

Adequate provision for parking or housing the automobiles of persons using dwellings and other buildings has become of general public concern. Public convenience and safety are adversely affected by crowded streets. Available street spaces are limited and unable to accommodate the increasing number of automobiles. Street parking regulations are ineffective. These, as general phenomena, are matters of common knowledge. . . . The reasonable premise of a requirement for off-street parking spaces for new buildings is that parking automobiles nearby is an established function of the use of any building wherein people live, work, study or congregate for other purposes. Such a requirement is analogous to the statutory requirements of public corridors and exits of certain size and number and somewhat analogous to requirements of fire walls, fire escapes and fireproof construction. . . .

Providing for the parking or housing of the automobiles of students, instructors, and employees of an educational institution is within the broad scope of the educational powers of the institution just as is providing for the feeding and housing of such personnel. These are secondary functions incidental to the main educational purpose. Hence, a regulation that requires that some of the college land be used for parking does not lessen the availability of all or any of the institution's land for some appropriate educational purpose. We think the statute does not bar such regulation. Plainly the statute does not do so in express terms. At most the Cambridge ordinance requires choices among the proper educational purposes of the institution. In so doing it does not impede the reasonable use of the college's land for its educational purposes. We rule, therefore, that it does not limit "the use of [its] land for any . . . educational purpose" within the meaning of [the statute]. . . .

§ 15:3. Intent of an Individual

Many legal transactions arise as the result of the act of one individual. Thus a lawsuit may turn on the question, such as did the owner intend to make a gift of his property, did he intend to transfer his property by his will, did he intend to release his claim.

PIERCE'S PETITION

153 Maine 180, 136 A.2d 510 (1957)

By his will dated 1870, Joseph How bequeathed his residuary estate in trust to pay the income therefrom to certain persons for their respective lives and upon their deaths to be used by his trustee to found a "home for indigent seamen." Joseph had been the master and the captain of Ellen Stevens, a three-masted sailing vessel. At the time of his death his estate was valued at $1,500. Thereafter certain investments that Joseph had made which were regarded as worthless increased in value to more than $300,000 and income of $100,000 was received by the trustee. A petition was then filed with the court for instructions as to how this fund should be expended under the will. From the decision directing certain uses of the money, an appeal was taken.

OPINION BY DUBORD, J. . . .

The doctrine of cy-pres does not apply to private trusts. . . .
Before the cy-pres doctrine will be applied, three prerequisites must be met. First, the court must find that the gift creates a valid charitable trust. Second; it must be established that it is to some degree impossible or impractical to carry out the specific purpose of the trust, for the cy-pres doctrine is inapplicable when the particular purpose of the settlor can be effectively carried out. The third prerequisite is the requirement of a general charitable intention. . . .
    . . . The bequest in the How will is in terms a good charitable bequest. . . .
    It is . . . clear that the trust fund now available is in an amount too large to permit its application for the relief of indigent seamen of the class to which the testator belonged. . . .

The important issue, therefore, for determination is whether or not the testator expressed in his will a general charitable intent. If so, then the application of the cy-pres doctrine would be in order and the scope of the beneficiaries seemingly covered in the trust can be broadened and enlarged. In other words, seamen of a type different from that to which the testator belonged can be included as beneficiaries.

We give our attention, therefore, to the issue of determining whether or not Captain How manifested a general charitable intention when he created the trust which is now before us for consideration.

Legal authors describe this general charitable intention as a desire to give to charity generally, rather than to any one party, object, or institution. . . .

If we endeavor to project ourselves into the past and contemplate upon the intention of Captain How, we may well suppose that while he was perhaps primarily interested in crewmen of ships such as he was master of, he nevertheless had in mind that wider group of men whose major means of livelihood was gained from the sea. . . .

It is, therefore, our opinion that the scope of the beneficiaries of this kindly gift should be widened and enlarged. . . .

The trustee is, therefore, authorized to use and employ the income for the benefit of indigent seamen not only of the class to which Captain How belonged, but to other classes, by way of illustration and not of limitation, such as crewmen of merchant vessels, oil tankers, and fishing vessels. . . .

[Cause remanded.]

§ 15:4. Intent of the Contracting Parties

When two or more parties make an agreement or enter into a transaction, it is necessary to determine what they intended as the law seeks to carry out that intention. This is merely a particular aspect of the freedom of contract. As the parties were free to contract on such terms as they chose, a court cannot impose on them any obligation which they had not assumed by their agreement. The difficulty that arises in this connection most frequently is merely a matter of communications. The parties for one reason or another fail to express what they had in mind, or they fail to clearly understand what they were doing and necessarily their agreement was as vague as they were.

MOFFITT v. HIEBY

149 Tex. 161, 229 S.W.2d 1005 (1950)

Mrs. Hieby sold growing grapefruit to Moffitt. The written contract specified: "All terms of this agreement have been reduced to writing herein." The contract provided for the harvesting of the crop nine weeks later and stated: "Seller agrees that if harvesting is paid by buyer, it is to be charged to seller's account." The crop was damaged by the failure of Mrs. Hieby to care for and water the orchards after making the sale. Moffitt refused to take the grapefruit. Mrs. Hieby sued him for damages for the breach of the contract. From a judgment for the plaintiff, the defendant appealed.

OPINION BY HARVEY, J. . . .

The agreement entered into by the parties appears on its face to be an executed contract. . . .

Inasmuch as title to the grapefruit on the trees passed to the buyer as of the date of the contract, with a consequent delivery thereof made in the orchards, and there was nothing on the part of the seller that remained to be done in the matter, there was no implied obligation on the part of the seller to water the orchards or perform any other act with reference thereto. Had the parties so desired and had so agreed, it would have been quite easy for them to have inserted a stipulation in the contract to the effect that the seller should do whatever might have been deemed advisable under the circumstances with reference to the care to be taken of the orchards, as well as in regard to any other matters. This they did not do, and there is no occasion for the courts to add to the contract as made by them. . . .

[Judgment for plaintiff affirmed.]

DISSENTING OPINION BY HART, J. . . .

The defendants pleaded that the breach of the implied obligation of the plaintiff to care for the orchards, resulting in the failure of the fruit to reach normal or full size, was a material breach of the contract which released the defendants from the obligation to harvest and pay for the fruit. . . .

Assuming the facts to be as pleaded and testified to by the defendants and their witnesses, an obligation should be implied in fact that the seller would, after the date of the contract, with reasonable diligence and prudence continue to water and otherwise properly care for the orchards so that the fruit would attain the size and quality which would normally be expected. Otherwise, it seems apparent that the intention of the parties would not be accomplished but, on the other hand, would be defeated. The contract discloses on its face that the buyer would be permitted a period of more than two months in which to gather the fruit and that the seller would pay the expense of harvesting. Aside from their right to enter the orchards for the purpose of gathering the fruit, the buyers were given no control over the orchards; and it would follow that if the trees were to be watered and otherwise cared for, this would have to be done by the seller. Regardless of whether, as a matter of law, the title to the grapefruit had passed to the buyers, the seller, since she remained in charge of the orchards, should be under an obligation implied in fact (assuming the defendant's testimony to be true) to care for the orchards so that the fruit would normally develop and not be rendered unfit for the purposes for which the defendants were buying it.

While courts will avoid enforcing a contract when they feel that the contract is unreasonable or unconscionable, the courts are reluctant to so avoid a contract. This reluctance can be explained for several reasons: (a) the court should carry out the intent of the parties as expressed, (b) the parties had the freedom of contract to express their intent, (c) the stability of relationship is furthered if effect is given to the terms of the contract, and (d) trade is thus furthered.

INMAN v. CLYDE HALL DRILLING CO.

369 P.2d 498 (Alaska, 1962)

Inman was employed by Clyde Hall Drilling Co. The written contract of employment specified that if Inman had any claim against Clyde, he must give "written notice" thereof within thirty days and could not bring suit on such claim until after the lapse of six months and that compliance with these provisions was a "condition precedent" to recovery against Clyde. After the expiration of the employment contract, Inman sued Clyde for damages for an alleged breach of the contract. Clyde defended on the ground that Inman had not complied with the notice provisions.

OPINION BY DIMOND, J. . . .

A fulfillment of the thirty-day notice requirement is expressly made a "condition precedent to any recovery." Inman argues that this provision is void as against public policy. In considering this first question we start with the basic tenet that competent parties are free to make contracts and that they should be bound by their agreements. In the absence of a constitutional provision or statute which makes certain contracts illegal or unenforceable, we believe it is the function of the judiciary to allow men to manage their own affairs in their own way. As a matter of judicial policy the court should maintain and enforce contracts, rather than enable parties to escape from the obligations they have chosen to incur.

We recognize that "freedom of contract" is a qualified and not an absolute right, and cannot be applied on a strict, doctrinal basis. An established principle is that a court will not permit itself to be used as an instrument of inequity and injustice. As Justice Frankfurter stated in his dissenting opinion in *United States* v. *Bethlehem Steel Corp.,* "The fundamental principle of law that the courts will not enforce a bargain where one party has unconscionably taken advantage of the necessities and distress of the other has found expression in an almost infinite variety of cases." [1] In determining whether certain contractual provisions should be enforced, the court must look realistically at the relative bargaining positions of the parties in the framework of contemporary business practices and commercial life. If we find those positions are such that one party has unscrupulously taken advantage of the economic necessities of the other, then in the interest of justice—as a matter of public policy—we would refuse to enforce the transaction. But the grounds for judicial interference must be clear. Whether the court should refuse to recognize and uphold that which the parties have agreed upon is a question of fact upon which evidence is required.

The facts in this case do not persuade us that the contractual provision in question is unfair or unreasonable. Its purpose is not disclosed. The requirement that written notice be given within thirty days after a claim arises may have been designed to preclude stale claims; and the further requirement that no action be commenced within six months thereafter may have been intended to afford the Company timely opportunity to rectify the basis for a

---

[1] 315 U.S. 289, 327-328, 62 S.Ct. 581, 600, 86 L.Ed. 855, 877 (1942).

just claim. But whatever the objective was, we cannot find in the contract anything to suggest it was designed from an unfair motive to bilk employees out of wages or other compensation justly due them.

There was nothing to suggest that Inman did not have the knowledge, capacity or opportunity to read the agreement and understand it; that the terms of the contract were imposed upon him without any real freedom of choice on his part; that there was any substantial inequality in bargaining positions between Inman and the Company. Not only did he attach a copy of the contract to his complaint, which negatives any thought that he really wasn't aware of its provisions, but he also admitted . . . that at the time he signed the contract he had read it, had discussed it with a Company representative, and was familiar with its terms. And he showed specific knowledge of the thirty-day notice requirement when, in response to a question as to whether written notice had been given prior to filing suit, he testified:

"A. Well, now, I filed—I started my claim within 30 days, didn't I, from the time I hit here. I thought that would be a notice that I started suing them when I first came to town.

"Q. You thought that the filing of the suit would be the notice?

"A. That is right."

Under these circumstances we do not find that such a limitation on Inman's right of action is offensive to justice. We would not be justified in refusing to enforce the contract and thus permit one of the parties to escape his obligations. It is conceivable, of course, that a thirty-day notice of claim requirement could be used to the disadvantage of a workman by an unscrupulous employer. If this danger is great, the legislature may act to make such a provision unenforceable.[2] But we may not speculate on what in the future may be a matter of public policy in this state. It is our function to act only where an existent public policy is clearly revealed from the facts and we find that it has been violated. That is not the case here.

Inman's claim arose on March 24, 1960. His complaint was served on the Company on April 14. He argues that since the complaint set forth in detail the basis of his claim and was served within thirty days, he had substantially complied with the contractual requirement.

Service of the complaint probably gave the Company actual knowledge of the claim. But that does not serve as an excuse for not giving the kind of written notice called for by the contract. Inman agreed that no suit would be instituted "prior to six (6) months *after the filing of the written notice of claim.*" (emphasis ours) If this means what it says (and we have no reason to believe it does not), it is clear that the commencement of an action and service of the complaint was not an effective substitute for the kind of notice called for by the agreement. To hold otherwise would be to simply ignore an explicit provision of the contract and say that it had no meaning. We are not justified in doing that. . . .

---

[2] In Oklahoma the constitution (art. XXIII, § 9) provides: "Any provision of any contract or agreement, express or implied, stipulating for notice or demand other than such as may be provided by law, as a condition precedent to establish any claim, demand, or liability, shall be null and void." See *Brakebill* v. *Chicago, R. I. & P. Ry.,* 37 Okla. 140, 131 P. 540 (1913).

§ 15:5. Formal Requirements as to Intent

Some statutes require that the intent of the parties be shown in a particular manner in order to be effective. Thus a sale of goods for a contract price of $500 or more must, with certain exceptions, be evidenced by a writing. Likewise a will is generally not effective unless written by the testator in the manner required by statute, and, in some states, witnessed.

What happens where the party or parties fail to follow the statutory requirements? In many instances the law holds that the intent is not effective. Thus, if a written will signed by the testator is required, an oral will is not effective. Likewise, there is no will when the dying man reads the written draft handed to him and approves it but then dies before he actually signs it. In these instances, the desire of the law to maintain stability and to prevent fraud is sufficient ground to overcome the desire of the law to give effect to intent. To illustrate the hazard of fraud, the law is afraid that witnesses will falsely testify that a dying man had approved the will but died before he could sign it. Actually, the fact could be that he was never shown the will, and that the witnesses who benefited by the will were merely waiting for him to die before they produced the false will and fraudulently claimed that it had been approved by the dying man. In order to avoid this great danger of fraud, the law takes the flat position that if the will is not signed as required by statute, it has no effect; even though it is possible or even admitted that in a given case, there was no fraud and that the will had in fact been approved by the decedent. Thus the law establishes certain minimum evidentiary standards and just ignores anything else that does not live up to these standards. To some extent, this furthers practical expediency because it eliminates the difficult problem of determining whether the person presenting the unsigned will is telling the truth. The court in less than a minute can determine whether the will was signed, whereas it could take several hours or even days to present evidence in court as to whether the unsigned will had been approved or not, and there would still remain the difficult question of sifting facts and determining from conflicting evidence what had been the actual truth.

Apart from the question of mechanical requirements as to manifesting intent, as above described, the law, through repeated usage, has come to give particular meanings to particular words and will not find a particular intent unless it is expressed in the standardized words that the law recognizes. This attitude of the law is encouraged by the social force of practical expediency for it reduces many a lawsuit down to a relatively simple issue; namely, have the "official" words been used, rather than throwing open the judicial door to seeking to probe into the mind of the actor to determine just what was intended. For example, if land is given to you to be used as a school, does this mean (a) the land is yours and I give it to you because I believe you will use it for a school; or does it mean (2) the land is yours only if you use it for school purposes and if you do not, the gift is forfeited and the land comes back to me? Rather than become involved in the difficult question of the subjective intent of the donor, it is much easier for the law to take the strict view, which it does, that when property is given, it is an absolute gift and any statement of contemplated or desired use does not in any way attach a condition to the gift. Notice that when this problem is placed in its real life setting, the practical expediency of this approach often becomes more apparent. That is, in most instances the question does not arise when the gift is made but may occur 40 years later when the school is abandoned and the heirs of the original donor then step in to claim the land. At that time there is probably no one living who had any direct contact with the original transaction, and all that the court can do is to look at the paper written by the donor.

If the court would attempt to conjecture what had been intended 40 years before, it is apparent that it would be faced with difficult problems as to which its judgment would, in effect, be merely a guess. Notice also that the conclusion reached by the court strengthens or protects the title to the property. If land is given, it is given and that title is to be protected even as against possible reduction by the vague language of the very man who gave the property. If he wants to give property with a string attached to the gift, he must be explicit on that point. Otherwise, the recipient of the gift, the donee, will have a final and definitive title.

§ 15:6.   The Unforeseen Event

The intent, whether it be of the legislature, or of one of the parties, or of two parties, may have failed to anticipate the situation which ultimately arises. For example, in a will which an attorney had prepared for himself careful provision was made for the 19 possible situations that could arise upon his death. Of course, the situation that occurred was a twentieth which was not foreseen and for which no provision was made.

As a legal matter, the courts when faced with these unforeseen situations may enforce the intent as it was expressed, reaching the conclusion that no provision was made by the legislature, the individual, or the two parties; and that it is not the function of the court to rewrite what they had done and make a provision for the situation for which they had neglected to provide. The court may, however, do just the opposite and fill in the gap by "implying a term" or finding "a general intent," which indicates to them the way in which the situation is to be handled.

WOLF v. HOME INSURANCE CO.

100 N.J.S. 27, 241 A.2d 28 (1968)

Wolf owned an apartment house in New Jersey, which was about to be condemned for use in highway construction. Instead of going through condemnation proceedings, Wolf agreed to sell the building to the state of New Jersey. The building was covered by a fire insurance policy issued by the Home Insurance Company. Thereafter the building was destroyed by fire. Some five months later, the sale of the ruined building and the land to the state was completed, and the state paid Wolf the amount that it had originally agreed to pay him. Wolf brought a suit to recover on the fire insurance policy. The insurance company raised the defense that when the building was destroyed, Wolf was under a contract obligation to sell it to the state and that he had not sustained any harm from the fire because the state had paid him the full purchase price, and therefore the insurance company was not liable as there had been no loss.

OPINION BY STAMLER, J. S. P. . . .

The insuring provisions in the case at bar conform precisely with the language found in the [New Jersey statute], N.J.S.A. 17:36-5.19:

"Every such fire insurance policy shall insure, limited to the amounts of insurance specified therein, the named insured and legal representatives, to the extent of the *actual cash value of the property at the time of loss,* but not exceeding the amount which it would cost to repair or replace the property with material of like kind and quality within a reasonable time after such loss, without allowance for any increased cost of repair or reconstruction by reason of any ordinance or law regulating construction or repair and without compensation for loss resulting from interruption of business or manufacture, *nor in any event for more than the interest of the insured, against all direct loss by fire,* lightning, and by removal from premises endangered by the perils insured against in such policy, except as thereinafter provided, *to the property described therein* while located or contained as described in such policy, or pro rata for 5 days at each proper place to which any of the property shall necessarily be removed for preservation from the perils insured against in such policy, but not elsewhere." (Emphasis added.)

There can be no dispute that an insured must sustain a loss before he can recover on a standard form fire insurance policy. The question before this court is: precisely when does one measure or ascertain whether a fire loss has occurred? What is the "time of the loss" referred to in N.J.S.A. 17:36-5.19? Does the "loss" become fixed as of the date of the fire so that, as long as the insured has an insurable interest at that time, the insurer becomes obligated to pay under its policy; or can subsequent collateral events, such as the fact that the sale between insureds and the State of New Jersey was ultimately consummated nearly five months after the fire, with insureds receiving the full previously agreed upon contract price, be taken into account in determining the existence of an insurable "loss"?

This is a controversy which "has been raging in Anglo-American law since 1801." . . . As noted in *First National Bank of Highland Park* v. *Boston Ins. Co.,* 17 Ill.2d 147, 150, 160 N.E.2d 802, 804 (Sup.Ct.1959):

"The problem that the case presents is not an easy one. When insured property is in a single ownership, it is not hard to hold to the orthodox concept of an insurance contract as a personal contract of indemnity. But there are inherent difficulties when there are multiple interests in the property. Those inherent difficulties are augmented because the effect given to an executory contract to sell realty, and to the doctrine of equitable conversion, differs significantly from one jurisdiction to another. . . .

It would appear that there are two broad lines of authority upon this question. What may be referred to as the "New York Rule" . . . to the effect that in the absence of any contractual agreement to the contrary, a fire insurance policy is a contract of indemnification, the premiums for which are computed according to the value of the property and the risk involved without the knowledge of collateral remedies, so that recovery on the policy will not be denied as long as the insured has a valuable insurable interest at the time of the casualty, even though there is an executory contract for the sale of the real property outstanding which is later consummated. A large majority of the courts . . . adhere to the New York Rule. . . . The contrary view, known as the "Wisconsin Rule" . . . also regards a contract of fire insurance as a contract of indemnity but it denies recovery to the vendor-insured where the existence of a collateral executory contract for the sale of the real property eventually results in shielding the vendor from sustaining any actual pecuniary loss from the casualty. . . .

The topic has received judicial attention in one reported New Jersey case. *Tauriello* v. *Aetna Insurance Co.,* 14 N.J.Super. 530, 82 A.2d 226 (Law Div. 1951) dealt squarely with the same factual situation now before this court. There is no relevant distinction. In holding for the defendant insurer on the theory that the plaintiffs had not been able to show any loss, the court in Tauriello in effect followed that line of cases referred to as the Wisconsin Rule, when it said:

"The general rule is that a contract for insurance against fire is ordinarily one of indemnity under which the insured is entitled to receive indemnity or to be reimbursed for any loss that he may have sustained and cannot recover if he has sustained no loss. . . . A fire insurance policy is a contract not to insure the property against fire but to insure the owner against loss by fire, and that the insurance company can be called upon when, and only when, the insured has sustained a loss which under the terms of the policy calls for indemnification. . . .

Plaintiffs submit that in light of the persuasive appellate authority from other states before and after Tauriello, that holding is erroneous. Our system of jurisprudence envisions that while the opinions of courts of coordinate jurisdiction be taken into consideration, they are nevertheless not binding on a court of equivalent rank. . . .

The difficulty with the opinion in Tauriello may lie in its stress on the term "indemnity." In talking about labels, Chief Justice Weintraub observed in *Spina* v. *Consolidated Police, etc., Pension Fund Com.,* 41 N.J. 391, 197 A.2d 169 (1964) that:

"There is no profit in dealing in labels such as 'gratuity,' 'compensation,' 'contract,' and 'vested rights.' None fits precisely, and it would be a mistake to choose one and be driven by that choice to some inevitable consequence." (at p. 401, 197 A.2d at p. 174)

This is exactly what the court did in Tauriello. Instead of analyzing and determining just what interest of the insured was protected by the policy in force, it applied the label "indemnity" and was thus bound by what it considered to be the "general rule" for contracts of indemnity.

The concept is a nebulous one and simple solutions are not necessarily in order. . . . Nothing illustrates this better than a comparison of two 1959 decisions of the Supreme Court of Minnesota. In *Marshall Produce Co.* v. *St. Paul Fire & Marine Ins. Co.,* 256 Minn. 404, 98 N.W.2d 280 (Sup.Ct. 1959), the court presents all the usual language about a fire insurance contract being a personal contract of indemnity with the insured . . . and that there can be no recovery if there is no loss to the insured. But when the same court, just three months earlier, in the case of *Board of Trustees, etc.* v. *Cream City Mutual Ins. Co.,* supra, deals with a fact situation much closer to that in the case at bar, it cites with approval (96 N.W.2d at p. 696) the view that: "the rights of an insurer and an insured are established as of the time of the fire, and those rights are not affected if the insured eventually is compensated for the loss from another source. The recovery of an insured will not be diminished because of the fact that he might have collateral contracts with third persons which operate to relieve the insured from the loss for which the insurer agreed to compensate him."

If the two Minnesota cases mean anything, it would seem to be that there is nothing inherent in the language of "indemnity" that should commit a state, in all instances, only to a particular result.

The cases of *United Bond & Mortgage Co. of Hackensack* v. *Concordia Fire Ins. Co.,* 113 N.J.L. 28, 172 A. 373 (E. & A. 1934) and *Power Building & Loan Association* v. *Ajax Fire Ins. Co.,* 110 N.J.L. 256, 164 A. 410 (E. & A. 1933), cited by the court in *Tauriello* v. *Aetna Insurance Co.,* 14 N.J.Super. 530 at p. 532, 82 A.2d 226 (Law Div. 1951), deal with a situation where the insured is a mortgagee who had insured his interest in the mortgaged premises. The test utilized by the two cases in determining whether the insured had suffered any loss is whether the debt represented by the mortgagee was subsequently fully satisfied or not. Any analysis of this topic must also consider the opinion of our Supreme Court in *Flint Frozen Foods, Inc.* v. *Firemen's Ins. Co. of Newark, N.J.,* 8 N.J. 606, 86 A.2d 673 (1952). In that case Einhorn's Inc., a creditor of the plaintiff, held warehouse receipts as collateral security upon a debt and obtained fire insurance which insured the creditor to the extent of its interest in groceries stored in a subsidiary of the plaintiff. A fire occurred which destroyed the goods covered by the warehouse receipts. Within a month after the fire the plaintiff-debtor had paid the debt in full. The insurance policy was assigned to plaintiff, which sued thereon notwithstanding that the assignor-creditor had never filed any claim under the policy. Plaintiff recovered below and the judgment was reversed on appeal. In holding that the plaintiff, as loss-claim assignee, could not recover because its assignor had suffered no loss, the Supreme Court made the following observations:

"A policy of fire insurance is a contract the terms of which are prescribed by statute, N.J.S.A. 17:36-5.7 [presently found in N.J.S.A. 17:36-5.20]. Like any contract, when its terms are clear the court must enforce the contract as it finds it, *James* v. *Federal Insurance Co.,* 5 N.J. 21, 24, 73 A.2d 720 (1950). Its meaning 'is to be governed by its own terms without recourse to other documents unless its own language so requires,' *Herbert L. Farkas Co.* v. *New York Fire Ins. Co.,* 5 N.J. 604, 609, 76 A.2d 895, 897 (1950).

By the policy here in litigation the insurance company insured Einhorn's to the extent of its interest against loss by fire with respect to groceries which Einhorn's held as collateral security for a debt owed it by the plaintiff. The debt having been paid in full by the plaintiff, it necessarily follows that Einhorn's suffered no loss. Therefore, neither Einhorn's nor the plaintiff as its assignee can recover on the policy which expressly provides that there shall be no recovery 'in any event for more than the interest of the insured.' This conclusion, reached under the clear terms of the policy, is consonant with the fundamental principle of all insurance on property that the policy is a contract of indemnity. If the insured has suffered no loss with respect to the property covered by the policy, there is, of course, no liability on the policy, for there is nothing for the insurer to indemnify." (at p. 610, 86 A.2d at p. 674)

Defendant argues that the above-mentioned authorities place New Jersey under what has been referred to as the Wisconsin Rule and that, pursuant to this rule, this court must look to related transactions to determine whether the insured plaintiffs have sustained a loss. The contention is that even if the plaintiffs had an insurable interest at the time of fire, the subsequent culmination of the sale of the insured property to the New Jersey Highway Department nearly five months after the fire for the same amount the plaintiffs had agreed to accept prior to the fire "wiped out" any loss; and in this State if there is no loss, there is nothing to indemnify. Plaintiffs maintain, on the other hand, that the New Jersey cases are distinguishable from the present set of facts because there it was the debt due the property owner that was insured while here, pursuant to the terms of the contract and N.J.S.A. 17:36-5.19, the property itself is insured. Furthermore, they insist that any collateral arrangements or outside agreements a vendor may have are of no concern to the insurance company and that to make the payment of claims which are ostensibly due dependent on extraneous matters does violence to the express terms of the insurance policy.

This court is, of course, bound by all pronouncements of the present or former high tribunal of New Jersey. A fair and proper reading of *Flint Frozen Foods, Inc.* v. *Firemen's Ins. Co. of Newark, N.J.*, supra, and the earlier opinions of the Court of Errors and Appeals, cited previously, can only mean that when the insured in a contract of fire insurance is a creditor, mortgagee, lienholder or the like who is insuring the obligation due to him, related transactions occurring subsequent to the fire can be taken into account in determining whether the insured has sustained a loss. The question before this court is whether the same rule obtains in noncreditor situations when the insured is simply an individual insuring himself against damage loss to property that he owns.

This court is aware of the seemingly broad import given the words "loss" and "indemnity" in Flint Frozen Foods, supra. But the court would also like to focus on p. 612, 86 A.2d on p. 675 of the same opinion. There the Supreme Court, after stating that it is now entirely appropriate for a person having merely a security interest to take out a fire insurance policy in his own name covering property in which he has an interest, finds that recovery by the plaintiff (the debtor and assignee of the former assured) "is precluded by the fact that the policy did not purport to insure its interest as owners of the property destroyed *and* because as assignee its claim could rise no higher than that of its assignor, Einhorn's, which suffered no loss." (Emphasis added.)

The intimation is that had the policy therein purported to insure a full ownership interest in the property, as does the one now before this court, the result might well have been different. . . .

When the underlying nature of the respective interests being insured by a creditor and by an owner are examined, it becomes completely logical and consistent that a different rule should prevail in each instance. A creditor is interested only in having the debt or obligation owing to him assured. He seeks to have his *status* as creditor protected. An owner, on the other hand, already holds what our law considers to be the most complete type of interest and he wishes to insure his *physical property* rather than his status. In short, if a piece of property held as security burns down, the "loss" is not yet a proven fact because the creditor may still be able to pursue successfully his underlying obligation; but if the same property held in outright ownership burns, the "loss" is then complete because the "owner" has nothing left to his ownership status except the ashes and rubble unless he can collect insurance that will enable him to rebuild or purchase some new property to evidence his ownership. . . .

In accordance with the mandate of N.J.S.A. 17:36-5.19, the present policy insures, but not "for more than the *interest of the insured, against all direct loss by fire, . . . to the property* described therein." (Emphasis added.) Here, unlike in Flint Frozen Foods, Inc., supra, the policy does purport to insure an ownership interest in the property. It is undisputed that plaintiffs held full legal title to the insured premises on the date of the fire. Did they also sustain a "loss" as of that date? The statute and policy allow for a recovery up to the maximum coverage specified "to the extent of the actual cash value of the property at the time of loss." The "time of loss" can only intend the time of fire damage or destruction. If any other meaning were inferred, then the time for valuing the loss would be uncertain in every case. Defendant insurer offers this court no fixed standard for determining when a casualty loss is to be measured and argues only that *here,* after taking cognizance of collateral events not involving the insurer which came to be realized nearly five months after the fire, there was no loss. . . . The time of the fire is the common, usual and expected time for valuing "loss." It is axiomatic that the words used in an insurance policy will be construed in accordance with common usage. . . .

To give any meaning other than "time of fire" to the words "time of loss," moreover, results in totally contradictory interpretations to the word "loss" in the several sections of this fire insurance policy. The insurance contract provides that:

"The insured shall give immediate written notice to this Company of any *loss, . . .* and within sixty days after the *loss,* unless such time is extended in writing by this Company, the insured shall render to this Company a *proof of loss, . . .*" (Emphasis added.)

. . . The insurance company maintains that if we look at the closing date between insureds and their vendee, nearly five months after the date of the fire, it becomes apparent that the plaintiffs have ultimately sustained no "loss" within the intendment of the policy. If this is the time of determining "loss," then, consistently, the "immediate" written notice to the Company of any loss and the sixty day requirement for filing a proof of loss only come into play as of the closing date. The defendant cannot have it both ways. A contract of insurance must be construed as a whole. . . . Certainly the only conceivable day meant by the terms of the policy after which notice of any loss must be given and proof of loss filed is the day on which the casualty occurred. Consistency dictates that the "time of loss" for purposes of arriving at the "actual cash value of the property" also be taken as the date of fire. . . .

This court submits that the fallacy of the so-called Wisconsin Rule is well illustrated by the following hypothetical example suggested in the dissenting opinion in *Paramount Fire Ins. Co.* v. *Aetna Casualty & Surety Co.,* 163 Tex. 250, 353 S.W.2d 841 at p. 846 (Sup.Ct. 1962):

"Suppose the vendor and purchaser had entered into a contract providing for $5,000 cash payment, the balance to be paid in monthly installments of $125 each due on the 10th day of each successive succeeding month. This would require 82 months, or approximately seven years, to pay the deferred payments. Vendor could not be forced to take his balance in one lump sum. He could insist on the monthly payments as set out in the contract in order to earn the interest. Under the majority holding Paramount's liability would not be known until the last payment had been made."

In the instant case, the State did not take title until nearly five months following the fire. The delay might well have been even longer. Should the determination of an insured's loss in the vendor-vendee-insurer context be made to await the outcome of such matters? The insurer is not being damaged by being compelled to pay the insured who is owner as of the date of the fire. Its premiums are assumed to represent the fair equivalent of the obligation it contracted to incur without knowledge of the existence of collateral remedies. . . . And the evil of the chance possibility of an ultimate collection by the vendor of the full purchase price from his vendee and also the insurance payment for the damage sustained does not outweigh the disruptions and harassments closely associated with delays in settlement of fire loss claims. . . .

In dealing with the problem at hand, some courts have recognized a theory of constructive trust whereby the vendor-insured can collect for the loss from the insurance company but only so as to hold the payment in trust for his vendee. . . . This issue may perhaps turn on whether the contract of sale requires the vendee to obtain fire insurance. . . .

This court expresses no opinion as to the applicability of the theory when the suit, as here, is only between the vendor-insured and the insurer. The question of disposition of the insurance proceeds once they are in plaintiffs' hands is not now before the court. . . . The only point to be emphasized is that any equitable title in the vendee cannot be set up as a defense by the fire insurer in a suit brought against it on its contract with the vendor. . . .

Questions for Review

1. Define the social force of enforcement of intent.

2. Give illustrations of its application.

3. Analyze each opinion in this chapter in terms of the social forces involved in the decision. See § 5:5 for a list of the social forces. With respect to each opinion, explain why the prevailing social forces prevailed and why those rejected did not. In each case in which there is a dissenting opinion, also make this analysis for the dissenting opinion.

4-8. On the basis of the social forces involved, what decision should be. made in each of the following cases?

4. *Assumption of liability. Hotel.* If a hotel agrees with a linen supply company that the hotel will be responsible for all articles lost or damaged and shall reimburse the company therefor, is the hotel liable where linens were destroyed by a hotel fire? *Consolidated Laundries* v. *Regis Operators,* 26 App.Div.2d 383, 274 N.Y.S.2d 815.

5. *Insurance. Double indemnity.* Is an unintentional death following a voluntary dose of narcotics an "accidental death" within the meaning of an insurance policy? *Beckham* v. *Travelers Insurance Co.,* 424 Pa. 107, 225 A.2d 532.

6. *Agency. Delegation.* Can an attorney delegate his authority to represent his client to another attorney with whom he shares the same suite of offices? *People* v. *Betillo,* 53 Misc.2d 540, 279 N.Y.S.2d 444.

7. *Release. Rejection of settlement check.* When a settlement is agreed to and a release is executed, does the fact that the insured refuses to accept the settlement check thereafter delivered in accordance with the term of the release agreement impair the effectiveness of the release? *Mannke* v. *Benjamin Moore & Co.,* [C.A.3rd] 375 F.2d 281.

8. *Insurance. Theft.* Does the presence of a stranger's padlock on the insured's warehouse satisfy the insurance policy requirement of proof of "physical damage" to premises? *Kretschmer's* v. *U.S.F. & G. Co.,* Ky., 410 S.W.2d 617.

9-13. What social forces were involved, which prevailed, and which were defeated in the following decisions?

9. *Release. Coverage of personal injury claim.* A literate, intelligent adult cannot avoid the effect of a "full settlement" release which clearly shows that it covers both personal and property damage claimed, where he knew when he signed the release that he was personally injured, and the amount paid was greater than the property damage claim, and the claimant waited four days before he cashed the insurer's draft; as against the contention that the adjuster had stated that only the property claim was being settled, which statement was denied by the adjuster. *Thigpen* v. *Guarisco,* La., 197 So.2d 904.

10. *Labor relations. Rehabilitation school.* A private school designed to further the rehabilitation of children with brain damage is an "employer" within a state labor relations law where such a statute is not limited to such relations in industrial plants. *Industrial Commission* v. *Wallace Village,* Colo., 437 P.2d 62.

11. *Insurance. Noncoverage.* A policy that does not cover a given peril does not provide coverage beyond its terms, even though the insured felt that it would and even though the insurer issued a settlement check in payment of a claim not within the policy coverage, but stopped payment thereon before payment was made. *Aptaker* v. *Centennial Insurance Co.,* Fla., 198 So.2d 188.

12. *Insurance. Struck by automobile.* Coverage for medical expenses from "being struck by automobile" exists where the insured's motor scooter ran into a turning automobile, the insured striking the automobile, as against the contention that "struck by automobile" required that the automobile run into the insured. *Foundation Reserve Insurance Co.* v. *McCarthy,* 77 N.Mex. 118, 419 P.2d 963.

13. *Insurance. Rubber stamp.* Presence of rubber stamp "double indemnity" and "waiver of premiums" does not establish right of insured to such coverage where not provided for in body of policy. *Niewoehner* v. *Western Life Insurance Co.,* 149 Mont. 57, 422 P.2d 644.

Chapter 16

PROTECTION FROM EXPLOITATION

§ 16:1.   Generally

Many rules of law have developed in the courts and many statutes have been enacted to protect certain groups or individuals from exploitation by others. Thus, the law developed that a minor, a person under legal age, could set aside his contract, subject to certain exceptions, in order to give the minor an opportunity to avoid a bad bargain.

§ 16:2.   Consumer Protection

Many statutes and decisions are explained in terms of the legislature's or the court's desire to protect the consumer from some exploitation against which he is unable to defend himself because of his ignorance, lack of funds, or lack of credit. In many instances, the buyer is unaware of what is taking place. This condition is remedied to some extent by statutes requiring that all the details of a transaction be set forth in a contract, that the contract specify certain particular matters, that the contract be printed in type of a certain size, and that a copy of the contract be given to the buyer.

Up to the middle of this century, the theory of the law, relying upon the concept of laissez-faire, was that if the buyer did not like the terms on which the seller was willing to do business, the buyer could go elsewhere. The difficulty faced by the poor buyer is that he does not have cash and cannot obtain bank credit so that if he goes elsewhere, he will find other sellers either unwilling to do business with him or only willing to do business on the same terms as the seller from whom he flees. The Adam Smith concept that the buyer was a mobile agent and could move around until he found a seller who would sell on terms suitable to the buyer collapses in the modern era in which competition makes all credit sellers sell on identical terms.

WILLIAMS v. WALKER-THOMAS FURNITURE CO.

350 F.2d 445 (C.A.Dist.Col., 1965)

The Walker-Thomas Furniture Co. sold furniture on credit under contracts which contained a provision that a customer did not own his purchase as long as any balance on the purchase remained due. It sold goods to Williams. At the time when the balance of her account was $164, Walker-Thomas Furniture Co. sold her a $514 stereo set with knowledge that she was supporting herself and seven children on a government relief check of $218 a month. From 1957 to 1962 Williams had purchased $1,800 worth of goods and made payments of $1,400. When she stopped making payments in 1962, Walker-Thomas sought to take back everything she had purchased since 1957. From a judgment in favor of Walker-Thomas, Williams appealed.

OPINION BY WRIGHT, J. . . .

[Williams'] contention, rejected by both the trial and the appellate courts below, is that these contracts . . . are unconscionable and, hence, not enforceable. In its opinion in *Williams* v. *Walker-Thomas Furniture Company,* 198 A.2d 914, 916 (1964), the District of Columbia Court of Appeals explained its rejection of this contention as follows: . . . "We cannot condemn too strongly appellee's conduct. It raises serious questions of sharp practice and irresponsible business dealings. A review of the legislation in the District of Columbia affecting retail sales and the pertinent decisions of the highest court in this jurisdiction disclose, however, no ground upon which this court can declare the contracts in question contrary to public policy. We note that were the Maryland Retail Installment Sales Act, Art. 83 §§ 128—153, or its equivalent, in force in the District of Columbia, we could grant appellant appropriate relief. We think Congress should consider corrective legislation to protect the public from such exploitive contracts as were utilized in the case at bar."

We do not agree that the court lacked the power to refuse enforcement to contracts found to be unconscionable. In other jurisdictions, it has been held as a matter of common law that unconscionable contracts are not enforceable. While no decision of this court so holding has been found, the notion that an unconscionable bargain should not be given full enforcement is by no means novel. In *Scott* v. *United States,* 79 U.S. (12 Wall) 443, 445 (1870), the Supreme Court stated: "If a contract be unreasonable and unconscionable, but not void for fraud, a court of law will give to the party who sues for its breach damages, not according to its letter, but only such as he is equitably entitled to." Since we have never adopted or rejected such a rule, the question here presented is actually one of first impression.

Congress has recently enacted the Uniform Commercial Code, which specifically provides that the court may refuse to enforce a contract which it finds to be unconscionable at the time it was made. 28 D.C. Code § 2—302 (Supp. IV 1965). The enactment of this section, which occurred subsequent to the contracts here in suit, does not mean that the common law of the District of Columbia was otherwise at the time of enactment, nor does it preclude the court from adopting a similar rule in the exercise of its powers to develop the common law for the District of Columbia. In fact, in view of the absence of prior authority on the point, we consider the congressional adoption of § 2—302 persuasive authority for following the rationale of the cases from which the section is explicitly derived. Accordingly, we hold that where the element of unconscionability is present at the time a contract is made, the contract should not be enforced.

Unconscionability has generally been recognized to include an absence of meaningful choice on the part of one of the parties together with contract terms which are unreasonably favorable to the other party. Whether a meaningful choice is present in a particular case can only be determined by consideration of all the circumstances surrounding the transaction. In many cases the meaningfulness of the choice is negated by a gross inequality of bargaining power. The manner in which the contract was entered is also relevant to this consideration. Did each party to the contract, considering his obvious education or lack of it, have a reasonable opportunity to understand the terms of the contract, or were the important terms hidden in a maze of fine print and minimized by deceptive sales practices? Ordinarily, one who signs an agreement without full knowledge of its terms might be held to assume the risk that he has entered a one-sided bargain. But when a party of little bargaining power, and hence little real choice, signs a commercially unreasonable contract with little or no knowledge of its terms, it is hardly likely that his consent, or even an objective manifestation of his consent, was ever given to all the terms. In such a case the usual rule that the terms of the agreement are not to be questioned should be abandoned and the court should consider whether the terms of the contract are so unfair that enforcement should be withheld.

In determining reasonableness or fairness, the primary concern must be with the terms of the contract considered in light of the circumstances existing when the contract was made. The test is not simple, nor can it be mechanically applied. The terms are to be considered "in the light of the general commercial background and the commercial needs of the particular trade or case." Corbin suggests the test as being whether the terms are "so extreme as to appear unconscionable according to the mores and business practices of the time and place." 1 Corbin, [Contracts § 128 (1963)]. We think this formulation correctly states the test to be applied in those cases where no meaningful choice was exercised upon entering the contract.

Because the trial court and the appellate court did not feel that enforcement could be refused, no findings were made on the possible unconscionability of the contracts in these cases. Since the record is not sufficient for our deciding the issue as a matter of law, the cases must be remanded to the trial court for further proceedings.

[So ordered.]

DISSENTING OPINION BY DANAHER, J. . . .

The District of Columbia Court of Appeals obviously was as unhappy about the situation here presented as any of us can possibly be. Its opinion in the Williams case, quoted in the majority text, concludes: "We think Congress should consider corrective legislation to protect the public from such exploitive contracts as were utilized in the case at bar."

My view is thus summed up by an able court which made no finding that there had actually been sharp practice. Rather the appellant seems to have known precisely where she stood.

There are many aspects of public policy here involved. What is a luxury to some may seem an outright necessity to others. Is public oversight to be required of the expenditures of relief funds? A washing machine, e.g., in the hands of a relief client might become a fruitful source of income. Many relief clients may well need credit, and certain business establishments will take long chances on the sale of items, expecting their pricing policies will afford a degree of protection commensurate with the risk. Perhaps a remedy when necessary will be found within the provisions of the "Loan Shark" law, D.C. Code § 26—601 et seq. (1961).

I mention such matters only to emphasize the desirability of a cautious approach to any such problem, particularly since the law for so long has allowed parties such great latitude in making their own contracts. I dare say there must annually be thousands upon thousands of installment credit transactions in this jurisdiction, and one can only speculate as to the effect the decision in these cases will have. . . .

§ 16:3. Domination by the Seller

In some situations there is unequal bargaining power because the seller is so large economically that it dominates the situation. The problem here is much like that considered under § 16:2 in that disparity of economic strength between the seller and the buyer is the significant element. The difference is largely a matter of point of view in that in the consumer protection case the court is thinking primarily of the poor little buyer, whereas in the seller domination case the court is thinking primarily of the big bad seller.

The net result is in many cases the same whether the court looks at the smallness of the buyer or the bigness of the seller. It is more likely to do the latter where the buyer is a businessman who may be regarded as understanding what is going on, while the little buyer approach is generally taken in connection with consumers.

SIMPSON v. UNION OIL CO.

377 U.S. 13 (1964)

The Union Oil Company leased a gas service station to Simpson. As in the case of its other gas stations, the lease was for a year and was renewable thereafter until terminated by either party upon notice. Gas was not sold outright by Union to Simpson, but instead was delivered on "consignment" by which the title of the gas was retained by Union. The consignment agreement specified the resale prices for the gas. Simpson sold below these prices because of which Union terminated the lease at the end of the year. Simpson sued for an injunction to prevent Union from terminating the lease because of its price-cutting. From adverse decisions of the District Court and the Court of Appeals, he appealed to the United States Supreme Court.

OPINION BY DOUGLAS, J. . . .

If the "consignment" agreement achieves resale price maintenance in violation of the Sherman Act, it and the lease are being used to injure interstate commerce by depriving independent dealers of the exercise of free judgment whether to become consignees at all, or remain consignees, and, in any event, to sell at competitive prices. The fact that a retailer can refuse to deal does not give the supplier immunity if the arrangement is one of those schemes condemned by the antitrust laws. . . .

The exclusive requirement contracts struck down in *Standard Oil Co.* v. *United States,* 337 U.S. 293, 93 L.Ed. 1371, 69 S.Ct. 1051, were not saved because the dealers need not have agreed to them, but could have gone elsewhere. If that were a defense, a supplier could regiment thousands of otherwise competitive dealers in resale price maintenance programs merely by fear of nonrenewal of short-term leases.

. . . A supplier may not use coercion on its retail outlets to achieve resale price maintenance. We reiterate that view, adding that it matters not what the coercive device is. . . .

Consignments perform an important function in trade and commerce, and their integrity has been recognized by many courts, including this one. . . .

One who sends a rug or a painting or other work of art to a merchant or a gallery for sale at a minimum price can, of course, hold the consignee to the bargain. A retail merchant may, indeed, have inventory on consignment, the terms of which bind the parties inter se. . . .

The interests of the Government . . . frequently override agreements that private parties make. Here we have an antitrust policy expressed in Acts of Congress. Accordingly, a consignment, no matter how lawful it might be as a matter of private contract law, must give way before the federal antitrust policy. . . . [And] § 1 of the Sherman Act [does not] tolerate agreements for retail price maintenance. . . .

Resale price maintenance of gasoline through the "consignment" device is increasing. The "consignment" device in the gasoline field is used for resale price maintenance. . . .

Dealers, like Simpson, are independent businessmen; and they have all or most of the indicia of entrepreneurs, except for price fixing. The risk of loss of the gasoline is on them, apart from acts of God. Their return is affected by the rise and fall in the market price, their commissions declining as retail prices drop. Practically the only power they have to be wholly independent businessmen, whose service depends on their own initiative and enterprise, is taken from them by the proviso that they must sell their gasoline at prices fixed by Union Oil. By reason of the lease and "consignment" agreement dealers are coercively laced into an arrangement under which their supplier is able to impose noncompetitive prices on thousands of persons whose prices otherwise might be competitive. The evil of this resale price maintenance program, . . . is its inexorable potentiality for and even certainty in destroying competition in retail sales of gasoline by these nominal "consignees" who are in reality small struggling competitors seeking retail gas customers.

As we have said, an owner of an article may send it to a dealer who may in turn undertake to sell it only at a price determined by the owner. There is nothing illegal about that arrangement. When, however, a "consignment" device is used to cover a vast gasoline distribution system, fixing prices through many retail outlets, the antitrust laws prevent calling the "consignment" an agency. . . .

Reliance is placed on *United States* v. *General Electric Co.,* 272 U.S. 476, 71 L.Ed. 362, 47 S.Ct. 192, where a consignment arrangement was utilized to market patented articles. Union Oil correctly argues that the consignment in that case somewhat parallels the one in the instant case. The Court in the General Electric case did not restrict its ruling to patented articles; it, indeed, said that the use of the consignment device was available to the owners of articles "patented or otherwise." . . . But whatever may be said of the General Electric case on its special facts, involving patents, it is not apposite to the special facts here. . . .

The patent laws which give a 17-year monopoly on "making, using, or selling the invention" are in pari materia with the antitrust laws and modify them pro tanto. That was the ratio decidendi of the General Electric case. . . . We decline the invitation to extend it. . . .

DISSENTING OPINION BY STEWART, J. . . .

In *United States* v. *General Electric,* 272 U.S. 476, 71 L.Ed. 362, 47 S.Ct. 192, this Court held that a bona fide consignment agreement of this kind does not violate the Sherman Act. . . . Possession of patent rights on the article allegedly consigned has no legal significance to an inquiry directed to ascertaining whether the burdens, risks, and rights of ownership actually remain with the principal or have passed to his agent. Nor is the power of a consignor to fix the prices at which his consignee sells augmented in any respect by the possession of a patent on the goods so consigned. It is not by virtue of a patent monopoly that a bona fide consignor may control the price at which his consignee sells; his control over price flows from the simple fact that the owner of goods, so long as he remains the owner, has the unquestioned right to determine the price at which he will sell them. . . .

It is clear, therefore, that the Court today overrules General Electric. . . . Today's upsetting decision carries with it the most severe consequences to a large sector of the private economy. We cannot be blind to the fact that commercial arrangements throughout our economy are shaped in reliance upon this Court's decisions elaborating the reach of the antitrust laws. Everyone knows that consignment selling is a widely used method of distribution all over the country. By our decision today outlawing consignment selling if it includes a price limitation, we inject severe uncertainty into commercial relationships established in reliance upon a decision of this Court explicitly validating this method of distribution. We create, as well, the distinct possibility that an untold number of sellers of goods will be subjected to liability in treble damage suits because they thought they could rely on the validity of this Court's decisions. . . .

§ 16:4. Domination by Employer

At the turn of the century, the modern economic world was beginning to come into existence. Expansion and industrialization following the Civil War were followed by the new production techniques of the assembly line and mass production. The shift of population from the country to the city and the rise of the factory owner to a position of bargaining dominance brought problems that law had never known before. Under decisions of the United States Supreme Court, which in effect declared freedom of contract to be the law of the land, legislative attempts to better the position of the workman were held invalid. Gradually new decisions and new laws changed the position of the employee. Safety and sanitary laws protected him from physical harm. Workmen's compensation gave him a form of insurance against physical accidents and later also against occupational diseases. Statutes protected him with respect to the payment of wages, the time and method of payment, and eventually assured him of a minimum wage. Gradually unions came to be recognized, and then statutes required the employer to bargain with the union when it was selected by his employees as their representative. It was also made an unfair labor practice for the employer to refuse to hire an applicant because of union membership, to require an employee to agree not to join a union, or to discriminate against an employee because of union membership, or later because of race or sex.

An employer is naturally afraid of an employee's leaving and going to work for a competitor or starting up a business of his own. It is, therefore, common for employers to specify in employment contracts that an employee shall not in any way compete after leaving his employment.

WOOD v. MAY

438 P.2d 587 (Wash.2d, 1968)

May went to work as an apprentice for Wood. The contract of employment specified that May would not set up his own place of business within five years after leaving his employment nor within 100 miles of his employer's place of business. When May left Wood's employment, he opened his own shop in a city five miles away. Wood sued for a court order to stop May from breaking his agreement.

OPINION BY FINLEY, C.J. . . .

In November 1961 appellant, Gordon S. Wood, a master horseshoer with some 15-years experience, employed respondent, William R. May, as an apprentice horseshoer. On January 3, 1962 the parties signed a written contract wherein appellant agreed to teach respondent the art of horseshoeing. Respondent agreed that:

"[F]or a period of five years from and after the time he shall leave the first party employer, either if by resignation or by discharge, that he shall not engage directly or indirectly in any business or enterprise the nature of which is competitive to the employers business, that is to say he shall not engage in the practice of Horseshoeing or Blacksmithing, within a radius of one hundred (100) miles from the Oakwood Horseshoeing presently situated at Route 1, Box 1491, or any branch of the Oakwood Horseshoeing during the tenure of this time."

The contract further provided that in the event of breach of the agreement not to compete, respondent could be enjoined by a court of equity from engaging in the trade of horseshoeing in the territory and during the time covered by the agreement.

Respondent displayed marked aptitude for horseshoeing, and during the two years he worked for appellant he progressed rapidly from the apprenticeship stage. He was soon on his own, so to speak, in shoeing the horses of a substantial number of appellant's customers. Actually, respondent became the only contact appellant had with many of his customers, and these customers gained confidence in respondent's ability as a horseshoer. Consequently, when respondent terminated his employment in March, 1964, and immediately set up his own horseshoeing business in Tacoma, five miles distance from Spanaway, he secured a substantial number of appellant's customers in Pierce County and on Vashon Island. Appellant began this action to enjoin respondent from engaging in horseshoeing in violation of the agreement.

The bulk of appellant's horseshoeing business was located in Pierce County and on Vashon Island, although he regularly shod a few horses as far north as Lynden, nearly 100 miles from Spanaway.

The trial court dismissed the case at the close of appellant's evidence, finding that although the rest of the contract was reasonable, it was unreasonable to restrict respondent from engaging in horseshoeing within a radius of 100 miles from Spanaway, an area which includes all or part of 22 counties in Washington, and parts of Oregon and Canada. The trial court determined the contract to be indivisible and for that reason refused to modify the restrictive covenants as to time and area.

There are four issues on appeal: (1) Are restrictive covenants not to compete after termination of employment void for reasons of public policy? (2) If such covenants are not void, were the covenants in this contract supported by adequate consideration? (3) If supported by adequate consideration, were the restrictions reasonable as to time and areas as to both the parties and the public? (4) If the restrictions were unreasonable, can a court exercising its equity jurisdiction modify such restrictive covenants and enforce them against respondent in a more reasonable manner? . . .

The general rule applied in construing such contracts is that restrictions therein are upheld if they meet the test of showing that they are not greater than are reasonably necessary to protect the business or goodwill of the employer, even though they restrain the employee of his liberty to engage in a certain occupation or business, and deprive the public of the services, or restrain trade. . . .

"The validity of covenants by employees not to engage in a similar or competing business for a definite period of time, following the termination of the contract of employment in which the covenant is incorporated, may be sustained, although the contract is recognized to be in restraint of trade. The test generally applied in determining the validity of such a covenant is whether or not the restraint is necessary for the protection of the business or goodwill of the employer, and, if so, whether it imposes on the employee any greater restraint than is reasonably necessary to secure to the business of the employer, or the goodwill thereof, such protection, regard being had to the injury which may result to the public, by restraining the breach of the covenant, in the loss of the service and skill of the employee, and the danger of his becoming a charge upon the public.

"It is clear that if the nature of the employment is such as will bring the employee in personal contact with the patrons or customers of the employer, or enable him to acquire valuable information as to the nature and character of the business and the names and requirements of the patrons or customers, enabling him, by engaging in a competing business in his own behalf, or for another, to take advantage of such knowledge of or acquaintance with the patrons or customers of his former employer, and thereby gain an unfair advantage, equity will interfere in behalf of the employer and restrain the breach of a negative covenant not to engage in such competing business. . . ."

The restrictive covenants in the instant matter are not void for reasons of public policy. The evidence indicated that there are some 3,000 horses in the Pierce County area, and some 8 competent horseshoers residing in the immediate area. Although customers may prefer respondent to other horseshoers in the area, his services are not indispensable. The law presumes that the services can be performed by someone else. . . . And, it was not shown that respondent will not be able to find work as a horseshoer without competing with appellant.

The contract, although somewhat vague and poorly drawn, was supported by adequate consideration. Respondent promised not to compete with appellant upon termination of his employment in return for appellant's promise to teach respondent the skill of horseshoeing. Over the period of two years during which the parties operated under the contract, appellant did indeed teach respondent the trade or art of horseshoeing. The evidence showed that there are two methods of becoming a skilled horseshoer. One may either attend a college course in horseshoeing, followed by experience under a master horseshoer, or he may learn by the apprenticeship method as respondent did in this case. During the two years respondent worked for appellant he earned approximately $3,800 the first year and approximately $6,500 the second year. After he left appellant's service respondent grossed from $500 to $1,800 per month, horseshoeing being somewhat seasonal in nature. Appellant obviously fulfilled his part of the bargain. He taught respondent to be a proficient horseshoer, a trade at which he has been able to earn a good living. This is adequate consideration for a promise not to compete in a trade which involves a unique personal relationship between tradesman and customer.

The trial court correctly found the area restriction in the contract to be unreasonable. It was correct to refuse to enforce this restriction as written, since it is both unduly harsh to respondent in curtailing his legitimate efforts to earn a livelihood and unnecessary for the protection of the legitimate interests of appellant. . . . The trial judge found the time restriction to be more acceptable, stating that he felt the time involved was "particularly lengthy," but that "[t]he Court could accept the restriction in terms of five-years."

However, on the basis of the evidence presented, we are constrained to believe that the restrictions were probably unreasonable *both* as to area and time. The trial judge felt he was obligated to either accept or reject the restrictions *in toto* rather than to modify them on the basis of his factual findings. We do not believe he could properly decide the issues before him while operating under this assumption. We are granting a new trial in this matter so that reasonable restrictions upon respondent's competitive activities, both as to time and area, can be determined and imposed. We note in passing that counsel for appellant admitted in oral argument that an area of 25-mile radius from Spanaway would be reasonable. . . . We offer no suggestion without more evidence than the record reveals whether a period of one year, three years or some other period of time is reasonable under the facts in this case. Neither do we suggest that it would be improper to restrict respondent only as to those customers with whom he came in contact while in the service of appellant. See *Columbia College of Music* v. *Tunberg,* 64 Wash. 19, 116 P. 280 (1911), in which such a restriction was found adequate to protect the employer. We do not limit the court upon new trial to any given formula for determining reasonable restrictions, nor do we read any of the cases cited in this opinion as so limiting a trial court. While guidelines set down in similar cases are helpful, the facts of a given case must determine the reasonableness of the restrictions imposed.

It is well settled that a court of equity will use its power to enforce a restriction against a former employee's competition only to the extent that such restriction is reasonable and necessary to protect a legitimate business interest of the employer. . . . But it does not follow that an entire contract must fail because of an unreasonable restriction as to time and area. One line of authority holds that unless the contract is divisible, the court will not write a new contract and will refuse to grant any equitable relief against competition. . . . However, a substantial number of American courts in later cases have adopted a new and different rule that a contract in restraint of trade will be enforced to the extent it is reasonable and lawful. . . .

We adopt the reasoning in the second line of cases. The enforcement of such a contract does not depend upon mechanical divisibility, meaning that offending portions of the covenant can be lined out and still leave the remainder grammatically meaningful and thus enforceable. This is the so-called "blue pencil test." The better test is whether partial enforcement is possible without injury to the public and without injustice to the parties. . . .

Professor Corbin, in approving the latter test, says:

"An agreement restricting competition may be perfectly reasonable as to a part of the territory included within the restriction but unreasonable as to the rest. Will the courts enforce such an agreement in part while holding the remainder invalid? It renders no service to say that the answer depends upon whether or not the contract is 'divisible.' 'Divisibility' is a term that has no general and invariable definition; instead the term varies so much with the subject-matter involved and the purposes in view that its use either as an aid to decision or in the statement of results tends to befog the real issue.

"With respect to partial illegality, the real issue is whether partial enforcement is possible without injury to the public and without injustice to the parties themselves. It is believed that such enforcement is quite possible in the great majority of cases. If a seller whose business and goodwill do not extend beyond the city limits of Trenton promises not to open a competing business anywhere within the state of New Jersey, the restriction is much greater than is reasonable. This is a good reason for refusing to enjoin the seller from doing business in Newark; but it is not a good reason for permitting him to open up a competing store within the same block in Trenton." 6A Corbin, Contracts § 1390 at 66 (1962).

. . .

"As in the case of contracts restraining the seller of a business with its goodwill, the fact that the restriction on an employee goes too far to be valid as a whole does not prevent a court from enforcing it in part insofar as it is reasonable and not oppressive. The injunction may be made operative only as to reasonable space and time; . . ." 6A Corbin, Contracts § 1394 (1962).

Professor Williston's comments on the subject are as follows:

"If a sharply defined line separated a restraint which is excessive territorially from such restraint as is permissible, there seems no reason why effect should not be given to a restrictive promise indivisible in terms, to the extent that it is lawful. If it be said that the attempt to impose an excessive restraint invalidates the whole promise, a similar attempt should invalidate a whole contract, though the promises are in terms divisible. Questions involving legality of contracts should not depend on form. Public policy surely is not concerned to distinguish differences of wording in agreements of identical meaning." 5 Williston, Contracts § 1660 (rev. ed. 1937).

We are in accord with the views expressed by Corbin and Williston. Under the circumstances of this case we find it just and equitable to protect appellant by injunction to the extent necessary to accomplish the basic purpose of the contract insofar as such contract is reasonable. The trial court erred in granting dismissal at the close of appellant's case. A new trial must be afforded to determine what is reasonable regarding time and space in limiting respondent's competitive horseshoeing activities, wherein both parties may offer evidence bearing thereon. Since we do not have the benefit of respondent's evidence, we cannot decide whether the restriction should be as to area, i.e., a certain number of miles from appellant's business, or as to those customers which respondent came to know during his employment with appellant. Neither can we decide a precise limitation as to time.

The judgment should be reversed and remanded for new trial consistent with the views expressed herein. It is so ordered.

DISSENTING OPINION BY ROSELLINI, J. . . .

The respondent was born and raised in the small community of Cleveland, Tennessee. When he was 17 years old, he entered the United States Army and had not completed his high school studies. While in the army, he was awarded an army high school diploma.

The respondent, prior to army service, had no special training for employment and had not held any compensable employment.

After his discharge from the army, the respondent married and lived with his wife at Eatonville, Pierce County, Washington. He was 25 years old at the time of trial.

Prior to beginning his apprenticeship as a horseshoer, he served four months as a deputy sheriff for Pierce County. In November, 1961, the respondent began apprenticeship with the appellant and was paid $1 for each horse shod. Nothing was said in regard to an agreement not to compete. In the latter part of 1961, the appellant asked the respondent to go to his accountant's office, stating that he had a contract which he desired the respondent to sign. The respondent signed the contract described by the majority.

Evidence discloses that horseshoeing can be taught in college in a five-weeks' course. The apprenticeship under the appellant lasted from November, 1961, to the middle of July, 1962, approximately an eight-months' period. From July, 1962, the respondent was considered a journeyman horseshoer. He was permitted to and did shoe horses without direction or advice from appellant.

The record shows that there are approximately 3,000 horses in Pierce County. The appellant had approximately 130 customers. There is no contention that these customers' owned all or even a substantial percentage of these horses.

When the respondent terminated his employment with the appellant, he began shoeing horses. Eleven months after his departure, he had only 13 rotating customers who had been customers of the appellant. A rotating customer is defined as one who, by agreement, has his horse shod for a period of a year; during that period his horse will be shod every six to eight weeks without the necessity of the owner asking for the service.

The majority, in reversing the trial court, fails to note that courts are reluctant to enforce contracts which prohibit individuals from continuing to work. It holds that the contract is enforceable even though the restriction of engaging in the business of horseshoeing for a period of five years and within 100 miles' vicinity of Pierce County is unreasonable. The majority has failed to observe that there is a different test applied where restrictions are contained in bargains for transfer of land or business and to where they are contained in bargains for employment. A restriction which may be upheld as reasonable in the sale of land or a business, may be found unduly harsh where the relationship between the parties has been that of employer and employee. This is rightly so because by an improvement contract entered into by an employee may deny him the opportunity to earn a livelihood which is every man's right.

"2 Restatement of Contracts, § 515 (1932), and the comments beginning at 988, illustrates this rule:

"A restraint of trade is unreasonable, in the absence of statutory authorization or dominant social or economic justification, if it

(a) is greater than is required for the protection of the person for whose benefit the restraint is imposed, or

(b) imposes undue hardship upon the person restricted, or

(c) tends to create, or has for its purpose to create, a monopoly, or to control prices or to limit production artificially, or

(d) unreasonably restricts the alienation or use of anything that is a subject of property, or

(e) is based on a promise to refrain from competition and is not ancillary either to a contract for the transfer of goodwill or other subjects of property or to an existing employment or contract of employment. . . .

b. No identical test of reasonableness applies to bargains for the transfer of land or goods or of a business, on the one hand, and to bargains for employment on the other. The elements that must be considered in order to determine reasonableness differ in the two cases, especially where the employment is of a specialized character, and familiarity and skill in it are assets of the employee. Limitations of his use of these assets are less readily supported than limitations of the use of property or in carrying on a business. . . .

" *Illustrations of Clause* (b):

"5. *A,* a lawyer, employs *B,* a young lawyer, as his clerk, who as part of the bargain covenants not to engage in the practice of law within the State after the termination of the employment. Although *A's* practice extends throughout the State, the covenant is illegal, since it imposes undue hardship upon *B.*

"6. *A* employs *B* for five years as manager of a clothing store. *B* covenants as part of the bargain not to engage or to be employed in similar business in any city where *A* has a store. *A* has stores in five of the principal cities in the State. The covenant is illegal, as imposing an undue hardship on *B.*

"7. *A* and *B* enter into a contract of employment in which *B* promises not to engage in a similar business anywhere within the State after the termination of the employment. *A's* business does not extend throughout the State but he hopes that it may later do so. *B's* promise to refrain from entering into a similar occupation is illegal.

Also, when the restraint is excessive as to time, the court will not enforce the restriction. Thus in *Schneller* v. *Hayes,* 176 Wash. 115, 28 P.2d 273 (1934), the court refused to enforce the restriction because it was unlimited as to time. . . .

"Such contracts were regarded with high disfavor under the old common law. And they are so regarded, in general, by modern courts, though apparently with some amelioration of the ancient disfavor. Modern courts have usually, in passing on these contracts, employed three criteria: (1) Is the restraint, from the standpoint of the employer, reasonable in the sense that it is no greater than is necessary to protect the employer in some legitimate business interest? (2) From the standpoint of the employee, is the restraint reasonable in the sense that it is not unduly harsh and oppressive in curtailing his legitimate efforts to earn a livelihood? (3) Is the restraint reasonable from the standpoint of a sound public policy?"

. . .

"Even if the restrictive covenant be not void, so that a suit at law for damages arising out of a breach of the covenant might lie, we think this covenant here might fairly be characterized as harsh and oppressive. And equity is slow to enforce such contracts through its extraordinary remedies such as specific performance and injunction, remedies that normally rest in the sound discretion of the trial judge. . . ."

In the leading case of *Herbert Morris, Ltd.* v. *Saxelby,* [1916] A.C. 688, 702 (H.L.), Lord Atkinson said that an employer

"[I]s undoubtedly entitled to have his interest in his trade secrets protected, such as secret processes of manufacture which may be of vast value. . . . He is also entitled not to have his old customers by solicitation or such other means enticed away from him. But freedom from all competition per se apart from both these things, however lucrative it might be to him, he is not entitled to be protected against. He must be prepared to encounter that even at the hands of a former employee."

Lord Parker pointed out that there is a distinction between restrictions placed upon a vendor and equal restrictions placed upon an employee. He said, at 709:

"It is quite different in the case of an employer taking such a covenant from his employee or apprentice. The goodwill of his business is, under the conditions in which we live, necessarily subject to the competition of all persons (including the servant or apprentice) who choose to engage in a similar trade. The employer in such a case is not endeavoring to protect what he has, but to gain a special advantage which he could not otherwise secure. I cannot find any case in which a covenant against competition by a servant or apprentice has, as such, ever been upheld by the Court. Wherever such covenants have been upheld it has been on the ground, not that the servant or apprentice would, by reason of his employment or training, obtain the skill and knowledge necessary to equip him as a possible competitor in the trade, but that he might obtain such personal knowledge [or] an influence over the customers of his employer, or such an acquaintance with his employer's trade secrets as would enable him, if competition were allowed, to take advantage of his employer's trade connection or utilize information confidentially obtained."

The restriction of five years and 100 miles' vicinity are unreasonable as to time and area. The court should be slow to enforce an agreement restraining an employee from engaging in his occupation. In the instant case the respondent does not know and has never worked at any other occupation than horseshoeing. If an injunction is granted, it will be necessary for respondent to sell his home and move elsewhere. The great hardship to the respondent seems oppressive and harsh when it is compared to benefits the contract bestows upon the appellant. There is no showing of irreparable harm to the appellant if the contract is not enforced. The damage he may sustain is minute in comparison to the respondent's damage. From the record it appears that the restraint is not reasonable and necessary for the protection of the appellant. This is so because there are 3,000 horses in the vicinity and the appellant has only 130 customers. Thus he has ample opportunity and potential to increase his business, while the respondent is prevented from earning his livelihood in the only manner for which he is trained.

The cross-examination of the appellant suggests that the reason some of his customers left him was because he was inattentive to his business and some of his work was not satisfactory to them. The public interest is a factor to be considered. The public has a right to obtain the best services possible and should not be forced by the court to accept services which may be inferior.

When the equity power of the court is invoked, it is the duty of the court to weigh the consideration of the contract. It must find that the bargain is fair and equitable between the parties. If it is unfair or the consideration of the party seeking injunctive relief is small in comparison to the penalty he seeks to impose on the other party, the court should refrain from using its injunctive powers.

Since horseshoeing can be taught in five weeks in college, and an apprentice can become a journeyman horseshoer in eight months, it is not an occupation that is special, unique, or extraordinary. Thus a restriction such as that imposed on the respondent is not a reasonable [exchange] for being taught the occupation of horseshoeing.

I believe this contract should not be enforced. I would affirm the trial court. In any event if it is enforced, it should be governed by the rule in *Columbia College of Music* v. *Tunberg*, 64 Wash. 19, 116 P. 280 (1911), where the court refused to enforce a contract by a music teacher not to teach elsewhere except to restrain him from soliciting clients of his employer. Any other result would be unjust and would prevent the respondent from earning a livelihood by the only occupation for which he is trained.

§ 16:5.   Exploitation of Minors

The law has traditionally sought to protect minors, as well as other persons under an incapacity, from exploitation by persons seeking to take advantage of their immaturity or lack of experience. This has led to the emergence of the traditional rule that a minor may disaffirm or set aside his ordinary contracts.

Notice that in so doing the intent of the parties is defeated in that the intent was expressed by the contract which is disaffirmed. To that extent, trade is hindered and the seller as a creditor is not protected. Notice also that the very definition of a minor as a person under 21, and even more specifically as a person one day younger than the 21st anniversary of his birth, is a matter of practical expediency. Rather than make it an open question in each case as to whether a person is "too" young to be bound by his contract, the law has fixed a flat date applicable to all persons. Note further the arbitrary character of the selection. Why not 20 years of age? Why not 22 years? Note the contrast in the field of criminal law that a minor under 7 years of age is deemed incapable of criminal intent; between 7 and 14 he is presumed incapable, although the contrary may be shown; while over 14, it is presumed that he has the same capacity as an adult and he has the burden of proving that he had such mental disability as would make him not responsible for his crimes. A similar subdivision is made in the field of tort law, although there is more variation as to the terminal or dividing years.

The power of a minor to avoid his contracts is subject to the limitations that when the contract relates to that which the law regards as "necessary" for the minor, he must keep the goods and pay the seller the reasonable value thereof, as distinguished from the contract price.

Originally necessaries were limited to those things absolutely necessary for the sustenance and shelter of the minor. Thus limited, the term would extend only to the most simple foods, clothing, and lodging. In the course of time, the rule was relaxed to extend generally to things relating to the health, education, and comfort of the minor. Thus the rental of a house used by a married minor, his wife, and child, is a necessary. The rule has also been relaxed to hold that whether an item is a necessary in a particular case depends upon the financial and social status or station in life of the minor. The rule does not treat all minors equally. To illustrate, college education may be regarded as necessary for one minor but not for another, depending upon their stations in life.

KIEFER v. FRED HOWE MOTORS
39 Wis.2d 20, 158 N.W.2d 288 (1968)

Kiefer purchased an automobile from Fred Howe Motors to use to drive to work. He was 20 years, 7 months old. He was married and had one child. When he purchased the car he signed a contract which stated that he was over 21. Later Kiefer notified the dealer that he disaffirmed the sales contract and thereafter he sued the dealer to get back the purchase price.

OPINION BY WILKIE, J. . . .

The law governing agreements made during infancy reaches back over many centuries. The general rule is that ". . . the contract of a minor, other than for necessaries, is . . . voidable at his option." The only other exceptions to the rule permitting disaffirmance are statutory or involve contracts which deal with duties imposed by law, such as a contract of marriage or an agreement to support an illegitimate child. The general rule is not affected by the minor's status as emancipated or unemancipated.

Appellant [seller] does not advance any argument that would put this case within one of the exceptions to the general rule, but rather urges that this court, as a matter of public policy, adopt a rule that an emancipated minor over 18 years of age be made legally responsible for his contracts.

The underpinnings of the general rule allowing the minor to disaffirm his contracts were undoubtedly the protection of the minor. It was thought that the minor was immature in both mind and experience and that, therefore, he should be protected from his own bad judgments as well as from adults who would take advantage of him. The doctrine of the voidability of minors' contracts often seems commendable and just. If the beans that the young naive Jack purchased from the crafty old man in the fairy tale "Jack and the Bean Stalk" had been worthless rather than magical, it would have been only fair to allow Jack to disaffirm the bargain and reclaim his cow. However, in today's modern and sophisticated society the "infancy doctrine" seems to lose some of its gloss.

Paradoxically, we declare the infant mature enough to shoulder arms in the military, but not mature enough to vote; mature enough to marry and be responsible for his torts and crimes, but not mature enough to assume the burden of his own contractual indiscretions. In Wisconsin, the infant is deemed mature enough to use a dangerous instrumentality—a motor vehicle —at 16, but not mature enough to purchase it without protection until he is 21.

No one really questions that a line as to age must be drawn somewhere below which a legally defined minor must be able to disaffirm his contracts for nonnecessities. The law over the centuries has considered this age to be 21. Legislatures in other states have lowered the age. We suggest that the appellant might better seek the change it proposes in the legislative halls rather than this court. A recent law review article in the Indiana Law Journal explores the problem of contractual disabilities of minors and points to three different legislative solutions leading to greater freedom to contract. The first approach is one gleaned from the statutes of California and New York, which would allow parties to submit a proposed contract to a court which would remove the infant's right of disaffirmance upon a finding that the particular contract is fair. This suggested approach appears to be extremely impractical in light of the expense and delay that would necessarily accompany the procedure. A second approach would be to establish a rebuttable presumption of incapacity to replace the strict rule. This alternative would be an open invitation to litigation. The third suggestion is a statutory procedure that would allow a minor to petition a court for the removal of disabilities. Under this procedure a minor would only have to go to court once, rather than once for each contract as in the first suggestion.

Undoubtedly, the infancy doctrine is an obstacle when a major purchase is involved. However, we believe that the reasons for allowing that obstacle to remain viable at this point outweigh those for casting it aside. Minors require some protection from the pitfalls of the market place. Reasonable minds will always differ on the extent of the protection that should be afforded. For this court to adopt a rule that the appellant suggests and remove the contractual disabilities from a minor simply because he becomes emancipated, which in most cases would be the result of marriage, would be to suggest that the married minor is somehow vested with more wisdom and maturity than his single counterpart. However, logic would not seem to dictate this result especially when today a youthful marriage is oftentimes indicative of a lack of wisdom and maturity. . . .

Appellant's last argument is that the respondent should be held liable in tort for damages because he misrepresented his age. Appellant would use these damages as a setoff against the contract price sought to be reclaimed by respondent.

The Nineteenth Century view was that a minor's lying about his age was inconsequential because a fraudulent representation of capacity was not the equivalent of actual capacity. This rule has been altered by time. There appear to be two possible methods that now can be employed to bind the defrauding minor: He may be estopped from denying his alleged majority, in which case the contract will be enforced or contract damages will be allowed; or he may be allowed to disaffirm his contract but be liable in tort for damages. Wisconsin follows the latter approach.

In *Wisconsin Loan & Finance Corp.* v. *Goodnough,*[1] the defendant minor was a copartner in a business who had defaulted on a note given to the plaintiff in exchange for a loan. The defendant had secured the loan by fraudulently representing to the plaintiff that he was 21 years old. In adopting the tort theory and declining to adopt the estoppel theory, Mr. Chief Justice Rosenberry said:

"It is a matter of some importance, however, to determine whether an infant who secures benefits by misrepresenting his age to the person from whom he secured them is estopped to set up his infancy in order to defeat the contract or whether he becomes liable in an action for deceit for damages. In this case, if there is an estoppel which operates to prevent the defendant from repudiating the contract and he is liable upon it, the damages will be the full amount of the note plus interest and a reasonable attorney's fee. If he is held liable, on the other hand, in deceit, he will be liable only for the damages which the plaintiff sustained in this case, the amount of money the plaintiff parted with, which was $352 less the $25 repaid. There seems to be sound reason in the position of the English courts that to hold the contract enforceable by way of estoppel is to go contrary to the clearly declared policy of the law. But as was pointed out by the New Hampshire court, that objection lies no more for wrongs done by a minor by way of deceit than by way of slander or other torts. The contract is not enforced. He is held liable for deceit as he is for other torts such as slander, trover, and trespass.

---

[1] (1930), 201 Wis. 101, 228 N.W. 484, 67 A.L.R. 1259.

"It is considered that the sounder rule is that which holds an infant under such circumstances liable in tort for damages."

Having established that there is a remedy against the defrauding minor, the question becomes whether the requisites for a tort action in misrepresentation are present in this case. . . .

The "motor vehicle purchase contract" signed by Steven Kiefer contained the following language just above the purchaser's signature:

"I represent that I am 21 years of age or over and recognize that the dealer sells the above vehicle upon this representation."

Whether the inclusion of this sentence constitutes a misrepresentation depends on whether elements of the tort have been satisfied. They were not. In *First National Bank in Oshkosh* v. *Scieszinski* [2] it is said:

"A party alleging fraud has the burden of proving it by clear and convincing evidence. The elements of fraud are well established:

" ' "To be actionable the false representation must consist, first of a statement of fact which is untrue; second, that it was made with intent to defraud and for the purpose of inducing the other party to act upon it; third, that he did in fact rely on it and was induced thereby to act, to his injury or damage." ' "

No evidence was adduced to show that the plaintiff had an intent to defraud the dealer. To the contrary, it is at least arguable that the majority of minors are, as the plaintiff here might well have been, unaware of the legal consequences of their acts.

Without the element of scienter being satisfied, the plaintiff is not susceptible to an action in misrepresentation. Furthermore, the reliance mentioned in Scieszinski must be, . . . "justifiable reliance." We fail to see how the dealer could be justified in the mere reliance on the fact that the plaintiff signed a contract containing a sentence that said he was 21 or over. The trial court observed that the plaintiff was sufficiently immature looking to arouse suspicion. The appellant never took any affirmative steps to determine whether the plaintiff was in fact over 21. It never asked to see a draft card, identification card, or the most logical indicium of age under the circumstances, a driver's license. Therefore, because there was no intent to deceive, and no justifiable reliance, the appellant's action for misrepresentation must fail.

DISSENTING OPINION BY HALLOWS, J. . . .

The majority opinion on the issue of whether an emancipated minor legally should be responsible for his contracts "doth protest too much." After giving very cogent reasons why the common-law rule should be abandoned, the opinion refrains from reshaping the rule to meet reality. Minors are emancipated by a valid marriage and also by entering military service. If they are mature enough to become parents and assume the responsibility of raising other minors and if they are mature enough to be drafted or volunteer to bear arms and sacrifice their life for their country, then they are mature enough to make binding contracts in the market place.

---

[2] (1964), 25 Wis.2d 569, 131 N.W.2d 308.

The magical age limit of 21 years as an indication of contractual maturity no longer has a basis in fact or in public policy.

My second ground of the dissent is that an automobile to this respondent was a necessity and therefore the contract could not be disaffirmed. Here, we have a minor, aged 20 years and 7 months, the father of a child, and working. While the record shows there is some public transportation to his present place of work, it also shows he borrowed his mother's car to go to and from work. Automobiles for parents under 21 years of age to go to and from work in our current society may well be a necessity and I think in this case the record shows it is. An automobile as a means of transportation to earn a living should not be considered a nonnecessity because the owner is 5 months too young. I would reverse.

§ 16:6. Exploitation by Minors

Historically persons under 21, as noted in § 16:5, have been afforded a special protection from contracts which they believed exploited them by giving them the power to avoid any contract.

As society moved into the Twentieth Century, many situations arose in which the person under age 21 was part of the economic system, and it became unreasonable to permit him to avoid his contract. Accordingly, it was held that a minor who took a cross-country air trip could not thereafter avoid the contract and recover back the plane fare that he had paid. Likewise, a minor of 20 running a grocery store as his own business was denied the right to avoid the contract and was required to pay the supply house from which he had purchased the goods that he sold. In many states, statutes now provide that certain contracts when made by a minor or a minor of 18 or over shall be as binding as though made by an adult, such as loans for education, contracts for the purchase of a home, life insurance contracts, and bank account contracts. Here we see the change in social values; the minor of 18 or more is no longer in danger of being exploited and should not be permitted to turn around and oppress the other party to the contract by asserting his minority.

PANKAS v. BELL

413 Pa. 494, 198 A.2d 312 (1964)

Bell, age 20 years and 7 months, went to work in the beauty parlor of Pankas and agreed that when he left the employment, he would not work in or run a beauty parlor business within a ten-mile radius of downtown Pittsburgh, Pennsylvania, for a period of two years. Contrary to this provision, Bell and another employee of Pankas opened up a beauty shop three blocks from his shop and advertised themselves as former employees of Pankas. Pankas sued Bell to stop the breach of the noncompetition or restrictive covenant. Bell claimed that he was not bound because he was a minor when he had agreed to the covenant. From a decision in favor of Pankas, Bell appealed.

OPINION BY JONES, J. . . .

It would appear that this issue is one of first impression in our appellate courts. On four occasions common pleas courts in this Commonwealth have been presented with somewhat similar issues: *Harbison* v. *Mawhinney,* 8 Pa. Dist.R. 697; *Harshbarger Dairy* v. *Hoover,* 13 Pa.Dist. & Co.R. 701; *Bradley* v. *Cool et al.,* 18 Dist. & Co.R. 404; *Niedland* v. *Kulka,* 64 Dist. & Co.R. 418.

In Harbison the court held that a minor could be enjoined from breaching his covenant not to serve milk to his former employer's customers within a year after his discharge from service. The court . . . said: "But [other minor's contracts] have been recognized by the courts and held binding on the grounds that they are clearly beneficial to the infant. Among these are his contracts of service. The test of validity is, 'Is the contract as a whole beneficial to the infant? If so, it will be enforced. If not, he may avoid it.' " . . .

In Bradley, the court refused to enjoin a professional boxer, who was a minor, from boxing under the auspices of persons other than a person with whom he had contracted as his manager. The court held that, while equity can restrain a minor from violating a contract not to compete in business with his employer for a certain number of years after leaving the employment, yet, if there is no element of competition involved, equity will not enforce a minor's contract for personal services by an injunction compelling him not to render similar services for others. In Harshbarger Dairy, the court, . . . stated that, while infants are liable on their contracts for necessaries, there are "numerous decisions . . . that minors are not liable *on any other form of contract.*" (Emphasis supplied.)

In Niedland, the rule in Harbison was approved and applied. Although it was pointed out to the court that Harbison constituted a dangerous precedent in that it tended to strip from minors the "protective cloak" which the law has always thrown about them, the court stated: ". . . the law should not allow a so-called 'protective cloak' to be used by a minor as an instrument for deliberately evading the dictates of common sense, good conscience, and a sense of justice. Where the contract is without taint of fraud or overreaching and is for the benefit of a minor, the minor should not be permitted to disaffirm where such action would result in injustice and damage to the other contracting party." . . .

The court in *Mutual Milk & Cream Co.* v. *Prigge,* 112 App.Div. 652, 98 N.Y.S. 458 adopted a sensible, logical, and practical approach to a situation somewhat similar to the case at bar. Therein, a 19-year old minor had entered the employ of the plaintiff as the driver of a milk delivery wagon and had signed a contract agreeing . . . not to solicit business from plaintiff's customers or deliver dairy products to them within three years after leaving plaintiff's employ; the contract was terminable by either party upon one week's notice; several months later the minor quit and entered the employment of a rival milk dealer and solicited business from the plaintiff's customers. In upholding the issuance of an injunction against the minor who had pleaded infancy to avoid the contract, the court stated: "Although he had not arrived at the age at which all contracts with him would be binding,

he was of sufficient age to appreciate the nature of this contract, and to know whether or not it was for his benefit." The court considered that the issue was not one of the liability of a minor for a breach of his contract but whether a minor should be thereunder permitted to repudiate his contract without restoring what he had received and, if restoration cannot be made, without being enjoined from making use of the information he had gained from his employment by the plaintiff to the latter's damage. The court held that the minor should be enjoined "from making use of that information, in violation of his agreement made at the time when he desired and obtained employment, and upon the faith of which he obtained the information and acquaintance" and the court further observed: "No man would engage the services of an infant if he could not impose the same condition for his own protection against the use of his formulas, trade secrets, and lists of customers that he could exact of an adult."

In the case at bar, we need not nor do we decide that a contract for the employment of a minor is an exception to the general rule that the contracts of minors are voidable. What we do determine is that, although this contract is voidable, the minor should not be permitted to utilize any benefits, training, or knowledge derived from such contract to the damage and detriment of his former employer. As a practical matter, to hold otherwise would deter the employment of minors because no person would care to run the risk of employing a person who could not only avoid the contract but also utilize that which he has derived from the contract to compete with his former employer.

Behind the rule rendering voidable the contracts of a minor is the very laudable purpose of the law to protect minors from contracts which may be disadvantageous to them and to protect them "against their own lack of discretion and against the snares of designing persons." . . . This "protective cloak" is to safeguard the interests of the minor; it is not to be employed as a vehicle whereby the minor is enabled to practice unconscionable business methods. It is a shield for defense, not a sword for offense. In enjoining this minor from using to his own benefit and to the detriment of his former employer that which he has gained from his former employment, we declare that, even though the contract is voidable, the minor is prohibited from exploiting that which he gained from the contract and that equity should restrain such exploitation.

There is no evidence of any fraud or overreaching on Pankas' part, the contract as a whole was beneficial to Bell, and Bell should be enjoined from exploiting that which he gained from his employment by Pankas. . . .

[Decree affirmed.]

§ 16:7. Mitigation of Damages

The law is concerned by the exploitation of the situation not only when the actor acts for the purpose of taking advantage of another but also even when a person omits acting when the failure to act aggravates the liability of another person. This concept is seen in the operation of the principle of mitigation of damages. By this principle, a plaintiff who is injured by the conduct of the defendant must take reasonable steps to reduce or keep down the damages that he sustained. Thus a person who is injured by the negligence of another must obtain reasonable medical care to cure himself. A person who by contract is entitled to the services of another must make reasonable efforts to obtain similar services elsewhere in order to reduce damages that the other party's breach of the contract causes him. Similarly, if an employer improperly fires an employee, the employee must seek similar employment elsewhere.

What is the penalty or consequence of the plaintiff's failing to keep down or mitigate the damages? The plaintiff is not entitled to recover from the defendant the damages that the plaintiff could have avoided had he taken reasonable steps to mitigate the harm. Thus, if reasonable care would have reduced the loss of working time down to a week but the plaintiff's neglect of his condition caused him to lose several months, the plaintiff is only entitled to recover from the defendant for the loss of the pay for the week that could not have been avoided by the plaintiff; and under a contract for services, the plaintiff cannot recover for the damages caused by the failure to furnish the services beyond what it would have cost him to procure them elsewhere. Likewise, the claim of the employee who was improperly discharged is reduced by the pay which the employee could have earned elsewhere.

GREEN v. SMITH

67 Cal.Rptr. 796 (Cal.App.2d, 1968)

Green ran a tree nursery. It was irrigated by a concrete ditch that ran over the land, which was thereafter acquired by Smith. Smith had a contractor destroy the concrete irrigation ditch. When Green sued Smith, the latter claimed that Green could not recover from him for the full amount of the damages which Green had sustained because Green had failed to mitigate the damages.

OPINION BY TAMURA, A.J. . . .

Plaintiff, a wholesale grower of ornamental nursery trees brought this action for damages for crop loss allegedly sustained by him by reason of defendant's destruction of a concrete irrigation pipeline. . . . Following a nonjury trial the court found that defendants unlawfully and intentionally, though not maliciously, demolished the pipeline and that as a consequence plaintiff was unable to harvest nursery stock having an "alleged market value in excess of $17,000." However, it found that plaintiff could have avoided the loss by utilizing a substitute means of conveying water to the land at a cost of not more than $600 and, hence, limited plaintiff's recovery to a judgment for that sum. . . . Plaintiff appeals.

Plaintiff contends that the court "abused its discretion" in applying the doctrine of mitigation of damages. To state it more accurately his contention

appears to be that on the findings made, the court erred in concluding that plaintiff failed to mitigate damages.

Plaintiff was the owner of a leasehold interest in a parcel of land on which he planted and grew, among other items, 110 rows of ornamental nursery trees, each row containing approximately 425 trees. A cement pipeline which he used to irrigate the trees and to water the ground preparatory to harvesting them ran along the northerly edge of the premises. Plaintiff's lease was due to expire on December 31, 1962.

On December 13, 1962, defendant Richard B. Smith, Inc. (Smith, Inc.), acquired title to the land, subject to the lease, and contracted with Kirchnavy Brothers, a partnership composed of defendants James R. Kirchnavy and William Kirchnavy, to clear the land for subdivision development. Some time in December, 1962, pursuant to instructions from Smith, Inc., but without plaintiff's permission or consent, Kirchnavy Brothers demolished the pipeline.

In December, prior to the destruction of the pipeline, plaintiff had commenced harvesting the trees. The procedure required the trees to be cut by running a U-shaped blade, mounted on a tractor, through the ground at a depth of 18-24 inches. On December 26 plaintiff discovered that he was unable to continue harvesting because the soil had become too dry and hard to operate the cutter. He immediately attempted to irrigate the land by constructing a ditch along the site of the demolished pipeline, but because of a swale the berms failed to contain the water. After waiting for a few days to permit the soil to dry, he constructed a larger ditch with higher and thicker berms and was thereby able to convey water to approximately 19 rows which he subsequently harvested. However, because of the swale he was unable to convey water to approximately 25 rows. On January 8 or 9 he left the premises stating that he was unable to harvest the remaining 25 rows. As soon as plaintiff left the premises, defendants plowed under the remaining trees.

Defendants introduced evidence to show that plaintiff could have conveyed water to the remaining 25 rows at a cost not exceeding $600 either (1) by constructing a ditch with higher or thicker berms; (2) by renting portable irrigation equipment and connecting it to a standpipe located at the edge of the property; (3) by obtaining water from a city fire hydrant located near the property; (4) by obtaining water from a domestic water meter; (5) by requesting use of defendant's water tank trucks which were on the land for subdivision work. Plaintiff admitted that he had the financial ability to incur an expenditure of $600 for substitute service.

On the issue of mitigation the court found:

"Plaintiff's nursery stock was ready for market in December of 1962 and prior to the demolition of said pipeline plaintiff had commenced the harvesting of his nursery stock; from and after the date of demolition of said pipeline plaintiff was unable to irrigate his nursery stock preparatory to harvesting as he had done theretofore. That as soon as plaintiff discovered that the land was dry and his nursery stock could not be harvested without irrigating, he immediately thereafter with the use of his equipment and employees endeavored to irrigate said nursery stock through an open ditch or trench which he constructed along the site of the demolished pipeline; when this operation was unsuccessful as the open ditch or berm broke, plaintiff again endeavored to irrigate said nursery trees by constructing another ditch or trench higher and thicker than the previous one and upon turning the water thereon was able to irrigate 19 rows of nursery trees and subsequently harvested them, but because of a swale in the land the open ditch could not carry the water to the remaining 25 rows of nursery trees and the berm again collapsed—resulting in approximately 9,300 trees having an alleged fair market value in excess of $17,000 from being harvested.

"That instead of using the open ditch or trench, plaintiff could have effected the delivery of the water to said remaining 25 rows of trees by other means at his disposal, to wit, from water available at a standpipe at the edge of said Minnick property by means of portable irrigation equipment or by installing a temporary line of water available from the City of Chino. Therefore, plaintiff's actual and real loss for which he is entitled to compensation was the cost of effecting the delivery of such water from other sources and the cost of said delivery would not have exceeded the sum of $600."

From the findings the court concluded that defendants intentionally, though not maliciously, destroyed the pipeline and that as a result plaintiff sustained damages but that he "failed to mitigate his damages as he was required to do."

It has been the policy of the courts to promote the mitigation of damages. . . . The doctrine applies in tort, willful as well as negligent. . . . A plaintiff cannot be compensated for damages which he could have avoided by reasonable effort or expenditures. . . . The frequent statement of the principle in the terms of a "duty" imposed on the injured party has been criticized on the theory that a breach of the "duty" does not give rise to a correlative right of action. . . . It is perhaps more accurate to say that the wrongdoer is not required to compensate the injured party for damages which are avoidable by reasonable effort on the latter's part. . . .

The doctrine does not require the injured party to take measures which are unreasonable or impractical or which would involve expenditures disproportionate to the loss sought to be avoided or which may be beyond his financial means. . . . The reasonableness of the efforts of the injured party must be judged in the light of the situation confronting him at the time the loss was threatened and not by the judgment of hindsight. . . . The fact that reasonable measures other than the one taken would have avoided damage is not, in and of itself, proof of the fact that the one taken, though unsuccessful, was unreasonable. . . . "If a choice of two reasonable courses presents itself, the person whose wrong forced the choice cannot complain that one rather than the other is chosen." . . . The standard by which the reasonableness of the injured party's efforts is to be measured is not as high as the standard required in other areas of law. . . . It is sufficient if he acts reasonably and with due diligence, in good faith. . . .

Plaintiff contends that the court erred in determining that under the facts of the instant case, plaintiff failed to act reasonably to mitigate damages. Defendants, on the other hand, urge that the issue was one of fact and that the trial court's determination may not be disturbed on appeal if there is any substantial evidence to support it.

It has been held that the question whether an injured party acted reasonably to mitigate damages is a matter to be determined by the trier of fact and
that the scope of review on appeal is circumscribed by the "any substantial
evidence rule." . . . However, in the instant case the court made specific
probative findings concerning the efforts made by plaintiff to save his crop as
well as the feasibility and cost of providing an alternate means of irrigating
the land and from those findings concluded that plaintiff failed to mitigate
damages as required by law. Where a conclusion, whether it be characterized
as a finding of "ultimate fact" or a legal conclusion, is drawn from specific
probative findings, it cannot stand if it is not supported or is inconsistent
with the specific probative findings. . . . The question whether probative
facts support the conclusion drawn from them does not involve weighing
or resolving conflicts in the evidence or judging the credibility of witnesses.
It is a question of law reviewable on appeal. . . .

In the instant case the probative findings do not support the conclusion
that plaintiff failed to make a reasonable effort to avoid the consequences of
defendants' tortious act. According to the specific findings, when plaintiff
discovered that he could not continue harvesting without moistening the soil,
he immediately endeavored to irrigate the land by constructing a ditch along
the site of the demolished pipeline and, when the first attempt failed, he
reconstructed the ditch with thicker and higher berms and was thereby able
to irrigate and salvage 19 rows. Those findings are wholly inconsistent with
the necessarily implied conclusion that plaintiff failed to take reasonable
measures to avoid injury; they establish the fact that he made a reasonable
good faith effort to save his crop. The court's conclusion cannot stand on
the finding that instead of using the open ditch, plaintiff, at a cost of not
more than $600, could have conveyed water to the land by renting portable
irrigation equipment and connecting it to a standpipe located at the edge of
the property or by connecting a temporary line to a city fire hydrant. The
fact that in retrospect a reasonable alternative course of action is shown
to have been feasible is not proof of the fact that the course actually pursued
by plaintiff was unreasonable. Significantly, defendants sought to prove that
one of the alternatives which was available to plaintiff was the construction
of an open ditch, albeit, they sought to prove that plaintiff should have constructed one with higher and thicker berms.

Plaintiff's response to the threatened damage was in sharp contrast to
the conduct of the injured party in *Henrici* v. *South Feather Land, etc., Co.,*
177 Cal. 442, 170 P. 1135; *Mabb* v. *Stewart,* supra, 147 Cal. 413, 81 P.
1073; *Severini* v. *Sutter-Butte Canal Co.,* 59 Cal.App. 154, 210 P. 49. In
those cases, plaintiffs, through passive indifference or stubborn insistence
upon a conceived legal right, failed to take any reasonable steps to avoid
damage.

We conclude that for the foregoing reasons that portion of the judgment
from which the appeal has been taken must be reversed. Since damages were
not specifically ascertained and additional evidence may be necessary on that
issue, it is our opinion that the interests of justice would best be served by
an unqualified reversal rather than a reversal with directions.

[Judgment reversed.]

Questions for Review

1. Define the social force of protection from exploitation.

2. Give illustrations of its application.

3. Analyze each opinion in this chapter in terms of the social forces involved in the decision. See § 5:5 for a list of the social forces. With respect to each opinion explain why the prevailing social forces prevailed and why those rejected did not. In each case in which there is a dissenting opinion, also make this analysis for the dissenting opinion.

4-8. On the basis of the social forces involved, what decision should be made in each of the following cases?

4. *Limitation of liability. Residential lease.* Is a lease provision that the landlord shall not be liable for damage caused by water, snow, or ice valid? *Feldman* v. *Stein Building & Lumber Co.,* 6 Mich.App. 180, 148 N.W.2d 544.

5. *Unjust enrichment. Contract with tenant.* May a contractor installing heating and air conditioning unit in building under a contract with the tenant recover the cost thereof from the landlord who had no knowledge of the installation until it was completed; where the contractor had contracted with the tenant who held a lease of the entire building under a long-term lease. *Kemp* v. *Majestic Amusement Co.,* 427 Pa. 429, 234 A.2d 846.

6. *Forfeiture. Lease.* The O'Fallon Development Co. built a shopping center and rented one of the stores to Reinbold and others. In the lease the tenant agreed to keep the store open daily from 8 to 5 with the exception of Sunday and agreed to "abide by the rules to be hereafter promulgated by the lessor or an Association of Tenants . . . for the betterment of the Southview Plaza Shopping Center." A year later the O'Fallon Development Co. adopted some rules, one of which required the stores to stay open from 9 to 9, six days a week. When Reinbold did not comply with this rule, O'Fallon declared the lease forfeited, locked Reinbold out of the store, and sued him for breach of the lease. Was O'Fallon entitled to do this? *O'Fallon Development Co.* v. *Reinbold,* 62 Ill.App.2d 169, 216 N.E.2d 9.

7. *Release from liability. Validity.* Charles Fedor, a minor, went to a summer camp. His father signed an agreement as a condition to his being admitted to the camp that the minor would not make any claim against the camp for any injury. When Charles was injured at the camp, he sued the camp claiming that the injury was caused by the camp's negligence. It raised the defense that the waiver agreement barred the suit. Was the camp correct? *Fedor* v. *Mauwehu Council,* 21 Conn.Supp. 38, 143 A.2d 466.

8. *Antitrust. Price maintenance.* A manufacturer of drug products wished to maintain the resale prices of its products. It informed retailers selling below a suggested list price that it would not deal with them thereafter. The manufacturer also told wholesalers that it would not sell its products to the wholesalers if they resold them to retailers selling below the list price. It was claimed that this was unlawful. Decide. *United States* v. *Parke, Davis & Co.,* 362 U.S. 29.

9-13. What social forces were involved, which prevailed, and which were defeated in the following decisions?

9. **Contracts. Minor.** If a minor may disaffirm his purchase of an automobile, he must allow a deduction from the purchase price representing depreciation in value; but the existence of a right to disaffirm is not affected by the fact that the minor appeared to have been an adult or that the disaffirmance was made for a trivial reason. *Rose* v. *Sheehan Buick,* Fla., 204 So.2d 903.

10. **Liquidated damage clause. Excessive payment.** Kuznicki made a contract for the installation of a fire detection system by Security Safety Corp. for $498. The contract was made one night and cancelled at 9:00 a.m. the next morning. Security then claimed one third of the purchase price from Kuznicki by virtue of a provision in the contract that "in the event of cancellation of this agreement . . . the owner agrees to pay 33⅓ percent of the contract price, as liquidated damages." It was held that Security Safety was not entitled to recover the amount claimed because the amount was out of proportion to any damages that it could have sustained by such cancellation. *Security Safety Corp.* v. *Kuznicki,* 350 Mass. 157, 213 N.E.2d 866.

11. **Limitation of liability. Invalid.** A provision in a public housing authority's lease to a tenant in a lowcost housing project is void as against public policy where it relieves the authority from liability for its own negligence. *Thomas* v. *Housing Authority,* Wash.2d, 426 P.2d 836.

12. **Limitation of liability. As is.** An exclusion of liability for negligence must be clearly made to have effect, and the use of "as is" merely disclaims warranty liability but has no effect upon liability for negligence. *Fleming* v. *Stoddard Wendle Motor Co.,* 70 Wash.2d 465, 423 P.2d 926.

13. **Agency. Debt of husband.** A wife is not liable for the maintenance of her husband in a state institution to which he has been committed for the purpose of a pretrial examination to determine his sanity, where the state constitution prohibited making a wife liable for the debts of her husband. *Rowe* v. *Department of Mental Hygiene,* 247 Md. 542, 233 A.2d 769.

Chapter 17

PROTECTION FROM HARDSHIP SITUATIONS

§ 17:1. Generally

The hardship situation here considered arises in which a party is exposed to a hardship without any particular intent or fault of any party. That is, no one seeks to exploit anyone, but the situation just arises that imposes a hardship. Will the court modify the law to protect the victim from such hardship? This is not as simple a matter to determine as where one party is consciously exploiting the other, for here the law feels no reluctance in rescuing the victim from the situation which the wrongdoer has intentionally created. In the hardship from the situation case, there is no intentional wrongdoer and while one might be negligent or more negligent than the other, both parties stand on the same or substantially the same footing with respect to moral fault.

§ 17:2. The Nonresident Defendant

In this modern day of interstate travel and engaging in interstate business, problems often arise with respect to bringing suit against a defendant who is a nonresident defendant or a corporation that was incorporated or formed in another state.

Historically, a lawsuit could only be brought in a state in which service could be made on the defendant. This created an obvious problem where a nonresident motorist lived in another state and, while driving through the victim's state, ran into the victim but thereafter left. In such case, when the victim sued the nonresident, it was impossible for the victim to serve the defendant who by definition was no longer in the state. In order to sue the defendant, it was necessary for the plaintiff to go to the state where the defendant lived and in which service could be obtained upon the defendant. By statute this problem has been solved; and it has been generally provided that when a nonresident drives in another state, he thereby appoints the secretary of state or some other official of that state to act as his agent so that service can be made on that officer. As to mechanics, these statutes provide an original copy of the process that is to be served is to be mailed to the state official and a copy thereof is mailed to the defendant in the other state by either the plaintiff or by the state official. This permits the plaintiff to sue in the state in which he was injured. This is generally important because it is that state in which the witnesses are located, and, in many instances, it will also be the state in which the plaintiff lives so that the burden and expense of bringing the lawsuit is reduced.

The problem of the nonresident defendant remains in the case of a suit for breach of contract. If a nonresident owes you a sum of money, you must generally go to his home state in order to sue him. As an exception, if the debt to you arose from business locally transacted by the nonresident, many states permit you to serve the person in charge of the place of business.

What of the foreign corporation which does business within the state? Generally it is required to obtain permission to do business within the state and as part of the process of obtaining permission, the corporation pays a license fee or tax and also expressly authorizes a state official or a named person to act as its agent to receive the service of process. When this is done, no question arises as to suing the foreign corporation within the state for service is made upon the statutory agent.

What happens if the foreign corporation has not appointed an agent? Under some statutes, service may be made upon a state official similar to the case of the nonresident motorist. In many instances, the question of the suability of the corporation within the state is answered in terms of whether the corporation is "present" within the state. In view of the fact that a corporation is an artificial nonexistent person, this is obviously merely a matter of playing with words, the object of the game being to determine whether the corporation has become so involved in local activity that it is fair to require it to answer to the local courts.

Many states have adopted what are nicknamed "long arm" statutes, which provide that when a foreign corporation does certain acts within the state, the courts of the state may reach out into the home state of the foreign corporation and subject the corporation to a local suit.

GRAY v. AMERICAN RADIATOR & STANDARD SANITARY CORP.

22 Ill.2d 432, 176 N.E.2d 761 (1961)

Gray lived in Illinois. She purchased a hot water heater manufactured by the American Radiator & Standard Sanitary Corp. of Pennsylvania. The heater had a safety valve made by the Titan Valve Co. of Ohio. The heater exploded. Gray sued both American Radiator and Titan in Illinois, claiming that the safety valve was defective. Titan claimed that suit against it could not proceed because it did not do business within the state of Illinois and had not been served in Illinois.

OPINION BY KLINGBIEL, J. . . .

The complaint charges, . . . that the Titan company, a foreign corporation, had negligently constructed the safety valve; and that the injuries were suffered as a proximate result thereof. Summons issued and was duly served on Titan's registered agent in Cleveland, Ohio. The corporation appeared specially, filing a motion to quash on the ground that it had not committed a tortious act in Illinois. Its affidavit stated that it does no business here; that it has no agent physically present in Illinois; and that it sells the completed valves to defendant, American Radiator & Standard Sanitary Corporation, outside Illinois. . . .

Section 16 of the Civil Practice Act provides that summons may be personally served upon any party outside the State; and that as to nonresidents who have submitted to the jurisdiction of our courts, such service has the force and effect of personal service within Illinois. . . . Under section 17(1)(b) a nonresident who, either in person or through an agent, commits a tortious act within this State submits to jurisdiction. . . . The questions in this case are (1) whether a tortious act was committed here, within the meaning of the statute, despite the fact that the Titan corporation had no agent in Illinois; and (2) whether the statute, if so construed, violates due process of law.

The first aspect to which we must direct our attention is one of statutory construction. Under section 17(1)(b) jurisdiction is predicated on the committing of a tortious act in this State. It is not disputed, for the purpose of this appeal, that a tortious act was committed. The issue depends on whether it was committed in Illinois, so as to warrant the assertion of personal jurisdiction by service of summons in Ohio.

The wrong in the case at bar did not originate in the conduct of a servant physically present here, but arose instead from acts performed at the place of manufacture. Only the consequences occurred in Illinois. It is well established, however, that in law the place of a wrong is where the last event takes place which is necessary to render the actor liable. Restatement, Conflict of Laws, sec. 377. A second indication that the place of injury is the determining factor is found in rules governing the time within which an action must be brought. In applying statutes of limitation our court has computed the period from the time when the injury is done. . . . We think it is clear that the alleged negligence in manufacturing the valve cannot be separated from the resulting injury; and that for present purposes, like those of liability and limitations, the tort was committed in Illinois.

Titan seeks to avoid this result by arguing that instead of using the word "tort," the legislature employed the term "tortious act"; and that the latter refers only to the act or conduct, separate and apart from any consequences thereof. We cannot accept the argument. To be tortious an act must cause injury. The concept of injury is an inseparable part of the phrase. . . . We think the intent should be determined less from technicalities of definition than from considerations of general purpose and effect. To adopt the criteria urged by defendant would tend to promote litigation over extraneous issues concerning the elements of a tort and the territorial incidence of each, whereas the test should be concerned more with those substantial elements of convenience and justice presumably contemplated by the legislature. . . .

The Titan company contends that if the statute is applied so as to confer jurisdiction in this case it violates the requirement of due process of law. . . . In [a prior] case the validity of the statute was upheld in an action against a nonresident whose employee, while physically present in Illinois, allegedly caused the injury. The *ratio decidendi* was that Illinois has an interest in providing relief for injuries caused by persons having "substantial contacts within the State." A standard of fairness or reasonableness was announced, within the limitation that defendant be given a realistic opportunity to appear and be heard. The case at bar concerns the extent to which due process permits substituted service where defendant had no agent or employee in the State of the forum.

Under modern doctrine the power of a State court to enter a binding judgment against one not served with process within the State depends upon two questions: first, whether he has certain minimum contacts with the State . . . , and second, whether there has been a reasonable method of notification. Defendant's argument on constitutionality is confined to the proposition that applying section 17(1)(b), where the injury is defendant's only contact with the State, would exceed the limits of due process.

A proper determination of the question presented requires analysis of those cases which have dealt with the quantum of contact sufficient to warrant jurisdiction. Since the decision in *Pennoyer* v. *Neff*, 95 U.S. 714, 24 L.Ed. 565, the power of a State to exert jurisdiction over nonresidents has been greatly expanded, particularly with respect to foreign corporations. See Annotations, 2 L.Ed.2d 1664; 94 L.Ed. 1167. *International Shoe Co.* v. *State of Washington*, 326 U.S. 310, 66 S.Ct. 154, 90 L.Ed. 95, was a proceeding to collect unpaid contributions to the unemployment compensation fund of the State of Washington. A statute purported to authorize such proceedings, where the employer was not found within the State, by sending notice by registered mail to its last known address. The defendant foreign corporation, a manufacturer of shoes, employed certain salesmen who resided in Washington and who solicited orders there. In holding that maintenance of the suit did not violate due process the court pointed out that the activities of the corporation in Washington were not only continuous and systematic but also gave rise to the liability sued on. It was observed that such operations, which resulted in a large volume of business, established "sufficient contacts or ties with the state of the forum to make it reasonable and just according to our traditional conception of fair play and substantial justice to permit the state to enforce the obligations which appellant has incurred there." . . .

Where the business done by a foreign corporation in the State of the forum is of a sufficiently substantial nature, it has been held permissible for the State to entertain a suit against it even though the cause of action arose from activities entirely distinct from its conduct within the State. . . . But where such business or other activity is not substantial, the particular act or transaction having no connection with the State of the forum, the requirement of "contact" is not satisfied. . . .

In the case at bar the defendant's only contact with this State is found in the fact that a product manufactured in Ohio was incorporated in Pennsylvania, into a hot water heater which in the course of commerce was sold to an Illinois consumer. The record fails to disclose whether defendant has done any other business in Illinois, either directly or indirectly; and it is argued, in reliance on the International Shoe test, that since a course of business here has not been shown there are no "minimum contacts" sufficient to support jurisdiction. We do not think, however, that doing a given volume of business is the only way in which a nonresident can form the required connection with this State. Since the International Shoe case was decided, the requirements for jurisdiction have been further relaxed so that at the present time, it is sufficient if the act or transaction itself has a substantial connection with the State of the forum.

In *McGee* v. *International Life Insurance Co.,* 355 U.S. 220, 78 S.Ct. 199, 201, 2 L.Ed.2d 223, suit was brought in California against a foreign insurance company on a policy issued to a resident of California. The defendant was not served with process in that State but was notified by registered mail at its place of business in Texas, pursuant to a statute permitting such service in suits on insurance contracts. The contract in question was delivered in California, the premiums were mailed from there and the insured was a resident of that State when he died, but defendant had no office or agent in California nor did it solicit any business there apart from the policy sued on. After referring briefly to the International Shoe case, the court held that "it is sufficient for purposes of due process that the suit was based on *a contract* which had substantial connection" with California. (Emphasis supplied.)

In *Smyth* v. *Twin State Improvement Corp.,* 116 Vt. 569, 80 A.2d 664, 666, 25 A.L.R.2d 1193, a Vermont resident engaged a foreign corporation to reroof his house. While doing the work the corporation negligently damaged the building, and an action was brought for damages. Service of process was made on the Secretary of State and a copy was forwarded to defendant by registered mail at its principal place of business in Massachusetts. A Vermont statute provided for such substituted service on foreign corporations committing a tort in Vermont against a resident of Vermont. In holding that the statute affords due process of law, the court discussed the principal authorities on the question and concluded, *inter alia,* that "continuous activity within the state is not necessary as a prerequisite to jurisdiction."

In *Nelson* v. *Miller,* 11 Ill.2d 378, 143 N.E.2d 673, the commission of a single tort within this State was held sufficient to sustain jurisdiction under the present statute. The defendant in that case, a resident of Wisconsin, was engaged in the business of selling appliances. It was alleged that in the process of delivering a stove in Illinois, an employee of the defendant negligently caused injury to the plaintiff. In holding that the defendant was not denied due process by being required to defend in Illinois, this court observed at page 390 of 11 Ill.2d, at page 680 of 143 N.E.2d: "The defendant sent his employee into Illinois in the advancement of his own interests. While he was here, the employee and the defendant enjoyed the benefit and protection of the laws of Illinois, including the right to resort to our courts. In the course of his stay here the employee performed acts that gave rise to an injury. The law of Illinois will govern the substantive rights and duties stemming from the incident. Witnesses, other than the defendant's employee, are likely to be found here, and not in Wisconsin. In such circumstances, it is not unreasonable to require the defendant to make his defense here."

Whether the type of activity conducted within the State is adequate to satisfy the requirement depends upon the facts in the particular case. . . . The question cannot be answered by applying a mechanical formula or rule of thumb but by ascertaining what is fair and reasonable in the circumstances. In the application of this flexible test the relevant inquiry is whether defendant engaged in some act or conduct by which he may be said to have invoked the benefits and protections of the law of the forum. . . . The relevant decisions since *Pennoyer* v. *Neff* show a development of the concept of personal jurisdiction from one which requires service of process within the State to one which is satisfied either if the act or transaction sued on occurs there or if defendant has engaged in a sufficiently substantial course of activity in the State, provided always that reasonable notice and opportunity to be heard are afforded. As the Vermont court recognized . . . , the trend in defining due process of law is away from the emphasis on territorial limitations and toward emphasis on providing adequate notice and opportunity to be heard: from the court with immediate power over the defendant, toward the court in which both parties can most conveniently settle their dispute.

In the McGee case the court commented on the trend toward expanding State jurisdiction over nonresidents, observing that: "In part this is attributable to the fundamental transformation of our national economy over the years. Today many commercial transactions touch two or more States and may involve parties separated by the full continent. With this increasing nationalization of commerce has come a great increase in the amount of business conducted by mail across state lines. At the same time modern transportation and communication have made it much less burdensome for a party sued to defend himself in a State where he engages in economic activity."

It is true that courts cannot "assume that this trend heralds the eventual demise of all restrictions on the personal jurisdiction of state courts." . . . An orderly and fair administration of the law throughout the nation requires protection against being compelled to answer claims brought in distant States with which the defendant has little or no association and in which he would be faced with an undue burden or disadvantage in making his defense. It must be remembered that lawsuits can be brought on frivolous demands or groundless claims as well as on legitimate ones, and that procedural rules must be designed and appraised in the light of what is fair and just to both sides in the dispute. Interpretations of basic rights which consider only those of a claimant are not consonant with the fundamental requisites of due process.

In the case at bar defendant does not claim that the present use of its product in Illinois is an isolated instance. While the record does not disclose the volume of Titan's business or the territory in which appliances incorporating its valves are marketed, it is a reasonable inference that its commercial transactions, like those of other manufacturers, result in substantial use and consumption in this State. To the extent that its business may be directly affected by transactions occurring here, it enjoys benefits from the laws of this State, and it has undoubtedly benefited, to a degree, from the protection which our law has given to the marketing of hot water heaters containing its valves. Where the alleged liability arises, as in this case, from the manufacture of products presumably sold in contemplation of use here, it should not matter that the purchase was made from an independent middleman or that someone other than the defendant shipped the product into this State.

With the increasing specialization of commercial activity and the growing interdependence of business enterprises, it is seldom that a manufacturer deals directly with consumers in other States. The fact that the benefit he derives from its laws is an indirect one, however, does not make it any the less essential to the conduct of his business; and it is not unreasonable, where a cause of action arises from alleged defects in his product, to say that the use of such products in the ordinary course of commerce is sufficient contact with this State to justify a requirement that he defend here.

As a general proposition, if a corporation elects to sell its products for ultimate use in another State, it is not unjust to hold it answerable there for any damage caused by defects in those products. Advanced means of distribution and other commercial activity have made possible these modern methods of doing business, and have largely effaced the economic significance of State lines. By the same token, today's facilities for transportation and communication have removed much of the difficulty and inconvenience formerly encountered in defending lawsuits brought in other States.

Unless they are applied in recognition of the changes brought about by technological and economic progress, jurisdictional concepts which may have been reasonable enough in a simpler economy lose their relation to reality, and injustice rather than justice is promoted. Our unchanging principles of justice, whether procedural or substantive in nature, should be scrupulously observed by the courts. But the rules of law which grow and develop within those principles must do so in the light of the facts of economic life as it is lived today. Otherwise the need for adaptation may become so great that basic rights are sacrificed in the name of reform, and the principles themselves become impaired.

The principles of due process relevant to the issue in this case support jurisdiction in the court where both parties can most conveniently settle their dispute. The facts show that the plaintiff, an Illinois resident, was injured in Illinois. The law of Illinois will govern the substantive questions, and witnesses on the issues of injury, damages and other elements relating to the occurrence are most likely to be found here. Under such circumstances, the courts of the place of injury usually provide the most convenient forum for trial. . . .

We are aware of decisions, cited by defendant, wherein the opposite result was reached on somewhat similar factual situations. . . . Little purpose can be served, however, by discussing such cases in detail, since the existence of sufficient "contact" depends upon the particular facts in each case. In any event we think the better rule supports jurisdiction in cases of the present kind. We conclude accordingly that defendant's association with this State is sufficient to support the exercise of jurisdiction.

We construe section 17(1)(b) as providing for jurisdiction under the circumstances shown in this case, and we hold that as so construed the statute does not violate due process of law. . . .

§ 17:3.   The Poorly Written Contract

In some instances, a party finds himself in an unexpected hardship because the contract into which he has entered failed to provide for the situation that has occurred. Sometimes this failure is understandable, as when the situation which had arisen is the one-in-a-million situation that no one could reasonably have been expected to anticipate. Sometimes the failure represents the taking of a calculated risk, the one party fearing to demand the inclusion of a particular contract term because the other party might then refuse to make any contract at all. In situations such as these, the court is often faced with the problem that if the contract is read just as written, that is, if the intent of the parties as expressed in the contract is given effect, an undue hardship will result to the one party. On the other hand, if the court modifies the contract by reading in a clause to protect the victim, the court is rewriting the contract of the parties, is enforcing the court's intent and not the intent of the parties, and is to that extent undermining the stability of contracts and retarding trade.

PERKINS v. STANDARD OIL CO.

235 Ore. 7, 383 P.2d 107 (1963)

Standard Oil made a jobbing or wholesale dealership contract with Perkins, which limited him to selling Standard's products and required Perkins to maintain certain minimum prices. Standard Oil had the right to approve or disapprove of Perkins' customers. In order to be able to perform under this contract, Perkins had to make a substantial money investment, and his only income was from the commissions on the sales of Standard's products. Standard Oil made some sales directly to Perkins' customers. When Perkins protested, Standard Oil pointed out that the contract did not contain any provision making his rights exclusive. Perkins sued Standard Oil to compel it to stop dealing with his customers. From a decision in Standard's favor, Perkins appealed.

OPINION BY ROSSMAN, J. . . .

The contract authorized the plaintiff [Perkins] to sell without Standard's written consent "on a nonexclusive basis" the products which Standard consigned to him but only to service stations or consuming accounts. Standard's written consent was required before the plaintiff could sell to any other account. The plaintiff promised in the contract to use his "best efforts to promote the sale of products consigned hereunder" and to sell a specified minimum amount during each year. . . . The plaintiff was required to deliver to Standard a complete list of the names and addresses of all his distributors and submit to it the names of any new potential distributors. . . .

The plaintiff claims that the contract by its very nature contains an implied condition that Standard would not solicit business directly from his (plaintiff's) customers. Standard protests that such an implied condition would be contrary to the express terms of the contract since the latter (1) provides that the plaintiff was authorized to sell Standard's products only "on a nonexclusive basis" and (2) reserved to Standard the "right to select its own customers." Plaintiff proposes a more restricted interpretation of the terms of the contract that we just took from Standard's quotation. He concedes that the contract reserved to Standard the right to sell to any new accounts which it found, and to accept or reject any new accounts which he (the plaintiff) might obtain, but he insists that it does not permit Standard to solicit accounts which it had approved as his customers. . . .

In order to be successful in his business and to comply with the terms of his contract, the plaintiff was obliged to make substantial investments in storage facilities, delivery trucks, and other equipment. He was also obliged to hire employees. He was required to use his "best efforts" to promote the sale of Standard's products. Only if he sold Standard's products exclusively could it be said that he was using his best efforts to promote their sale. It is clear, then, that the contract limited his dealership to Standard products. Plaintiff was also required to sell a minimum quantity of other designated Standard petroleum products. If he at any time failed to sell the minimum quantity, Standard was at liberty to terminate its contract with him. Plaintiff's compensation was based exclusively on the sales he made to customers, which he secured through his own efforts. No compensation was available for the plaintiff if he obtained customers for Standard who bought directly from it. Nor does the contract obligate Standard to compensate him for sales made directly by Standard to plaintiff's customers. Yet, it reserves to Standard the right to exercise a strict surveillance over a substantial segment of plaintiff's business. In the exercise of this surveillance, Standard had access to the names of a large number of the plaintiff's customers and the amounts that the plaintiff sold to them.

The foregoing elements of the contract between plaintiff and Standard convince us that a condition must be implied that Standard would not solicit customers which had been obtained through plaintiff's efforts. The interpretation of the contract for which Standard contends would leave plaintiff and others in a position similar to his completely at the mercy of Standard. . . .

"We cannot accept [Standard's] construction of its meaning. An intention to make so one-sided an agreement is not readily to be inferred. . . .

"In every contract there is an implied covenant that neither party shall do anything that will have the effect of destroying or injuring the right of the other party to receive the fruits of the contract, which means that in every contract there exists a covenant of good faith and fair dealing." . . .

The implication of a condition finds support in many circumstances. . . . Plaintiff's only source of return on his substantial investments in the business was the sales he made to his customers. If Standard was at liberty to solicit as direct customers, as it contends . . . plaintiff was in a state of economic servility; we do not believe that the parties intended such a result at the time the contract was signed.

Standard argues that the provisions that plaintiff could sell only "on a nonexclusive basis" and that Standard had the "right to select its own customers" conflict with a condition which would limit its liberty to appropriate the customers of its jobbers. Perhaps Standard's position would be tenable if the two clauses upon which it depends stood alone. But we have noticed that the instrument must be construed in its entirety. From the considerations which have gone before, we must conclude that Standard was limited in its selection of customers to those which were not already customers of plaintiff. . . .

The contract before us is obviously a form contract prepared by Standard. It is a contract of "adhesion" in the sense that it is a take-it-or-leave-it whole. Such contracts are regarded by some authorities as anachronistic or inconsistent with real freedom of contract. At least they should be construed with an awareness of the inequality of the bargainers. . . . There is nothing novel about an implied condition that Standard will not negotiate with Perkins' customers during the term of any contract between Perkins and his customer, even though Standard has reserved the right to compete in the territory. Competition in the territory must be presumed to mean competition for uncommitted accounts.

§ 17:4. Difficulty of Proof

In certain situations, the legal rights of the parties are clear if the facts are known but there is difficulty in proving the facts. In certain instances, the law denies any remedy to any party on the ground that nothing can be proven, whereas in other cases the rules of law are modified to protect from hardship arising from the inability to prove a case.

In some instances, the difficulty arises because there are no witnesses to say what actually happened. The law admits circumstantial evidence of what happened whether or not there are actual witnesses. If the circumstantial evidence were not admitted, it would be necessary to throw many cases out of court that are now decided in favor of the plaintiff on the basis of the circumstantial evidence.

Consider the case of the air crash in which there will ordinarily be no surviving witnesses and very little, if any, circumstantial evidence beyond the scattered bits of wreckage. If the law insists on proof of what happened, it is apparent that the plaintiff will ordinarily lose and an airline defendant will automatically win. To avoid this hardship to plaintiffs, many states modify the ordinary rule of law as by placing upon the airline the burden of showing that it was not at fault.

The problem of proof arises where there are two or more successive wrongdoers and it is not possible to determine how much damage each one did. For example, when a coal mine unlawfully discharges mine refuse in a river which washes downstream and damages lower-lying farmland, the farmland owner may sue the coal mine. Suppose that three mines do this with the result that the farmer's land is worth $9,000 less than it was worth before. It is obviously impossible to prove how much of this $9,000 loss was caused by each of the three coal mines. It is unfair to require any mine to pay more than the share of damages which it had caused. At the same time, if the plaintiff is required to prove what portion of the damage was caused by each mine, he will never win.

MADDUX v. DONALDSON

362 Mich. 425, 108 N.W.2d 33 (1961)

Maddux was injured when the car in which she was riding was hit by a skidding truck, which was driven by Donaldson, and then by the car following the truck. Maddux sued Donaldson for injuries caused by both collisions. Donaldson claimed that he could only be sued for those injuries which Maddux could show were caused by him and not for the total amount of damages. Because Maddux could not show what part of her injuries were caused by Donaldson, the trial court dismissed the action. Maddux appealed.

OPINION BY SMITH, J. . . .

This is one of the most baffling of our current legal problems, critical because of the extensive use of expressways upon which large numbers of cars travel at high speeds in close proximity to one another. . . . The difficulty arises from the fact that we do not have a "joint" tort in the ordinary sense of the word, and thus it is argued that there cannot be joint and several liability. . . . Actually what we have is injury to plaintiffs resulting from the independent and tortious acts of two tort-feasors.

There is authority, in this situation, that plaintiff must separate the injuries, ascribing some to one tort-feasor and the balance to the other. much as a housewife separates the colored and the white goods before laundering. Such authority concludes that if plaintiff cannot make such differentiation, he cannot recover from either. This type of decision is well illustrated by the case of *Adams* v. *Hall,* 1829, 2 Vt. 9. In this case an owner of sheep suffered loss to his flock through the depredations of two dogs. The owners he sued jointly. It was shown at the trial, however, that they were not joint owners. In addition, there was no testimony as to which dog killed which sheep. In approving a [dismissal of the action] it was held that neither owner was liable for the actions of the other's dog, merely because they "did the mischief in company."

However defensible such a result may have been in this and cases similar in principle in an agrarian economy shortly after the American Revolution (and even this is open to question), we do not regard it as precedent governing the liability of automobile owners in what are known as "chain collisions" on today's highways. It should be unnecessary to spell out the differences between the social problems presented or the judicial policies involved in their solution. When we impose upon an injured plaintiff the necessity of proving which impact did which harm in a chain collision situation, what we are actually expressing is a judicial policy that it is better that a plaintiff, injured through no fault of his own, take nothing, than that a tort-feasor pay more than his theoretical share of the damages accruing out of a confused situation which his wrong has helped to create. . . . It is . . . utterly inconsistent with the [basis] of precedents going back at least to the year 1613 when the rule of joint and several liability dispensed with the necessity of plaintiff's proof of just which ruffian inflicted which injury when he was set upon by three. The reason behind the rule was impossibility, the impossibility of plaintiff's proving the origin of each of his injuries. Where the same impossibility exists today, our sensitivity to plaintiff's injury should be no less than that of the King's Bench to its plaintiff, whose "wounding . . . in a cruel and barbarous manner" was held to impose joint and several liability upon the defendants. It is clear that there is a manifest unfairness in "putting on the injured party the impossible burden of proving the specific shares of harm done by each. . . . Such results are simply the law's callous dullness to innocent sufferers. One would think that the obvious meanness of letting wrongdoers go scot free in such cases would cause the courts to think twice and to suspect some fallacy in their rule of law." . . .

It is our conclusion that if there is competent testimony, adduced either by plaintiff or defendant, the injuries are factually and medically separable, and that the liability for all such injuries and damages, or parts thereof, may be allocated with reasonable certainty to the impacts in turn, the jury will be instructed accordingly and mere difficulty in so doing will not relieve the triers of the facts of this responsibility. This merely follows the general rule that "where the independent concurring acts have caused distinct and separate injuries to the plaintiff, or where some reasonable means of apportioning the damages is evident, the courts generally will not hold the tort-feasors jointly and severally liable."

But if, on the other hand, the triers of the facts conclude that they cannot reasonably make the division of liability between the tort-feasors, this is the point where the road of authority divides. Much ancient authority, not in truth precedent, would say that the case is now over, and that plaintiff shall take nothing. Some modern courts, as well, hold that this is merely the case of the marauding dogs and the helpless sheep relitigated in the setting of a modern highway. The conclusion is erroneous. . . .

Is it better, as we asked heretofore, that a plaintiff, injured through no fault of his own, take nothing, rather than that a tort-feasor pay no more than his theoretical share of the damages accruing out of a confused situation which his wrong has helped to create? . . .

Here, then, is the essence of the problem—Where is the likelihood of injustice? We think it is in denying the blameless victim of traffic chain collision any recovery whatever. We perceive no reason why his tort-feasors should escape liability because of the very complexity of the injury created by their wrong. . . .

[Judgment reversed and new trial ordered.]

CONCURRING OPINION BY BLACK, EDWARDS, KAVANAGH and SOURIS, JJ., with SMITH, J. . . .

DISSENTING OPINION BY CARR, J. . . .

The rule has been consistently recognized in Michigan, as well as in other states, that a tort-feasor may not be held liable for damages for an injury not caused by such defendant's wrongful conduct. In 15 Am. Jur., p. 404, it is said:

"A defendant is liable only to the extent to which his acts have caused the injury complained of, and it follows that separate wrongs done by independent agents cannot be joined together to increase the responsibility of one of the wrongdoers, notwithstanding any difficulty there may be in determining what part of the injury or loss was the result of the acts or omissions of the defendant, and what part was the result of other causes." . . .

CONCURRING OPINION BY DETHMERS, C. J., and KELLY, J., with CARR, J. . . .

CONCURRING OPINION IN REVERSAL BY BLACK, J. . . .

Until now the Michigan rule has been settled. Where two or more wrongdoers separately cause the plaintiff to suffer an unknown or uncertain part or portion of the damages he has shown, each—hitherto—stood responsible to the plaintiff only for the harm caused by his tort, however difficult it may have been to establish the same. . . .

Now we affirm that, where the trier or triers of fact find they cannot ascertain the amount of damages each wrongdoer has inflicted, then such trier or triers are authorized to assess the plaintiff's damages against any one or all of such wrongdoers on ground that the latter have—in law—participated in the infliction of "a single, indivisible injury." . . .

These sentiments are recorded solely that lawyers may know that the former rule is now definitely modified to the extent, and only to the extent, we now attest by majority vote. Otherwise such former rule remains in full force.

§ 17:5. The Buyer of Real Estate

Traditionally the buyer of real estate is subject to the rule of "Let the buyer beware." Thus he gets nothing more than what the deed gives him.

In the absence of an express provision in the deed guaranteeing title or the fitness of a building, no such guarantee exists. No warranties are implied as in the sale of goods.

Historically, the difference between the law as to the sale of goods and the sale of real estate is explained in terms of the fact that the real estate law became rigidly fixed when feudalism existed, whereas the legal consequences of a sale of goods did not become established until centuries later when feudalism had gone and the then more "modern" social forces began to operate. In terms of practical expediency, the difference can be justified or at least explained in terms of the n factor. Compare the number of tracts of land that are sold in a 24-hour period to the number of cans of food sold in the same period of time. In the course of your entire life you will only buy a few homes, yet you will purchase literally thousands of cans of food. This suggests that there is more time to spend per land transaction so that no harm will be done if the real estate transaction gives the buyer only what he expressly contracted for, as he had all the time he needed to specify what he needed. Furthermore, the n factor comes into play in terms of the value of the transaction, the ordinary real estate transaction will involve many more dollars than any purchase of food transaction, with the result that society can leave it to the buyer to have an attorney to protect his interests, whereas it would be absurd to frame the rule of law so that you could not buy a can of soup from the supermarket without the presence of your attorney.

In spite of these possible rationalizations to support separate rules as to goods and real estate, the dividing line is beginning to break down and eventually the merchant-seller of homes will be held to the same responsibility as the merchant-seller of goods. To the man in the street it is becoming absurd to say that the merchant impliedly warrants that the umbrella which he sells will not leak, whereas the real estate developer does not make any implied warranty that the roof on the house that he sells will not leak. Increasingly the contents of a house becomes a mystery that cannot be determined by a mere inspection of the finished product. Today's home is a far cry from either the castle or the hut of the Eleventh Century, and the ordinary buyer cannot readily determine what he is getting when he buys a house.

HUMBER v. MORTON

426 S.W.2d 554 (Tex., 1968)

Humber purchased a new house from Morton who was in the business of building and selling new houses. The first time that she lit a fire in the fireplace, the house caught on fire because of a defect in the fireplace and the house was partially damaged. She sued Morton who defended in part on the theory that the rule of caveat emptor, or "Let the buyer beware," barred the suit.

OPINION BY NORVELL, J. . . .

We are of the opinion that the courts below erred in holding as a matter of law that Morton was not liable to Mrs. Humber because the doctrine of caveat emptor applied to the sale of a new house by a "builder-vendor" and consequently no implied warranty that the house was fit for human habitation arose from the sale. Accordingly, we reverse the judgments of the courts below and remand the cause to the district court for a . . . trial upon the merits.

It is undisputed that Morton built the house and then sold it as a new house. Did he thereby impliedly warrant that such house was constructed in a good workmanlike manner and was suitable for human habitation? We hold that he did. Under such circumstances, the law raises an implied warranty. . . .

Does the doctrine of caveat emptor apply to the sale of a new house by a builder-vendor?

Originally, the two great systems of jurisprudence applied different doctrines to sales of both real and personal property. The rule of the common law—caveat emptor—was fundamentally based upon the premise that the buyer and seller dealt at arm's length, and that the purchaser had means and opportunity to gain information concerning the subject matter of the sale which were equal to those of the seller. . . .

In 1884, the Supreme Court of the United States applied the doctrine of implied warranty, the antithesis of caveat emptor, to a real property situation involving false work and pilings driven into the bed of the Maumee River. The case of *Kellogg Bridge Company* v. *Hamilton,* 110 U.S. 108, 3 S.Ct. 537, 28 L.Ed. 86, arose in connection with the construction of a bridge. The Supreme Court . . . said:

"Although the plaintiff in error (Kellogg Bridge Company, defendant in the trial court) is not a manufacturer, in the common acceptation of that word, it made or constructed the false work which it sold to Hamilton. The transaction, if not technically a sale, created between the parties the relation of vendor and vendee. The business of the company was the construction of bridges. By its occupation, apart from its contract with the railroad company, it held itself out as reasonably competent to do work of that character. Having partially executed its contract with the railroad company, it made an arrangement with Hamilton whereby the latter undertook, among other things, to prepare all necessary false work, and, by a day named, and in the best manner, to erect the bridge then being constructed by the bridge company— Hamilton to assume and pay for such work and materials as that company had up to that time done and furnished. Manifestly, it was contemplated by the parties that Hamilton should commence where the company left off. It certainly was not expected that he should incur the expense of removing the false work put up by the company and commence anew. On the contrary, he agreed to assume and pay for, and therefore it was expected by the company that he should use, such false work as it had previously prepared. It is unreasonable to suppose that he would buy that which he did not intend to use, or that the company would require him to assume and pay for that which it did not expect him to use, or which was unfit for use. . . . In the cases of sales by manufacturers of their own articles for particular purposes, communicated to them at the time, the argument was uniformly pressed that, as the buyer could have required an express warranty, none should be implied. But, plainly, such an argument impeaches the whole doctrine of implied warranty, for there can be no case of a sale of personal property in which the buyer may not, if he chooses, insist on an express warranty against latent defects.

"All the facts are present which, upon any view of the adjudged cases, must be held essential in an implied warranty. The transaction was, in effect, a sale of this false work, constructed by a company whose business it was to do such work; to be used in the same way the maker intended to use it, and the latent defects in which, as the maker knew, the buyer could not, by any inspection or examination, at the time discover; the buyer did not, because in the nature of things he could not, rely on his own judgment; and, in view of the circumstances of the case, and the relations of the parties, he must be deemed to have relied on the judgment of the company, which alone of the parties to the contract had or could have knowledge of the manner in which the work had been done. The law, therefore, implies a warranty that this false work was reasonably suitable for such use as was contemplated by both parties. . . ."

In Texas, the doctrine of caveat emptor began its fade-out at an early date. In *Wintz* v. *Morrison,* 17 Tex. 369 (1856), involving a sale of personal property, the Texas Supreme Court quoted with approval the following from Story on Sales as to the trend of Nineteenth Century decisions:

"[T]he tendency of all the modern cases of warranty is to enlarge the responsibility of the seller, to construe every affirmation by him to be a warranty, and frequently to imply a warranty on his part, from acts and circumstances, wherever they were relied upon by the buyer. The maxim of *caveat emptor* seems gradually to be restricted in its operation and limited in its dominion, and beset with the circumvallations of the modern doctrine of implied warranty, until it can no longer claim the empire over the law of sales, and is but a shadow of itself. . . ."

While in numerous common-law jurisdictions, the caveat emptor doctrine as applied to the vendor-builder—new house situation has overstayed its time, it was said by way of dicta in a Texas Court of Civil Appeals case in 1944 that: "By offering the (new) house for sale as a new and complete structure appellant impliedly warranted that it was properly constructed and of good material and specifically that it had a good foundation, . . ."

This decision has been described as "a preview of things to come." . . . See also, Williston on Contracts (3rd Ed. Jaeger) § 926A, wherein it is said: "It would be much better if this enlightened approach (implied warranty, *Jones* v. *Gatewood,* 381 P.2d 158 [Okl.]) were generally adopted with respect to the sale of new houses for it would tend to discourage much of the sloppy work and jerry-building that has become perceptible over the years." . . .

The Glisan case (*Glisan* v. *Smolenske*), 153 Colo. 274, 387 P.2d 260 (1963), was factually similar to the hypothetical example heretofore set out in this opinion. Smolenske had agreed to purchase a house from Glisan while it was under construction. The court propounded and answered the implied warranty question, thusly:

"Was there an implied warranty that the house, when completed, would be fit for habitation? There is a growing body of law on this question, which, if followed, requires an answer in the affirmative.

"It is the rule that there is an implied warranty where the contract relates to a house which is still in the process of construction, where the vendor's workmen are still on the job, and particularly where completion is not accomplished until the house has arrived at the contemplated condition—namely, finished and fit for habitation. . . ."

In the next year, 1964, the Colorado Supreme Court in *Carpenter* v. *Donohoe,* 154 Colo. 78, 388 P.2d 399, extended the implied warranty rule announced by it in Glisan to cover sales of a new house by a builder-vendor. The court said: "That a different rule should apply to the purchaser of a house which is near completion than would apply to one who purchases a new house seems incongruous. To say that the former may rely on an implied warranty and the latter cannot is recognizing a distinction without a reasonable basis for it. . . . We hold that the implied warranty doctrine is extended to include agreements between builder-vendors and purchasers for the sale of newly constructed buildings, completed at the time of contracting. There is an implied warranty that builder-vendors have complied with the building code of the area in which the structure is located. Where, as here, a home is the subject of sale, there are implied warranties that the home was built in workmanlike manner and is suitable for habitation."

While it is not necessary for us to pass upon a situation in which the vendor-purchaser relationship is absent, the case of *Schipper* v. *Levitt & Sons,* 44 N.J. 70, 207 A.2d 314 (1965), is important as much of the reasoning set forth in the opinion is applicable here. The Supreme Court of New Jersey recognized "the need for imposing on builder-vendors an implied obligation of reasonable workmanship and habitability which survives delivery of the deed." This was a case in which a person other than a purchaser had been injured by a defective water heater which had been installed in a new house by Levitt, the builder-vendor. The opinion cited and quotes from *Carpenter* v. *Donohoe* but proceeded upon the theory of strict liability in tort. The court placed emphasis upon the close analogy between a defect in a new house and a manufactured chattel. The opinion states:

"The law should be based on current concepts of what is right and just and the judiciary should be alert to the never-ending need for keeping its common law principles abreast of the times. Ancient distinctions which make no sense in today's society and tend to discredit the law should be readily rejected. . . .

"When a vendee buys a development house from an advertised model, as in a Levitt or in a comparable project, he clearly relies on the skill of the developer and on its implied representation that the house will be erected in reasonably workmanlike manner and will be reasonably fit for habitation. He has no architect or other professional adviser of his own, he has no real competency to inspect on his own, his actual examination is, in the nature of things, largely superficial, and his opportunity for obtaining meaningful protective changes in the conveying documents prepared by the builder-vendor is negligible. If there is improper construction, such as a defective heating system or a defective ceiling, stairway and the like, the well-being of the vendee and others is seriously endangered and serious injury is foreseeable. The public interest dictates that if such injury does result from the defective construction, its cost should be borne by the responsible developer who created the danger and who is in the better economic position to bear the loss rather than by the injured party who justifiably relied on the developer's skill and implied representation."

In *Bethlahmy* v. *Bechtel*, 415 P.2d 698 (Idaho, 1966), it appeared that the trial court had rendered judgment in accordance with the 1959 holding of the Supreme Court of Oregon in *Steiber* v. *Palumbo*, a much cited case which is relied upon by the defendant here. The specific finding of the trial court was: "There are no implied warranties in the sale of real property. *Steiber* v. *Palumbo*, 219 Oreg. 479, 347 P.2d 978 [78 A.L.R.2d 440] (1959); Annot., 78 A.L.R.2d 446. The sale of this home carried with it, absent an express warranty, no promise that the floor would not leak."

The Idaho court was then called upon to deal with the Oregon decision and the later decisions of the Colorado Supreme Court in Carpenter and that of the New Jersey Supreme Court in Schipper. After a careful review of many decisions, including the Oregon, Colorado, and New Jersey cases mentioned, the court said: "The Schipper decision is important here because: (1) it illustrates the recent change in the attitude of the courts toward the application of the doctrine of caveat emptor in actions between the builder-vendor and purchaser of newly constructed dwellings; (2) it draws analogy between the present case and the long-accepted application of implied warranty of fitness in sales of personal property; and (3) the opinion had the unanimous approval of the participating justices. . . .

"The foregoing decisions all (except for one case) rendered subsequent to the 1959 Oregon decision, relied upon by the trial court, show the trend of judicial opinion is to invoke the doctrine of implied warranty of fitness in cases involving sales of new houses by the builder. The old rule of caveat emptor does not satisfy the demands of justice in such cases. The purchase of a home is not an everyday transaction for the average family, and in many instances is the most important transaction of a lifetime. To apply the rule of caveat emptor to an inexperienced buyer, and in favor of a builder who is daily engaged in the business of building and selling houses, is manifestly a denial of justice. . . ."

We see no reason for any distinction between the sale of a new house and the sale of personalty, especially in a suit between the original parties to the contract, one of whom constructed the house in question. It was the seller's duty to perform the work in a good and workmanlike manner and to furnish adequate materials, and failing to do so, we believe the rule of implied warranty of fitness applies. . . .

If at one time in Texas the rule of caveat emptor had application to the sale of a new house by a vendor-builder, that time is now past. The decisions and legal writings herein referred to afford numerous examples and situations illustrating the harshness and injustice of the rule when applied to the sale of new houses by a builder-vendor. . . . Obviously, the ordinary purchaser is not in a position to ascertain when there is a defect in a chimney flue, or vent of a heating apparatus, or whether the plumbing work covered by a concrete slab foundation is faulty. . . . The common law is not afflicted with the rigidity of the law of the Medes and the Persians "which altereth not," and as stated in Cardozo in "The Nature of the Judicial Process," pp. 150-151 (quoted in 415 P.2d 698):

"That court best serves the law which recognizes that the rules of law which grew up in a remote generation may, in the fullness of experience, be found to serve another generation badly, and which discards the old rule when it finds that another rule of law represents what should be according to the established and settled judgment of society, and no considerable property rights have become vested in reliance upon the old rule. . . ."

The caveat emptor rule as applied to new houses is an anachronism patently out of harmony with modern home buying practices. It does a disservice not only to the ordinary prudent purchaser but to the industry itself by lending encouragement to the unscrupulous, fly-by-night operator and purveyor of shoddy work.

The judgments of the courts below are reversed and the cause remanded for trial in accordance with this opinion.

§ 17:6. Production of Evidence

As will be discussed in Chapter 30, modern procedure permits parties to a lawsuit to obtain discovery to learn the facts of the case. Ignoring the details of the procedure involved, a party is permitted to ask the other party and third person various questions, and the person asked is required to answer to the same extent as though he were a witness at a regular trial.

SECURITY INDUSTRIES v. FICKUS

439 P.2d 172 (Alaska, 1968)

Fickus purchased a camper unit and a camping furnace, an oven, and a gas lamp manufactured by four different manufacturers. Members of his family were killed or injured by fumes which emanated from this equipment. When Fickus sued the manufacturers, one of them, Security Industries, requested the court to require the production of all written reports furnished to or in the possession of any of the parties with respect to the testing and operation of the items of camping equipment so that it could determine whether the harm had been caused by its product or the product of one of the other defendants.

OPINION BY RABINOWITZ, J. . . .

The superior court entered an order denying petitioner's discovery motion. From the text of the superior court's order, it appears that the denial was [in part] based upon the court's belief that . . . the reports were beyond the reach of discovery procedures because they were the work products of the attorneys involved.

Before discussing in detail the issues which appertain to the discoverability of reports of expert witnesses, we believe reference to two decisions of this court concerning our rules of discovery is necessary. In our view the discovery philosophy and principles we espoused in *Miller* v. *Harpster* [1] and *Mathis* v. *Hilderbrand* [2] control resolution of the questions raised in this review proceeding.

In *Miller* v. *Harpster* we granted review of a Civil Rule 34 order which required a party and his attorney to produce for inspection all written statements of witnesses to the automobile collision there in question. At the superior court level, the motion to produce was opposed on the grounds that production of the written statements would violate the attorney work-product rule of *Hickman* v. *Taylor;* [3] would unfairly give opposing counsel the benefit of defense counsel's preparation; and was unwarranted since there was a lack of compliance by movant with Civil Rule 34's requirement of a showing of good cause.

In rejecting the unfairness contention, . . . we said in part that:

"The question should not be decided on the basis of what is fair or unfair to petitioner's counsel, but rather on the basis of what is most likely to attain the objectives of the rule.

"The broad policy of all of our rules permitting discovery is to eliminate surprise at the trial and to make it convenient for the parties to find and preserve all available evidence concerning the facts in issue, thereby encouraging the settlement or expeditious trial of litigation. . . .

"Counsel have been retained by their clients to bring about an early favorable end to the litigation. They do not acquire property rights in the contents of the written statements they obtain. Experience has proved that the ends of justice are more likely to be served by liberal rules of discovery requiring full disclosure of all unprivileged relevant matter. No purpose of the rule is to reward diligent counsel in a manner that could result in the suppression of knowledge of relevant facts. . . ."

Mathis v. *Hilderbrand* is also of significance to the resolution of the discovery questions raised in the case at bar. There the issue presented for review was whether an attending physician of the plaintiff in a personal injury action could be deposed prior to trial. From an analysis of the historical antecedents of the physician-patient privilege, the precedents, and legal commentary regarding the privilege, it was concluded that the commencement of a personal injury action constituted a waiver of the physician-patient privilege and that it was therefore permissible to take the deposition of plaintiff's attending physician prior to trial. In reaching this conclusion, we said:

"Courts commonly hold that the plaintiff waives the privilege when he voluntarily testifies concerning the injuries being sued upon. Increasingly it is being held that common sense dictates against enforcing the privilege until it has actually been waived during trial, as it almost invariably must be, and then in fairness being required to grant the defendant's request for a continuance to meet the new matter disclosed.

---

[1] 392 P.2d 21 (Alaska, 1964).

[2] 416 P.2d 8 (Alaska, 1966).

[3] 329 U.S. 495, 67 S.Ct. 385, 91 L.Ed. 451 (1947).

"We are convinced that a rigid enforcement of the privilege under the facts of this case would serve no useful purpose and might result in injustice. We accordingly hold that the plaintiffs in this personal injury action waived the physician-patient privilege by the commencement of the action to the extent that attending physicians may be required to testify on pretrial deposition with respect to the injuries sued upon."

Tested against the criteria and discovery philosophy pronounced in the *Mathis* v. *Hilderbrand* and *Miller* v. *Harpster* cases, the trial court's denial of petitioner's discovery motion is erroneous.

Courts have developed three separate rationales for precluding discovery of reports of experts or the taking of their depositions prior to trial. We are not persuaded that any of the reasons advanced in the decisions thus far, either in and of themselves, or collectively, warrant holding discovery procedures inapplicable to experts or their reports. Upholding of the lower court's denial of discovery in the case at bar would be tantamount to repudiation of the Mathis and Miller decisions, and would negate what appears to us to be a logical extension of the rationale of these cases.

Miller v. *Harpster* anticipated our present rejection of the work-product explanation which has been employed to deny discovery of expert witnesses' reports. In *Hickman* v. *Taylor,* the Supreme Court of the United States first enunciated the "work product" doctrine. The rationale for the work-product rule was formulated in the following manner:

"In performing his various duties, however, it is essential that a lawyer work with a certain degree of privacy, free from unnecessary intrusion by opposing parties and their counsel. . . . This work is reflected, of course, in interviews, statements, memoranda, correspondence, briefs, mental impressions, personal beliefs, and countless other tangible and intangible ways— aptly though roughly termed by the Circuit Court of Appeals in this case as the 'work product of the lawyer.' Were such materials open to opposing counsel on mere demand, much of what is now put down in writing would remain unwritten. *An attorney's thoughts, heretofore inviolate, would not be his own. . . . The effect on the legal profession would be demoralizing. And the interests of the clients and the cause of justice would be poorly served."* (Emphasis supplied.)

Several lower federal court decisions have extended the Hickman work-product doctrine to bar discovery of the contents of experts' reports which have been furnished to the party or to his attorney. According to one authority, the reasoning underlying these decisions is that:

"At the root of the more protective attitude evinced in this situation has been a long-standing inclination to consider an expert practically an assistant counsel and, therefore, to treat him for purposes of discovery similarly to an attorney."

On the other hand, extension of the work-product doctrine to experts has been criticized by commentators. One writer states:

"Although most of the cases which have considered the application of the work product doctrine to experts have rejected such an extension, it has been applied to preclude discovery in a number of cases. Extension of this doctrine to experts without qualification appears to be unsound. Unlike an attorney's, client's or investigator's recollection of potential witnesses' conversations or even the statements obtained from potential witnesses, expert information in the form of opinions and conclusions and the support therefor constitute evidence. . . ."

We are in agreement with the authorities which have declined to extend the Hickman work-product rule to shelter reports of experts from discovery. In our view, discovery of an expert's report does not violate the lawyer-privacy rationale of the Hickman rule. The conclusions and opinions of an expert, unlike those of an attorney, constitute relevant evidence and should be made subject to discovery procedures.

In addition to the work-product doctrine, several decisions have based denial of discovery of the reports of experts upon the theory of the existence of an attorney-client privilege. . . .

The attorney-client privilege should be applied only to protect communications, not facts. . . . [T]he experts' observations and conclusions themselves, whether or not contained within a report, and even if based to some extent on communications of the client, are facts which, if relevant, constitute evidence.

We hold that the attorney-client privilege is not available to insulate the expert or his reports from discovery. As a matter of policy, the communication of relevant facts by an expert to an attorney should not place such facts beyond the ambit of discovery procedures. To hold otherwise would be contrary to the objectives of our discovery rules and result in an indefensible extension of the attorney-client privilege.

The third foundation for denial of discovery of experts and of their reports which has been advanced is the "unfairness" argument: . . .

"While the Rules of Civil Procedure were designed to permit liberal examination and discovery, they were not intended to be made the vehicle through which one litigant could make use of his opponent's preparation of his case. To use them in such a manner would penalize the diligent and place a premium on laziness."

Another facet of the unfairness argument places emphasis upon the financial aspects of the problem in addition to the diligence factor. It is argued that the party has a property interest in the conclusions his expert has prepared for litigation, and that to permit their discovery would amount to the taking of another's property without compensation. . . .

We believe *Miller* v. *Harpster* to be dispositive of these "unfairness" contentions. Miller subordinated any potential element of unfairness to opposing counsel to the paramount criterion of the attainment of the objectives of our discovery rule (i.e., elimination of surprise at trial, location and preservation of evidence, and the encouragement of settlement or expeditious trial of litigation). In Miller, we specifically held that counsel did not possess any property rights in reports of nonexpert witnesses.

In fashioning an order to guard against any element of unfairness, trial judges are vested with sufficient discretion and flexibility to minimize or eliminate the possibility of any unfairness actually occurring. Under our rules of procedure, the trial judge can condition discovery upon payment of the experts' expenses or any reasonable part thereof. The court is also empowered to make discovery of experts or their reports reciprocal by providing for simultaneous exchanges of reports as well as appropriate timing of the taking of depositions. A further possibility is the deferral of any action on discovery motions until all parties to the litigation have disclosed the identity of the experts they intend to call at trial. Imaginative and creative action by the trial judge is called for in administering the discovery ruling we have enunciated in this case. . . .

We, therefore, conclude that reports of experts and experts themselves are within the ambit of our discovery rules. Adhering to the discovery principles which were articulated in Miller and Mathis, we believe that the ends of justice and the attainment of the objectives of our rules of discovery will be furthered by permitting the discovery of reports of experts as well as the taking of their pretrial depositions.

The superior court's order denying petitioner's Civil Rule 34 motion is reversed and the case remanded for further proceedings not inconsistent with the foregoing.

Questions for Review

1. Define the social force of protection from hardship situations.

2. Give illustrations of its application.

3. Analyze each opinion in this chapter in terms of the social forces involved in the decision. See § 5:5 for a list of the social forces. With respect to each opinion, explain why the prevailing social forces prevailed and why those rejected did not. In each case in which there is an dissenting opinion, also make this analysis for the dissenting opinion.

4-8. On the basis of the social forces involved, what decision should be made in each of the following cases?

4. *Release. Unknown condition.* Does a release bar suit for a condition unknown to the releasor when the release was executed, where the release stated that it covered "any and all known and unknown, foreseen and unforeseen bodily and personal injuries . . . and the consequences thereof . . . ?" *Ranta* v. *Rake*, 91 Idaho 376, 421 P.2d 747.

5. *Product liability. Existence of defect.* Is a tire manufacturer liable for injury sustained when an automobile tire collapsed without any blowout? *Markwell* v. *General Tire and Rubber Co.* [C.A.7th] 367 F.2d 748.

6. *Impossibility. Contract performance.* The Transatlantic Financing Corp. made a contract with the United States to haul a cargo of wheat from the United States to a safe port in Iran. The normal route lay through the Suez Canal. As the result of the nationalization of the Canal by Egypt and the subsequent international crisis which developed, the Canal was closed and it was necessary for Transatlantic to go around Africa to get to the destination. It then sued for additional compensation because of the longer route on the theory that it had been discharged from its obligation to carry to Iran for the amount named in the contract because of "impossibility." Was this correct? *Transatlantic Financing Corp.* v. *United States,* [C.A.Dist.Col.] 363 F.2d 312.

7. *Premises liability. After hours escape.* Is a theater liable for the harm sustained by a young child patron who fell asleep during the show and was injured when he attempted to escape through a bathroom window after the theater had been closed for the night? *Love* v. *Hudson,* 115 Ga.App. 222, 154 S.E.2d 419.

8. *Insurance. Consortium.* May a husband recover on an insurance policy for loss resulting to injury to his wife where she had recovered up to policy limit which was stated as a specified maximum as to "each person" and limited recovery with respect to "all damages sustained because of injury to one person, including damages for . . . loss of services . . . ?" *Napier* v. *Banks,* 9 OhioApp.2d 265, 224 N.E.2d 158.

9-12. What social forces were involved, which prevailed, and which were defeated in the following decisions?

9. *Enterprise liability. House settling damage.* Although earth on which house was built was satisfactory foundation for house, the contractor is liable for settling damage to house that resulted from shrinkage of earth because a number of large trees near the house absorbed excessive moisture from the soil, on theory that contractor should have foreseen that this could result. *Wurst* v. *Pruyn,* 250 La. 1109, 202 So.2d 268.

10. *Indemnity. Own negligence.* A provision that the "safety of all persons . . . shall be the sole responsibility of the contractor" is not to be construed as an agreement by the contractor to indemnify the owner for his negligence that causes harm to the contractor or his employees, for such a provision violates public policy where there is a great disparity of bargaining power between the large owner and the small local contractor. *United States Steel* v. *Warner* [C.A.10th] 378 F.2d 995.

11. *Banks. Fiduciary funds.* Where a depositor authorized her son to sign checks on her account, the son's authority was not limited to the use of checks but included instructions to the bank to transfer funds from the checking account to another account in the bank in the name of the son in trust for the parent; and the bank is not liable to the mother when the son thereafter misappropriated such funds, as long as the bank had acted in good faith without knowledge that the son was committing a breach of any fiduciary obligation. *Rheinberger* v. *First National Bank,* 276 Minn. 194, 150 N.W.2d 37 (Uniform Fiduciaries Act).

12. *Successive tort-feasors. Apportionment.* Where a motorist is involved in four collisions over a period of years, the jury may roughly apportion the damage among the four defendants but if this cannot be done, it is proper to hold each defendant liable for an equal share of the total damages. *Loui* v. *Oakley,* Hawaii, 438 P.2d 393.

Chapter 18

PROTECTION FROM GOVERNMENT ACTION

§ 18:1. Generally

Protection from oppression by the government has loomed large in the culture and legal system of our country. In addition to the limitations on the power of government in the Constitution, the first ten Amendments evidence the great concern of the framers of the Constitution for protection from oppression by the government. Although the era of rebellion against George III has long since passed, much of the fear of government oppression continues. In some instances, it is the fear of local police rather than the fear of "official" government which underlies the particular decision.

In this connection, it is important to note again the fact that beginning in 1937 the Supreme Court of the United States held that the more fundamental guarantees of the Bill of Rights of the United States Constitution, which limited action by Congress, were also limitations upon action by the states. This is important because it marks the beginning of a new era of concern over the desire to protect the dignity and freedom of the individual from all dangers—including official oppression.

§ 18:2. Rules of Evidence

Many of the rules of evidence are designed to protect the parties, and particularly the defendant in a criminal prosecution from being prejudiced. Thus it is generally not permitted to show that the defendant had committed

258

other crimes for fear that the jury will tend to think that since the defendant was a bad man, he must necessarily be guilty of the crime with which he was charged; or even that if he were innocent of the crime in question, it was about time that he paid for some of his crimes.

Likewise, hearsay evidence is excluded. This means that a witness generally cannot state in court that someone told him that the defendant had committed the crime in question. Such a statement is not admissible because there is a great likelihood that the jury will believe that it is true; and since the declarant whose statement would thus be repeated is not himself in court, it is impossible to cross examine the absentee to show that he was mistaken or lying or was not present at the scene of the crime. Likewise, it is very difficult to show that the witness who is in court was lying as by showing that in fact no one ever told him that the defendant had committed the crime. Prejudice may also arise through the use of scientific tests and experiments unless their accuracy has been sufficiently established. There is the danger that anything which looks like a scientific device will be believed to be true and infallible.

ARIZONA v. VALDEZ

91 Ariz. 274, 371 P.2d 894 (1962)

Valdez was indicted for the crime of possessing narcotics. He agreed to take a lie detector test and further agreed that the results of the test could be admitted in evidence at his trial. The test indicated his guilt and he objected to the introduction of such results in evidence. He was convicted and then appealed.

OPINION BY UDALL, V.C.J. . . .

"In a criminal case, if prior to trial the defense attorney, on behalf of his client and with his client's consent, and the deputy county attorney agrees in a written stipulation that the results of a polygraph test, to be taken by the defendant, will be admissible as evidence at the trial, on behalf of either the State of Arizona or the accused, may the trial court admit the results of the test over the objection of defense counsel?" . . .

The polygraph or lie-detector is a pneumatically operated device which simultaneously records changes in a subject's blood pressure, pulse, respiration rate and depth, psychogalvanic skin reflex (skin resistance to electrical current) and, in some cases, muscular activity. "The basis for the use of the so-called lie-detector . . . is the hypothesis that conscious deception can be deduced from certain involuntary physiological responses in the same manner as physicians diagnose various diseases. The thesis is that lying engenders emotional disturbances which are transmuted into tangible bodily manifestations." The machine itself reflects and records only the subject's physiological responses to the questions propounded by the operator. He then interprets the poly*graph* (meaning, literally, "many pictures") and determines whether the subject is lying.

I *Admissibility in General*

The first reported American case involving admissibility of lie-detector evidence was *Frye* v. *United States,* 54 App. D.C. 46, 293 F. 1013, 34 A.L.R. 145 (1923). Frye, convicted of murder in the second degree, appealed alleging as his sole assignment of error the trial court's refusal to allow an expert to testify as to the results of a systolic blood pressure test to which Frye had submitted. In affirming the conviction and in upholding the trial court's refusal of the proffered testimony the Circuit Court observed:

"Just when a scientific principle or discovery crosses the line between the experimental and demonstrable stages is difficult to define. Somewhere in this twilight zone the evidential force of the principle must be recognized, and while courts will go a long way in admitting expert testimony deduced from a well-recognized scientific principle or discovery, the thing from which the deduction is made must be sufficiently established to have gained general acceptance in the particular field in which it belongs.

"We think the systolic blood pressure deception test has not yet gained such standing and scientific recognition among physiological and psychological authorities as would justify the courts in admitting expert testimony deduced from the discovery, development, and experiments thus far made." . . .

And the judicial attitude toward lie-detector evidence expressed in Bohner has not changed. . . . Thus, in 1961 a New Jersey appellate court was correct in pointing out:

". . . that there is not a single reported decision where an appellate court has permitted the introduction of the results of a polygraph or lie-detector test as evidence in the absence of a sanctioning agreement or stipulation between the parties." *State* v. *Arnwine,* 67 N.J.Super. 483, 495, 171 A.2d 124, 131 (1961). . . . Appellate courts have reversed convictions in cases where lie-detector results unfavorable to defendants were placed before the juries inferentially. . . . Further, it is uniformly held that a defendant is not permitted to introduce evidence of his willingness to take a lie-detector test. . . . Nor can a defendant's refusal to submit to polygraphic interrogation be shown by the state directly . . . or indirectly. . . .

But judicial reluctance to recognize generally the worth of lie-detector evidence in the court room has not been due to mere inertia. . . . " '. . . . factors which occasion the chief difficulties in the diagnosis of deception by the lie-detector technique. . . ."

" '(1) Emotional tension—"nervousness"—experienced by a subject who is innocent and telling the truth regarding the offense in question, but who is nevertheless affected by

" '(a) fear induced by the mere fact that suspicion or accusation has been directed against him, and particularly so in instances where the subject has been extensively interrogated or perhaps physically abused by investigators prior to the time of the interview and testing by the lie-detector examiner; and

" '(b) a guilt complex involving another offense of which he is guilty.

" '(2) Physiological abnormalities, such as

" '(a) excessively high or excessively low blood pressure;

" '(b) diseases of the heart;

" '(c) respiratory disorders, etc.

" '(3) Mental abnormalities, such as

" '(a) feeblemindedness, as in idiots, imbeciles, and morons;

" '(b) psychoses or insanities, as in manic depressives, paranoids, schizophrenics, paretics, etc.;

" '(c) psychoneuroses, and psychopathia, as among so-called "peculiar" or "emotionally unstable" persons—those who are neither psychotic nor normal, and who form the borderline between these two groups.

" '(4) Unresponsiveness in a lying or guilty subject, because of

" '(a) lack of fear of detection;

" '(b) apparent ability to consciously control responses by means of certain mental sets or attitudes;

" '(c) a condition of "subshock" or "adrenal exhaustion" at the time of the test;

" '(d) rationalization of the crime in advance of the test to such an extent that lying about the offense arouses little or no emotional disturbance;

" '(e) extensive interrogation prior to the test.

" '(5) Unobserved muscular movements which produce ambiguities or misleading indications in the blood pressure tracing.' " . . . And in addition to the above enumerated scientific shortcomings of the polygraph technique the following objections to the unrestricted use of its results in the court room have been registered:

(1) The supposed tendency of judges and juries to treat lie-detector evidence as conclusive on the issue of defendants' guilt. . . .

(2) Lack of standardization of test procedure, . . . examiner qualifications and instrumentation.

(3) Difficulty for jury evaluation of examiners' opinions.

Finally, it appears ". . . that at the present time the technique is not an 'accepted' one among the scientists whose approval is a prerequisite to judicial recognition." . . . Of course absolute infallibility is not the standard for admissibility of scientific evidence. But at this time it seems wise to demand greater standardization of the instrument, technique and examiner qualifications and the endorsement by a larger segment of the psychology and physiology branches of science before permitting general use of lie-detector evidence in court. Accordingly, in the absence of a stipulation lie-detector evidence should not be received in an Arizona court for the present.

II *Admissibility Upon Stipulation*

. . . .

Generally speaking, even those experts who warn against admissibility in the absence of a stipulation favor admission of lie-detector evidence upon a proper stipulation. And although polygraphic interrogation has not attained that degree of scientific acceptance in the fields to which it belongs to be admissible at the instance of either the state or defendant . . . it has been considerably improved since *Frye* v. *United States,* supra, was decided in 1923. A conservative estimate of the accuracy of such tests is as follows:

(1) In 75-80 percent of the cases the examination correctly indicates the guilt or innocence of the accused;

(2) in 15-20 percent of the cases the results are too indefinite to warrant a conclusion by the examiner one way or the other; and

(3) 5 percent or less is the margin of proven error.

With improvement in and standardization of instrumentation, technique and examiner qualifications the margin of proven error is certain to shrink. "Modern court procedure must embrace recognized modern conditions of mechanics, psychology, sociology, medicine, or other sciences, philosophy, and history. The failure to do so will only serve to question the ability of courts to efficiently administer justice." Chappell, J., concurring in *Boeche* v. *State,* 151 Neb. 368, 383, 37 N.W.2d 593, 596, 600 (1949). Although much remains to be done to perfect the lie-detector as a means of determining credibility we think it has been developed to a state in which its results are probative enough to warrant admissibility upon stipulation. . . .

Accordingly, and subject to the qualifications announced herein, we hold that polygraphs and expert testimony relating thereto are admissible upon stipulation in Arizona criminal cases. And in such cases the lie-detector evidence is admissible to corroborate other evidence of a defendant's participation in the crime charged. If he takes the stand, such evidence is admissible to corroborate or impeach his own testimony.

The "qualifications" are as follows:

(1) That the county attorney, defendant and his counsel all sign a written stipulation providing for defendant's submission to the test and for the subsequent admission at trial of the graphs and the examiner's opinion thereon on behalf of either defendant or the state.

(2) That notwithstanding the stipulation the admissibility of the test results is subject to the discretion of the trial judge, i.e. if the trial judge is not convinced that the examiner is qualified or that the test was conducted under proper conditions he may refuse to accept such evidence.

(3) That if the graphs and examiner's opinion are offered in evidence, the opposing party shall have the right to cross-examine the examiner respecting:

(a) the examiner's qualifications and training;

(b) the conditions under which the test was administered;

(c) the limitations of and possibilities for error in the technique of polygraphic interrogation; and

(d) at the discretion of the trial judge, any other matter deemed pertinent to the inquiry.

(4) That if such evidence is admitted, the trial judge should instruct the jury that the examiner's testimony does not tend to prove or disprove any element of the crime with which a defendant is charged but at most tends only to indicate that at the time of the examination defendant was not telling the truth. Further, the jury members should be instructed that it is for them to determine what corroborative weight and effect such testimony should be given. . . .

§ 18:3.   Obtaining Evidence

When evidence is obtained by police officers by illegally entering a building without a search warrant, any evidence that they find is not admissible in evidence. Here the fear is that the officers will falsely plant incriminating evidence after unlawfully entering the premises and will then pretend to find it in order to obtain a conviction of the defendant. As the counter-argument, it can be said that if the incriminating evidence is in fact found on the premises, the law should not be required to shut its eyes to the existence of such evidence once it is found to exist.

KATZ v. UNITED STATES

389 U.S. 347 (1967)

Katz was suspected of making bets by telephone. FBI agents placed an electronic listening device on the top of the roof of a public telephone booth and recorded statements made by Katz into the phone. These recordings of his half of the telephone conversations were admitted in evidence at a trial in spite of his objections. He was convicted of placing bets by phone and appealed.

OPINION BY STEWART, J. . . .

The petitioner [Katz raises two] questions as follows:
"A. Whether a public telephone booth is a constitutionally protected area so that evidence obtained by attaching an electronic listening recording device to the top of such a booth is obtained in violation of the right to privacy of the user of the booth.
"B. Whether physical penetration of a constitutionally protected area is necessary before a search and seizure can be said to be violative of the Fourth Amendment to the United States Constitution."
We decline to adopt this formulation of the issues. In the first place, the correct solution of Fourth Amendment problems is not necessarily promoted by incantation of the phrase "constitutionally protected area." Secondly, the Fourth Amendment cannot be translated into a general constitutional "right to privacy." That Amendment protects individual privacy against certain kinds of governmental intrusion. . . . But the protection of a person's *general* right to privacy—his right to be let alone by other people—is, like the protection of his property and of his very life, left largely to the law of the individual States.
Because of the misleading way the issues have been formulated, the parties have attached great significance to the characterization of the telephone booth from which the petitioner placed his calls. The petitioner has strenuously argued that the booth was a "constitutionally protected area." The Government has maintained with equal vigor that it was not. But this effort to decide whether or not a given "area," viewed in the abstract, is "constitutionally protected" deflects attention from the problem presented by this case. For the Fourth Amendment protects people, not places. . . .

The Government stresses the fact that the telephone booth from which the petitioner made his calls was constructed partly of glass, so that he was as visible after he entered it as he would have been if he had remained outside. But what he sought to exclude when he entered the booth was not the intruding eye—it was the uninvited ear. He did not shed his right to do so simply because he made his calls from a place where he might be seen. . . . One who occupies [the booth], shuts the door behind him, and pays the toll that permits him to place a call, is surely entitled to assume that the words he utters into the mouthpiece will not be broadcast to the world. To read the Constitution more narrowly is to ignore the vital role that the public telephone has come to play in private communication.

The Government contends, however, that the activities of its agents in this case should not be tested by Fourth Amendment requirements, for the surveillance technique they employed involved no physical penetration of the telephone booth from which the petitioner placed his calls. It is true that the absence of such penetration was at one time thought to foreclose further Fourth Amendment inquiry, *Olmstead* v. *United States,* 277 U.S. 438, 457, 464, 466, 72 L.Ed. 944, 947, 950, 951, 48 S.Ct. 564, 66 A.L.R. 376; *Goldman* v. *United States,* 316 U.S. 129, 134-136, 86 L.Ed. 1322, 1327, 1328, 62 S.Ct. 993, for that Amendment was thought to limit only searches and seizures of tangible property. But "[t]he premise that property interests control the right of the Government to search and seize has been discredited." . . . Thus, although a closely divided Court supposed in Olmstead that surveillance without any trespass and without the seizure of any material object fell outside the ambit of the Constitution, we have since departed from the narrow view on which that decision rested. Indeed, we have expressly held that the Fourth Amendment governs not only the seizure of tangible items, but extends as well to the recording of oral statements, overheard without any "technical trespass under . . . local property law." . . . Once this much is acknowledged, and once it is recognized that the Fourth Amendment protects people—and not simply "areas"—against unreasonable searches and seizures, it becomes clear that the reach of that Amendment cannot turn upon the presence or absence of a physical intrusion into any given enclosure.

We conclude that the underpinnings of Olmstead and Goldman have been so eroded by our subsequent decisions that the "trespass" doctrine there enunciated can no longer be regarded as controlling. The Government's activities in electronically listening to and recording the petitioner's words violated the privacy upon which he justifiably relied while using the telephone booth and thus constituted a "search and seizure" within the meaning of the Fourth Amendment. The fact that the electronic device employed to achieve that end did not happen to penetrate the wall of the booth can have no constitutional significance.

The question remaining for decision, then, is whether the search and seizure conducted in this case complied with constitutional standards. In that regard, the Government's position is that its agents acted in an entirely defensible manner: They did not begin their electronic surveillance until investigation of the petitioner's activities had established a strong probability that he was using the telephone in question to transmit gambling information to persons in other states, in violation of federal law. Moreover, the surveillance was limited, both in scope and in duration, to the specific purpose of establishing the contents of the petitioner's unlawful telephonic communications. The agents confined their surveillance to the brief periods during which he used the telephone booth, and they took great care to overhear only the conversations of the petitioner himself.

Accepting this account of the Government's actions as accurate, it is clear that this surveillance was so narrowly circumscribed that a duly authorized magistrate, properly notified of the need for such investigation, specifically informed of the basis on which it was to proceed, and clearly apprised of the precise intrusion it would entail, could constitutionally have authorized, with appropriate safeguards, the very limited search and seizure that the Government asserts in fact took place. Only last term we sustained the validity of such an authorization, holding that, under sufficiently "precise and discriminate circumstances," a federal court may empower government agents to employ a concealed electronic device "for the narrow and particularized purpose of ascertaining the truth of the . . . allegations" of a "detailed factual affidavit alleging the commission of a specific criminal offense." . . . Here, too, a similar judicial order could have accommodated "the legitimate needs of law enforcement" by authorizing the carefully limited use of electronic surveillance.

The Government urges that, because its agents . . . did no more here than they might properly have done with prior judicial sanction, we should retroactively validate their conduct. That we cannot do. It is apparent that the agents in this case acted with restraint. Yet the inescapable fact is that this restraint was imposed by the agents themselves, not by a judicial officer. They were not required, before commencing the search, to present their estimate of probable cause for detached scrutiny by a neutral magistrate. They were not compelled, during the conduct of the search itself, to observe precise limits established in advance by a specific court order. Nor were they directed, after the search had been completed, to notify the authorizing magistrate in detail of all that had been seized. In the absence of such safeguards, this Court has never sustained a search upon the sole ground that officers reasonably expected to find evidence of a particular crime and voluntarily confined their activities to the least intrusive means consistent with that end. Searches conducted without warrants have been held unlawful "notwithstanding facts unquestionably showing probable cause," . . . for the Constitution requires "that the deliberate, impartial judgment of a judicial officer . . . be interposed between the citizen and the police. . . ." . . . "Over and again this Court has emphasized that the mandate of the [Fourth] Amendment requires adherence to judicial processes," . . . and that searches conducted outside the judicial process, without prior approval by judge or magistrate, are per se unreasonable under the Fourth Amendment—subject only to a few specifically established and well-delineated exceptions.

It is difficult to imagine how any of those exceptions could ever apply to the sort of search and seizure involved in this case. Even electronic surveillance substantially contemporaneous with an individual's arrest could hardly be deemed an "incident" of that arrest. Nor could the use of electronic surveillance without prior authorization be justified on grounds of "hot pursuit." And, of course, the very nature of electronic surveillance precludes its use pursuant to the suspect's consent.

The Government does not question these basic principles. Rather, it urges the creation of a new exception to cover this case. It argues that surveillance of a telephone booth should be exempted from the usual requirement of advance authorization by a magistrate upon a showing of probable cause. We cannot agree. Omission of such authorization "bypasses the safeguards provided by an objective predetermination of probable cause, and substitutes instead the far less reliable procedure of an after-the-event justification for the . . . search, too likely to be subtly influenced by the familiar shortcomings of hindsight judgment." . . .

Wherever a man may be, he is entitled to know that he will remain free from unreasonable searches and seizures. The government agents here ignored "the procedure of antecedent justification . . . that is central to the Fourth Amendment," a procedure that we hold to be a constitutional precondition of the kind of electronic surveillance involved in this case. Because the surveillance here failed to meet that condition, and because it led to the petitioner's conviction, the judgment must be reversed.

Dissenting Opinion by Black, J. . . .

My basic objection is twofold:

(1) I do not believe that the words of the Amendment will bear the meaning given them by today's decision, and (2) I do not believe that it is the proper role of this Court to rewrite the Amendment in order "to bring it into harmony with the times" and thus reach a result that many people believe to be desirable.

While I realize that an argument based on the meaning of words lacks the scope, and no doubt the appeal, of broad policy discussions and philosophical discourses on such nebulous subjects as privacy, for me the language of the Amendment is the crucial place to look in construing a written document such as our Constitution. The Fourth Amendment says that "The right of the people to be secure in their persons, houses, papers, and effects, against unreasonable searches and seizures, shall not be violated, and no Warrants shall issue, but upon probable cause, supported by Oath or affirmation, and particularly describing the place to be searched, and the persons or things to be seized."

The first clause protects "persons, houses, papers, and effects, against unreasonable searches and seizures. . . ." These words connote the idea of tangible things with size, form, and weight, things capable of being searched, seized, or both. The second clause of the Amendment still further establishes its Framers' purpose to limit its protection to tangible things by providing that no warrants shall issue but those "particularly describing the place to be searched and the person or things to be seized." A conversation overheard by eavesdropping whether by plain snooping or wiretapping, is not tangible and, under the normally accepted meanings of the words, can neither be searched nor seized. In addition the language of the second clause indicates that the Amendment refers to something not only tangible so it can be seized but to something already in existence so it can be described. Yet the Court's interpretation would have the Amendment apply to overhearing future conversations which by their very nature are nonexistent until they take place. How can one "describe" a future conversation, and if not, how can a magistrate issue a warrant to eavesdrop one in the future? It is argued that information showing what is expected to be said is sufficient to limit the boundaries of what later can be admitted into evidence; but does such general information really meet the specific language of the Amendment which says "particularly describing?" Rather than using language in a completely artificial way, I must conclude that the Fourth Amendment simply does not apply to eavesdropping.

Tapping telephone wires, of course, was an unknown possibility at the time the Fourth Amendment was adopted. But eavesdropping (and wiretapping is nothing more than eavesdropping by telephone) was, . . . , "an ancient practice which at common law was condemned as a nuisance. 4 Blackstone, Commentaries 168. In those days the eavesdropper listened by naked ear under the eaves of houses or their windows, or beyond their walls seeking out private discourse." . . . There can be no doubt that the Framers were aware of this practice, and if they had desired to outlaw or restrict the use of evidence obtained by eavesdropping, I believe that they would have used the appropriate language to do so in the Fourth Amendment. They certainly would not have left such a task to the ingenuity of language-stretching judges. No one, it seems to me, can read the debates on the Bill of Rights without reaching the conclusion that its Framers and critics well knew the meaning of the words they used, what they would be understood to mean by others, their scope and their limitations. Under these circumstances, it strikes me as a charge against their scholarship, their commonsense and their candor to give the Fourth Amendment's language the eavesdropping meaning the Court imputes to it today.

I do not deny that common sense requires and that this Court often has said that the Bill of Rights' safeguards should be given a liberal construction. This principle, however, does not justify construing the search and seizure amendment as applying to eavesdropping or the "seizure" of conversations. The Fourth Amendment was aimed directly at the abhorred practice of breaking in, ransacking and searching homes and other buildings and seizing people's personal belongings without warrants issued by magistrates. The Amendment deserves, and this Court has given it, a liberal construction in order to protect against warrantless searches of buildings and seizures of tangible personal effects. But until today this Court has refused to say that eavesdropping comes within the ambit of Fourth Amendment restrictions. . . .

Since I see no way in which the words of the Fourth Amendment can be construed to apply to eavesdropping, that closes the matter for me. In interpreting the Bill of Rights, I willingly go as far as a liberal construction of the language takes me, but I simply cannot in good conscience give a meaning to words which they have never before been thought to have and which they certainly do not have in common ordinary usage. I will not distort the words of the Amendment in order to "keep the Constitution up to date" or "to bring it into harmony with the times." It was never meant for this Court to have such power, which in effect would make us a continuously functioning constitutional convention.

With this decision the Court has completed, I hope, its rewriting of the Fourth Amendment, which started only recently when the Court began referring incessantly to the Fourth Amendment not so much as a law against *unreasonable* searches and seizures as one to protect an individual's privacy. By clever word juggling the Court finds it plausible to argue that language aimed specifically at searches and seizures of things that can be searched and seized may, to protect privacy, be applied to eavesdropped evidence of conversations that can neither be searched nor seized. Few things happen to an individual that do not affect his privacy in one way or another. Thus, by arbitrarily substituting the Court's language, designed to protect privacy, for the Constitution's language, designed to protect against unreasonable searches and seizures, the Court has made the Fourth Amendment its vehicle for holding all laws violative of the Constitution which offend the Court's broadest concept of privacy.

The Fourth Amendment protects privacy only to the extent that it prohibits unreasonable searches and seizures of "persons, houses, papers and effects." No general right is created by the Amendment so as to give this Court the unlimited power to hold unconstitutional everything which affects privacy. Certainly the Framers, well acquainted as they were with the excesses of governmental power, did not intend to grant this Court such omnipotent lawmaking authority as that. The history of governments proves that it is dangerous to freedom to repose such powers in courts. . . .

§ 18:4.   Treatment of the Accused

The great concern of the law for the protection of the accused from government persecution is seen in the recent decisions of the Supreme Court relating to the rights of the person accused of crime. His right to be warned when arrested that what he states may be admitted as evidence against him, his right to be informed that he may remain silent and that he has the right to counsel, the necessity of appointing counsel for the indigent defendant before trying him for a serious offense, and various other rights are all based on the premise that the defendant is to be assumed innocent until shown to be guilty and that in his contest with the government, he must be given every possible protection.

JACKSON v. DENNO

378 U.S. 368 (1964)

Jackson was tried for murder. At the trial his confessions were admitted in evidence. Jackson contended that the confessions were not voluntary because at the time he made them to the police he was in the hospital, suffering from two bullet wounds and the loss of blood, and had received medication. He claimed that at the time he was also in pain, was gasping for breath, was refused water, and was told that he would be questioned by the police until they got the answers they wanted. Under the New York practice, the trial judge instructed the jury to decide whether the confessions were voluntary, and therefore admissible, and whether, if admissible, they were worthy of belief. Jackson was convicted. He claimed that the conviction was illegal because of the procedure with respect to the confessions and petitioned for a writ of habeas corpus directed against Denno, the warden of the penitentiary where he was confined.

OPINION BY WHITE, J. . . .

The jury was told that if it found the confession involuntary, it was to disregard it entirely, and determine guilt or innocence solely from the other evidence in the case; alternatively, if it found the confession voluntary, it was to determine its truth or reliability and afford it weight accordingly.

It is now axiomatic that a defendant in a criminal case is deprived of due process of law if his conviction is founded, in whole or in part, upon an involuntary confession, without regard for the truth or falsity of the confession . . . and even though there is ample evidence aside from the confession to support the conviction. . . . Equally clear is the defendant's constitutional right at some stage in the proceedings to object to the use of the confession and to have a fair hearing and a reliable determination on the issue of voluntariness, a determination uninfluenced by the truth or falsity of the confession. . . . In our view, the New York procedure employed in this case . . . cannot withstand constitutional attack under the Due Process Clause of the Fourteenth Amendment. . . .

The New York jury returns only a general verdict upon the ultimate question of guilt or innocence. It is impossible to discover whether the jury found the confession voluntary and relied upon it, or involuntary and supposedly ignored it. Nor is there any indication of how the jury resolved disputes in the evidence concerning the critical facts underlying the coercion issue. Indeed, there is nothing to show that these matters were resolved at all, one way or the other. . . .

This method of trying the coercion issue to a jury is not informative as to its disposition. Sometimes the record permits a guess or inference, but where other evidence of guilt is strong a reviewing court cannot learn whether the final result was to receive or to reject the confessions as evidence of guilt. Perhaps a more serious, practical cause of dissatisfaction is the absence of any assurance that the confessions did not serve as make-weights in a compromise verdict, some jurors accepting the confessions to overcome lingering doubt of guilt, others rejecting them but finding their doubts satisfied by other evidence, and yet others or perhaps all never reaching a separate and definite conclusion as to the confessions but returning an unanalytical and impressionistic verdict based on all they had heard."

A defendant objecting to the admission of a confession is entitled to a fair hearing in which both the underlying factual issues and the voluntariness of his confession are actually and reliably determined. But did the jury in

Jackson's Case make these critical determinations, and if it did, what were these determinations? . . .

In those cases where without the confession the evidence is insufficient, the defendant should not be convicted if the jury believes the confession but finds it to be involuntary. The jury, however, may find it difficult to understand the policy forbidding reliance upon a coerced, but true, confession, a policy which has divided this Court in the past . . . and an issue which may be reargued in the jury room. That a trustworthy confession must also be voluntary if it is to be used at all, generates natural and potent pressure to find it voluntary. Otherwise the guilty defendant goes free. Objective consideration of the conflicting evidence concerning the circumstances of the confession becomes difficult and the implicit findings become suspect.

The danger that matters pertaining to the defendant's guilt will infect the jury's findings of fact bearing upon voluntariness, as well as its conclusion upon that issue itself, is sufficiently serious to preclude their unqualified acceptance upon review in this Court, regardless of whether there is or is not sufficient other evidence to sustain a finding of guilt. In Jackson's case, he confessed to having fired the first shot, a matter very relevant to the charge of first degree murder. The jury also heard the evidence of eyewitnesses to the shooting. Jackson's testimony going to his physical and mental condition when he confessed and to the events which took place at that time, bearing upon the issue of voluntariness, was disputed by the prosecution. The obvious and serious danger is that the jury disregarded or disbelieved Jackson's testimony pertaining to the confession because it believed he had done precisely what he was charged with doing. . . .

It is now inescapably clear that the Fourteenth Amendment forbids the use of involuntary confessions not only because of the probable unreliability of confessions that are obtained in a manner deemed coercive, but also because of the "strongly felt attitude of our society that important human values are sacrificed where an agency of the government, in the course of securing a conviction, wrings a confession out of an accused against his will" . . . and because of "the deeprooted feeling that the police must obey the law while enforcing the law; that in the end life and liberty can be as much endangered from illegal methods used to convict those thought to be criminals as from the actual criminals themselves." Where pure factual considerations are an important ingredient, which is true in the usual case, appellate review in this Court is, as a practical matter, an inadequate substitute for a full and reliable determination of the voluntariness issue in the trial court and the trial court's determination, pro tanto, takes on an increasing finality. The procedures used in the trial court to arrive at its conclusions on the coercion issue progressively take on added significance as the actual measure of the protection afforded a defendant under the Due Process Clause of the Fourteenth Amendment against the use of involuntary confessions. These procedures must, therefore, be fully adequate to insure a reliable and clear-cut determination of the voluntariness of the confession, including the resolution of disputed facts upon which the voluntariness issue may depend. In our view, the New York procedure falls short of satisfying these constitutional requirements. . . .

We turn to consideration of the disposition of this case. Since Jackson has not been given an adequate hearing upon the voluntariness of his confession he must be given one, the remaining inquiry being the scope of that hearing and the court which should provide it.

This is not a case where the facts concerning the circumstances surrounding the confession are undisputed and the task is only to judge the voluntariness of the confession based upon the clearly established facts and in accordance with proper constitutional standards. Here there are substantial facts in dispute: Jackson said that he was in pain from his wounds, gasping for breath and unable to talk long. A state witness described Jackson as in strong condition despite his wounds. According to Jackson, the police told him he could have no water and would not be left alone until he gave the answers the authorities desired. These verbal threats were denied by the State. Whereas Jackson claimed his will was affected by the drugs administered to him, the State's evidence was that the drugs neither had nor could have had any effect upon him at all. Whether Jackson is entitled to relief depends upon how these facts are resolved, for if the State is to be believed we cannot say that Jackson's confession was involuntary, whereas if Jackson's version of the facts is accepted, the confession was involuntary and inadmissible. . . .

As reflected in the cases in this Court, police conduct requiring exclusion of a confession has evolved from acts of clear physical brutality to more refined and subtle methods of overcoming a defendant's will. . . .

Expanded concepts of fairness in obtaining confessions have been accompanied by a correspondingly greater complexity in determining whether an accused's will has been overborne—facts are frequently disputed, questions of credibility are often crucial, and inferences to be drawn from established facts are often determinative. The overall determination of the voluntariness of a confession has thus become an exceedingly sensitive task, one that requires facing the issue squarely, in illuminating isolation and unbeclouded by other issues and the effect of extraneous but prejudicial evidence. . . .

As we have already said, Jackson is entitled to a reliable resolution of these evidentiary conflicts. If this case were here upon direct review of Jackson's conviction, we could not proceed with review on the assumption that these disputes had been resolved in favor of the State for as we have held we are not only unable to tell how the jury resolved these matters but, even if the jury did resolve them against Jackson, its findings were infected with impermissible considerations and accordingly cannot be controlling here. . . . At the very least, *Townsend* v. *Sain,* 372 U.S. 293, 9 L.Ed.2d 770, 83 S.Ct. 745, would require a full evidentiary hearing to determine the factual context in which Jackson's confession was given.

However, we think that the further proceedings to which Jackson is entitled should occur initially in the state court . . . Jackson's trial did not comport with constitutional standards and he is entitled to a determination of the voluntariness of his confession in the state courts in accordance with valid state procedures; the State is also entitled to make this determination before this Court considers the case on direct review or a petition for habeas corpus is filed in a Federal District Court. . . .

It is New York, therefore, not the federal habeas corpus court, which should first provide Jackson with that which he has not yet had and to which he is constitutionally entitled—an adequate evidentiary hearing productive of reliable results concerning the voluntariness of his confession. It does not follow, however, that Jackson is automatically entitled to a complete new trial including a retrial of the issue of guilt or innocence. Jackson's position . . . is that the issue of his confession should not have been decided by the convicting jury but should have been determined in a proceeding separate and apart from the body trying guilt or innocence. So far we agree and hold that he is now entitled to such a hearing in the state court. But if at the conclusion of such an evidentiary hearing in the state court on the coercion issue, it is determined that Jackson's confession was voluntarily given, admissible in evidence, and properly to be considered by the jury, we see no constitutional necessity at that point for proceeding with a new trial, for Jackson has already been tried by a jury with the confession placed before it and has been found guilty. True, the jury in the first trial was permitted to deal with the issue of voluntariness and we do not know whether the conviction rested upon the confession; but if it did, there is no constitutional prejudice to Jackson from the New York procedure if the confession is now properly found to be voluntary and therefore admissible. If the jury relied upon it, it was entitled to do so. Of course, if the state court, at an evidentiary hearing, redetermines the facts and decides that Jackson's confession was involuntary, there must be a new trial on guilt or innocence without the confession's being admitted in evidence.

Obviously, the State is free to give Jackson a new trial if it so chooses, but for us to impose this requirement before the outcome of the new hearing on voluntariness is known would not comport with the interests of sound judicial administration and the proper relationship between federal and state courts. We cannot assume that New York will not now afford Jackson a hearing that is consistent with the requirements of due process. Indeed, New York thought it was affording Jackson such a hearing, and not without support in the decisions of this Court, when it submitted the issue of voluntariness to the same jury that adjudicated guilt. It is both practical and desirable that in cases to be tried hereafter a proper determination of voluntariness be made prior to the admission of the confession to the jury which is adjudicating guilt or innocence. But as to Jackson, who has already been convicted and now seeks collateral relief, we cannot say that the Constitution requires a new trial if in a soundly conducted collateral proceeding, the confession which was admitted at the trial is fairly determined to be voluntary. Accordingly, . . . the case is remanded to the District Court to allow the State a reasonable time to afford Jackson a hearing or a new trial, failing which Jackson is entitled to his release.

[Reversed and remanded.]

DISSENTING OPINION IN PART BY BLACK, J., in which CLARK, J. concurs . . .

The court rests its challenge to the reliability of jury verdicts in this field on its belief that it is unfair to a defendant, and therefore unconstitutional, to have the question of voluntariness of a confession submitted to a jury until the trial judge has first canvassed the matter completely and made a final decision that the confession is voluntary. . . .

Another reason given by the Court for invalidating the New York rule is that it is inherently unfair and therefore unconstitutional to permit the jury to pass on voluntariness, since the jury, even though finding a confession to have been coerced, may nevertheless be unwilling to follow the court's instruction to disregard it, because it may also believe the confession is true, the defendant is guilty, and a guilty person ought not be allowed to escape punishment. This is a possibility, of a nature that is inherent in any confession fact-finding by human factfinders—a possibility present perhaps as much in judges as in jurors. There are, of course, no statistics available, and probably none could be gathered, accurately reporting whether and to what extent factfinders (judges or juries) are affected as the Court says they may be.

Though able to cite as support for its holding no prior cases suggesting that the New York practice is so unfair to defendants that it must be held unconstitutional, the Court does refer to commentators who have made the suggestion. None of these commentators appears to have gathered factual data to support his thesis, nor does it appear that their arguments are at all rooted in the actual trial of criminal cases. Theoretical contemplation is a highly valuable means of moving toward improved techniques in many fields, but it cannot wholly displace the knowledge that comes from the hard facts of everyday experience. With this in mind it is not amiss to recall that the New York method of submitting the question of voluntariness to the jury without first having a definitive ruling by the judge not only has more than a century of history behind it but appears from the cases to be the procedure used in 15 States, the District of Columbia, and Puerto Rico, has been approved by this Court as a federal practice, . . . and has been approved in 6 of the 11 United States Court of Appeals Circuits. Fourteen other States appear to require full-scale determinations as to voluntariness both by the trial court and the jury. Another 20 States require the trial judge first to decide the question of voluntariness for purposes of "admissibility" but have him then submit that question for the jury to consider in determining "credibility" or "weight." Yet no matter what label a particular State gives its rule and no matter what the purpose for which the rule says the jury may consider the confession's voluntariness, it is clear that all the States, in the end, do let the jury pass on the question of voluntariness for itself, whether in deciding "admissibility" or "credibility."

The Court . . . indicates that a State may still, under the new constitutional rule announced today, permit a trial jury to determine voluntariness if first the trial judge has "fully and independently resolved the issue against the accused." . . . In other words, the Constitution now requires the judge to make this finding, and the jury's power to pass on voluntariness is a mere matter of grace, not something constitutionally required. If, as the Court assumes, allowing the jury to pass on the voluntariness of a confession before the judge has done so will "seriously distort" the jury's judgment, I fail to understand why its judgment would not be similarly distorted by its being allowed to pass on voluntariness after the judge has decided that question.

Yet, of course, the jury passing on guilt or innocence must, under any fair system of criminal procedure, be allowed to consider and decide whether an offered confession is voluntary in order to pass on its credibility. But it should be obvious that, under the Court's new rule, when a confession does come before a jury it will have the judge's explicit or implicit stamp of approval on it. This Court will find it hard to say that the jury will not be greatly influenced, if not actually coerced, when what the trial judge does is the same as saying "I am convinced that this confession is voluntary, but, of course, you may decide otherwise if you like." . . .

The Court's new constitutional doctrine is, it seems to me, a strange one when we consider that both the United States Constitution and the New York Constitution . . . establish trial by jury of criminal charges as a bedrock safeguard of the people's liberties. The reasons given by the Court for this downgrading of trial by jury appears to me to challenge the soundness of the Founders' great faith in jury trials. Implicit in these constitutional requirements of jury trial is a belief that juries can be trusted to decide factual issues. Stating the obvious fact that "it is only a *reliable* determination on the voluntariness issue which satisfies the constitutional rights of the defendant . . . ," . . . the Court concludes, however, that a jury's finding on this question is tainted by inherent unreliability. In making this judgment about the unreliability of juries, the Court, I believe, overlooks the fact that the Constitution itself long ago made the decision that juries *are* to be trusted.

Today's holding means that hundreds of prisoners in the State of New York have been convicted after the kind of trial which the Court now says is unconstitutional. The same can fairly be said about state prisoners convicted in at least 14 other States . . . and federal prisoners convicted in 6 federal judicial circuits. . . . The disruptive effect which today's decision will have on the administration of criminal justice throughout the country will undoubtedly be great. . . . Nevertheless, if I thought that submitting the issue of voluntariness to the jury really denied the kind of trial commanded by the Constitution, I would not hesitate to reverse on that ground even if it meant overturning convictions in all the States, instead of in just about one-third of them. But for the reasons already stated, it is impossible for me to believe that permitting the jury alone to pass on factual issues of voluntariness violates the United States Constitution, which attempts in two different places to guarantee trial by jury. My wide difference with the Court is in its apparent holding that it has constitutional power to change state trial procedures because of its belief that they are not fair. There is no constitutional provision which gives this Court any such lawmaking power. I assume, although the Court's opinion is not clear on this point, that the basis for its holding is the "due process of law" clause of the Fourteenth Amendment. The Court appears to follow a judicial philosophy which has relied on that clause to strike down laws and procedures in many fields because of a judicial belief that they are "unfair," are contrary to "the concept of ordered liberty," "shock the conscience," or come within the various other vague but appealing catch phrases. . . . I have repeatedly objected to the use of the Due Process Clause to give judges such a wide and unbounded power, whether in cases involving criminal procedure, . . . or economic legislation. . . . I believe that "due process of law" as it applies to trials means, . . .

a trial, according to the "law of the land," including all constitutional guarantees, both explicit and necessarily implied from explicit language, and all valid laws enacted pursuant to constitutionally granted powers. . . . I think that the New York law here held invalid is in full accord with all the guarantees of the Federal Constitution and that it should not be held invalid by this Court because of a belief that the Court can improve on the Constitution. . . .

Questions for Review

1. Define the social force of protection from government action.

2. Give illustrations of its application.

3. Analyze each opinion in this chapter in terms of the social forces involved in the decision. See § 5:5 for a list of the social forces. With respect to each opinion, explain why the prevailing social forces prevailed and why those rejected did not. In each case in which there is a dissenting opinion, also make this analysis for the dissenting opinion.

4-5. On the basis of the social forces involved, what decision should be made in each of the following cases?

4. *Presence of crime. Blood.* Several drops of blood were found near the scene of the crime. This blood was of the same type as the blood of the defendant. Does this establish that the defendant was at the scene of the crime? *Commonwealth v. Mussoline*, 429 Pa. 464, 240 A.2d 549.

5. *Evidence illegally obtained. Divorce action.* A husband seeking grounds for divorce obtained evidence of adultery of his estranged wife by illegally entering her apartment. She objected to the use of this evidence in the divorce action. Should such evidence be excluded from the divorce action? *Sackler v. Sackler*, 16 App.Div.2d 423, 229 N.Y.S.2d 61.

6-10. What social forces were involved, which prevailed, and which were defeated in the following decisions?

6. *Traffic violation. Search of automobile.* The defendant was arrested for a traffic violation and taken to the police station. While he was there, his automobile was searched and marijuana was found therein. When he was prosecuted for illegal possession of marijuana, he claimed that this evidence could not be used against him because it involved an offense unrelated to that for which he had been arrested. It was held that this did not make the evidence of finding marijuana in the automobile inadmissible if the initial arrest had been made in good faith and not merely for the ulterior purpose of obtaining possession of the automobile in order to search it. *Washington v. Montague*, Wash.2d, 438 P.2d 571.

7. *Representation by counsel. Indigent defendant.* A state court must appoint an attorney to represent an indigent defendant tried for a serious crime on the theory that the Sixth Amendment's guarantee of the right to

counsel in federal courts extends to state courts as an element of due process guaranteed by the Fourteenth Amendment. *Gideon* v. *Wainwright,* 372 U.S. 335.

8. *Jury. Capital punishment.* A defendant is denied a fair trial if prospective jurors are excluded from the jury because they state that they have scruples against inflicting capital punishment. *Witherspoon* v. *Illinois,* 391 U.S. 510.

9. *Hearsay evidence. Business records.* A driver was convicted of drunken driving. Part of the evidence presented at the trial against him was the police log on which the arresting officer had made a notation that another driver had been forced off the road by the defendant's automobile. It was held that the conviction must be reversed because the statement from the police log was not admissible in evidence, as it was merely a repetition of a hearsay statement; and, therefore, could not be admitted as a business record since it was not based on the observations made by the recorder of the statement in the course of a "business." *Fairmont* v. *Sjostrom,* Minn., 157 N.W.2d 849.

10. *Privileged communication. Letter.* The defendant, while awaiting trial, wrote a letter to his wife. It was not sealed or folded in any way to indicate that it was confidential. The defendant handed the letter to the sheriff to deliver to his wife and after she saw the letter, she gave it to a deputy sheriff. At the trial the letter was held admissible in evidence over the objection of the defendant that the letter was a confidential communication, since there was nothing in the above-stated facts to indicate that there was any confidential communication of anything. *Guyette* v. *Nevada,* Nev., 438 P.2d 244.

Chapter 19

PROTECTION FROM OPPRESSION GROUPS

§ 19:1. Generally

Groups may oppress an individual in three situations: (a) the group takes action against a particular outsider or outsiders generally; (b) the group refuses to permit the outsider to become a member; or (c) the group or persons within the group act in a way that is harmful to the individual member of the group.

§ 19:2. Group Action Against an Outsider

Historically, the monopoly is an early illustration of group action directed against an outsider. Here the objective of protecting the outsider joins with the objective of preventing oppression, holding that the group action is illegal. When the action contemplated by the group is itself illegal, the objective of stability joins in reaching the conclusion that the group activity is illegal. Thus since it is illegal for A to murder B, it follows that a combination by which C and D agree to murder E is likewise illegal.

When we move away from intended harm to person or property and enter into the area of intended economic harm, an analytical difficulty is met. To start with the situation of individual action, if I own one store and you own another store across the street, there is basically nothing wrong with my lowering my prices and running special bargain sales, although I do so with the intention of attracting all available customers to my store and ultimately succeed in doing so with the result that you are driven out of business. Now suppose that I and others agree to cut prices below those that you charge so that our group will obtain all of the customer trade. Stability, in the sense of consistency, would suggest that our conduct is lawful, even though we must recognize or appreciate that the consequence of our succeeding in our objective will be to drive you out of business. In this case, however, the law holds that our conspiracy or combination is unlawful, even though its objective is to do something which would be lawful if done or intended by anyone of us individually.

Thus, we see the interesting fact that while society is willing to permit the individual merchant to be destroyed by the competition of another individual merchant, it objects to such a destruction when brought about by group action—in union not only is there strength, there is also illegality. The conclusion that the group action is illegal does violence to the concept of stability by departing from the rule of what is lawful merely because of the number of persons involved in doing the act. It can be explained, however, on the ground that society deems that a man's property, in the form of his business, should be protected from the oppressive force of combined competition.

Is it necessary that those combining intend to cause harm to the victim? Here the answer is now "no," since combinations, contracts, trusts, and mergers are condemned merely because they have the tendency of harming competition. Not only is there no requirement that there be any intent to harm the victim but also there is no requirement of proof of actual harm. Group activity in the economic field finds itself condemned merely because it may have the effect of suppressing competition.

To some extent this view may be regarded as advancing the objective of practical expediency. It would be so difficult to prove that given conduct would suppress competition that it would be virtually impossible to ever bring the law to bear. Moreover, by the time that it could be shown that there was an actual suppression of competition, the harm would have been done, and it would be impossible to turn back the economic clock and put everyone back in his original position. For example, suppose that the effect of a merger of two corporations is to cut you out of a market to which you would otherwise have access. Assume that the courts declare the merger unlawful and direct it to be set aside. It is not possible for the courts to turn back the clock to give you access to the market from which you were already excluded. Therefore, if anything is to be done, practical expediency dictates that it be done before the combination is effective to cause the harm and that the law not wait until the harm has already been done. It is the difference between locking the barn before the horse is stolen and locking it afterwards.

The problem of protecting the individual from possible economic harm, which may result from group activity, is seen not only in the obvious group of conspirators who form a trust in violation of the antitrust law but also in the more subtle form of group action as shown by the interlocking stock ownership or the acquisition by one corporation of the assets of another. The Supreme Court held in *United States* v. *Columbia Steel Co.,* 344 U.S. 495 (1948), that the acquisition of the assets of another corporation is lawful even though the effect thereof may be to reduce competition. It is interesting to note that the dissenting opinion of four of the nine judges objected on the philosophic ground that "size can become a menace—both industrial and social. It can be an industrial menace because it creates gross inequalities against existing or putative competitors. It can be a social menace because of its control of prices. Control of prices in the steel industry is powerful leverage on our economy, for the price of steel determines the price of hundreds of other articles. Our price level determines in large measure whether we have prosperity or depression—an economy of abundance or scarcity. Size in steel should therefore be jealously watched. In final analysis, size in steel is the measure of the power of a handful of men over our economy. That power can be utilized with lightning speed. It can be benign, or it can be dangerous. The philosophy of the Sherman Act is that it should not exist. For all power tends to develop into a government in itself. Power that controls the economy should be in the hands of elected representatives of the people, not in the hands of an industrial oligarchy. Industrial power should be decentralized. It should be scattered into many hands so that the fortunes of the people will not be dependent on the whim or caprice, the political prejudices, the emotional stability of a few self-appointed men. The fact that they are not vicious men but respectable and social minded men is irrelevant. That is the philosophy and the command of the Sherman Act. It was founded on a theory of hostility to the concentration in private hands of power so great that only a government of the people should have it." The dissent, addressing itself to the acquisition by United States Steel of certain plants, stated: "This acquisition gives it unquestioned domination [on the Pacific Coast] and protects it against growth of the independents in that developing region. That alone is sufficient to condemn the purchase. Its serious impact on competition and the economy is emphasized when it is recalled that United States Steel has one third of the rolled steel production of the entire country. The least I can say is that a company that has that tremendous leverage on our economy is big enough. . . ."

It is significant that the dissenting opinion above stated did not contend that any harm was done to anyone as the result of the merger, but the fear that harm might be done was sufficient to persuade the dissenters that the merger should be condemned. The view of the dissenters became the law by the 1950 Amendment to Section 7 of the Clayton Act by which the Congress provided, in effect, that no corporation of any significant size may acquire the stock or assets of another corporation "where in any line of commerce in any section of the country, the effect of such acquisition may be substantially to lessen competition, or to tend to create a monopoly."

Notice that as we move from the traditional concept of "restraint of trade" into combinations and contracts that affect competition, there is also a change from an identified actual victim to unidentified potential victims. Thus where *A* and *B* conspire to drive *C* out of business, or to refuse to deal with him, the identity of the victim is clear. Where the question is whether *D* and *E* can merge, the victim ceases to be a defined enterprise and becomes merely a floating or indefinite class of such other persons or enterprises as would ordinarily have a share in the competitive market.

UNITED STATES v. VON'S GROCERY CO.

384 U.S. 270 (1966)

Two supermarket chain food stores in the Los Angeles area, Von's Grocery Co. and Shopping Bag Stores, proposed to merge. The United States government brought an action to enjoin the merger on the ground that it would lessen competition and thus violate § 7 of the Clayton Act.

OPINION BY BLACK, J. . . .

The District Court . . . concluded . . . that there was "not a reasonable probability" that the merger would tend "substantially to lessen competition" or "create a monopoly" in violation of § 7. . . .

The market involved here is the retail grocery market in the Los Angeles area. In 1958 Von's retail sales ranked third in the area and Shopping Bag's ranked sixth. In 1960 their sales together were 7.5 percent of the total $2.5 billion of retail groceries sold in the Los Angeles market each year. For many years before the merger both companies had enjoyed great success as rapidly growing companies. From 1948 to 1958 the number of Von's stores in the Los Angeles area practically doubled from 14 to 27, while at the same time the number of Shopping Bag's stores jumped from 15 to 34. During that same decade, Von's sales increased fourfold and its share of the market almost doubled while Shopping Bag's sales multiplied seven times and its share of the market tripled. The merger of these two highly successful, expanding and aggressive competitors created the second largest grocery chain in Los Angeles with sales of almost $172,488,000 annually. In addition the findings of the District Court show that the number of owners operating a single store in the Los Angeles retail grocery market decreased from 5,365 in 1950 to 3,818 in 1961. By 1963, three years after the merger, the number of single-store owners had dropped still further to 3,590. During roughly the same period from 1953 to 1962 the number of chains with two or more grocery stores increased from 96 to 150. While the grocery business was being concentrated into the hands of fewer and fewer owners, the small companies were continually being absorbed by the larger firms through mergers. According to an exhibit prepared by one of the government's expert witnesses, in the period from 1949 to 1958, nine of the top 20 chains acquired

126 stores from their smaller competitors. Figures of a principal defense witness . . . illustrate the many acquisitions and mergers in the Los Angeles grocery industry from 1953 through 1961 including acquisitions made by Food Giant, Alpha Beta, Fox, and Mayfair, all among the 10 leading chains in the area. Moreover, a table prepared by the Federal Trade Commission . . . shows that acquisitions and mergers in the Los Angeles retail grocery market have continued at a rapid rate since the merger. These facts alone are enough to cause us to conclude contrary to the District Court that the Von's-Shopping Bag merger did violate § 7. Accordingly, we reverse.

From this country's beginning there has been an abiding and widespread fear of the evils which flow from monopoly—that is the concentration of economic power in the hands of a few. On the basis of this fear, in 1890, when many of the Nation's industries were already concentrated into what Congress deemed too few hands, it passed the Sherman Act in an attempt to prevent further concentration and to preserve competition among a large number of sellers. Several years later in 1897 this Court emphasized this policy of the Sherman Act by calling attention to the tendency of powerful business combinations to restrain competition "by driving out of business the small dealers and worthy men whose lives have been spent therein, and who might be unable to readjust themselves to their altered surroundings." . . . The Sherman Act failed to protect the smaller businessmen from elimination through the monopolistic pressures of large combinations which used mergers to grow ever more powerful. As a result in 1914 Congress, viewing mergers as a continuous, pervasive threat to small business, passed § 7 of the Clayton Act which prohibited corporations under most circumstances from merging by purchasing the stock of their competitors. Ingenious businessmen, however, soon found a way to avoid § 7 and corporations began to merge simply by purchasing their rivals' assets. This Court in 1926, over the dissents of Justice Brandeis, Chief Justice Taft, Justices Holmes, and Stone approved this device for avoiding § 7 and mergers continued to concentrate economic power into fewer and fewer hands until 1950 when Congress passed the Celler-Kefauver Anti-Merger Bill now before us.

Like the Sherman Act in 1890 and the Clayton Act in 1914, the basic purpose of the 1950 Celler-Kefauver Bill was to prevent economic concentration in the American economy by keeping a large number of small competitors in business. In stating the purposes of the bill, both of its sponsors, Representative Celler and Senator Kefauver, emphasized their fear, widely shared by other members of Congress, that this concentration was rapidly driving the small businessman out of the market. The period from 1940 to 1947, which was at the center of attention throughout the hearings and debates on the Celler-Kefauver bill, had been characterized by a series of mergers between large corporations and their smaller competitors resulting in the steady erosion of the small independent business in our economy. As we said in *Brown Shoe Co.* v. *United States,* 370 U.S. 294, 315, 82 S.Ct. 1502, 1518, 8 L.Ed2d 510, "The dominant theme pervading Congressional consideration of the 1950 amendments was a fear of what was considered to be a rising tide of economic concentration in the American economy." To arrest this "rising tide" toward concentration into too few hands and to halt the gradual demise of the small businessman, Congress decided to clamp down with vigor on mergers. It both revitalized § 7 of the Clayton Act by "plugging its loophole" and broadened its scope so as to prohibit not only mergers between competitors, the effect of which "may be substantially to lessen competition, or to tend to create a monopoly" but to prohibit all mergers having that effect. By using these terms in § 7, which look not merely to the actual present effect of a merger but instead to its effect upon future competition, Congress sought to preserve competition among many small businesses by arresting a trend toward concentration in its incipiency before that trend developed to the point that a market was left in the grip of a few big companies. Thus, where concentration is gaining momentum in a market, we must be alert to carry out Congress' intent to protect competition against ever increasing concentration through mergers.

The facts of this case present exactly the threatening trend toward concentration which Congress wanted to halt. The number of small grocery companies in the Los Angeles retail grocery market had been declining rapidly before the merger and continued to decline rapidly afterwards. This rapid decline in the number of grocery store owners moved hand in hand with a large number of significant absorptions of the small companies by the larger ones. In the midst of this steadfast trend toward concentration, Von's and Shopping Bag, two of the most successful and largest companies in the area, jointly owning 66 grocery stores, merged to become the second largest chain in Los Angeles. This merger cannot be defended on the ground that one of the companies was about to fail or that the two had to merge to save themselves from destruction by some larger and more powerful competitor. What we have on the contrary is simply the case of two already powerful companies merging in a way which makes them even more powerful than they were before. If ever such a merger would not violate § 7, certainly it does when it takes place in a market characterized by a long and continuous trend toward fewer and fewer owner-competitors which is exactly the sort of trend which Congress, with power to do so, declared must be arrested.

Appellee's primary argument is that the merger between Von's and Shopping Bag is not prohibited by § 7 because the Los Angeles grocery market was competitive before the merger, has been since, and may continue to be in the future. Even so, § 7 "requires not merely an appraisal of the immediate impact of the merger upon competition, but a prediction of its impact upon competitive conditions in the future; this is what is meant when it is said that the amended § 7 was intended to arrest anticompetitive tendencies in their 'incipiency.' " *United States* v. *Philadelphia National Bank,* 374 U.S., at p. 362, 83 S.Ct., at 1741. It is enough for us that Congress feared that a market marked at the same time by both a continuous decline in the number of small businesses and a large number of mergers would, slowly but inevitably gravitate from a market of many small competitors to one dominated by one or a few giants, and competition would thereby be destroyed. Congress passed the Celler-Kefauver Bill to prevent such a destruction of competition. Our cases since the passage of that bill have faithfully endeavored to enforce this Congressional command. We adhere to them now. . . .

Since appellees "have been on notice of the antitrust charge from almost the beginning . . . we not only reverse the judgment below but direct the District Court to order divestiture without delay." . . .

[Reversed.]

DISSENTING OPINION BY STEWART, J. in which HARLAN, J. concurs. . . .

We first gave consideration to the 1950 amendment of § 7 of the Clayton Act in *Brown Shoe Co.* v. *United States,* 370 U.S. 294, 82 S.Ct. 1502, 8 L.Ed.2d 510. The thorough opinion the Chief Justice wrote for the Court in that case made two things plain: First, the standards of § 7 require that every corporate acquisition be judged in the light of the contemporary economic context of its industry. Second, the purpose of § 7 is to protect competition, not to protect competitors, and every § 7 case must be decided in the light of that clear statutory purpose. Today the Court turns its back on these two basic principles and on all the decisions that have followed them.

The Court makes no effort to appraise the competitive effects of this acquisition in terms of the contemporary economy of the retail food industry in the Los Angeles area. Instead, through a simple exercise in sums, it finds that the number of individual competitors in the market has decreased over the years, and, apparently on the theory that the degree of competition is invariably proportional to the number of competitors, it holds that this historic reduction in the number of competing units is enough under § 7 to invalidate a merger within the market, with no need to examine the economic concentration of the market, the level of competition in the market, or the potential adverse effect of the merger on that competition. This startling *per se* rule is contrary not only to our previous decisions, but contrary to the language of § 7, contrary to the legislative history of the 1950 amendment, and contrary to economic reality.

Under § 7, as amended, a merger can be invalidated if, and only if, "the effect of such acquisition may be substantially to lessen competition, or to tend to create a monopoly." No question is raised here as to the tendency of the present merger to create a monopoly. Our sole concern is with the question whether the effect of the merger may be substantially to lessen competition. . . .

The legislative history leaves no doubt that the applicable standard for measuring the substantiality of the effect of a merger on competition was that of a "reasonable probability" of lessening competition. The standard was thus more stringent than that of a "mere possibility" on the one hand and more lenient than that of a "certainty" on the other. I cannot agree that the retail grocery business in Los Angeles is in an incipient or any other stage of a trend toward a lessening of competition, or that the effective level of concentration in the industry has increased. Moreover, there is no indication that the present merger, or the trend in this industry as a whole, augurs any danger whatsoever for the small businessman. The Court has substituted bare conjecture for the statutory standard of a reasonable probability that competition may be lessened.

The Court rests its conclusion on the "crucial point" that, in the 11-year period between 1950 and 1961, the number of single-store grocery firms in

Los Angeles decreased 29 percent from 5,365 to 3,818. Such a decline should, of course, be no more than a fact calling for further investigation of the competitive trend in the industry. For the Court, however, that decline is made the end, not the beginning, of the analysis. In the counting-of-heads game played today by the Court, the reduction in the number of single-store operators becomes a yardstick for automatic disposition of cases under § 7.

I believe that even the most superficial analysis of the record makes plain the fallacy of the Court's syllogism that competition is necessarily reduced when the bare number of competitors has declined. In any meaningful sense, the structure of the Los Angeles grocery market remains unthreatened by concentration. Local competition is vigorous to a fault, not only among chain stores themselves but also between chain stores and single-store operators. The continuing population explosion of the Los Angeles area, which has outrun the expansion plans of even the largest chains, offers a surfeit of business opportunity for stores of all sizes. Affiliated with cooperatives that give the smallest store the buying strength of its largest competitor, new stores have taken full advantage of the remarkable ease of entry into the market. And, most important of all, the record simply cries out that the numerical decline in the number of single-store owners is the result of transcending social and technological changes that positively preclude the inference that competition has suffered because of the attrition of competitors.

Section 7 was never intended by Congress for use by the Court as a charter to roll back the supermarket revolution. Yet the Court's opinion is hardly more than a requiem for the so-called "Mom and Pop" grocery stores —the bakery and butcher shops, and vegetable and fish markets—that are now economically and technologically obsolete in many parts of the country. No action by this Court can resurrect the old single-line Los Angeles food stores that have been run over by the automobile or obliterated by the freeway. The transformation of American society since the Second World War has not completely shelved these specialty stores, but it has relegated them to a much less central role in our food economy. Today's dominant enterprise in food retailing is the supermarket. Accessible to the housewife's automobile from a wide radius, it houses under a single roof the entire food requirements of the family. Only through the sort of reactionary philosophy that this Court long ago rejected in the Due Process Clause area can the Court read into the legislative history of § 7 its attempt to make the automobile stand still, to mold the food economy of today into the market pattern of another era.

This is not a case in which the record is equivocal with regard to the status of competition in the industry in question. To the contrary, the record offers abundant evidence of the dramatic history of growth and prosperity of the retail food business in Los Angeles.

The District Court's finding of fact that there was no increase in market concentration before or after the merger is amply supported by the evidence if concentration is gauged by any measure other than that of a census of the number of competing units. Between 1948 and 1958, the market share of Safeway, the leading grocery chain in Los Angeles, declined from 14 percent to 8 percent. The combined market shares of the top two chains declined from 21 percent to 14 percent over the same period; for the period

1952-1958, the combined shares of the three, four, and five largest firms also declined. It is true that between 1948 and 1958, the combined shares of the top 20 firms in the market increased from 44 percent to 57 percent. The crucial fact here, however, is that seven of these top 20 firms in 1958 were not even in existence as chains in 1948. Because of the substantial turnover in the membership of the top 20 firms, the increase in market share of the top 20 as a group is hardly a reliable indicator of any tendency toward market concentration.

In addition, statistics in the record for the period 1953-1962 strongly suggest that the retail grocery industry in Los Angeles is less concentrated today than it was a decade ago. During this period, the number of chain store firms in the area rose from 96 to 150, or 56 percent. That increase occurred overwhelmingly among chains of the very smallest size, those composed of two or three grocery stores. Between 1953 and 1962, the number of such "chains" increased from 56 to 104, or 86 percent. Although chains of 10 or more stores increased from 10 to 24 during the period, seven of these 24 chains were not even in existence as chains in Los Angeles in 1953. . . .

In fashioning its *per se* rule, based on the net arithmetical decline in the number of single-store operators, the Court completely disregards the obvious procreative vigor of competition in the market as reflected in the turbulent history of entry and exit of competing small chains. . . .

The irony of this case is that the Court invokes its sweeping new construction of § 7 to the detriment of a merger between two relatively successful, local, largely family-owned concerns, each of which had less than 5 percent of the local market and neither of which had any prior history of growth by acquisition. In a sense, the defendants are being punished for the sin of aggressive competition. The Court is inaccurate in its suggestions . . . that the merger makes these firms more "powerful" than they were before, and that Shopping Bag was itself a "powerful" competitor at the time of the merger. There is simply no evidence in the record, and the Court makes no attempt to demonstrate, that the increment in market *share* obtained by the combined stores can be equated with an increase in the market *power* of the combined firm. . . .

With regard to the "plight" of the small businessman, the record is unequivocal that his competitive position is strong and secure in the Los Angeles retail grocery industry. The most aggressive competitors against the larger retail chains are frequently the operators of single stores. The vitality of these independents is directly attributable to the recent and spectacular growth in California of three large cooperative buying organizations. Membership in these groups is unrestricted; through them, single-store operators are able to purchase their goods at prices competitive with those offered by suppliers even to the largest chains. The rise of these cooperative organizations has introduced a significant new source of countervailing power against the market power of the chain stores, without in any way sacrificing the advantages of independent operation. In the face of the substantial assistance available to independents through membership in such cooperatives, the Court's implicit equation between the market power and the market share resulting from the present merger seems completely invalid.

Moreover, it is clear that there are no substantial barriers to market entry. The record contains references to numerous highly successful instances of entry with modest initial investments. Many of the stores opened by new entrants were obtained through the disposition of unwanted outlets by chains; frequently the new competitors were themselves chain-store executives who had resigned to enter the market on their own. Enhancing free access to the market is the absence of any such restrictive factors as patented technology, trade secrets, or substantial product differentiation.

Numerous other factors attest to the pugnacious level of grocery competition in Los Angeles, all of them silently ignored by the Court in its emphasis solely on the declining number of single-store competitors in the market. 3,590 single-store firms is a lot of grocery stores. The large number of separate competitors and the frequent price battles between them belie any suggestion that price competition in the area is even remotely threatened by a descent to the sort of consciously interdependent pricing that is characteristic of a market turning the corner toward oligopoly. The birth of dynamic new competitive forces—discount food houses and food departments in department stores, bantams and superettes, deli-liquor stores and drive-in dairies—promises unremitting competition in the future. In the more than four years following the merger, the District Court found not a shred of evidence that competition had been in any way impaired by the merger. Industry witnesses testified overwhelmingly to the same effect. By any realistic criterion, retail food competition in Los Angeles is today more intense than ever.

The harsh standard now applied by the Court to horizontal mergers may prejudice irrevocably the already difficult choice faced by numerous successful small and medium-sized businessmen in the myriad smaller markets where the effect of today's decision will be felt, whether to expand by buying or by building additional facilities. And by foreclosing future sale as one attractive avenue of eventual market exit, the Court's decision may over the long run deter new market entry and tend to stifle the very competition it seeks to foster. . . .

The Court pronounces its work consistent with the line of our decisions under § 7 since the passage of the 1950 amendment. The sole consistency that I can find is that in litigation under § 7, the government always wins. . . .

§ 19:3.   Admission to the Group

Historically groups of all kinds were free associations that could determine their own membership. Thus a labor union, a medical association, a church society were all the masters of their own admissions. When there was no economic consequence or significance to membership, society was not concerned with which persons were permitted by an association to become its members. After all, the worst that the excluded applicant sustained was hurt feelings. In the course of time, membership in the group became essential to employment or professional opportunity. For example, it became necessary to belong to the union in order to get work. At the professional level, it was necessary to belong to the local medical association in order to be permitted to use the facilities of the local hospital.

When the voluntary association thus became a door to economic opportunity, the person who was unjustifiably kept out not only had hurt feelings but also might not be able to earn a living, thus being deprived of the use of his knowledge and skill. At this point, society steps in to monitor or oversee the admission practices of the voluntary association. Here the social force seeking to protect the individual from oppression by an improper exclusion is joined by the social objective of furthering the general welfare, for society suffers if, through the association regulation, society is deprived of the services or labor of a person whose labor or service is needed.

To illustrate the foregoing supervision of the group, the National Labor Management Relations Act permits an employer to agree that if a new employee is not a union member, he must join a union within 30 days or he will be discharged. It is obvious that in such case the union must be required to admit the new employee to membership, or the new employee is placed in a trap from which he cannot escape. Thus the same federal statute that permits the union to hold the key to employment by means of a union shop contract also makes it an unfair labor practice for the union to charge an "excessive or discriminatory" fee for joining the union.

FALCONE v. MIDDLESEX COUNTY MEDICAL SOCIETY

34 N.J. 582, 170 A.2d 791 (1961)

Dr. Falcone was admittedly a licensed and qualified physician and surgeon, holding degrees from a Philadelphia school and from the College of Medicine of the University of Milan, who practiced surgery and obstetrics. He met all the requirements of the bylaws of the Middlesex County Medical Society. The Society, however, refused him membership on the ground that it had an unwritten rule requiring that every applicant have four years of study in a medical school recognized by the American Medical Association. Dr. Falcone did not meet this requirement since the Philadelphia school was not AMA-approved and, although the University of Milan was so approved, the course was not four years. Dr. Falcone brought suit against the Society for refusing to admit him to membership.

OPINION BY JACOBS, J. . . .

The Society's declaration of his ineligibility and its refusal to admit him to membership have had seriously adverse economic and professional effects on Dr. Falcone. He was a member of the medical staffs of the Middlesex General Hospital and St. Peter's General Hospital in New Brunswick but was dropped because they, like other hospitals in the area, require that their staff physicians be members of the County Medical Society. It seems entirely evident that Dr. Falcone cannot successfully continue his practice of surgery and obstetrics or properly serve his surgical and obstetric patients without the use of local hospital facilities; he testified that in order to earn a livelihood it is necessary "to belong to the local society" for "otherwise, you cannot use the hospitals." The virtual monopoly which the Society possesses in fact over the use of local hospital facilities results from the well-known inter-relationship between the County Society, the State Medical Society, the American Medical Association, and the Joint Commission on Accreditation of Hospitals. . . .

Over thirty years ago Professor Chafee, in his discussion of nonprofit associations, pointed to the distinction between the customary social and fraternal organizations on the one hand and trade unions and professional societies on the other hand; he noted that whereas exclusion or expulsion from a social or fraternal organization may result in little more than hurt feelings, exclusion or expulsion from a trade union or a professional society may result, as here, in deprivation of the invaluable opportunity "to earn a livelihood." . . . In a more recent discussion addressed specially to medical societies, the editors of the Yale Law Journal, after pointing out that ex-clusion or expulsion from a local medical society results, as a practical matter, in the deprivation of hospital facilities, descriptively noted that "non-membership amounts to a partial revocation of licensure to practice medi-cine." 63 Yale L.J. at p. 953. . . .

. . . Holmes repeatedly stressed the vital part played by public policy considerations in the never ending growth and development of the common law. Over eighty years have passed since he expressed his now well known thought that "every important principle which is developed by litigation is in fact and at bottom the result of more or less definitely understood views of public policy." See Holmes, "Common Carriers and the Common Law," 13 Am.L.Rev. 609, 631 (1879); Holmes, The Common Law 35 (1881). . . .

We are here concerned with . . . an organization, membership in which may . . . be viewed as "an economic necessity"; in dealing with such an organization, the court must be particularly alert to the need for truly pro-tecting the public welfare and advancing the interests of justice by reasonably safeguarding the individual's opportunity for earning a livelihood while not impairing the proper standards and objectives of the organization. . . .

When courts originally declined to scrutinize admission practices of membership associations, they were dealing with social clubs, religious organizations, and fraternal associations. Here the policies against judicial intervention were strong, and there were no significant countervailing policies. When the courts were later called upon to deal with trade and professional associations exercising virtually monopolistic control, different factors were involved. The intimate personal relationships which pervaded the social, religious, and fraternal organizations were hardly in evidence and the individual's opportunity of earning a livelihood and serving society in his chosen trade or profession appeared as the controlling policy considera-tion. . . .

It must be borne in mind that the County Medical Society is not a private voluntary membership association with which the public has little or no concern. It is an association with which the public is highly concerned and which engages in activities vitally affecting the health and welfare of the people. . . . Through its interrelationships, the County Medical Society possesses, in fact, a virtual monopoly over the use of local hospital facilities. As a result it has power, by excluding Dr. Falcone from membership, to preclude him from successfully continuing in his practice of obstetrics and surgery and to restrict patients who wish to engage him as an obstetrician or surgeon in their freedom of choice of physicians. Public policy strongly dictates that this power should not be unbridled but should be viewed judicially as a fiduciary power to be exercised in reasonable and lawful manner for the advancement of the interests of the medical profession and the public generally. . . .

In the light of all of the foregoing, the effort of the County Society to apply its unwritten requirement of four years' attendance at an AMA approved medical college so as to exclude Dr. Falcone from membership, must be viewed as patently arbitrary and unreasonable and beyond the pale of the law. When the County Society engages in action which is designed to advance medical science or elevate professional standards, it should and will be sympathetically supported. When, however, as here, its action . . . runs strongly counter to the public policy of our State and the true interests of justice, it should and will be stricken down. . . .

[Admission ordered.]

§ 19:4. Protection of Group Member from Group Action

Assume that the individual is a member of the group but that he is improperly treated by the group or deprived of some benefit to which he is entitled. Historically, there was no remedy for the individual since the law regarded the voluntary association and the rights of the member therein much the same as the case of the guest you invite to your home. If you don't like the way things turn out, you will not invite the guest again; but you cannot bring a lawsuit against him because you are disappointed or even because your feelings are hurt. Conversely, your guest has no claim against you because you do not invite him again. Likewise, if you were improperly treated by a voluntary association, it was merely a risk that you ran when you initially, of your own free will, became a member of that association.

In the course of time, equity would step in to protect the member "wrongfully" treated when such conduct would cause a loss of money or property. For example, when working men formed a fraternal benefit society and provided that from the dues paid a certain sum would be paid on the sickness of a member, a member had a "money" interest in the proper handling of sickness claims. If his claim were wrongfully rejected, the law would then step in to protect his rights to the money.

The concept of protecting the member from unfair treatment by the group is further seen as the underlying policy of the 1959 Federal Labor-Management Reporting and Disclosure Act. Under the Act, unions operating in or affecting interstate commerce must adopt constitutions and bylaws and file copies of them, together with detailed reports on administrative and financial matters. Each officer and key employee is required to file a report that sets forth any interest he or a member of his family has which conflicts with his duties to the union. Reports are required of labor relations consultants, and employers must report payments to union officers. The grounds on which a national union may exercise control or trusteeship power over a local union or its funds are specified to prevent abuse of that power.

The Act protects rights of union members within their unions by guaranteeing equality, the right to vote on specified matters, and information on union matters and contracts; and it protects members from interferences with the enjoyment of these rights. The terms of office and the process of election are regulated to provide democratic elections by secret ballot by members in good standing. Communists and persons convicted of major crimes are barred as officers or employees of unions until a specified period of time has elapsed since termination of membership or conviction.

How much farther will the member of the group be protected from hardship arising through the conduct of the group or its members? Assume, for example, that you are the head of a corporation's sales department and that under the ordinary pattern of salary increases you would be entitled to receive certain increases this year. Assume that because of the mistakes of the shipping department, several important sales are canceled with the result that you do not make the good showing for the year and do not receive the salary increase that you would otherwise receive. Can you bring any action against either your superior who has refused to give you the raise or against the head of the shipping department for his conduct that has led to your loss of the raise? Are you entitled to a hearing to prove that you are justified in receiving the raise and that it was wrong to deprive you of it? At the present time, you have no right to proceed against anyone, and it is just your misfortune that you have lost the raise because of someone else's bungling. It is quite likely that in the course of time the possibility of receiving an expectable raise will be regarded as so much a matter of right that you will be entitled to a hearing to determine whether there was justification for denying you that right. There will be a hearing similar to that in civil service to determine whether you are entitled to the wage increase.

If this change comes about, it will be the result of a wider recognition given to the objective of protecting property in the diluted form of the expectancy of receiving a raise, and the objective of protecting from the oppression which results when you are deprived of a raise because of the conduct of another. Conversely, when viewed from the standpoint of the employer, the objective in favor of his freedom of action and the freedom of the use of his property will be defeated.

SILVER v. NEW YORK STOCK EXCHANGE
373 U.S. 341 (1963)

The New York Stock Exchange directed some of its members to discontinue private wire connections with two nonmember brokers who dealt in over-the-counter securities. No reason was given by the Exchange for this action, and it was taken without any notice or opportunity to be heard being given to the nonmembers in spite of repeated requests therefor. The brokers brought a Sherman Act suit against the Stock Exchange. The Exchange claimed that it had not violated the Sherman Act because it was exempt therefrom by the Securities Exchange Act of 1934. The District Court decided the case against the Exchange. The Court of Appeals then reversed that decision, and an appeal was taken to the United States Supreme Court.

OPINION BY GOLDBERG, J. . . .

The fundamental issue confronting us is whether the Securities Exchange Act has created a duty of exchange self-regulation so pervasive as to constitute an implied repealer of our antitrust laws, thereby exempting the Exchange from liability in this and similar cases.

It is plain, to begin with, that removal of the wires by collective action of the Exchange and its members would, had it occurred in the context free from other federal regulation, constitute a per se violation of § 1 of the Sherman Act. The concerted action of the Exchange and its members here was, in simple terms, a group boycott depriving petitioners of a valuable business service which they needed in order to compete effectively as brokers-dealers in the over-the-counter securities market. . . .

The exchanges are by their nature bodies with a limited number of members, each of which plays a certain role in the carrying out of an exchange's activities. The limited-entry feature of exchanges led historically to their being treated by the courts as private clubs, . . . and to their being given great latitude by the courts in disciplining errant members. . . . As exchanges became a more and more important element in our Nation's economic and financial system, however, the private-club analogy became increasingly inapposite and the ungoverned self-regulation became more and more obviously inadequate, with accelerating grave consequences. . . .

It was, therefore, the combination of the enormous growth in the power and impact of exchanges in our economy, and their inability and unwillingness to curb abuses which had increasingly grave implications because of this growth, that moved Congress to enact the Securities Exchange Act of 1934. . . .

The pattern of governmental entry, however, was by no means one of total displacement of the exchanges' traditional process of self-regulation. . . . It is only where they fail adequately to provide protection to investors that the Commission is authorized to step in and compel them to do so. . . . The House Committee Report added the hope that the bill would give the exchanges sufficient power to reform themselves without intervention by the Commission. . . .

Thus arose the federally mandated duty of self-policing by exchanges. . . .

One aspect of the statutorily imposed duty of self-regulation is the obligation to formulate rules governing the conduct of exchange members. § 6(b). . . .

In addition, the general requirement of § 6(d) that an exchange's rules be "just and adequate to insure fair dealing and to protect investors" has obvious relevance to the area of rules regulating the conduct of an exchange's members. . . .

The Exchange's constitutional provision and rules relating to private wire connections are unquestionably part of this fulfillment of the § 6(b) and § 6(d) duties. . . .

But it does not follow that the case can be disposed of, as the Court of Appeals did, by holding that since the Exchange has a general power to adopt rules governing its members' relations with nonmembers, particular applications of such rules are therefore outside the purview of the antitrust laws. Contrary to the conclusions reached by the courts below, the proper approach to this case, in our view, is an analysis which reconciles the operation of both statutory schemes with one another rather than holding one completely ousted.

The Securities Exchange Act contains no express exemption from the antitrust laws or, for that matter, from any other statute. This means that any repealer of the antitrust laws must be discerned as a matter of implication, and "[i]t is a cardinal principle of construction that repeals by implication are not favored." . . . Repeal is to be regarded as implied only if necessary to make the Securities Exchange Act work, and even then only to the minimum extent necessary. This is the guiding principle to reconciliation of the two statutory schemes.

Although the Act gives to the Securities and Exchange Commission the power to request exchanges to make changes in their rules, § 19(b), . . . and impliedly, therefore, to disapprove any rules adopted by an exchange, see also § 6(a)(4), . . . it does not give the Commission jurisdiction to review particular instances of enforcement of exchange rules. . . .

The issue is only that of the extent to which the character and objectives of the duty of exchange self-regulation contemplated by the Securities Exchange Act are incompatible with the maintenance of an antitrust action. . . .

The absence of Commission jurisdiction, besides defining the limits of the inquiry, contributes to its solution. There is nothing built into the regulatory scheme which performs the antitrust function of insuring that an exchange will not in some cases apply its rules so as to do injury to competition which cannot be justified as furthering legitimate self-regulative ends. By providing no agency check on exchange behavior in particular cases, Congress left the regulatory scheme subject to "the influences of . . . [improper collective action] over which the Commission has no authority but which if proven to exist can only hinder the Commission in the tasks with which it is confronted." . . . Enforcement of exchange rules, particularly those of the New York Stock Exchange with its immense economic power, may well, in given cases, result in competitive injury to an issuer, a nonmember broker-dealer, or another when the imposition of such injury is not within the scope of the great purposes of the Securities Exchange Act. Such unjustified self-regulatory activity can only diminish public respect for and confidence in the integrity and efficacy of the exchange mechanism. Some form of review by exchange self-policing, whether by administrative agency or by the courts, is therefore not at all incompatible with the fulfillment of the aims of the Securities Exchange Act. . . . Since the antitrust laws serve, among other things, to protect competitive freedom, i.e., the freedom of individual business units to compete unhindered by the group action of others, it follows that the antitrust laws are peculiarly appropriate as a check upon anticompetitive acts of exchanges which conflict with their duty to keep their operations and those of their members honest and viable. Applicability of the antitrust laws, therefore, rests on the need for vindication of their positive aim of insuring competitive freedom. Denial of their applicability would defeat the congressional policy reflected in the antitrust laws without serving the policy of the Securities Exchange Act. Should review of exchange self-regulation be provided through a vehicle other than the antitrust laws, a different case as to antitrust exemption would be presented. . . .

The final question here is, therefore, whether the act of self-regulation in this case was so justified. The answer to that question is that it was not, because the collective refusal to continue the private wires occurred under totally unjustifiable circumstances. Notwithstanding their prompt and repeated requests, petitioners were not informed of the charges underlying the decision to invoke the Exchange rules and were not afforded an appropriate opportunity to explain or refute the charges against them.

Given the principle that exchange self-regulation is to be regarded as justified in response to antitrust charges only to the extent necessary to protect the achievement of the aims of the Securities Exchange Act, it is clear that no justification can be offered for self-regulation conducted without provision for some method of telling a protesting nonmember why a rule is being invoked so as to harm him and allowing him to reply in explanation of his position. No policy reflected in the Securities Exchange Act is, to begin with, served by denial of notice and an opportunity for hearing. Indeed, the aims of the statutory scheme of self-policing—to protect investors and promote fair dealing—are defeated when an exchange exercises its tremendous economic power without explaining its basis for acting, for the absence of an obligation to give some form of notice and, if timely requested, a hearing creates a great danger of perpetration of injury that will damage public confidence in the exchanges. The requirement of such a hearing will, by contrast, help in effectuating antitrust policies by discouraging anticompetitive applications of exchange rules which are not justifiable as within the scope of the purposes of the Securities Exchange Act. In addition to the general impetus to refrain from making unsupportable accusations that is present when it is required that the basis of charges be laid bare, the explanation or rebuttal offered by the nonmember will in many instances dissipate the force of the ex parte information upon which an exchange proposes to act. The duty to explain and afford an opportunity to answer will, therefore, be of extremely beneficial effect in keeping exchange action from straying into areas wholly foreign to the purposes of the Securities Exchange Act. And, given the possibility of antitrust liability for anticompetitive acts of self-regulation which fall too far outside the scope of the Exchange Act, the utilization of a notice and hearing procedure with its inherent check upon unauthorized exchange action will diminish rather than enlarge the likelihood that such liability will be incurred and hence will not interfere with the Exchange's ability to engage efficaciously in legitimate substantive self-regulation. Provision of such a hearing will, moreover, contribute to the effective functioning of the antitrust court, which would be severely impeded in providing the review of exchange action which we deem essential if the exchange could obscure rather than illuminate the circumstances under which it has acted. Hence the affording of procedural safeguards not only will substantively encourage the lessening of anticompetitive behavior outlawed by the Sherman Act but will allow the antitrust court to perform its function effectively.

Our decision today recognizes that the action here taken by the Exchange would clearly be in violation of the Sherman Act unless justified by reference to the purposes of the Securities Exchange Act, and holds that that statute affords no justification for anticompetitive collective action taken without according fair procedures. . . . The point is not that the antitrust laws impose the requirement of notice and a hearing here, but rather that, in acting without according petitioners these safeguards in response to their request, the Exchange has plainly exceeded the scope of its authority under the Securities Exchange Act to engage in self-regulation and therefore has not even reached the threshold of justification under that statute for what would otherwise be an antitrust violation. Since it is perfectly clear that the Exchange can offer no justification under the Securities Exchange Act for its collective action in denying petitioners the private wire connections without notice and an opportunity for hearing, . . . the Exchange has therefore violated § 1 of the Sherman Act, . . . and is thus liable to petitioners under §§ 4 and 16 of the Clayton Act. . . .

§ 19:5. Expulsion from the Group

Historically, courts would not interfere with the expulsion of a person from a group or association unless such exclusion deprived him of property rights. Consider again the example where membership in a fraternal society entitled a person to receive certain sick benefits. Here, in the course of time, an exclusion from membership could be reviewed by the courts in order to avoid the member's being unjustly deprived of the benefit rights. In the absence of such a direct property interest, the courts did not interfere.

As the "property" in the above illustration is primarily a contract right to receive money rather than the co-ownership of a specific fund, the next step was for courts to interfere with expulsion cases on the ground that contract rights of the expelled member were violated. When membership in the group was essential to employment, as in the case of a labor union where employers agreed to employ only union labor, it was logical to require fairness in expulsion of members, as the reverse of the Falcone case considered under § 19:3. In some instances, statutes may declare an improper exclusion to be an unfair labor practice or an unfair discrimination. Thus the Federal Labor Management Relations Act makes it an unfair labor practice for a union to cause or attempt to cause an employer to discriminate against an employee whose membership in the union has been terminated for any reason other than the nonpayment of union dues.

The next step in the evolution of the concept of what might be called "the right to belong" involves the case of membership which, although not essential to employment, confers a status that has a competitive advantage in that ordinarily it enables the member to obtain better employment than could be obtained without such status recognition.

HIGGINS v. AMERICAN SOCIETY OF CLINICAL PATHOLOGISTS

51 N.J. 191, 238 A.2d 665 (1968)

Higgins was a medical technician who was a member of the American Society of Clinical Pathologists. It adopted rules prohibiting its members from working in laboratories operated by nonphysicians. Higgins violated this rule and was expelled from the society. She brought an action to compel her reinstatement.

OPINION BY PROCTOR, J. . . .

ASCP is a nonprofit corporation of the State of Colorado whose membership is composed primarily of physicians specializing in pathology. Its purposes, as set forth in its constitution, are: ". . . (a) to promote the practice of scientific medicine by a wider application of pathology to the diagnosis and treatment of disease, (b) to stimulate research in all branches of pathology, (c) to establish standards for performance of various laboratory procedures, (d) to elevate the scientific and professional status of those specializing in this branch of medicine, and (e) to encourage closer cooperation of pathologists with other physicians and with medical technologists." . . .

ASCP has created, as one of its standing committees, a Board of Registry which . . . has promulgated a Code of Ethics and Standards of Conduct which . . . contains the following rules.

"A medical technologist will work at all times under the direction or supervision of a pathologist or other duly qualified and licensed doctor of medicine, such qualifications being determined on the basis of accepted medical ethics. . . .

"A medical technologist will not act as owner, co-owner, advisor or employee, or by means of any subterfuge, participate in an arrangement whereby an individual not regularly licensed to practice medicine is enabled to own or operate a laboratory of clinical pathology." . . .

In May, 1964, the plaintiff left her position at Mercer Hospital to accept her present employment at Egan Laboratories, where her salary and working hours were better than they had been at the hospital. Egan Laboratories is an independent bioanalytic laboratory located in Trenton. Its director, although not a physician, is duly licensed by the State of New Jersey pursuant to the Bio-Analytical Laboratory and Laboratory Director's Act. . . . Nevertheless, because the laboratory operation is not supervised by a pathologist or other duly qualified and licensed doctor of medicine, plaintiff's employment conflicts with the proscription contained in the ASCP Standards of Conduct quoted above. For this reason, ASCP's Board of Registry refused to renew the plaintiff's certification for 1965. The plaintiff was aware that her acceptance of employment at Egan Laboratories violated the ASCP Standards and Code and that this violation would result in the loss of her certification. . . .

Plaintiff admitted that she had suffered no present economic loss as a result of the termination of her certification. She conceded that there had been no requirement at Mercer Hospital, her former place of employment, that a medical technologist be certified by defendant, nor did she know of any hospital having such requirement. . . . Because of the absence of an economic necessity for membership as a *sine qua non* to employment or advancement, . . . the [lower court] concluded that there was no basis for judicial intervention. . . .

However, plaintiff contends that . . . "the primary injury which she has sustained as a result of defendant's action relates to her professional identity, reputation and status, and such unforeseeable affects therefrom on her future career in the field of medical technology."

In the present case we do not believe that, in order to obtain relief, the plaintiff must show an injury resulting from the economic necessity for membership in an organization exercising monopolistic control. . . . The courts have emphasized the distinction between reinstating an expelled member and ordering the admission of an applicant in the first place. While the general rule is that courts will not compel admission of an individual into a voluntary association, they have been willing to intervene and compel the reinstatement of a member who has been wrongfully expelled: "The law accords important rights and status to members of voluntary organizations not extended to mere aspirants to membership therein." . . .

The rights accorded to members of an association traditionally have been analyzed either in terms of property interests—that is, some interest in the assets of the organization, . . . or in terms of contract rights—that is, reciprocal rights and duties laid down in the constitution and bylaws. . . . These theories, however, are incomplete since they often prevent the courts from considering the genuine reasons for and against relief . . . and have been extensively criticized. . . . Leading commentators have pointed out that the real reason for judicial relief against wrongful expulsion is the protection of the member's valuable personal relationship to the association and the status conferred by that relationship. . . .

The loss of *status* resulting from the destruction of one's relationship to a professional organization ofttimes may be more harmful than a loss of property or contractual rights and properly may be the subject of judicial protection. . . .

Though it may be conceded that the plaintiff in the present case has suffered neither tangible economic loss nor any loss remediable under the traditional contract and property theories, we believe that her membership represented an interest of sufficient value to warrant judicial protection if it has been subjected to an unjust interference. Certification of the plaintiff by ASCP conferred upon her the standing of a competent professional. Her membership in this professional society gave her recognition and status, two important elements of professional success. . . . According to the defendant's pamphlet, quoted earlier in this opinion, the Registry "has elevated the status of the medical laboratory worker to a high professional level." From the record it is clear that the designation M.T. (ASCP) is the hallmark of competence in the field of medical technology. Plaintiff's status as a certificate holder imparts a certain cachet which distinguishes her from those noncertified laboratory workers who presumably are not as well trained or well qualified as is the plaintiff. Certification by ASCP and listing in its registry is the concrete and authoritative recognition of high professional attainment in the field. Because the Registry has come to be recognized by the leading medical and hospital groups as the only authoritative qualifying body for medical technologists, the certificate gives to its holder a valuable distinction. It is beyond doubt that plaintiff's standing in her profession has been impaired by the loss of this distinction. We conclude that the plaintiff's stake in her professional status is substantial enough to warrant at least limited judicial examination of the reason for her expulsion. . . .

In determining whether the deprivation of plaintiff's status was justified, our examination of the reason for her expulsion must be limited. Courts ordinarily ought not to intrude upon areas of associational decision involving specialized knowledge. . . . Private associations must have considerable latitude in rule-making in order to accomplish their objectives and their private law generally is binding on those who wish to remain members. However, courts will relieve against any expulsion based on rules which are in conflict with public policy. . . .

We are satisfied that the ASCP rules asserted as a justification for plaintiff's expulsion conflict with the public policy of this State and therefore can provide no proper basis for the refusal to renew her certification. The bioanalytical laboratory at which the plaintiff is employed is operated pursuant to a license granted by the State of New Jersey under [its licensing statutes]. This statute evinces a legislative policy determination that the operation of bioanalytical laboratories by qualified nondoctors, as well as by physicians, is in the public interest.

Defendant's rules by their terms forbid a certified medical technologist to be an employee of a person not licensed to practice medicine, even though that person is duly licensed by the State to operate a bioanalytical laboratory. The readily apparent purpose of the rules is to place a nonphysician in a position where he is not "enabled to own or operate a laboratory of clinical pathology." . . . That the rules are aimed at eliminating laboratories owned or operated by nonphysicians—rather than at elevating the standards and work performance of the certificate holder himself—is made apparent by the fact that the rules do not deny recertification to one who is engaged in work unrelated to the field. Moreover, if a medical technologist were employed by a laboratory which was supervised by—although not owned by —a licensed physician, the technologist apparently would be in contravention of the defendant's rules. Such employment would be "an arrangement whereby an individual not regularly licensed to practice medicine is enabled to *own* or operate a laboratory of clinical pathology." . . . The record shows that the best qualified medical technologists are those who have met the educational requirements of ASCP and have been certified by it. Defendant's restrictive employment rules have a logical tendency to deprive licensed bio-analytical directors who are not physicians of certified medical technologist employees, since the certified technologist can accept such employment only at the loss of the professional status conferred by her ASCP certification. Not only do these rules detract from the exercise of the privilege granted to the director by his license, but more importantly, they tend to deprive the public of obtaining from these laboratories services of the highest quality and reliability as are scientifically possible. As noted above, the Bio-Analytical Laboratory and Laboratory Director's Act . . . authorizes the operation of clinical laboratories by licensed nonphysicians. Such laboratories, of course, should be staffed by the best qualified technologists available. Any rule which restricts the availability of such technologists for work in this type of laboratory only can be viewed as being against the public interest and contrary to public policy.

We therefore hold that, on the record before us, the professional status conferred on plaintiff by her certificate is an interest of sufficient substance to warrant the protection of the court, and that because the ASCP rules underlying the plaintiff's expulsion violate the policy of this State they can provide no valid basis for ASCP's refusal to recertify her. . . .

Questions for Review

1. Define the social force of protection from oppression groups.

2. Give illustrations of its application.

3. Analyze each opinion in this chapter in terms of the social forces involved in the decision. See § 5:5 for a list of the social forces. With respect to each opinion, explain why the prevailing social forces prevailed and why those rejected did not. In each case in which there is a dissenting opinion, also make this analysis for the dissenting opinion.

4-5. *On the basis of the social forces involved, what decision should be made in each of the following cases?*

4. *Merger. Potential competition.* The El Paso Natural Gas Company acquired the stock and assets of the Pacific Northwest Pipe Line Company. El Paso, although not a California enterprise, supplied over half of the natural gas used in California; all the other natural gas was supplied by California sources. No gas was sold in California by Pacific Northwest, although it was a strong experienced company within the Northwest area and had attempted several times to enter the California market. United States claimed that the acquisition of Pacific by El Paso constituted a violation of § 7 of the Clayton Act, as amended, because the effect would be to remove competition between the two companies within California. The defense was raised that (a) California was not a "section" of the country within the Clayton Act, and (b) the sale of natural gas was not a line of commerce, and (c) the acquisition did not lessen competition when there had not been any prior sales by Pacific within the area. Was this defense valid? *United States* v. *El Paso Natural Gas Co.,* 376 U.S. 651.

5. *Mergers. Joint venture.* Two chemical corporations formed a third corporation to produce and sell for the Southeastern United States market, each owning one half of the new corporation's stock and supplying half of its officers and directors. The United States sought the dissolution of this new corporation under amended Section 7 of the Clayton Act. It was claimed that the Act did not apply because by its express wording, it was only applicable when one corporation "acquired" the assets of another corporation that was "engaged" in interstate commerce, whereas the new corporation was not "engaged" in any activity as it had been newly formed, and its assets were not acquired by either of the participating chemical companies. Was this defense valid? *United States* v. *Penn-Olin Chemical Co.,* 378 U.S. 158.

6-8. What social forces were involved, which prevailed, and which were defeated in the following decisions?

6. *Merger. Effect on competition.* Kinney Shoe Company and the Brown Shoe Company proposed to merge by giving the Kinney shareholders shares of the Brown Shoe Company stock in exchange for their shares. By dollar value, Brown was the third largest seller of shoes in the United States and fourth largest manufacturer. Kinney was the eighth largest seller and owned and operated the largest independent chain of family shoe stores in the nation. It was claimed that the merger would not lessen competition as Kinney manufactured less than ½ percent of shoes in the United States and Brown produced about 4 percent. It was held that the merger was prohibited because it would tend to lessen competition in a line of commerce. *Brown Shoe Company* v. *United States,* 370 U.S. 294.

7. *Competition. Provision against.* A provision by which buyer of unpatented machine agrees with the manufacturer that he will not permit its use by nor make any resale to anyone else is an anticompetitive attempt to create the effect of a patent for an unpatentable article and is invalid as a violation of the antitrust law, with the result that a competitor who made a copy of the machine when it was made available to it by the buyer will not be enjoined from marketing such copies. *Merchant Suppliers Paper Co.* v. *Photo-Marker Corp.,* 29 App.Div.2d 94, 285 N.Y.S.2d 932.

8. *Grand jury. Secrecy.* Where the defendant is accused of causing a witness to testify falsely before a grand jury, the defendant is entitled to see all of the testimony of the witness before the grand jury, as opposed to the contention that the rule of secrecy guarding grand jury proceedings prevented examination of any evidence presented to the grand jury or of any part other than the very statements claimed by the government to be false. *New Jersey* v. *Moffa,* 36 N.J. 219, 176 A.2d 1.

FURTHERANCE OF TRADE

§ 20:1. Generally

Society may seek to further trade in a variety of ways, as by establishing a currency as a medium of payment; by recognizing and giving legal effect to installment sales; by adopting special rules for checks, notes, and similar instruments so that they can be widely used as credit devices and substitutes for money; or by enacting laws to mitigate the harmful effects of alternating periods of depression and inflation.

Laws that have been considered in connection with other objectives may also serve to further trade. For example, laws protecting against unfair competition have this objective, as well as the objective of protecting certain classes from exploitation by others. And in a very general sense, trade would be impossible on the Twentieth Century scale without such areas of law as contract law, insurance and suretyship law, partnership and corporation law.

§ 20:2. Protection of the Buyer

A number of laws have as their aim the protection of the buyer from harm against which he cannot protect himself. Foremost in this area is the implication of warranties in the case of the sale of goods. The law could theoretically continue to follow a principle of "let the buyer beware" so that the buyer who did not go to the trouble of obtaining a guarantee from his seller would be taking his chances as to what it was that he was buying and the extent to which it was fit for anything. Instead, the modern law has abandoned this concept and has shifted to the seller the burden of, in effect, guaranteeing the product unless the seller makes an adequate disclaimer of the warranty. Thus, the law has shifted from the position of let the buyer beware to that of let the seller beware.

In the case that follows, this modern attitude of the law is applied to hold responsible a seller who was innocent and ignorant of any defect and had no better knowledge than the buyer. Were the law to proceed upon the theory of liability based on fault, the seller in the following case would have been held not liable because there was no fault on his part, but this did not excuse him from liability.

SAMS v. EZY-WAY FOODLINER COMPANY

157 Maine 10, 170 A.2d 160 (1961)

Sams purchased some frankfurts at Ezy-Way's Self Service Food supermarket. They were contained in a sealed plastic bag labeled "Jordan's Hot Dogs." The manufacturer had a good reputation and there was no evidence of any negligence. In eating one of the hot dogs, Sams was cut by pieces of glass which it contained. He sued Ezy-Way for his damages. From a judgment in favor of the supermarket, Sams appealed.

OPINION BY WILLIAMSON, C.J. . . .

The controlling issue in this action of a plaintiff purchaser-consumer against a defendant-retailer is whether there is a "sealed container exception" from the implied warranty of merchantability. . . .

A "hot dog" containing glass is, of course, not fit to eat and is therefore not of merchantable quality. . . .

The fact that the frankfurts were sold in a self-service market does not affect the result. The sign, or label, effectively described the goods in the market and in the package. The printed word was the silent salesman. . . . Compare *Mead* v. *Coca Cola Bottling Co.,* [329 Mass. 440, 108 N.E.2d 757] holding a warranty of merchantability . . . attached to the sale of coca cola in an automatic vending machine. . . .

We come to the issue of whether the retailer of food in a sealed container is insulated from an implied warranty of merchantability. . . . We make no distinction between [a] can of asparagus . . . , [a] package of macaroni . . . , bread wrapped in paper and sealed [referring to cases involving such containers], and the "hot dogs" in the sealed plastic bag. In each instance we have a sealed container or an original package effectively preventing inspection by the retailer at any time and by the purchaser until the container is opened. The basis of the "sealed container exception" is that the purchaser could not have placed reliance upon the retailer's skill or judgment in determining that the contents were fit to eat. . . .

Vast changes have taken place in the manufacture and distribution of food products. . . . The purchase of food in a can, jar, package, or sealed bag under brand or trade name is commonplace. The pantry shelf, the refrigerator, and the "deep freeze" evidence the fact. Sales are made over the counter, at self-service markets, and by vending machines. Inspection of such products which will uncover the defect within the container, as the defective asparagus, or the pin in the bread, is impossible as a practical matter until at least the container is opened, or in many instances, as here, until the product is eaten.

There is as well the problem of the latent defect in the product not sold in a container. The pin in the unwrapped loaf of bread may be, and probably is, hidden from the retailer and buyer no less than the pin in the wrapped loaf of "Ward's bread." . . .

If the frankfurts here had not been sold in a sealed bag, inspection would not have disclosed the glass within the edible casing. . . .

[Judgment for defendant reversed and remanded.]

The principle recognized in the above case of liability of the market-place to the victim has been expanded far beyond the fact situation there involved so that the day will soon arrive when the person injured by a product, whether or not he is a buyer, a person to whom a buyer has made the product available, or a third person injured when the defect in the product causes him harm, as when the defect in an automobile causes it to run out of control, will be able to sue any and all prior sellers and the remote manufacturer on one theory or another—some courts calling the theory by its historical name of implied warranty, while others employ the term of strict tort liability.

As present, it is declared essential that there be a defect in the product in order to impose liability, but this requirement is being relaxed and eventually it is likely that it will be ignored and liability will be imposed if the product "caused" the harm.

§ 20:3. Protection from Restrictions

In some cases the owner of property will attempt to put restrictions on his property when it is given or sold to another.

While the law is willing to protect a person in the use of his property, such limitations will sometimes be ignored in order to keep the property more readily "marketable." In some cases, the court will evade a limitation by so narrowly construing it that the limitation is destroyed. For example, a gift of land to a school "to be used for the purposes of education and no other purposes" is not a limitation that binds the school and thus, when such use is terminated, the school may sell the land free and clear of the limitation, in a sense sending the land into the channels of ordinary commerce rather than returning it to the original giver. This would appear to the ordinary person to defeat the intention of the donor of the land who would appear to have made a conditional gift of the land. One could very well argue that since the donor of the land was not required to make any gift in the first place, he should certainly be allowed to make a gift with a string attached if he so chose. The only difficulty with this argument is that the law does not recognize it.

In other instances, the law recognizes the limitation imposed upon property as a limitation, but then holds that the limitation is void. For example, a provision in your will that your house should go to your unborn child, and upon his death to your unborn grandchild, and upon the death of the grandchild to the unborn great-grandchild, and so on through successive generations will not be held binding. The law does not want to see property held up in one family line for an indefinite period of time, during which time the land cannot be sold because the person who is the owner in the future is not yet known or has not yet been born. To some extent the law will recognize provisions tying up the disposition of property in the future, but it will hold the limitations void when they reach too far into the future—the courts then holding that there is a violation of the rule against perpetuities.

RAFE v. HINDIN

29 App.Div.2d 481, 288 N.Y.S.2d 662 (1968)

Rafe and Hindin each owned 50 percent of the stock of a small corporation. Each agreed that he would not sell his stock without the consent of the other, and this agreement was expressly stated in the stock certificates each of them owned. Later Rafe found a buyer for his shares of stock, but Hindin would not consent to the sale. Rafe sued Hindin to have the restriction declared void.

Opinion by Beldock, P.J. . . .

The plaintiff and the . . . defendant . . . each owned one certificate for 50 percent of the outstanding stock. There was a legend on each certificate, signed by the parties, which made it nontransferable except to the other stockholder; and written permission from the other stockholder was required to transfer the stock to a third party on the books of the corporation. . . .

The legend on the stock certificate was not contained either in the certificate of incorporation or in the bylaws of the corporation, but was the result of agreement between the parties. That fact is not a sufficient ground for invalidating the restriction. A restriction on the alienation of stock made between all the stockholders of a corporation may be enforced, if reasonable, even though it is not contained in the certificate of incorporation or the bylaws. . . .

The legend contained two separate restrictions: (a) each stockholder is required to sell to the other stockholder, but no price is stated at which the offeror is required to sell or the offeree to purchase, and no time limit is set for the offeree to exercise his option to purchase; and (b) each stockholder is required to obtain the consent of the other stockholder to a proposed transfer of the stock to a third party, but there is no provision that the second stockholder may not unreasonably withhold his consent. We are concerned on this appeal solely with the validity of the second restriction.

There is a conflict of authority in other states on the subject of the validity of a restriction on the transfer of stock in a close corporation without the consent of either all or a stated percentage of the other stockholders or the board of directors of the corporation.

In *Longyear* v. *Hardman,* 219 Mass. 405, 106 N.E. 1012, it was held that a provision in a certificate of incorporation that none of the shares of stock shall be sold without the consent of the holders of three-quarters of the stock was not palpably unreasonable or unconscionable because in a small business corporation there is a personal relation analogous to a partnership and there should be retained the right to choose one's associates; harmony of purpose and of business methods and ideals among stockholders may be a significant element in success. . . .

In *Wright* v. *Iredell Tel. Co.,* 182 N.C. 308, 108 S.E. 744, it was held that a provision in a certificate of incorporation that shares of stock shall not be transferred unless approved by the directors was valid, where the board of directors had acted in good faith and in the absence of allegation or proof of arbitrary, oppressive, or unreasonable conduct.

In *Tracey* v. *Franklin,* 31 Del.Ch. 477, 67 A.2d 56, 11 A.L.R.2d 990, affg. 30 Del.Ch. 407, 61 A.2d 780, it was held that a provision whereby two stockholders in a close corporation agreed not to sell their shares, except on the consent of both, was invalid because a restraint on alienation of property is against public policy; and that the fact that two stockholders wish to solidify ownership in themselves is not a legally sufficient purpose to justify the restraint on alienation. To the same effect, see for example, *People ex rel. Malcom* v. *Lake Sand Corp.,* 251 Ill.App. 499; *Steele* v. *Farmers' & Merchants' Mut. Tel. Assn.,* 95 Kan. 580, 148 P. 661; *Miller* v. *Farmers Milling & Elevator Co.,* 78 Neb. 441, 110 N.W. 995; *Matter of Klaus,* 67 Wis. 401, 29 N.W. 582.

In New York certificates of stock are regarded as personal property and are subject to the rule that there be no unreasonable restraint on alienation . . . . "[t]he general rule that ownership of property cannot exist in one person and the right of alienation in another . . . has in this State been frequently applied to shares of corporate stock . . . and cognizance has been taken of the principle that 'the right of transfer is a right of property, and if another has the arbitrary power to forbid a transfer of property by the owner that amounts to annihilation of property.' " . . .

The legend on the stock certificate at bar contains no provision that the individual defendant's consent may not be unreasonably withheld. Since the individual defendant is thus given the arbitrary power to forbid a transfer of the shares of stock by the plaintiff, the restriction amounts to annihilation of property. The restriction is not only not reasonable, but it is against public policy and, therefore, illegal. It is an unwarrantable and unlawful restraint on the sale of personal property, the sale and interchange of which the law favors, and in restraint of trade.

The individual defendant argues that there was an oral agreement between the parties that his consent would not be unreasonably withheld and that, in fact, the withholding of his consent to the transfer to the plaintiff's prospective purchaser was reasonable. Assuming that there was such an oral agreement prior to the issuance of the shares of stock and assuming further that the inclusion of such a provision in the written legend on the stock certificate would make reasonable what we hold to be an unreasonable restraint on alienation, it is our opinion that proof of such an oral agreement would be inadmissible at the trial as in violation of the parol evidence rule. Such an agreement relates so closely to the stockholder relationship and the subject dealt with in the written legend that it would be expected to be embodied in the writing; therefore, if it is contained merely in an oral agreement, it may not be proved. . . .

It is further noted that, because the individual defendant is given by the legend on the stock certificate the arbitrary right to refuse for any reason or for no reason to consent to the transfer of the plaintiff's stock to a prospective purchaser, and since no price is stated at which the plaintiff must sell to the individual defendant and which the latter is required to pay to the plaintiff for the plaintiff's stock, the legend may be construed as rendering the sale of the plaintiff's stock impossible to anyone except to the individual defendant at whatever price he wishes to pay. This construction makes the restriction illegal. . . .

In the Penthouse Properties case (256 App.Div. 685, 11 N.Y.S.2d 417, supra), it was held that a provision in stock certificates of a corporation operating a cooperative apartment house and in the proprietary leases of apartments therein, barring the transfer of any certificate or the assignment of any lease without the written consent of the board of directors of the corporation or of two thirds of its stockholders, is neither invalid nor unenforcible as in restraint of alienation, where it appeared that the restrictions imposed, viewed in the light of the permanency of the individual occupants as tenant owners, were legal, reasonable, and appropriate to the lawful purpose to be attained; and that the special nature of the ownership of cooperative apartment houses by tenant owners required that they not be included in the general rule against restraint on the sale of stock of corporations organized for profit. The case at bar involves the sale of stock of a corporation organized for profit and, therefore, does not come within the principle of that holding. . . .

Judgment should be . . . entered (1) declaring void the legend on the certificate requiring the consent of the individual defendant to the transfer of the plaintiff's stock to a third-party and (2) directing the corporate defendant, upon submission to it of a properly endorsed assignment of the stock and appropriate payment to it on account of any taxes on the transfer, to record the transfer in its stock transfer book, to cancel the plaintiff's stock certificate, to issue a new stock certificate to the plaintiff's transferee, and to record the plaintiff's transferee in its stock book as the present holder of the stock.

§ 20:4.   Protection of Buyer from Seller's Financer

The modern world of financing and credit transactions has added another element to the problem of protecting the buyer; that is, assuring the buyer that when he buys, he will in fact obtain the ownership of the goods and that rights in them held by third persons will be cut off. Today, the merchant or dealer typically purchases his inventory on credit. This may be credit extended to him by his source of supply as in the form of a provision for 90 days, or longer, in which to make payment. It may be credit extended by a third person, as in the case when the dealer borrows money from a bank with which to pay his supplier. In either case, the extender of credit, whether the original supplier or the third person, will ordinarily have a claim to or security interest in the goods while still held by the dealer as inventory. As a practical matter, when viewed from the standpoint of the ultimate buyer or consumer, this security interest must be cut off without regard to whether the dealer has paid the amount that he owed. For example, when you purchase an automobile, you do not want some bank to repossess the automobile because the dealer from whom you purchased the automobile owes money to the bank and had a security interest in the car.

If creditor protection were the only force in operation, the law would conclude that until the original security interest holder was paid, he could follow the car wherever it went and take it back regardless of the good faith of the ultimate buyer and the fact that the buyer had paid in full. If this seems extreme, notice that this is exactly what is done if the automobile is stolen. That is, the true owner can follow the car and recover it from the innocent buyer who had paid value for the car and had acted in good faith. In the stolen car case, the protection of title prevails over the argument that the honest buyer should be protected in order to further trade.

Society, however, wishes the honest buyer to prevail in the financed sale transaction earlier described. Here the objective of furthering trade looms greater than the protection of the original creditor. Notice also that the n factor becomes important. The number of cars that are purchased from a dealer who has purchased his inventory on credit is many times greater than the number of cars that are stolen and sold to buyers in good faith. Therefore, the stolen car rule with its occasional burden on the honest buyer would have only slight effect upon trade, in contrast with the dampening effect to a large area of trade that would result from permitting the seller of the inventory to the dealer to recover an automobile purchased by the ultimate buyer. Society, through the law, has therefore tipped the scales in favor of the good-faith buyer from a dealer so that the buyer holds clear of the original security interest.

CHRYSLER CREDIT CORP. v. SHARP

56 Misc.2d 261, 288 N.Y.S.2d 525 (1968)

Heintzman-McCrea Motors was an automobile dealer. It financed the purchase of its inventory of cars by loans from the Marine Midland Trust Company, giving the trust company a security interest in its inventory to protect such loans. Heintzman sold an automobile on credit to Dorothy Sharp. This sale was financed by Chrysler Credit Corporation, which was given a security interest in the car by Sharp. When Heintzman did not pay its loan to Marine Midland, the latter took possession of all cars of Heintzman, including the car which had been sold to Sharp. Meanwhile Sharp had stopped making payments on her car, and Chrysler Credit Corporation sought to repossess the car. Chrysler then brought suit to recover the balance due by Sharp on her contract and to recover damages from Marine Midland for converting Chrysler's interest in the car by repossessing it. Marine Midland defended on the ground that Sharp was not a "buyer in ordinary course of business" and therefore the transaction between Heintzman and Sharp did not cut off Marine's security interest, which it would have done if Sharp were a buyer in ordinary course.

OPINION BY SERRA, J. . . .

This is an action brought against Dorothy Mae Sharp, as buyer, upon a retail installment contract to recover the amount due upon an automobile sales contract and also to recover against the Marine Midland Trust Company of Western New York, the bank which provided floor plan financing to the automobile dealer on the theory of conversion for the reasonable market value of an automobile seized and sold by the said defendant bank. . . . The defendant, Dorothy Mae Sharp, has never been served and her whereabouts are unknown. The determinations are based on a nonjury trial of the issues. . . .

A formal printed instrument entitled, "Retail Installment Contract," was signed by Mrs. Sharp and by the dealer's office manager. . . . On the following day, it was endorsed by the president of the dealer corporation to the plaintiff. Payment of the cash balance received by the dealer from the sale of the retail finance contract to the plaintiff was deposited by the dealer in its deposit account with the defendant bank on February 17, 1966. On February 24, 1966, a financing statement . . . was filed . . . to perfect the security interest of the plaintiff. . . . The retail installment contract contained, in a printed portion, an acknowledgment of delivery and acceptance of the car by the buyer. In fine print on the reverse side under the assignment portion of the contract, the dealer warrants, among other things, that the buyer paid the down payment as stated in the contract. The contract, by its terms, provides for a trade-in, which was actually delivered to the dealer at or about the time of signing the contract. It further provided for a cash down payment of $443, a payment of $100 to be due March 16, 1966, and a 30-payment deferred balance of $1710.70. The $443 in cash was in fact not paid on the signing of the contract despite the form recitations. The arrangement between the sales manager and of Mrs. Sharp was that she, as retail purchaser, was to make the cash payment when she received an income tax refund which she expected to receive in the immediate future and that the car was to be left on the lot until the cash payment was made. On or about March 18, 1966, and before the delivery of the car, the defendant, Marine Midland Trust Company of Western New York seized all of the dealer's automobiles then remaining on its lot, including the 1963 Chevrolet automobile described in the Sharp contract. The automobile was sold by the bank and the rights to the proceeds is the issue to be determined herein. . . .

Situations such as this are . . . commonplace . . . in insolvent automobile dealerships and with major appliance dealers. . . .

The New York State car registration was never transferred in the instant case. . . .

This Court is inclined to feel that while title questions may be of significance in determining many issues under the UCC, the theory of the act and its relation to the problem relegates the issue of title in this case to a subordinate position. The UCC is the result of the rapid expansion of credit operations in the business world, both wholesale and retail, to the position where traditional paper in the form of chattel mortgages, conditional sales forms, and even trust receipt floor planning do not in large, fast moving operations meet the needs of a rapid flow of credit. The financing of inventories, particularly, has long baffled those accustomed to the country store with its annual inventory and slow movement of goods. A car dealer with hundreds of transactions a month, or a major appliance shop with transactions running into the thousands must keep inventory controls by modern business machinery and has a constant flow of cash and credit. To meet these demands the UCC provides for greater flexibility and in some respects to the uninitiate, will, during the transition of its ultimate form, seem to create new risks. To aid in this transition, guidelines of interpretation have been set forth in Article 1 and carefully prepared definitions are found throughout the Act. The purposes of the Act, to be liberally construed, are specified as the simplification, clarification, and modernization of the law governing commercial transactions to permit the continued expansion of commercial practices through custom, usage, and agreement of the parties. . . . Of critical interest to the question at hand is whether Mrs. Sharp was a buyer in the ordinary course of business out of inventory.

Under UCC 1-201, GENERAL DEFINITIONS, such a buyer is defined in Subdivision 9 as follows: "(9) 'Buyer in ordinary course of business' means a person who in good faith and without knowledge that the sale to him is in violation of the ownership rights or security interest of a third party in the goods buys in ordinary course from a person in the business of selling goods of that kind but does not include a pawnbroker. 'Buying' may be for cash or by exchange of other property or on secured or unsecured credit and includes receiving goods or documents of title under a preexisting contract for sale but does not include a transfer in bulk or as security for or total or partial satisfaction of a money debt." . . .

Mrs. Sharp entered into a contract with the dealer to purchase the car by (1) delivery of her trade-in or exchange of property; (2) by cash, not actually paid but secured by a deferred delivery of the vehicle under a collateral oral agreement; (3) by cash, unsecured, to be paid at a later date; and (4) by a secured credit agreement sold by the dealer to the plaintiff. The dispute, arising out of the attempt to enforce the secured credit agreement or retail installment contract, comes from the contention of the defendant bank that the entire transaction with Mrs. Sharp was executory only, that it was never consummated, title did not pass, and it was null and void.

The plaintiff, as a retail financer, on the other hand, contends that Mrs. Sharp was a buyer out of inventory in the ordinary course of business on her partly performed contract. . . .

It may be said that Mrs. Sharp entered into a specific written contract to purchase the car owned by the dealer. She gave valuable consideration in goods, she traded in her old vehicle, and she signed a binding installment contract. She agreed to pay in cash a down payment and a deferred payment. By agreement, orally, she specified the source of her down payment, an anticipated income tax refund, and she certainly, in good faith expected to receive the car and to make her payments. . . . According to the testimony, she attempted to pay her cash deficiency a few days after the repossession by the bank, but, finding the car gone, abandoned her rights. The sales manager testified without contradiction that they frequently took and negotiated contracts with the car to be held for a time for the cash down payment, that it was common practice in his twenty years experience in the car business to take contracts without actual receipt of the recited cash down payment. He said he would fire a salesman who failed to do so and that in his experience and opinion a number of dealers would go out of business if they failed to follow this practice.

It is agreed by the parties that both the plaintiff and the defendant have formally perfected security interests and that the value of the collateral is $1,200. The question, therefore, becomes one of the priority of rights in the proceeds of the sale of the 1963 Chevrolet automobile. . . .

It is clear that the automobiles of the dealer were inventory held for sale to the public. . . . Under the agreement between the defendant bank and the dealer entitled "Floor-Plan Agreement and Signatory Authorization (Inventory)," it is provided in the opening paragraph that the purpose is to finance the dealer's acquisition and/or holding goods, i.e., motor vehicles for use and resale in the course of the dealer's business. It further provides, paragraph 8, as follows; "(8) The Dealer agrees that when any item of Goods is sold or otherwise disposed of, the Dealer will account to the Bank for the Proceeds and will deliver to the Bank such Proceeds and such assignments or indorsements as may be requisite or requested by the Bank. The Bank shall be entitled to the Proceeds and shall have a security interest in them. Pending such accounting and delivery, the Dealer will hold the Proceeds in trust for the Bank as the Bank's property, but at the Dealer's risk, in the identical form received and separate and apart from the Dealer's property. Proceeds as used herein means cash and noncash proceeds, immediate and remote, and includes any debts owing to the Dealer by reason of the sale or other disposition of any Collateral and any cash, checks, trade-ins, accounts, chattel paper, notes, drafts, or other instruments whenever received and any items of Collateral disposed of by the Dealer which are returned to or repossessed by the Dealer."

This is the very type of floating lien contemplated by UCC 9-204, and by UCC 9-205, which offsets the restrictive rulings of *Benedict* v. *Ratner*, 268 U.S. 353, 45 S.Ct. 566, 69 L.Ed. 991. Pursuant to this clause in the contract, the dealer received the funds obtained by assignments of Mrs. Sharp's retail installment contract and deposited these moneys to the dealer's account in the defendant bank. If it became comingled by the time of the insolvency, having, however, been traced into the bank account, it still remained a part of the gross remaining assets of the dealer enuring to the benefit of the bank on its seizure. . . . The bank should, then, have a prior right to such funds even against the trustee in bankruptcy, since the claim is an equitable substitution authorized by the statute for the original inventory lien and relates back to the perfection of such lien. . . .

Under its floor plan agreement, paragraph 12, the bank is completely [substituted] to all rights of the dealer in the business transactions and assets of the dealer on insolvency in implementation of the "floating lien" type transaction and for the protection of its rights thereunder. This includes its rights in and to the trade-in and its proceeds, if any, in the rights, if any, and in the contract rights of the dealer against Mrs. Sharp, had they been pursued on the contract, or for damages. . . .

By the same token, the plaintiff finance company, having furnished new value, which has been paid to the dealer on the assignment, and having purchased the chattel paper in due course, is entitled to the returned or repossessed goods under UCC 9-306(5)(b), (c), and (d) and UCC 9-308, provided, as in this case, its interest has been perfected, UCC 9-306(5)(d), UCC 9-302(1)(d), UCC 9-401(1)(b) and UCC 9-312(1). See also William D. Hawkland, a *Transactional Guide on Uniform Commercial Code,* pages 730 to 732, pages 700 to 701; *Anderson's Uniform Commercial Code,* pages 562 to 566 inclusive, for discussions of this point.

In making this determination, the Court has, of course, by inference, determined that the buyer of goods was a buyer in the ordinary course of business out of inventory. A discussion of this has been left to the close of this memorandum by reason of the fact that the entire relation of the parties as indicated above relates to whether the irregularities of the transaction would make Mrs. Sharp other than such a buyer. As indicated at the beginning, UCC 1-102 requires a construction of all terms to carry out the underlying purposes and policies set forth in the statute. . . . Any interpretation of the entire transaction, where both the retail financer and bank entruster acted in good faith which became so technical as to abort the intention of the Act and where a dealer has acted in relation to all the other parties, buyer, entruster, and financer, in such manner as to leave each with damage would undermine the ultimate success of the Act. If there is a usage of trade, which exposes an entruster on floor plan to certain risks, these are risks against which he can guard by audits and accounting procedures or he can refuse to knowingly expose himself to the risk with the particular dealer. To fail to place the exposure of such risk with the entruster in such situation would make it impossible for retail finance companies to do business with any dealer unless the entruster were directly a participant. To hold otherwise, would expose the retail financer to a double loss as against at most a partial loss for both. The proliferation of paper work would be a giant step backwards in modern commercial practice. The Court feels a buyer who makes a purchase on a printed form contract in good faith with a full understanding it is a binding contract, who knowingly signs a retail installment payment obligation and trades in an old car in addition must, certainly as to a retail financer furnishing new value on the strength of such contract and as to an entruster giving the dealer wide latitude of sale goods, be deemed a buyer in the ordinary course of business, without regard to the technicalities of when title is to pass pursuant to collateral oral agreements or as to time of delivery and without the necessity of determining whether such delay brings about technically, a bailment, a nondelivery, a repossession or whatever. . . . This is especially so where Article 9, UCC provides such a finely integrated plan for the determination of the priorities and equities of the parties to secured transactions. . . .

The plaintiff shall have judgment against the defendant, Marine Midland Trust Company of Western New York in the amount of $1,200 and interest from the 18th day of March, 1966.

Questions for Review

1. Define the social force of furtherance of trade.

2. Give illustrations of its application.

3. Analyze each opinion in this chapter in terms of the social forces involved in the decision. See § 5:5 for a list of the social forces. With respect to each opinion, explain why the prevailing social forces prevailed and why those rejected did not. In each case in which there is a dissenting opinion, also make this analysis for the dissenting opinion.

4-8. *On the basis of the social forces involved, what decision should be made in each of the following cases?*

4. *Premises liability. Adequacy of inspection.* Is a hotel protected from liability when a porcelain faucet handle crushes in the guest's hand by reason of the fact that the cleaning maid regularly reported defects observed? *Brown Hotel Co.* v. *Marx, Ky.,* 411 S.W.2d 911.

5. *Product liability. Safety device broken.* Is an equipment manufacturer required to give warning of a danger that would arise if the safety catch on the door of the equipment would break? *Westerburg* v. *School District,* 276 Minn. 1, 148 N.W.2d 312.

6. *Assignment. Right of assignee.* The City of Moab owed Holder for construction work. Holder assigned his claim against the city to Cooper. Cooper gave the city notice that the claim had been assigned to him and demanded payment. The city refused to make payment. Was Cooper entitled to recover? *Cooper* v. *Holder,* 21 Utah 40, 440 P.2d 15.

7. *Insurance. Cancellation.* May an insurance policy validly provide that the mere act of mailing a notice of cancellation shall be effective to cancel the policy? *Olson* v. *Hardware Dealers Mutual Fire Insurance Co.,* 38 Wis.2d 175, 156 N.W.2d 429.

8. *Assignment. Payment to assignor.* When a buyer is aware of an assignment because the installment contract signed by him contains a printed assignment clause, may the buyer make payment to the seller-assignor where

the contract states that payment may be made "in the office of the seller and/or its assigns?" *General Acceptance Corp.* v. *Guintini*, 115 Ga.App. 723, 155 S.E.2d 722.

9-13. What social forces were involved, which prevailed, and which were defeated in the following decisions?

9. **Premises liability. Carry-out service.** The fact that a store discontinues practice of having its employees assist customers in carrying out large packages does not constitute fault so as to impose liability where the customer, knowing that package was large and assistance not available, fell while carrying out the package. *Mick* v. *Kroger Co.*, 37 Ill.2d 148, 224 N.E.2d 859.

10. **Product liability. Free sample.** Distributor of product whose salesman gives a beauty shop operator a sample is liable on strict liability theory where the sample, a permanent wave preparation, is unfit for use; although no privity of contract was present, the preparation was in a sealed container, and there was not a sale of the sample but merely an expectation of future sales. *McKisson* v. *Sales Affiliates*, Tex., 416 S.W.2d 787.

11. **Product liability. Warning.** A manufacturer of a dangerous instrumentality satisfies the requirement of giving warning of its dangerous quality if he informs his purchaser, and an employee of the purchaser cannot bring suit for absence of a warning. *West* v. *Hydro-Test Inc.*, La., 196 So.2d 598.

12. **Usury. Resale profit.** Profit made on resale of property, after repossession, by secured credit seller is not "interest" within prohibition of the usury law. *Mong* v. *Bass*, Cal.App.2d, 56 Cal.Rptr. 579.

13. **Definiteness. Divisibility of contract.** Fincher was employed by Belk-Sawyer Co. as fashion coordinator for the latter's retail stores. The contract of employment also provided for additional services of Fincher to be thereafter agreed upon in connection with beauty consultation and shopping services to be established at the stores. After Fincher had been employed as fashion coordinator for several months, Belk-Sawyer Co. refused to be bound by the contract on the ground that it was too indefinite. It was held that the work of fashion coordinator was separate from future plans and that the contract was sufficiently definite and could be enforced with respect to the services as fashion coordinator, although there was no binding contract yet formed with respect to the additional services. *Fincher* v. *Belk-Sawyer Co.*, Fla., 127 So.2d 130.

Chapter 21

CREDITOR PROTECTION

§ 21:1. Generally

Society seeks to protect the rights of creditors and to protect them from dishonest or fraudulent acts of debtors. Initially creditors are protected by the law which declares that contracts are binding and which provides the machinery for the enforcement of contracts, and by the provision of the federal Constitution that prohibits states from impairing the obligation of contracts. Further, creditors may compel a debtor to come into bankruptcy in order to settle his debts as far as his property permits. If the debtor has concealed his property or transferred it to a friend in order to hide it from his creditors, the law permits the creditors to claim the property for the payment of the debts due them.

§ 21:2.   Transfers Harmful to Creditors

(a) *Generally.* The more property that a debtor owns, the more likely it is that he would be able to pay his debts. Society, therefore, seeks to protect creditors from transfers made by their debtors for the purpose of concealing their assets or otherwise putting them beyond the reach of the creditors.

(b) *Fraudulent conveyances.* Following an English statute, it is held in most states that a conveyance for the purpose of hindering, delaying, or defrauding creditors is voidable as against such creditors. The rule is applicable in the case of subsequent creditors, as well as those existing at the time of the conveyance. For example, when one, just before entering into debt, makes a conveyance that he knows is likely to render him unable to pay his obligations, the subsequent creditor may avoid the conveyance. When the transfer is made to a bona fide purchaser without notice, the title passes under a deed free from the demands or claims of either existing or subsequent creditors. In any case the person who claims that a transfer of title has been made in fraud of creditors has the burden of proving that fact.

Under the Uniform Fraudulent Conveyance Act [1] conveyances in certain situations are classified as being in fraud of creditors. If the claim of a defrauded creditor of the grantor is due, he may have the fraudulent conveyance set aside or he may disregard the conveyance and attach or levy execution upon the property conveyed, subject to whatever consideration has been paid by the grantee. If his claim has not matured, he may have the conveyance set aside or a receiver appointed or obtain such relief as may be appropriate.

NEUBAUER v. CLOUTIER

265 Minn. 539, 122 N.W.2d 623 (1963)

In 1958, Conrad Cloutier executed and delivered a promissory note to his then wife. Thereafter she sued him for divorce, which she obtained on December 8, 1961. On December 26, 1961, Conrad conveyed all his interest in his real estate to his mother and sister, Emma Cloutier and Mildred Stasik. The ex-wife then sued the mother and sister to have the deed to them set aside as a conveyance made in fraud of her claim based upon the promissory note.

---

[1] This Act has been adopted in Arizona, California, Delaware, Maryland, Massachusetts, Michigan, Minnesota, Montana, Nevada, New Hampshire, New Jersey, New Mexico, New York, North Dakota, Ohio, Oklahoma, Pennsylvania, South Dakota, Tennessee, Utah, Virgin Islands, Washington, Wisconsin, and Wyoming.

OPINION BY SHARAN, J. . . .

The question for determination is whether the trial court correctly decided that the evidence introduced by the creditor was, as a matter of law, inadequate to establish fraud in a conveyance by a deed dated December 26, 1961, and recorded on the following day whereby grantor conveyed to his mother and his sister his interest in a building located in Grand Rapids, Minnesota.

The complaint served on or about January 19, 1962, is based on a promissory note executed by the grantor and delivered to the creditor on January 2, 1958. . . . Judgment is prayed against the grantor for the amount due by the terms of the note and against the grantees that the conveyance be declared void and subject to a lien to enforce payment. . . .

Following the inception of the divorce proceedings between the grantor and his wife, which came up for trial in February, 1960, the grantor's mother had taken care of his child. Both the mother and the sister had advanced money in an unspecified amount to the grantor over a period of years prior to December 26, 1961, and he was then indebted to them. The amount of the indebtedness at the time of trial was not explained although the testimony indicated that it was at least $1,700. There was no written evidence to support the existence of this claimed obligation. There is no testimony as to whether interest on the obligation had ever been requested or paid.

The parties to the conveyance testified that the consideration for the transfer was the preexisting indebtedness, the amount of which, except as stated, was never specified.

The grantor was indebted to the plaintiff at the time of the conveyance on account of the promissory note of January 2, 1958, no payment on it having been made subsequent to December 24, 1959. The note was secured by a second mortgage on fixtures and equipment used in a restaurant business, the purchase of which gave rise to the debt.[1] The amount of the first mortgage does not appear in the record. The value, if any, of the security afforded by the second mortgage is unknown.

Although the note involved was not offered or received in evidence, admissions made by the attorneys for the grantor at the inception of the trial (April 24, 1962) constituted an acknowledgment that it was delinquent as of that date. Whether it was delinquent on December 26, 1961, when the conveyance involved was made, cannot be determined either from the record or from an examination of the chattel mortgage attached to the complaint.[2]

As of December 26, 1961, the grantor's interest in the realty involved was subject to a lien to secure payment of fees he owed the attorney who had represented him in the divorce proceedings. By the terms of the divorce decree his wife had been granted a lien to secure a debt grantor owed her also, although the record does not establish whether that debt was still a lien at the time of the conveyance. He had additional debts, the amount and character of which does not appear in the evidence.

---

[1] A mortgagee is a "creditor" and a mortgagor a "debtor" within definitions of "creditor" and "debt" under the Uniform Fraudulent Conveyance Act as respects a mortgagee's right to set aside as fraudulent conveyances of property not included in the mortgage. . . .

[2] See page 316.

There was no evidence as to the value of the grantor's interest in the realty involved as of December 26, 1961. In the course of the divorce proceedings in February, 1960, the grantor expressed the opinion that the realty was worth $75,000. Under cross-examination in this action he stated that it had been appraised at $50,000. However, the record is barren of evidence as to whether at the time the opinion was expressed the realty so valued was encumbered or subject to liens and there is nothing in the record showing the relationship, if any, between the opinion expressed as to the value of the realty in February, 1960, and the value of the grantor's interest therein on December 26, 1961.

1. Minn.St. 513.23 provides:

"Every conveyance made and every obligation incurred by a person who is or will be thereby rendered insolvent is fraudulent as to creditors without regard to his actual intent if the conveyance is made or the obligation is incurred without a fair consideration."

The fact that a conveyance was made and that plaintiff was then a creditor having been conceded, the burden of proof remains on the plaintiff [3] to show (a) that on December 26, 1961, defendant grantor was insolvent either at the time he made the conveyance here involved or as a result of it, and (b) that defendant grantor did not receive fair consideration in exchange.

2. A person is insolvent when the present fair salable value of his assets is less than the amount that will be required to pay his probable liabilities on his existing debts as they become absolute and mature.[4] There is no evidence whatever in the record from which the fair salable value of the grantor's assets on December 26, 1961, can be determined, and evidence as to the amount of his debts over and above his obligation to plaintiff was never developed. While it has been held in some jurisdictions that proof of

---

[2] The fact that the note was delinquent on December 26, 1961, does not appear specifically from the evidence. The grantor, at trial, admitted "that part of the complaint wherein a cause of action is alleged on a promissory note and chattel mortgage to the amount of the chattel mortgage and note as alleged . . . ." Delinquency on December 26, 1961, is not alleged. The chattel mortgage, a copy of which is attached to the complaint, is on a standard form and describes the note secured as follows: "Note for $4,206.47 dated January 2, 1958, 19—, due in ———— installments of $—— each with interest at 6% included in payments, percent per annum until paid, the first installment to be paid on the —— day of ————, 19—, and a like and equal sum on the —— day of each succeeding ———— thereafter until ——, 19—, when the balance remaining unpaid shall become due and payable."

[3] A creditor who assails a conveyance of his debtor for fraud must show it. . . . Ordinarily the burden is on the creditor to show the fraudulent character of the conveyance which he attacks. . . . Where a son conveys realty to his mother, no presumption of fraud arises from the relationship of the parties. . . . "Transfers between husband and wife are presumptively fraudulent as to existing creditors. . . . They are not so considered between parent and child, although scrutinized." . . . A different rule may apply if it is established that the conveyance was "voluntary," i.e., without consideration. . . . In the instant case there was consideration for the conveyance and no proof that the amount was disproportionate.

[4] Minn.St. 513.21(1) provides: "A person is insolvent when the present fair salable value of his assets is less than the amount that will be required to pay his probable liability on his existing debts as they become absolute and matured."

the delinquency of the debtor's obligation to the creditor at the time of the contested transfer makes a prima facie showing of insolvency, the rule is otherwise where the only proof is that of an existing debt without evidence of default as of the date the transfer is made. There is insufficient evidence, therefore, either to sustain the burden of proving insolvency or to raise a presumption which would support an affirmative finding in the absence of direct evidence on the point.

3. Apart from the defect of proof on the question of insolvency, there is no evidence that the quitclaim deed was executed and delivered "without a fair consideration." "Fair consideration" is given for property when in exchange for such property, as a fair equivalent therefor, and in good faith, an antecedent debt is satisfied.[5] To determine whether the antecedent debt satisfied by the conveyance was fairly equivalent in value to the interest quitclaimed we must know, first, the market value of the interest conveyed at the time of the transfer and, secondly, the amount of the antecedent debt thereby satisfied. On the record before us we have no way of determining what the value of the grantor's interest on the crucial date might have been. The rule that has been adopted in some jurisdictions to the effect that the revenue stamps affixed to deeds establish prima facie the amount of the consideration paid would, in the absence of any other evidence, support a finding that the grantor received consideration in an amount of less than $1,000.[6] This presumption continued only so long as there was no direct evidence on the point and dissolved upon proof that the antecedent debt satisfied was in the amount at least $1,700. Whether the consideration was approximately $1,000 or $1,700 or some amount in excess of $1,700 is of no aid to us where we lack competent evidence of the value of the interest quitclaimed against which to compare the consideration received.

---

[5] Minn.St. 513.22 provides: "Fair consideration is given for property, or obligation,

"(1) When in exchange for such property, or obligation, as fair equivalent therefor, and in good faith, property is conveyed or an antecedent debt is satisfied, or

"(2) When such property, or obligation, is received in good faith to secure a present advance or antecedent debt in amount not disproportionately small as compared with the value of the property, or obligation obtained."

[6] 26 USCA § 4361, reads as follows: "There shall be imposed a tax on each deed, instrument, or writing (unless deposited in escrow before April 1, 1932), whereby any lands, tenements, or other realty sold shall be granted, assigned, transferred, or otherwise conveyed to, or vested in, the purchaser or purchasers, or any other person or persons, by his, her, or their direction, when the consideration or value of the interest or property conveyed, exclusive of the value of any lien or encumbrance remaining thereon at the time of sale, exceeds $100 and does not exceed $500, in the amount of 55 cents; and at the rate of 55 cents for each additional $500 or fractional part thereof."

Minn.St. 287.21 reads as follows: "There is hereby imposed on each deed, instrument, or writing by which any lands, tenements, or other realty in this state shall be granted, assigned, transferred, or otherwise conveyed, a tax determined in the following manner. When there is no consideration or when the consideration, exclusive of the value of any lien or encumbrance remaining thereon at the time of sale, is $1,000 or less, the tax shall be $1.10. When the consideration, exclusive of the value of any lien or encumbrance remaining thereon at the time of sale, exceeds $1,000, the tax shall be $1.10 plus 55 cents for each $500 or fractional part of $500 in excess of $1,000."

4. There was no direct evidence in the case of actual intent to hinder, delay, or defraud creditors.[7] The defendant grantees testified that they did not know of the existence of the indebtedness to plaintiff at the time of the transfer. The answers of the defendant grantor suggest, if anything, an impression on his part that the security afforded by the second mortgage was protection for the plaintiff. Although the statement "Now let them file their liens" was made at the time that the deed was recorded, it can be assumed, and plaintiff in her brief suggests, that this statement was made with reference to the lien for attorney's fees filed against the property by the attorney who had represented the grantor in the divorce proceedings. Plaintiff had no lien on the real estate at the time. Action on the note was not commenced until the following month. The intent to which reference is made in Minn.St. 513.26 must exist at the time that the transfer was made. . . . To void the transfer, as in fraud of creditors, it is necessary in a case where the conveyance is not voluntary to show fraudulent intent of both debtor-grantor and creditor-grantee. . . . The fact that the grantor may have intended to give a preference to the debt owed his mother and sister is not evidence of an intent to hinder, delay, and defraud creditors within the meaning of § 513.26. . . . A conveyance is not "voluntary" if made in exchange for a valuable or fair consideration. . . .

5. Plaintiff contends that a finding of fraud on creditors could be based on the circumstance that the conveyance was made by a man, recently divorced, to his mother and sister. This relationship could not support a finding that the grantor was insolvent on December 26, 1961. It does not raise a presumption that the conveyance was "voluntary," i.e., without consideration, or that it was made "with actual intent, as distinguished from intent presumed in law, to hinder, delay, or defraud . . . creditors" within the meaning of § 513.26.[8] Where, as here, the uncontradicted evidence shows that consideration was in fact paid to the grantor by the grantees in the form of extinguishment of a preexisting debt, and there is a complete absence of evidence indicating a disparity between the consideration transferred and the value of the property received, the necessity which permits application of presumptions does not come into play.

6. The weakness of the plaintiff's proof in this case was probably due to the fact that she was taken by surprise when the defendant grantor, who had denied the indebtedness in his answer, admitted the debt after the jury had been selected, putting plaintiff in a position where it was necessary for her to proceed at once with such proof as she had available on the issue of fraud. In the court below, we note that plaintiff professed to have been deprived of the testimony of one possible witness because of this development. There is a suggestion—but no evidence—that the note involved was in fact

---

[7] Minn.St. 513.26 reads as follows: "Every conveyance made and every obligation incurred with actual intent, as distinguished from intent presumed in law, to hinder, delay, or defraud either present or future creditors, is fraudulent as to both present and future creditors."

[8] See footnote 3, supra.

delinquent on December 26, 1961, and, if this had been proved, a prima facie case of insolvency would have been established.[9] Interrogatories to the defendants could have fixed precisely the amount of the consideration claimed and the basis of it. Testimony as to the value of this building on the date of the transfer must be readily available. Liens and encumbrances are a matter of public record. There may be a reason why the essential evidence, so readily obtainable, was not presented to the trial court. Disposition of the rights of a creditor on a record which hints at but does not prove the essential elements of the plaintiff's case is not satisfactory. We are limited to the evidence before us. The same restriction confronted the trial court. Whether relief is possible under Rule 60.02, Rules of Civil Procedure, is a matter to be addressed to its discretion. Our decision of the case is without prejudice to application for such relief and without suggestion that, upon application, relief should or should not be granted.

[Affirmed.]

(c) Federal Bankruptcy Act. Another situation in which the claims of creditors may defeat the passing of title is that in which the conveyance violates a provision of the Federal Bankruptcy Act. Under the provisions of that statute, a conveyance that operates to give a preference to one creditor as against another may be set aside if the conveyance was made within four months prior to the time when the grantor was adjudged a bankrupt. The trustee in bankruptcy is also authorized to avoid any conveyance that is a fraud upon creditors.

§ 21:3. Surety Not Released

(a) Generally. In many transactions it is common for one of the parties to demand additional protection. Thus a bank lending money to the small corporation may want the promise of the corporation's president to pay the corporation debt if the corporation does not do so. In former years, it would appear that almost all of such guarantors or sureties were persons who were not paid for their assuming this supporting obligation, but were rather persons who did so out of friendship or because there was a common business objective, as in the corporation case above noted. It was not until the Twentieth Century that the insurance company went into the business of being a surety on any large scale. As may be expected, the switch in the character of the surety from an uncompensated, amateur friend to a compensated, professional stranger has influenced judicial decision.

---

[9] . . . Some courts construing § 4 of the Uniform Fraudulent Conveyance Act (Minn.St. 513.23) have held that the debtor need not be in default, but where there is a showing that he is heavily in debt the burden of going forward with the evidence is on the grantor or the grantee to show solvency at the time of the conveyance. . . . The burden rests upon the creditor, however, where the grantor or transferor is not in default. . . .

(b) Modification of the primary obligation. What if the primary debtor and the creditor make some change in the primary obligation, such as extending the time for payment, without the approval of the surety? In the earlier days, and many decisions still evidence this approach, the courts interpreted the surety's obligation very strictly and held that any modification thereof made without the consent of the surety discharged his liability as such. To take a simple case, if you guaranteed the note signed by a friend for 30 days and your friend and the holder of the note extended the time for payment to 60 days, this modification, if made without your consent, would release you as surety. Furthermore, the law did not consider whether the extension of the note was done in the exercise of good faith or good business judgment. In the eyes of the law the only significant fact was that you had only agreed to back up a 30-day note and, when that note ceased to exist because of the extension, your undertaking ceased to exist. With the advent of the paid corporate surety, the courts are not so eager to release the surety just because some change has taken place. Here the desire of protecting the creditor rises above the desire of protecting the surety, and it is frequently held that unless the surety can show that it had been harmed by what the parties have done, it is not released.

RELIANCE INSURANCE CO. v. COLBERT

365 F.2d 530 (C.A. Dist.Col., 1966)

Colbert and other trustees of a church made a contract with a contractor to build a church building. He was required to obtain a performance bond to indemnify the trustees in case he did not complete and satisfactorily perform the contract. The contractor obtained such a performance bond from the Reliance Insurance Co. After the bond was obtained, the trustees of the church and the contractor changed the terms of the original contract by a separate writing, which they called Addendum No. 3. The contractor failed to perform. Colbert and the trustees sued Reliance, which raised the defense that it was released by the modification made by the addendum without its consent. From an adverse decision, Reliance appealed.

OPINION BY McGOWAN, J. . . .

We return to the first—and primary—ground advanced by the District Court, *i.e.,* its conclusion that the alterations made by Addendum No. 3 were not material in relation to the risk assumed by the surety. The payment schedule contained in the contract before the advent of Addendum No. 3 called for an initial deposit of $7,450, and for successive payments of $12,500 upon completion of certain described phases of the construction. The comparative payment schedules provided by Addendum No. 2 and Addendum No. 3 are as follows:

	Addendum No. 2	Addendum No. 3
Initial Deposit	$ 7,450	$ 7,500
Completion of first floor shell to joists	12,500	10,000
Completion of second floor joists	12,500	10,000
Roofed in	12,500	5,000
Completion of job	12,500	25,000

It was because of financing difficulties that Addendum No. 3 was formulated. Under it the trustees were themselves to provide current financing in the amount of $32,500, consisting of the preconstruction first payment of $7,500, and $25,000 to be paid in escrow. The contractor was to produce $25,000 against the receipt by him of a negotiable note for $25,000 signed by the trustees and secured by real and chattel mortgages on the Church property. Addendum No. 3 said that the initial deposit of $7,500 [sic] called for by the original contract was to be met by an immediate payment of $1,450, plus $50, and release of $6,000 which the trustees had already deposited in escrow some time before Addendum No. 3 was signed. The $25,000 to be paid into escrow by the trustees was to be released in successive amounts of $10,000, $10,000, and $5,000 as the three phases of construction prior to final completion were reached. Addendum No. 3 then added a new undertaking by the trustees to pay the contractor a 5 percent commission on the $25,000 (or $1,250) which the contractor undertook in Addendum No. 3 to supply as a loan against the note.

Little discussion by way of comparison of Addendum Nos. 2 and 3 is necessary to demonstrate that the contract terms had undergone a substantial change, certainly of such a nature as to enable a surety to claim with reason that it should have had an opportunity to review its risk before deciding whether to adhere to its commitment to guarantee performance. A surety company is not a public utility. It may, for any or no reason, conclude not to furnish its bond with respect to a particular contract. When it has committed itself with respect to one contract, amendments which convert that agreement into a significantly different one should be brought to the attention of the surety so that it may exercise its own business judgment as to whether it wishes to continue its commitment. It is not for the parties to the contract to decide among themselves that their amendments are of no interest to the surety, at least when, as here, those amendments go beyond mere matters of form.

It may, of course, be entirely possible that notice to the surety of Addendum No. 3 would have evoked no cancellation of its bond. But the changes in the contract made by Addendum No. 3 are not such as to make this hypothesis a reasonably reliable one. Even a surety company as casual in its methods of operation as appellant appears on this record to have been might well have had second thoughts when it examined Addendum No. 3. We do not, therefore, feel warranted in attributing no significance to the fact that appellant was without opportunity to reappraise its commitment in the light of the contract as it took final shape through the instrumentality of Addendum No. 3. We do not, in sum, think that liability can be imposed upon the surety in this case. . . .

[Judgment reversed and case remanded.]

§ 21:4. Mortgages

(a) Recording. Creditors are protected in a number of ways in connection with mortgages. First in importance is undoubtedly the protection that each creditor has that a secret mortgage cannot be shown by a third person. For example, suppose that a bank lends $1 million to a corporation. On default, the bank proceeds against the corporation and directs the sheriff to sell the property of the debtor corporation to raise this amount. At that point, in walks another creditor who has a piece of paper of undisputed validity showing that he had loaned $1 million to the corporation before the bank had done so and that such other lender also has a mortgage. In order to protect lenders, the law provides that any unrecorded mortgage has no effect as against third persons not charged with knowledge thereof. Thus, the bank is protected from a surprise mortgage because the bank, having checked the records in city hall and not finding the recording of any mortgage, is entitled to rely on that record and all rights are disposed of as though in fact there were no mortgage.

(b) Future advances. When a mortgage is properly recorded, the debt it covers is a lien or claim against the mortgaged land. Thus, ordinarily the holder of the first mortgage gets paid first from any available proceeds arising from the sale of the land, the second mortgage holder gets paid second, and so on.

What if the first mortgage holder had made a further loan to the debtor after the second mortgage had been made? If the law adhered to the principle that it has followed thus far, the later loan made by the first mortgagee would be inferior to the second mortgage and would come third in priority. To give the first mortgagee greater protection, it is possible for the first mortgage to declare on its face that it covers future advances. In that case, the subsequent loan may be tacked onto the priority of the first mortgage and thus comes before the second mortgage.

The fact that the later loan by the first mortgagee cuts ahead of the second mortgagee would, at first glance, appear to be harming that creditor who had made the second mortgage loan on the basis of the facts as they existed at that time and not those facts as altered by increasing the amount of the prior mortgage. Here the practical answer is that the later advances cannot be added to the first mortgage or to any other earlier mortgage unless the earlier mortgage expressly states that it covers future advances; and since this mortgage must have been recorded in order to bind the subsequent parties, the second mortgagee makes his loan with his eyes open that there is the possibility of additional advances being added to the first mortgage, and thereby taking priority over his second mortgage.

BATTEN v. JURIST

306 Pa. 64, 158 A. 557 (1932)

Jurist mortgaged certain land to Freeman to secure a debt of $13,000. Jurist subsequently mortgaged the same property to Sutro to secure payment of $5,000 and "future advances." Thereafter, the Northwestern National Bank & Trust Co., believing the property to be mortgaged for only $18,000, extended credit to Jurist from time to time until the indebtedness amounted to more than $41,000. The Freeman mortgage was assigned to Batten, who brought suit against Jurist to foreclose the mortgage. After payment of the Freeman debt, there remained $16,339.76 in the hands of the sheriff. Sutro, who had advanced an additional $15,000 to Jurist, claimed this money. The Northwestern National Bank & Trust Co. contended that Sutro was entitled only to the amount specifically set out in the mortgage, $5,000, and interest. From a judgment in favor of Sutro with respect to the additional $15,000, the bank appealed.

OPINION BY MAXEY, J. . . .

A mortgage to secure a specific sum and also further advances unlimited as to time and amount is . . . valid against subsequent lien creditors. . . .

"It is also established that when such a contract obligates the mortgagee either to make advances or assume future responsibilities on behalf of the mortgagor, this lends a sufficient consideration to the mortgage and the lien of payments made under such an agreement relates back to the date of the mortgage; furthermore, this is true even though the advances or liquidation of assumed responsibilities occur after the date of a subsequent or junior encumbrance placed upon the mortgaged premises."

. . . A mortgagee cannot make voluntary additional advances after knowledge of an intervening claim and then have priority as to such advances. "Actual notice to the mortgagee will cut off his priority as to all optional future advances thereafter made." . . . However, the rule thus variously stated had no application . . . here.

There is much logic in the argument that the judicial recognition accorded mortgages for unlimited future advances offends the spirit of our modern recording acts. For example, the Act of April 29, 1909, . . . provides that the recorder shall deliver at stated intervals to the board of revision of taxes or other officials charged with the assessment of state tax a list of the mortgages recorded, assignments, etc., with the names and residences of the mortgagees, assignees, or persons entitled to interest, with the amount and date of the mortgages, etc. A mortgage given for future advances would put the recorder to the trouble of ascertaining the amount of such advances, and this information might be withheld from him. However, the act quoted would

not in itself justify us in departing from the judicial precedents long established in cases like this and in cases of cognate character. . . . If public
policy is to condemn such mortgages, it must find statutory expression, as it
has in Maryland and New Hampshire. . . .

[Judgment in favor of Sutro sustained.]

§ 21:5. Workers' Claims

(a) Generally. The law ordinarily prefers the claims of workingmen to a
certain extent. Thus, by statute most states provide that workers or particular kinds of workers shall have laborers' or mechanics' liens. Some of
these statutes only apply when the employer is insolvent or when the work
done results in the improvement or alteration of a building, such as in the
case of the work of plasterers, bricklayers, and stonemasons. In spite of
the traditional limited liability of corporate shareholders, statutes frequently
impose upon shareholders liability for unpaid wages of employees. In bankruptcy proceedings, a priority is given to wages due to workmen, clerks,
traveling or city salesmen, or servants earned within the three months preceding the filing of the bankruptcy petition, and not exceeding $600 as to
each claimant. In most states, when a person dies owing wages, the wage
claimant is generally given some degree of priority for his claim.

Various criminal laws are designed to protect the wage claimant, as by
making it a crime to pay wages in scrip or to pay less frequently than every
other week. On federal construction work, it is a crime to require the employee to kick back part of his wage as the "fee" for letting him have the job.
In a number of states, money paid by an owner to a contractor for the
payment of the construction work covered by the contract is deemed a
"trust fund" that must be used by the contractor for paying off all claims
for the labor and material used in the construction, and the contractor is
guilty of a crime if he fails to do so.

DAUGHERTY v. TENNESSEE

216 Tenn. 666, 393 S.W.2d 739 (1965)

Vermillion made a contract with Daugherty by which the latter was to
construct a house. Daugherty did not pay for all the labor and material used
in the construction and was prosecuted and convicted under a construction
trust fund statute.

OPINION BY DYER, J. . . .

The defendant entered into a written contract with Roy Vermillion, the
prosecutor, on March 26, 1963, for the construction of a house for the consideration of $19,000. By the terms of the contract the defendant, a build-
ing contractor, was to furnish the materials, supplies, and labor. Defendant
stopped construction on the house about November 15, 1963, without com-

pleting it after making a demand for $3,200, which demand was not granted. There was a difference of opinion as to the percentage of completion at this time with estimates ranging from 45 percent completion to 80 percent completion. When construction stopped Mr. Vermillion had paid the defendant $14,644 of the $19,000 contract price, lacking some $4,300, which was to be paid when the house was completed. Mr. Vermillion had paid the defendant an additional $820 for changes and alterations made in the contract specifications, making a total paid of $15,464. Liens were filed by materialmen and laborers who had worked on the house against both Roy Vermillion and the defendant in the amount of $7,401.14.

While building the house, the defendant expended $7,243.93 for materials and $8,364.21 for labor making a total expenditure for materials and labor of $15,608.14. Evidence was introduced that the defendant issued two checks to the Smith Hardware Store; one for $100 and the other for $75, marked "Materials, Vermillion Job" as payment on his account there. The only things shown to have been bought from Smith was a roto-tiller and a skill saw, which things would not ordinarily be considered materials for a house construction.

There was additional evidence that defendant issued two checks to Harris Supply Company; one for $300 and the other for $500, although no material was sent to the Vermillion job from Harris. Defendant explained by saying these materials were sent to another job by mistake. All of the checks issued by the defendant including the ones to Smith and Harris had notations on them indicating their uses, i.e. "Material Vermillion Job," but defendant was unable to testify at what time these notations were placed on the checks.

Defendant kept no records of the work done by his laborers that is, he didn't keep any time records nor did he have a set rate of pay. The laborers kept their own time according to the defendant, and they were paid according to the value of the work they did. Defendant did keep canceled checks and receipts, although the receipt dates did not correspond to the date of actual payments. One of the laborers was defendant's brother and two of them were his cousins.

The statute the defendant was convicted under, TCA § 64-1140, reads as follows:

"Any contractor, subcontractor, or other person who, with intent to defraud, shall use the proceeds of any payment made to him on account of improving certain real property for any other purpose than to pay for labor performed on, or materials furnished by his order for, this specific improvement, while any amount for which he may be or become liable for such labor or materials remains unpaid, shall be guilty of a felony and punished accordingly. 64-1140."

This statute should be read in conjunction with TCA § 64-1142 which states:

"Such use of the proceeds mentioned in §§ 64-1139—64-1141 for any purpose other than the payment of such unpaid amount shall be prima facie evidence of intent to defraud. 64-1142."

Under this statute, it is a criminal offense for a contractor to retain or appropriate to his own use payments made to him on a contract for realty improvements without paying the amounts due for labor and materials which may become a lien on the realty. A statute of this nature is intended to make the payments to the contractor trust funds for the payment of labor and materials, and to afford protection against contractors who receive money for construction or repair of buildings and divert it to other uses prior to payment of claims for labor, materials, or other charges in connection with the work on the buildings. The legislative purpose is to punish for a fraudulent conversion and not for failure to comply with a contractual obligation. The essential elements for the commission of the offense are the payment of the money to a contractor by the owner for the construction of a building and a diversion of the money to other purposes by the contractor prior to the payment of all claims for which the money constitutes a trust fund. . . .

It is assigned here as error the evidence preponderates against the verdict and in favor of the innocence of the accused. Under a long line of decisions we have held the verdict of the jury determines the credibility of the witnesses and resolves all conflicts in their testimony. In this case the jury verdict is against defendant and there is ample evidence to support such finding. This assignment of error is overruled.

The determinative issue, in this appeal, is the constitutionality of the statute in question. Generally, statutes which, in effect, make it an offense for a contractor to retain or appropriate to his own use payments made to him on a contract for realty improvements without paying amounts due for labor and materials which may become a lien on the realty have been sustained although some statutes of that nature, but having different phraseology, have been held to violate constitutional provisions. . . .

Several recent Tennessee cases have involved this statute although they have not ruled on the precise issues in point here. *State* v. *Overton,* 193 Tenn. 171, 245 S.W.2d 188 (1951), held that the statute in question was not unconstitutional on the grounds that it was ambiguous or meaningless. This is apparently the only Tennessee case that has ruled on the statute's constitutionality. The court pointed out that the offense very closely approaches embezzlement since there exists a confidential relation and the person who is charged by reason of such relationship misappropriates or diverts the funds paid to him for a specific purpose.

As mentioned previously, several states, including California and South Dakota, with similar statutes, have held these statutes unconstitutional for various reasons. Two California cases . . . held similar statutes unconstitutional on the grounds of imprisonment for debt and interfering with the right to contract. These courts held that the legislature did not have the power to tell the contractor how to spend his own money nor could it provide that "a contractor who breaches his agreement to pay a certain class of debts with money that is his own shall, for that reason alone, be deemed guilty of a crime punishable with imprisonment." This California position was followed in South Dakota. . . .

By far the majority of courts that have ruled on this question in this country, however, have held the statutes constitutional. The Delaware case, *State* v. *Tabasso Homes,* 42 Del. 110, 28 A.2d 248 (1943), held:

"While there is, subject to limitations, an inalienable right of parties to contract one with another, there is no inalienable right to embezzle or misappropriate money paid pursuant to a contract for the erection of a building, and it is this latter act that the statute attempts to prevent. The statute does not interfere with the right to contract, but contractors enter into their engagements with a knowledge of the statute, in the same manner as they do with reference to the Mechanics Lien Statute, and numerous other statutory provisions. . . .

"[T]he penalty of the statute is not invoked by any reason of the contract, but only in case of the misapplication of money, subsequently committed by one of the contractors. The penalty of the statute only arises if and when the offense is committed. . . ."

The Delaware court interpreted their statute to mean money paid to a contractor, to be used in a building operation, should constitute a trust fund for those who by labor or materials have erected the building. The Tennessee case of *Hammer-Johnson Supply, Inc.* v. *Curtis,* 51 Tenn.App. 72, 364 S.W. 2d 496 (1962), used similar language in saying a trust fund was set up.

The following states have held similar statutes to be constitutional: Georgia . . . ; Washington . . . ; Virginia . . . ; South Carolina . . . ; Minnesota . . . ; [and] Wisconsin. . . .

Defendant first cites Article 1, Section 8, of the Tennessee Constitution which is the "law of the land" section. This is, of course, synonymous with the "due process of law" used in the Fifth Amendment and in the First Section of the Fourteenth Amendment to the Constitution of the United States. . . . The right to contract is subject to curtailment, limitation, and destruction by the legislature, when such is done pursuant to "the law of the land." . . . In *Motlow* v. *State,* 125 Tenn. 547, 145 S.W. 177 (1911), it was held that this section of the constitution forbade that any mere individual be singled out for legislative action, but did not deny the right to the legislature to make proper classification for purposes of legislation. Such legislation has to rest upon some natural or reasonable basis, having some substantial relation to the public welfare, and the same provisions must approximately apply in the same way to all the members of the class. TCA § 64-1140 does not violate this section of the Constitution since it applies to all contractors. As was said in *Henley* v. *State,* 98 Tenn. 665, 41 S.W. 352 (1897):

"A statute is the "law of the land," which embraces all persons who are already or who may thereafter come into similar situations, conditions, and circumstances. If classifications are resorted to, they must be natural and reasonable, not arbitrary and capricious. 98 Tenn. 665, 41 S.W. 352."

Defendant next cites Article 1, Section 9, which deals with the right of the accused in criminal prosecutions. Although not cited by name, defendant was apparently referring to the case of *Duncan Mayes* v. *State,* 50 Tenn. 430, 441 (1871), which held:

"It is not in the power of the legislature to so regulate the proof as to throw the burden on the accused, and thereby change the legal presumption that every man is innocent until the contrary appears from the proof. 50 Tenn. 441."

The above statement is correct but we do not think it applicable to the case at bar. More nearly in point is the following:

"The right of trial by an impartial jury is not impaired or abridged by a provision in a statute that proof of certain enumerated facts shall constitute prima facie evidence of fraudulent intent to commit the offense created by the statute. Legislation prescribing rules of evidence, and declaring what shall be evidence is practically unrestricted and will be upheld, if impartial and uniform, and not operating to preclude a party from exhibiting his rights. . . .

"In every case the defendant is entitled to trial by an impartial jury, and to the benefits of a presumption of innocence, but that right and that presumption can no more preclude a presumption of guilty intent from sufficient proof adduced than they can preclude the introduction of proof altogether. . . ."

(b) Conflict with other creditors. The interest of a small creditor may come into conflict with the interest of a large creditor, and then the law must determine whether all creditors are to be treated equally or whether the court is to protect the smaller creditor in some way.

In today's circumstances, this problem arises frequently when the owner of a financed car takes it to a repair shop and has repairs made for which he does not pay. It is clear that the financer of the car contemplated the possibility that the car would be taken in for repairs. If the buyer used the car to earn money, it might even be surmised that the financer would approve of making the repairs in order to enable the debtor to earn the money with which the financer would be paid. At the same time, the concept of stability would argue that the prior security interest of the financer, being prior in point of time, should prevail, unless the financer authorized or approved the making of the repairs.

Here the argument as to practical expediency comes into the picture. It would be very annoying if the repairman had to identify, locate, and consult with the secured creditor before he could safely take any action as to making repairs on credit. In the interest of bypassing much delay over what repairs are needed and the reasonable cost for them, the Uniform Commercial Code has flatly declared that the lien of the repairman is superior.[2]

Intercreditor conflict is also found when the employer owes money to the employee and the employee owes money to a third person, such as a department store. If wages were not involved, the debt owed by a third person to the claimant's debtor may be reached by the claimant by means of an attachment or garnishment. In the wage situation above described, many states prohibit any attachment of wages or limit the amount of percentage of the wage claim which the creditor of the employee may reach. By the Federal Consumer Credit Protection Act of 1968, garnishment of wages is ordinarily limited to (a) 25 percent of the worker's weekly take-home pay, or (b) the difference between his weekly take-home pay and 30 times the federal minimum hourly wage—whichever is less.

---

[2] Uniform Commercial Code § 9-310. The only exception is when the repairman's lien is based on a statute which expressly declares that it is subordinated to or inferior to the prior perfected security interest of the financer.

Questions for Review

1. Define the social force of creditor protection.

2. Give illustrations of its application.

3. Analyze each opinion in this chapter in terms of the social forces involved in the decision. See § 5:5 for a list of the social forces. With respect to each opinion, explain why the prevailing social forces prevailed and why those rejected did not. In each case in which there is a dissenting opinion, also make this analysis for the dissenting opinion.

4-8. On the basis of the social forces involved, what decision should be made in each of the following cases?

4. *Wages. Exemption.* Jones was employed by American Messer Corporation. Jones owed money to Laurencic who attached Jones' wages. Under the local law, 80 percent of the wages was exempt from attachment. Laurencic claimed that he was entitled to attach all of the wages on the theory that the exemption from attachment had ended because Jones (a) had quit his job, and (b) had abandoned his family. Decide. *Laurencic v. Jones,* La., 180 So.2d 803.

5. *Mechanics' lien. Nature of services.* The applicable statute provided that ". . . all persons . . . bestowing skill or other necessary services on, or furnishing materials to be used . . . or furnishing appliances, teams, or power contributing to, the construction, . . . or other work of improvement . . ." upon the real estate was entitled to a mechanics' lien. Contractors Dump Truck Service was in the business of contacting owners of equipment and then making contracts for the use of their equipment with contractors doing actual construction work. It made such an equipment brokerage contract with Gregg Constr. Co., furnishing it with equipment owned by other persons. When Gregg did not pay the amount due, Contractors claimed that it was entitled to a lien under the above quoted statute. Was it correct? *Contractors Dump Truck Service v. Gregg Constr. Co.,* Cal.App.2d, 46 Cal.Rptr. 738.

6. *Bankruptcy. Fraudulent transfer.* The Brankruptcy Act provides "every transfer made . . . by a debtor within one year prior to the filing of [the petition of bankruptcy] is fraudulent as to creditors existing at the time of such transfer . . . if made . . . without fair consideration by a debtor who is . . . insolvent, without regard to his actual intent." Stone and other employees of Estes were given two months' pay as a Christmas bonus. Within one year thereafter, Estes went into bankruptcy. Was the Christmas bonus a fraudulent transfer? *Stone v. Moore,* [C.A.5th] 375 F.2d 110.

7. *Bankruptcy. Discharge of codebtor.* Wolken and Brown were the principal officers of Wolbrown, Inc. Bertash Market Company sold goods to the corporation. Later Bertash claimed that Brown and Wolken owed for the goods thus sold. They raised the defense that the claim for the bill could not be made against them because Wolbrown, Inc., had gone through bankruptcy and Bertash's bill had been proven and discharged in the bankruptcy proceeding. Was this a valid defense? *Bertash Market Co. v. Brown,* 10 Ill.App.2d 8, 217 N.E.2d 362.

8. ***Bankruptcy. Refinancing.*** Barnes borrowed money from the Seaboard Finance Company. He executed a note covering the loan. Sometime thereafter he borrowed additional money and executed a new note to take the place of the original note. The finance company showed that the original loan was obtained by false statements. The finance company claimed that this falsity barred granting Barnes a discharge for the total amount of the debt. Barnes claimed that it only barred a discharge as to the original loan but not the additional loan. The Bankruptcy Act states: "a discharge in bankruptcy shall release a bankrupt from all of its provable debts . . . except such as . . . are liabilities for obtaining money or property by false pretenses or false representations, or for obtaining money or property on credit or obtaining an extension or renewal of credit in reliance upon materially false statement in writing respecting his financial condition made or published or caused to be made or published in any manner whatsoever with intent to deceive." *Seaboard Finance Co.* v. *Barnes,* 378 Mich.2d 627, 148 N.W.2d 756.

9-11. *What social forces were involved, which prevailed, and which were defeated in the following decisions?*

9. ***Fraudulent conveyance. Presumption of fraud.*** Where an insolvent debtor transfers accounts receivable without receiving consideration therefor, a presumption of fraudulent intent arises that entitles the creditor to avoid the transfer unless the presumption is rebutted. *Gafco, Inc.* v. *H.D.S. Mercantile Corp.,* 47 Misc.2d 661, 263 N.Y.S.2d 109.

10. ***Mortgages. Future advances.*** A mortgage was obtained to finance a building construction. It provided for optional future advances up to a stated maximum. After this amount had been fully loaned, persons entitled to mechanics' liens claimed that they were entitled to share the priority of the mortgage as to their claims because their work was essential to performing the construction that was the object of the mortgage loan. It was held that the mortgagee who was not notified by the lien claimants until after the advances had been made was entitled to priority over all their claims. *Regold Mfg. Co.* v. *Maccabees,* Tex.Civ.App., 348 S.W.2d 864.

11. ***Commercial paper. Value.*** A father sold a promissory note to his son. The note was in the amount of $6,900. The son paid for the note by giving the father a check for $3,000, a note for $1,000, and six head of cattle worth at least $1,000. It was held that the son was a purchaser of the note for value and in good faith, as against the argument that the difference between the note and the amount paid required a contrary conclusion. *Bolten* v. *Colburn,* Mo.App., 389 S.W.2d 384.

Chapter 22

DEBTOR PROTECTION

§ 22:1. Generally

Society has come to regard as unsound the fact that debtors should be ruined forever by the burden of their debts. The passing centuries have seen the debtor's prison abolished. Bankruptcy laws have been adopted to provide the debtor with a means of settling his debts as best he can and then starting upon a new economic life. In times of widespread depression, the same objective has been served by special laws that prohibit the foreclosure of mortgages and regulate the amount of the judgments that can be entered against mortgage debtors.

The object of debtor rehabilitation is seen in laws designed to prevent debtors from getting too deeply into debt or from paying too much when they borrow money. For example, the usury law acts as a limitation on the "cost" of a debt to the borrower. In some states, limitations or prohibitions are placed on the assigning of wages. Other states limit the extent to which subsequent loans may be added to a prior mortgage, thereby limiting the extent to which the mortgagee or other lenders would be willing to lend money to the debtor, since the subsequent loans would not have the priority of the original mortgage.

§ 22:2.   Bankruptcy

Under a survival-of-the-fittest system, society could ignore those who become insolvent. However, our society is not willing to do so. It has accordingly provided a system by which the honest debtor can, in substance, pay into court what he has, be relieved of all unpaid debts, and start economic life anew. This is achieved by means of bankruptcy laws in the case of the federal government and insolvency laws in the case of the states.

Historically these laws were not concerned with benefiting the debtor as much as they were with benefiting creditors. In their origin bankrutcy laws were designed to enable creditors to compel a fraudulent debtor to bring his property into court and pay it to his creditors, thus preventing him from concealing his property or from paying it only to some of his creditors. Today, bankruptcy and insolvency proceedings partake of both features as can be seen from the fact that such a proceeding may be started by the debtor himself or by his creditors.

State insolvency laws have only a limited sphere of operation today because the federal bankruptcy laws have superseded them to a large degree, but state statutes relating to voluntary assignments made by a debtor for the benefit of all of his creditors may still be in force.

CONTINENTAL & ILLINOIS NATIONAL BANK & TRUST CO. v. CHICAGO, R.I. & P. RY.

294 U.S. 648 (1935)

By an amendment to the Federal Bankruptcy Law, Section 77 was added providing for the corporate reorganization of railroads. The validity of this law was challenged on the ground that it was not a bankruptcy law.

Opinion by Sutherland, J. . . .

The English law of bankruptcy, as it existed at the time of the adoption of the Constitution, was conceived wholly in the interest of the creditor and proceeded upon the assumption that the debtor was necessarily to be dealt with as an offender. Anything in the nature of voluntary bankruptcy was unknown to that system. The persons who were permitted to fall within the term "bankrupt" were limited to traders. But the notion that the framers of the Constitution, by the bankruptcy clause, intended to limit the power of Congress to the then existing English law and practice upon the subject long since has been dispelled.

. . . It was definitely decided that the extent of the power of Congress was not limited to the principle upon which the English bankruptcy system was founded. . . .

But, while it is true that the power of Congress under the bankruptcy clause is not to be limited by the English or Colonial law in force when the Constitution was adopted, it does not follow that the power has no limitations. Those limitations have never been explicitly defined. . . . Probably the most satisfactory approach to the problem of interpretation here involved is to examine it in the light of the acts, and the history of the acts, of Congress which have from time to time been passed on the subject. . . .

The first act, that of 1800 so far ignored the English law, which was confined to traders, as to include bankers, brokers, and underwriters as well. The act of 1841 added merchants; and other additions have been made by later acts until now practically all classes of persons and corporations are included. . . . The act of 1800 was one exclusively in the interest of the creditor. But the act of 1841 took what then must have been regarded as a radical step forward by conferring upon the debtor the right by voluntary petition to surrender his property, with some exceptions, and relieve himself of all future liability in respect of past debts. The act of 1800, like the English law, was conceived in the view that the bankrupt was dishonest; while the act of 1841 and the later acts proceeded upon the assumption that he might be honest but unfortunate. One of the primary purposes of these acts was to "relieve the honest debtor from the weight of oppressive indebtedness, and permit him to start afresh free from the obligations and responsibilities consequent upon business misfortunes," and to give him "a new opportunity in life and a clear field for future effort, unhampered by the pressure and discouragement of preexisting debt." . . .

By the Act of March 2, 1867, as amended by the Act of 1874, . . . the debtor for the first time was permitted, either before or after an adjudication in bankruptcy, to propose terms of composition to his creditors to become binding upon their acceptance by a designated majority and confirmation by the judge.

The fundamental and radically progressive nature of these extensions becomes apparent upon their mere statement; but all have been judicially approved or accepted as falling within the power conferred by the bankruptcy clause of the Constitution. Taken altogether, they demonstrate in a very striking way the capacity of the bankruptcy clause to meet new conditions as they have been disclosed as a result of the tremendous growth of business and development of human activities from 1800 to the present day. And these acts, far-reaching though they be, have not gone beyond the limit of congressional power; but rather have constituted extensions into a field whose boundaries may not yet be fully revealed.

Section 77 advances another step in the direction of liberalizing the law on the subject of bankruptcies. Railway corporations had been definitely excluded from the operation of the law in 1910 . . . , probably because such corporations could not be liquidated in the ordinary way or by a distribution of assets. A railway is a unit; it cannot be divided up and disposed of piecemeal like a stock of goods. It must be sold, if sold at all, as a unit and as a going concern. Its activities cannot be halted because its continuous, uninterrupted operation is necessary in the public interest; and, for the preservation of that interest, as well as for the protection of the various private interests involved, reorganization was evidently regarded as the most feasible solution whenever the corporation had become "insolvent or unable to meet its debts as they mature."

Equity receiverships, resorted to for that purpose, have never been satisfactory for many reasons. Partly, no doubt, in recognition of that situation, Congress, by § 77, added railroad corporations to the category of those who might have relief by legislation passed in virtue of the bankruptcy clause of the Constitution; and determined, after consideration, that such relief to be effectual should take the form of a reorganization, and should extend to cases where the corporation is "unable to meet its debts as they mature." The last phrase, since it is used as an alternative for the word "insolvent," obviously means something less than a condition of "bankruptcy" or "insolvency" as those words are employed in the law. See Bankruptcy Act, § 1(15), which defines an "insolvent" as one whose assets, at a fair valuation, are not sufficient to pay his debts. It may be construed to include a debtor who, although unable to pay promptly, may be able to pay if time to do so be sufficiently extended. Obviously, § 77 does no more than follow the line of historical and progressive development projected by previous acts.

As outlined by that section, a plan of reorganization, when confirmed, cannot be distinguished in principle from the composition with creditors authorized by the act of 1867, as amended by the act of 1874. It is not necessary to the validity of either that the proceeding should result in an adjudication of bankruptcy. The constitutionality of the old provision for a composition is not open to doubt. . . . That provision was . . . sustained upon the broad ground that the "subject of bankruptcies" was nothing less than "the subject of the relations between an insolvent or nonpaying or fraudulent debtor, and his creditors, extending to his and their relief." That it was not necessary for the proceedings to be carried through in bankruptcy was held not to warrant the objection that the provision did not constitute a law on the subject of bankruptcies. The same view sustains the validity of § 77. Both contemplate an adjustment of a failing debtor's obligations; and although actual bankruptcy may not supervene in either, they are none the less laws on the subject of bankruptcies. With due regard for consistency, the constitutional validity of the one cannot well be sustained and that of the other denied. . . .

§ 22:3.   Protection of Wages and Employee Benefits

Many states prohibit or restrict an employee from assigning his wages or rights in various pension and retirement funds. Here the object of debtor protection dominates at the expense of creditor protection. This is stated because ordinarily the assignment is made to someone else to whom money is owed, and the conclusion that the interest in question cannot be assigned means that such person is not paid from the assigned fund or claim but must pursue his ordinary remedies for collection. In the case of the ordinary employee, this may mean as a practical matter that the creditor may never get paid because there may be no fund other than the one assigned from which the creditor can obtain payment, even after the creditor has gone to the expense and trouble of obtaining a judgment against the debtor.

The rule of nonassignability may also deter trade in that it means that the employee has less available assets than if he could assign such interest. Correspondingly, the creditor will be less willing to deal with the employee on a credit basis if such funds are not assignable, although this negative effect with respect to furtherance of trade has been offset by the development of the secured transactions in personal property.

SAN JOSE v. FORSYTHE

261 Cal.App.2d 131, 67 Cal.Rptr. 754 (1968)

A declaratory judgment action was brought to determine whether a former city employee had, in effect, made an assignment of his rights in a retirement fund and whether such assignment was valid.

OPINION BY SHOEMAKER, P. J. . . .

Plaintiffs City of San Jose, the Retirement Board of the Federated City Employees' Retirement System, and Jack Marzluft, the city auditor, brought this action for declaratory relief against defendants Chester Forsythe and the Municipal Employees' Credit Union of San Jose. . . .

Defendant Forsythe was an employee of plaintiff city from March 1, 1962, until March 2, 1964, and while so employed was a member of the retirement system. During the period of his employment, monthly sums were deducted from his salary and deposited in the retirement fund. On July 17, 1963, defendant Forsythe was granted a loan of $1,650 by credit union and executed an installment note and a special power of attorney authorizing defendant credit union "to receive, endorse, or collect checks payable to [Forsythe] issued by any person, firm, or corporation whatsoever, and to give a full discharge for the same. . . ." Upon the termination of his employment, plaintiff retirement board authorized the return to Forsythe of his accumulated contributions in the sum of $524.71. Plaintiff city auditor drew a warrant in that amount in Forsythe's favor, and he and defendant credit union demanded delivery of the warrant.

Under section 2904.128 of the San Jose Municipal Code, the right of any person to money in the retirement fund was unassignable. Plaintiffs assert that section 2904.128 prohibited plaintiff city auditor from delivering the warrant to defendant credit union.

Defendant credit union asserts that the power of attorney was in full force and effect and that it was entitled to Forsythe's accumulated contributions in the retirement fund.

Forsythe failed to appear in the action, either in person or by counsel, and his default was entered.

At the trial it developed that the proceeds of the warrant, if received by credit union, would be paid to the comakers of the note who had already paid defendant credit union the amount due under the note.

The trial court made findings of fact in accord with the foregoing statement, and further found that defendant Forsythe's default had been duly entered; that Forsythe's accumulated contributions in the retirement fund were not wages or salary within the meaning of Government Code, section 1155; that section 2904.128 of the San Jose Municipal Code did not prohibit plaintiff city auditor from delivering the warrant to defendant credit union; that the power of attorney, which had never been revoked, was a valid instrument as between plaintiffs and defendants; and that defendant credit union was entitled to delivery of the warrant.

The court concluded as a matter of law that by allowing his default to be entered, defendant Forsythe had consented to the making and entering of any judgment with respect to the issues raised by the pleadings, and that defendant credit union was entitled to judgment in its favor.

Plaintiffs point out that section 2904.128 of the San Jose Municipal Code prohibits the assignment of "any benefit or other right under this Part and the money in the Retirement Fund" and that section 2904.28 of said code defines the term "benefit" as inclusive of a "refund of accumulated contributions." Plaintiffs further note that the trial court found that Forsythe's accumulated contributions in the retirement fund were not wages or salary within the meaning of Government Code, section 1155, and that the court based its judgment in favor of defendant credit union upon a narrow and literal interpretation of section 2904.128 as applying only to an "assignment" and not to a "power of attorney." Plaintiffs assert that such a construction of the section in question is erroneous because the legal effects of an assignment and a power of attorney are the same, in that both accomplish a transfer to the creditor of the right to collect moneys owed the debtor.

Defendant credit union contends that an assignment and a power of attorney are not the same in legal effect and asserts that the latter term means "a written authorization to an agent to perform specified acts in behalf of his principal," and further asserts that since Forsythe himself certainly possessed the capacity to receive, endorse or collect his own checks, he was also entitled to execute a power of attorney authorizing defendant, as his agent, to perform these acts. Defendant additionally urges that the execution of such a power of attorney cannot be deemed an assignment within the meaning of section 2904.128 of the San Jose Municipal Code, and does not agree that public policy favors protection of sums, which an employee withdraws from a pension fund prior to retirement age, upon termination of his employment.

The law of California favors the enforceability of clauses protecting retirement benefits from the claims of creditors. In *Thomas* v. *Thomas* (1961) 192 Cal.App.2d 771, 780, 783, 13 Cal.Rptr. 872, the court commented upon this policy and noted that in almost every instance where retirement programs are the subject of regulation by the legislature, the rights granted by such programs are preserved against creditors' claims. The Thomas case and the instant case present a similar situation in that the party whose funds are sought to be applied to the creditor's demands has disappeared, and the protection of the funds is asserted by the retirement agency. The Thomas case discusses the prevalence of nonassignability clauses respecting benefits both under public and private programs and finds that the rule in each case is the same, namely: that restrictions on assignability are valid and prevent the transfer to third parties of any rights held by the beneficiary of the plan.

In view of the policy favoring a provision such as that contained in section 2904.128 of the San Jose Municipal Code, the language therein employed should be liberally construed. . . .

Although the statute construed in the Lande case restricted the assignability of wages or salary, whereas the code section in the instant case prohibits the assignment of retirement benefits or accumulated contributions, it is apparent that both provisions are remedial in nature and ought to be accorded an equally liberal interpretation. In our view, if defendant credit union were permitted to exercise its power of attorney upon Forsythe's accumulated contributions in the retirement fund, said contributions would be transferred to said defendant just as effectively as if Forsythe had assigned to it his interest therein. Under such circumstances, we are satisfied that while a power of attorney is not an assignment, in strict legal parlance, nevertheless the City of San Jose intended, by the enactment of section 2904.128, to prevent an employee from utilizing either device as a means of transferring his interest in the retirement fund.

We find no merit in defendant's contention that accumulated contributions in the retirement fund are not entitled to protection when the employee terminates his employment prior to attaining retirement age. Sections 2904.-128 and 2904.28 of the city code are both too broadly worded to support any such construction. The former section prohibits the assignment of "any benefit or other right under this Part and *the money in the Retirement Fund*." . . . The latter section includes in its definition of "benefit" a "refund of accumulated contributions."

The judgment is reversed, with directions to the trial court to enter a declaratory judgment decreeing that defendant credit union is not entitled, under the power of attorney given to it by Chester Forsythe, to the refund of the contributions to the retirement system made by him.

§ 22:4.　Liquidity of Assets

Can the contract debtor borrow on the strength of his assets or convert them into cash? Because of the social force in favor of rehabilitating the debtor, the law has gradually moved in the direction of making it easier for the debtor to raise money. Thus, the prohibition against assigning contract rights was gradually destroyed in most instances. Likewise, the ability to transfer a claim by the device of negotiating commercial paper arose. And for the same reason, it is now possible for a debtor to borrow money on the strength of a shifting inventory. For reasons here not important, the law before the adoption of the Uniform Commercial Code deemed it improper for a creditor to have a security interest in or a lien upon a stock of goods or inventory, which shifted continually as the result of sales from and the purchase of new inventory. In the case of the small merchant who might have a large part of his capital invested in inventory, this created a burden in the sense that he could not effectively borrow on the strength of what he had on his shelves.

The problem of liquidity of assets arises also in the sense of a salvage operation. For example, if you buy a house on credit and then decide to move to another city, how can you get out of the purchase transaction by having someone else take over? The ideal thing of course would be to effect a novation and have the seller agree that you were released and that the seller would only look to a new buyer for payments. In the case that follows, the question arises as to whether a tenant can require the landlord to accept a new tenant in his place. If the case were decided solely on the basis of free enterprise, intent of the parties as expressed in the original lease, and protection of the landlord's property, the answer would be that the landlord's freedom of action is not subject to any restraint.

SCHEINFELD v. MUNTZ TV, INC.

67 Ill.App.2d 8, 214 N.E.2d 506 (1966)

Scheinfeld, doing business as Greenleaf Investors, leased a warehouse to Muntz TV, Inc. Thereafter, with Greenleaf's written consent, Muntz sublet the warehouse to Breuer Electric Mfg. Co. It later decided to sublet to Calumet Mfg. Co., but Greenleaf refused to consent thereto. Breuer vacated the premises. Scheinfeld then proceeded against Muntz TV for the full rent. Muntz TV claimed that it was only liable for the difference between the full rent and the rent that Calumet would have paid. From a decision in favor of Scheinfeld, Muntz appealed.

Opinion by Dempsey, J. . . .

The controlling question is whether a lessor has the duty to mitigate damages if a suitable subtenant is secured and tendered by the lessee. . . .
. . . Application of the mitigation of damages rule is consistent with the landlord-tenant relationship; for example: the property relations between Greenleaf and Muntz and between Muntz and Breuer would not have been affected had the Calumet sublease been consented to; Greenleaf could still have looked solely to Muntz and Muntz solely to Breuer for performance of the covenants of the lease and sublease. . . .

The argument that the landlord's duty to mitigate arises only if the lease so provides is relevant where the provisions of the lease cover the landlord's duty to mitigate damages; where, however, there is no provision in the lease expressing the intent of the parties on this specific subject matter, it is the law of contracts which implies that duty. . . . Since neither the prime lease nor the sublease in the instant case provides that the respective landlords shall have no duty to mitigate damages, this court would not be eliminating any of the express provisions of either lease in applying the mitigation rule.

We reaffirm, therefore, our holding . . . that the contractual rule compelling mitigation of damages applies to leases. In doing so, we emphasize the validity of the provisions of the lease and sublease in the present case prohibiting assignment and subletting without the landlord's consent and giving the landlord the option to rerent on such terms as he sees fit is not in question. We do not mean that the landlord must accept any subtenant submitted by the lessee, that he must grant a new lease to the proposed subtenant, that he must release the lessee from further responsibility for rent, or that he must rent his property for a purpose which might damage it. The landlord's duty to mitigate damages does not prevent him from exercising his choice of tenants in rerenting the premises. But when the duty to mitigate is raised by the tender of a suitable sublessee, the option of the landlord lies between consenting to the sublease or crediting the tenant with the amount which would have been paid by the sublessee had he been accepted. The landlord may not arbitrarily reject a suitable sublessee and yet continue to hold the tenant liable for the whole rental in default. Thus, in the case at bar, Breuer should be credited on its indebtedness to Muntz with the rental it could have received from Calumet, and Muntz should receive like credit on its indebtedness to Greenleaf, if it is established that Calumet would have been a reputable and responsible tenant. . . .

Questions for Review

1. Define the social force of debtor protection.

2. Give illustrations of its application.

3. Analyze each opinion in this chapter in terms of the social forces involved in the decision. See § 5:5 for a list of the social forces. With respect to each opinion, explain why the prevailing social forces prevailed and why those rejected did not. In each case in which there is a dissenting opinion, also make this analysis for the dissenting opinion.

4-8. *On the basis of the social forces involved, what decision should be made in each of the following cases?*

4. *Customer credit. Coupon plan.* A store adopted a plan by which coupons worth $200 as payment on purchases would be issued to a customer who would be required to pay $246.01 over a 24-month period. Payment of this amount was required whether or not any purchases were made and whether the coupons were lost or destroyed. Was this plan valid? *W. T. Grant Co.* v. *Walsh*, 100 N.J.S. 60, 241 A.2d 46.

5. *Insurance. Commissions.* When an insurer's agent is entitled to commissions improperly denied by the insurer, is the agent entitled to recover for "embarrassment and humiliation" on proof of failure to pay commissions? *Gilson* v. *Continental Casualty Co.*, La., 196 So.2d 820.

6. *Credit sales. Repossession and resale.* After the goods sold on credit are repossessed and a resale is made to a subsequent buyer, is the liability of the original buyer for a deficiency fixed at the time of the resale when the resale was made on credit? The seller claimed that the original buyer should be liable in case the second buyer should thereafter default, causing an ultimate loss to the seller. *Elster's Sales* v. *El Bodrero Hotel*, Cal.App.2d, 58 Cal. Rptr. 402.

7. *Deed. Parol evidence of mortgage.* Castleberry executed a deed conveying land to Ehrlich. Thereafter Castleberry sued to prove that the deed was not meant to transfer title absolutely but merely as security for Castleberry's paying for construction work done by Ehrlich. Can the deed be contradicted

by showing that it was to terminate when the debt was paid? *Ehrlich* v. *Castleberry*, Ark., 299 S.W.2d 38.

8. *Contracts. Stranger to contract.* The Republic National Bank made a short-term loan to a customer in reliance upon the agreement made by the National Bankers Life Insurance Company with the customer to furnish long-term financing to the customer, from which Republic contemplated it would be repaid. Republic was not a party to the contract between the customer and National Bankers. National Bankers later refused to furnish the long-term financing with the result that the customer did not have the money to repay Republic. Republic then sued National Bankers for the loss that it thereby sustained. Was Republic entitled to recover? *Republic National Bank* v. *National Bankers Life Insurance Co.*, Tex.Civ.App., 427 S.W.2d 76.

9-13. What social forces were involved, which prevailed, and which were defeated in the following decisions?

9. *Damages. Breach of contract.* Where violation of contract by building contractor could readily be corrected, the homeowner may recover only the pecuniary loss sustained and cannot recover damages for "mental anguish." *Jankowski* v. *Mazzotta*, 7 Mich.App. 483, 152 N.W.2d 49.

10. *Agency. Excess advances.* When an agent is allowed to take advances to be charged against future commissions, the principal cannot recover the excess of the advances over commissions in the absence of an express or implied agreement to that effect. *Valoco Building Products* v. *Chafee*, 4 Conn.Cir. 322, 231 A.2d 101.

11. *Retail installment sale. House construction.* A secured contract for the construction of a house with payment in monthly installments is a "sale" within the scope of a retail installment sales statute. *Morgan* v. *Reasor Corp.*, Cal.App.2d, 67 Cal.Rptr. 577.

12. *Bankruptcy. False representation.* Where a borrower signs in blank a statement of outstanding indebtedness, he does not make a false representation that will bar his subsequent discharge in bankruptcy when the blank form was incorrectly filled in by the lender's agent and there was no authority from the borrower to fill in erroneous information. *Household Finance Corp.* v. *Gilliam*, 12 Ohio.App.2d, 199 N.E.2d 417.

13. *Jurisdiction. Chain hotels.* As management corporation operating a hotel chain is distinct from independent corporate hotels, which are members of the chain, the service of process upon the manager of one of the hotels is not a service that binds the management corporation in the chain. *Young* v. *Albert Pick Hotels*, [C.A.Dist.Col.] 375 F.2d 331.

Chapter 23

STABILITY

§ 23:1. Generally

Stability is particularly important in business transactions. When you buy a house, for example, you not only want to know the exact meaning of the transaction under today's law but you also hope that the transaction will have the same meaning in the future. When the businessman invests money, he desires that the law will remain the same as it was when he acted.

Because of the objective of stability, the courts will ordinarily follow former decisions unless there is some valid reason to depart from them. When no former case directly bears on the point involved, the desire for stability will influence the courts to reach a decision that is a logical extension of some former decision or which follows a former decision by analogy rather than to strike off on a fresh path and to reach a decision unrelated to the past. Thus stability is achieved through continuity based on the assumption that many problems of today and tomorrow will be basically the same as those that were settled yesterday.

If stability were an absolute objective of the law, the cause of justice would often be thwarted. The reason that originally gave rise to a rule of law may have ceased to exist. The rule then appears unjust because it reflects a concept of justice that is outmoded or obsolete. For example, a rule of law, such as capital punishment, which one age believes just may be condemned by another age as unjust. We must not lose sight of the fact that the rule of law under question was created to further the sense of social justice existing at that time, but since our concepts of justice may change, the law may not always coincide with current concepts.

§ 23:2. Constitutional Interpretation

By one school of thought, and undoubtedly the thought which the framers had in mind in adopting the Constitution, that document should be interpreted to further stability. Thus the Constitution should stand as the bedrock on which the government is based, unchanging unless expressly amended in the manner specified by the Constitution itself.

As seen in § 24:2, this view has not been held by the Supreme Court for some time but was formally enunciated by Chief Justice Marshall in the case that follows.

MARBURY v. MADISON

1 Cranch 137 (1803)

Marbury was appointed a justice of the peace for the District of Columbia, but the commission by which his appointment would become effective was not delivered to him. He brought an action to compel the Secretary of State, Madison, to deliver the commission. This action was brought in the Supreme Court, which had been given authority to hear such cases by the Judiciary Act of 1789. The Constitution did not permit the bringing of actions of this nature in the Supreme Court. The Supreme Court therefore had to consider whether the Constitution or the statute was the superior authority.

OPINION BY MARSHALL, C.J. . . .

That the people have an original right to establish, for their future government, such principles as, in their opinion, shall most conduce to their own happiness, is the basis on which the whole American fabric has been erected. . . .

This original and supreme will organizes the government, and assigns to different departments their respective powers. It may either stop here, or establish certain limits not to be transcended by those departments.

The government of the United States is of the latter description. The powers of the legislature are defined and limited; and that those limits may not be mistaken, or forgotten, the Constitution is written. To what purpose are powers limited, and to what purpose is that limitation committed to writing, if these limits may, at any time, be passed by those intended to be restrained? The distinction between a government with limited and unlimited powers is abolished, if those limits do not confine the persons on whom they are imposed, and if acts prohibited and acts allowed are of equal obligation. It is a proposition too plain to be contested, that the Constitution controls any legislative act repugnant to it; or, that the legislature may alter the Constitution by an ordinary act.

Between these alternatives there is no middle ground. The Constitution is either a superior paramount law, unchangeable by ordinary means, or it is on a level with ordinary legislative acts, and, like other acts, is alterable when the legislature shall please to alter it.

If the former part of the alternative be true, then a legislative act contrary to the Constitution is not law; if the latter part be true, then written constitutions are absurd attempts, on the part of the people, to limit a power in its own nature illimitable.

Certainly all those who have framed written constitutions contemplate them as forming the fundamental and paramount law of the nation, and, consequently, the theory of every such government must be, that an act of the legislature, repugnant to the constitution, is void. . . .

If an act of the legislature, repugnant to the Constitution, is void, does it, notwithstanding its invalidity, bind the courts, and oblige them to give it effect? Or, in other words, though it be not law, does it constitute a rule as operative as if it was a law? . . .

It is emphatically the province and duty of the judicial department to say what the law is. . . . If two laws conflict with each other, the courts must decide on the operation of each.

So if a law be in opposition to the Constitution; if both the law and the Constitution apply to a particular case, so that the court must either decide that case conformably to the law, disregarding the Constitution, or conformably to the Constitution, disregarding the law, the court must determine which of these conflicting rules governs the case. This is of the very essence of judicial duty.

If, then, . . . the Constitution is superior to any ordinary act of the legislature, the Constitution, and not such ordinary act, must govern the case to which they both apply. . . .

Why does a judge swear to discharge his duties agreeably to the Constitution of the United States, if that Constitution forms no rule for his government? . . .

It is also not entirely unworthy of observation, that in declaring what shall be the supreme law of the land, the Constitution itself is first mentioned; and not the laws of the United States generally, but those only which shall be made in pursuance of the Constitution, have that rank.

Thus, the particular phraseology of the Constitution of the United States confirms and strengthens the principle, supposed to be essential to all written constitutions, that a law repugnant to the Constitution is void; and that courts, as well as other departments, are bound by that instrument. . . .

§ 23:3.   Judicial Determination

Once a matter is determined by a court, the social force in favor of stability leans heavily in favor of accepting the action of the court as final. If the same question comes up between the parties at a later date, they are bound by the earlier decision. For example, if you and your neighbor have a dispute as to the location of the boundary line between your properties and go to court, the final decision of the court will bind you. Moreover, it will also bind persons who buy your land from you or your neighbor's land from him; that is, the decision of the court has stabilized or put to rest once and for all the question of the location of the boundary line.

In this illustration there is an element of protecting title, since the title once determined by the court is final and cannot be attacked. There is also an element of furthering trade because everyone knows just what is being bought when there is a purchase of the land after the case has been decided.

In the illustration it was stated that the final judgment of the court was binding. The judgment is final when there is no further chance of review, reversal, appeal, or rehearing. But even before that stage is reached, the operation of the force of stability is apparent. Thus the court that hears an appeal does not go into the case from the beginning and does not listen to the witnesses. Instead, it takes the case as presented to the lower court and merely reads what was said at the trial from the record or papers that are filed on appeal. If there is a jury verdict, the court reviewing the verdict goes no further than to determine that the verdict was supported by the evidence and does not look to see if the court agrees with the verdict. If it is claimed that the proper procedure was not followed, it is presumed that the procedure was proper until it is shown otherwise. While a defendant is presumed innocent, once he is convicted it is presumed that he is guilty and was properly convicted, and the defendant on appeal must therefore prove that there was some error.

Thus, in one way or another, the procedural side of the law seeks to put an end to disputes—first, by flatly closing the door on any further litigation, and last, in narrowing the scope of issues that may be raised in attacking the action of the court.

BEAR v. ALASKA

439 P.2d 432 (Alaska, 1968)

Bear was convicted of involuntary manslaughter. He was sentenced to twelve years. Although this was a lawful length of sentence, he appealed on the ground that the trial judge had abused his discretion in imposing the sentence and requested that the case be sent to a different judge for a resentencing.

OPINION BY NESBETT, C.J. . . .

Appellant does not question the validity of his conviction nor the fact that the sentence was within the maximum established by law for the offense. . . .

In support of his request, appellant urges that a statement made by the court at the time it denied the motion to reduce sentence clearly demonstrates that it disregarded the jury's finding that the killing was unintentional and viewed it instead as an intentional killing and sentenced accordingly. Appellant quotes and emphasizes the statement of the trial judge, who is reported to have said:

"I considered this a very vicious case; the jury found manslaughter. . . . They found him guilty of manslaughter and certainly the evidence indicated that he had this pistol; he fired into the floor one time and during the course of punching his wife in the ribs with the pistol it went off; and I think it was a very vicious type of thing."

Appellant argues that the court clearly displayed its prejudice when it referred to what the jury had found to be an involuntary act of manslaughter as a vicious killing. According to appellant, the trial court's prejudice was caused by incompetent hearsay statements made by the prosecutor at the time of sentencing to the effect that appellant had threatened to kill two of the State's witnesses after trial.

Appellee contends that the court obviously did not consider the prosecutor's statement that appellant had threatened two witnesses. Appellant denied making the statement, according to appellee, whereupon the prosecutor offered to support his statement with affidavits. The court is then reported to have stated, when it denied the prosecutor's offer, that it had heard all that it wished to on that point. According to appellee, the above facts clearly support the inference that the court did not consider the statement, otherwise it would have accepted the prosecutor's offer to prove the threats and would have referred to them when passing sentence.

Appellee argues that the trial court's characterization of the offense as "vicious" and its statement that it could not "give the man a license to kill his wife" were comments appropriate to the nature of the offense.

Appellee points out that most of the dictionary definitions of the adjective "vicious" such as, "violative of moral rectitude," "immorality or depravity," and "corrupt or dissolute in conduct," do appropriately describe the unintentional homicide under the particular facts of this case. The trial judge concluded his statement by saying:

"I don't think we could give a man a license to kill his wife because he has children and he has to look after the children. I don't go along with that argument."

According to appellee, this is nothing more than an explanation by the court that it could not excuse appellant's conduct merely because of his responsibility to his children, and in brief, there is no support for the argument of appellant that the judge considered the homicide other than involuntary manslaughter.

We shall defer consideration of appellant's claim that the facts related amounted to an abuse of discretion and examine first the question of whether this court has jurisdiction to review a legal criminal sentence.

The majority of federal jurisdictions follow the rule that an appellate court has no authority to act on a sentence which is within the limits allowed by a statute, because such a sentence is not cruel and unusual punishment and any relief therefrom must be obtained by act of Congress. The same rule appears to be followed in a majority of the state jurisdictions on the ground that it would be improper to interfere, or to seem to interfere, with the executive branch's power to pardon and commute sentences.

According to Professor B. J. George, the rule of the state courts is a carry-over from the common law where, in feudal times, the chief variations in punishments lay more in the methods by which an offender was to be executed than in any other respect; the role of the judiciary being to determine the question of guilt and to enter judgment. When this had been done the penalties of the law were exacted as a matter of course, unless royal pardon was forthcoming. Professor George suggests that immunity of criminal sentences from review is also explainable by the fact that under the common-law system, appeals are based on questions of law exclusively whereas under the civil law, appeals may be based on questions of law or fact.

States which review sentences in criminal cases, such as Arizona, California, New York, Nebraska, Iowa, and Hawaii, generally do so under statutory authority.

A few states have inferred the power to review and reduce sentences from statutes which permit appellate courts to "reverse or modify the judgment" appealed from, but none have found in this language the power to increase a sentence. . . .

This court is of the opinion that it does not have jurisdiction to review and remand or to review and revise a criminal sentence for abuse of discretion.

There is no provision of the constitution or of the statutes of Alaska specifically giving this court the power to "reverse, affirm, or modify the judgment." Article IV, section 2 of the Alaska Constitution states that, "The supreme court shall be the highest court of the State, with final appellate jurisdiction." . . .

Our decision is influenced to some extent by the history of the doctrine of immunity of review of criminal sentences and by the absence of specific constitutional or statutory authority in this area.

It is true that this court has exercised appellate authority to review the many aspects of criminal matters mentioned in our colleague's dissenting opinion. For the most part such review is confined to questions of law or mixed questions of law and fact and is therefore within the traditionally recognized sphere of appellate court jurisdiction. The review of an otherwise legal criminal sentence, which is within the maximum established by the legislature, is not a question of law and is not within the traditional sphere of appellate court jurisdiction.

As is pointed out in the dissent, approximately fifteen states now undertake to review criminal sentences. In thirteen of these states, the authority to review criminal sentences stems from specific statutory provisions.

The legislature of Alaska has established by statute the maximum and minimum sentences for each offense. The determination of the exact period of time that a convicted defendant should serve is basically a sociological problem to be resolved by a careful weighing of the principle of reformation and the need for protecting the public. The trial judge, by reason of his personal observation of the defendant and the complete personal history report prepared for him by the probation officer, is expected to be prepared to impose sentence.

The trial judge's sentence is subject, however, to the following overriding statutory provisions:

"(1) that the State Board of Parole may, if its investigation and the defendant's rehabilitation prognosis appears to warrant, release the defendant on parole after only a portion of the sentence has been served,

(2) that by statute the defendant is entitled to three to fifteen days per month reduction of sentence for good behavior and prison camp activity, and (3) that the defendant may be granted a commutation of sentence or a pardon by the governor."

The chairman of the State Board of Parole is required by statute to be an official in the Department of Health and Welfare with training in the field of probation and parole. This Board, through its continued reports on the prisoner's conduct, psychological outlook, and rehabilitation prognosis, is intended to be suited to exercise the authority imposed on it by the legislature to adjust downward the prisoner's sentence within the limits allowed by statute.

The foregoing serves to illustrate that the legislature of Alaska has assumed and now exercises a substantial control over the length of criminal sentences. It may perhaps be advisable that this control be extended so as to place the responsibility for establishing the initial sentence, as well as the ultimate sentence to be served, in a board composed of persons trained in the social sciences appropriate to the responsibility. Appellate judges do not have an expertise, because of training, experience or otherwise, that qualifies them to be reviewers of criminal sentences.

It is the view of this court that review of legal criminal sentences should be provided for by statute only after a careful study of the efficacy of reviewing techniques now in force in other jurisdictions has been made, and the need for the procedure determined. Reviewing authority should perhaps include the power to modify a sentence upward as well as downward in order to achieve the full advantage of the procedure and decrease or eliminate disparity in sentences.

In view of our decision herein it becomes unnecessary to consider the question of abuse of discretion.

[The judgment below is affirmed.]

DISSENTING OPINION BY RABINOWITZ, J. . . .

I dissent from the majority's holding that the Supreme Court of Alaska lacks jurisdiction to review criminal sentences. I reach this conclusion on the basis of this court's own prior precedents and upon analysis of the policy considerations inherent in the question. [The dissenting Justice discussed four cases in which the Supreme Court had exercised the power of review.] . . .

Thus, without any real discussion of our own precedents, the majority has abruptly shunted aside any considerations of stare decisis and now holds that the Supreme Court of Alaska lacks jurisdiction to review criminal sentences. When experience and compelling reasons require the overruling of explicit precedent, I would agree that this court is not inhibited by the rule of stare decisis from taking such action. Here I can perceive no compelling policy considerations, or history of adverse experience under our prior decisions, which call for today's refusal to review the sentence which was imposed upon appellant. . . .

Appellate review of criminal sentences has been undertaken and is generally available in approximately fifteen states. In thirteen of these states authority to review sentences is derived from statutes. It is true that the weight of precedent is in favor of those courts which have concluded they lacked the authority to review criminal sentences. Despite the foregoing, I believe that our court rightly held in [prior] cases that it did possess the authority to review criminal sentences.

Pursuant to article IV, section 2 of the Alaska Constitution, this court is vested with "final appellate jurisdiction." I interpret the phrase "final appellate jurisdiction" as embodying the power to review the merits of a criminal sentence. . . . To me it is an indefensible anomaly that in the carrying out of our obligation to supervise the administration of criminal justice in our courts, we have the appellate authority to review questions pertaining to prearrest matters, (i.e., search warrants, admissions, confessions, et cetera) complaints, preliminary hearings, bail, grand jury proceedings, indictments, composition of petit juries, errors occurring during the trial itself, deliberations of the petit jury, sentencing procedures, legality of the sentence, but are powerless to review the actual sentence which is imposed by the trial judge. This hiatus in our review jurisdiction is illogical and in my view cannot be defended on the traditional grounds that appellate review would interfere with exercise of executive clemency. Sentencing is a discretionary judicial function and the judiciary itself should have the power to correct abuses of such discretion. The alternative course, and the one which has been adopted by the majority, is to abdicate review of judicial discretion. In my view the more reasonable and logical construction of our constitutional grant of final appellate jurisdiction is to hold that this provision authorizes appellate review of criminal sentences.

Today's ruling results in the unsatisfactory situation that this court will now review all facets of criminal proceedings to insure the integrity of the fact-finding process, to zealously protect the rights of the accused and the public in the administration of criminal justice, and to insure adherence to our constitutional mandate that penal administration "shall be based on the principle of reformation and upon the need for protecting the public," but will refuse to review the merits of the sentence which the trial judge has determined. Based on this court's own prior decisions, the decisions I have referred to in this separate opinion, and the absence of any persuasive reasons for holding that an exception for review of criminal sentences should be carved out of our general appellate jurisdiction, I conclude that this court possesses jurisdiction to review criminal sentences.

Of all the stages in a criminal proceeding, sentencing is one area in which there is a most compelling need for the development of appropriate criteria. Having had the privilege of serving as a trial judge in the superior court of this state, I am fully cognizant of the uncertainties and extraordinary responsibilities which confront the sentencing judge in his quest to determine a just sentence. This same experience has convinced me of the need for appellate review of the sentencing judge's discretion and the formulation of appropriate sentencing standards.

Now that it has been determined that the problem is one which must be answered by our legislature, it is my hope that Alaska's Legislature will resolve the issue in favor of empowering the Supreme Court of Alaska to exercise appellate review of criminal sentences.

§ 23:4. Property Law

The field of property law is the last stronghold for the objective of stability. Here transactions are entered into on the basis that certain legal consequences will follow and the economic disorder that a change of the law could produce is readily apparent. Assume that you purchase a tract of land believing that you acquire a full title thereto and then after you have built a factory thereon, the law is changed and it is held that you do not own the land until the heir of a former owner had died. Mindful of the consequences of such changing of property law, the courts have generally been reluctant to make any change thereto.

Stability is also recognized in property law in the case of restrictive covenants. For example, if you agree with the person selling you your land that you will not erect certain kinds of buildings on the land, you are bound by that agreement. Likewise, if the agreement was made by a remote seller and a remote buyer, you would ordinarily be bound by their restrictive agreement, although you were not a party to that agreement and had not agreed with your seller that you would observe that agreement. Here the law could have taken the position that if you did not make any agreement, your intent was that there should be no agreement and that you are not bound by the agreement that some other persons have made. Moreover, the objective of protecting your freedom of the use of property argues in favor of your using your land as you choose, subject only to restrictions imposed by government or general principles of law, as contrasted with the agreement of strangers. In many instances, however, the law ignores these social forces and declares that you hold the land subject to the same limitations as have been imposed by the former parties. Thus the pattern of private rights, which they created, is given a stability that survives the resale of the land and travels with the land into the hands of a subsequent buyer.

Such a restriction will not be enforced when enforcement of the restriction would amount to a discrimination prohibited by the Fourteenth Amendment of the Constitution of the United States, or when the circumstances and neighborhood have so changed that it would be absurd to continue to enforce the restriction. Thus restrictions in deeds delivered sixty years ago stipulating that no private automobile garages could be erected or maintained have frequently been held invalid in recent years because the auto is now so commonplace that its exclusion would be ridiculous and would now make the ownership of the property less valuable. Restrictions requiring that premises be used only for residential purposes may often be ignored when stores and other commercial or industrial enterprises have entered the neighborhood in such a large number that the character of the neighborhood is no longer predominantly residential. However, every change in character does not warrant an abandonment of a restrictive covenant. Likewise the mere fact that the owner can make more money from the use of his property for commercial purposes is not in itself sufficient to justify ignoring the restriction that it be used only for residential purposes.

COCHRAN v. LONG

294 S.W.2d 503 (Ky.App., 1956)

Long owned real estate in what was designated as Block 2 of Harrodsburg, Kentucky. All lots in this block were subject to a restrictive covenant that they could only be used for residential purposes. A state highway was relocated so that it ran through Block 2, and from 400 to 500 motor vehicles passed on the highway per hour. A number of commercial enterprises had been built outside of but near Block 2. Long and others brought an action against Cochran and others owning property in Block 2 to determine whether this change of conditions released their land from the covenant that it be used only for residential purposes. From a judgment that the covenant was not binding, Cochran appealed.

OPINION BY STEWARD, J. . . .

The decisive issue in this case is whether there has been such a radical change in the status of lots 1, 2, 3, 4, 5, and 28 in Block 2, affected by the restrictive covenant, as to relieve them in the burden of this covenant. . . .

"A change of conditions which will . . . annul . . . a restrictive covenant is a change of such a character as to make it impossible longer to secure in a substantial degree the benefits sought to be realized through the performance of a promise respecting the use of the land. If it is still possible, despite a change in conditions, to secure the anticipated benefit in a substantial, though lessened, degree, the change of conditions will not alone be sufficient to warrant the refusal of injunctive relief against breach of the obligation arising from the promise." . . .

The problem before us is simply one of deciding whether the facts in this case disclose there has been such a basic change in the character of the restricted property as to cause the covenant in question to be inapplicable to what appellees claim is a new situation. . . .

The chancellor, in finding for appellees [Long and others], held there had been such a complete change in the territory under scrutiny that the restriction as to residential use applicable to lots 1 through 5 and to lot 28 in Block 2 was no longer of any substantial value to these lots. This conclusion was reached primarily, because of the location of the new highway through this block, over which much traffic proceeds and from which considerable noise ensues. For this reason, it was believed the trend is toward a business district in this area, although in Block 2 only two commercial establishments have been built since the completion of the highway. It is true there was testimony to the effect that some distance to the north and outside of Block 2, particularly at a street intersection about a block distant, several business places have been located within the last year or so, but we do not believe this changes the basic picture at the present time.

It does not follow that the mere presence of a highway that has become one of the principal arteries of travel through the city of Harrodsburg automatically alters the character of property involved here to the extent that this property is released from the restrictions that adhere to it. . . .

Nor are we convinced that the evidence in this record shows there has been such a transition over to business in Block 2 and the surrounding area as to interfere in any material respect with the enjoyment by appellant lot owners of the benefit of the neighborhood as a place of residence. This is especially true where, as here, the restricted property, though it be small in extent, has not been invaded. Appellants do not claim that the approach of business on either side of the restricted lots along the highway has affected the restricted area's desirability for residential purposes or materially changed its character as a residential district. . . .

[Judgment reversed and case remanded.]

DISSENTING OPINION BY SIMS, J. . . .

This case is easily distinguished from *Bickell* v. *Moraio,* 117 Conn. 176, 167 A. 722. . . . There, the restricted property was already located on the Post Road which was merely widened, which resulted in an increase of traffic. While here, the trunk line highway was put through the restricted property which theretofore had not abutted any road and had suffered no annoyance or inconvenience from any traffic.

To my mind putting this highway through the property protected by the restricted covenant makes such a change in conditions of the property as to neutralize the benefits of the restriction and to defeat the purpose of the covenant. . . .

Questions for Review

1. Define the social force favoring stability.

2. Give illustrations of its application.

3. Analyze each opinion in this chapter in terms of the social forces involved in the decision. See § 5:5 for a list of the social forces. With respect to each opinion, explain why the prevailing social forces prevailed and why those rejected did not. In each case in which there is a dissenting opinion, also make this analysis for the dissenting opinion.

4-8. *On the basis of the social forces involved, what decision should be made in each of the following cases?*

4. *Contract validity. Change of law.* A contractor and a subcontractor made a contract. The contractor claimed that a provision of the contract required the subcontractor to pay liability claims even though they arose from the negligence of the contractor. By a statute, which was adopted after the contract was made, this kind of clause was declared "against public policy and . . . void and unenforceable." Would this statute invalidate the clause in the contract between the contractor and the subcontractor? *Whitmire* v. *Ferguson,* Cal.App.2d, 68 Cal.Rptr. 78.

5. *Corporate reorganization. Identity of employer.* A labor union made a collective bargaining agreement with Interscience Publishers, Inc. The contract made no provision that it was binding on successors of the contracting parties. Later, for general business reasons and not as an antilabor measure, Interscience merged with and disappeared into another publishing corporation, John Wiley & Sons, Inc. The former's employees, with a few exceptions, worked for Wiley. Thereafter the labor union claimed that Wiley was required to submit to arbitration, in accordance with the terms of the contract with Interscience, certain questions relating to employees who had worked for Interscience but were working for Wiley after the merger. Wiley claimed that it was not bound by the arbitration agreement with Interscience. Was it correct? *John Wiley & Sons* v. *Livingston,* 376 U.S. 543.

6. *Federal courts. What law governs.* An action may be brought in a federal district court when it is between citizens of different states and the amount in controversy exceeds $10,000. When such an action is brought, should the federal court follow (a) general federal principles of law in order to establish uniformity and stability throughout the nation; or (b) the principles of law that would have been applied had the action been brought in the local state court in order to maintain stability unaffected by the circumstance of whether the action is brought in a federal or a state court? *Erie Railroad Co.* v. *Tompkins,* 304 U.S. 64.

7. *Liquidated damages clause. Validity.* Melodee Lane Lingerie Co. was a tenant in a building that was protected against fire by a sprinkler and alarm system maintained by the American District Telegraph Co. Because of the fault of the latter, the controls on the system were defective and allowed the discharge of water into the building, which damaged Melodee's property. When Melodee sued A.D.T., it raised the defense that its service contract limited its liability to 10 percent of the annual service charge made to the customer. Was this limitation valid? *Melodee Lane Lingerie Co.* v. *American District Telegraph Co.,* 271 N.Y.S.2d 937, 18 N.Y.2d 57, 218 N.E.2d 661.

8. *Release. Exceptions.* A real estate development ran into financial difficulties in the course of construction. The parties adjusted matters by having the plaintiffs assign their stock in the development corporation to the defendants who allegedly promised that they would "put all the necessary capital into the projects to complete them as quickly as possible," and the plaintiffs gave the defendants releases "of all claims and demands arising out of any transactions between" the parties. Later the plaintiffs sued the defendants on the ground that they failed to put up the capital as allegedly promised. Could the plaintiffs assert this claim against the defendants? *Schuster* v. *Baskin,* Mass., 236 N.E.2d 205.

9-13. *What social forces were involved, which prevailed, and which were defeated in the following decisions?*

9. *Restrictive covenant. Promotion contract.* A restrictive covenant against competition contained in a contract with an employee promoted to supervisor is void because it is not ancillary to the "taking of employment," with the

result that the different restrictive covenant in the original contract of employment was alone valid. *Capital Bakers* v. *Townsend,* 426 Pa. 188, 231 A.2d 292.

10. *Statute of limitations. Minor claimant.* The statute of limitations for personal injuries runs against the minor where no exception is expressly made in the statute, and the fact that a settlement was made of the minor's claim, which settlement the minor may avoid because it was not made by an authorized representative of the minor, does not alter such conclusion. *Schmucker* v. *Naugle,* 426 Pa. 203, 231 A.2d 121.

11. *Insurance. Interstate risks.* Where liability policy covers risks in several states, the policy is to be deemed governed by the law of the state in which the risk in question is located, as though separate policies were written for the risk in each state. *Consolidated Mutual Insurance Co.* v. *Radio Foods Corp.,* 108 N.H. 494, 240 A.2d 47.

12. *Finality of decision. Failure to object.* Where the state department of highways taking an appeal failed to ask for a review of a judgment which had been entered against it for $2,000, the appellate court cannot decrease or affect that award even though the appellate court believes that there was no liability for any amount. *Cox* v. *Department of Highways,* 22 La. 252, 209 So.2d 9.

13. *Prior action. No bar to issues.* Where first action was brought by employer-owner of automobile against defendant, defendant was not barred when thereafter he was sued by the employer's driver from relitigating issues of own negligence and the negligence of the driver, even though driver had testified in first action. *Kayler* v. *Gallimore,* 269 N.C. 405, 152 S.E.2d 518.

Chapter 24

FLEXIBILITY

§ 24:1. Generally

The law itself may be flexible in that it makes provision for changes in rules to meet situations that cannot be anticipated or for which an explicit set of rules cannot be developed satisfactorily in advance. Our constitutions state the procedures for their amendment. Such changes in constitutional law are purposely made difficult in order to serve the objective of stability, but they are possible when the need for change is generally recognized by the people of the state or nation.

Changes by legislative action in federal and state statutes and local ordinances are relatively easier to make. Furthermore, some statutes recognize the impossibility of laying down in advance a hard and fast rule that will do justice in all cases. The typical modern statute, particularly in the field of regulation of business and enterprise, will therefore contain "escape clauses" by which a person can escape from the operation of the statute under certain circumstances. Thus a rent control law may impose a rent ceiling, that is, a maximum above which landlords cannot charge; but it may also authorize a greater charge when special circumstances make it just to allow such exception, as when the landlord has made expensive repairs to the property or when his taxes have increased materially.

The rule of law may be stated in terms of what a reasonable or prudent man would do. Thus, whether you are negligent in driving your automobile is determined in court by whether you exercised the same degree of care that a prudent man would have exercised had he been driving your car under the circumstances in question. This is a vague and variable standard as to how you must drive your car, but it is the only standard that is practical. The alternative would be a detailed motor code specifying how you should drive your car under every possible situation that might arise: a code that obviously could not foresee every possible situation and which obviously would be too long for any driver to know by heart.

§ 24:2.   Constitutional Interpretation

The concept of flexibility dominates the field of modern constitutional interpretation. While there is authority, as discussed in § 23:2, that the Constitution of the United States and any constitution is a bedrock upon which all action must be based, the dominant view, at least since 1937, has been to regard the Constitution as a "living document" which has the flexibility to permit it to be expanded to meet the needs of the situation. This is opposed to the bedrock view that only that which is authorized by the Constitution may be done, and that if the Constitution is not in harmony with the times, it must be amended in the manner specified in the Constitution and not by the action of the Supreme Court.

McCULLOCH v. MARYLAND

4 Wheat. 316 (1819)

The first bank of the United States was chartered for twenty years in 1791 and again in 1816. Hostile state legislation attempted to drive it out of existence. In 1818, Maryland adopted a law imposing a tax on bank notes issued by any bank not chartered by the state legislature. McCulloch, the cashier of the Baltimore branch of the National Bank, issued bank notes on which this tax had not been paid. Suit was brought by the State of Maryland against him to recover the statutory penalties imposed for violation of the statute. The opinion of the Supreme Court is the classic statement of the right of the federal government to exercise powers not expressly granted to it by the Constitution, that is, a classic statement of the liberal construction of the Constitution.

OPINION BY MARSHALL, C.J. . . .

The first question . . . is, has Congress power to incorporate a bank? . . .
This government of the Union . . . is acknowledged by all to be one of enumerated powers. . . .
Among the enumerated powers, we do not find that of establishing a bank or creating a corporation. . . . A constitution, to contain an accurate

detail of all the subdivisions of which its great powers will admit, and of all the means by which they may be carried into execution, would partake of the prolixity of a legal code, and could scarcely be embraced by the human mind. It would probably never be understood by the public. Its nature, therefore, requires, that only its great outlines should be marked, its important objects designated, and the minor ingredients which compose those objects be deduced from the nature of the objects themselves. . . .

Although, among the enumerated powers of government, we do not find the word "bank" or "incorporation," we find the great powers to lay and collect taxes; to borrow money; to regulate commerce; to declare and conduct a war; and to raise and support armies and navies. The sword and the purse, all the external relations, and no inconsiderable portion of the industry of the nation, are intrusted to its government . . . a government, intrusted with such ample powers, on the due execution of which the happiness and prosperity of the nation so vitally depends, must also be intrusted with ample means for their execution. The power being given, it is the interest of the nation to facilitate its execution. It can never be their interest, and cannot be presumed to have been their intention, to clog and embarrass its execution by withholding the most appropriate means. Throughout this vast republic, . . . revenue is to be collected and expended, armies are to be marched and supported. The exigencies of the nation may require that the treasure raised in the North should be transported to the South, that raised in the East conveyed to the West, or that this order should be reversed. Is that construction of the Constitution to be preferred which would render these operations difficult, hazardous, and expensive? Can we adopt that construction (unless the words imperiously require it) which would impute to the framers of that instrument, when granting these powers for the public good, the intention of impeding their exercise by withholding a choice of means? If, indeed, such be the mandate of the Constitution, we have only to obey; but that instrument does not profess to enumerate the means by which the powers it confers may be executed; nor does it prohibit the creation of a corporation, if the existence of such a being be essential to the beneficial exercise of those powers. It is, then, the subject of fair inquiry, how far such means may be employed. . . .

The government which has a right to do an act, and has imposed on it the duty of performing that act, must, according to the dictates of reason, be allowed to select the means; and those who contend that it may not select any appropriate means, that one particular mode of effecting the object is excepted, take upon themselves the burden of establishing that exception. . . .

But the Constitution of the United States has not left the right of Congress to employ the necessary means, for the execution of the powers conferred on the government, to general reasoning. To its enumeration of powers is added that of making "all laws which shall be necessary and proper, for carrying into execution the foregoing powers, and all other powers vested by this Constitution, in the government of the United States, or in any department thereof."

. . . This provision is made in a constitution intended to endure for ages to come, and, consequently, to be adapted to the various crises of human affairs. To have prescribed the means by which government should, in all future time, execute its powers, would have been to change, entirely, the character of the instrument, and give it the properties of a legal code. It would have been an unwise attempt to provide, by immutable rules, for exigencies which, if foreseen at all, must have been seen dimly, and which can be best provided for as they occur. [The Court rejected the contention that "necessary" means "absolutely necessary."] . . . Sound construction of the Constitution must allow to the national legislature that discretion, with respect to the means by which the powers it confers are to be carried into execution, which will enable that body to perform the high duties assigned to it, in the manner most beneficial to the people. Let the end be legitimate, let it be within the scope of the Constitution, and all means which are appropriate, which are plainly adapted to that end, which are not prohibited, but consist with the letter and spirit of the Constitution, are constitutional.

. . . It can scarcely be necessary to say, that the existence of state banks can have no possible influence on the question. No trace is to be found in the Constitution of an intention to create a dependence of the government of the Union on those of the states, for the execution of the great powers assigned to it. . . . The choice of means implies a right to choose a national bank in preference to state banks, and Congress alone can make the election.

§ 24:3. Trade Regulation

The field of trade regulation is most clearly an area in which the law is stated in flexible terms. On the one hand, this flexibility or vagueness is desirable because it would be most difficult to anticipate just what should be permitted and what should be prohibited before an actual case arose. On the other hand, the flexibility makes it very difficult for management and for lawyers to plan an intelligent course of action.

UNITED STATES v. E. I. DU PONT DE NEMOURS & COMPANY

353 U.S. 586 (1957)

In 1917 to 1919, Du Pont acquired 23 percent stock interest in General Motors. During the following years, General Motors bought all its automotive finishes and fabrics from Du Pont. In 1949, the United States claimed the effect of the stock acquisition had been to lessen competition in interstate commerce on the theory that the sales to General Motors had not been the result of successful competition but were the result of the stock ownership, and therefore such stock ownership violated the Clayton Act. The United States brought an action against Du Pont, General Motors, and others. From a decision in their favor, the United States appealed.

OPINION BY BRENNAN, J. . . .

The primary issue is whether Du Pont's commanding position as General Motor's supplier of automotive finishes and fabrics was achieved on competi-

tive merit alone, or because its acquisition of relationship, led to the insulation of most of the General Motors' market from free competition, with the
resultant likelihood, at the time of suit, of the creation of a monopoly of a
line of commerce [contrary to § 7 of the Clayton Act]. . . .

Section 7 is designed to arrest in its incipiency not only the substantial
lessening of competition from the acquisition by one corporation of the whole
or any part of the stock of a competing corporation, but also to arrest in
their incipiency restraints or monopolies in a relevant market which, as a
reasonable probability, appear at the time of suit likely to result from the
acquisition by one corporation of all or any part of the stock of any other
corporation. The section is violated whether or not actual restraints or
monopolies, or the substantial lessening of competition, have occurred or are
intended. Acquisitions solely for investment are excepted, but only if, and so
long as, the stock is not used by voting or otherwise to bring about, or in
attempting to bring about, the substantial lessening of competition. . . .

The first paragraph of § 7 plainly is framed to reach not only the
corporate acquisition of stock of a competing corporation, where the effect
may be substantially to lessen competition between them, but also the
corporate acquisition of stock of any corporation, competitor or not, where
the effect may be either (1) to restrain commerce in any section or community, or (2) tend to create a monopoly of any line of commerce. . . .

We hold that any acquisition by one corporation of all or any part of
the stock of another corporation, competitor or not, is within the reach of
the section whenever the reasonable likelihood appears that the acquisition
will result in a restraint of commerce or in the creation of a monopoly of
any line of commerce. Thus, although Du Pont and General Motors are not
competitors, a violation of the section has occurred if, as a result of the
acquisition, there was at the time of suit a reasonable likelihood of a
monopoly of any line of commerce. . . .

Appellees argue that there exists no basis for a finding of a probable
restraint or monopoly within the meaning of § 7 because the total General
Motors market for finishes and fabrics constituted only a negligible percentage
of the total market for these materials for all uses, including automotive uses.
It is stated in the General Motors brief that in 1947 Du Pont's finish sales to
General Motors constituted 3.5 percent of all sales of finishes to industrial
users, and that its fabrics sales to General Motors comprised 1.6 percent of
the total market for the type of fabric used by the automobile industry.

Determination of the relevant market is a necessary predicate to a finding
of a violation of the Clayton Act because the threatened monopoly must be
one which will substantially lessen competition "within the area of effective
competition." Substantiality can be determined only in terms of the market
affected. The record shows that automotive finishes and fabrics have sufficient
peculiar characteristics and uses to constitute them products sufficiently distinct from all other finishes and fabrics to make them a "line of commerce"
within the meaning of the Clayton Act. . . . Thus, the bounds of the relevant
market for the purposes of this case are not coextensive with the total market
for finishes and fabrics, but are coextensive with the automobile industry, the
relevant market for automotive finishes and fabrics.

The market affected must be substantial. . . . Moreover, in order to establish a violation of § 7 the Government must prove a likelihood that competition may be "foreclosed in a substantial share of . . . [that market]." Both requirements are satisfied in this case. The substantiality of a relevant market comprising the automobile industry is undisputed. The substantiality of General Motors' share of that market is fully established in the evidence.

General Motors . . . accounts annually for upwards of two fifths of the total sales of automotive vehicles in the Nation. . . . Du Pont supplied 67 percent of General Motors' requirements for finishes in 1946 and 68 percent in 1947. In fabrics Du Pont supplied 52.3 percent of requirements in 1946, and 38.5 percent in 1947. Because General Motors accounts for almost one half of the automobile industry's annual sales, its requirements for automotive finishes and fabrics must represent approximately one half of the relevant market for these materials. Because the record clearly shows that quantitatively and percentagewise Du Pont supplies the largest part of General Motors' requirements, we must conclude that Du Pont has a substantial share of the relevant market.

The appellees argue that the Government could not maintain this action in 1949 because § 7 is applicable only to the acquisition of stock and not to the holding or subsequent use of the stock. This argument misconceives the objective toward which § 7 is directed. The Clayton Act was intended to supplement the Sherman Act. Its aim was primarily to arrest apprehended consequences of intercorporate relationships before those relationships could work their evil, which may be at or any time after the acquisition, depending upon the circumstances of the particular case. . . . The Government may proceed at any time that an acquisition may be said with reasonable probability to contain a threat that it may lead to a restraint of commerce or tend to create a monopoly of a line of commerce. . . .

We agree with the trial court that considerations of price, quality, and service were not overlooked by either Du Pont or General Motors. Pride in its products and its high financial stake in General Motors' success would naturally lead Du Pont to try to supply the best. But the wisdom of this business judgment cannot obscure the fact, plainly revealed by the record, that Du Pont purposely employed its stock to pry open the General Motors market to entrench itself as the primary supplier of General Motors' requirements for automotive finishes and fabrics.

Similarly, the fact that all concerned in high executive posts in both companies acted honorably and fairly, each in the honest conviction that his actions were in the best interests of his own company and without any design to overreach anyone, including Du Pont's competitors, does not defeat the Government's right to relief. It is not requisite to the proof of a violation of § 7 to show that restraint or monopoly was intended.

The statutory policy of fostering free competition is obviously furthered when no supplier has an advantage over his competitors from an acquisition of his customer's stock likely to have the effects condemned by the statute. We repeat, that the test of a violation of § 7 is whether, at the time of suit, there is a reasonable probability that the acquisition is likely to result in the condemned restraints. The conclusion upon this record is inescapable that such likelihood was proved as to this acquisition. . . .

§ 24:4. Choice of Law

The problem of selecting the law that shall govern in the case of interstate transactions and occurrences is becoming increasingly important. In the case which follows, an Illinois to Illinois round trip by automobile ended in a crash in Wisconsin. Should the law of Illinois or of Wisconsin govern?

Historically, the answer to this question was made in terms favoring stability. It was the law of the state where the occurrence took place or the accident occurred. The more modern approach, gaining prominence in the last ten years, has been to apply the law of the state that has the most significant contacts with the transactions. This gives the court a flexible hand to "do justice" as it sees "justice."

This view has been strongly criticized by attorneys on the ground that it destroys stability and makes it impossible to know how to settle a case out of court. The two big questions that arise in settling a case are with whom can the settlement be made and what is the extent of the damages. The answers to these questions may be different if the law of State X is applied than if the law of State Z is applied. If the lawyers cannot know in advance which law applies, it will be necessary in every case to bring a lawsuit and require the court to decide which law applies before the parties can safely settle the case. This has the bad effect of increasing the workload of the courts, adding to the expense and delay of claim adjustment, and seems to the practicing lawyer most absurd when everyone is willing to settle the case provided a safe settlement can be made. These problems will encourage the adoption of a federal statute on the subject, as has already been urged in the case of air crash claims.

CONKLIN v. HORNER

38 Wis.2d 468, 157 N.W.2d 579 (1968)

Horner lived in Illinois. He went for a motor trip which took him into Wisconsin and was to end in Illinois. On the trip, Conklin, a resident of Illinois, was his guest. In Wisconsin, Horner's car left the road, hit a tree and Conklin was injured. When Conklin sued Horner, the latter claimed that the Illinois guest statute applied under which he would only be liable for "willful and wanton" misconduct. Conklin claimed that the law of Wisconsin governed under which Horner would be liable for ordinary negligence. Conklin sued Horner in Wisconsin.

OPINION BY HEFFERNAN, J. . . .

The defendant's claim is based upon our decision in *Wilcox* v. *Wilcox* (1965), 26 Wis.2d. 617, 133 N.W.2d 408, where we abandoned the choice-of-law rule of *lex loci delicti* and adopted in its stead a more flexible methodology based upon the qualitative analysis of the contacts that one or more jurisdictions might have with the relevant facts. We adopted the general approach of *Babcock* v. *Jackson* (1963), 12 N.Y.2d 473, 240 N.Y.S.2d 743, 191 N.E.2d 279, 95 A.L.R.2d 1, and the basic principle of Tentative Draft No. 9, Restatement, Conflicts of Laws 2d, which may be denominated as the "center of gravity," "grouping of contacts," "dominant interest," "interest oriented," or "interest analysis" approach. We emphasized that what we adopted was not a rule, but a method of analysis that permitted dissection of the jural bundle constituting a tort and its environment to determine what elements therein were relevant to a reasonable choice of law.

When the Wilcox Case is so viewed, it is apparent that we cannot conclude that, when one set of facts leads logically to the law of the forum, the reverse, or the apparent reverse, of these facts will lead to the opposite conclusion. It has often been remarked in scientific experimentation that the mere observation of a phenomenon in itself constitutes a relevant fact in the history of the phenomenon. The same is true in a choice-of-law problem, for the observation, or to put it in the Wilcox context, the methodology, the analysis, and the evaluation of contacts can only be made by the forum, and the relationship of the forum to the other facts is a significant factor in the analysis. Thus, the exact factual, mirror image in a conflicts case is substantially an impossibility.

The appellants point out that in *Wilcox* v. *Wilcox* the journey of Mr. and Mrs. Wilcox to California commenced in Wisconsin and was intended to continue until their vacation was ended upon their return to Wisconsin. Using one of the favorite cliches of conflicts jurisprudes, we referred to the happening of the accident in Nebraska as "fortuitous." We stated the automobile was licensed and garaged in Wisconsin and concluded that the protection afforded by the Nebraska guest statute was designed to benefit Nebraska hosts and the host in Wilcox was a Wisconsin resident. Since the standard of care required by the guest statute of Nebraska would only penalize gross negligence, we concluded that no Nebraska purpose in promoting safety on its highways would be served by applying the lesser-care standard of the Nebraska law.

We said later in *Heath* v. *Zellmer* (1967), 35 Wis.2d 578, 589, 151 N.W.2d 664, Wilcox was an easy case that revealed no serious conflict with the laws of another jurisdiction. We resolved Wilcox by resorting solely to the law of Wisconsin, the only concerned jurisdiction.

The reverse situation, argued by the appellants—that Illinois is the only seriously concerned jurisdiction—is not, however, to be found under the facts of this case.

Wisconsin is a seriously concerned jurisdiction. While in Wilcox, Nebraska was merely the site of the tort and not the forum, in the instant case, Wisconsin is not only the state where the tortious conduct and the injury occurred, . . . but it is the forum as well. Thus, this court is specially charged as an instrument of the Wisconsin government to further the interests of Wisconsin, if to do so furthers the underlying policies of our law. We are obliged to examine the policies of our law. We are obliged to examine the policies behind the relevant laws to determine qualitatively whether their significance is great enough to warrant finding a serious conflict, which would

in turn require making a conscious choice of law, using the "choice-influencing considerations" adopted in Heath, supra. In Wilcox, supra, page 634 of
26 Wis.2d, page 416 of 133 N.W.2d, we expressed this duty of the forum
court as an instrument of state policy as a presumption, "that the law of the
forum should presumptively apply unless it becomes clear that nonforum
contacts are of the greater significance."

It is thus obvious that Wilcox is not controlling. This case is not the
reverse of Wilcox, for the place of conduct, the place of injury, and the
forum coincide. Accordingly, the whole gamut of the responsibilities of a
concerned forum court come into play.

The law of Illinois allows recovery only if the negligence of the host is
"willful and wanton," while Wisconsin would allow recovery if the host fails
to exercise ordinary care. In Heath we summarized some of the policy factors
motivating a guest statute. We stated in Heath, supra, pages 590, 591 of 35
Wis.2d, page 669 of 151 N.W.2d, that such a statute:

". . . evinces a desire to (a) prevent collusive suits between hosts and
guests; (b) prevent the ingratitude of the guest who sues his kindly host (bites
the hand that feeds him); (c) protect the host from being obligated for more
than he bargained for (a judgment when he only offered a ride); and (d) keep
intact a fund (the host's assets) so it can be reached by other parties to the
accident whose claims are assumed to have some vague moral priority over
the claims of the gratuitous guest. It is clear that the policy of the Indiana
statute is to shield the host, and therefore his insurer, from some liability.
The lower standard of conduct (a lesser duty) required in the host-guest
situation is for the benefit of defendants.

"The law of Wisconsin imposes liability in the host-guest situation when
there is proof of ordinary negligence:

" 'It is the policy of our law to provide compensation to a person when
he has been negligently injured. The reasons for this policy are manifold.
Among them are that the wrongdoer should bear the cost of an injury because
of his causal fault and not the injured party (unless he is equally at fault)
or the state authorities or those who have furnished medical services, and
that to the extent that damages in a negligence action are punitive, it is
hoped that the burden of a judgment may deter like conduct by others.'
Wilcox v. *Wilcox,* supra, page 631, 133 N.W.2d page 415.

"The purposes of the Wisconsin law are compensatory, admonitory, and
deterrent."

If Illinois law is used, the Wisconsin policy of compensating those who
are injured by ordinary negligence will be defeated. We stated in Heath, at
page 601, 151 N.W.2d at page 674, that our compensatory policy extends
to ". . . persons whether they be residents of this state or whether they come
from another jurisdiction."

If we accept the Illinois guest law, we accept a legal standard that gives
sanction to wrongful conduct. The deterrent effect that it is hoped our negligence laws exercise upon driver misconduct will be defeated by allowing
negligent misconduct to go unpunished. This is of particular importance in
this case, where the misconduct occurred on a Wisconsin highway.

On the other hand, if Wisconsin law is applied, the Illinois policies of protecting the host and his insurer will be defeated and those whom Illinois would shield will be answerable in damages.

It is thus apparent that a serious conflict arises. Both states have substantial physical contacts with the tort. The place of conduct, injury, and the forum are all in Wisconsin, while the parties and the vehicle came from Illinois and intended to return there. It could arguably be contended that the law of either jurisdiction could apply.

Accordingly, this court is obligated to evaluate the competing laws to determine which is most consonant with the considerations that we have determined to be relevant to the choice of law. . . .

These choice-influencing considerations are:

Predictability of results,
Maintenance of interstate and international order,
Simplification of the judicial task,
Advancement of the forum's governmental interests,
Application of the better rule of law.

As in Heath, supra, and Zelinger, supra, we find the element of predictability inapplicable under these facts. We said in Zelinger, page 470 of 156 N.W.2d: ". . . the choice influencing consideration of predictability is minimal . . . since parties do not plan to be negligent or to commit torts relying on interspousal or host-guest immunity. . . ."

Moreover, it can hardly be imagined, in these days of tourism and extensive interstate automobile traffic, that a motor vehicle will be confined strictly to the jurisdiction where it is licensed, garaged, or insured. After all, Winnebago county, Illinois, the residence of both the plaintiffs and the defendant, is located on the Wisconsin border. No doubt, frequent automobile travel in the neighboring state was contemplated by all concerned. As the respondents point out, the appellant insurance company is called the "Nationwide Mutual Insurance Co.," a name consistent with the wide territorial area of insurance company responsibility, hardly indicative that it relied solely upon local laws for setting its rates. Moreover, this accident occurred prior to Wilcox, when Wisconsin followed the rule of *lex loci delicti*, and the contemplation of the parties at that time would have been that Wisconsin law would apply if the accident occurred on Wisconsin highways. As we have stated before, however, a tort which is not intended can never, by definition, be the subject of advance planning with reference to a particular state's law.

While we conclude that predictability is not an element of preselection that controls the choice of law in an automobile accident, we do not thereby mean that there should be any uncertainty in respect to which law should be applied after all the facts relevant to the occurrence are available and subject to analysis. We pointed out that such analysis leads to a reasonable certainty based upon rational considerations as contrasted to the irrational, though certain (as viewed following the adventitious situs of the tort), rule of *lex loci*.

We are also obliged to consider whether the choice of Wisconsin law will impede the maintenance of interstate order and comity or whether the free flow of persons and commerce between Illinois and Wisconsin will be facilitated by the choice of Illinois law. This criterion requires that a state that is minimally concerned defer to the interests of a state that is substantially concerned. Wisconsin is more than minimally concerned, for the negligent conduct occurred on its highways.

Nor do we think it likely that Illinois' governmental interests are so concerned that retaliatory conduct would ensue. In fact, while in this case, at least, we are willing to accept the premise that the Illinois host-guest law results in a marked difference in the outcome of a particular negligence case, we have strong doubts that this is literally true.

The Illinois Personal Injury Jury Instructions provide:

" 'Willful and wanton conduct' means a cause of action which, if not intentional, shows an utter indifference to or conscious disregard for a person's own safety and the safety of others."

However, the decided cases take on a decidedly different flavor.

All studies indicate that the term, "willful and wanton," refers to a degree of negligence less than that indicated by a literal construction of the term. The commentator in 54 Northwestern University Law Review, 263, 267 (1959), reviewed recent cases and pointed out the refusal of the Illinois Supreme Court to exactly define the words of the statute, "willful and wanton." He observed that the court stated that the term expressed an area between ordinary negligence and actual malice. The commentator stated at page 268:

"Whether this was within the contemplation of the legislature or whether it indicates a trend towards compensation for every injury, the Illinois Guest Statute has evolved as something quite different from what the original proponents of guest statute legislation evidently had in mind."

A recent appellate division opinion, *Spivack* v. *Hara* (1966), 69 Ill.App. 2d 22, 216 N.E.2d 173, 175, would equate the words of the statute to something akin to ordinary negligence. That opinion stated:

"The words willful and wanton used in the charge and in the finding against Hara no longer have the connotation of willfulness or even utter lack of restraint, but have been used to define a vague and somewhat shadowy area close to ordinary negligence. They do not imply that the defendant *intentionally* disregarded the safety of another."

While a fair evaluation of the Illinois cases would lead to the conclusion that something more than ordinary negligence is generally required to place liability upon a host, yet it is clear that the immunity contemplated by the statute is rendered but grudgingly by the Illinois courts. Wisconsin's position on host-guest is not as much opposed to the position of the Illinois courts as one would conclude from the literal reading of the statute.

We thus see no great violence done to Illinois policy in the event Wisconsin law is applied. However, assuming, as we do, that "willful and wanton" means just that—negligence substantially in excess of ordinary lack of care— we nonetheless conclude that our interest is not so minimal that the application of Wisconsin law to the case would be merely a matter of forum preference. Moreover, it is obvious that the imposition of liability upon an Illinois host is not likely to reduce the likelihood that Illinois hosts will continue to drive into Wisconsin with their guests. We see no burden upon interstate movement as the result of the choice of Wisconsin law.

We pointed out in Heath and Zelinger that the third choice-influencing consideration—simplification of the judicial task—is of little importance in the host-guest situation. Although the previous discussion indicates some doubt about the exact posture of the Illinois host-guest law, and no doubt we would be surer of our own law, the courts of this state, though more accustomed to trying cases under the law of the forum, would find little difficulty in applying the Illinois law. We said in Heath, supra, page 600 of 35 Wis.2d, page 674 of 151 N.W.2d, " 'the wanton or willful' test . . . could be applied easily by any Wisconsin lawyer or judge." Additional complications posed by the possible use of Illinois law are so insignificant that they may be ignored.

One of the most relevant considerations is the duty of the courts to further the legitimate governmental policies of the forum. The policy of our tort law is to compensate those who are injured by negligent acts. We pointed out in Heath, page 601, 151 N.W.2d page 674, that this policy applies to all who come within our borders:

"To deny recovery for ordinary negligence is to defeat Wisconsin's policy of compensating victims of ordinary negligence. It is the policy of Wisconsin to provide compensation to those persons whether they be residents of this state or whether they come from another jurisdiction. To deny nonresidents recovery for damages occasioned by the same tort that creates liability to a resident would not only defeat Wisconsin's policy and its governmental interest, but could perhaps be challenged as a denial of equal protection of the laws to nonresidents."

Mr. Chief Justice Hallows stated in Zelinger, supra, page 472 of 156 N.W.2d: ". . . Wisconsin's interest in the nonexistence of such rules [interspousal and host-guest immunity] is to promote the spreading of the risk and fasten liability in torts on a moral basis of fault."

We have also stated that, in addition to the compensatory aspect of our tort law, liability for ordinary negligence is deemed to be admonitory and deterrent in nature. Heath, supra, page 591, 151 N.W.2d 664. We stated therein, at page 602, 151 N.W.2d at page 675, that to employ the Indiana host-guest law: ". . . would remove the deterrent effect of our law of negligence, while the choice of Wisconsin law would further this state's interest in regulating conduct on Wisconsin highways and penalizing that conduct when it is negligent. It would promote safe driving on Wisconsin highways."

To the extent that our laws of negligence serve that purpose, this court would seriously breach its duty to its forum obligations by applying a foreign host-guest rule when the Wisconsin rule of ordinary negligence could reasonably be applied. Wisconsin is a tourist state, and large numbers of vehicles from immunity jurisdictions visit our state each year. In 1965, 14,213 out-of-state vehicles were involved in accidents in Wisconsin. Twenty-nine percent of these, or 4,129 were from Illinois. In 1966, 21,699 of all the vehicles involved in Wisconsin's accidents were from out of state. Seventeen percent of these, or 3,655, were Illinois automobiles. It is apparent that we are dealing with an area of major concern to the state of Wisconsin. While it is obvious that the host-guest rule may not be relevant to all or to even a large number of these instances (statistics are not available), the concern of this court that the application of a rule that would, in its potential, substantially dilute the deterrent (as well as the compensatory) effect of our negligence law is obviously well founded. Our legislature has recently spoken out strongly for strict enforcement of highway safety rules. In ch. 292, Laws of 1967, it referred to the "immensity of the state's traffic problem" and called for "rigid enforcement" of all traffic laws. The preamble of this new legislative act concluded:

"The gravity of the problem, and the devastating power of the machine no longer permits countenance of the myriad excuses of *careless* drivers which were, in an earlier day, tiresome, but which now become lethal." (Emphasis supplied.)

It is in the interest of this state and of its citizens to retain where possible those laws which require motorists to refrain from acts of ordinary negligence.

We also conclude that Wisconsin's law is the "better law" to apply under the circumstances. We have in Heath, supra, and Zelinger, supra, pointed out that the guest statutes are anachronistic vestiges of the early days of the development of the law-of-enterprise liability and do not reflect present day socioeconomic conditions. Earlier in this opinion we said the application of the host-guest rule defeats the Wisconsin objective of highway safety. We also conclude that such a law is bad law; for its application in those states where a legislature has put a guest law in effect results in a haven—a sanctuary—for those who wrongfully cause harm with impunity. We see only legal retrogression in extending the pernicious effects of such a law to Wisconsin.

We emphasize that we prefer the Wisconsin rule of ordinary negligence not because it is Wisconsin's law, but because we consider it to be the better law. In three cases within a year, Heath, Zelinger, and this case, we have preferred Wisconsin law, but it should be noted that the merits of the competing rules of law were carefully considered, and the choice was made not as a matter of parochial preference but in the honest belief that, given the opportunity to apply either a forum or nonforum law, the better law in each case proved to be that of the forum. We said in Zelinger, supra, page 473 of 156 N.W.2d, "We would apply the law of a nonforum state if it were the better law."

This analysis leads to the conclusion that Wisconsin, not Illinois, law should be applied to the case. We are satisfied that the contacts of Wisconsin with the tort are substantial and the application of Wisconsin law is fully justified by the facts. We are not mere intruders in a non-Wisconsin situation. The two most relevant choice-influencing considerations lead inevitably to the selection of Wisconsin law. The use of Wisconsin law will significantly advance the interests of the forum, while its nonapplication will be detrimental to Wisconsin's policy; and, in addition, we select Wisconsin's law as the better law and reject that of Illinois as a "creed outworn."

Illinois is not so significantly concerned with his case that its law should replace Wisconsin's better law in derogation of the interests of the forum. . . .

DISSENTING OPINION BY HALLOWS, C.J. . . .

The majority has overemphasized the Wisconsin contacts and has favored Wisconsin governmental interests and better law in determining that this state had the most significant relationship to the host-guest issue in this personal injury action. Wisconsin has only two contacts, the forum and the place of accident [here, the place of conduct and injury coincide]. Illinois has substantial contacts, the domicile of all the parties and the center of the host-guest relation, which is the very issue involved. To paraphrase *Wilcox* v. *Wilcox* (1965), 26 Wis.2d 617, 631, 133 N.W.2d 408, we are concerned with the situation in which the plaintiff guest and the defendant host are Illinois residents who were on a trip which commenced in Illinois and was intended to end there. The policy of insurance was issued by an Illinois licensed company, delivered in Illinois, to afford coverage on an automobile licensed in Illinois and usually garaged and operated in Illinois.

Of the five choice-influencing considerations, we have little difficulty with predictability and the simplification of the judicial task. They are of little significance in tort cases. However, predictability was stressed as being most important in an antenuptial-agreement case which adopted the grouping-of-contacts theory for contact issues prior to the application of such rule in Wilcox to torts. See *Estate of Knippel* (1959), 7 Wis.2d 335, 96 N.W.2d 514. However, on the issue of whether the host-guest law of Illinois should apply to protect the host, the factor of maintenance of interstate and international order has some significance. Illinois may have little basis to be offended when Wisconsin applies its law to protect its own residents in their right to recover in an automobile accident case when an Illinois resident is also involved. . . .

Illinois, however, is greatly concerned when its law governing a relationship existing solely between its residents is at issue and is not applied to its residents who are temporarily in Wisconsin simply because a court of Wisconsin thinks its law is better than that of Illinois. The court of the forum must not only evaluate the factual contacts in relation to the issue to determine whether they give rise to a legitimate governmental interest but also evaluate the strength of these local concerns or interest in relation to the factual contacts. Thus three ingredients must be weighed with each choice-influencing factor—the factor itself, the importance of the factual contact in relation to the choice factor and the relevancy of both in relation to the precise issue involved.

The facts in the instant case are the converse of *Wilcox* v. *Wilcox,* supra, and its reasoning for not applying *lex loci* should be applied to be consistent and to further the hope expressed in that case that, page 635 of 26 Wis.2d, page 417 of 133 N.W.2d, "on a case-by-case-basis generalizations will soon become apparent and will take its place as a guide to the future to provide a uniform common law of conflicts." If this reasoning were used, the place of the accident contact would not support the application of our local concerns to the specific issue. The Wilcox reasoning is not to be depreciated, because in truth and in fact the happening of the accident in this case in Wisconsin was fortuitous and "should not now inure as a windfall to any of the defendants" [plaintiffs, here]. The Wilcox reasoning also relied on the argument that the law of Wisconsin was the law of the place whose application was "anticipated and insured against," . . . the application of the Illinois law because Wisconsin law is not a "foreseeable and insurable law." Certainly, the mobility of modern society must be considered but the question is how much compelling force or influence should this factor be given.

The only other factual contact in the instant case is that Wisconsin is the forum, but we said in Zelinger that the application of the law of the forum was merely a weak presumption to be used as a starting point in evaluating the choice-influencing factors in relation to the specific issue and not to the tort as a unitary entity. If the advancement of the local concerns of the forum is to be the controlling factor, as the majority seems to indicate, then we have deserted in fact, if not in word, our newly adopted method of deciding choice-of-law questions and are committed to applying the law of the forum because it is always our duty to advance Wisconsin governmental interest and to apply our better law in every conflicts case before us.

I think Illinois contacts and interests in relation to the host-guest issue here presented are substantially greater and more relevant than Wisconsin's. I do not think the underpinnings of contacts of forum and place of accident on these facts are sufficient to entitle nonresidents to reject the governmental interest of their domicile state and the law under which their relationship was created and to claim what we consider and undoubtedly the plaintiff considers to be the better law. . . .

§ 24:5. Contractual Flexibility

The law is moving away from the common-law view that a contract must be definite or it will not be binding. Instead the law is beginning to let the parties work out their own arrangements, and if they are satisfied with them, the law will not hold their agreement invalid because it is indefinite. This permits the parties to establish a flexible working relationship when from the nature of the circumstances, it is impractical for them to be specific— primarily because no one can anticipate what will happen, and it is more practical to wait and see and then work out each day's problems as they arise rather than to make a binding commitment in advance that would seek to anticipate every combination of events which might thereafter arise.

GRISWOLD v. HEAT INCORPORATED

108 N.H. 119, 229 A.2d 183 (1967)

Griswold was an accountant. He made a contract with Heat Incorporated by which it agreed to pay him $200 a month for rendering such accounting services "as he in his sole discretion should render." When he sued for payment under the contract, the corporation refused to pay on the ground that the contract was so indefinite that it was not binding.

Opinion by Lampron, J. . . .

When Heat was incorporated in New Hampshire in 1956 its stockholders and directors were Kretschmar, Harris and the defendant Illig, each holding 500 shares. Its business, the distribution of heating equipment and boilers, was based in Nashua and operated by Kretschmar, as Harris and Illig had businesses of their own, the former in Portland, Maine, the latter in Fitchburg, Massachusetts.

Plaintiff Griswold, a certified public accountant, was associated with Heat from its beginning. He installed its accounting system, kept the stock book records, the records of meetings of the directors and the stockholders, counseled and advised on bookkeeping and accounting procedures, and on the financial operation of the company. The Trial Court found that Griswold is a 78-year old man with a life expectancy in excess of the remainder of the contract in dispute, who is somewhat deaf, has sciatica, but is alert, moves briskly and he presently is still active in his profession as a certified accountant as a member of a large Portland firm of accountants.

When Kretschmar died in May, 1957, the corporation bought his 500 shares of stock. The remaining stockholders, Harris and Illig, because of their own full time interests, agreed to continue Heat only if a manager could be obtained and if Griswold agreed to continue to serve the corporation as he had in the past. This was arranged and thereafter Griswold, who became the holder of one share of stock, served as director, assistant treasurer, clerk, and continued as financial advisor to the corporation. For these services Griswold received $300 per month, which was reduced to $100 per month in 1960, when Heat had financial reverses, and continued at that rate until January 1, 1964.

Prior to December 2, 1963, Harris notified Illig that he was interested in disposing of his stock in Heat to him. On that date Harris transferred his shares to Illig who became owner of 998 of the 1,000 shares outstanding, Mrs. Illig owning one share and Griswold the other. Illig testified that in connection with this purchase he was desirous that Griswold continue to serve Heat in the same manner as he had in the past and that Griswold agreed to do so for $200 per month which Illig agreed to pay. Both Harris and Griswold, who with Illig then constituted the board of directors of Heat, testified that was the agreement between Illig and Griswold.

Although Illig admitted that the above was an agreement he sought and obtained, he denied that the agreement was in writing, stating that it rested on his "verbal agreement." However the Trial Court properly found as a fact that the contract on which plaintiff relies appears in the corporate records of the December 2, 1963, special meeting of Heat's board of directors.

The Corporate minutes relating thereto read as follows:

"*Voted:* That Heat Incorporated, a New Hampshire corporation or its successor or successors, if any, by this vote of the directors of the corporation here assembled, does contract to pay monthly to Ernest H. Griswold not less than two hundred dollars beginning January 1, 1964, for such services as he, in his sole discretion may render, the term of the contract to be not less than five years from January 1, 1964, unless terminated earlier by the death of Ernest H. Griswold. A copy of this vote attested by a majority or all of the directors of this corporation shall constitute the written contract to be delivered forthwith to the said Ernest H. Griswold."

The Trial Court properly found that copies of the above vote were signed on that day by all the three directors of Heat, including defendant Illig, and constituted a written contract, copies of which were retained by the plaintiff.

The Court further found as follows: "The plaintiff during the year 1964 performed approximately the same services as he had previously performed and was paid by the corporation for the entire twelve months of 1964. On December 8, 1964, the defendant, Ernest E. Illig, notified the plaintiff, who was then in Florida, of his intention to have the corporation terminate any further payments to the plaintiff as of January 1, 1965, and further stating that in the event of any other employment of the plaintiff by the corporation it would be on a fee basis. There was a substantial acrimonious exchange of letters and telegrams between the plaintiff and the defendant during this period, and the defendant called a Special Meeting of the Directors on December 29, 1964, at his home, at which two of the then three Directors (the Director replacing Harris being Mrs. Illig), terminated the employment of the plaintiff by vote, and the plaintiff has not been asked to do any duties since then, nor has he received any compensation since then."

The Trial Court in transferring without ruling plaintiff's right to recover on the contract found "specifically that the only question in which the Court has not found for the plaintiff on the contract is whether or not the language 'for such services as he,' (the plaintiff) 'in his sole discretion may render,' renders this contract voidable."

If plaintiff is entitled to recover on this contract, the Trial Court found "that at the present time there would be due on the contract $2,200, and that . . . he is entitled to $2,200, plus the value as of the present date of the right to receive $200 per month for 37 months more forthwith, plus interest on the $2,200 to date."

Defendants take the position that Griswold's promise by its terms gives the plaintiff such an option in regard to the performance required of him as to render his promise illusory and insufficient to constitute consideration for a bilateral contract between the parties. . . .

Does Griswold's promise or obligation "for such services as he, in his sole discretion, may render" constitute sufficient consideration for Heat's promise to pay him $200 per month for 5 years in accordance with the terms of their agreement?

It has long been the rule in this state that "the proper interpretation of a contract is that which will make it speak the intention of the parties at the time it was made." . . . It follows that in construing the written agreement of these parties, all of its provisions, its subject matter, the situation of the parties at the time, and the object intended to be effected will be considered in arriving at the sense of the words they used. . . .

There was evidence that the nature of the services rendered by Griswold to Heat from its origin in 1956 to December 2, 1963, the date of the agreement, were well known to both Griswold and Illig. The latter testified that on the above date when he purchased Harris' interest he wanted Griswold to continue to serve the corporation as "he had over the years." He asked Griswold if he was willing to continue in "this fashion," at $200 a month and Griswold said he would. The latter testified that Illig agreed to pay him $200 per month for his "usual services" the nature of which was known to Illig. This insight of the object intended to be effected by the agreement is an important factor in determining the sense of the words used therein by these parties. . . .

The course of conduct of the parties for the first year following their agreement is further evidence "of their common understanding of the meaning of their contract and the result they expected to accomplish thereby." . . . The Trial Court properly found that "the plaintiff during the year 1964 performed approximately the same services as he had previously performed and was paid by the corporation for the entire twelve months." Griswold was paid $200 per month as provided for by the agreement. During that period Illig owned all of the shares of Heat except two, one owned by his wife, the other by Griswold. The three of them constituted the board of directors.

Since this agreement was made by businessmen, it is reasonable to assume that it was made for business reasons and was intended to have business efficacy. . . . It should be so construed. . . . In all such business undertakings an obligation of good faith is implied. . . . An interpretation which makes the agreement fair and reasonable will be preferred to one which leads to harsh and unreasonable results. . . . Similarly "[a]n interpretation that would place one party at the mercy of another should, if at all possible, be avoided." . . .

Construing the language of the agreement in the light of all the criteria previously mentioned, we hold that the provision "for such services as he (Griswold), in his sole discretion, may render" obligated Griswold to render some services to Heat and imposed on him the duty to exercise good faith in the determination of their amount. . . . We further hold that these obligations constituted detriment to Griswold and benefit to Heat and were sufficient consideration for Heat's promises in the agreement. . . .

The plaintiff is entitled to recover on the contract.

Questions for Review

1. Define the social force of flexibility.

2. Give illustrations of its application.

3. Analyze each opinion in this chapter in terms of the social forces involved in the decision. See § 5:5 for a list of the social forces. With respect to each opinion, explain why the prevailing social forces prevailed and why those rejected did not. In each case in which there is a dissenting opinion, also make this analysis for the dissenting opinion.

4-6. On the basis of the social forces involved, what decision should be made in each of the following cases?

4. **Contracts. Definite.** May a contract for the construction of a swimming pool validly provide for the construction of the pool according to the "plans to be submitted by the National Pool Company," although such plans are not in existence at the time the contract is made? *Martinson* v. *Brooks Equipment Leasing,* 36 Wis.2d 207, 152 N.W.2d 849.

5. **Contracts. Requirements.** Is a contract by which "buyer agrees to purchase all . . . gas for above listed points" an "illusory" contract, and therefore not binding, because it does not impose an obligation to purchase any specific amount of gas? *United Butane Sales* v. *Bessemer-Suburban Gas Co.,* Ala., 207 So.2d 416.

6. **Punishment. Jury mercy.** Where a statute gives the jury power to determine whether punishment should be death or life imprisonment, may the jury make its choice on the basis of its view as to the social value of the death sentence? *California* v. *Love,* Cal.2d, 17 Cal.Rptr. 481, 366 P.2d 809.

7-10. What social forces were involved, which prevailed, and which were defeated in the following decisions?

7. **Scholastic standing. Judicial review.** When a student is dropped from medical school because of unsatisfactory scholastic standing, a court will not review the action of the school authorities where the student does not prove that their action was arbitrary, capricious, or taken in bad faith. *Mustell* v. *Rose,* Ala., 211 So.2d 489.

8. **Deceptive practice. "Free."** The court will not reverse the conclusion of the Federal Trade Commission that a deceptive practice was engaged in when a paint seller advertised that with every can of paint purchased, the buyer would receive one "free" can, where the price paid for the one can was greater than the seller's ordinary single-can purchase price. *Federal Trade Commission* v. *Carter Paint Co.,* 382 U.S. 46.

9. **Premises liability. Snow.** The occupier of premises is permitted to wait until the end of a storm and has a reasonable time thereafter in which to remove snow from the public walking areas. *Hovden* v. *Decorah City,* Iowa, 155 N.W.2d 534.

10. **Parol evidence. Condition precedent.** Parol evidence is admissible to show that a written agreement for sale of mining rights was not to become effective if Atomic Energy Commission allocation did not permit sufficient mining to make operations economically practical. *Cosper* v. *Hancock,* Colo., 430 P.2d 80.

Chapter 25

PRACTICAL EXPEDIENCY

§ 25:1. Generally

Frequently the law is influenced by what is practical and expedient in the situation. In some of these situations, the law will strive to make its rules fit the business practices of society.

The concept of practical expediency may also apply when the courts are influenced by the effect upon the courts themselves of the adoption of a particular rule of law. For example, courts will not ordinarily render advisory opinions, that is, give legal advice to people when there is no real lawsuit. It would not be practical for courts to perform that function because if they did, the courts would be overburdened with "advice" work.

§ 25:2. Mailed Acceptance of Contract

When an offer to enter into a contract is made by one person to another and the latter makes an acceptance by mailing, the question once arose as to whether the acceptance was effective when mailed or when received by the offeror. The law, guided by the concept of practical expediency, has settled on the rule that the acceptance of the offer is effective when mailed.

Any decision on this point is obviously one which is arbitrary or one which can only find justification in terms of practical expediency. If the offer is effective when mailed, there is a time interval when the contract exists but the offeror does not yet know that he is bound by a contract. If the receipt of the acceptance were made the controlling time, the offeree mailing an acceptance would never know just when he had a contract and would have to wait until he received word from the offeror indicating that the acceptance had been received.

MORRISON v. THOELKE

155 So.2d 889 (Fla., 1963)

Thoelke and his wife owned land which Morrison and his wife offered to buy. The Morrisons mailed an offer to the Thoelkes, which they accepted by mailing back a completed contract for the sale of the land. While this letter of acceptance was in transit, the sellers notified the buyers that the acceptance was revoked. The sellers brought an action to declare the contract void. The lower court decided in favor of the sellers and the buyers appealed.

OPINION BY ALLEN, A.C.J. . . .

A number of undisputed facts were established by the pleadings, including the facts that appellees are the owners of the subject property, located in Orange County; that on November 26, 1957, appellants, as purchasers, executed a contract for the sale and purchase of the subject property and mailed the contract to appellees who were in Texas; and that on November 27, 1957, appellees executed the contract and placed it in the mails addressed to appellants' attorney in Florida. It is also undisputed that after mailing said contract, but prior to its receipt in Florida, appellees called appellants' attorney and canceled and repudiated the execution and contract. Nonetheless, appellants, upon receipt of the contract caused the same to be recorded. . . .

The question is whether a contract is complete and binding when a letter of acceptance is mailed, thus barring repudiation prior to delivery to the offeror, or when the letter of acceptance is received, thus permitting repudiation prior to receipt. Appellants, of course, argue that posting the acceptance creates the contract; appellees contend that only receipt of the acceptance bars repudiation. . . .

The appellant, in arguing that the lower court erred in giving effect to the repudiation of the mailed acceptance, contends that this case is controlled by the general rule that insofar as the mail is an acceptable medium of communication, a contract is complete and binding upon posting of the letter of acceptance. . . . Appellees, on the other hand, argue that the right to recall mail makes the Post Office Department the agent of the sender, and that such right coupled with communication of a renunciation prior to receipt of the acceptance voids the acceptance. In short, appellees argue that acceptance is complete only upon receipt of the mailed acceptance. . . .

Turning first to the general rule relied upon by appellant, some insight may be gained by reference to the statement of the rule in leading encyclopedias and treatises. Accordingly, attention is directed to 12 Am.Jur., Contracts §§ 46, 49 (1938) for the following:

"§ 46. Acceptance by Mail.—The formation of the contract may be made dependent upon the communication of the acceptance to the offeror, and in such a case there will be no contract if for any reason the offeror is not notified of the acceptance according to the agreement. In cases in which such an arrangement has not been made, the courts have been confronted by the rather difficult question whether the contract is completed when the letter of acceptance is mailed or when it is received by the offeror. There is no doubt that the implication that a complete, final, and absolutely binding contract is formed as soon as the acceptance of an offer is posted may in some cases lead to inconvenience and hardship. At the same time, it has been pointed out that an offeror, if he chooses, may always make the formation of the contract which he proposes dependent upon the actual communication to himself of the acceptance and that if no answer to his offer is received by him and the matter is of importance to him, he can make inquiries of the person to whom his offer was addressed. It has been suggested, moreover, that if the offeror is not to be bound by the acceptance until it is received by him, the party accepting the offer ought not to be bound when his acceptance is received, because he does not know of the meeting of the minds, for the offer may have been withdrawn before his acceptance was received. Upon balancing convenience and inconvenience, the courts have deemed it more consistent with the acts and declarations of the parties to consider the contract complete and absolutely binding on the transmission of the acceptance through the post, as the medium of communication which the parties themselves contemplate, instead of postponing its completion until the acceptance has been received by the offeror. By treating the post office as the agency of both parties, the courts have managed to harmonize the legal notion that it is necessary that the minds of the parties meet with the equally well-established principle that a determination to accept is ineffectual if it is not communicated either actually or by legal implication. Accordingly, if acceptance by mail is authorized, the contract is completed at the moment the acceptor deposits in the post office the letter of acceptance directed to the offeror's proper address and with the postage prepaid, provided he does so within the proper time and before receiving any intimation of the revocation of the offer. . . . "Of course, a letter which is written, but remains in the writer's hands or under his control, is not an acceptance. . . .

"§ 49.—Effect of Withdrawal of, or Right to Withdraw, Letter from Mail.—Since 1887, at least, postal regulations have permitted the withdrawal, under certain conditions, of letters from the mail. . . .

"The authorities are not entirely harmonious as to the effect of such right to withdraw letters or of the withdrawal of letters pursuant to such regulations upon the acceptance of contracts. A leading authority on contracts states that it is not important that the acceptor has the power to withdraw his acceptance from the mail. Moreover, there are several decisions holding that an acceptance duly deposited in the mail is effective, although the acceptor intercepts the letter of acceptance and secures its return before it has reached the addressee. There are also numerous recent cases in which no question of withdrawal or the right to withdraw the acceptance from the mail arose, applying or recognizing the rule that a contract is complete at the time of the depositing of a proper letter of acceptance in the mail, where acceptance in this manner is authorized. On the other hand, the view is held that a contract is not deemed consummated by a deposit in the mail of a letter accepting an offer, so long as the sender has a right to withdraw the letter. The position has been taken that in view of the postal regulations permitting the withdrawal of a letter from the mail by the depositor, the post office should be regarded as the latter's agent, so long as the letter may be withdrawn by him, unless it appears, expressly or by implication, that the parties intended that the sender of the communication after mailing, should have no right to withdraw it."

A near identical statement of the general rule is found in 1 Williston, Contracts § 81 (3rd ed. 1957): . . . . The same work, in Section 86, negatives the possible effect of a power to recall an acceptance after mailing. In the author's words:

"By the United States Postal Regulations, the sender of a letter may regain it by complying with certain specified formalities, and yet a contract is completed by mailing an acceptance in the authorized channel. Since the acceptance is binding when it is mailed, the fact that the sender of a letter may regain possession of it should have no effect on the validity of the acceptance. . . .

A second leading treatise on the law of contracts, Corbin, Contracts §§ 78 and 80 (1950 Supp. 1961), also . . . negates the effect of the offeree's power to recall his letter:

"The postal regulations have for a long period made it possible for the sender of a letter to intercept it and prevent its delivery to the addressee. This has caused some doubt to be expressed as to whether an acceptance can ever be operative upon the mere mailing of the letter, since the delivery to the post office has not put it entirely beyond the sender's control.

"It is believed that no such doubt should exist. . . . In view of common practices, in view of the difficulties involved in the process of interception of a letter, and in view of the decisions and printed discussions dealing with acceptance by post, it is believed that the fact that a letter can be lawfully intercepted by the sender should not prevent the acceptance from being operative on mailing. If the offer was made under such circumstances that the offeror should know that the offeree might reasonably regard this as a proper method of closing the deal, and the offeree does so regard it, and makes use of it, the contract is consummated even though the letter of acceptance is intercepted and not delivered."

Significantly, Corbin expressly distinguishes cases involving bank drafts or bills of exchange from cases involving bilateral contracts. He writes:

"It should be borne in mind that whenever the receipt of the letter is necessary to produce some legal effect, the interception, and resulting non-delivery of the letter will prevent that effect. For almost all purposes, other than the acceptance of an offer, the mere mailing of a letter is not enough to attain the purpose. Unless it is clearly otherwise agreed, the mailing of a letter is not a sufficient notice to quit a tenancy, it is not actual payment of money that is inclosed, it does not transfer title to a check or other document; it will not ordinarily be sufficient notice required by a contract as a condition precedent to some contractual duty of immediate performance." . . .

The position adopted by the lower court is succinctly expressed in the excellent memorandum opinion of the lower court as follows: ". . . the decisions of the Courts seem to hinge upon the question of whether or not the party has lost control of the instrument prior to the time of its renunciation by him. Formerly, the Courts took the position that once a letter had been deposited in the U.S. Mail, it was beyond retrieve and the depositor no longer had control over it; that the Post Office Department became, in fact, the agent of the addressee so that any attempt to cancel or repudiate the written document was beyond the power and authority of the sender and without effect once it had been deposited in the mail. U.S. Postal Regulations, Sec. 153.5, provide, and for some years has provided, that mail deposited in a post office may be recalled by the sender before delivery to the addressee.

"In the Court decisions cited by the parties here, wherever this Postal Regulation has been brought to the attention of the Court, they have held that the Post Office is the agent of the sender, rather than the addressee, and his right to withdraw mail after deposit gives him the right to repudiate a document signed and mailed by him but not yet received by the addressee."

An examination of the cases relied upon by appellees sustains their contention that these decisions represent a departure from the general rule. In *Traders National Bank* v. *First National Bank,* 1920, 142 Tenn. 229, 217 S.W. 977, 9 A.L.R. 382, the Court held, when appellant bank, in response to receipt of a check drawn on it, mailed a draft to appellee bank but phoned and requested return of the draft prior to its receipt by appellee, that appellant had not accepted the check. This holding was predicated on the existence of a power in appellant to recall the draft from the mails. The Court concluded:

"In ordinary cases we will adhere to the old rule that the mailing of a letter amounts to a delivery of its contents to the person to whom it is addressed. This, however, is subject to the power of the person sending the letter to recover it from the mails, under the Postal Regulations of 1913. Such a delivery is therefore subject to be defeated by the proper exercise of such power."

In *Guardian National Bank* v. *Huntington County State Bank,* 1933, 206 Ind. 185, 187 N.E. 388, 92 A.L.R. 1056, the appellant bank sued to recover on checks drawn on appellee bank. The checks had been deposited in appellant bank and forwarded to a second bank, which bank notified appellee bank. Appellee prepared and mailed a letter indicating that it had credited the second bank with the amount of the checks. Later in the day, however, this letter was withdrawn from the mail and the credit changed to exclude the amount of the subject checks. The Court held that the original mailing had not constituted acceptance of the checks. Citing the Traders National Bank case, supra, and Ex parte Cote, L.R. 9 Ch. 27, (1873), the Court determined that the Post Office was an agent of the sender and that until delivery to the addressee, mail remained in control of the sender. Discussing the rule that deposit in the mail constitutes acceptance, the Court said: . . .

"But in 1913 the Post Office Department adopted a regulation by the terms of which, under certain conditions, a communication which has been mailed may be recovered as a matter of right and without the consent or authority of the addressee. Under this regulation, when a communication is mailed, it is as though it is intrusted to the sender's agent or servant for delivery, and is subject to recall at any time before actual delivery."

Referring to the Traders National Bank case, the Court said:

"If the post office is the agent of the sender in a case involving the mailing of a draft, because of the fact that the sender may recover the same, how can it be said that it is not the agent of the sender in the case of an acceptance of an offer which is subject to the same regulation? No rule of construction has been suggested that would permit of treating a messenger from whom a message may be recalled as the agent of any one but the sender.

"The time at which payment would become effective or a contract consummated by acceptance of an offer is controlled by contract, express or implied. The parties are bound to know the rules and regulations of the Post Office Department, and must be considered as acting in the light of those rules, and unless it appears by expression or implication that the parties intended that the acceptor or remittor should have no right to withdraw his communication after mailing, it must be assumed that they intended that he should continue to exercise control of it, and that therefore, following the normal rules of interpretation, the post office should be his agent.

"We conclude that the post office is the agent of the sender so long as the communication may be withdrawn by him, regardless of whether the transaction be treated as a payment or an acceptance of an offer to contract, and therefore the evidence supports the verdict of the jury."

A third case cited by appellee, *Dick* v. *United States,* 82 F.Supp. 362, 113 Ct.Cl. 94 (1949), involved mistaken acceptance of an offer evidenced by a government purchase order. The appellant, after mailing his acceptance wired a repudiation of the acceptance. The repudiation was received prior to the acceptance. Although remanding the cause for proofs, the court inferred that the fact of a mailed acceptance did not, as a matter of law, bar subsequent repudiation. In an opinion paralleling the opinion in the Guardian National Bank case, the Court, over a vigorous dissent, concluded that the Post Office was the sender's agent and that "delivery" was incomplete so long as the acceptance had not been received.

The same court, in *Rhode Island Tool Company* v. *United States,* 128 F.Supp. 417, 130 Ct.Cl. 698 (1955), extended the principle that a contract was made only upon receipt of the acceptance to permit revocation of an offer after an acceptance had been posted but prior to its receipt. Again predicating its decision on the postal regulations, the court concluded:

"Does any one believe that if the mistake had been the other way, . . . that through oversight the defendant had mailed an acceptance for too high a price and the same day had wired withdrawing and cancelling the acceptance before it left the sending post office the defendant would nevertheless have been held to an excessive price? Or again, if after mailing such an acceptance the defendant, discovering its mistake, had gone to the sending post office and withdrawn the letter, the plaintiff on hearing of it, could have enforced an excessive contract on the ground that the acceptance actually had been posted and became final and enforceable, notwithstanding its withdrawal and nondelivery?

"We cannot conceive of such an unjust enforcement. No, under the new regulation, the Post Office Department becomes, in effect, the agency of the sender until actual delivery.

"We are living in a time of change. The theories of yesterday, proved by practice today, give way to the improvements of tomorrow.

"To apply an outmoded formula is not only unjust, it runs counter to the whole stream of human experience. It is like insisting on an oxcart as the official means of transportation in the age of the automobile. The cart served a useful purpose in its day, but is now a museum piece.

"The old rule was established before Morse invented the telegraph as a means of communication. Commerce must have a breaking point upon which it may rely for the completion of a contract. At that time no faster mode of communication was known. But in the light of the faster means of communication the Post Office Department wisely changed the rule. The reason for the old rule had disappeared. This does not change any principle, it simply changes the practice to suit the changed conditions, but leaves unchanged the principle of finality, which is just as definite as ever, though transferred to a different point by the new regulation.

"This change seems to have been recognized by the Government officials who prepared the Invitation for Bids. The offer by the defendant stated that when the award was 'received' by the bidder it would 'thereupon' become a binding contract. This it would seem clinches the correctness of our interpretation."

It is clear then, as aforesaid, that these cases represent a departure from the general rule. . . .

As is abundantly clear from the quoted material excerpted from appellees' cases, the decision in each is predicated on an assumption, correct or incorrect, that the basis of the rule they reject was invalidated by changed postal regulations. The opinions cited by appellees each proceed on the theory that the "deposited acceptance" rule was based on a theory that the depositor lost control of his acceptance when it was deposited and that this fact rendered the acceptance complete upon deposit. To the extent that "loss of control" was the significant element in the "deposited acceptance" rule, the logic of appellees' cases is impeccable. On the other hand, if the rule is, in fact, not based on the "loss of control" element, the fact that this element has been altered may in no way affect the validity of the rule. Determination of the question presented in this appeal cannot then be had merely by adoption or rejection of the logic of appellees' cases. Rather, the source and justification of the "deposited acceptance" rule must be found and appellees' argument considered in light of this finding. Should the proffered justification for the rule be other than the "loss of control" theory, adoption or rejection of the rule must be based on considerations other than those relied upon in appellees' cases. . . .

The rule that a contract is complete upon deposit of the acceptance in the mails, hereinbefore referred to as "deposited acceptance rule" and also known as the "rule in *Adams* v. *Lindsell*," had its origin, insofar as the common law is concerned, in *Adams* v. *Lindsell*, 1 Barn. & Ald. 681, 106 Eng. Rep. 250 (K.B. 1818). In that case, the defendants had sent an offer to plaintiffs on September 2nd, indicating that they expected an answer "in course of post." The offer was misdirected and was not received and accepted until the 5th, the acceptance being mailed that day and received by defendant-offerors on the 9th. However, the defendants, who had expected to receive the acceptance on or before the 7th, sold the goods offered on the 8th of September. It was conceded that the delay had been occasioned by the fault of the defendants in initially misdirecting the offer.

Defendants contended that no contract had been made until receipt of the offer on the 9th.

". . . They relied on *Payne* v. *Cave*, 3 T.R. 148, and more particularly on *Cooke* v. *Oxley*, [ibid., 653]. In the case Oxley, who had proposed to sell goods to Cooke, and given him a certain time at his request, to determine whether he would buy them or not, was held not liable to the performance of the contract, even though Cooke, within the specified time, had determined to buy them, and given Oxley notice to that effect. So here the defendants who have proposed by letter to sell this wool, are not to be held liable, even though it be now admitted that the answer did come back in due course of post. Till the plaintiffs' answer was actually received there could be no binding contract between the parties; and before then the defendants had retracted their offer by selling the wool to other persons.

"But the court said that if that were so, no contract could ever be completed by the post. For if the defendants were not bound by their offer when accepted by the plaintiffs till the answer was received, then the plaintiffs ought not to be bound till after they had received the notification that the defendants had received their answer and assented to it. And so it might go on ad infinitum. The defendants must be considered in law as making, during every instant of the time their letter was traveling, the same identical offer to the plaintiffs, and then the contract is completed by the acceptance of it by the latter. Then as to the delay in notifying the acceptance, that arises entirely from the mistake of the defendants, and it therefore must be taken as against them that the plaintitffs' answer was received in course of post."

Examination of the decision in *Adams* v. *Lindsell* reveals three distinct factors deserving consideration. The first and most significant is the court's obvious concern with the necessity of drawing a line, with establishing some point at which a contract is deemed complete and their equally obvious concern with the thought that if communication of each party's assent were necessary, the negotiations would be interminable. A second factor, again a practical one, was the court's apparent desire to limit but not overrule the decision in *Cooke* v. *Oxley*, 3 T.R. 653 [1790] that an offer was revocable at any time prior to acceptance. In application to contracts negotiated by mail, this latter rule would permit revocation even after unqualified assent unless the assent was deemed effective upon posting. Finally, having chosen a point at which negotiations would terminate and having effectively circumvented the inequities of *Cooke* v. *Oxley*, the court, apparently constrained to offer some theoretical justification for its decision, designated a mailed offer as "continuing" and found a meeting of the minds upon the instant of posting assent. Significantly, the factor of the offeree's loss of control of his acceptance is not mentioned.

The "meeting of the minds" justification advanced in *Adams* v. *Lindsell* is repeated in the first of two leading American cases on point. In *Mactier's Adm'rs* v. *Frith,* New York, 1830, 6 Wendell 103, 21 Am.Dec. 262, the offeree died while an acceptance was in the post. Since, if a "meeting of the minds" was essential to the contract, the contract could have been completed only during the offeree's lifetime, the court found it necessary to determine the effective date of acceptance. They deemed the posting of the assent sufficient and wrote:

"All the authorities state a contract or an agreement (which is the same thing) to be *aggregatio mentium*. Why should not this meeting of the minds, which makes the contract, also indicate the moment when it becomes obligatory? I might rather ask, is it not and must it not be the moment when it does become obligatory? If the party making the offer is not bound until he knows of this meeting of minds, for the same reason the party accepting the offer ought not to be bound when his acceptance is received because he does not know of the meeting of the minds, for the offer may have been withdrawn before his acceptance was received. If more than a concurrence of minds upon a distinct proposition is required to make an obligatory contract, the definition of what constitutes a contract is not correct. Instead of being the meeting of the minds of the contracting parties, it should be a knowledge of this meeting. It was said on the argument that if concurrence of minds alone would make a valid contract, one might be constructed out of mere volitions and uncommunicated wishes; I think such a result would not follow. The law does not regard bare volitions and pure mental abstractions. When it speaks of the operations of the mind, it means such as have been made manifest by overt acts; when it speaks of the meeting of minds, it refers to such a meeting as has been made known by proper acts; and when thus made known it is effective, although the parties who may claim the benefit of, or be bound by a contract thus made, may for a season remain ignorant of its being made."

"However, the court went beyond this justification and proceeded to consider what facts constituted acceptance.

"What shall constitute an acceptance will depend, in a great measure, upon circumstances. The mere determination of the mind, unacted on, can never be an acceptance. Where the offer is by letter, the usual mode of acceptance is the sending of a letter announcing a consent to accept; where it is made by messenger, a determination to accept, returned through him, or sent by another, would seem to be all the law requires, if the contract may be consummated without writing. There are other modes which are equally conclusive upon the parties: keeping silence, under certain circumstances, is an assent to a proposition; anything that shall amount to a manifestation of a formed determination to accept, communicated or put in the proper way to be communicated to the party making the offer, would doubtless complete the contract; *but a letter written would not be an acceptance so long as it remained in the possession or under the control of the writer.* An acceptance is the distinct act of one party to the contract as much as the offer is of the other; the knowledge by the party making the offer, of the determination of the party receiving it, is not an ingredient of an acceptance. It is not compounded of an assent by one party to the terms offered, and a knowledge of that assent by the other." (Emphasis added.)

Thus, the element of loss of control was introduced, not as a primary legal requisite to the existence of a contract but as a factual matter affecting the sufficiency of the manifestation of assent. But see, *Dunlop* v. *Higgens,* 1 H.L.C. 381 (1848). Significantly, in the second leading American case, *Tayloe* v. *Merchants' Fire Insurance Co. of Baltimore,* 9 How. [50 U.S.] 390, 13 L.Ed. 187 (1850), the Supreme Court did not advert to the "loss of control" but closely followed the reasoning of *Adams* v. *Lindsell.* Holding an insurance contract complete upon posting of an acceptance, the Court wrote:

"The negotiation being carried on through the mail, the offer and acceptance cannot occur at the same moment of time; nor, for the same reason, can the meeting of the minds of the parties on the subject be known by each at the moment of concurrence; the acceptance must succeed the offer after the lapse of some interval of time; and, if the process is to be carried further in order to complete the bargain, and notice of the acceptance must be received, the only effect is to reverse the position of the parties, changing the knowledge of the completion from the one party to the other.

"It is obviously impossible, therefore, under the circumstances stated, ever to perfect a contract by correspondence, if a knowledge of both parties at the moment they become bound is an essential element in making out the obligation. And as it must take effect, if effect is given at all to an endeavor to enter into a contract by correspondence, in the absence of the knowledge of one of the parties at the time of its consummation, it seems to us more consistent with the acts and declarations of the parties, to consider it complete on the transmission of the acceptance of the offer in the way they themselves contemplated; instead of postponing its completion till notice of such acceptance has been received and assented to by the company.

"For why make the offer, unless intended that an assent to its terms should bind them? And why require any further assent on their part, after an unconditional acceptance by the party to whom it is addressed?

"We have said that this view is in accordance with the usages and practices of these companies, as well as with the general principles of law governing contracts entered into by absent parties."

Whereas *Mactier's Adm'rs* v. *Frith,* supra, had made "loss of control" *an* operative fact, later courts tended to make this *the* operative fact of conclusive legal significance. Thus, in *Dunlop* v. *Higgens,* 1 H.L.C. 381 (1848) one Justice wrote:

"If a party does all that he can do, that is all that is called for. If there is a usage of trade to accept such an offer, and to return an answer to such an offer, and to forward it by means of the post, and if the party accepting the offer puts his letter into the post on the correct day, has he not done everything he was bound to do? How can he be responsible for that over which he has no control?"

The significance attached to "loss of control" in the Dunlop case must be considered a departure from the original reasoning of *Adams* v. *Lindsell* similarly so considered is the suggestion in another leading English case that the post is a common agent or agent of the offeror. This suggestion (and it can be considered nothing more) is found in *Household Fire & Carriage Acc. Ins. Co. Ltd.* v. *Grant,* 4 Exch. Div. 216 (Ct.App. 1879). In that case, one Justice, speaking for a majority, held a contract complete upon posting acceptance and justified this with the observation, *inter alia,* that:

". . . It is impossible in transactions which pass between parties at a distance, and have to be carried on through the medium of correspondence, to adjust conflicting rights between innocent parties, *so as to make the consequences of mistake on the part of a mutual agent fall equally upon the shoulders of both.* At the same time I am not prepared to admit that the implication in question will lead to any great or general inconvenience or hardship. An offeror, if he chooses, may always make the formation of the contract which he proposes dependent upon the actual communication to himself of the acceptance. If he trusts to the post, he trusts to a means of communication which, as a rule, does not fail, and if no answer to his offer is received by him and the matter is of importance to him, he can make inquiries of the person to whom his offer was addressed. . . .

"Upon balance of conveniences and inconveniences it seems to me, applying with slight alterations the language of the Supreme Court of the United States in *Tayloe* v. *Merchants' Fire Insurance Co.,* 9 How. 390, 13 L.Ed. 187, more consistent with the acts and declarations of the parties in this case to consider the contract complete and absolutely binding on the transmission of the notice of allotment through the post, *as the medium of communication that the parties themselves contemplated,* instead of postponing its completion until the notice had been received by the defendant. . . ." (Emphasis added.) . . .

Similarly, the "loss of control" theory, having its origin in the observation that under general contract principles an acceptance is manifest only when the offeree loses the power to suppress the manifestation, has, by a process of extension, come to be urged as a factor of primary legal significance. Yet, as was discussed earlier, the "loss of control" was not deemed controlling in the earliest cases. Nor is the general principle that a manifestation of assent must be beyond the party's control to be effective any more sacred than the general rule that assent in contract must be communicated. Yet the latter is obviously qualified in the "deposited acceptance" rule and in many instances of unilateral contract. Why then should the "loss of control" principle not also be— or have been—qualified?

The unjustified significance placed on the "loss of control" in the cases relied upon by appellee follows from two errors. The first error is failure to distinguish between relinquishment of control as a factual element of manifest intent, which it is, and as *the* legal predicate for completion of contract, which it is not. The second error lies in confusing the "right" to recall mail with the "power" to recall mail. Under current postal regulations, the sender has the "power" to regain a letter, but this does not necessarily give him the "right" to repudiate acceptance. The existence of the latter right is a matter of contract law and is determinable by reference to factors which include, but are not limited to the existence of the power to recall mail. In short, the power to recall mail is a factor, among many others, which may be significant in determining when an acceptance is effective, but the right to effectively withdraw and repudiate an acceptance must be dependent upon the initial determination of when that acceptance is effective and irrevocable.

From the foregoing it is clear that a change in postal regulations does not, *ipso facto,* alter or effect the validity of the rule in *Adams* v. *Lindsell.* To the extent that the cases relied upon by appellee mistakenly assumed that "loss of control" and "agency" were determinative of the validity of the rule, they are not authority for rejecting the rule. Rather, the adoption of the rule in this jurisdiction must turn on an evaluation of its justifications, quite apart from the fallacious theories of agency and control sometimes advanced in its support. . . .

The justification for the "deposited acceptance" rule proceeds from the uncontested premise of *Adams* v. *Lindsell* that there must be, both in practical and conceptual terms, a point in time when a contract is complete. In the formation of contracts *inter praesentes* this point is readily reached upon expressions of assent instantaneously communicated. In the formation of contracts *inter absentes* by post, however, delay in communication prevents concurrent knowledge of assents and some point must be chosen as legally significant. The problem raised by the impossibility of concurrent knowledge of manifest assent is discussed and a justification for the traditional rule is offered in Corbin, Contracts § 78 (1950).

"A better explanation of the existing rule seems to be that in such cases the mailing of a letter has long been a customary and expected way of accepting the offer. It is ordinary business usage. More than this, however, is needed to explain why the letter is operative on mailing rather than on receipt by the offeror. Even though it is business usage to send an offer by mail, it creates no power of acceptance until it is received. Indeed, most notices sent by mail are not operative unless actually received.

"The additional reasons for holding that a different rule applies to an acceptance and that it is operative on mailing may be suggested as follows: When an offer is by mail and the acceptance also is by mail, the contract must date either from the mailing of the acceptance or from its receipt. In either case, one of the parties will be bound by the contract without being actually aware of that fact. If we hold the offeror bound on the mailing of the acceptance, he may change his position in ignorance of the acceptance; even though he waits a reasonable time before acting, he may still remain unaware that he is bound by contract because the letter of acceptance is delayed, or is actually lost or destroyed, in the mails. Therefore this rule is going to cause loss and inconvenience to the offeror in some cases. But if we adopt the alternative rule that the letter of acceptance is not operative until receipt, it is the offeree who is subjected to the danger of loss and inconvenience. He cannot know that his letter has been received and that he is bound by contract until a new communication is received by him. His letter of acceptance may never have been received and so no letter of notification is sent to him; or it may have been received, and the letter of notification may be delayed or entirely lost in the mails. One of the parties must carry the risk of loss and inconvenience. We need a definite and uniform rule as to this. We can choose either rule; but we must choose one. We can put the risk on either party; but we must not leave it in doubt. The party not carrying the risk can then act promptly and with confidence in reliance on the contract; the party carrying the risk can insure against it if he so desires. The business community could no doubt adjust itself to either rule; but the rule throwing the risk on the offeror has the merit of closing the deal more quickly and enabling performance more promptly. It must be remembered that in the vast majority of cases the acceptance is neither lost nor delayed; and promptness of action is of importance in all of them. Also it is the offeror who has invited the acceptance."

The justification suggested by Corbin has been criticized as being anachronistic. Briefly, critics argue that the evident concern with risk occasioned by delay is premised on a time lag between mailing and delivery of a letter of acceptance, which lag, in modern postal systems is negligible. Opponents of the rule urge that if time is significant to either party, modern means of communication permit either party to avoid such delay as the post might cause. . . . At the same time critics of the rule cannot deny that even in our time delay or misdirection of a letter of acceptance is not beyond the realm of possibility.

Another justification offered for the rule, related to the argument of expediency discussed by Corbin, is the mixed practical and conceptual argument attributed to Holmes but in reality being manifest in *Adams* v. *Lindsell* itself. See Holmes, The Common Law, 305-307 (1881); Note, 38 Geo.L.J. 106, 110 (1949). This argument proposes that the making of an offer constitutes an expression of assent to the terms of the contract and that the "overt act" of depositing a written acceptance in the post represents the offeror's assent, whereupon the "concluding prerequisite" of a contract, mutual assent, is formed and the contract is complete. Critics of the rule respond by pointing out that the deposit of a letter in the mail is, in and of itself, a neutral factor, charged with legal significance only because the rule makes this particular "overt act" significant: signing a contract but then pocketing it could be, they argue, viewed as equally conclusive.

At this point and upon the "overt act" theory issue is clearly joined. On the one hand proponents of the rule insist that contracts *inter absentes* are *sui generis* and require consideration not in terms of the secondary principles of contract law relating to the necessity of communicating assent and the necessity of an unrecoverable expression of acceptance, but in terms of the essential concept of manifest intent and assent. Opponents of the rule, though no longer encountering conceptual difficulty in the abandonment of the principle of communication, . . . argue that absent overriding practical considerations the law relating to acceptance by mail should be harmonized with the law regarding offers by mail and contracts generally, i.e. that the acceptance is ineffective until received. Ultimately then the weight given the "practical considerations" and the emphasis accorded the reliance—expectation factors determine the view adopted as to the "deposited acceptance" rule. . . .

Outmoded precedents may, on occasion, be discarded and function of justice should not be the perpetuation of error, but, by the same token, traditional rules and concepts should not be abandoned save on compelling ground.

In choosing to align this jurisdiction with those adhering to the deposited acceptance rule, we . . . hold that an acceptance is effective upon mailing and not upon receipt. . . .

In the instant case, an unqualified offer was accepted and the acceptance made manifest. Later, the offerees sought to repudiate their initial assent. . . . Adopting the view that the acceptance was effective when the letter of acceptance was deposited in the mails, the repudiation was . . . invalid. . . .

§ 25:3. Signing

One ordinarily thinks of "signing" as requiring the writing by hand of one's own name. Both the speed and volume of modern commercial transactions have caused the law to abandon such concept so that any writing, stamping, printing, or typing of one's name is his signature when placed on the paper for the purpose of identifying it as his paper. The necessity for reaching this conclusion is seen by considering how impractical it would be if the rule of law required a personal signing of checks so that every paycheck issued by every corporation would require the actual signature of the treasurer by hand.

It is true that by permitting a rubber stamp signature on a check the door is open to fraud as anyone may procure a rubber stamp and it is easy to "forge" a rubber stamp. However, experience shows that the great majority of persons dealing with checks and other commercial paper are honest so that the danger of fraud and forgery exists only for a very small percent of the transactions. To guard against such small percentage of total transactions by adopting a rule requiring handwritten signatures would impose a greater cost of operation on every transaction for the sake of preventing harm in only a few. It is more conducive to trade to permit the easier and practically expedient methods of "artificial" or mechanical signing, with the risk of loss which it creates, rather than impose upon the business world the great burden of using handwritten signatures only.

Of diminishing importance is the problem of what is a sufficient signature when the signer is unable to sign his name. Here it has been traditional that he may "sign" by merely making his mark, typically a large "X" on the paper. This problem also arises in the case of physical disability as well as the case of lack of education. While the allowance of the "X" signature opens the door to fraud, a contrary conclusion would mean that persons mentally or physically unable to make a handwritten signature could not make an effective writing: and their intent would thus be defeated.

WILLIAMS ESTATE

182 So.2d 10 (Fla., 1966)

Williams died. The proper official refused to admit his will to probate because it was signed only with a large "X" and nothing more.

OPINION BY O'CONNELL, J. . . .

The single issue for decision is whether, under the wording of Sec. 731.07, a testator may execute his will by making his mark, as distinguished from writing his alphabetical name. The county judges and the district court held that a will could not be validly executed in this manner. We cannot agree.

The pertinent portions of the controlling statute read:

"731.07 Execution of Wills.—Every will, other than a noncupative will, must be in writing and must be executed as follows:

"(1) The testator must sign his will at the end thereof, or some other person in his presence and by his direction must subscribe the name of the testator thereto.

"(2) The testator, in the presence of at least two attesting witnesses present at the same time, must sign his will or cause his name to be signed as aforesaid or acknowledge his signature thereto."

We are here concerned only with the requirement that the "testator must sign his will at the end thereof. . . ." The county judges and the district court were of the view that in order to "sign" the testator must write his alphabetical name. The respondents, of course, agree with this, while the petitioners argue that one may "sign" by making his mark.

In the construction of any statute it is always our duty to give effect to the legislative intent where such is ascertainable. However, we find nothing in the statute itself which gives support to either of the definitions urged to be given the word "sign."

This being so, we think we must then decide in that way which gives effect to the will of the testators involved unless some countervailing factor of public policy prevents.

We are surprised that the question here presented is one of first impression in this state. The only Florida case dealing with the question of signing by mark is *Bruner* v. *Hart*, 1910, 59 Fla. 171, 51 So. 593, in which this court held that a witness to a deed could subscribe as a witness by affixing his mark, rather than by writing his alphabetical name. In so holding this court stated that a person could witness by mark unless such method was forbidden by statute and noted that the applicable statute did not forbid a witness "subscribing his name by making his mark." A witness to a will is now required to actually sign his name to the will. F.S. Sec. 731.03(16), F.S.A.

It is interesting to note that in *Bruner* v. *Hart*, supra, the two grantors also signed the questioned deed by mark. Surprisingly the deed was not attacked on this ground. This would seem to indicate that the parties in that case conceded that a grantor could "sign" by mark, but questioned only whether a witness could "subscribe" by mark. It is not unreasonable to assume that a like and widely held concession that a testator could sign his will by mark may account for the fact that no case in point has previously been presented to the appellate courts of this state.

We have carefully read the three cases cited by this court in support of the holding in *Bruner* v. *Hart* that a witness could subscribe by mark. Two of the cited cases decided that a witness to a will could subscribe as an attesting witness by mark. *Garrett* v. *Heflin*, 1893, 98 Ala. 615, 13 So. 326; and *Pridgen* v. *Pridgen's Heirs*, 1852, 13 Ired. 259, 35 N.C. 259. In the

Pridgen case that court discussed the early English cases and statutes dealing with the execution of wills, explained that the word "signum" (from which our word sign is derived) meant no more than a mark, and expressed the view that sign and subscribe meant essentially the same thing when used in a statute. This seems to be the prevailing view in this country.

There can be no doubt that the effect of this court's decision in *Bruner* v. *Hart* is that a person can meet the statutory mandate of subscribing his name by making his mark rather than writing his alphabetical name. If there is a difference in meaning in the words "sign" and "subscribe" it is that "subscribe" is more limited than "sign." This logically leads to the conclusion that if one can subscribe by making his mark he can certainly sign by the same means. We so hold.

The great majority of the courts which have dealt with cases like these involving similar statutes hold as we do here, that a mark made by the testator at the proper place on his will with the intent that it constitute his signature and evidence his assent to the will is sufficient to satisfy the statutory requirement that he "sign" his will. . . .

We have not ignored respondent's contention that public policy, which is to protect testators and their heirs from fraud, would be best served by refusing to accept as properly executed under the statute a will signed by the testator with only his mark. In support of this contention respondents argue that it is impossible for handwriting experts to determine the authenticity of a mark as might be done with a handwritten alphabetical name. They also argue that if a testator cannot write his name and is not permitted to sign by mark, he will be forced to have another person subscribe his name for him. This they say will be added protection because a person requested to sign the name of another will not be likely to do so without first determining the identity of the purported testator.

It is true that even a handwriting expert would have difficulty determining who made a mark in the absence of distinguishing characteristics by which certain comparisons can reasonably be made. If proof of the execution of a will rested entirely upon the identification of the mark or signature of the testator the respondents' argument would be difficult to overcome. But such is not the case. The greatest protection against fraud, and the greatest aid in proof that a testator did in any manner sign his will as his, is furnished by the statutory requirement that it be done in the presence of, or acknowledged in the presence of, at least two attesting witnesses.

Furthermore, the alternative method for the execution of a will, by which some other person may subscribe the testator's name, really seems to offer even less protection than the testator's mark.

This is so because the statute does not require the person signing for the testator to be identified in the document. True, a careful lawyer supervising the execution of a will would see that such person's identity was reflected in some manner at the end of the will. Nevertheless, the statute does not require it nor does it prescribe how it shall be made known that the testator's name was subscribed by another or how such person is to be identified in the document.

Therefore, we fail to see how fraud on testators would be prevented in any meaningful way by a holding that our statute requires that a person must either subscribe his alphabetical name or have another person to do so for him. Rather, we hold, as do most jurisdictions, that a testator may "sign" his will by making a mark. It is a matter of fact to be proved in proper proceedings whether the testator made the mark with the intention that it evidence his assent to the document.

If this cause accomplishes nothing more than to call attention to the inadequacies of Section 731.07(1) and (2) it will have served a useful purpose. We have no doubt that the appropriate committees of The Florida Bar and the Legislature will give attention to making the changes which are necessary to make clear whether a person should be able to sign his will by mark, and to prescribe the formalities to be followed and recorded as a part of the will when the testator signs by mark or another person subscribes the name of the testator at the testator's direction. . . .

DISSENTING OPINION BY ERVIN, J. . . .

F.S. Section 731.07, F.S.A. appears to require the testator to either sign (write) his name at the end of his will or if he is unable to write his name to get some other person in his presence and by his direction to sign his (testator's) name for him. This appears to preclude the use of an "X" or other mark to legally execute a will. The policy of the statute is to require the testator's name to be written either in his handwriting or in another's handwriting at the end of the will to serve the purpose of authenticity and to avoid as far as possible fraud or forgery.

§ 25:4.   Procedural Irregularities

In the stress and strain of trial, minor irregularities often occur or things are taken for granted rather than being directly proven. It would be very inconvenient and wasteful of everyone's time and money if a lawsuit had to be tried over a second time whenever some irregularity had occurred. The force of practical expediency, therefore, urges the law to forget the matter unless it is of a very serious nature, in which case there will be some other social force that will urge a reexamination of the matter.

In the interest of reducing to a minimum the matters which it must consider, the law erects a presumption against irregularity. By this presumption, any person claiming that there was an irregularity in a legal proceeding has the burden of convincing the court; and if it cannot be shown whether there was or was not any irregularity, the objection is lost. For example, if it is claimed that the jury improperly ignored the instructions given to it by the trial judge, it will be presumed that the jury performed its duty properly and was guided by the judge's instructions; and unless the objector can affirmatively show that the jury had violated its duty, the objection is lost. For practical purposes, this means that in the ordinary sense the objection that the jury ignored the instructions given to it can never be proven.

The area for objection is further reduced by requiring that the objection be made at the time the irregularity occurs. Thus, if the judge gives an improper instruction to the jury, the attorney must object to the charge before the jury retires for deliberation and must suggest to the judge what the charge should have been. If he waits until later, he has lost his opportunity for objecting and his objection will ordinarily be ignored. Similarly, if improper evidence is admitted at the trial, the opposing attorney must object then and there. If he waits until later, it is too late. All of this makes sense to us because the concept of practical expediency fits in with our idea of orderly procedure and justice. Yet a mistake is a mistake; and if we applied cold logic, we would say that whether or not an objection was made, there is still a defect in the proceedings. And this is what the law does when there is a mistake of sufficient gravity.

Thus, if an indigent defendant is not represented by counsel in a murder prosecution, the higher court will not overlook the fact on the theory that no request was made for the appointment of an attorney. Here the law regards representation by counsel as so vital that the judge must inform the defendant of his rights. The court records must also clearly show that this was done and that, if there is no attorney, the defendant intelligently declined or waived his right to be represented by counsel. If this is not done, the basic error makes the proceedings voidable.

Similarly, in an ordinary lawsuit, the judge has the duty of explaining the essential issues to the jury. If the instruction or charge that he gives to the jury is so confusing and contradictory that it is fundamentally wrong, the higher court will reverse the lower court, even though no request was made for better instructions to the jury.

In some instances, irregularities at the trial are ignored on the theory that everyone understood what was involved. For example, in many actions an essential element of the power of the court to act is that some events took place within the county, such as the crime was committed in the county; or service was made on the defendant in the county. Suppose that it is shown that the event occurred in Chicago, but no evidence is presented that Chicago is in Cook County, Illinois. This irregularity is ignored because, of course, the judge of a Cook County court knows that Chicago is in Cook County. Therefore, it is deemed proper for him to recognize or accept that fact as part of the common knowledge, without requiring separate proof of that fact, and above all, without requiring that there be a new trial to establish that fact. This technique by which the court takes for granted well-known geographic, historical, and scientific facts, is called "judicial notice."

Theoretically, the jury can decide a case only on the basis of the evidence before it. In some instances, minor matters may be noticed by the jury, in much the same manner as judicial notice.

GUPTILL v. BERGMAN
108 N.H. 507, 240 A.2d 55 (1968)

Schellinger and Bergman were involved in an automobile accident. The former died and suit was brought on behalf of his estate by Guptill. In order to determine the visibility at the time of the collision, evidence was offered to show that the sun had already set. A farmer's almanac was introduced in evidence to show that the sun had set at 6:08 p.m. Standard Time. No evidence was offered to show that this was the same as 7:08 p.m. Daylight Saving Time, and the jury was not instructed that these two times were the same.

OPINION BY DUNCAN, J. . . . .

The Trial Court properly permitted the plaintiff to use the "Old Farmers' Almanac" to establish that the sun set on the day of the accident at 6:08 p.m. Standard Time. . . . We do not assume that the jury was so unfamiliar with the effect of daylight saving time as to require the Court to instruct the jury that the evidence thus received meant 7:08 p.m. Eastern Daylight Saving Time, as requested by the plaintiff's 25th and 26th requests for instructions.

The plaintiff offered to show by the same almanac that twilight on the day in question had a duration of one hour and thirty-three minutes after sunset. To the exclusion of this evidence, the plaintiff excepted. We think the exclusion was discretionary with the Trial Court. There was direct evidence that the weather was "cloudy-clear," and that fog patches had been encountered beyond where the accident happened. There was also evidence that the defendant operated with his lights on low beam from the time he and Schellinger left the officers' club. The defendant testified that this was approximately 7:20 p.m., Portsmouth time, and conceded that twilight would precede dark. The evidence did not disclose how much time was consumed in reaching the scene of the accident, although the defendant thought the scene was about two miles from the club. In this state of the record, we are not prepared to hold that the Court erred in considering that evidence of the length of twilight as reported by the "Old Farmers' Almanac" would not add materially to the jury's common knowledge, or aid them in reconstructing existing conditions as to which they had direct evidence before them. . . . .

§ 25:5. Jury Verdict

Various forces have come into play in moulding the significance or effect of a jury verdict. If stability were the sole concern, the law would be that once a verdict was returned by a jury, the case was at an end and nothing could be done to upset the jury's verdict. The danger of oppression through error or intentional wrongdoing on the part of the jury is obviously great and, therefore, the rule of law early developed that the verdict of a jury could be set aside where there was some manifest error or miscarriage of justice. In the field of civil law, this also meant that there would be a new trial of the case. In the field of criminal law, a new trial is generally barred on the basis of double jeopardy, society believing that the danger of oppression from government was so great that the government should only be allowed one chance to prove its case. Here society was fearful that a government might hound the defendant through trial after trial until the defendant was either financially ruined or convicted by a verdict that could be upheld.

Confining our attention to the verdict in the civil trial, while the device of awarding a new trial protected from the hardship and oppression of mistake or misconduct on the part of the jury, it was often not the most efficient solution for the problem. To explain, in a civil action the verdict is based upon two elements: (1) the existence of liability of the defendant, and (2) the extent of damages to be allowed the plaintiff because of the defendant's breach. In a given case, the first element, liability of the defendant, may be clear but the jury was in error in awarding either too much or too little in money damages. For example, assume that there is no question but that the defendant negligently killed another driver in an automobile collision case. If the jury should award the plaintiff $100 in an action for such wrongful death, it is obvious that the verdict would be inadequate. To make the contrast, assume that one person without justification or privilege struck another with his fist, causing only temporary pain, and the jury awarded damages of $10 million. It is equally obvious that these damages are excessive.

If the law were guided solely by the principle of protection from oppression, it would say in both cases that the amount of the damages was so improper that a new trial should be required. This would not be efficient for the reason that as assumed there was no error with respect to the liability of the defendant in each case. The verdicts were wrong only as to the amount of damages to be paid. It is, therefore, wasteful of time and money to require that there be a new trial of the entire case.

Gradually the force of practical expediency led to techniques to meet this problem. One of them was a new trial limited to the issue of damages. While this is clearly the practical thing, it did violence to stability that would urge that the jury trial be retained forever as the jury trial had been known before.

The second device to meet the situation was to give the adverse party the choice of agreeing to a change in the jury's verdict; or if he refused, the court would order a new trial. For example, if the plaintiff recovered too much money, the court could give the plaintiff the choice of taking a new trial or of voluntarily agreeing to reduce the verdict to an amount suggested by the judge. This device, known as a remittitur, gave the plaintiff the ability to retain his victory on the liability issue by compromising his claim as to damages. If the plaintiff did not accept the compromise offer, a new trial would be ordered and the case would be tried from the beginning as though there never had been a first trial. The verdict in the first trial would not have any effect on the second jury, and the second jury might even decide against the plaintiff. In the face of this peril, the tendency is strong for the plaintiff to accept the remittitur, particularly in a doubtful case.

As the complementary procedure, the additur developed to increase inadequate verdicts. Again the party, now the defendant, had the choice of agreeing to the suggestion of the judge or of going to a new trial. Here the defendant ran the risk that on the new trial the second jury might return a verdict substantially higher than that of the first jury and, in any case, he would be again subjected to the delay and expense of a second trial. If the case of liability is clear so that the defendant feels that he will probably lose the second trial anyway, it is likely that the defendant will agree to the suggestion of the judge and thus eliminate the hazards above indicated.

JEHL v. SOUTHERN PACIFIC CO.

59 Cal.Rptr. 276, 427 P.2d 988 (Cal., 1967)

Jehl was employed by a railroad, the Southern Pacific. He was injured and sued the railroad under the Federal Employers Liability Act and Safety Appliance Act. These statutes applied instead of a state workmen's compensation law because he was injured in interstate commerce. A verdict was returned in favor of Jehl but only in the sum of $100,000. The trial judge felt that this amount was shockingly inadequate and granted the plaintiff a new trial on the issue of damages. The railroad appealed from this order.

OPINION BY TRAYNOR, C.J. . . .

On June 19, 1962, at approximately 3:25 a.m., plaintiff was working in defendant's railroad yard at South Gate, California. He was then 19 years old and had been working for defendant for about 6 weeks. His job that night was to work as a field man. As railroad cars were switched onto the track he was working, plaintiff secured them by placing wooden blocks under the wheels. The blocking was necessary because the track was on a grade. Two cars failed to couple properly with cars already secured and began to roll back. The foreman told plaintiff to climb on the moving cars and secure them by means of the handbrake on each car. As plaintiff was doing so two other cars that had been sent up the track collided with the cars coming down the track. The impact threw plaintiff from the car he was riding and he fell under the wheels of one of the moving cars, receiving severe injuries to the lower part of both legs. It was necessary to amputate his right leg below the knee. The left leg remains in jeopardy of amputation because osteomyelitis has developed in it.

The jury returned a verdict for $100,000, and plaintiff successfully moved for a new trial on the issue of damages on the ground that the evidence was insufficient to sustain the verdict in that the damages awarded were inadequate. . . . Defendant contends that the trial court erred in concluding that the damages were inadequate and therefore abused its discretion in granting plaintiff's motion. . . .

Plaintiff's right leg was amputated below the knee; his left leg was so seriously injured that it may also have to be amputated. There is permanent, chronic osteomyelitis in the left leg that has required repeated surgical treatment and may require recurrent treatment well into the future, and there is permanent limitation of motion in the left ankle. Plaintiff continues to suffer pains in his right leg. He was hospitalized for 16 months following the accident and underwent 18 operations. Throughout this time he suffered great pain, necessitating extensive administration of pain-killing drugs. Had he not been injured, plaintiff's projected gross income from the date of the accident to the age of 65 would have exceeded $500,000. By substantially impairing his ability to compete in the labor market, his injuries materially reduced this expectable earning power. The projected costs of his prosthetic appliances exceeded $15,000. It thus appears that the trial court could reasonably have concluded that plaintiff's pecuniary losses alone would exceed the amount of the verdict and that a substantial additional amount should be allowed for pain and suffering. Accordingly, the trial court did not abuse its discretion in granting a new trial on the ground of inadequate damages. . . .

Defendant contends that the trial court should have given defendant the option to consent to an additur [1] before granting plaintiff's motion for a new trial. We consider this contention even though defendant did not directly request an additur in the trial court, for such a request would have been an idle act. . . . Indeed, in light of this court's decision in *Dorsey* v. *Barba,* 38 Cal.2d 350, 240 P.2d 604, holding additur to be unconstitutional, the trial court would have been bound to deny an additur even if it had been specifically and directly requested. . . . Should the decision in *Dorsey* v. *Barba,* supra, 38 Cal.2d 350, 240 P.2d 604, be overruled? . . .

In Dorsey this court held that additur would deny a plaintiff's right to jury trial as guaranteed by article I, section 7, of the California Constitution.[2] Although the Seventh Amendment to the United States Constitution is not binding on the states and differs significantly in language from the California constitutional provision,[3] Dorsey relied in large part on *Dimick* v. *Schiedt,* 293 U.S. 474, 55 S.Ct. 296, 79 L.Ed. 603. . . . Dimick was a five-to-four decision and has been vigorously criticized. Like Dorsey, Dimick was based on an historical and logical analysis that was open to serious question. Since additur did not exist at common law when the relevant constitutional provisions were adopted and since a plaintiff is guaranteed the right of jury trial as it existed at common law, additur was deemed a denial of that right. . . .

Both courts were confronted with the argument that additur is no more a denial of a plaintiff's right to jury trial than remittitur is a denial of a defendant's right. Although some faint historical foundation was found for this difference in treatment, Dimick further relied on the tenuous ground that remittitur left standing a part of the jury's award, whereas additur constituted "a bald addition" to the verdict.

We have reassessed Dorsey and overrule it, finding its arguments unpersuasive when considered in the light of the demands of fair and efficient

---

[1] "Additur" is used here to describe an order by which a plaintiff's motion for a new trial on the ground of inadequate damages is granted unless the defendant consents to a specified increase of the award within a prescribed time.

[2] Article I, section 7, provides: "The right of trial by jury shall be secured to all, and remain inviolate; . . . ."

[3] The Seventh Amendment provides: "In Suits at common law, where the value in controversy shall exceed twenty dollars, the right of trial by jury shall be preserved, and no fact tried by a jury, shall be otherwise reexamined in any Court of the United States, than according to the rules of the common law." (Compare fn. 2, supra.)

administration of justice. We do not believe that defendants should be denied the advantages of additur when they are required to submit to remittitur.

Even in Dorscy this court noted that the "constitutional guarantee does not require adherence to the letter of common-law practice, and new procedures better suited to the efficient administration of justice may be substituted if there is no impairment of the substantial features of a jury trial." . . . We have concluded that additur is such a procedure. The demands of an "efficient administration of justice" must be considered in context. Since 1952, the year Dorsey was decided, there has been a tremendous increase in filings in civil cases including contested matters. Total dispositions in ordinary civil litigation increased more than fourfold during the 1952-1964 period.[4] . . . Of course, such practical considerations would be immaterial if additur impaired the right to a jury trial. We do not believe it does.

In assessing the precedents, we search for the meaning and substance of jury trial and are not rigidly bound by exacting rules that happen to be found on "the legal scrap heap of a century and a half ago." . . . The guarantee of jury trial in the California Constitution operates at the time of trial to require submission of certain issues to the jury. Once a verdict has been returned, however, the effect of the constitutional provision is to prohibit improper interference with the jury's decision. At the time of the American Revolution, the English courts seldom interfered with the amount of the jury's verdict in actions involving torts against the person. . . . The reason for their refusal to grant new trials in such cases was their view that determination of the amount of damages was within the exclusive province of the jury. . . .

By the end of the 18th century, however, the Court of King's Bench accepted the doctrine that new trials would be granted in cases of torts against the person under appropriate circumstances . . . but until the middle of the 19th Century, the English courts refused to grant new trials on the ground of inadequate damages. . . . The unwillingness to interfere with the jury's decision, exemplified by the English courts, was a controlling consideration in the first California case to discuss the constitutional function of the jury with respect to the assessment of damages, *Payne* v. *Pacific Mail S.S. Co.,* 1 Cal. 33, where this court reversed an order granting a new trial unless plaintiff remit some of the jury's award. The plaintiff refused and appealed from the order granting a new trial. The court held that this interference with the right of trial by jury would result in "great abuse, if not the destruction of this right. . . ." (*Payne* v. *Pacific Mail S.S. Co.,* supra, 1 Cal. at 37.) Although Payne was approved the following year in *George* v. *Law,* 1 Cal. 363, 365, the court held that the plaintiff's consent authorized remittitur and that defendants could not complain, because "the judgment stands for but one-half the amount, for which the verdict of the jury was rendered." (*George* v. *Law,* supra, 1 Cal. at 365.) These early English and

---

[4] The social and economic costs of crowded dockets increase every year. Additur's practical advantage in reducing these costs prompted the California Law Revision Commission to recommend legislation permitting some forms of additur thought not to be inconsistent with *Dorsey* v. *Barba.* (See California Law Revision Commission Study at pp. 607-614.)

California cases illustrate that the right to jury trial was regarded as a protection to parties relying upon a verdict. The modern practice of granting new trials because of excessive or inadequate damages constitutes a limitation on the former broad powers of the jury.

It is true that the practical effect of additur is to give the plaintiff an award based upon a finding made ultimately by the trial court. Courts often determine fact issues, however, and the acceptance of this practice over many years refutes the argument that the framers of the Constitution regarded the jury as the only competent finder of facts. Decisions by the court admitting or excluding evidence at trial involve factual determinations as do those pertaining to the court's jurisdiction, the sufficiency of pleadings, and the interpretation of documents. Other instances of judicial or quasi-judicial fact-finding are found in equity, admiralty, probate, divorce, bankruptcy, and administrative proceedings.

At the time of the American Revolution, there was no clear standard or practice governing the relationship between judge and jury. . . . If any reliable conclusion can be drawn from the practice at that time, it is that plaintiff would not have had the right to a reassessment of damages by a second jury; the first jury's determination of the amount of damages was conclusive. Reexamination of the damages issue following an inadequate verdict is a modern development. Had the English judges in the late 18th Century been willing to give a plaintiff's motion for new trial any consideration at all, as judges do time and again today, there is good reason to believe that they would have used additur.[5]

Remittitur happened to develop earlier than additur because courts undertook to grant new trials for excessive damages long before they took similar action on the ground of inadequacy. . . . The issue of additur was not presented until modern times, but it is a logical step in the growth of the law relating to unliquidated damages as remittitur was at an earlier date. Its acceptance, though still somewhat retarded, is growing. It should not be treated differently from other modern devices aimed at making the relationship between judge and jury as to damages [6] as well as to other matters, one that preserves the essentials of the right to jury trial without shackling modern procedure to outmoded precedents. Additur does not detract from the substance of the common-law trial by jury. Like its fraternal twin remittitur, now over 100 years old in this state, it promotes economy and efficiency in judicial proceedings.

There is no essential difference between the procedures appropriate for remittitur and additur, and we may therefore look to remittitur cases to determine the proper procedure for additur.

Upon a motion for new trial grounded on insufficiency of the evidence because the damages are inadequate, the court should first determine whether the damages are clearly inadequate and, if so, whether the case would be a

---

[5] A practice similar to additur was employed for some time prior to 1791 in actions for mayhem. . . .

[6] For example, both remittitur and a new trial limited to damages have been held not to deny the right to jury trial. . . .

proper one for granting a motion for new trial limited to damages. . . .[7] If both conditions exist, the court in its discretion may issue an order granting the motion for new trial unless the defendant consents to an additur as determined by the court. The court's power extends to all such cases. It is not limited to those cases in which an appellate court would sustain either the granting or denial of a motion for new trial on the ground of insufficiency of the evidence. The court shall prescribe the time within which the defendant must accept the additur, and in no case may this time be longer than the jurisdictional period for granting a new trial. . . . If the defendant fails to consent within the prescribed time, the order granting the new trial becomes final.

If the court decides to order an additur, it should set the amount that it determines from the evidence to be fair and reasonable. In this respect it should exercise its completely independent judgment. It need not fix either the minimum or maximum amount that it would have sustained on a motion for new trial or the minimum or maximum amount that would be supported by substantial evidence and therefore sustainable on appeal. If the defendant deems the additur excessive, he may reject it and seek to sustain the jury's award on an appeal from the order granting a new trial. If the plaintiff deems the additur insufficient, he may raise the issue on an appeal from the judgment as modified by the additur. . . .

Questions for Review

1. Define the social force of practical expediency.

2. Give illustrations of its application.

3. Analyze each opinion in this chapter in terms of the social forces involved in the decision. See § 5:5 for a list of the social forces. With respect to each opinion, explain why the prevailing social forces prevailed and why those rejected did not. In each case in which there is a dissenting opinion, make this analysis for the dissenting opinion.

4-8. *On the basis of the social forces involved, what decision should be made in each of the following cases?*

4. *Releases. Payment delay.* After forwarding a release, does a delay of seven days before payment is received affect the release? *Sosa* v. *Velvet Dairy Stores,* Mo.App., 407 S.W.2d 615.

5. *Release. Fraudulent procurement.* Will a release be set aside because fraudulently procured where the Statute of Limitations would bar a suit on the claim covered by the release? *McKinley* v. *Greyhound Park,* 5 Ariz. 93, 423 P.2d 368.

6. *Release. Avoidance.* Boman and Johnson were in an automobile collision. Boman released Johnson from liability and was paid a sum of money. On

---

[7] There is no contention in the present case that the jury's verdict was the result of passion or prejudice or that it was tainted by prejudicial error occurring at trial.

the theory that the release was not binding, Boman thereafter sued Johnson to recover greater damages. Johnson claimed that this could not be done without first having the settlement set aside and the payment made to Boman being returned to Johnson. Was Johnson correct? *Boman* v. *Johnson,* S.D., 158 N.W.2d 528.

7. *Minors. Capacity.* Should a 19-year old boy whose motorcycle collided with the defendant's automobile be judged by the same standard of care as an adult? *Daniels* v. *Evans,* 107 N.H. 407, 224 A.2d 63.

8. *Animals. Zebra.* Is a tame zebra a "wild animal" so that its owner or keeper is liable for any harm caused by it without regard to any claimed vicious disposition of the animal or knowledge thereof? *Smith* v. *Jalbert,* 351 Mass. 432, 221 N.E.2d 744.

9-13. What social forces were involved, which prevailed, and which were defeated in the following decisions?

9. *Contracts. Acceptance of offer.* The cashing of a check accompanying a written offer is an acceptance of the offer where nothing beyond cashing of check is shown, and it would be immaterial whether the cashing was the result of the offeree's mistake. *Crouch* v. *Marrs,* 199 Kan. 387, 430 P.2d 204.

10. *Hospital record. Nurse.* The hospital record made by a hospital nurse is admissible under the Uniform Business Records as Evidence Act, even though she is not called as a witness. *Plank* v. *Heirigs,* S.D., 156 N.W.2d 193.

11. *Determination of facts. Medical knowledge.* In a suit to recover for personal injuries, the court held that "while there was some conflict on the medical testimony concerning the X-rays, it was for the jury to determine which was right." *United States* v. *Dudley,* [C.A.9th] 64 F.2d 743.

12. *Nuisance. Realty.* Landowner harmed by dust from cement plant would be limited to recovery of money damages and would be denied injunction where defendant's plant cost over $40 million, was one of the largest and most modern plants in the world, and the most efficient antiair pollution controls had been installed. *Boomer* v. *Atlantic Cement Co.,* 55 Misc.2d 1023, 287 N.Y.S.2d 112.

13. *Product liability. Professional market.* Where beauty preparation is labeled for professional use only, the sufficiency of the instructions on the package to avoid harm and the foreseeability of danger from the use of the product are to be determined in the light of use by a professional beautician, and the manufacturer is not liable because a nonprofessional might not be aware of the danger that would be involved if used by one not possessing the knowledge of a professional operator. *Helene Curtis* v. *Pruitt,* [C.A.5th] 385 F.2d 841.

PART III. THE LAW IN OPERATION

<u>Chapter</u> **26**

CONTRACTS

§ 26:1.   Generally

(a) Commercial importance. Most legal rights arise from a contract or from a situation that was formed or grew out of a contract. To illustrate the latter, you own your car because title to the car was transferred to you by the seller, but such transfer was part of a contract of sale between the dealer and you. Part of the importance of contract law lies in the fact that it is the mainstream of law from which many other special branches of law have flowed. For example, the law governing the sale of goods is merely a specialized branch of contract law. Likewise, the law of insurance is a particular kind of contract law. Thus, contract law either directly or indirectly, is the basis for most of our legal rights today. This fact is more readily appreciated when you think of the number of contracts that you make in a year, contrasted with the number of crimes or torts in which you are involved in the same period of time. Each time that you buy a newspaper, pay your fare on a bus, or buy a watch or a house, you are taking part in a contract. Contracts are thus part of your daily life in a Twentieth Century community.

(b) Definition of contract. A contract is ordinarily defined as (1) an agreement, (2) between competent parties, (3) based upon the genuine assent of the parties, (4) supported by consideration, (5) made for a lawful

object, and (6) in the form, if any, required by law. This definition for the most part has not changed, but the definitions of the elements have been modified.

While there must be an agreement, the sufficiency of the agreement has been modified. Historically, the emphasis was on whether there was a meeting of the minds as to the terms of the contract. The emphasis is now on what the agreement appeared to be to a reasonable man in the position of the contracting parties. The most significant change relating to the agreement has been the extent to which the agreement must be definite. The competency or capacity of parties to make a contract has been modified, particularly in tending to limit the extent to which a minor can avoid his contract, as discussed in § 16:6. The identity of the parties has sometimes been changed to embrace the multiple-party contract, such as the labor union contract discussed in § 26:2. The requirement of consideration has been modified or eliminated in a variety of circumstances (see § 26:3). A nonlawful purpose, which will impair or invalidate a contract, has been expanded (see § 26:7). The absence of a required writing is excused in instances when there is present some fact element that the law regards as sufficient to take the place of the writing, or when to refuse to enforce the agreement would work a particular hardship or be deemed fraudulent.

(c) The n factor. A difference in the approach of traditional and modern contract law is the modern recognition of the fact that the contract before the court is not one in a million but is one *of* a million. That is, *n,* or the number of times this particular contract is likely to arise, is considered by the modern court. The earlier law regarded each contract to a large degree as though it were an isolated contract—no other such contract was made between the same parties nor by either of the parties with others, nor would other persons make similar contracts. This statement may tend to exaggerate, but there was a marked feeling of "isolation" for many years, with each contract being viewed as though it were the only contract of its kind.

Today, the situation may be one in which the court will recognize the fact that the contract in question is merely one of many. Three situations may arise:

(1) *A* and *B* are a manufacturer and the supplier of raw materials, respectively. The contract between them is similar to many others that they have made before and will undoubtedly continue to make in the future. Here there is an understandable feeling on the part of the court to leave the parties to themselves. Although the contract that they make might not be exactly the way a lawbook says it should be theoretically, it is apparently good enough for *A* and *B.* Hence, the court should not create any difficulty between them where none exists. Furthermore, the continuance of business relations will undoubtedly supply an element of good faith that may be relied upon by the courts to correct omissions and defects in the contract,

just as the parties themselves have ignored such matters as evidenced by their continuing to do business under such a contract form.

(2) *C* is a dealer or a bank or other "business," which not only makes the one contract with *D* but makes similar contracts with *E, F, G,* and *H.* There is recognition on the part of the modern court that what the court determines must be determined carefully lest it make an error that would jeopardize an entire enterprise.

In addition, the fact that *C* is "in business" and that *D, E,* and *F* apparently are not, suggests that *C* knows what he is doing and that the others may not be fully aware of the legal consequences of their respective contracts. This appreciation of the unequal knowledge and experience of the parties underlies the distinction made in the Uniform Commercial Code between the merchant party and the casual party.

(3) *T* makes a contract with *J,* which is of the same nature as the contract which *K* makes with *L,* and which *M* makes with *N.* Thus, the insurance policy that the insurer *T* makes with insured *J* is similar to the insurance policy which insurer *M* makes with *N,* and so on. The same similarity or industry-wide pattern is seen in the case of the bank loan made by bank *O* to borrower *P,* by bank *Q* to borrower *R,* and so on.

The appreciation that a particular contract is merely one of many has not only influenced the courts in the interpretation of such contracts but has also been held to justify regulation of the contract by statute. The view has been adopted that "when a widely diffused public interest has become enmeshed in a network of multitudinous private arrangements, the authority of the state 'to safeguard the vital interests of its people' . . . is not to be gainsaid by abstracting one such arrangement from its public context and treating it as though it were an isolated private contract constitutionally immune from impairment." [1]

Otherwise stated, what was a private contract between *A* and *B* ceases to be a private contract when there are many other such contracts being made between other persons; and when there are many other such contracts, the particular kind of contract may be regulated. The significance of this concept cannot be underestimated, for in a nation of millions of people possessing a standard of living sufficiently high that they can enter into hundred of thousands of transactions, it is apparent that there are few types of contracts which are so rare that they still retain their "private" character.

HOME BUILDING & LOAN ASS'N v. BLAISDELL

290 U.S. 398 (1934)

OPINION BY HUGHES, J. . . .

Appellant contests the validity of . . . the Minnesota Mortgage Moratorium Law, as being repugnant to the contract clause . . . [which limits state legislative action].

---

[1] *East New York Savings Bank* v. *Hahn,* 326 U.S. 230 (1945).

The Act provides that, during the emergency declared to exist, relief may be had through authorized judicial proceedings with respect to foreclosures of mortgages, and execution sales, of real estate; that sales may be postponed and periods of redemption may be extended.

[A state cannot] . . . adopt as its policy the repudiation of debts or the destruction of contracts or the denial of means to enforce them. But it does not follow that conditions may not arise in which a temporary restraint of enforcement may be consistent with the spirit and purpose of the constitutional provision and thus be found to be within the range of the reserved power of the State to protect the vital interests of the community. It cannot be maintained that the constitutional provision should be so construed as to prevent limited and temporary interpositions with respect to the enforcement of contracts if made necessary by a great public calamity such as fire, flood, or earthquake. . . . The reservation of state power appropriate to such extraordinary conditions may be deemed to be as much a part of all contracts, as is the reservation of state power to protect the public interest in the other situations to which we have referred. And if state power exists to give temporary relief from the enforcement of contracts in the presence of disasters due to physical causes such as fire, flood or earthquake, that power cannot be said to be nonexistent when the urgent public need demanding such relief is produced by other and economic causes. . . .

It is manifest . . . that there has been a growing appreciation of public needs and of the necessity of finding ground for a rational compromise between individual rights and public welfare. The settlement and consequent contraction of the public domain, the pressure of a constantly increasing density of population, the interrelation of the activities of our people and the complexity of our economic interests, have inevitably led to an increased use of the organization of society in order to protect the very bases of individual opportunity. Where, in earlier days, it was thought that only the concerns of individuals or of classes were involved, and that those of the State itself were touched only remotely, it has later been found that the fundamental interests of the State are directly affected; and that the question is no longer merely that of one party to a contract as against another, but of the use of reasonable means to safeguard the economic structure upon which the good of all depends.

It is no answer to say that this public need was not apprehended a century ago, or to insist that what the provision of the Constitution meant to the vision of that day it must mean to the vision of our time. . . . We must never forget it is a *constitution* we are expounding . . . , a constitution intended to endure. . . .

DISSENTING OPINION BY SUTHERLAND, J. . . .

The present exigency is nothing new. From the beginning of our existence as a nation, periods of depression, of industrial failure, of financial distress, of unpaid and unpayable indebtedness, have alternated with years of plenty . . . and the attempt by legislative devices to shift the misfortune of the debtor to the shoulders of the creditor without coming into conflict with the contract impairment clause has been persistent and oft-repeated.

The defense of the Minnesota law is made upon grounds which were discountenanced by the makers of the Constitution and have many times been rejected by this court. That defense should not now succeed, because it constitutes an effort to overthrow the constitutional provision by an appeal to facts and circumstances identical with those which brought it into existence. . . .

A statute which materially delays enforcement of the mortgagee's contractual right of ownership and possession does not modify the remedy merely; it destroys, for the period of delay, *all* remedy so far as the enforcement of that right is concerned. The phrase, "obligation of a contract," in the constitutional sense imports a legal duty to perform the specified obligation of *that* contract, not to substitute and perform, against the will of one of the parties, a different, . . . obligation. . . .

§ 26:2.   The Parties to a Contract

(a) Minors. The standard law as to minority has undergone a change. By the traditional common-law rule, a person under 21 years of age could avoid his contract. Inroads have been made upon this doctrine so that a minor who engages in business is often now treated as over 21 and cannot avoid his contract. In addition, statutes commonly provide that with respect to various types of transactions, such as bank accounts, educational loans, insurance policies, and stock transfers, a minor is to be treated as an adult.

(i) *Necessaries.* The concept that a minor must pay the reasonable value for necessaries is an inroad on the concept of the voidability of a minor's contract. The category of "necessaries" has been steadily broadening and, as it does, the inroad on the concept of the voidability of the minor's contract becomes that much greater; that is to say, there are fewer contracts which may be completely set aside without any liability remaining on the minor.

If it became known to merchants and sellers that they could not take the chance of selling on credit to minors because they would stand to lose everything, they would be less willing to sell on credit to minors. Under the reasonable-value rule, the merchant is taking less of a risk for he knows that under the rule he would at least be entitled to the reasonable value of his goods, although he cannot recover the contract price. If merchants are not willing to take the chance that a minor will pay, the court sees in its mind's eye the picture of the poor starving minor unable to get a meal or shelter from the merchant because no one will take the chance of trusting a minor.

In contrast, if minors must at least pay the reasonable value for their necessaries, the court sees the greater probability of merchants trusting the minor. Otherwise stated, it is the desire to protect minors as a class which makes the court impose upon the individual minor in the case before it the duty to pay the reasonable value for his necessaries. Thus, the interest of the particular minor conflicts with the interests of minors generally. Here again the n factor comes into play. Since there are many minors and only one minor before the court, it is desirable to make the rule of law do justice in the case of the many, rather than to tailor it to the case of the one.

(ii) *Recovery of property after avoidance.* By the basic concept, when a minor avoids his contract, the other contracting party must return all the money or the property that he had received from the minor or its money equivalent.

What happens when the person dealing with a minor has resold the property to a third person who buys in good faith in the ordinary course of business? In the modern era of trade-in sales, this can readily happen. Furthermore, it can happen under circumstances in which the person dealing with the minor is also acting in good faith in that he did not take any advantage of the minor and made the resale in the belief that the minor would not be seeking to avoid the transaction thereafter. Can the minor recover his property from the third person?

Here we have the familiar seesaw phenomenon of two persons free of moral fault, and inevitably any decision will make an innocent party suffer. Specifically, is the good-faith purchaser to be protected at the expense of the minor by refusing to allow the minor to recover his property? Or conversely, is the minor to be protected by regaining his property at the expense of the good-faith purchaser? Notice that the social force in favor of protecting title and perhaps that of avoiding oppression will argue in favor of the minor. But in support of the buyer is furtherance of trade as well as the desire to avoid the oppression that would result should the minor regain the property. At the common law, the minor was entitled to regain his property. Today the other social forces prevail and the decision is in favor of the purchaser.

(b) Merchants. At the common law, there was technically no distinction made in terms of being in the business or being merely a casual buyer or seller. In appreciation of the realities of the Twentieth Century, the courts in a growing number of instances have treated a person differently because he was not an amateur but was a professional who had experience with the type of contract that was employed. In some instances, this approach of the court had the additional support that the contract itself had been prepared by the professional party.

The "merchant" is recognized by name by the Uniform Commercial Code, which in connection with the sale of goods places higher duties upon the merchant. In nontechnical terms, the merchant is the person in the business of buying or selling goods. Although not called a "merchant," the general body of contracts and insurance law has come to treat the insurer as a "merchant" in the sense that it is in the business and knows what it is doing. In some instances, this concept is taken a step further and the contract prepared by the merchant is criticized as a "contract of adhesion" on the theory that the other person is faced with a "take-it-or-leave-it" situation in which he must accept or adhere to the contract as offered by the other party and cannot bargain as to its terms. This approach recognizes not only the greater knowledge of the merchant but also his superior bargaining power.

A further illustration of the classifying of parties to a contract according to their bargaining power may be noted in the National Labor Management Relations Act, which gives employees the right to unionize and to bargain collectively.[2]

Such legislation is based upon the principle that the nonunionized employee is too weak to bargain effectively with a large employer and that it is, therefore, necessary to permit the workers to organize so that their combined bargaining power will offset the greater bargaining power of the employer.

(c) Corporations. The fact that a party is a corporation may make a difference in the interpretation of a contract. Sometimes the difference is explained in terms of a feeling of the court that the corporation is either a "merchant" or has the superior bargaining power. In many states, corporations cannot raise the defense of usury to a contract. This is apparently based upon the premise that individuals are poor little debtors who need protection—the social force of debtor protection, while corporations are rich and should not be permitted to deny the creditor what has been promised him as the price for his loan—the social force of creditor protection.

With the modern expansion of the use of the corporate form of organization in order to obtain limited liability, the factual distinction above lacks validity. That is, there are many small poor corporations that need help just as much as the little debtor, and there are many rich debtors who do not need the protection of the usury law. The distinction between corporate and noncorporate debtors has given rise to litigation involving the question whether a loan is really made to a corporation or whether the corporation loan is merely a sham with an individual actually receiving the benefit of the loan. When the transaction is a sham, it is generally held that the interposition of the corporation is to be ignored so that the individual can, as the true debtor, raise the defense of usury.

§ 26:3.   Consideration

(a) Generally. By the common law, a promise was not deemed binding unless it was supported by consideration. Consideration in simple terms is the price that a person demands for his promise or performance. Thus, if

---

[2] See for example Taft-Hartley Act § 7.

I say that I will paint your house for $1,000, your promise to pay that sum is the price which I demand for my promise to paint your house. Traditionally, the law was not concerned with whether $1,000 was too much, too little, or just right. Technically stated, the law was not concerned with the adequacy of the consideration unless the consideration was so small that, when coupled with other circumstances, it was evidence of fraud.

It would appear that the original function of consideration was to distinguish "serious" agreements that the parties intended to be enforceable at law from the nonserious agreements which were not; that is, the agreements which the law should not enforce because they had not been made seriously, were made in jest, or were made as a mere social undertaking. To illustrate, consider the case where a friend agrees to drive you downtown tomorrow. If he fails to do so, you might be angry with him but you cannot sue him. The law so holds because there was no consideration for his promise to drive you. Actually, this result is reached because neither of you contemplated that the agreement to drive you downtown was of such a serious nature that if there was a breach thereof you could sue your friend. If you feel that there is a binding obligation, what if you should tell your friend that you do not want to go downtown. Can he sue you for breach of a contract to be his guest?

Now by way of contrast, consider the case where you phone a car rental agency and promise to pay a specified number of dollars if the agency will supply a driver and an automobile tomorrow. Here there is no difficulty in concluding that if the agency does not provide the driver and the car or if you do not pay, the injured party may bring suit for breach of contract.

This is true because it is clear that in the car rental agreement situation, a serious business transaction was entered into which society should enforce through its courts. The law will, however, disguise this underlying reason by stating that the promise to supply the driver and car was binding because it was supported by consideration in the form of the customer's promise to pay the specified rental fee, and his promise to pay the fee was supported by the consideration of the promise to supply the car and driver.

Most "consideration" problems could be readily and properly disposed of by stating the problem in terms of whether the parties were serious and intended to be bound by a legal obligation. When approached from this point, the fact that the promisor was given something for his promise would be merely evidence that the parties were serious. Unfortunately, the common-law lawyers, with their great reverence for form, took the presence of consideration which was merely evidence of the serious character of the agreement and elevated it to the status of an essential element of a binding contract. Unfortunately, because the result was that an agreement regardless of its serious character or how much the parties intended to be bound did not constitute a contract unless a court could find "consideration." The common-law doctrine of consideration has fallen into disrepute partly because it seems so meaningless as anything, however trivial, is accepted as consideration; partly because insistence on the higher standards of consideration denies to modern business the flexibility that it would need for its operation, and partly because, in some instances, hardship results when promises are held not binding for want of consideration.

(b) Flexibility. The necessity of "open end terms" in repeating transactions runs into difficulty with the concept of consideration. For example, a promise to purchase all the coal that you need in your factory was once held not to be consideration to sell you the coal at a stated price. This was for the reason that there was no positive obligation on your part to purchase coal or any coal at all. That is to say, you could convert to oil or gas or go out of business. The modern business world soon recognized the desirability of "requirements" contracts and desired that they be recognized by the law. While it was true that the requirer under such a contract for one reason or another might not require, the odds were that he would continue to require and that he would not go out of business just to avoid requiring. The risk that there be no requirements was therefore in a sense minimal, and if the supplier was willing to enter into the transaction on that basis, the court should not block two "merchants" from making the kind of working arrangement that they desired. If the vague floating requirements contract was good enough for the men in the business, the law should not handicap them by declaring such a contract not binding. Thus requirements and output contracts came to be recognized and have been held binding for many years.

The Uniform Commercial Code gives greater freedom of action in contracting by providing that written firm offers of merchants are binding without consideration, and the requirement of consideration is abolished as to a written discharge of a claim or an alleged breach of a commercial contract, or for a modification of a contract for the sale of goods.

As further illustration of the emphasis upon the flexibility of relationships, which in turn places greater emphasis upon the intent or belief of the parties, rather than the formal requirements of the law, is the provision of the Code under which a sales contract can be found to exist if the parties believe that there is a sales contract between them. Thus, it is provided with respect to all sales of goods that "conduct by both parties which recognizes the existence of a contract is sufficient to establish a contract for sale although the writings of the parties do not otherwise establish a contract." [3]

(c) Promissory estoppel. In the interest of furthering fairness, the social force of preventing oppression, many courts are adopting the doctrine of promissory estoppel. By this doctrine, if a person makes a promise to

---

[3] Uniform Commercial Code § 2-207(3). See also the "open price" clause, UCC § 2-305.

another and that other person acts upon the promise, the promisor is barred from setting up the absence of consideration in order to avoid his promise. The enforcement of the promise, even though there is no consideration is deemed proper when the promisor should reasonably expect to induce and does induce action or forbearance of a definite and substantial character on the part of the promisee, and injustice can be avoided only by the enforcement of the promise.

HOFFMAN v. RED OWL STORES, INC.

26 Wis.2d 683, 133 N.W.2d 267 (1965)

Hoffman wanted to acquire a franchise as a Red Owl Grocery Store, Red Owl being a corporation that maintained a system of chain stores. The agent of Red Owl informed Hoffman and his wife that if they would sell their bakery in Wautoma, acquire a certain tract of land in Chilton, another city, and put up a specified amount of money, he would be given a franchise as desired. Hoffman sold his business, acquired the land in Chilton, but was never granted a franchise. He and his wife sued Red Owl, which raised the defense that there had only been an assurance that Hoffman would receive a franchise but no promise supported by consideration and therefore no binding contract to give him a franchise. From a judgment in the Hoffmans' favor, Red Owl appealed.

OPINION BY CURRIE, C.J. . . .

The development of the law of promissory estoppel "is an attempt by the courts to keep remedies abreast of increased moral consciousness of honesty and fair representations in all business dealings." . . .

The Restatement avoids use of the term "promissory estoppel," and there has been criticism of it as an inaccurate term. . . . Use of the word "estoppel" to describe a doctrine upon which a party to a lawsuit may obtain affirmative relief offends the traditional concept that estoppel merely serves as a shield and cannot serve as a sword to create a cause of action. . . .

Because we deem the doctrine of promissory estoppel, as stated in Sec. 90 of Restatement, 1 Contracts, is one which supplies a needed weapon which courts may employ in a proper case to prevent injustice, we endorse and adopt it.

The record here discloses a number of promises and assurances given to Hoffman by Lukowitz in behalf of Red Owl upon which plaintiffs relied and acted upon to their detriment. . . .

There remains for consideration the question of law raised by defendants that agreement was never reached on essential factors necessary to establish a contract between Hoffman and Red Owl. Among these were the size, cost, design, and layout of the store building; and the terms of the lease with respect to rent, maintenance, renewal, and purchase options. This poses the question of whether the promise necessary to sustain a cause of action for promissory estoppel must embrace all details of a proposed transaction between promisor and promisee so as to be the equivalent of an offer that

would result in a binding contract between the parties if the promisee were
to accept the same.

Originally the doctrine of promissory estoppel was invoked as a substitute for consideration rendering a gratuitous promise enforceable as a
contract. . . . In other words, the acts of reliance by the promisee to his
detriment provided a substitute for consideration. If promissory estoppel
were to be limited to only those situations where the promise giving rise to
the cause of action must be so definite with respect to all details that a
contract would result were the promise supported by consideration, then the
defendants' instant promises to Hoffman would not meet this test. However,
Sec. 90 of Restatement, 1 Contracts, does not impose the requirement that
the promise giving rise to the cause of action must be so comprehensive in
scope as to meet the requirements of an offer that would ripen into a contract if accepted by the promisee. Rather the conditions imposed are:

(1) Was the promise one which the promisor should reasonably
expect to induce action or forbearance of a definite and substantial character
on the part of the promisee?

(2) Did the promise induce such action or forbearance?

(3) Can injustice be avoided only by enforcement of the promise?

We deem it would be a mistake to regard an action grounded on promissory estoppel as the equivalent of a breach of contract action. . . . While
the first two of the above listed three requirements of promissory estoppel
present issues of fact which ordinarily will be resolved by a jury, the third
requirement, that the remedy can only be invoked where necessary to avoid
injustice, is one that involves a policy decision by the court. Such a policy
decision necessarily embraces an element of discretion.

We conclude that injustice would result here if plaintiffs were not granted
some relief because of the failure of defendants to keep their promises which
induced plaintiffs to act to their detriment. . . .

§ 26:4. Interpretation of Contracts

(a) Generally. By traditional principles, a contract is to be enforced
according to its terms. It is the intent that is expressed in the contract which
controls, and a secret intention or reservation of one party that is not
expressed in the contract has no effect.

In interpreting a contract, the court must seek to give meaning to every
word and to construe the contract as a whole. In the absence of proof that
a word has a peculiar meaning or that it was employed by the parties with
a particular meaning, a common word is given its ordinary meaning and
a technical word is given its ordinary technical meaning.

(b) Divisibility of contracts. When the contract consists of two or
more parts and calls for corresponding performances of each part by the
parties, a question arises whether the parties intended a group of separate,
divisible contracts or whether there was to be a "package deal" under which
a complete performance by each party is essential.

If the law chose to do so, it could say that whichever party claims that the contract is or is not divisible has the burden of convincing the court. Instead the court will step into the situation and determine which alternative will be more nearly just. In such case, the social force of furthering intent is, in effect, inoperative because while it is desired to enforce the intent, the difficulty is that the intent of the parties has not been expressed and the court must rewrite the contract for the parties, in spite of the time-honored rule that the courts will not rewrite contracts. When the court is faced with the question whether a contract is divisible or not divisible, it is clear that the court is seeking to balance the oppression that will be caused one party against the oppression that might be caused the other.

ARROW GAS CO. v. LEWIS

71 N. Mex. 232, 377 P.2d 655 (1963)

Richard and Ruby Lewis owned separated tracts of land, designated as Section 1 and Section 18, which they leased to Gailey and Sredanovich. The lease specified that the Lewises would convey to the tenants a one-half interest in the land if the tenants or lessees developed water on the land suitable for irrigation. The tenants developed such a water supply on Section 18 but not on Section 1. Arrow Gas Co. acquired the interest of the lessees and claimed that it was entitled to a one-half interest in Section 18. The Lewises contended that Arrow was not entitled to any interest in the land because the lessees had not developed nor made any effort to develop water on Section 1. From a judgment in their favor, Arrow appealed.

OPINION BY CHAVEZ, J. . . .

The lease agreement provides:
"It is agreed and understood that the purpose of this Lease is to develop the above described area for irrigation purposes and that the consideration passing from [lessees] to [lessors] for this Lease is the development of water or the effort of [lessees] to develop water upon said premises for irrigation purposes. The [lessors] recognize the value to them of exploration for water to be used for irrigation.

"It is agreed and understood between the parties hereto that in the event that water is developed in sufficient quantities and quality for irrigation purposes that [lessors] shall convey to [lessees] one-half of the above described premises; the division shall be made at the time it is determined that water of sufficient quantity and quality for irrigation purposes has been developed, and such division shall be made upon an equitable basis. . . ." . . .

This brings us to the question of whether the lessees, Gailey and Sredanovich, upon developing water in Section 18, acquired a one-half interest in the lands covered by the lease, or at least a one-half interest in Section 18 where water was developed. . . .

The next question is whether the lease agreement is severable. . . .

In determining whether or not a contract is divisible, the governing principle is the manifested intention of the parties in view of the nature of the contract, that is, their intention to have performance of the contract in parts and have the performance of a part on one side the price or exchange of a corresponding part on the other. . . .

A severable or divisible contract has been defined as one under which the whole performance is divided into two sets of partial performances, each part of each set being the agreed exchange for a corresponding part of the set of performances to be rendered by the other promisor. . . .

Restatement of the Law, Contracts, § 266(3) e, p. 385, defines divisible contracts as follows: "A contract is divisible where by its terms (1) performance of each party is divided into two or more parts, and (2) the number of parts due from each party is the same, and (3) the performance of each part by one party is the agreed exchange for a corresponding part by the other party."

We hold that the intention of the parties is clearly expressed in the lease agreements, i.e., the development of water for irrigation purposes and the vesting of an interest in the land upon its having been determined that water has been developed. It is clear from the evidence presented in the trial that the lessees executed their part of the agreements with respect to Section 18. It is uncontradicted that the well developed by lessees was adequate to provide water of sufficient quantity and quality to irrigate that section, or such part of it as is practicable to farm by irrigation. This performance by lessees entitled them to . . . an undivided one-half interest in Section 18. This is true even though lessees made no effort to develop a water supply in Section 1 because the lease agreements are severable. Under their express terms, the parties assented separately to several things in a single contract. The performance by the lessees in developing water on Section 18 is the separate consideration for the corresponding performance provided for in the lease agreements on the part of appellees.

[Judgment reversed.]

DISSENTING OPINION BY NOBLE, J. . . .

The majority opinion proceeds upon a construction that when water sufficient in quantity and quality to irrigate Section 18 was produced, Sredanovich and Gailey became immediately entitled to a deed to one half of the land to which water had been beneficially applied. . . .

This brings me immediately to the question whether the lessees were required to develop water sufficient to irrigate all of the land described in the contract, or at least, make an effort to do so before lessees were entitled to a division of the lands. Stated otherwise, was the contract divisible or entire? Primarily, the question of whether a contract is severable or entire is one of intention of the parties and is to be determined by the language used by the parties and the subject matter of the agreement. . . . Each case must be determined upon its own facts. If the terms of the agreement clearly show the intention of the parties, the inquiry is at once ended and no construction is required. But, in many instances, the language used does not clearly settle the question. Resort is then had to the subject matter of the agreement.

The provision for conveyance of an interest in the land, standing alone, leaves some uncertainty as to when the lessees are entitled to receive conveyance; but when the whole instrument is read together and the purpose and nature of the subject matter considered, I have no doubt as to the intention of the parties. . . .

It is plain to me that the parties themselves expressed their purpose or intention "to develop the above described area for irrigation purposes," and the consideration as "the development of water or the effort of second parties to develop water upon said premises for irrigation purposes." A reading of the purpose clause and the nature of the subject matter indicates that it was the intention of the parties that the entire area described in the contract be developed, or that an effort be made to develop it. . . . This contract does not apportion the consideration to the separate tracts of land nor to less than the whole, until there has been at least an effort to develop water on both tracts. . . . As I view the contract, when read as a whole, and considering its subject matter and expressed purpose, this was an entire and indivisible contract requiring the development of, or an honest effort to develop, the entire tract. No provision was made for partial performance until, at least, there was an effort to develop water for both tracts. Since Sredanovich and Gailey made no effort to develop water on any part of Section 1, they were not entitled to conveyance of either a portion of the land developed nor of the whole tract. . . .

(c) *Implied terms.* When a contract is not explicit as to a particular matter, the courts may imply terms. In some instances, the term is so clearly what the persons had in mind that the implication of terms may be regarded as motivated by the social force of enforcing the intent of the parties. In other instances, no intent has in fact been expressed, and it is clear that the implication is made merely to protect from the oppression which would result were it not made. Illustrative of the former situation is the implication that a sale for $50 means $50 in cash, and it is that kind of cash which is legal tender at the time and place for payment, as contrasted with $50 in money of the Second Continental Congress. Likewise, in a contract to perform work, there is an implied promise to use such skill as is necessary for the proper performance of the work; and in a "cost-plus" contract, there is an implied undertaking that the costs will be reasonable and proper.

Illustrative of the antioppression implication, is the case of implying a term to refrain from competing with the other contracting party as seen in § 17:3.

§ 26:5.   Voluntary

(a) *Generally.* By hypothesis, a contract is based upon the voluntary agreement of the parties. What is "voluntary" has to some extent been redefined in the case of duress, giving rise to the doctrine of economic duress. Likewise there is an appreciation by the courts that under modern methods of marketing a free choice might not be as voluntary as it sounds.

(b) What is voluntary? The courts are coming to appreciate that sometimes the party with the weaker bargaining power has no choice although, as far as the rule of law is concerned, his contract is binding as the voluntary act of a free adult person.

Underlying the traditional concept of the law of contracts is the belief that a person can go elsewhere to contract and therefore when he stays and makes a given contract, his contract is necessarily voluntary. But "going elsewhere" may be meaningless when better terms cannot be obtained elsewhere because the industry does business on the basis of the terms in question, or when the particular person cannot obtain better terms elsewhere because of his inferior economic standing or bargaining position.

This "appreciation" of the practical inability to go elsewhere has not been formalized into a rule of law that states that when that condition is present, the case shall be decided a particular way. Rather, when the condition of relative immobility of either party exists, there is a tendency to find that the party might be oppressed or exploited and the social forces which oppose such result come into play.

In some instances, the bargaining scales are sought to be balanced by rules of construction. Thus, the insurance contract is strictly construed because it is regarded as a standardized "contract of adhesion" to which the insureds must adhere if they want to obtain any insurance. In an earlier decade, the same conclusion could be reached and is still reached as a matter of construction on the ground that the contract of insurance having been prepared by the insurer should be construed strictly against it. That is, no stigma is attached to the contract that the insurer offered in terms of the insurer's being bigger or of its adopting a "take it or leave it" attitude.

The adoption of legislation to create equality of bargaining power has already been noted; namely, the Uniform Commercial Code provision establishing different standards for merchants, and the right given to labor by the labor management relations statutes. To these may be added statutes permitting exporters to combine for the purpose of the exporting trade so that they can meet the competition of foreign dealers, such privilege creating an exception to the federal antitrust law under which such combinations in foreign commerce would be prohibited.

HENNINGSEN v. BLOOMFIELD MOTORS
32 N.J. 358, 161 A.2d 69 (1960)

Henningsen purchased a Plymouth automobile from Bloomfield Motors. He did not read the fine print on the reverse side of the printed contract, and its terms were not called to his attention. Ten days later, while being driven by his wife, the car went out of control apparently because of some defect in the steering mechanism and she was injured in the resulting crash. Suit was brought by Henningsen and his wife against Bloomfield Motors and Chrysler Corporation, the manufacturer of the automobile. The defense was raised that the standard warranty on the back of the contract prevented suit for the wife's injuries.

OPINION BY FRANCIS, J. . . .

The reverse side of the contract contains 8½ inches of fine print. It is not as small, however, as the two critical paragraphs [set forth below]. The page is headed "Conditions" and contains 10 separate paragraphs consisting of 65 lines in all. The paragraphs do not have headnotes or margin notes denoting their particular subject, as in the case of the "Owner Service Certificate" to be referred to later. In the seventh paragraph, about two-thirds of the way down the page, the warranty, which is the focal point of the case, is set forth. It is as follows:

"7. It is expressly agreed that there are no warranties, express or implied, *made* by either the dealer or the manufacturer on the motor vehicle, chassis, of parts furnished hereunder except as follows.

" 'The manufacturer warrants each new motor vehicle (including original equipment placed thereon by the manufacturer except tires), chassis, or parts manufactured by it to be free from defects in material or workmanship under normal use and service. Its obligation under this warranty being limited to making good at its factory any part or parts thereof which shall, within ninety (90) days after delivery of such vehicle *to the original purchaser* or before such vehicle has been driven 4,000 miles, whichever event shall first occur, be returned to it with transportation charges prepaid and which its examination shall disclose to its satisfaction to have been thus defective; *this warranty being expressly in lieu of all other warranties expressed or implied, and all other obligations or liabilities on its part,* and it neither assumes nor authorizes any other person to assume for it any other liability in connection with the sale of its vehicles. . . .' "

In the ordinary case of sale of goods by description, an implied warranty of merchantability is an integral part of the transaction. . . . [This] simply means that the thing sold is reasonably fit for the general purpose for which it is manufactured and sold. . . .

The transcendent value of the [Sales Act], particularly with respect to implied warranties, rests in the fact that obligations on the part of the seller were imposed by operation of law, and did not depend for their existence upon express agreement of the parties. . . .

As the Sales Act and its liberal interpretation by the courts threw this protective cloak about the buyer, the decisions in various jurisdictions revealed beyond doubt that many manufacturers took steps to avoid these ever increasing warranty obligations. Realizing that the act governed the relationship of buyer and seller, they undertook to withdraw from actual and direct contractual contact with the buyer. They ceased selling products to the consuming public through their own employees and making contracts of sale in their own names. Instead, a system of independent dealers was established; their products were sold to dealers who in turn dealt with the buying public, ostensibly solely in their own personal capacity as sellers. In the past in many instances, manufacturers were able to transfer to the dealers burdens imposed by the act and thus achieved a large measure of immunity for themselves. But, as will be noted in more detail hereafter, such marketing practices, coupled with the advent of large scale advertising by manufacturers to promote the purchase of these goods from dealers by members of the public, provided a basis upon which the existence of express or implied warranties was predicated, even though the manufacturer was not a party to the contract of sale. . . .

The terms of the warranty are a sad commentary upon the automobile manufacturers' marketing practices. Warranties developed in the law in the interest of and to protect the ordinary consumer who cannot be expected to have the knowledge or capacity or even the opportunity to make adequate inspection of mechanical instrumentalities, like automobiles, and to decide for himself whether they are reasonably fit for the designed purpose. . . . But the ingenuity of the Automobile Manufacturers Association, by means of its standardized form, has metamorphosed the warranty into a device to limit the maker's liability. . . .

The manufacturer agrees to replace defective parts for 90 days after the sale or until the car has been driven 4,000 miles, whichever is first to occur, *if the part is sent to the factory, transportation charges prepaid, and if examination discloses to its satisfaction that the part is defective.* It is difficult to imagine a greater burden on the consumer, or less satisfactory remedy. Aside from imposing on the buyer the trouble of removing and shipping the part, the maker has sought to retain the uncontrolled discretion to decide the issue of defectiveness. . . .

Also suppose, as in this case, a defective part or parts caused an accident and that the car was so damaged as to render it impossible to discover the precise part or parts responsible, although the circumstances clearly pointed to such fact as the cause of the mishap. Can it be said that the impossibility of performance deprived the buyer of the benefit of the warranty?

Moreover, the guaranty is against defective workmanship. That condition may arise from good parts improperly assembled. There being no defective parts to return to the maker, is all remedy to be denied? One court met that type of problem by holding that where the purchaser does not know the precise cause of inoperability, calling a car a "vibrator" would be sufficient to state a claim for relief. It said that such a car is not an uncommon one in the industry. The general cause of the vibration is not known. Some part or parts have been either defectively manufactured or improperly assembled in the construction and manufacture of the automobile. In the operation of the car, these parts give rise to vibrations. The difficulty lies in locating the precise spot and cause. *Allen* v. *Brown,* 181 Kan. 301, 310 P.2d 923 (Sup.Ct. 1957). But the warranty does not specify what the purchaser must do to obtain relief in such case, if a remedy is intended to be provided. Must the purchaser return the car, transportation charges prepaid, over a great distance to the factory? It may be said that in the usual case the dealer also gives the same warranty and that as a matter of expediency the purchaser should turn to him. But under the law the buyer is entitled to proceed against the manufacturer. Further, dealers' franchises are precarious (see, Automobile Franchise Agreements, Hewitt (1956)). For example,

Bloomfield Motors' franchise may be cancelled by Chrysler on 90 days' notice. And obviously dealers' facilities and capacity, financial and otherwise, are not as sufficient as those of the primarily responsible manufacturer in his distant factory.

The matters referred to represent only a small part of the illusory character of the security presented by the warranty. Thus far the analysis has dealt only with the remedy provided in the case of a defective part. What relief is provided when the breach of the warranty results in personal injury to the buyer? . . . As we have said above, the law is clear that such damages are recoverable under an ordinary warranty. The right exists whether the warranty sued on is express or implied. . . . And, of course, it has long since been settled that where the buyer or a member of his family driving with his permission suffers injuries because of negligent manufacture or construction of the vehicle, the manufacturer's liability exists. . . . But in this instance, after reciting that defective parts will be replaced at the factory, the alleged agreement relied upon by Chrysler provides that the manufacturer's "obligation under this warranty" is limited to that undertaking; further, that such remedy is "in lieu of all other warranties, express or implied, and all other obligations or liabilities on its part." The contention has been raised that such language bars any claim for personal injuries which may emanate from a breach of the warranty. Although not urged in this case, it has been successfully maintained that the exclusion "of all other obligations and liabilities on its part" precludes a cause of action for injuries based on negligence. *Shafer* v. *Reo Motors,* 205 F.2d 685 (3 Cir. 1953). Another Federal Circuit Court of Appeals holds to the contrary. *Doughnut Machine Corporation* v. *Bibbey,* 65 F.2d 634 (1 Cir. 1933). There can be little doubt that justice is served only by the latter ruling. . . .

Under modern conditions the . . . obligation of the manufacturer should . . . be based . . . upon 'the demands of social justice.' " . . .

Accordingly, we hold that under modern marketing conditions, when a manufacturer puts a new automobile in the stream of trade and promotes its purchase by the public, an implied warranty that it is reasonably suitable for use as such accompanies it into the hands of the ultimate purchaser. . . .

What effect should be given to the express warranty in question which seeks to limit the manufacturer's liability to replacement of defective parts, and which disclaims all other warranties, express or implied? In assessing its significance we must keep in mind the general principle that, in the absence of fraud, one who does not choose to read a contract before signing it, cannot later relieve himself of its burdens. . . . And in applying that principle, the basic tenet of freedom of competent parties to contract is a factor of importance. But in the framework of modern commercial life and business practices, such rules cannot be applied on a strict, doctrinal basis. The conflicting interests of the buyer and seller must be evaluated realistically and justly, giving due weight to the social policy evinced by the Uniform Sales Act, the progressive decisions of the courts engaged in administering it, the mass production methods of manufacture and distribution to the public, and the bargaining position occupied by the ordinary consumer in such an economy. This history of the law shows that legal doctrines, as first expounded, often prove to be inadequate under the impact of later experience.

In such case, the need for justice has stimulated the necessary qualifications or adjustments. . . .

In a society such as ours, where the automobile is a common and necessary adjunct of daily life, and where its use is so fraught with danger to the driver, passengers, and the public, the manufacturer is under a special obligation in connection with the construction, promotion, and sale of his cars. Consequently, the courts must examine purchase agreements closely to see if consumer and public interests are treated fairly. . . .

"There is sufficient flexibility in the concepts of fraud, duress, misrepresentation and undue influence, not to mention differences in economic bargaining power" to enable the courts to avoid enforcement of unconscionable provisions in long printed standardized contracts. . . . Freedom of contract is not such an immutable doctrine as to admit of no qualification in the area in which we are concerned. . . .

Fraud and physical duress are not the only grounds upon which courts refuse to enforce contracts. The law is not so primitive that it sanctions every injustice except brute force and downright fraud. More specifically, the courts generally refuse to lend themselves to the enforcement of a 'bargain' in which one party has unjustly taken advantage of the economic necessities of the other. . . ."

The traditional contract is the result of free bargaining of parties who are brought together by the play of the market, and who meet each other on a footing of approximate economic equality. In such a society there is no danger that freedom of contract will be a threat to the social order as a whole. But in present-day commercial life the standardized mass contract has appeared. It is used primarily by enterprises with strong bargaining power and position. "The weaker party, in need of the goods or services, is frequently not in a position to shop around for better terms, either because the author of the standard contract has a monopoly (natural or artificial) or because all competitors use the same clauses. His contractual intention is but a subjection more or less voluntary to terms dictated by the stronger party, terms whose consequences are often understood in a vague way, if at all." . . .

The warranty before us is a standardized form designed for mass use. It is imposed upon the automobile consumer. He takes it or leaves it, and he must take it to buy an automobile. No bargaining is engaged in with respect to it. In fact, the dealer through whom it comes to the buyer is without authority to alter it; his function is ministerial—simply to deliver it. The form warranty is not only standard with Chrysler but, as mentioned above, it is the uniform warranty of the Automobile Manufacturers Association. Members of the Association are: General Motors, Inc., Ford, Chrysler, Studebaker-Packard, American Motors, (Rambler), Willys Motors, Checker Motors Corp., and International Harvester Company. . . . Of these companies, the "Big Three" (General Motors, Ford, and Chrysler) represented 93.5 percent of the passenger-car production for 1958 and the independents 6.5 percent. . . . And for the same year the "Big Three" had 86.72 percent of the total passenger vehicle registrations. . . .

The gross inequality of bargaining position occupied by the consumer in the automobile industry is thus apparent. There is no competition among the car makers in the area of the express warranty. Where can the buyer go to negotiate for better protection? Such control and limitation of his remedies are inimical to the public welfare and, at the very least, call for great care by the courts to avoid injustice through application of strict common-law principles of freedom of contract. Because there is no competition among the motor vehicle manufacturers with respect to the scope of protection guaranteed to the buyer, there is no incentive on their part to stimulate good will in that field of public relations. Thus, there is lacking a factor existing in more competitive fields, one which tends to guarantee the safe construction of the article sold. . . .

Although the courts, with few exceptions, have been most sensitive to problems presented by contracts resulting from gross disparity in buyer-seller bargaining positions, they have not articulated a general principle condemning, as opposed to public policy, the imposition on the buyer of a skeleton warranty as a means of limiting the responsibility of the manufacturer. They have endeavored thus far to avoid a drastic departure from age-old tenets of freedom of contract by adopting doctrines of strict construction, and notice and knowledgeable assent by the buyer to the attempted exculpation of the seller. . . . Accordingly to be found in the cases are statements that disclaimers and the consequent limitation of liability will not be given effect if "unfairly procured," . . . if not brought to the buyer's attention and he was not made understandingly aware of it, . . . or if not clear and explicit. . . .

The task of the judiciary is to administer the spirit as well as the letter of the law. On issues such as the present one, part of that burden is to protect the ordinary man against the loss of important rights through what, in effect, is the unilateral act of the manufacturer. The status of the automobile industry is unique. Manufacturers are few in number and strong in bargaining position. In the matter of warranties on the sale of their products, the Automotive Manufacturers Association has enabled them to present a united front. From the standpoint of the purchaser, there can be no arms length negotiating on the subject. Because his capacity for bargaining is so grossly unequal, the inexorable conclusion which follows is that he is not permitted to bargain at all. He must take or leave the automobile on the warranty terms dictated by the maker. He cannot turn to a competitor for better security.

Public policy is a term not easily defined. Its significance varies as the habits and needs of a people may vary. It is not static and the field of application is an ever increasing one. A contract, or a particular provision therein, valid in one era may be wholly opposed to the public policy of another. . . . Courts keep in mind the principle that the best interests of society demand that persons should not be unnecessarily restricted in their freedom to contract. But they do not hesitate to declare void as against public policy contractual provisions which clearly tend to the injury of the public in some way. . . .

The judicial process has recognized a right to recover damages for personal injuries arising from a breach of that warranty. The disclaimer of the implied warranty and exclusion of all obligations except those specifically assumed by the express warranty signify a studied effort to frustrate that protection. True, the Sales Act authorizes agreements between buyer and seller qualifying the warranty obligations. But quite obviously the Legislature contemplated lawful stipulations (which are determined by the circumstances of a particular case) arrived at freely by parties of relatively equal bargaining strength. The lawmakers did not authorize the automobile manufacturer to use its grossly disproportionate bargaining power to relieve itself from liability and to impose on the ordinary buyer, who in effect has no real freedom of choice, the grave danger of injury to himself and others that attends the sale of such a dangerous instrumentality as a defectively made automobile. . . . We are of the opinion that Chrysler's attempted disclaimer of an implied warranty of merchantability and of the obligations arising therefrom is so inimical to the public good as to compel an adjudication of its invalidity. . . .

§ 26:6.   Isolation of Disputes and Avoidance of Litigation

(a) *Generally.* The common law apparently had much litigation time available and was much more concerned with legal rights than is the modern businessman. Today, the emphasis is upon getting the job done and moving on. This change in social attitude has resulted in there arising a number of contract techniques and rules of law, the object of which is to iron out anything which might become a dispute or to isolate the dispute when it arises so that performance may continue without interruption and the matter can be determined later.

(b) *Reference to third person.* The modern contract, with the approval of the courts, recognizes the right to provide that certain matters shall be governed by the decision of a third person. Thus a buyer and seller who are unable to agree as to price but in whose minds the making of a sale is a primary objective, may contract that the price shall be determined by a third person. In the case of construction work, it is common to provide that an architect in charge of the job shall have the final word as to certain matters relating to the construction.

In these cases, the law could have taken a flat view that until all terms had been agreed to there was no contract. An intermediate position could be that before the third person has acted, there was no contract but, in effect, merely an agreement to make an agreement in the future. The great practical advantage of the techniques of letting a third person decide later is too great to reject because of a "technical" rule of law requiring that a contract set forth all of its material terms. Thus, the social force in favor of furthering trade, aided by that of practical expediency, comes into play to give rise to a variation to the standard rule of law.

It is significant that the law is not much concerned with the possibility that the third person may be acting in collusion with one of the contracting parties. Theoretically, this danger is particularly great in the case of the architect who is ordinarily paid by the owner and could therefore be expected to decide in favor of the owner. It could consequently be argued that the social force which seeks to prevent fraud would not permit the kind of provision discussed above. The danger of fraud is minimal, however, as a practical matter. In the case of the third person setting the price, it is likely that he is either an expert or a merchant and probably would be unwilling to jeopardize his reputation for the sake of "helping" one of the parties to the contract in question. Similarly, the architect has a professional status and would not want to jeopardize his reputation for the sake of the one construction job.

Therefore, the law takes the approach, which is practically expedient, by deciding in favor of the rule that will further trade, which will be present in all cases, rather than deciding to protect against fraud that might be present in only a few cases. This does not mean that the law is ignoring fraud; but only that there is a valid contract in spite of the possibility of fraud and if either party wishes to avoid the effect of the contract provision on the ground of fraud, it is necessary that he assume the burden of proving that there was fraud present in the given case.

(c) Arbitration. The various hazards of litigation that will be discussed in Chapter 30 did much to accelerate the growth of arbitration.

(i) *Nature of arbitration.* By the use of arbitration, a dispute is brought before one or more arbitrators who make a decision which the parties have agreed to accept as final.

When a case is tried in court, the members of the jury and the judge are ordinarily not familiar with the business practices involved. The attorneys find it necessary, therefore, to explain these business practices before presenting the facts and the law of the case. Arbitration, in contrast, enables the parties to select as arbitrators trained experts who come to the arbitration panel already educated in the business transactions involved. This permits the attorneys to get down to the facts of the case immediately and assures a more understanding analysis of the case.

The parties to a contract, which is to be in effect for some time, may specify in the contract that any disputes arising thereunder shall be submitted to arbitrators to be selected by the parties. In some instances, the contract will name the arbitrators, who will then be a standing board of arbitrators for the duration of the contract, in advance. Frequently, the parties provide their own remedy against failure to obey the award of the arbitrators as by executing a mutual indemnity bond by which each party agrees to indemnify the other for any loss caused by his failure to carry out the arbitration award.

(ii) *Validity of arbitration.* Arbitration has become such an accepted way of modern commercial life that it is strange to recognize that less than a century ago an agreement to arbitrate was deemed contrary to public policy on the ground that it ousted the jurisdiction of the courts. Accordingly, it was deemed socially undesirable and therefore unlawful for parties to agree to settle a case by some means outside of court, rather than to take the dispute into court.

With the rise of technical problems and the great rise of the volume of litigation, the modern court is quite happy to have arbitrators shoulder part of the workload so that the early view that arbitration was illegal has been replaced by the new rule that it is legal. In many states, vestiges of the old rule of illegality may still be found, some states still holding invalid an agreement to submit in advance all disputes that may thereafter arise, as distinguished from submitting each dispute at the time that it arises. In some states, disputes under contracts relating to personal services, such as labor union contracts, cannot be made the subject of arbitration or cannot be made subject to an arbitration clause in advance of the existence of a particular dispute.

(d) Practical operation of the new techniques. It will be helpful in understanding the new approach to a contract as a working arrangement for the doing of a job by giving thought to the interrelation of the above techniques. As a hypothetical illustration, consider the case of the coal supplier contracting to deliver 100 tons of coal to a buyer in the first week of each month. Assume that the buyer complains to the seller that there is too much slate in the first 100 tons. If the buyer is able to perceive the slate as the coal is being delivered to his plant, he has the technical right to reject the shipment and sue the seller for breach of the contract as to the installment. If the breach as to the installment is substantially material to the entire contract, he may treat the installment breach as a breach of the entire contract. But what about the coal needed by the buyer for his plant? Even though the shipment is of poorer quality than required by the contract, it might be the lesser of two evils for the buyer to take the coal, use it, and then fight out the differences with the seller, as opposed to rejecting the coal, suing the seller, and seeking to obtain this month's and future months' coal in the open market.

Traditional contract law gave the buyer the right to accept the installment to which he objected, but there was the danger that in doing so he would be deemed to have waived and lost his right to object. In modern times, the dilemma in which the buyer finds himself is all the more aggravated by the fact that a lawsuit for breach of the contract by the seller could take anywhere from two to five years in many of the larger urban areas. In the meantime, what is the buyer to be doing for coal for his plant? To meet these problems, the modern business world and business law have worked out the devices and techniques considered above in this section. Today the buyer could accept the first shipment with a reservation of his rights. This means that he would have his installment of coal and subsequent installments, but he would not have lost his right to complain and obtain a money indemnity if he could show thereafter that there was a defect or deficiency in the installment.

The buyer may also demand of the seller that the seller give the buyer reasonable assurance that future performances will be proper. This, depending upon the circumstances, the reputation of the parties, and so on, may range from a mere stated assurance that a particular mistake will not be repeated to the more formal technique of furnishing a surety bond or placing money on deposit to indemnify the buyer in the event that there is a future breach.

The above pattern could be added to by referring to an expert the question whether the first installment was defective and what price adjustment should be made if it were. As an alternative, the parties could agree to submit the matter to arbitrators if they did not wish one expert to have the final decision. Whatever pattern is used, notice that the significant thing is that business goes on in spite of the dispute. The buyer keeps getting coal and keeps running his plant, the seller keeps selling coal to the buyer, and in due course a money adjustment is made if it is found that there was any defect.

This contrasts with the attitude of the common law in which the guiding motto seems to have been "let's have a lawsuit" rather than "let's get the job done." Notice also that it removes the great hazard that the complaining party always ran the risk that the court might ultimately decide against him. To illustrate, in the example of the supplying of coal, if the jury should in a later lawsuit determine that there was nothing wrong with the first installment of coal, the buyer who rejected the shipment and refused to take the coal would then be the party who had broken the contract and the supplier could sue him for damages. This would naturally tend to make the buyer reluctant to assert his rights unless he was positive not only that his contract was broken but also that he had competent witnesses by whose testimony he could thereafter prove that fact. Under the modern device, as the performance of the contract goes on, the worst that can happen to the objecting party is that he loses his claim to a price reduction or for damages and must then pay according to the terms of the contract. He does not, however, find himself thrown into the position of being a wrongdoer who is required to indemnify the innocent seller.

§ 26:7. Good Faith and Fairness

The classic approach to contracts was that a contract made by an adult person without any fraud or actual deception by the other party was binding. Whether the contract was a good bargain or even a fair bargain was not a matter with which the courts were concerned. This was not an indication that the courts were nonhumanitarian. Rather, in the interest of practical expediency, in order to avoid the flooding of the court docket with contract evaluation cases, and in the interest of enforcing the intent of the parties, encouraging trade, and giving stability to business relationships, the courts took the position that the parties must live with the contract which they had made and that the court would not rewrite their contract by substituting the contract which the judge would have made had he been in their place.

To some extent, the law did not permit the parties to always have the exact contract that they agreed upon. The law has always and still does invalidate a contract which the law deems to be for an illegal purpose. By this criterion, the law declares not binding a contract which called for the commission of an act that viewed by itself was a crime, such as a contract to commit murder or to forge securities. The law soon began to expand this common-law limitation and began to, and still does, invalidate a contract which the court deems to be contrary to public policy. This, of course, is a vague concept and introduces uncertainty into the law for it can well be noted that the reason an act is classified as a crime is because it is deemed contrary to public policy, so that the object of illegality is merely an aspect of the broader concept of "public policy" rather than a separate criterion. In practical operation, contracts that a court deems contrary to public policy are, in effect, contracts relating to matters which, though technically not crimes because the legislature has not yet so declared them, the court deems to be of a criminal nature so that at least the court will not lend its aid to enforce the contract.

In addition to the limiting factors of illegality and contrary to public policy, the law is evolving toward requiring that contracts be not unfair nor manifest bad faith. Affirmatively stated, it is now required that contracts be fair and be made in good faith. This, of course, is a statement which begs the question because both according to Adam Smith and Blackstone, fundamental fairness would mean only that the contract was reached freely and voluntarily by adult persons. The law, however, is becoming increasingly concerned with whether *A* has utilized a superior bargaining power to obtain better terms from *B* than would otherwise be obtained.

This is seen in the case of the seller of goods. Under the Uniform Commercial Code, the contract that he makes must not be unconscionable; and he must act in good faith, which is defined as to merchant sellers as "honesty in fact and the observance of reasonable commercial standards of fair dealing in the trade." [4]

The burden or duty of exercising good faith is also given statutory recognition in the federal Automobile Dealers' Day in Court Act, providing

[4] See UCC § 2-103(1)(b) as to good faith; § 2-314, as to warranties; § 2-603, as to duties with respect to rightfully rejected goods; and § 2-509(3), as to the transfer of risk of loss. While the provisions of the Code above noted do not apply to contracts generally, there is a growing trend of courts to extend Article 2 of the Code, which relates only to the sale of goods, to contract situations generally, on the theory that it represents the latest restating of the law of contracts made by expert scholars and the legislators of the land.

that "an automobile dealer may bring suit against (an) automobile manu-facturer . . . (to) recover the damages by him sustained . . . by reason of the failure of said automobile manufacturer . . . to act in good faith in per-forming or complying with any of the terms of the franchise (which has been given by the manufacturer to the dealer) or in terminating, compelling, or not renewing the franchise with said dealer, providing that in such suit the manufacturer shall not be barred from asserting in defense of any such action the failure of the dealer to act in good faith." By the definition in Section (1)(e) of the Act, "good faith" is significantly stated to mean "the duty of each party to any franchise, and of officers, employees, or agents thereof to act in a fair and equitable manner to each other so as to guarantee the one party freedom from coercion, intimidation, or threats of coercion or intimidation from the other party: provided, that, . . . persuasion, . . . or argument shall not be deemed to constitute lack of good faith."[5]

The operation of the unconscionability concept has already been con-sidered in Chapter 14.

§ 26:8. Social Consequences

(a) Generally. The modern law gives greater consideration to the social consequences of a private contract than was given before. Under the tradi-tional common law, no consideration was given to the social consequences of a contract beyond the narrow scope of condemning contracts that were illegal or which violated the somewhat broader scope of being contrary to public policy. In the present century, the social consequences of a contract are now an important element in determining its validity and the power of govern-ment to regulate it.

(b) Unconscionability. The social consequences of a contract are re-lated to the concept of unconscionability, although the latter concept is narrower in that it seems to carry with it some element of oppression or exploitation. Also unconscionability would appear to be thinking of the effect of the contract as between the parties, whereas social consequences has a broader view of thinking of the effect of the contract and other similar con-tracts upon society in general.

The student should not be troubled by the way in which one concept appears to flow into or blend with another.

(c) The private contract in society. The law of contracts, originally oriented to private relations between private individuals, is moving from the field of bilateral private law to multiparty societal considerations. This con-cept that no man is an island unto himself is recognized by the Supreme Court in holding that private contracts lose their private and "do-not-touch" char-

---

[5] Act of August 8, 1956, Chapter 1038, § 2; 15 United States Code 1222.

acter when they become such a common part of our way of life that society deems it necessary to regulate them. The same view that private matters become a public concern in our Twentieth Century underlies the regulation of membership in and expulsion from professional societies and labor unions; the theory being that the position they occupy in the economic pattern of the Twentieth Century takes them out of the category of fraternal or social organizations which must be left to themselves, and, to the contrary, clothes them with such a character as justifies their regulation. The same concept underlies the requirement that procedures established by trade organizations and associations be fair.

The significance of the socioeconomic setting of the contract has already been seen in the minimum wage law decisions where the Supreme Court at first held such laws unconstitutional as an improper interference with the rights of two adult contracting parties, thereafter changing its point of view to sustain such laws because of the consequences of substandard wages upon the welfare of the individual, society, and the nation.

Another aspect of this approach is society's ability to step in and interrupt the performance of the contract because of its socioeconomic consequences. See for example, the Supreme Court's sustaining the validity of mortgage moratorium laws, that is, laws delaying or postponing the enforcement of mortgage contracts because of the "needs" of society. This conclusion was particularly significant because the contracts were not illegal when made nor were they declared illegal by the moratorium laws, and this result was sustained in spite of the clear mandate of the United States Constitution that no state shall pass any law impairing the obligation of contracts. The evaluation of a contract in terms of the effect upon society is further seen in such federal legislation as the Amendment to Section 7 of the Clayton Act, by which significant mergers are prohibited not because they are illegal, but because of their potential economic danger to society.

This reevaluation of old standards is part of the general move to make modern law more "just." While no one can quarrel with this objective, it is manifest that difficulties arise when each court considers itself free to decide as it chooses, ignoring the social force favoring stability, as discussed in Chapter 23.

§ 26:9. Suits by Third Persons

(a) Generally. Originally a third person could not sue on a contract. This was based on the theory that only the parties to the contract itself could sue each other and that third persons could not acquire any right which would permit them to sue for breach of contract. The persons who were parties to the contract and were thus entitled to sue for its breach were described as being in privity.

The rule requiring privity of contract has been, to a very large degree, abandoned and persons not in privity may sue for breach of the contract on either the theory that it was intended they be benefited by the contract or on the ground that they have been harmed by its breach.

(b) Third party beneficiary contracts.

(i) *Creditor and donee beneficiaries.* The third person may be either a creditor beneficiary or a donee beneficiary. A creditor beneficiary is a creditor of the promisee whose obligation will be discharged to the extent that the promisor performs his promise. A donee beneficiary is a person to whom no legal duty was owed by the promisee and as to whom the performance of the promise is a gift. The right of the beneficiary to sue on a life insurance policy is the most common application of the principle of third party beneficiary suits.

(ii) *Incidental beneficiaries.* Although the right of a third party beneficiary to sue is now generally recognized, not everyone who benefits from the performance of a contract between others is such a beneficiary. If a city makes a contract with a contractor to pave certain streets, property owners living along those streets will naturally receive a benefit from the performance. This fact, however, does not confer upon them the status of third party beneficiaries. Accordingly, the property owners cannot sue the contractor if he fails to perform. The courts reason that such beneficiaries are merely incidentally benefited. The city contracted for the building of the streets to further the general public interest, not primarily to benefit individual property owners.

(c) Tort liability for nonperformance.

(i) *Generally.* By the general rule, a complete failure to perform gives rise only to a suit for breach of contract as above noted and does not confer a right to sue for tort whether the plaintiff is the other contracting party or a third person.

(ii) *Discharge of obligee's duty.* An exception is made to the above rule when the obligee, that is, the other party to the contract who will receive the benefit of performance, owes a duty to the third person or the general public, and the performance by the contractor will discharge that duty. Here the breach of the duty by the contractor gives rise to a tort liability in favor of the injured third person against the contractor. To illustrate, the operator of an office building owes the duty to third persons of maintaining its elevators in a safe operating condition. In order to discharge this duty the building management may make a contract with an elevator maintenance contractor. If the latter fails to perform its contract, and the plaintiff is injured because of the defective condition of an elevator, the plaintiff may sue the elevator maintenance contractor for the damages sustained.

(iii) *Partial nonperformance.* Confusion exists in the law as to the classification to be made of conduct involved when the contracting party has entered upon the performance of the contract but omits some act or measure in consequence of which harm is sustained. The problem is the same as that involved in determining when the negligent actor who omits a particular precaution has "acted" negligently or has been guilty of a negligent "omission." In many of the older cases the courts have disposed of the matter with a broad sweep by stating that no tort arises by the breach of a contract between other persons.

A strong factor in favor of no tort liability is the vast, unlimited, and unpredictable liability that a contrary rule would impose. Some courts have not deemed this factor controlling and have held water companies liable in such situations on the theory that having erected hydrants and having entered upon the performance of the contract to supply water, they caused property owners to rely on the appearance of the availability of adequate water and were therefore liable to them if that appearance was not lived up to, as by failing to maintain proper pressure or to keep hydrants in working condition.

(d) Tort liability for improper performance.

(i) *Service contract.* When the defendant contracts to perform a service for another person and his defective or improper performance causes harm to a third person, such third person may sue the contractor. This is at least true where the performance of the contract would discharge an obligation or duty which is owed to the injured plaintiff by the person dealing with the contractor.

(ii) *Repair or alteration of personal property.* When the contractor fails to perform properly his contract for the repair or alteration of an automobile or any other thing, there is a conflict of authority as to whether he is liable to a third person who is injured as the result thereof. For example, suppose that an automobile repairman negligently repairs the brakes of an automobile with the result that it does not stop in time when driven by the customer and runs into the plaintiff. Can the plaintiff sue the repairman for tort damages?

By the older view, the injured plaintiff was automatically barred because he was not a party to the contract with the repairman. That is, the privity of contract rule earlier noted in connection with product liability was applied to exclude liability. The modern view, however, emphasizes the fact that the person who makes a poor repair of the brakes is launching a dangerous instrumentality on the highway just as much as the manufacturer who manufactures an automobile with defective brakes. Both should recognize that their negligence will expose persons on the highway to an unreasonable risk of foreseeable harm. The modern view accordingly holds the negligent repairman liable to the injured third person.

INVESTMENT CORP. v. BUCHMAN

208 So.2d 291 (Fla., 1968)

Buchman and others were certified public accountants. They prepared financial statements of the condition of Belcher-Young Company. Relying on the accuracy of these statements, Investment Corporation purchased a large block of stock of the company. The statements were erroneous and Investment Corporation lost money and then sued the accountants to recover their loss.

OPINION BY LILES, C.J. . . .

The defendants, certified public accountants, had served as auditors for Belcher-Young Company and in that capacity defendants had prepared an uncertified financial statement depicting the condition of Belcher-Young as of September 30, 1963. The plaintiff desired to purchase an interest in Belcher-Young, and an agreement was made whereby plaintiff was to buy a large block of Belcher-Young stock. However, a proviso in the agreement called for Belcher-Young to provide a certified financial statement as of December 31, 1963. Furthermore, this proviso stated that if the certified statement disclosed as of December 31, 1963, had changed adversely in a material manner from its position as shown by the September 30, 1963, statement, then plaintiff could rescind the purchase.

The certified statements were subsequently prepared and forwarded to plaintiff, and plaintiff elected to stand by the transaction. In November of 1964, Belcher-Young failed financially and thereafter the shareholders of Belcher-Young received nothing for their stock. Plaintiff then brought suit against defendants asserting that it had relied upon defendants' certified statement in electing not to rescind the purchase of Belcher-Young's stock and further asserting that due to defendants' gross negligence in preparation of the statement, the financial condition of Belcher-Young was grossly misstated. . . . Plaintiff . . . alleged . . . that Belcher-Young and defendants entered into a contract to prepare the certified statement, and plaintiff was a third party beneficiary of that contract; that defendants knew plaintiff intended to rely on the certified statement and defendants owed a duty of due care to known third parties. . . . Plaintiff contends that the trial court erred in dismissing plaintiff's count which alleged that defendants violated their duty of care to plaintiff in that defendants were negligent in the preparation of the financial statement when they knew plaintiff intended to act in reliance upon this statement.

The leading case involving the duty of certified public accountants to parties with whom they were not in privity of contract is *Ultramares Corp.* v. *Touche*, 255 N.Y. 170, 174 N.E. 441, 74 A.L.R. 1139 (1931). The defendants in Ultramares had no knowledge that the statements would be shown to plaintiff, however, the defendants did know "that in the usual course of business the balance sheet when certified would be exhibited by the Stern Company to banks, creditors, stockholders, purchasers, or sellers, according to the needs of the occasion as the basis of financial dealings." *Ultramares* v.

Touche, supra, 174 N.E. at 442. The plaintiff relied on defendants' financial statement in lending money to the Stern Company. Subsequently, the corporation went bankrupt and it became apparent that the statement had portrayed the corporation as being sound when it was actually insolvent.

The New York Court of Appeals in an opinion written by Justice Cardozo held that in the absence of privity of contract the plaintiff had no right to recovery under the theory of negligence even though the acts complained of amounted to gross negligence. However, the court did permit the plaintiff to recover under the theory of fraud stating "that negligence or blindness, even when not equivalent to fraud, is none the less evidence to sustain an inference of fraud." *Ultramares* v. *Touche,* supra at 449.

In *State Street Trust Co.* v. *Ernst,* 278 N.Y. 104, 15 N.E.2d 416, 120 A.L.R. 1250 (1938), the New York Court of Appeals again had before it a case involving the duty of certified public accountants to third parties. However, in this case, unlike Ultramares, defendants knew that a certain third party intended to rely on their certified statements in deciding whether to extend credit to defendants' client. Despite this knowledge on the part of defendants, the court denied the plaintiff's claim for relief based on negligence saying:

"We have held that in the absence of a contractual relationship or its equivalent, accountants cannot be held liable for ordinary negligence in preparing a certified balance sheet even though they are aware that the balance sheet will be used to obtain credit. *Ultramares Corporation* v. *Touche,* 255 N.Y. 170, 174 N.E. 441, 74 A.L.R. 1139." *State Street Trust Co.* v. *Ernst,* supra, 15 N.E.2d at 418.

The court went on to add, however, that negligence "if sufficiently gross, may furnish evidence leading to an inference of fraud so as to impose liability for losses suffered by those who rely on the balance sheet." *State Street Trust Co.* v. *Ernst,* supra at 419. . . .

The Florida Supreme Court in commenting upon the liability of a title abstractor to third parties enunciated a rule of law which is applicable to the present issue. The court stated in *Sickler* v. *Indian River Abstract & Guaranty Co.,* 1940, 142 Fla. 528, 195 So. 195, 198, that:

"The weight of authority is that an abstractor does not render himself liable to any and every person who may be injured by reason of his negligence, ignorance, or want of skill in preparing abstracts, but that such liability exists only in favor of the person employing him or those in privity with him. The negligence or unskillfulness of an abstractor does not render him liable to the alienee, devisee, or other successor in interest employing him, or *other persons with whom there is no privity of contract.* . . ."

Plaintiff, in support of its position, relied upon *Glanzer* v. *Shepard,* 233 N.Y. 236, 135 N.E. 275, 23 A.L.R. 1425 (1922) and Section 552 of the Restatement of Torts.

In Glanzer the seller of beans hired a public weigher to weigh the goods and supply the buyer with a certified copy of the weight sheets. The weigher knew that these weight certificates would be relied upon by the buyer in paying the seller. The weigher was paid by the seller. It was later learned that the actual weight was less than that certified by the weigher and the buyer sued the weigher for the amount overpaid. In an opinion by Justice Cardozo the New York Court of Appeals said:

"We think the law imposes a duty toward buyer as well as seller in the situation here disclosed. The plaintiff's use of the certificates was not an indirect or collateral consequence of the action of the weighers. It was a consequence which, to the weighers' knowledge was the end and aim of the transaction. . . . They sent a copy to the plaintiffs for the very purpose of inducing action. All this they admit. In such circumstances, assumption of the task of weighing was the assumption of a duty to weigh carefully for the benefit of all whose conduct was to be governed. We do not need to state the duty in terms of contract or of privity. Growing out of a contract, it has none the less an origin not exclusively contractual. Given the contract and the relation, the duty is imposed by law. . . ."

Plaintiff also relies on Restatement of Torts § 552, which states:

"One who in the course of his business or profession supplies information for the guidance of others in their business transactions is subject to liability for harm caused to them by their reliance upon the information if:

(a) he fails to exercise that care and competence in obtaining and communicating the information which its recipient is justified in expecting, and

(b) the harm is suffered

(i) by the person or one of the class of persons for whose guidance the information was supplied, and

(ii) because of his justifiable reliance upon it in a transaction in which it was intended to influence his conduct or in a transaction substantially identical therewith."

Section 552 appears to be in conflict with State Street Trust and Sickler, and although we realize there are public policies in support of the arguments advanced by both plaintiff and defendants, we feel obliged to follow the precedent established by State Street Trust and Sickler. Thus, we hold that the trial court was correct in ruling that plaintiff's count failed to state a cause of action. . . .

Questions for Review

1. Analyze each opinion in this chapter in terms of the social forces involved in the decision. See § 5:5 for a list of the social forces. With respect to each opinion, explain why the prevailing social forces prevailed and why those rejected did not. In each case in which there is a dissenting opinion, also make this analysis for the dissenting opinion.

2-6. *On the basis of the social forces involved, what decision should be made in each of the following cases?*

2. *Formation of contract. Subsequent request.* An offer to sell land to the buyer was accepted. The buyer then requested the seller to make out the deed

to a third person. This was refused by the seller and then the buyer dropped the request. Later the seller refused to perform the contract and when sued for its breach raised the defense that there was no contract because of the rejection of the request to make out the deed to a third person. Was this defense valid? *Wallerius* v. *Hare,* 200 Kan. 578, 438 P.2d 65.

3. *Contracts. Indefinite.* Is the promise of an independent insurance adjuster that the insurer would pay the cost of repairs to the insured automobile, the rental of another car, and be responsible for all expenses incurred, too indefinite to be binding? *Southern Pine Superior Stud Corp.* v. *Herring,* Miss., 207 So.2d 632.

4. *Breach of contract. Lost profits.* May the seller of custom-built kitchens recover lost profits when the homeowner breaks his contract by refusing to take the kitchen if the seller cannot prove the exact cost of fabricating and installing the kitchen? *Stuart Kitchens* v. *Stevens,* 248 Md. 71, 234 A.2d 749.

5. *Insurance. Medical payments.* Where the insured has received medical payments for his injuries by virtue of the policy covering one automobile, can he recover payments for the same injuries from another insurer under a different policy? *Wyman* v. *Allstate Insurance Co.,* 29 App.Div.2d 319, 288 N.Y.S.2d 250.

6. *Termination. Notice.* The lease by a supermarket to individual stores provided that if a tenant should be in default under the terms of the lease for 10 days, the landlord could terminate the lease by giving notice to the tenant of such intent. A tenant failed to install a sprinkler system as required by the fire department and after 10 days was given notice by the landlord that the lease was terminated. The tenant claimed that the court should give him additional time, such as 20 days, in which to cure the default, because the 10-day provision was harsh and inequitable. Decide. *First National Stores* v. *Yellowstone Shopping Center,* 21 N.Y.2d 630, 290 N.Y.S.2d 721.

7-11. What social forces were involved, which prevailed, and which were defeated in the following decisions?

7. *Malpractice. Contract liability.* Where a patient contracts with a specialist, the specialist must take care of the patient. If without justification the specialist leaves the patient to the care of a resident, the specialist is liable for breach of his contract; and the specialist is not excused on the ground that the resident used reasonable care under the circumstances, because the patient by contracting with a specialist was entitled to receive a specialist's care and not merely the skill ordinarily possessed. *Alexandridis* v. *Jewett,* [C.A.5th] 388 F.2d 829.

8. *Premises liability. Covenant to repair.* Where landlord does not make any repair in breach of his covenant to repair, he is liable in tort for damages sustained by employee of tenant because of defect in floor. *Rampone* v. *Wanskuck Buildings, Inc.,* R.I., 227 A.2d 586.

9. *Insurance. Financial condition of applicant.* Insurer selling air flight insurance through vending machines is not liable to surviving heirs of passengers killed when the insured caused the plane to crash, there being no negligence liability on the theory that insurer should have screened persons purchasing flight insurance to determine suicide and murder potential. *Galanis* v. *Mercury International Insurance Underwriters,* Cal.App., 55 Cal. Rptr. 890.

10. *Service station. State certification of automobile.* Service station certifying automobile as passing state motor vehicle inspection requirements is liable to the employee of the automobile owner who was injured thereafter while driving the automobile, where the injury resulted because of a defective condition of the brakes which the service station neglected to discover, as against the contention that lack of privity barred recovery. *Buszta* v. *Souther,* R.I., 232 A.2d 396.

11. *Architect. Faulty construction.* An architect is liable to a pedestrian injured when wall fell in high wind, where the wall did not comply with the city building code, although (a) the designing of the wall had been performed by an independent contracting engineer, and (b) the work had been approved by the city inspector. *Johnson* v. *Salem Title Co.,* Ore., 425 P.2d 519.

Chapter 27

TORTS

§ 27:1. Nature of Torts

In simple terms, a tort is any civil wrong other than a breach of contract. By civil wrong, we indicate that a suit will be brought by the injured person, the plaintiff, against the wrongdoer, the defendant, as contrasted with a prosecution brought by the government against the wrongdoer for the purpose of imposing a fine or a term of imprisonment. When the tort is defined in terms of a wrong other than a breach of contract, the term is made to embrace a wide range of conduct or situations as discussed below. For the purpose of classification, distinctions may be made in terms of the theory of liability involved.

§ 27:2.   Liability-Imposing Conduct

(a) Negligence. The widest range of tort liability today arises in the field of negligence, which exists whenever the defendant had acted with less care than would be exercised by a reasonable man under the circumstances. More specifically stated, the defendant has failed to exercise that degree of care which a reasonable man would exercise under the circumstances, and such negligence is the proximate cause of harm to a person to whom the defendant owed the duty to exercise due care.

(i) *The imaginary man.* The reasonable man whose behavior is made the standard is an imaginary man. In a given case which is tried before a jury, the reasonable man becomes the ideal man as he appears to the composite or combined minds of the twelve jurors.

This reasonable man is not any one of the jurors nor an average of what the jurors would do. The law is not concerned with what the jurors would do in a like situation, for it is possible that they may be more careful or less careful than the abstract reasonable man. Likewise it is not what is done in the community, for again, the community may live above or below the standard of the reasonable man.

(ii) *Variable character of the standard.* By definition, the standard is a variable standard for it does not tell you specifically in any case what should have been done. This flexibility is confusing to everyone, in the sense that you never know the exact answer in any borderline case until after the lawsuit is over. From the standpoint of society, however, this very flexibility is desirable because it is obviously impossible to foresee every possible variation that might arise in the facts and even more impossible to keep such a code of conduct up-to-date. Imagine how different the reasonable man must act while driving today's automobile on today's superhighways than he did when he drove a model T more than a half century ago.

(iii) *Administrative difficulty.* The very elements of abstractness and flexibility that make the reasonable man concept desirable also create administrative difficulty. This is so because it is obviously difficult for the twelve people in the jury or anyone else to think of a reasonable man's standard in the abstract as unrelated to what the jurors themselves personally do or know. There is naturally a strong tendency for a juror to say "The defendant acted like a reasonable man because he did just what I would do."

(b) Intentional harm. In the more elementary forms, intentional harm involves wrongs such as a battery; an assault; intentionally causing mental distress; and intentional wrongs directed against property, such as stealing another's automobile, cutting timber from his land, or setting his house on fire. Notice that most of these "elementary" torts are also crimes.

At a slightly higher level are the torts of fraud, slander and libel, the invasion of privacy, and the intentional interference with contract rights or business relations of others.

In some of these cases, the defendant's wrong gives not only the immediate victim the right to sue but also his conduct is a tort to persons standing in certain relationships to the victim. Thus under certain circumstances, a husband can sue for an injury to his wife, or a parent can sue for an injury to the child. In the wrongful death action, the surviving group, typically the spouse, child, or parents of the person who has been killed, have a right to sue the wrongdoer for such death.

To those who may question the conclusion that legal rights exist only when they are recognized, it is worth noting that many of the torts above specified did not exist 100 to 150 years ago. In terms of liability, the action for wrongful death did not exist until created by statute in the middle of the last century. Prior to that time, the common-law rule was followed that death extinguished all claims. Now it does not. Thus before the middle of the last century, there was no right to sue for a death. Now there is such a right.

(c) Absolute liability.

(i) *Generally.* In some areas of the law, liability for harm exists without regard to whether there was any negligence or intention to cause harm. For example, in most states when a contractor blasts with dynamite and debris is hurled onto the land of another, the latter landowner may sue the contractor even though the contractor had used due care, was not negligent, and did not intend to cause the plaintiff any harm by committing an intentional trespass on the plaintiff's land.

By this concept of absolute liability, society is in effect taking a middle position between (a) liability based on moral fault and (b) illegality. That is, society is saying that the activity is so dangerous to the public that liability must be imposed even though no fault is present. Yet society will not go so far as to say that the activity is so dangerous that it must be outlawed. Instead the compromise is made to allow the activity but make it pay for its victims regardless of the circumstances under which the injuries were sustained. By virtue of statutes the area of absolute liability is expanding.

(ii) *Industrial activity*. There is generally absolute liability for harm growing out of the storage of inflammable gas and explosives in the middle of a populated city; crop dusting, where the chemical used is dangerous to life and the dusting is likely to spread on the wind; factories emitting dangerous fumes, smoke, and soot in populated areas. By statute, the concept of absolute liability has been extended to certain areas of industrial activity, the social justification being that the industry that benefits from the activity and which can the better procure insurance against loss or shift the incidence of economic loss to the consuming public should be required to bear the loss as against the employee. Specifically, this philosophy underlies workmen's compensation in which the liability of the employer is not predicated upon his fault but upon the fact that the accident or occupational disease is employment-related. Child labor statutes frequently provide for absolute liability when harm arises from a violation of its provisions. Similar provision is made by the Federal Safety Appliance Act.

In the United States there is no liability for the nonnegligent spread or origination of fire. This rule has been changed by statutes, such as those imposing liability when locomotives are not equipped with spark arresters, or when a fire is started during a dry period, or a prairie fire is intentionally started. By a decision or statute, approximately one fourth of the states have imposed the standard of absolute liability upon aircraft with respect to damage caused to persons or property on the ground.

(iii) *Consumer protection*. Pure foods statutes may impose absolute liability upon the seller of foods in favor of the ultimate consumer who is harmed by them. Under the doctrine of implied warranties and strict tort liability, decisions and statutes have imposed to a certain extent a pseudo-absolute liability on the manufacturer and on the seller of goods.

Statutes, commonly called Dram Shop Acts, which prohibit the sale of intoxicating liquors to persons who are visibly intoxicated, may impose absolute liability upon the seller in favor of an innocent third person who is injured by the intoxicated customer to whom the seller has made prohibited sales.

MAGRINE v. KRASNICA

94 N.J.S. 228, 227 A.2d 539 (1967)

Magrine was treated by Krasnica, a dentist. He used a hypodermic needle that broke for no apparent reason, leaving a fragment which had to be removed from her gum by surgery. Magrine believed the needle had been sold to the dentist by a supply house owned by Spector. Krasnica did not know from which of several houses he had purchased it. Magrine sued Krasnica and Spector for the damages she sustained.

OPINION BY LYNCH, J.S.C. . . .

In all of our recent cases strict liability was imposed (except with respect to a retail dealer) upon those who were in "a better position" in the sense that they *created* the danger (in making the article) . . . or possessed a better capacity or expertise to control, inspect, and discover the defect . . . than the party injured. In these respects the dentist here was in no better position than plaintiff. He neither created the defect nor possessed any better capacity or expertise to discover or correct it than she.

It is further very clear that strict liability was imposed in our New Jersey cases for the *essentially basic reason* that those so held liable put the product "in the stream of trade and promote its purchase by the public." . . . Defendant dentist did not put the needle in the stream of commerce or promote its purchase.

It may be logically argued that the foregoing analysis does not effectively distinguish defendant from the retail dealer who, for example, sells food in a sealed container, or otherwise has no opportunity to discover a defect in the article he sells, and who nevertheless is liable for breach of warranty. . . . In this respect such retail dealer is in no better position to discover the defect than the dentist here. Nevertheless, the situations are distinct. In the first place, the Uniform Sales Act and the Uniform Commercial Code, *legislative* enactments, apply to sales and there can be no judicial construction which could deny a warranty against a retail seller. . . .

We must consider, also, the consequences if we were to adopt the rule of strict liability here. The same liability, in principle, should then apply to any user of a tool, other equipment or any article which, through no fault of the user, breaks due to a latent defect and injures another. It would apply to any physician, artisan, or mechanic and to any user of a defective article —even to a driver of a defective automobile. In our view, no policy consideration positing strict liability justifies application of the doctrine in such cases. No more should it here. . . .

[On appeal, the above decision was affirmed, 100 N.J.S. 223, 241 A.2d 637 (1968):]

PER CURIAM. . . .

The sole issue presented here is whether a dentist is strictly liable to a patient injured by a defective instrument used in the course of treatment. In our opinion, the imposition of liability on the defendant-dentist cannot be justified on the basis of any of the accepted policies which underlie the doctrine of strict liability as it is presently understood. Nor are we persuaded that that doctrine should be extended under the circumstances of this case so as to render the defendant-dentist liable without fault for a defect in a needle which he merely purchased and used.

DISSENTING OPINION BY BOTTER, J.S.C. . . .

Plaintiff does not charge defendant with negligence, but asserts strict liability in tort, relying on *Henningsen* v. *Bloomfield Motors, Inc.*, 32 N.J. 358, 161 A.2d 69, 75 A.L.R.2d 1 (1960); *Santor* v. *A. & M. Karagheusian,*

Inc., 44 N.J. 52, 207 A.2d 305, 16 A.L.R.3d 670 (1965); *Cintrone* v. *Hertz Truck Leasing & Rental Service,* 45 N.J. 434, 212 A.2d 769 (1965); and *Schipper* v. *Levitt & Sons, Inc.,* 44 N.J. 70, 207 A.2d 314 (1965).

The trial court denied recovery. Strict liability was refused because the dentist was engaged in a profession, not a large-scale business; he was not a manufacturer or supplier of the needle, but a user of it; he could not discover a latent defect in the needle; and precedent in this state has not yet applied the doctrine beyond manufacturers (Henningsen and Santor, supra), retailers (Henningsen, supra), suppliers such as rental companies (Cintrone, supra) and mass producers of homes (Schipper, supra). The majority of this court affirms.

I disagree with the views of my colleagues. As between an innocent patient and a dentist who causes injury by using a defective instrument the law should require the loss to be borne by the dentist even if he is not negligent.

The issue posed is as old as jurisprudence: when an innocent person is injured through the inadvertent conduct of another, who should bear the loss? The answer has varied with the epoch and environment. From ancient times until the 19th Century, the answer given generally was in favor of strict liability. Thereafter, with some exceptions, the basic rule has been to deny recovery against a defendant who is free of negligence. In the 20th Century no liability without fault has been the basic premise, but it has been replaced through legislation by strict liability for industrial accidents (workmen's compensation) and for other specific activities, such as ground damage by airplanes (N.J.S.A. 6:2-7) and dog bites (R.S. 4:19-16, N.J.S.A.). In addition, the courts have restored strict liability in a broad area where a defective product or device has caused injury.

We may ask ourselves what objectives did the law seek in fashioning these rules of liability? In primitive cultures vengeance against the offending thing or person, not compensation, was a primary objective. . . . If a man fell from a tree and died the tree was delivered to his relatives or was chopped to pieces. . . . Liability was visited upon the offending source, animate or inanimate, as well as persons connected with it, as if evil inhered in the instrument of harm. . . . The reason may have been revenge or superstition or fear of an instrument of evil. It may have seemed just that "the damage which we have inflicted on others must be made good." . . .

This sweeping rule caught all harm-doers; but the difference between intentional and accidental harm was recognized at an early age in criminal law for the purpose of punishment [1] and in civil wrongs for the purpose of mitigating damages. If a man's ox was killed by an ox whose owner was ignorant of its propensity "to push in time past," then "They shall sell the live ox, and divide the money of it; and the dead ox also they shall divide." Exodus 21:35, 36. This is one solution where both parties are blameless:

---

[1] Misadventure and self-defense were grounds for mercy or pardon in a criminal case. . . . Exile to a city of refuge, but not death, was decreed for one who "killeth his neighbour ignorantly, whom he hated not in time past"; and this rule clearly included accidental killing. Deuteronomy 19:4, 5; Numbers 35:15-25. Lack of knowledge of prior harmful proclivities excused an owner for a death caused by his ox. Exodus 21:28-30.

have them share the loss. This approach has some parallel to workmen's compensation laws of the 1900's and to various suggestions made since the 1920's to compensate victims of motor vehicle accidents by a strict liability plan.

In the 19th Century fault—the failure to act as an ordinary prudent man—became the central condition of liability for unintentional harm. . . . The purpose that was championed was the right of individuals and corporations to act freely and unburdened unless harm is done through their negligence. Some areas of strict liability continued at common law, but the spirit of laissez faire and the momentum of the industrial revolution prevailed. "We must have factories, machinery, dams, canals and railroads," the court said in *Losee* v. *Buchanan,* 51 N.Y. 476, 484-485 (Ct.App. 1873), denying recovery without proof of negligence for damage to property caused by an exploding boiler. "By becoming a member of civilized society," the court said, "natural rights" must be surrendered, but a benefit is gained through the surrender by others of the same rights. "I hold my property subject to the risk that it may be unavoidably or accidentally injured by those who live near me; and as I move about upon the public highways and in all places where other persons may lawfully be, I take the risk of being accidentally injured in my person by them without fault on their part." In 1881 Holmes shared these views; however, he also suggested that deterrence of harmful behavior was a product of the rule that makes fault a condition of liability. . . .

In those days the problem was considered "on the assumption that plaintiff and defendant were alone involved and that what happened between them was the real issue—that tort liability was paid for out of the defendant's own pocketbook." . . . The irony is that the fault rule, which was partly inspired by the desire to protect the growth of industry, was undone by the results of that very growth, namely, an increase in the harmful capacity of mechanized facilities, the inevitability of accidents in their use and the consequent toll of human life and losses.[2] The expansion of the economy, the broadening of distribution of goods and services and the new pervasiveness of liability insurance are all part of the environment for the tort law of the 20th Century. In this environment new views have taken shape about the objectives of the law. What has become dominant in our time is the need to compensate victims of normal conditions of daily life. "There is a tendency to revive the idea of liability without fault not only in the frame of wide responsibility for agencies employed, but in placing upon an enterprise the burden of repairing injuries, without fault of him who conducts it, which are an incident to the undertaking. . . . There is a strong and growing tendency, where there is no blame on either side, to ask in view of the exigencies of social justice, who can best bear the loss." . . .

Assuring compensation for victims of accidents is a matter of public policy which legislatures have promoted in various ways. Very recently the courts have come to serve this purpose by expanding liability without proof of negligence in the area of "product liability." This result followed naturally

---

[2] In World War II 313,000 soldiers were killed, but 386,000 people were killed in accidents during the same period. . . .

the change in economic and social organization. So long as direct sales brought goods from a manufacturer to a consumer the law had little difficulty in affording relief in contract or in tort. When the process of manufacturing and distribution became extended and diversified, determining liability seemed more complicated. In contract the requirement of privity insulated the obligor on the belief that business transactions would become treacherous if liability were extended to persons beyond the immediate parties; and in tort, arising from contractual relations, the same fear of creating uncertain burdens was used to limit the scope of the duty of care to the immediate parties in the transaction. . . .

With changes in production and marketing methods the courts looked for techniques to extend liability in favor of the ultimate consumer. The courts came to realize that the public interest required protection against defects in products which consumers must buy or use and against which they are helpless to protect themselves. . . . Representations of quality, express or implied, were held to run in favor of the consumer. The courts used various devices to overcome lack of privity, such as implied agency, third-party beneficiary and the like. . . . Intricacies in the law of sales involving privity, warranties and disclaimer rights forced the courts to turn to the law of torts for a solution. . . .

Through the Henningsen, Santor, Cintrone, and Schipper cases, supra, our Supreme Court has expressed the principles on which the doctrine of strict liability in tort is based. "The demands of social justice," the court said in Henningsen, supra, 32 N.J. at p. 384, 161 A.2d at p. 83, require a rule of law that holds manufacturers and dealers liable for a defect in an automobile which causes injury to a consumer who, "has neither the opportunity nor the capacity to inspect or to determine the fitness of an automobile for use. . . ." In Santor, supra, 44 N.J. at pp. 65-66, 207 A.2d at p. 312, the court pointed out that the obligation is "an enterprise liability" [3] that does not depend upon "the intricacies of the law of sales" and that this "strict liability in tort is not conditioned upon advertising to promote sales." Cintrone, supra, makes it clear that there is no reason to restrict the rule to sales transactions. The obligation is implied in law, "as an incident of a transaction because one party to the relationship is in a better position than the other to know and control the condition of the chattel . . . *and to distribute the losses* which may occur because of a dangerous condition the chattel possesses." . . .

The injured patient should have the option of suing the dentist directly. It is the dentist with whom plaintiff has dealt and in whose hands and confidence the patient has put herself. It may be more difficult to sue a manufacturer or supplier located in a distant state or a foreign country. The dentist chose the instrument. The dentist is in a better position to know and prove the identity of the manufacturer or distributor. If he cannot, the patient should not be denied recovery on that account. The dentist should also know the quality of the instrument and the reliability of his source of supply. This rule

---

[3] "A new law of enterprise liability is in the making." Ehrenzweig, Negligence Without Fault, p. 2 (1951).

may encourage greater caution in purchasing equipment and examining for defects. . . .

Shifting the loss from *A* to *B* may not produce a net gain for society as a whole, but distribution of the loss does. . . . Liability insurance is recognized as a means of distributing losses among the group involved in risk-producing activity. . . . But the trial judge agreed . . . that insurance cannot and should not be used "to determine whether the group shall bear them (losses) in the first instance—and whether, for example, consumers shall be compelled to accept substantial price increases on everything they buy in order to compensate others for their misfortunes." [4] . . . The argument is unrealistic and unpersuasive. . . .

98.8 percent of all payments for motor vehicle injury claims are received from insured sources. It is pointless to say that those who purchase goods should not be compelled to pay an item of cost for insurance to protect others. The protection is for the whole group. No one knows which consumer will be injured. The cost paid by each consumer assures his own satisfaction of a judgment if he gets one. The fact is that through the cost of goods and services consumers today do pay indirectly for insurance covering losses caused by the negligent activities of their suppliers. If this is just, granting consumer protection against defective products cannot be unjust.

The total compensation awarded for accidental loss by reason of tort liability and workmen's compensation is $3,178,000,000 annually. . . . These losses would be devastating without loss distribution. Corporations (such as some public utilities) which are large enough to insure themselves distribute the loss to the public through the price of goods and services. Businessmen, professionals and individuals, who have sufficient assets to protect, are likely to carry insurance under existing law. It must be remembered that even with strict liability the exposure to liability for negligence continues as before. The extension of strict liability for defective goods and utensils merely expands the concept of tort liability. It has been called "negligence without fault." . . . Those who do not carry insurance and are judgment proof will probably be unaffected by this rule of law.

Insurance plays another role in the formulation of a desirable rule. It interferes with the achievement of the objectives sought by the fault principle. An injuror was to pay damages because he was negligent. With insurance, however, the negligent man pays no damages, although he pays for his insurance. The loss is shared by all who insure with the same company, or by its stockholders or by those who are participants in the activity. It was also believed that the threat of liability for negligence would encourage prudent conduct. The existence of insurance diminishes this threat. Moreover, the strict liability rule does not discourage prudence but may actually encourage examination for defects which are not obvious. Workmen's Compensation

---

[4] Similarly, in 1881, Holmes said it was no more justifiable for a man to indemnify a neighbor against injury from his faultless acts than it would be to require him to insure his neighbor against lightning. . . . Holmes derided the idea that the state might insure its citizens against accidents and distribute the burden amongst all citizens as well as provide "a pension for paralytics, and state aid for those who suffered in person or estate from tempest or wild beasts." But the state has come to do these very things in the form of medicare, disaster aid and unsatisfied judgment funds.

laws have spurred safety consciousness by employers whose insurance rates depend upon loss experience. . . . Insurance companies themselves have applied some of their resources to safety goals. . . . In any case, the threat of liability for fault continues where strict liability applies. Lastly, the fear that lawful activities and growing industry would be unduly burdened by liability without fault is minimized by the loss-spreading effect of insurance.

Occasionally we are told that it violates a natural sense of justice to require a defendant to pay damages when he is not at fault, . . . answering current proposals for completely abolishing fault as a basis for liability in motor vehicle accident cases. . . . In my view our sense of justice is better served by the principle that holds a dentist accountable for injuries caused by a defective instrument which he has selected and used. The risk of harm to which an innocent patient is exposed by a defective instrument far exceeds the risk of burden which the dentist is asked to bear. The point may be made by reference to the automobile. . . . It seems more unjust to leave the loss with the victim of an accident caused by a defective instrumentality which has the potential for harm. It does not offend our sense of justice to place the loss on the one responsible for the instrument. The law has done this very thing throughout its history. Justice requires only that we apply the rule in appropriate cases. A retailer who sells a can of beans containing a latent defect is no more culpable than a dentist who uses an instrument with a latent defect. The patient probably places more reliance upon the dentist than he does on the retailer. Yet in the case of a sale the legislature has expressed the public policy of our state to compensate the victim by holding the seller to a warranty of fitness for use despite his blamelessness. It is not unjust to hold a dentist to the same responsibility. . . .

In France liability would attach in a case of this kind. Under Art. 1384 of the Civil Code an individual is liable for damage caused by the act of things in his charge, and this is interpreted to apply absolute liability for accidental injury due to a defect in the thing, such as a fracture of a metal part. Esmein, "Liability in French Law for Damages Caused by Motor Vehicle Accidents," 2 Am.J.Comp.L. 156, 158 (1953); Conard, supra, at p. 467. In England there are several cases in which recovery has been allowed for defective materials furnished as part of service contracts. In *G. H. Myers & Co.* v. *Brent Cross Service Co.,* (1934) 1 K.B. 46, 150 L.T.R. 96 (1933) the court held that if an automobile repairman selects the supplier of a connecting rod he is liable for damage caused by a defect in the rod which he installed in a motor. In *Watson* v. *Buckley,* (1940) 1 All E.R. 174 (K.B., 1939) plaintiff was allowed recovery against Mrs. Buckley, a hairdresser, for dermatitis resulting from a defective hair dye. The court held that there was an implied warranty from Mrs. Buckley that the dye was fit for use on plaintiff's hair, although she is not held to have warranted that the dye would work well or produce a given shade of color. In *Dodd* v. *Wilson* (1946) 2 All E.R. 691 (K.B.) a veterinary surgeon was held liable for injury caused by defective serum which defendant had purchased and injected into plaintiff's cattle. The court held that it was an implied "condition" in the contract between the parties that defendant would furnish a substance reasonably fit for the required purpose. The court reasoned that if the serum had been sold to plaintiff and plaintiff had used it himself, recovery would have been allowed under the Sale of Goods Act. Accordingly, the court saw no reason why the same obligation should not apply when the materials were furnished as part of a service. . . .

Courts should abandon the search for the qualities of a sale in a transaction and should apply strict liability in nonsales cases by analogous reasoning. . . .

Defendant's brief states that there is a "lack of scholarly comment" supporting the cause of action. It is true that few writers have focused on the specific area of service transactions as distinguished from sales, leases and bailments. However, I know of no academic comment opposing the application of strict liability to this type of case. . . . Significantly, however, most current scholarly comment urges the total abolition of the negligence-fault principle in accidental injury cases. . . . The scholars, therefore, go far beyond the needs of this case.

The law of torts should seek to compensate the injured, to encourage safety practices and to distribute losses justly. . . . These objectives may be taken to express the needs of justice. In my view these objectives are advanced by granting plaintiff an award in this case. Dentistry as an enterprise should pay its own way. Denying compensation is to require an injured person who bears the loss alone to subsidize the risk-creating activities by which others profit.

For the foregoing reasons strict liability in tort should apply to a dentist who injures his patient by a latently defective instrument.

§ 27:3. Interference with Contract

(a) Generally. The tort law relating to interference with contracts and other economic relationships has increased greatly in recent years, as the result of the law's seeking to impose upon the marketplace higher ethical standards to prevent the oppression of victims of "improper" practices. In general terms, when the defendant interferes with and brings about the breach of a contract between a third person and the plaintiff, the circumstances may be such that the plaintiff has an action in tort against the defendant for interfering with his contractual relations. Likewise, the plaintiff may have such a claim for the defendant's interfering with performance by the plaintiff of his contract.

Any lawful contract may be the heart of an action for interference with contractual relations. It is immaterial whether it relates to the performance of personal services or labor.

(b) Contracts terminable at will. The fact that a contract is terminable at will does not deprive it of the right to protection from interference. While by hypothesis it is true that the defendant could terminate the agreement whenever he chose, the fact remains that there was no reason to believe that he would have terminated the agreement in the absence of the action or urging of the defendant. That is, the defendant has interfered with the

great likelihood that the third person would continue to perform for the benefit of the plaintiff, as he had originally agreed to do.

(c) Prospective contracts. In addition to protecting existing contracts from intentional interference, it is also held that there is tort liability based upon acts intentionally committed to prevent the making of a contract.

To illustrate, an action may be brought for slander of title where the malicious false statements of the defendant as to the plaintiff's ownership of property scared a buyer away and prevented the plaintiff from making the sale. In recent years the concept of protection from interference with expected economic gain has been expanded to protect prospective or possible contracts relating to all subjects.

HARRIS v. PERL

41 N.J. 455, 197 A.2d 359 (1964)

A real estate broker brought a prospective buyer and the owner of a house into negotiations for the sale of the house. Later in the course of the negotiations the buyer learned through an officer of a bank that the bank had acquired title to the property in part payment of the owner's debt to the bank. The buyer made a secret offer directly to the bank for the purchase of the property at $125,000 free of brokerage to anyone. This was accepted by the bank. The broker sued the buyer for what would have been the commissions on $125,000. The buyer raised the defense that (1) at the time the buyer dealt with the bank the broker was not entitled to commissions as the parties had not agreed on a price, (2) the bank had never dealt with or recognized the broker as acting in the transaction, and (3) the sale to the bank would never have been made if commissions had been allowed because the bank would not have gone below $125,000 net and the buyer would not have paid more than that, so that the broker could not recover for the breach of a contract that never was, and never would have been if commissions were to be paid.

OPINION BY WEINTRAUB, C.J. . . .

Plaintiff, Florence Harris, is a licensed real estate broker. Knowing that defendant Cronin wished to sell his home, plaintiff suggested the property to the defendants Perl. Plaintiff arranged with Cronin for inspection of the property by the Perls and they visited the premises on three occasions, June 5, July 2, and July 18, 1959. In negotiations through plaintiff, Cronin came down from a demand of $175,000 to $135,000, while the Perls moved from an offer of $100,000 to $125,000, at which point Perl told plaintiff that if she was "a smart girl," she would reduce her commission.

Meanwhile, on July 2, the defendant Union County Trust Company recorded a deed from Cronin to it, dated May 26. The deed probably was not delivered until on or after June 22. It appears that Cronin and his father were indebted to the bank for some $600,000, secured by a mortgage on

a number of properties including the one in question and that the conveyance was made to satisfy that obligation in part. By an agreement dated
June 22, the Cronins were permitted to remain in possession on a rental
basis until December 31, with the express understanding that the bank could
show the property to interested buyers at all times. Thus Cronin was the
owner during only part of the period of the negotiations.

On September 3, Mrs. Cronin telephoned plaintiff. According to plaintiff,
Mrs. Cronin said she felt her husband would accept $125,000 if the Perls
were still willing to pay that sum. Mrs. Cronin says she called only to find
out if the property was or would be sold because she had the problem of
enrollment of her children for the ensuing school year. Whatever the conversation, plaintiff that day telephoned Perl, who abruptly said he was too
busy to talk with her but would after the Labor Day weekend. In fact Perl
did not intend any further discussion. The reason was that, having learned
the day before through a Dr. Wallach that the bank had title, Perl had
hurriedly submitted an offer directly to the bank for $125,000, free of
brokerage to anyone. A contract on that basis was signed by the bank on
September 4, the day after plaintiff's call.

Plaintiff learned of the contract when she telephoned Mrs. Perl on
September 8, the day after Labor Day. It was then that plaintiff discovered
that Cronin had conveyed to the bank. Prior thereto she knew only that the
bank held the mortgage and that a *lis pendens* indicated foreclosure proceedings had been instituted in 1957, but there was no reason for plaintiff to
suppose that Cronin could not complete a sale. . . .

The issues as between plaintiff and the Perls are (1) whether they
breached a duty owing to plaintiff, and (2) whether the breach in fact deprived plaintiff of commissions on the sale. The Appellate Division did not
decide the first question, saying that although "the Perls doubtless treated
plaintiff shabbily," it could not find the bank would have recognized her as a
broker if the Perls had given her a chance to approach the bank and hence
there was no injury. In this connection the Perls had also urged that, since
they would not have gone above $125,000 and the bank would not have
taken less than that sum net to it, there would never have been a sale if
the bank had given plaintiff a brokerage agreement, and accordingly plaintiff
was not hurt. . . .

It should be stressed that plaintiff was not a meddlesome interloper. She
did not intrude upon either the Perls or Cronin. The Perls wanted her to find
a home for them. Indeed, through the efforts of plaintiff the Perls were
actively considering still another property only a few days before they quietly
submitted their offer to the bank through Dr. Wallach. Cronin too was interested in making a deal and of course expected plaintiff to receive a commission if a deal was made.

And although plaintiff had no arrangement with the bank, we are satisfied one could readily have been made. The bank was not opposed to dealing
through a broker. One of its officers testified the directors had authorized
a sale at "a net to us of $125,000" and that he told Dr. Wallach "if there
were no brokerage fees involved, that it would be $125,000." In fact the
bank had already asked a firm of brokers to try to move the property. And
Perl doubtless believed the bank would deal with plaintiff, for when she

telephoned him on September 3, he put her off, lest she learn of the bank's interest before a deal was made and spoil his plan. And we note also that Dr. Wallach objected to the inclusion in the contract of a standard clause used by the bank's attorney to the effect that there was no broker, explaining, without however disclosing plaintiff's identity, that someone had shown the property to the Perls at some time in the past. As a result the clause was changed to read:

"The purchaser represents that at no time did any real estate broker show the premises to him on behalf of Union County Trust Company, the present owner, and so far as he has knowledge, no one is entitled to be paid real estate commissions on said sale."

The negotiations over the form of the contract thus further revealed that the bank had no policy against sales through brokers and that the emissary of the Perls knew that was so. And finally, the Perls were the only prospect and the bank was anxious to sell.

We think it perfectly clear that the bank would have recognized plaintiff as broker if she had sought recognition before the identity of her prospect was revealed. The question then is whether a person who accepts the services of a broker may surreptitiously appropriate those services to his own profit by buying directly from the owner and justify that action on the ground that the broker had not established some relationship with the seller.

The law protects a man in the pursuit of his livelihood. True, he cannot complain of every disappointment; others too may further their equal interests, and if the means are fair, the advantage should remain where success has put it. But if the act complained of does not rest upon some legitimate interest or if there is sharp dealing or overreaching or other conduct below the behavior of fair men similarly situated, the ensuing loss should be redressed.

Hence one who unjustifiably interferes with the contract of another is guilty of a wrong. And since men usually honor their promises no matter what flaws a lawyer can find, the offender should not be heard to say the contract he meddled with could not have been enforced. "Accordingly, it usually is held that contracts which are voidable by reason of the Statute of Frauds, formal defects, lack of consideration, lack of mutuality, or even uncertainty of terms, still afford a basis for a tort action when the defendant interferes with their performance." . . .

Protection is not limited to contracts already made. The law protects also a man's interest in reasonable expectations of economic advantage. . . .

[As stated in an earlier case:] "It is no answer to say that the contractual relations were not complete because [the plaintiff] had not gone through the formality of signing the agreement. This status should not stand in the way of the existence of the right of action. Treating the case (on the facts here) in terms of unlawful interference with prospective economic advantage, the cause of action exists. . . . 'By analogy to interference with existing contractual relations, tort liability has been imposed for interference with prospective advantage.' . . . 'In a civilized community, which recognizes the right of private property among its institutions, the notion is intolerable that a man should be protected by the law in the enjoyment of property, once it is acquired, but left unprotected by the law in his efforts to acquire

it. . . . ,' . . . 'since a large part of what is most valuable in modern life depends upon the "probable expectancies," as social and industrial life becomes
more complex the courts must do more to discover, define, and protect them
from undue interference.' . . ."

With these principles in mind, let us turn to the present scene. The
economic facts and the expectations of fair men with respect to real estate
brokerage are clear enough. The role of the broker is to bring buyer and
seller together at terms agreeable to both, and both know the broker expects
to earn a commission from the seller if he succeeds. The broker's stock in
trade is his knowledge of what property is or can be made available and
who is or can be interested in a given parcel. The inherent uniqueness of
each parcel distinguishes the real estate broker from the salesman of automobiles or cutlery, for the very act of identifying real property or the
prospective purchaser is itself both a rendition of a valuable service and an
opportunity for a dishonest man to make off with the broker's stock in trade.
In a practical world the broker must trust that those who seek or willingly
accept his services will not cheat him of the fruit of his industry. The courts
should protect him from that abuse, except insofar as the countervailing
policy of the statute of frauds may insulate the owner from liability.

Of course a broker must accept competition from other brokers. . . .
Frequently, especially when property is listed widely, several brokers will
try to interest the same prospect. In such circumstances, a dispute as to who
was the procuring cause should be fought out with the owner, and the
purchaser should not be burdened with the quarrel in the absence of fraudulent conduct on his part. But if the purchaser beats the broker out of his
commission by buying from the owner directly or through a front, thus
appropriating to himself the value of the services of the broker, he should pay
for that mischief. . . .

In *Louis Kamm, Inc.* v. *Flink,* 113 N.J.L. 582, 175 A. 62, 99 A.L.R. 1,
the complaint alleged that plaintiff broker revealed the name of his prospect
to an officer of the owner corporation with the express understanding that
the disclosure was in confidence, and that the officer funneled the information
to his brother who with others closed the deal and obtained the commission.
The court held the complaint was sufficient. Although there an express pledge
of confidence was alleged, the court pointed out that a like obligation may be
implied in appropriate circumstances. . . .

And so here, when the Perls accepted plaintiff's services, it was with the
obligation which all decent men would recognize, that they would not line
their purse with the money value of those services. It is of no moment that
Cronin was not the agent of the bank and hence plaintiff had no authorization from the record owner. That fact provided an opportunity for overreaching rather than a justification for it. As we pointed out above, the law
protects not only contracts but also the reasonable expectations of economic
gain. In these circumstances fair play would require a prospective purchaser
to permit the broker to seek recognition by the owner, unenticed by the
purchaser's offer to deal directly. As we have already said, we have no doubt
the bank would have dealt with plaintiff, but the Perls did not give her
that opportunity. More than that, Perl lured plaintiff from stumbling upon

the truth by deceitfully saying he would discuss the sale after the Labor Day weekend.

The remaining point is that both the bank and the Perls were adamant at $125,000 and hence, if plaintiff had been recognized by the bank, there would have been no deal. *Ergo,* no damage. It must be noted at once that if a wrongdoer could advance this position, it could be equally a haven for a seller whose brokerage obligation is plainly set forth in a written contract, since he too could disclaim liability for anything beyond nominal damages upon the premise that he and the buyer would never have reached agreement if the price to be paid included the amount of the promised commission.

Defendants' point is unsound. Even under a brokerage contract carefully drawn from a seller's point of view, the broker earns his commission when title is closed. Here that event occurred and hence plaintiff established the final ingredient of her claim. What the Perls seek to do is to generate an uncertainty which but for their . . . assertion would not be in the case. They ask that the Court accept their belief that under no circumstances would they have budged from the figure of $125,000. The claim, of course, is wholly hypothetical and even the Perls cannot really know how high they would have gone. The question is whether a wrongdoer should be permitted to avoid real damages by raising an issue made hypothetical by his very wrong. We think he should not. The same contention was rejected in *Johnson* v. *Gustafson,* 201 Minn. 629, 277 N.W. 252, 255 (Supp.Ct. 1938): "It seems to us that Clarity's assertion that he would not have paid more than he did ($5,700) in any event comes with poor grace. He was willing to and did concoct a fraudulent scheme. He procured the necessary assistance to bring about a result which, had it not been discovered, would have given him an advantage to the extent of the commission plaintiff was in common honesty entitled to receive. No man should be permitted to reap a profitable crop from seed of the kind here used."

§ 27:4. What Constitutes Interference with Contract

(*a*) *Generally.* The interference with the plaintiff's contract may be an interference with the performance by a third person of his contract with the plaintiff or it may be an interference with the plaintiff in his performance of his contract with another person. That is, the defendant may be either (1) persuading or causing another person to break his contract, or (2) preventing or hindering the plaintiff from performing his contract.

(*b*) *Action directed to third person.* There is a tort when the defendant persuades a person who has a contract with the plaintiff to break that contract and to render to the defendant the performance which should have been rendered to the plaintiff. For example, the defendant persuades the superintendent of the plaintiff to breach his contract with the plaintiff and to become the superintendent of the defendant's plant.

If it can be concluded that the defendant has acted maliciously for the purpose of interfering with the plaintiff's contract, liability can be easily found. The difficulty arises where the defendant did not actively seek to persuade the third person to breach his contract but merely made an offer, or informed him of a job opening, which the third person chose to accept, thereby incidentally and necessarily repudiating his contract with the plaintiff.

The action of the defendant directed to the third person may also be such as to make it difficult or impossible for him to perform his contract with the plaintiff, as contrasted with the pattern just discussed in which the third person chooses voluntarily to break his contract with the plaintiff. So it has been held that where the defendant refused to supply a materialman who contracted with the plaintiff to deliver goods to the plaintiff and thereby prevented the middleman from performing his contract to supply the plaintiff with such goods, the plaintiff could recover from the defendant for such "interference."

§ 27:5. Requirement of Malice

(a) Generally. There is no liability for interference with contractual relations unless such interference be deemed "malicious." The term "malicious" is misleading because it may mean either (1) acting with actual malice, that is, the desire to harm for the sheer sake of causing harm, or (2) the infliction of harm only as a matter of competition in order to advance the actor's personal interest, rather than to inflict injury on the plaintiff for its own sake. The fact that the defendant knows that he is harming the plaintiff by his actions is not an easy solution to the problem for the defendant may still be not liable when he is acting to further his own interests, even though he is well aware that by doing so he will interfere with the plaintiff's contract. The problem is even more acute when, as in the case of a striking labor union, the defendant union acts for the purpose of advancing its own interests and does so by intentionally interfering with the performance of the plaintiff employer's contracts as by striking and making it impossible for him to fill such contracts.

(b) Advancement of defendant's legitimate interests. The mere fact that the defendant's voluntary conduct has the effect of interfering with the plaintiff's contract does not establish that the defendant is liable to the plaintiff. Conversely, when the defendant is acting for what the law regards as his own legitimate economic end, the fact that there results a breach of contract between a third person and the plaintiff does not impose liability on the defendant.

The legitimate self-interest, the existence of which protects the defendant from liability, may be a duty on the part of the defendant to act to protect others. Accordingly, an officer of a corporation or an employee is not liable for inducing a breach of contract when in good faith he persuades the corporation to refuse to recognize the contract, when it is his responsibility to give such advice and he honestly believes that there is no existing contract or that there is a valid defense to the contract.

WILSON v. McCLENNY

262 N.C. 121, 136 S.E.2d 569 (1964)

Before a new corporation, Gateway Life Insurance Co., was formed, an agreement was made between the plaintiff, Wilson, and the defendants, McClenny and others, that the plaintiff should be the president of Gateway and the defendants should be directors and that all should acquire certain amounts of stock. The plaintiff was hired by the corporation as president in consequence of this agreement but on a yearly contract. When the contract came up for renewal, the directors who had signed this agreement and the other directors voted against renewal of the contract because the plaintiff had a serious drinking problem and had voluntarily committed himself to an institution for inebriates for 21 days. The plaintiff sued the defendants for breach of the contract and in tort because, as directors, they had interfered with his contract by voting against its renewal when, in fact, his drinking had not interfered with the conduct of the business. From a judgment against Wilson as to both claims, he appealed.

Opinion by Sharp, J. . . .

The first question presented by this appeal is whether the agreement . . . was void as against public policy. This preincorporation contract between the parties was intended to serve as a stockholders' agreement after incorporation. Such agreements are governed by the general principles of contract law. . . . Whatever may have been the legal status of such an agreement prior to the enactment of the Business Corporation Act of 1955, . . . it is clear that this contract is not now prohibited by law. Under G.S. § 55-24(a) the board of directors is given the right to manage the affairs of the corporation "[s]ubject to the provisions of the charter, the bylaws *or agreements* between the shareholders otherwise lawful. . . ." (Italics ours.) G.S. § 55-73(a) permits two or more shareholders of a North Carolina corporation to enter into a written agreement to vote the shares held by them as a unit for the election of directors. This section provides: "An otherwise valid contract between two or more shareholders that the shares held by them shall be voted as a unit for the election of directors shall, if in writing and signed by the parties thereto, be valid and enforceable as between the parties thereto, but for not longer than ten years from the date of its execution. Nothing herein shall impair the privilege of the corporation to treat the shareholders of record as entitled to vote the shares standing in their names, as provided in G.S. § 55-59 nor impair the power of a court to determine voting rights as provided in G.S. § 55-71."

Likewise, the contract to elect plaintiff president of the corporation at a specified salary is not subject to the usual objection that it interferes with the discretion of the directors in view of the provisions of G.S. § 55-73(c), to wit: "An agreement between all or less than all of the shareholders, whether solely between themselves or between one or more of them and a party who is not a shareholder, is not invalid, as between the parties thereto, on the ground that it so relates to the conduct of the affairs of the corporation as to interfere with the discretion of the board of directors, but the making of such an agreement shall impose upon the shareholders who are parties thereto the liability for managerial acts that is imposed by this chapter upon directors."

Thus, the Business Corporation Act clearly aligns North Carolina with the majority of jurisdictions which hold that a contract entered into between corporate stockholders by which they agree to vote their stock in a specified manner—including agreements for the election of directors and corporate officers—is not invalid unless it is inspired by fraud or will prejudice the other stockholders. . . .

The rationale of this rule is aptly stated in *Mansfield* v. *Lang,* 293 Mass. 386, 200 N.E. 110, a case involving facts very similar to those here: ". . . [S]uch agreements as the one in the case at bar, even if regarded as open to the objection that they pledge in advance the action of officers or stockholders, may be sustained on the ground of the practical necessity that it would be impossible to organize a corporation if its proper management were not assured."

A competent person gainfully employed in his chosen field will not ordinarily give up a secure position to take another with a new enterprise without some assurance as to his future. No corporation could ever be created without a preliminary agreement between the parties proposing to form it as to the mode and manner of doing so. However, when such agreements providing for the future management and control of a corporation violate the express charter or statutory provision, contemplate an illegal object, involve any fraud, oppression, or wrong against other stockholders, or are made in consideration of a private benefit to the promisor, the courts will declare them invalid. . . . The promoters of a corporation occupy a relation of trust and confidence towards the corporation which they are calling into existence as well as to each other, and the law requires of them the same good faith it exacts from directors and other fiduciaries. . . . Both G.S. § 55-24 and G.S. § 55-73 require that the contemplated agreements be "otherwise lawful."

There is no evidence here that the contract between the plaintiff and defendants was not made in good faith or that, at the time it was made, it was not in the best interest of the corporation. *Prima facie,* it was a valid exercise of the promoter's right to contract. . . . Since the organization of the corporation, the defendants have not owned a majority of its stock. Therefore, they could not have forced their will upon either the stockholders or the other eight directors. To remove plaintiff from the board of directors and the presidency of the corporation, they ultimately required the proxies and votes of other stockholders.

The defendants' contention that the agreement was void as against public policy is not sustained. . . .

As justification for the abandonment of their agreement, defendants alleged that plaintiff's addiction to alcohol had caused him to neglect the business of Gateway. Plaintiff denied the allegation. It therefore became a question for the jury whether plaintiff used alcohol to an extent which would justify his discharge. . . .

Plaintiff's second cause of action is in tort for the wrongful interference by defendants with the contractual relation existing between him and Gateway. . . . "[T]he overwhelming weight of authority in this nation is that an action in tort lies against an outsider who knowingly, intentionally, and unjustifiably induces one party to a contract to breach it to the damage of the other party. . . ."

The contract here was for one year only, but it is a fair inference that both plaintiff and Gateway expected it to be renewed from year to year as long as plaintiff was able to perform his duties. . . . Defendants here are not *outsiders*. They are all stockholders and directors of Gateway. As stockholders, they had a financial interest in the corporation; as directors, they owed it fidelity and the duty to use due care in the management of its business. . . . As either directors or stockholders, they were privileged purposely to cause the corporation not to renew plaintiff's contract as president if, in securing this action, they did not employ any improper means and if they acted in good faith to protect the interests of the corporation. In other words, because of their financial interest and fiduciary relationship they had a qualified privilege to interfere with contractual relations between the corporation and a third party. . . . To hold otherwise, "would tend to hinder directors of a corporation from acting on their judgment for the interest of their corporation." . . .

The acts of a corporate officer in inducing his company to sever contractual relations with a third party are presumed to have been done in the interest of the corporation. "Individual liability may, however, be imposed where his acts involve individual and separate torts distinguishable from acts solely on his employer's behalf or where his acts are performed in his own interest and adverse to that of his firm." . . .

Directors of an insurance company may not be subjected to liability for acting on the assumption that it might prejudice the corporation to retain as president a man with a drinking problem who had been committed to a State institution as an inebriate. Plaintiff offered no evidence tending to show that the defendants abused their privilege as directors.

The question whether plaintiff's use of alcohol had *actually* rendered him unfit to perform his duties or prejudiced the business of Gateway is not determinative of the second cause of action. An error in judgment about this would not impose liability upon the directors. . . .

[Judgment affirmed as to tort claim but remanded for trial as to first claim.]

Similar to the foregoing, a lawyer is not liable for inducing his client to break a contract with the plaintiff when the lawyer believes that he is correct in advising the client that he is not bound by the contract with the plaintiff. And again, an insurance agent or broker is not liable when in good faith he persuades the insured to cancel a policy and change to another insurer because the latter's policy is better for the insured than the original policy.

In this connection, note that there are statutes specifically prohibiting such "twisting" or inducing shifting of insurers when the agent does not act in good faith but merely for the purpose of his own economic gain.

(c) Negligently-caused breach. When the plaintiff loses the value of a contract because of the defendant's negligence, there is no liability of the defendant to the plaintiff because of that fact alone. For example, a defendant who negligently causes the explosion of a factory which is then unable to perform its supply contract with the plaintiff is not liable to the plaintiff for loss which is thereby caused him.

§ 27:6. Federal Regulation

In some areas the law governing interference with business and economic relations is based on federal statutes which, by virtue of the general rule of the supremacy of federal law, displaces state law.

LOCAL 20 v. MORTON
377 U.S. 252 (1964)

The employer rented out trucks and drivers for highway construction work. Its employees were represented by Union Local 20 acting under an oral agreement. The union began negotiations to secure a written contract. Negotiation stalled and the union called a strike. The union sought to bring pressure on the employer by engaging in various nonviolent activities. The employer then sued the union for damages for the loss caused by the following: (1) persuasion by the union of employees of other enterprises dealing with the employer which caused such other enterprises to refrain from dealing with the employer; (2) persuasion by the union of the management of another enterprise to refrain from so dealing; (3) loss of profits resulting from the loss of a customer's account because the employer did not have sufficient employees left to do the work; and (4) punitive damages. The National Labor Management Relations Act of 1947 declares that item (1) above is unlawful and that damages may be recovered for harm caused thereby. The lower courts awarded the employer damages for item (1). The federal statute is silent as to the remaining items and therefore the lower courts awarded damages as to all such items on the ground that the law of the state in which the acts were committed authorized such recovery.

OPINION BY STEWART, J. . . .

The petitioner is a labor organization. The respondent is a company engaged in the business of providing dump trucks and drivers, as a subcontractor on highway construction, with its principal place of business at Tiffin, Ohio. The petitioner represented the respondent's employees from 1950 until 1956 under an oral agreement. In 1956 the parties engaged in negotiations for a written agreement. An impasse in bargaining precipitated a strike which lasted from August to October of that year. During the strike, the petitioner engaged in secondary activities involving some of the respondent's customers and suppliers, for the purpose of inducing them to cease doing business with the respondent. Claiming that these activities were unlawful both under § 303 of the Labor Management Relations Act of 1947, 29 USC § 187, and under the common law of Ohio, the respondent sued the petitioner in the United States District of Ohio, claiming damages for business losses caused by the petitioner's allegedly unlawful conduct during the strike.

After a trial without a jury, the District Court found that the petitioner had encouraged the employees of France Stone Co., a supplier of the respondent, and the employees of C. A. Schoen, Inc., and O'Connel Coal Co., customers of respondent, to force their employers to cease doing business with the respondent, in violation of § 303 of the federal Act. The court awarded the respondent some $1,600 damages for business losses caused by this violation of federal law. The court also determined that during the strike the petitioner had persuaded the management of Launder & Son, Inc., another of the respondent's customers, to refrain from doing business with the respondent. Since there had been no approach to Launder's employees, the court held that the request to Launder management was permissible activity under federal law, but ruled that this conduct violated the common law of Ohio, which, the court said, prohibits "making direct appeals to a struck employer's customers or suppliers to stop doing business with the struck employer. . . ." The respondent was accordingly awarded almost $9,000 as compensatory damages for this violation of Ohio law. In addition, the court awarded the respondent more than $9,000 for the loss of a contract to haul sand for the Wilson Sand & Gravel Co., which loss had resulted from an insufficient number of drivers available during the strike to perform the contract. This award was based upon the court's reasoning that the respondent was entitled to recover damages measured by all of the profits lost as a result of the petitioner's total strike activity, so long as some of that activity was unlawful. Finally, the court awarded punitive damages of $15,000, although expressly finding that the petitioner's conduct during the strike had at all times been free of any violence.

The Court of Appeals affirmed the award in all respects. . . .

At the outset we affirm the award of compensatory damages for the violation of § 303 of the federal Act. The District Court found that "the defendant encouraged the employees of the O'Connel Company to stop using plaintiff's trucks for the purpose of forcing or requiring the O'Connel Company to cease doing business with the plaintiff . . . ." This finding of a clear violation of § 303 was supported by the evidence, as was the amount of damages awarded therefor.

With respect to the remaining components of the money judgment recovered by the respondent, the central question to be decided is whether a court, state or federal, is free to apply state law in awarding damages resulting from a union's peaceful strike conduct vis-à-vis a secondary employer, or is confined in the field of damage actions brought for union secondary activities to the specifically limited provisions of § 303 of the federal Act. . . .

In cases involving union violence, state law has been permitted to prevail by reason of controlling considerations which are entirely absent in the present case. "[W]e have allowed the States to grant compensation for the consequences, as defined by the traditional law of torts, of conduct marked by violence and imminent threats to the public order. . . . State jurisdiction has prevailed in these situations because the compelling state interest, in the scheme of our federalism, in the maintenance of domestic peace is not overridden in the absence of clearly expressed congressional direction. . . . In the present case there is no such compelling state interest." . . .

It is the respondent's contention, however, that since the petitioner union's peaceful conduct was neither arguably protected under § 7 nor arguably prohibited under § 8 of the National Labor Relations Act, as amended, the trial court was free to award damages on the basis of state law for injuries caused by this conduct. But even though it may be assumed that at least some of the secondary activity here involved was neither protected nor prohibited, it is still necessary to determine whether by enacting § 303, "Congress occupied this field and closed it to state regulation." . . . The basic question, in other words, is whether "in a case such as this, incompatible doctrines of local law must give way to principles of federal labor law." . . . The answer to that question ultimately depends upon whether the application of state law in this kind of case would operate to frustrate the purpose of the federal legislation. . . .

Section 303(b) of the Labor Management Relations Act expressly authorizes state and federal courts to award damages to any person injured by certain secondary boycott activities described in § 303(a). The type of conduct to be made the subject of a private damage action was considered by Congress, and § 303(a) comprehensively and with great particularity "describes and condemns specific union conduct directed to specific objectives." . . . In selecting which forms of economic pressure should be prohibited by § 303, Congress struck the "balance . . . between the uncontrolled power of management and labor to further their respective interests," . . . "preserving the right of labor organizations to bring pressure to bear on offending employers in primary labor disputes and [by] shielding unoffending employers and others from pressures in controversies not their own." . . .

In this case, the petitioner's request to Launder's management to cease doing business with the respondent was not proscribed by the Act. "[A] union is free to approach an employer to persuade him to engage in a boycott, so long as it refrains from the specifically prohibited means of coercion through inducement of employees." . . . This weapon of self-help, permitted by federal law, formed an integral part of the petitioner's effort to achieve its bargaining goals during negotiations with the respondent. Allowing its use is a part of the balance struck by Congress between the conflicting interests of the union, the employees, the employer and the community. . . . If the Ohio law of secondary boycott can be applied to proscribe the same type of conduct which Congress focused upon but did not proscribe when it enacted § 303, the inevitable result would be to frustrate the Congressional determination to leave this weapon of self-help available, and to upset the balance of power between labor and management expressed in our national labor policy. "For a state to impinge on the area of labor combat designed to be free is quite as much an obstruction of federal policy as if the state were to declare picketing free for purposes or by methods which the federal Act prohibits." . . . We hold, therefore, that the damages awarded against the petitioner based upon its peaceful persuasion of Launder's management not to do business with the respondent during the strike cannot stand.

The same considerations require reversal of the award of punitive damages. Punitive damages for violations of § 303 conflict with the Congressional judgment, reflected both in the language of the federal statute and in its legislative history, that recovery for an employer's business losses caused by a union's peaceful secondary activities proscribed by § 303 should be limited to actual, compensatory damages. And insofar as punitive damages in this case were based on secondary activities which violated only state law, they cannot stand, because, as we have held, substantive state law in this area must yield to federal limitations. In short, this in an area "of judicial decision within which the policy of the law is so dominated by the sweep of federal statutes that legal relations which they affect must be deemed governed by federal law having its source in those statutes, rather than by local law." . . . Accordingly, we hold that since state law has been displaced by § 303 in private damage actions based on peaceful union secondary activities, the District Court in this case was without authority to award punitive damages.

There remains for consideration only the question of the damage award for the respondent's loss of the Wilson account. The respondent conceded at trial that there was "no evidence of unlawful activity in connection with this [the Wilson] job," and the record makes clear that the respondent lost the Wilson account because his drivers were discouraged from working during the strike by the petitioner's primary strike activity. Since § 303(b) authorizes an award of damages only in the event of injury "by reason of any violation of subsection (a)" and peaceful primary strike activity does not violate § 303(a), . . . the District Court was without power to award damages proximately caused by lawful, primary activities, even though the petitioner may have contemporaneously engaged in unlawful acts elsewhere. . . .

Questions for Review

1. Analyze each opinion in this chapter in terms of the social forces involved in the decision. See § 5:5 for a list of the social forces. With respect to each opinion, explain why the prevailing social forces prevailed and why those rejected did not. In each case in which there is a dissenting opinion, also make this analysis for the dissenting opinion.

2-6. On the basis of the social forces involved, what decision should be made in each of the following cases?

2. *Negligence. Rescue.* When a worker is injured in attempting to warn defendant of his negligence in unloading steel with a chain instead of a stronger cable, is the worker barred by assumption of risk or contributory negligence when the chain breaks and causes him injury? *Scott* v. *Hampshire,* 246 Md. 171, 227 A.2d 751.

3. *Premises liability. Split level.* Can a social guest recover for injuries sustained by falling because of a step down between an entrance hallway and the living room? *Bergman* v. *Cook,* Ore., 421 P.2d 382.

4. *Marital status. Remarriage after Mexican divorce.* May a first wife, claiming to have been invalidly divorced by a Mexican decree, claim tort damages from her husband and his second wife? *Weicker* v. *Weicker,* 28 App. Div.2d 138, 283 N.Y.S.2d 385, reversing 53 Misc.2d 570, 279 N.Y.S.2d 852.

5. *Negligence. Absence of duty.* Is a building inspector liable for the negligent inspection of a building which later collapses and kills a member of the public? *Modlin* v. *Miami Beach,* Fla., 201 So.2d 70.

6. *Malpractice. Organ donor.* A mother voluntarily donated one of her kidneys to her son who was dying of a kidney ailment. As the result of such donation, the son lived but the mother's health was impaired. The mother sued the doctor on the theory that his negligence had necessitated the donation of the kidney by the mother. If the doctor had been negligent, can the mother recover from him for the impairment of her health? *Sirianni* v. *Anna,* 55 Misc.2d 553, 285 N.Y.S.2d 709.

7-10. *What social forces were involved, which prevailed, and which were defeated in the following decisions?*

7. *False imprisonment. Hospital.* A hospital is not liable for false imprisonment where the mother of an 8-year old patient was required to see two employees to make financial arrangements for the release of the daughter without paying the hospital bill, as the delay involved was not an unreasonable detention and there was no evidence that the hospital had acted for an improper purpose. *Bailie* v. *Miami Valley Hospital,* 8 Ohio Misc. 193, 221 N.E.2d 217.

8. *Kidnapping. Finance company.* Where a finance company tells it young employee to bring an aged debtor into the finance company's office and the employee, without any authority to do so, brings the debtor over the latter's protest, the finance company and the employee are liable for the injury sustained when the debtor, after stating that he will jump from the car, does so, and is injured—as against the claim that the debtor by jumping from the moving car was guilty of contributory negligence. *Spears* v. *Southern Discount,* [C.A.2dLa.] 191 So.2d 751.

9. *Absolute liability. Rocket test.* Defendant testing rocket fuels under contract with United States is liable to adjoining landowner for vibration damage. *Smith* v. *Lockheed Propulsion Co.,* Cal.App.2d, 56 Cal.Rptr. 128.

10. *Automobiles. Darting child.* The fact that a 3-year old child darts from behind an ice cream vendor's truck and runs into the travel lane of street is not sufficient to impose liability upon the motorist then running into the child, where the motorist was driving slowly and carefully by the vending truck. *Hardy* v. *Bye,* [La.] 207 So.2d 198.

Chapter 28

MUST YOU PAY FOR YOUR DEEDS?

§ 28:1. Generally

There is no difficulty in deciding that you must pay for the harm you have caused and, conversely, that you are not liable for harm which you

459

have not caused. But to what extent are you required to pay for the consequences of your conduct? Is a person liable for every act that he does or
for every consequence that flows from his acts? To illustrate the problem, we
will concede that the defendant who negligently runs over and kills a person
is liable for the harm he has caused. But where does the harm end? Suppose
that the man is the keyman of a large industrial enterprise which, because
of his death, very quickly goes out of business. In that event, there are
innumerable employees, shareholders, and creditors who have lost money
in consequence of the unfortunate death of the keyman. Does this mean
that the negligent driver must pay for the economic loss which he has
caused to all of these other persons? And to take the question of causation
a step further, consider any one of the shareholders, creditors, or employees,
and assume that because of the crash of the enterprise such person is not in
a financial position to send his child to college. Can the child then sue the
negligent driver for the economic loss and the loss of future opportunities
which the child sustains thereby? To assume an even larger-scale pattern of
actual harm, consider the case of the negligent driver who runs over and
kills a great political leader, as the result of whose death the country is
plunged into a depression or a war. It is perfectly obvious that although it
can be said that the subsequent events and subsequent losses would not
have occurred or probably would not have occurred if the defendant had not
run over and killed the key man or the political leader, the law will just not
go to the extreme of imposing liability for the infinity of consequences which
flows from the defendant's wrongful act.

(a) Determining existence of proximate relationship. In order to
indicate when a causal relationship will impose liability, the law uses the
phrase "proximate cause." This merely means that the cause is sufficiently
close to the harm that society regards it proper to impose liability. A phrase
often used for the same purpose is "legal cause," which again merely means
that in the eyes of the law a given cause is regarded as imposing liability for
the result.

Two things are clear: (1) society does not want to impose endless liability
upon the actor, and (2) when harm is such that society wants to impose
liability it uses the label of "proximate" or "legal" cause. But how does
society determine how far liability should reach? How does it determine
when it has reached the cutoff point for liability?

(b) Foreseeability of harm.

KAUFMAN v. MILLER

414 S.W.2d 164 (Tex., 1967)

Miller was in an automobile collision. Some time thereafter he was in a
collision with Kaufman's truck. He was not physically injured in the second

collision and both vehicles were able to be driven away after the collision. The effect of the shock of the second collision caused the development of a neurosis that physically incapacitated Miller. He sued Kaufman for damages because of such disability.

OPINION BY CALVERT, C.J. . . .

Defendant argues under her first point of error that, as a matter of law, the evidence will not support the jury findings that her negligent acts or omissions were proximate causes of the plaintiff's injuries. In evaluating this argument, it should be stated at the outset that the evidence establishes conclusively that there was no physical impact with the plaintiff's body in the collision and that the only injury suffered by him was an injury to his nervous system, diagnosed by his psychiatrist-witness as a "conversion reaction" and "compensation neurosis." . . .

The force of the collision threw the defendant's automobile against the bridge railing. The damage to the automobile was insubstantial and no damage was done to the truck. Both vehicles later left the scene of the collision under their own power, and both drivers proceeded to their respective destinations in Louisiana.

Defendant had her mother and her aunt as passengers in her car. Plaintiff saw the car approaching on Pine Street but did not see it as it entered the highway. He did not know it had collided with his trailer. He "heard a little crash" which required him to use some effort to keep the truck under control, but he thought he had hit the curb of the bridge. He looked in his rear view mirror and saw the car against the bridge railing and then knew "that I had either hit her or she hit me." He stopped his truck some 150 feet from the place of collision and walked back to investigate.

When plaintiff reached the car, he found the three women. He was nervous. Defendant was nervous, excited and "shook up," but no one appeared to have been injured. Plaintiff discovered that his truck and trailer were undamaged, and he told the defendant he was not hurt. He testified, however, that he got "shocked" and "shook up at the accident." In his testimony he accounted for his shock thusly: "I didn't even know that I had hit her, for one thing, and that's what shook me up—or she hit me. When I went over there she told me that I had run into her and that's what got me all shook up, then, and shocked." He sent in an accident report to his employer in which he stated that he had received no injuries in the collision.

"Right after" the collision, the plaintiff began to have spells of nervousness and dizziness and blackout spells. He would have dizzy spells when he got nervous, and he would get nervous because he "was scared somebody would run into" him and was afraid he "might hurt somebody." His dizzy spells did not get "real bad" until about the time he went to see a doctor in May, 1962, some ten months after the collision. By that time, he was having nightmares and spells of nausea. His doctor would not let him go back to driving a truck. He consulted several doctors and was hospitalized for a week. From May, 1962, until the time of the trial in April, 1965, plaintiff had worked at various jobs at a considerable loss of earnings. His dizzy spells were less frequent at the time of trial.

Plaintiff is a son of farmer parents who separated when he was fourteen years old. He received an eighth grade education. He remained on the farm with his father until he was seventeen, at which time he went into the military service where he remained for six years. While in the army, he was a heavy truck driver, and, with study, achieved the equivalent of a tenth grade education. He left the military service in 1955, went to a mechanic's school for one year and then got a job driving a truck. He worked for various employers in different kinds of employment before he secured work as a truck driver with Herring Tank Lines for whom he was working at the time of the collision on July 15, 1961. He was 31 years of age at the time of trial. He could remember having had only one dizzy spell before the collision and that was on an occasion when he was doing off-shore work and "the heat hit" him.

The plaintiff had been in other accidents prior to the collision, only one of which needs to be noticed. In May, 1959, he had a serious accident. He hit a hole in the highway and broke the left front frame on his truck, causing the truck to jack-knife and turn over and catch fire at a trailer camp. One trailer house burned down and three occupants of it died in the fire. Two or three other trailer houses and a nearby residence and garage burned down. The plaintiff admitted that the accident was a "horrible" one, he suffered a severe shock from it, and he would always remember it; but he testified he recovered from that shock and it had no effect on him during the two years preceding the collision on July 15, 1961.

The testimony of the plaintiff has been set out in considerable detail because it also summarizes the history related by him to his psychiatrist and forms the basis for the opinion of the psychiatrist that plaintiff is suffering from a "conversion reaction" and "compensation neurosis" which were "triggered" by the collision of July 15, 1961.

The psychiatrist spent one hour with the plaintiff. His testimony will be summarized. The plaintiff is a "passive dependent personality" and "has two significant neurotic patterns, one of depression and the other conversion reaction." His neurosis "had its beginning on the farm" in "a hard, dreary existence," and the depressive part of the neurosis "was caused by this accident in 1959" when he could have been killed and "realized at the time of the accident that he was facing death." The witness testified that the 1959 accident left the plaintiff with a feeling of guilt and that the "horrible accident" would be with him "until the day he dies." It was the professional opinion of the witness that the plaintiff's condition was such that he was disabled from driving a truck; and it was his positive opinion that the accident of July 15, 1961, "triggered off" the conversion reaction and that the conversion reaction neurosis was the disabling factor.

The psychiatrist-witness explained the various technical terms and neuroses referred to in his testimony and the effect of the neuroses on the behavior of the plaintiff.

A "passive dependent personality" is "characterized by helplessness, indecisiveness, and a tendency to cling to others. . . . These individuals must, at all costs, conceal their energy and aggressive impulses from their own consciousness. . . . These are nice, quiet, gentle people, who would never hurt a fly. For such a person hurting a fly, without intending, and without any way of not inflicting the damage or hurting, is a frightening experience." It was his opinion that a person with a "passive dependent personality would be more susceptible to developing a conversion reaction."

The "depressive reaction" neurosis of the plaintiff was related to the accident in 1959. "The effect was that it left him with the realization that he could hurt people"; and "the danger for a person of this personality type is [from fear of] hurting someone else, and not [from fear of] being hurt himself." The "conversion reaction" neurosis was "triggered off" by the accident of July 15, 1961, the essential quality of which "was the complete absence of awareness that it was happening, and, therefore, the inability to make any attempt to prevent it from happening." It was "the experience of the danger of this massive vehicle which could kill, and which could cause damage, without knowing about it . . . that . . . triggered the conversion reaction in the man." The spells of nervousness, dizziness and blackout spells were symptomatic of the conversion reaction neurosis; the dizziness and fainting "in this man serve to prevent overwhelming anxiety." . . .

The witness distinguished a "traumatic neurosis" and a "conversion reaction neurosis." A traumatic neurosis "is a description of a neurosis which occurs in direct reaction to an emotionally traumatic experience, and it is characterized by the sudden incapacitation of a person." In a conversion reaction neurosis "the pattern of disability develops over a period of time." Asked, "Would that in any manner mean that this type of condition that this man suffers from is any less severe or less disabling than the traumatic or instant neurosis would have been?" the witness answered: "On the contrary, this type of pattern is more likely to be of a more permanent nature than traumatic neurosis."

From the evidence here set out, it is apparent that the jury could reasonably have concluded that the plaintiff had suffered a serious and disabling nervous disorder as a direct result of the collision which was caused by the defendant's negligent acts and omissions, and thus that the evidence supports the jury's finding of causal relation between the defendant's negligence and the plaintiff's injuries. The finding of the cause in fact element of proximate cause is supported by the evidence. But under the law of this State there is a second essential element of proximate cause, i.e., the foreseeability element. . . . The serious question is whether we should hold as a matter of law that the defendant could not reasonably have foreseen that the injuries to the plaintiff's nervous system would be a natural and probable consequence of her negligent conduct. We do so hold. . . .

It is generally recognized by writers in the field of tort law, as well as by courts of all jurisdictions, that the right of recovery for injuries from mental shock caused by negligent conduct cannot be an unlimited right; that an unlimited right of recovery would impose undue burdens on persons guilty of nothing more than simple negligence. Accordingly, some courts have imposed arbitrary limitations on the right. The limitations are generally keyed to foreseeability of consequences, whether foreseeability is treated as an element of negligence or an element of proximate cause. Two of the limitations will be noticed.

Courts have been virtually unanimous in recognizing that one who suffers injury from mental shock as a result of an injury or threatened injury to a third person cannot recover damages from the negligent tort-feasor. . . . Prosser states that the reason usually assigned for denying recovery for emotional shock because of fear of injury to a third person "is that the defendant could not reasonably anticipate any harm to the plaintiff, and therefore owes her no duty of care." See Prosser, The Law of Torts, 352 (3d ed. 1964). He recognizes that there is no logical reason for permitting recovery by a woman for shock because of fear of injury to herself and denying her recovery for shock because of fear of injury to her child, but states (pp. 353-354):

"It would be an entirely unreasonable burden on all human activity if the defendant who has endangered one man were to be compelled to pay for the lacerated feelings of every other person disturbed by reason of it, including every bystander shocked at an accident, and every distant relative of the person injured, as well as his friends. And obviously the danger of fictitious claims, and the necessity of some guarantee of genuineness, are even greater here than before. It is no doubt such considerations that have made the law extremely cautious." . . .

Recovery is also generally denied when the plaintiff is unusually or peculiarly susceptible to emotional trauma and that fact is unknown to the negligent tort-feasor. In *Haas* v. *Metz,* 78 Ill.App. 46 (1898), the plaintiff sought damages from the defendant because loud and angry talk by the defendant caused the plaintiff to have recurring spells of hysteria. Plaintiff's doctor testified that she had spells of hysteria before the incident. The court concluded its opinion denying recovery with this language: "We conclude . . . that defendant could not reasonably anticipate that the words she spoke and the tone of voice she used would cause the recurrence of an hysterical malady of whose very existence she was not aware . . . ." Somewhat analogous are the cases which hold that one's acts are not negligent toward a person with physical defects if the defects are unknown to the actor and his conduct would not have been negligent toward a normal person. . . .

An opposing view is illustrated by two Wisconsin cases. In *Sundquist* v. *Madison Rys. Co.,* 197 Wis. 83, 221 N.W. 392 (1928), the plaintiff was allowed to recover for hysterical paralysis caused by fright and shock even though all of the medical witnesses agreed that the fright would not have caused paralysis in a normally healthy person. And in *Colla* v. *Mandella,* 1 Wis.2d 594, 85 N.W.2d 345, 64 A.L.R.2d 95 (1957), a negligent defendant was held liable for the death of a man from a heart attack brought about by emotional shock even though the proof showed that unknown to the defendant the man had high blood pressure and a heart condition for which he was being treated by a doctor before the traumatic experience.

We need not approve either of the limitations discussed as an arbitrary limitation on the right of recovery for injuries resulting from emotional shock caused by negligent conduct. Both limitations are present in this case. There are also other factors which when combined with the limitations discussed impel a conclusion as a matter of law that the defendant could not reasonably have foreseen the injuries suffered by the plaintiff as a natural and probable consequence of her negligent conduct.

According to the testimony of his own expert witness, plaintiff's conversion reaction neurosis is his disabling condition. This developed from a fear, triggered by the collision, that the negligent defendant might have been injured under circumstances in which the plaintiff could not have prevented the injury. In other words, the emotional shock sustained by the plaintiff was not from fear that he might have been injured but from fear that another might have been injured, the other not being an innocent person subjected to injury by a wrongdoer but the wrongdoer herself. The plaintiff was unusually or peculiarly susceptible to a conversion reaction neurosis. We pass over the testimony of the psychiatrist that "a passive dependent personality would be more susceptible to developing a conversion reaction," but note that the sum total of the witness' testimony shows conclusively that the depressive reaction neurosis suffered by the plaintiff as a result of his accident experience in May, 1959, made him peculiarly susceptible to the conversion reaction neurosis suffered by him as a result of the trifling collision of July 15, 1961. Moreover, the disabling neurosis did not result from an immediate impact of the negligent conduct and collision on his senses, but from learning of it after it happened and after learning that apparently no one was injured in the collision. Finally, the disabling neurosis, although originating "right after" the collision, was a slowly developing type which did not incapacitate the plaintiff until after the lapse of several months.

We recognize that this field of law is in a developing process, as is the field of psychiatry, and we would be reluctant to hold at this time that any one of the enumerated factors would of and by itself be sufficient to require a judgment denying liability. We are satisfied, however, that public policy is better served by denying liability when all are combined. . . .

The difficulty with the foreseeability test as applied in the Kaufman case is that had Miller sustained only "ordinary" harm as the result of the collision, the law would find that the collision was the proximate cause of the harm. There is an element of unrealism in saying that conduct is the "proximate" cause of an expectable result but not when the result is unexpectable. Expectability should only be involved when the question is whether the actor had used the degree of care that a reasonable man would have exercised upon foreseeing the harm which could follow the failure to exercise such care. Whether an act or an event is a cause or proximate cause would appear to be a matter of fact without regard to whether the chain of events from cause to effect was a "reasonable" chain, or whether the result was foreseeable.

Furthermore, the law will allow recovery in some instances when the degree of foreseeability is merely a mathematical possibility rather than probability. For example, if you carelessly run over someone with your automobile and he goes to a doctor who improperly treats him, thereby aggravating his injury or his condition, you are liable for not only the harm you caused but also the additional harm caused by the doctor. Likewise, if a third person had rushed into the street to attempt to save your victim, you would have then been liable for the harm to the rescuer had he been injured instead of the initially apparent victim. Now of course, it is mathematically possible that a rescue would be made or that the victim would go to a doctor who might not treat him properly, but the degree of probability is so small that liability is obviously predicated upon some concept of social justice rather than upon a scientific determination of the existence of a causal relationship.

(c) Avoidance of oppression. As a further criticism of the foresee-abiltity test above discussed, it is held that the fact that harm is foreseeable does not always establish liability.

AMAYA v. HOME ICE & FUEL CO.

59 Cal.2d 295, 29 Cal.Rptr. 33, 379 P.2d 513 (1963)

A mother, 7 months pregnant, was on the sidewalk. Her 17-month old child was in the street when a truck negligently came down upon him. She attempted to warn the driver and the child but was helpless. The truck ran over the child. The shock caused the mother to miscarry and suffer actual physical and mental harm. She sued the driver and his employer for harm to herself and the infant child.

OPINION BY SCHAUER, J. . . .

The plaintiff suffered fright and shock as a result of being compelled to watch her infant child crushed beneath the wheels of an ice truck, and . . . the fright and shock she suffered was as a result of her fear for the safety of her child, and not out of fear for her own safety." . . .

May tort liability be predicated on fright or nervous shock (with consequent bodily illness) induced solely by the plaintiff's apprehension of negligently caused danger or injury to a third person? . . .

"As a general rule, no recovery is permitted for a mental or emotional disturbance, or for a bodily illness resulting therefrom, in the absence of a contemporaneous bodily contact or independent cause of action, or an element of willfulness, wantonness, or maliciousness, in cases in which there is no injury other than one to a third person, even though recovery would have been permitted had the wrong been directed against the plaintiff. The rule is frequently applied to mental or emotional disturbances caused by another's danger, or sympathy for another's suffering. It has been regarded as applicable to a mental or emotional disturbance resulting from an injury not only to a stranger, but also to a relative of the plaintiff, such as a child, sister, father, or spouse." . . .

The law of California as declared in *Reed* v. *Moore* (1957), 156 Cal. App.2d 43, 319 P.2d 80, is in complete accord with these authorities. . . . The Legislature has not seen fit to act in this connection, and has adopted no statute inconsistent with the common-law rule of nonliability. The remaining question is whether we should nevertheless now abrogate that rule in California by judicial decision. . . .

"The problem must be approached at the outset from the viewpoint of the duty of defendant and the right of plaintiff, and not from the viewpoint of proximate cause. The right of the mother to recover must be based, first, upon the establishment of a duty on the part of defendant so to conduct herself with respect to the child as not to subject the mother to an unreasonable risk of shock or fright, and, second, upon the recognition of a legally protected right or interest on the part of the mother to be free from shock or fright occasioned by the peril of her child." . . .

The determination of this question—the existence of a duty owed to the plaintiff by the defendant—is in the first instance for the court, not for the jury. The classic statement is that of Minturn, J., in *Morril* v. *Morril* (1928, N.J.) 104 N.J.L. 557, 142 A. 337, 339-340 [8-9], 60 A.L.R. 102: "Hence it becomes imperative before legal liability for conceded damages can be imposed upon a defendant, for the court in the first instance to inquire and determine the character of duty which the law under the facts imposed upon the defendant as the basis of liability; for manifestly, it cannot be conceded that the jury from their inner consciousness may evolve in every variety of tort-feasance a legal duty as the standard of liability." . . . Much confusion has been engendered in this connection by a misplaced reliance on the "foreseeability" formula. . . . [T]*here are many situations involving foreseeable risks where there is no duty."* . . .

There are sound reasons for the established rule that the determination of the existence and scope of the defendant's duty to the plaintiff is primarily a question for the court and does not depend only on "foreseeability." First it will be observed that the negligence issue, i.e., the *violation* of duty, is submitted to the jury under instructions couched in terms of how an ordinarily prudent person would view the "foreseeability of risk" created by the defendant's conduct; yet if the issue of the *existence* of duty is also submitted to the jury under a "foreseeability" formula, the jury will in effect be asked to determine two distinct issues in the case by means of the same "test." And if, as sometimes occurs, the jury are also instructed that the defendant's conduct is not the "proximate cause" of events that he could not reasonably have anticipated, then truly "analysis has played itself false, so that a case is seemingly to be subject thrice to the ponderous process of the 'foreseeability' formula." . . .

[The] second reason touches on the fundamental responsibility of the court to declare the law. There is a legal duty on any given set of facts *only if the court or the Legislature says there is a duty.* "Duty is only a word with which we state our conclusion that there is or is not to be liability; it necessarily begs the essential question." . . .

Turning to the factors that are to be weighed in the balance we consider, on the one hand, plaintiff's undoubted interest in freedom from invasion of her bodily security, and on the other, such factors as the following:

The Administrative Factor. Justice, we observed above, exists only when it can be effectively administered. . . . In circumstances such as those here shown, to impose liability would "open the way to fraudulent claims, and enter a field that has no sensible or just stopping point." It has become almost trite for legal writers to deprecate such reasoning; and we have not hesitated to reject it when we deemed that the problems of proof could be solved and the scope of liability could be delineated. . . . But is this necessarily true of the case at bench? . . .

Granted that simply because "naivete about the problem of proof has caused injustice in times past does not necessarily settle the matter for the future" . . . , we are left with the question of whether in this area of inquiry where emotions play so large a role the law has now become sufficiently responsive to scientific reality to redress the "net balance of justice." The question is a disturbing one, and cannot be answered merely by invoking the rule that a conflict of expert testimony is for the jury. . . . The parade of expert medical witnesses continues, ushered in by both plaintiff and defendant, and the juries are daily called upon to "resolve" the disputes thus engendered. This may be difficult enough when traumatic injuries to the body are involved; but as doctors well know, the "resolution" of such conflicts often borders on fancy when the causation of alleged psychoneural disorders is at issue. There are indications, moreover, that in this area the law continues to cling to cherished preconceptions of the layman, with bland disregard for the development of modern medical knowledge. Much timeliness remains in [the] warning . . . that "eagerness to be progressive may cause extravagant credulity and injury to scientific standards of proof." Extravagant credulity, of course, means ultimate injustice.

Another—and no less important—administrative factor to be weighed is the problem of setting some limits to such liability for fright or shock allegedly caused by the apprehension of danger or injury not to the plaintiff but to a third person. Here, at least, the legal writers are generally agreed that the problem is a real one. Professor Prosser suggests the following limitations on liability (Prosser, Torts (1955, 2d ed.) p. 182): First, "It is clear that the injury threatened or inflicted upon the third person must be a serious one, of a nature to cause severe shock to the plaintiff, and that the shock must result in actual physical harm." But what if the plaintiff was honestly mistaken in believing the third person to be in danger or to be seriously injured? And as we are dealing here with a *negligently* caused danger or injury to the third person, what if the latter was contributively negligent? Or assumed the risk involved? Second, "The action might well be confined to members of the immediate family, or perhaps to husband, wife, parent, or child, to the exclusion of bystanders, and remote relatives." But what if the third person was the plaintiff's beloved niece or nephew, grandparent, fiancé, or lifelong friend, as dear to the plaintiff as her more immediate family? Third, "the plaintiff must be present at the time of the accident, or at least the shock must be fairly contemporaneous with it, rather than follow at a later date." But how soon is "fairly contemporaneous"? What is the magic in the plaintiff's being "present"? Is the shock any less immediate if the mother does not know of the accident until the injured child is brought home? And what if the plaintiff is present at the scene but is nevertheless unaware of the danger or injury to the third person until shortly after the accident has occurred. . . .

As Professor Prosser concedes, such limitations are quite arbitrary. . . . But compelling moral and socioeconomic reasons, hereinafter discussed, require that a negligent defendant's liability have some stopping point. None has yet been proposed that would be fair to all parties concerned, and the failings of the above quoted limitations suggest that the quest may be an inherently fruitless one. There is an appealing simplicity in the view that difficulties in delimiting an area of liabilty do not justify a refusal to enter that area. But this court does not act in a vacuum; we cannot fashion a rule for the case at bench without reflecting on the fact that there will be other such cases, other plaintiffs. When, as here, a wholly new type of liability is envisioned, our responsibility extends far beyond the particular plaintiff before us, and touches society at large.

The Socio-Economic and Moral Factors. As just observed, there must be some stopping point to the liability of the negligent defendant. "It is still unthinkable that any one shall be liable to the end of time for all of the results that follow in endless sequence from his single act. Causation cannot be the answer; in a very real sense the consequences of an act go forward to eternity, and back to the beginning of the world." . . . There are two principal reasons why this is "unthinkable."

First, to the extent that the law intervenes in any area of human activity and declares that for certain consequences of that activity the actor shall be held civilly liable in damages, both the individual actor and society as a whole feel the effects of the restraint—a psychological effect in the form of a lessening of incentive, and an economic effect in the form of the cost of insurance necessary to enable the activity to continue. Yet it is recognized that no activity could survive an unlimited progression of such effects. Accordingly, when the general social utility of an activity is deemed to outweigh the particular interests with which it may clash, important policy reasons dictate that some limits be set to liability for its consequences. How do these considerations affect our problem? The law, both in California and in the many other jurisdictions which have passed on the question, now provides, as has been shown, that an actor who is merely negligent is not liable to one who claims injury through fright or shock induced by conduct directed not to the latter but to a third person. Thus, in cases where the defendant's conduct involved negligent driving of a motor vehicle the courts conclude that to extend liability to spectators who were not themselves in danger "would, in our opinion, place an unreasonable burden upon users of highways." . . .

As the industrial society in which we live becomes still more complex and the use of the streets and highways and airways increases, a certain percentage of accidents therefrom appears to become statistically inevitable. There will be losses, and our present system of insurance attempts to compensate for them, and, of course, to spread the cost of compensation over those who do not, as well as those who do, cause such losses. But could that system—imperfect at best—adequately and fairly absorb the far-reaching extension of liability that would follow from judicial abrogation of the rule before us? And what of the many other activities of everyday life that are either uninsurable or customarily uninsured, yet may well give rise to the type of "spectator injury" here alleged? We conclude, rather, that the social utility of such activities outweighs the somewhat speculative interest of individuals to be free from the risk of the type of injury here alleged.

The second reason for seeking a stopping point to the negligent defendant's liability is a related one. As long as our system of compensation is based on the concept of fault, we must also weigh "the moral blame attached to the defendant's conduct." . . . Here is felt the difference between the social importance of conduct that negligently causes harm and conduct that is intended to do so. It is often said that in the latter case the defendant will be held liable for a broader range of consequences because, as the consequences are intended, they are the more "foreseeable." But in many intentional tort cases the defendant has been held liable under this reasoning for consequences far beyond those which he actually intended. . . . It follows that, once more, "foreseeability" is not the real answer. Rather, the increased liability imposed on an intentional wrongdoer appears to reflect the psychological fact that solicitude for the interests of the actor weighs less in the balance as his moral guilt increases and the social utility of his conduct diminishes. . . .

Having weighed each of the foregoing factors in the balance, we hold that the complaint fails to state facts sufficient to constitute a cause of action.

DISSENTING OPINION BY PETERS, J. . . .

The majority opinion states the issue to be "whether liability may be predicated on fright or nervous shock (with consequent bodily illness) induced solely by the plaintiff's apprehension of negligently caused danger or injury to a third person." So stated, the answer to such a broad question might well be in the negative. But the issue now before us is not the one quoted above. The real issue is a much more limited one. The plaintiff is not just anyone. She is a *mother* of a 17-month-old *infant child*. The defendant, *in the presence of the mother,* negligently ran down and injured that *infant child*. As a proximate result the mother has suffered permanent injuries. Thus the real question is not the one stated by the majority, but is whether or not a mother may recover damages for physical injuries resulting from emotional shock caused by fear for her infant child who is negligently run down by the automobile of the defendant in the presence of the mother. I submit that the answer to that question, so limited, should be that liability for such injuries should exist.

The italicized words above create real limitations that are not merely matters of form. Common sense tells us that a defendant who negligently injures someone, should not be liable to every over sensitive person, whoever he or she may be, who is shocked by an accident, whether it happens in his or her presence or not, and happens to any person, whomsoever he or she may be, and whether plaintiff is related to or even known to the injured person or not. The line of legal causation cannot be stretched so thin. But the fact that, morally and legally, there should not be liability in any such general situation is no reason for holding that, morally and legally, there should not be liability in the limited situation. Now common sense tells us, and elementary principles of fairness command us, to impose liability against a negligent defendant who negligently injures an infant child in the presence of its mother, and the mother suffers serious emotional shock as a result. Admittedly, if we once create liability in the limited situation here involved, demands will inevitably be made upon us to extend the limits of the rule. Admittedly, it will be a difficult but not impossible task to draw the line between liability and nonliability in such situations. When we are called upon to draw that line the place we draw it may not, perhaps, be entirely logical. By necessity it will have to be arbitrary. It will be less arbitrary, however, than to deny liability entirely. But the fact that such a task may be difficult should not deter us from performing it. One of the main functions of appellate courts is to draw just such lines. We are constantly doing so. The law grows, develops, expands or is limited by a case by case consideration of particular facts, and not by deciding broad general principles not involved in the case under consideration. All that we are required to decide in the instant case, and it is submitted all we should decide, is whether a mother, who as a result of seeing her infant child run down by defendant's truck, suffers severe shock may recover. Whether anyone else, in a different relationship, can recover, should be left for future cases.

It must be conceded, as the majority opinion correctly points out, that the great weight of case authority denies liability even in the limited situation here involved. This is partly due to the sheer inertia caused by the doctrine of stare decisis, and the apparent reluctance of appellate courts to disturb the status quo. It is also in no small part due to the fear, expressed in many of the cases that have adopted the majority rule, that it will be difficult if not impossible to draw the line between liability and nonliabiliy in such cases. This point has already been discussed. So far as the doctrine of stare decisis is concerned, it is, of course, a sound doctrine, but it is not immutable. Old cases, no matter how numerous, should not stand, if, under modern and different conditions, they cannot withstand the impact of critical analysis. The doctrine of stare decisis should never be used as a substitute for such critical analysis. If an old rule cannot withstand such analysis, it should be overruled. This court has not hesitated to do so in other situations. It should not hesitate here. It seems obvious to me that anyone who objectively analyzes the problem will inevitably come to the conclusion that it is reasonably probable that a mother who observes her child being run over by a negligently operated truck will inevitably be shocked, and it is also reasonably probable that the effects of such shock may inflict serious and permanent injuries. To use the language of the cases, such result is "reasonably probable" and "reasonably foreseeable." The negligence of defendant is, obviously, the direct "proximate cause" of the accident. The resulting injuries should therefore be compensable. . . .

The early law was to the effect that shock was not a recoverable item of damage. That rule had the advantage, at least, of being clear, easily understood and easy to apply. Then many states, including California, started to limit that rule by holding that shock accompanied by impact was a proper element of damage . . . . The rule was further limited by the rule, now the law of California, that recovery for shock may properly be an item of damage even without impact if the plaintiff is in the "zone of danger." . . . Then the rule was further limited, if not abolished, by the several California cases holding that a plaintiff could recover for shock caused by the infliction of an intentional tort on a third person member of the family, even though the plaintiff was not in the "zone of danger." . . .

These gradual modifications of the original rule are of great significance. They at least suggest, if they do not compel, the conclusion that we have now reached the stage of development of the law that we should at long last take the intelligent and logical step forward of holding that a mother who sees her child run down by a negligent defendant, and who, as a proximate result thereof, suffers serious and permanent injuries should recover whether or not she was in the "zone of danger." The "zone of danger" test is illogical and unsound and should be abandoned.

It seems to me that when this court adopted the rule that in the case of an intentional tort committed against a member of the family, the plaintiff can recover for shock resulting in serious injuries whether she was in the "zone of danger" or not it necessarily undermined the rule that no such recovery should be allowed in the case of negligent torts. . . .

The intentional tort cases are important for another reason. The line between liability and nonliability in the intentional tort cases, that is who may sue for shock because they saw injuries to whom, is precisely the same as it is in the negligent tort cases. It is no more difficult to draw that line in the negligent tort cases than it is in the intentional tort cases. Yet the difficulty of drawing that line in the intentional tort cases did not deter this court from imposing liability, and adopting the modern, intelligent, logical, and humane rule of liability in this field. It should not be a deterrent in this, a negligent tort case. . . .

" 'It seems sufficiently obvious that the shock of a mother at danger or harm to her child may be both a real and a serious injury. All ordinary human feelings are in favor of her action against the negligent defendant.' . . . To understand the reluctance of some courts to give effect to that feeling we must glance backwards briefly to certain aspects of the development of the law of torts.

"In the early stages of that unfolding, the courts, . . . fastened a strict liability upon the actor who caused the damage. In the decisions, which set the rules of conduct for the enclosed feudal society, the actor bore responsibility for the damage he caused without regard to whether he was at fault or whether he owed a 'duty' to the injured person. Indeed, the defendant owed a duty to all the world to conduct himself without causing injury to his fellows. It may be that the physical contraction of the feudal society imposed an imperative for maximum procurable safety, and a corresponding absolute responsibility upon its members.

"The Industrial Revolution, which cracked the solidity of the feudal society and opened up wide and new areas of expansion, changed the legal concepts. Just as the new competitiveness in the economic sphere figuratively broke out of the walls of the feudal community, so it broke through the rule of strict liability. In the place of strict liability, it introduced the theory that an action for negligence would lie only if the defendant breached a duty which he owed to plaintiff. . . .

"The classic definition of duty has been in terms of foreseeability, but the definition itself is wide and general, and its application here becomes even more difficult because of the incursion of two other factors: the so-called 'unforeseeable' plaintiff and the infliction upon such plaintiff of emotional distress. . . . 'The rule that you are to love your neighbour becomes in law, you must not injure your neighbour; and the lawyer's question, Who is my neighbour? receives a restricted reply. You must take reasonable care to avoid acts or omissions which you can reasonably foresee would be likely to injure your neighbour. Who, then, in law is my neighbour? The answer seems to be—persons who are so closely and directly affected by my act that I ought reasonably to have them in contemplation as being so affected when I am directing my mind to the acts or omissions which are called in question.'

"But our question is the more difficult because we must determine if appellant is a person who is so 'closely and directly affected' by the act of the driver of the truck that he should have reasonably had her in contemplation when he directed his mind to performing the act. Respondents would contend here that the mother of the injured child, should, instead, be characterized as an 'unforeseeable' victim of the driver's negligence and outside the zone of any apparent danger. . . .

"We believe, . . . that the proper approach is to recognize, and grant, recovery for an injury caused to one who suffers emotional distress. We think, too, that such injury is foreseeable if a defendant's conduct encompasses potential risk of harm to a class of persons which includes the plaintiff. . . .

"The point in controversy crystallizes into the issue as to who falls within the class of persons to whom respondents owed a duty. Several dangers were present when the driver negligently operated respondent ice company's truck in the vicinity of the mother and her child. There was the danger that certain persons, including the child, and possibly the mother, although she did not fear for her own safety, might be struck by the truck. There was the danger that property might be destroyed. There was the danger that certain persons might suffer physical harm as a result of fright for their own safety or for the safety of others. The foreseeability of each of these dangers constitutes a question of fact which, within the limits we set forth *infra,* should be resolved by the trier of fact and not by a mechanical rule which, insensitive to individual situations, serves merely to establish an artificial and abstract simplicity.

"We cannot rule that, as a matter of law, the injury to appellant was not foreseeable. The only justification for holding that appellant cannot state a cause of action would be, not that the injury to her, due to emotional distress, was not foreseeable, as a matter of law, but rather that the courts must deny recovery for reasons of policy; that, otherwise, factual questions will arise which are too difficult for courts or juries to decide. . . . Various courts declare themselves unable to give relief because of the absence of such requirements as (1) *physical* impact. . . . Finally, (5) some courts hold that recovery would encourage a flood of fraudulent claims which, they say, they cannot successfully segregate from deserving ones. . . .

"Thus no immutable rule calls for physical impact to justify recovery for emotional distress. The courts have long held that the occupant of land who suffers a trespass or nuisance may recover for emotional distress caused by fear for the safety of a member of his family. In *Acadia, California, Ltd.* v. *Herbert* (1960), 54 Cal.2d 328, 5 Cal.Rptr. 686, 353 P.2d 294 the Supreme Court of California said, 'regardless of whether the occupant of land has sustained physical injury, he may recover damages for the discomfort and annoyance of himself and the members of his family and for mental suffering occasioned by fear for the safety of himself and his family when such discomfort or suffering has been proximately caused by a trespass or a nuisance.' (p. 337, 5 Cal.Rptr. p. 691, 353 P.2d p. 299.) Granted that the rule expressed here derives from the earlier sensitivity of the law to the rights of the property holder, no reason forbids a similar modern recognition of the individual's interest in the protection of his emotional stability. . . .

"Courts have said that 'to allow recovery in the absence of physical injury will open the door to unfounded claims and a flood of litigation . . . .' (*State Rubbish etc. Ass'n* v. *Siliznoff* (1952), 38 Cal.2d 330, 338, 240 P.2d 282, 286.) Yet the Supreme Court in Siliznoff, in the absence of physical manifestations, gave relief for emotional distress which followed threats of physical violence. While in that case plaintiff intentionally, rather than negligently, caused the emotional upset, the court recognized that mental distress could foreseeably lead to bodily harm. Thus the cause of action need not be 'founded on a right to be free from intentional interference with mental tranquillity, but on the right to be free from negligent interference with physical well-being.' (p. 336, 240 P.2d p. 285.)

"The court in Siliznoff, moreover, did not shy away from affording recovery for the bare emotional distress because it might be simulated, but held that the jurors '[f]rom their own experience' (p. 338, 240 P.2d 440) were competent to judge the effect of different acts upon the emotions. Indeed, in an age when the teachings of psychiatry have made clear the effect of emotional disturbance, it would be incongruous to hold that we must not allow recovery for such injury because it is hard to measure or because it may be simulated.

"The various bases for refusal of relief which we have discussed do not actually touch upon the central issue as to whether respondents owed appellant a duty of due care because of the foreseeability of the emotional trauma suffered by appellant. When one is negligent in the operation of a car he should, as a reasonable man, foresee that the class of persons who may suffer harm from his misconduct includes the parent whose emotional distress issues from the exposure of his child to injury by reason of the negligence. The above grounds for refusal of relief are in substance no more than court-inspired theories to restrict the range of liability of a defendant to narrow areas; they do not relate to the key question.

"We are sympathetic with courts which do not believe that redress should be afforded for the flutter of every heart at the sight of an accident. But the need for delineating the area of liability does not justify the obliteration of the liability. We think Prosser has suggested reasonable boundary lines; the instant case falls within them. As Prosser states: 'It is clear that the injury threatened or inflicted upon the third person must be a serious one, of a nature to cause severe shock to the plaintiff, and that the shock must result in actual physical harm. The action might well be confined to members of the immediate family, or perhaps to husband, wife, parent, or child, to the exclusion of bystanders, and remote relatives. As an additional safeguard, it has been said that the plaintiff must be present at the time of the accident, or at least that the shock must be fairly contemporaneous with it, rather than follow at a later date. Admittedly such restrictions are quite arbitrary, but they may be necessary in order not to "leave the liability of a negligent defendant open to undue extension by the verdict of sympathetic juries, who under our system must define and apply any general rule to the facts of the case before them." Within some such limits, it is still possible that a rule imposing liability may ultimately be adopted.' . . .

"Within those limits the trier of the fact in the instant case may find that the emotional distress suffered by appellant was foreseeable to respondents.

"It is not consonant with the reactions, or the mores, of the society of today to hold that the mother who suffers emotional distress upon the sight of her child's injury should not recover if the trier of fact finds such injury was reasonably foreseeable. The knowledge of potential emotional trauma to a parent who witnesses an injury to a child is too clear to the negligent driver to permit an escape upon the ground of unforeseeability. In this time of death and danger on the highway, it would be anachronistic to grant immunity to the negligent driver for such foreseeable emotional disturbance upon the basis of legal abstractions that do not relate to the issue of the case." . . .

Five years later, the Amaya case was overruled by the California Supreme Court, and a mother was allowed to recover for physical harm resulting from emotional shock sustained in an "Amaya" situation.

DILLON v. LEGG

Cal.2d, 69 Cal.Rptr. 72, 441 P.2d 912 (1968)

OPINION BY TOBRINER, J. . . .

That the courts should allow recovery to a mother who suffers emotional trauma and physical injury from witnessing the infliction of death or injury to her child for which the tort-feasor is liable in negligence would appear to be a compelling proposition. As Prosser points out. All ordinary human feelings are in favor of her [the mother's] action against the negligent defendant. If a duty to her requires that she herself be in some recognizable danger, then it has properly been said that when a child is endangered, it is not beyond contemplation that its mother will be somewhere in the vicinity, and will suffer severe shock." Prosser, Law of Torts (3d ed. 1964) page 353.

Nevertheless, past American decisions have barred the mother's recovery. Refusing the mother the right to take her case to the jury, these courts ground their position on an alleged absence of a required "duty" of due care of the tort-feasor to the mother. Duty, in turn, they state, must express public policy; the imposition of duty here would work disaster because it would invite fraudulent claims and it would involve the courts in the hopeless task of defining the extent of the tort-feasor's liability. In substance, they say, definition of liability being impossible, denial of liability is the only realistic alternative.

We have concluded that neither of the feared dangers excuses the frustration of the natural justice upon which the mother's claim rests. We shall point out that in the past we have rejected the argument that we should deny recovery upon a legitimate claim because other fraudulent ones may be urged. We shall further explain that the alleged inability to fix definitions for recovery on the different facts of future cases does not justify the denial of recovery on the specific facts of the instant case; in any event, proper guidelines can indicate the extent of liability for such future cases. . . .

Whatever the possibilities of fraudulent claims of physical injury by disinterested spectators of an accident, a question not in issue in this case, we certainly cannot doubt that a mother who sees her child killed will suffer physical injury from shock. "It seems sufficiently obvious that the shock of a mother at danger or harm to her child may be both a real and a serious injury." Prosser, Law of Torts, supra, at page 353. . . .

In the second instance, and more fundamentally, the possibility that fraudulent assertions may prompt recovery in isolated cases does not justify a wholesale rejection of the entire class of claims in which that potentiality arises. . . .

The possibility that some fraud will escape detection does not justify an abdication of the judical responsibility to award damages for sound claims: if it is "to be conceded that our procedural system for the ascertainment of truth is inadequate to defeat fraudulent claims . . . , the result is a virtual acknowledgment that the courts are unable to render justice in respect to them." . . .

Indubitably juries and trial courts, constantly called upon to distinguish the frivolous from the substantial and the fraudulent from the meritorious, reach some erroneous results. But such fallibility, inherent in the judicial process, offers no reason for substituting for the case-by-case resolution of causes an artificial and indefensible barrier. Courts not only compromise their basic responsibility to decide the merits of each case individually but destroy the public's confidence in them by using the broad broom of "administrative convenience" to sweep away a class of claims a number of which are admittedly meritorious. The mere assertion that fraud is possible, "a possibility [that] exists to some degree in all cases" . . . does not prove a present necessity to abandon the neutral principles of foreseeability, proximate cause and consequential injury that generally govern tort law. . . .

We deal here with a case in which plaintiff suffered a shock which resulted in physical injury and we confine our ruling to that case. In determining, in such a case, whether defendant should reasonably foresee the injury to plaintiff, or, in other terminology, whether defendant owes plaintiff a duty of due care, the courts will take into account such factors as the following: (1) Whether plaintiff was located near the scene of the accident as contrasted with one who was a distance away from it. (2) Whether the shock resulted from a direct emotional impact upon plaintiff from the sensory and contemporaneous observance of the accident, as contrasted with learning of the accident from others after its occurrence. (3) Whether plaintiff and the victim were closely related, as contrasted with an absence of any relationship or the presence of only a distant relationship.

The evaluation of these factors will indicate the *degree* of the defendant's foreseeability: obviously defendant is more likely to foresee that a mother who observes an accident affecting her child will suffer harm than to foretell that a stranger witness will do so. Similarly, the degree of foreseeability of the third person's injury is far greater in the case of his contemporaneous observance of the accident than that in which he subsequently learns of it. The defendant is more likely to foresee that shock to the nearby, witnessing mother will cause physical harm than to anticipate that someone distant from the accident will suffer more than a temporary emotional reaction. All these elements, of course, shade into each other; the fixing of obligation, intimately tied into the facts, depends upon each case.

In light of these factors the court will determine whether the accident and harm was *reasonably* foreseeable. Such reasonable foreseeability does not turn on whether the particular defendant as an individual would have in actuality foreseen the exact accident and loss; it contemplates that courts, on a case-to-case basis, analyzing all the circumstances, will decide what the ordinary man under such circumstances should reasonably have foreseen. The courts thus mark out the areas of liability, excluding the remote and unexpected.

In the instant case, the presence of all the above factors indicates that plaintiff has alleged a sufficient prima facie case. Surely the negligent driver who causes the death of a young child may reasonably expect that the mother will not be far distant and will upon witnessing the accident suffer emotional trauma. As Dean Prosser has stated: "when a child is endangered, it is not beyond contemplation that its mother will be somewhere in the vicinity, and will suffer serious shock." Prosser, The Law of Torts, supra, at page 353. See also 2 Harper & James, The Law of Torts, supra, at page 1039.

We are not now called upon to decide whether, in the absence or reduced weight of some of the above factors, we would conclude that the accident and injury were not reasonably foreseeable and that therefore defendant owed no duty of due care to plaintiff. In future cases the courts will draw lines of demarcation upon facts more subtle than the compelling ones alleged in the complaint before us. . . .

We . . . overrule *Amaya* v. *Home Ice, Fuel & Supply Co.,* supra, 59 Cal.2d 295, 29 Cal.Rptr. 33, 379 P.2d 513.

To deny recovery would be to chain this state to an outmoded rule of the Nineteenth Century which can claim no current credence. No good reason compels our capacity to an indefensible orthodoxy.

[The judgment is reversed.]

DISSENTING OPINION BY BURKE, J. . . .

As recently as 1963 this court, in *Amaya* v. *Home Ice, Fuel & Supply Co.,* 59 Cal.2d 295, 29 Cal.Rptr. 33, 379 P.2d 513, thoroughly studied and expressly rejected the proposition . . . that tort liability may be predicated on fright or nervous shock (with consequent bodily illness) induced solely by the plaintiff's apprehension of negligently caused danger or injury to a third person. . . .

Every one of the arguments advanced in today's opinion was considered by this court and rejected, expressly or by fair implication, in Amaya. . . .

In every jurisdiction in this country that had ruled on the point at issue the decisions up to that time (1963) were unanimous in upholding the rule of nonliability. . . .

The majority, obviously recognizing that they are now embarking upon a first excursion into the "fantastic realm of infinite liability" Amaya, at page 315 of 59 Cal.2d, 29 Cal.Rptr. 33, 379 P.2d 513, undertake to provide so-called "guidelines" for the future. But notwithstanding the limitations which these "guidelines" purport to impose, it is only reasonable to expect pressure upon our trial courts to make their future rulings conform to the spirit of the new elasticity proclaimed by the majority.

Moreover, the majority's "guidelines" (ante, 441 P.2d pages 920, 921) are simply a restatement of those suggested earlier by Professor Prosser, Prosser, Torts, 2d ed., 1955, page 182; they have already been discussed and expressly rejected by this court in Amaya, pages 312-313, 29 Cal.Rptr. 33, 379 P.2d 513. Upon analysis, their seeming certainty evaporates into arbitrariness, and inexplicable distinctions appear. As we asked in Amaya: What if the plaintiff was honestly *mistaken* in believing the third person to be in danger or to be seriously injured? What if the third person had assumed the risk involved? How "close" must the relationship be between the plaintiff and the third person? I. e., what if the third person was the plaintiff's beloved niece or nephew, grandparent, fiancé, or lifelong friend, more dear to the plaintiff than her immediate family? Next, how "near" must the plaintiff have been to the scene of the accident, and how "soon" must shock have been felt? Indeed, what is the magic in the plaintiff's being actually present? Is the shock any less real if the mother does not know of the accident until her injured child is brought into her home? On the other hand, is it any less real if the mother is physically present at the scene but is nevertheless unaware of the danger or injury to her child until after the accident has occurred? No answers to these questions are to be found in today's majority opinion. Our trial courts, however, will not so easily escape the burden of distinguishing between litigants on the basis of such artificial and unpredictable distinctions. . . .

The leading case of *Waube* v. *Warrington* (1935) 216 Wis. 603, 613, 258 N.W. 497, 501, . . . had this to say: . . . "The answer to this question cannot be reached solely by logic, nor is it clear that it can be entirely disposed of by a consideration of what the defendant ought reasonably to have anticipated as a consequence of his wrong. The answer must be reached by balancing the social interests involved in order to ascertain how far defendant's duty and plaintiff's right may justly and expediently be extended. It is our conclusion that they can neither justly nor expediently be extended to any recovery for physical injuries sustained by one out of the range of ordinary physical peril as a result of the shock of witnessing another's danger. Such consequences are so unusual and extraordinary, viewed after the event, that a user of the highway may be said not to subject others to an unreasonable risk of them by the careless management of his vehicle. Furthermore, the liability imposed by such a doctrine of the negligent tort-feasor, would put an unreasonable burden upon users of the highway, open the way to fraudulent claims, and enter a field that has no sensible or just stopping point."

As this court declared in Amaya, page 315 of 59 Cal.2d p. 45 of 29 Cal.Rptr., page 529 of 379 P.2d, there is good sense in the conclusion of the court in Waube that "the liability imposed by such a doctrine is wholly out of proportion to the culpability of the negligent tort-feasor"; further, to permit recovery by every person who might adversely feel some lingering effect of the defendant's conduct would throw us into "the fantastic realm of infinite liability." Yet the majority opinion in the present case simply omits to either mention or discuss the injustice to California defendants flowing from such a disproportionate extension of their liability—an injustice which plainly constituted a "prime hypothesis" for rejection of the liability sought to be imposed by the plaintiffs in Waube and in Amaya. See also *Jelley* v. *LaFlame* (N.H. 1968) supra, 238 A.2d 728, 730, citing with approval and following this ground of decision expressed in Waube and in Amaya.

Additionally, the majority fail to explain their bare assertion, ante, 441 P.2d page 916, that contributory negligence of Erin will defeat any recovery by plaintiff mother and sister.[1] The familiar and heretofore unquestioned principle is that the relationships of parent and child or of husband and wife *in themselves furnish no basis* for imputation of contributory negligence. Witkin, Summary of Cal.Law, Torts, § 341, page 1542; Rest., Torts 2d, § 488. Is this principle now abrogated in California? If so, it is a ruling extending far beyond the confines of the particular issue now before us, and reaches potentially every negligence action in which the plaintiffs are members of the same family.

It appears to me that in the light of today's majority opinion the matter at issue should be commended to the attention of the Legislature of this state. Five years have elapsed since our Amaya decision, during which that body has not undertaken to change the law we there declared. We may presume, therefore, that the limitations upon liability there affirmed comport with legislative views. But if all alleged California tort-feasors, including motorists, home and other property owners, and governmental entities, are now to be faced with the concept of potentially infinite liability beyond any rational relationship to their culpability, then surely the point has been reached at which the Legislature should reconsider the entire subject and allow all interests affected to be heard.

I would affirm the judgment.

McComb, J., concurs.

(d) *Substantial factor test.* Other courts, guided primarily by a concept of practical expediency, have cut the Gordian knot of determining the existence of "cause" by holding it sufficient that the act in question played a substantial part in bringing about the plaintiff's harm.

Notice that this does not require that the defendant's conduct be the only cause. Hence, when harm is caused by two actors, as when the plaintiff

---

[1] Neither does the majority opinion enlighten us as to how the contributory negligence of either (a) plaintiff mother or (b) plaintiff sister will assertedly, defeat any recovery *by the other.*

is harmed by being run over by two different automobiles, neither defendant can escape liability, if otherwise at fault, by asserting that his act did not cause the harm because the plaintiff would have been harmed anyway by the act of the other defendant. To the contrary, each defendant is liable for the harm which he causes to the plaintiff even though others cause similar harm. Likewise, a defendant's act is a liability-imposing cause although by itself it might not have caused harm had not some other person acted, so that the combined conduct "causes" the plaintiff's harm.

This theory has been applied in situations such as the following: Defendant #1 parked his truck in the street near the bottom of a ditch on a dark, foggy night. Iron pipes carried in the truck projected beyond the truck nine feet in back. Neither the truck nor the pipes carried any warning light or flag, thus violating both city ordinance and state statute. Defendant #2 was a taxicab owner whose taxicab was negligently driven at an excessive speed and ran into the pipes, thereby killing the passenger in the taxi. The plaintiff brought an action for the passenger's death. Defendant #1 claimed he was not liable because it was the negligent act of Defendant #2 which caused the harm. It was held that this defense was not valid as the negligence of each had been a cause of the decedent's harm and therefore neither defendant could be allowed to say that he was not liable because he was not the sole cause.

§ 28:2. Criminal Law

(a) Generally. In criminal law, a more strict test of "cause" is applied in some instances in order to protect the person and the liberty of the defendant.

PENNSYLVANIA v. ROOT

403 Pa. 571, 170 A.2d 310 (1961)

Root was challenged to an illegal auto race at night on a public highway. While the challenger was doing 70 to 90 miles an hour in a 50-mile-an-hour no-passing zone, he crossed the dividing line in attempting to pass Root, struck an oncoming truck, and was killed. Root was prosecuted for involuntary manslaughter. From a conviction, Root appealed.

OPINION BY JONES, C.J. . . .

While precedent is to be found for application of the tort law concept of "proximate cause" in fixing responsibility for criminal homicide, the want of any rational basis for its use in determining criminal liability can no longer be properly disregarded. When proximate cause was first borrowed from the field of tort law and applied to homicide prosecutions in Pennsylvania, the concept connoted a much more direct causal relation in producing the alleged culpable result than it does today. Proximate cause, as an essential element of a tort founded in negligence, has undergone in recent times, and is still undergoing, a marked extension. More specifically, this area of civil law has been progressively liberalized in favor of claims for damages for personal injuries to which careless conduct of others can in some way be associated. To persist in applying the tort liability concept of proximate cause to prosecutions for criminal homicide after the marked expansion of *civil* liability of defendants in tort actions for negligence would be to extend possible *criminal* liability to persons chargeable with unlawful or reckless conduct in circumstances not generally considered to present the likelihood of a resultant death. . . .

Legal theory which makes guilt or innocence of criminal homicide depend upon such accidental and fortuitous circumstances as are now embraced by modern tort law's encompassing concept of proximate cause is too harsh to be just. A few illustrations should suffice to so demonstrate.

In *Mautino* v. *Piercedale Supply Co.,* 1940, 338 Pa. 435, 12 A.2d 51—a civil action for damages—we held that where a man sold a cartridge to a person under 16 years of age in violation of a State statute and the recipient subsequently procured a gun from which he fired the cartridge injuring someone, the injury was proximately caused by the act of the man who sold the cartridge to the underage person. If proximate cause were the test for criminal liability and the injury to the plaintiff in the Mautino case had been fatal, the man who sold the bullet to the underage person (even though the boy had the appearance of an adult) would have been guilty of involuntary manslaughter, for his unlawful act would, according to the tort law standard, have been the proximate cause of the death. . . .

In *Marchl* v. *Dowling & Company,* 1945, 157 Pa.Super. 91, 41 A.2d 427, . . . where a truck driver had double parked his truck and the minor plaintiff was struck by a passing car when she walked around the double parked truck, the truck driver's employer was held liable in tort for the plaintiff's injuries on the ground that the truck driver's act of double parking, which violated both a State statute and a city ordinance, was the proximate cause of the plaintiff's injuries. Here, also, if proximate cause were the test for criminal liability and the plaintiff's injuries had been fatal, the truck driver would have been guilty of involuntary manslaughter since his unlawful act would have been the proximate cause of the death for which his employer was held liable in damages. . . . To be guilty of involuntary manslaughter for double parking would, of course, be unthinkable, yet if proximate cause were to determine criminal liability, such a result would indeed be a possibility. . . .

If the tort liability concept of proximate cause were to be applied in a criminal homicide prosecution, then the conduct of the person whose death is the basis of the indictment would have to be considered, not to prove that it was merely an *additional* proximate cause of the death, but to determine, under fundamental and long recognized law applicable to proximate cause, whether the subsequent wrongful act *superseded* the original conduct chargeable to the defendant. If it did in fact supervene, then the original act is so insulated from the ensuing death as not to be its proximate cause. . . .

In this case, the conduct of the defendant was not the proximate cause of the decedent's death as a matter of law. . . .

The deceased was aware of the dangerous condition created by the defendant's reckless conduct in driving his automobile at an excessive rate of speed along the highway but, despite such knowledge, he recklessly chose to swerve his car to the left and into the path of an oncoming truck, thereby bringing about the head-on collision which caused his own death.

To summarize, the tort liability concept of proximate cause has no proper place in prosecutions for criminal homicide and more direct causal connection is required for conviction. . . . In the instant case, the defendant's reckless conduct was not a sufficiently direct cause of the competing driver's death to make him criminally liable therefor. . . .

[Conviction reversed.]

DISSENTING OPINION BY EAGEN, J. . . .

If the defendant did not engage in the unlawful race and so operate his automobile in such a reckless manner, this accident would never have occurred. He helped create the dangerous event. He was a vital part of it. The victim's acts were a natural reaction to the stimulus of the situation. The race, the attempt to pass the other car and forge ahead, the reckless speed, all of these factors the defendant himself helped create. He was part and parcel of them. That the victim's response was normal under the circumstances, that his reaction should have been expected and was clearly foreseeable, is to me beyond argument. That the defendant's recklessness was a substantial factor is obvious. All of this, in my opinion, makes his unlawful conduct a direct cause of the resulting collision. . . .

Acts should be judged by their tendency under the known circumstances, not by the actual intent which accompanies their performance. Every day of the year, we read that some teen-agers, or young adults, somewhere in this country, have been killed or have killed others, while racing their automobiles. Hair-raising, death-defying, law-breaking rides, which encompass "racing," are the rule rather than the exception, and endanger not only the participants, but also every motorist and passenger on the road. To call such . . . [conduct] unlikely to result in death, is to ignore the cold and harsh reality of everyday occurrences. . . .

1 Wharton, Criminal Law and Procedure § 68 [Anderson Edition] (1957), speaking of causal connections, says: "A person is only criminally liable for what he has caused, that is, there must be a causal relationship between his act and harm sustained for which he is prosecuted. It is not essential to the existence of a causal relationship that the ultimate harm which has resulted was foreseen or intended by the actor. It is sufficient that the ultimate harm is one which a reasonable man would foresee as being reasonably related to the acts of the defendant." Section 295, in speaking about manslaughter, says: "When homicide is predicated upon the negligence of the defendant, it must be shown that his negligence was the proximate cause or a contributing cause of the victim's death. It must appear that the death was not the result of misadventure, but the natural and probable result of a reckless or culpably negligent act. To render a person

criminally liable for negligent homicide, the duty omitted or improperly performed must have been his personal duty, and the negligent act from which death resulted must have been his personal act, and not the act of another. But he is not excused because the negligence of someone else contributed to the result, when his act was the primary or proximate cause and the negligence of the other did not intervene between his act and the result."

Professor Joseph Beale, late renowned member of the Harvard Law School faculty, in an article entitled, The Proximate Consequence of an Act, 33 Harv.L.Rev. 633, 646, said, "Though there is an active force intervening after defendant's act, the result will nevertheless be proximate if the defendant's act actually caused the intervening force. In such a case the defendant's force is really continuing in active operation *by means of the force it stimulated into activity."* . . . 2 Bishop, New Criminal Law § 424 (1913), says: "He whose act causes in any way, directly or indirectly, the death of another, kills him, within the meaning of felonious homicide. It is a rule of both reason and the law that whenever one's will contributes to impel a physical force, whether another's, his own, or a combined force, proceeding from whatever different sources, he is responsible for the result, the same as though his hand, unaided, had produced it."

But, says the majority opinion, these are principles of tort law and should not in these days be applied to the criminal law. But such has been the case since the time of Blackstone. These same principles have always been germane to both crimes and tort. . . . They have been repeatedly so applied throughout the years and were employed in a criminal case in Pennsylvania as long as one hundred and seventeen years ago. See *Commonwealth* v. *Hare,* 1844, 2 Clark 467. In that case, two separate bands of men were fighting each other with firearms in a public street and, as a result, an innocent citizen was shot and killed. The person firing the fatal shot could not be ascertained. Hare, one of the rioters, was convicted of homicide and the judgment was affirmed. Can anyone question the logic or correctness of this decision? Under the rationale of the majority opinion, what would be the result in the Hare case? Certainly, under its reasoning, if the truck driver met death under the circumstances the case at hand presents, the defendant would not be legally responsible. Again with this conclusion, I cannot agree.

While the victim's foolhardiness in this case contributed to his own death, he was not the only one responsible and it is not he alone with whom we are concerned. It is the people of the Commonwealth who are harmed by the kind of conduct the defendant pursued. Their interests must be kept in mind. . . .

(b) Felony-murder rule. The strict definition of "cause" as seen in the Root case conflicts with the concept of the felony-murder. By this latter concept, if a person takes part in a felony and a homicide occurs in the course of its commission, such person is ordinarily guilty of murder, even though he took no actual part in the killing and even though no killing was intended. For example, assume that robbers plan to burglarize a house of which the owners are away on vacation. They do not have any guns or deadly weapons. One of their group waits outside the house in the getaway

car. Assume that a neighbor of the homeowner happened to be in the house checking the water pipes and the windows. The burglars encounter him. There is a minor scuffle during which the neighbor slips and falls to the ground, striking his head on a hard object, and such fall causes his death. The driver in the getaway car is guilty of murder because the homicide occurred in the commission of a felony.

If the strict doctrine of "cause" of the Root case were applied, it would be held that the driver in the getaway car was not guilty of murder and probably not guilty of any crime. This conflict between the Root case and the felony-murder rule cannot be explained, except in terms of the desire of society to protect persons who might be killed by deterring felonies by imposing the maximum liability upon any participant therein for any harm that occurs. That is to say, in the felony-murder rule, the person and life of the victim are valued more highly, while in the Root case the concern was greater for the life and person of the participant rather than the possible victim. Paralleling the felony-murder rule, the common law developed the principle that a homicide occurring in the commission of an ordinary misdemeanor was manslaughter.

NEW JERSEY v. McKEIVER

89 N.J.S. 52, 213 A.2d 320 (1965)

McKeiver entered a tavern and held it up. He fired a warning shot into the ceiling. One of the patrons died of fright. McKeiver was prosecuted for murder.

OPINION BY YANCEY, J.C.C. . . .

At about 1:30 a.m., October 29, 1963, defendant entered the Green Village Tavern in Newark, New Jersey. Tied around his head was a light gray handkerchief, which concealed the lower part of his face. Upon entering the tavern he immediately fired a shot into the ceiling and ordered the bartender and four other persons to move to the end of the bar. Defendant then commanded these persons to place their wallets on the bar, and they complied. He then went to the back of the bar and opened the cash register and took approximately $90. After so doing, defendant picked up the wallets and ordered the victims to walk toward the front door of the tavern. As they were doing this, Mrs. Julia Yuhas toppled over and fell to the floor. Defendant, on seeing this, ran out of the front door of the tavern and disappeared.

Minutes later Mrs. Yuhas was administered first aid by the Newark Emergency Squad and was subsequently taken to Newark City Hospital. She was pronounced dead at 2:05 a.m. by Dr. Evke of the hospital staff. An autopsy performed by the Chief Medical Examiner, Dr. Edwin H. Albano, disclosed, in the doctor's opinion, that Mrs. Yuhas' death was "due to fright during hold-up in tavern: cardiac arrest; occlusive arteriosclerotic coronary artery disease."

Defendant was subsequently apprehended and, as stated, indicted for murder. The indictment was returned on the theory that decedent met her death as a result of defendant's actions during the course of a robbery he was committing. The State, under this indictment, contends that since death resulted during the commission of a high misdemeanor (robbery), a charge of first degree murder is appropriate under the "felony-murder" theory. . . .

Defendant contends that his acts do not substantiate the State's charge of felony murder. He grounds this contention, and relies heavily, on the fact that there was no direct physical contact between himself and decedent, and therefore his acts were not those which would render him responsible for Mrs. Yuhas' death. . . .

The statute upon which the indictment was returned, declares:

"Murder which is perpetrated by means of poison, or by lying in wait, or by any other kind of willful, deliberate and premeditated killing, or which is committed in perpetrating or attempting to perpetrate arson, burglary, kidnapping, rape, robbery or sodomy, is murder in the first degree. . . ."

The statute is a codification of the so-called "felony-murder rule" which was developed in England under the common law. The rule places upon a man committing a felony, or attempting to commit a felony, the hazard of being guilty of murder if he creates any substantial human risk which would actually result in the loss of life; and it does this without excluding those homicides which occur so unexpectedly that no reasonable man would have considered any risk of this nature to be involved. The English jurists reasoned that certain felonies have been attended so frequently by death or great bodily harm, even when not intended or contemplated by the particular wrongdoer, that they must be classified as dangerous. Common experience points to the presence of a substantial human risk from the perpetration of such wrongful acts as arson, burglary, rape, and robbery. The intent to avoid all personal harm, formed in the mind of the transgressor at the time he embarks upon such a felony, is no reasonable safeguard that death will not result from his illegal actions. . . .

In the instant case, the death occurred during the perpetration of an act which created substantial human risk. Defendant had in his hand a pistol, which he fired to demonstrate to the patrons of the tavern that he meant to place them in fear of losing their lives or receiving great bodily harm if they did not immediately submit to his demands. It does not matter whether he intended to do actual harm, or whether he did not contemplate decedent's death by his acts.

The death occurred during the commission of a high misdemeanor. . . .

After careful consideration, I find that death occurred under circumstances which substantiate the theory of "felony-murder."

There still remains to be determined the more difficult question of whether or not defendant can be held responsible for the death of Mrs. Yuhas, since there appears to have been no actual physical contact with her that led to her demise.

Under early common law there could be no culpable homicide unless it was the result of some kind of bodily harm inflicted upon the victim. The reasoning for such holding was due to the dreaded fear, perhaps then justified, of prosecutions based on witchcraft or sorcery. . . . Modern courts have come to reject this view, and it has been considered unreasonable and possibly subversive of justice that criminal responsibility should not attach under circumstances where death resulted from nonphysical forces such as terror and grief. . . . See also Ex parte Heigho, 18 Idaho 566, 110 P. 1029 (Sup.Ct. 1910).

Fright, or other "mental force" as it has been called . . . will receive judicial recognition if it is accompanied by physical force. Physical force does not necessitate physical contact, because one can exert physical force over another by "working upon the fancy of another or treating him harshly or unkindly," as by certain actions which might cause him to "die of fear or grief." . . .

In the Heigho case, supra, defendant and another went to the home of a person named Barton to discuss a grievance. Heigho was wearing a gun in plain view on his person. During the ensuing argument blows were exchanged between Heigho and Barton. Present during the altercation was Barton's mother-in-law, Mrs. Riegleman. She became upset and excited due to the fight, and as a result expired shortly thereafter of aneurysm of the ascending aorta. No one had touched her during the struggle between Heigho and Barton. The Idaho Court held that Heigho could be tried for manslaughter.

In the instant case, defendant is charged with causing death while committing a robbery, a common-law felony. In Heigho death came to the woman while she witnessed a fight. In the case at bar, Mrs. Yuhas, who was also a victim of robbery, died.

The indictment as presented is sufficient in that it sets forth the necessary facts required to adequately charge defendant with the crime of murder, within the purview of the statute. The fact that there was no physical contact with decedent does not negate the premise that a homicide occurred as a result of fear and apprehension during defendant's commission of a robbery. . . .

§ 28:3. Immunity from Liability

(a) Generally. In certain instances, conduct that would otherwise impose liability upon the actor does not do so because he has some immunity which shields him. This concept has widest application in the field of tort law. It has a parallel in the field of contract law where certain persons, as minors, may avoid their contracts. There is also a parallel in the field of criminal law where persons who are deemed insane are not punishable for acts which would otherwise be criminal. A different type of exemption exists in the case of diplomatic representatives of foreign countries who, in varying degrees, are exempt from the operation of the criminal law.

(b) Tort immunity. Governments are generally immune from liability. This has been eroded by decision and in some instances by statutes, such as the Federal Tort Claims Act, which, subject to certain exceptions, permits the recovery of damages for property, personal injury, or death action claims arising from the negligent act or omission of any employee of the United

States under such circumstances that the United States "if a private person, would be liable to the claimant in accordance with the law of the place where the act or omission occurred."

Public officers, when acting within the sphere of their discretion, and higher public executive officials are immune from tort liability.

At common law, no suit could be brought by a husband against his wife and vice versa. By statute, this immunity has been abolished as to torts involving property. The immunity continues in most states with respect to personal torts, whether intentional or negligent, although some two fifths of the states now allow personal tort actions between spouses.

The common-law rule for the most part was based on the theory that the allowance of interspousal suits for personal torts would disturb domestic tranquility; even when the victim had left home or procured a divorce or brought a criminal prosecution because of such wrongful conduct. The modern view regards this reason as absurd. The trend of judicial decision also rejects the argument that the allowance of such suits would open the door to fraud and collusion between spouses when one of them was insured.

A similar immunity exists between parent and child in most states with respect to personal tort claims. A trend toward abolishing parental immunity, paralleling the rising abolition of the spousal immunity, has begun to appear.

Charities were once exempt from tort law. For example, a hospital could not be held liable for the negligent harm caused by its staff or employees to a patient. Within the last three decades this immunity has been rejected in nearly two thirds of the states. It is quite likely that with the coming years it will be repudiated generally.

HEBEL v. HEBEL

435 P.2d 8 (Alaska, 1967)

Douglas Hebel, aged six, was riding in an automobile driven by his mother, Sandra Hebel. Because of her negligence in driving, Douglas was injured. He brought suit against his mother in order to establish liability to enable him to proceed against her public liability insurer. The defense was raised that a minor could not sue his mother for tort injury.

OPINION BY RABINOWITZ, J. . . .

The subject of parental immunity encompasses controversial, complex, and delicate issues. The doctrine has received exhaustive treatment in law reviews, treatises, and opinions of numerous state courts. Generally the law review authors and treatise writers are extremely critical of the parental immunity doctrine and its concomitant disallowance of negligence actions on behalf of unemancipated minors. On the other hand, the weight of judicial authority is clearly in favor of refusing the unemancipated minor a remedy for any injury inflicted through the negligence of the minor's parents.

While fully cognizant of judicial antipathy to the allowance of suits by unemancipated minors against their parents, we are persuaded that on the facts of this record the minor child should be granted a remedy for any injuries sustained.

In *Ranson* v. *Haner* [1] we said we would not be bound by the mere weight of judicial precedent but rather by the rule which embodies the more persuasive reasoning. We adhere to the views expressed in this prior decision and in so doing have determined that the more persuasive reasoning favors allowance of this negligence action by the unemancipated minor. To a large extent today's decision was foreshadowed by our holding in *Cramer* [v. *Cramer*] [2] which allowed intraspousal negligence actions. Although our decision in Cramer involved, to some extent, construction of our Married Women's Statutes, we also relied upon the policy rationale of two, then recent, decisions of the courts of California in which the doctrine of intraspousal immunity for personal tort actions was abolished.

Since this is a question of first impression in our jurisdiction, we consider it appropriate to discuss briefly the historical antecedents of the parental or family immunity doctrine, as well as judicial precedents in this area.

At early common law in matters concerning property, there was no bar to actions between parents and minor children. As to a minor's suit involving a personal tort action based on the negligence of the parent, it appears that there are no reported early English common-law decisions on the subject.

American precedent begins in 1891 with the case of *Hewlett* v. *George* [3] where the family immunity doctrine was first announced. There the Mississippi court held that a minor child could not maintain a false imprisonment action against her mother for maliciously confining her in an insane asylum. In reaching this result the court cited no authority, basing its decision on the rationale that, "The peace of society . . . and a sound public policy, designed to subserve the repose of families and the best interests of society, forbid to the minor child a right to appear in court in the assertion of a claim to civil redress for personal injuries suffered at the hands of the parent." . . .

From this base the family immunity doctrine, after a relatively slow start, came to be applied almost uniformly by those jurisdictions which have ruled on the question, to bar negligence actions between an unemancipated minor and his parents. We consider it pertinent to discuss briefly the many exceptions and qualifications to the family immunity doctrine before explaining our rejection of the doctrine in the case at bar.

It is firmly established that the emancipated child may sue the parent, and the parent may sue the emancipated child, for negligent wrongs, and that an unemancipated minor child may sue his parents for his property. There are authorities which have permitted an unemancipated minor to maintain an action for personal injuries willfully or intentionally inflicted; authorities which have allowed suits where the injuries were caused by unintentional but willful, reckless, or grossly negligent conduct; and authorities which have held that the parental immunity rule does not prohibit a negligence action by an unemancipated minor against the estate of his deceased parent. Where

---

[1] 362 P.2d 282, 287 (Alaska, 1961).
[2] 379 P.2d 95 (Alaska, 1963).
[3] 68 Miss. 703, 9 So. 885, 13 L.R.A. 682 (1891).

the special circumstance of a carrier-passenger relationship existed between the minor and the parent, suit has been allowed. Similarly, when a master-servant relationship is present, the courts have allowed the action. And where the parent was not acting in a parental capacity but rather in his business or vocational capacity, suit has been allowed. Thus, it is apparent that there exists an ever increasing number of judicially fashioned qualifications and exceptions to the parental immunity doctrine.

As to the bases for the parental immunity doctrine in regard to ordinary negligence actions, the courts on various occasions have advanced the following explanations: Allowance of such causes of action would deplete the family exchequer; would encourage fraud and collusion; would disrupt domestic tranquility; and would interfere with parental care, discipline, and control. Additionally, some courts have analogized from the intraspousal immunity doctrine in adopting the rule of parental immunity.

As to reliance upon intraspousal immunity doctrine, our decision in *Cramer* v. *Cramer* disposes of this basis for the parental immunity rule. Concerning the depletion of the family exchequer rationale, the New Hampshire court in *Briere* v. *Briere*[4] made the following apposite comments:

"As to the depletion of the family exchequer, the court in the Dunlap case summarily rejected this argument as having no substantial weight and said that it ignored 'the parent's power to distribute favors as he will, and leaves out of the picture the depletion of the child's assets of health and strength through the injury.' . . . To this may be added today's reality that if the father has means, he will almost inevitably carry insurance, and if he has not, the chances of anyone bringing suit for the child are remote. . . . We agree that the existence of insurance should not impose a duty upon a parent where none existed before. . . . However, as a practical matter, the prevalence of insurance cannot be ignored in determining whether a court should continue to discriminate against a class of individuals by depriving them of a right enjoyed by all other individuals." . . .

In regard to the fraud-collusion-perjury argument, we are of the opinion that it does not warrant denial of a remedy to the child. . . . "One may not, of course, deny the hazard, but such a danger, being present in all liability insurance cases, furnishes reason not for denial of a cause of action, but for added caution on the part of court and jury in examining and assessing the facts. The danger is precisely the same when the injury is to a child who has attained 21 or to a brother or sister or, to a less degree, to a friend." . . .

This brings us to the frequently urged ground that allowance of the action by the unemancipated minor would be disruptive of family harmony. We are of the opinion that our decision in Cramer points to rejection of this argument for there we were unpersuaded by a similar argument which was advanced in regard to disruption of conjugal harmony. . . .

" 'It is reasonably clear that the domestic peace has already been disturbed beyond repair or where by reason of the circumstances it is not imperiled, and where the reasonableness of family discipline is not involved.' . . . One situation in which family harmony is not thereby disturbed arises where there is liability insurance coverage. . . .

---

[4] 107 N.H. 432, 224 A.2d 588, 590 (1966).

"We consider the wide prevalence of liability insurance in personal injury actions a proper element to be considered in making the policy decision of whether to abrogate parental immunity in negligence actions. This is because in a great majority of such actions, where such immunity has been abolished, the existence of insurance tends to negate any possible disruption of family harmony and discipline. . . .

"The problem, in short, comes to this: A child is seriously injured by his father's careless operation or maintenance of his automobile. As the law now stands, the judgment recovered against the parent is more than likely, in the vast majority of cases, to be paid by an insurer. If the crippled child may have the benefit of this insurance, a fund will be supplied the family to provide for him. If the fund is cut off, cripple as well as parent will have to stagger beneath the load. To tell them that the pains must be endured for the peace and welfare of the family is something of a mockery."

On the balance we believe that the scales should be weighed in favor of affording the injured child a remedy in this case. In reaching this decision we are not unaware of the pivotal role the family has assumed, and will continue to play, in our culture. Nor are we oblivious to the continuing need for parental discipline and control within the family grouping. And we are fully cognizant that there are large areas of activities within the family sphere involving parental discipline, care, and control which should and must remain free from judicial intrusion. . . .

At this time we believe it unnecessary to attempt to define precisely what scope should be given to the doctrine of parental immunity. Rather, we limit our decision to the factual situation before us, and hold that the unemancipated minor has a right of action against her mother for personal injuries allegedly sustained as a result of the parent's negligent driving.

We remain unpersuaded by the traditional explanations which have been proffered in favor of parental immunity. Analysis of them has convinced us that neither individually nor collectively do the arguments in support of the immunity rule outweigh the necessity of according the minor child a remedy for wrongful negligent injury to his person. And it is this factor of a negligent wrong that we believe to be of paramount significance. It appears to us illogical to sanction property actions between unemancipated minors and their children; to allow an action if the child happens to be emancipated; to permit an action if the parent inflicts intentional harm upon the child; or if that harm is inflicted through negligence characterized as gross or wanton; to permit an action should the child happen to be injured in the course of the parent's business or vocation; to permit an action if the parent is deceased; but, on the other hand, to deny the unemancipated child redress for his personal injuries when caused by the negligence of a living parent.

We are of the further view that although the existence of liability insurance does not create liability, its presence is of considerable significance here. To persist in adherence to family-harmony and parental-discipline-and-control arguments when there is automobile liability insurance involved is in our view unrealistic. If there is insurance, there is small possibility that parental discipline will be undermined, or that the peace of the family will be shattered by allowance of the action. . . .

§ 28:4.   Contributory Negligence and Assumption of Risk

(a) Generally. The doctrines of contributory negligence and assumption of risk serve to limit the liability of the defendant by narrowing the scope of the consequences that he has "caused." The net effect of these doctrines is to assure the defendant that he will only be required to answer for the consequences of his own conduct and that where damage in part is caused by the voluntary act of the plaintiff, the defendant will not be held liable for the consequence of such conduct even though the activity in which he was engaged contributed to the harm sustained.

(b) Effect of contributory negligence and assumption of risk. At common law, the plaintiff was barred from any recovery if he were in any degree negligent and such negligence contributed to the harm that he sustained. Whether he was more or less negligent than the defendant was immaterial.

In all cases, the assumption of a risk, as in the case of taking a job painting the side of a house from rope-held scaffolding, barred recovery for the "normal" harm resulting from the risk.

By statute, the doctrine of contributory negligence has been replaced in some states by the doctrine of comparative negligence in which a comparison is made of the negligence of the plaintiff and the defendant, and the negligence of the plaintiff merely reduces his recovery but does not bar it. In some types of proceedings, as workmen's compensation claims, the defense of assumption of risk has generally been abolished but still exists as between persons who are not employer and employee.

A modification has been made by the courts to the concept of contributory negligence by holding that if the defendant had the last clear chance to avoid harming the plaintiff, the defendant is liable for such harm although the negligence of the plaintiff had contributed to creating the harm-causing situation.

(c) Spectators. In most instances, a spectator will be held to assume the risks which were characteristic of the activity witnessed. The underlying basis for such holding is that of practical expediency. Namely, that it would be impossible as a practical matter to require the person conducting the activity to make a distinction between the great majority of spectators who would understand the hazards of the activity and the few who might not appreciate the risk involved.

PERRY v. SEATTLE SCHOOL DISTRICT

66 Wash.2d 800, 405 P.2d 589 (1965)

Tom played football on his high school team. In accordance with promotional efforts of the school to bring relatives to the games, he invited his grandmother, Louise Perry, aged 67, to see him play. She had seen one football game before from a grandstand seat. At this high school there were no seats available to the grandmother, and spectators stood along the playing field. Louise stood on the sideline a few feet from the playing field and was talking to her daughter and a friend of the latter. While so engaged, a player in the game was driven out of bounds and ran into Louise. She sued the school district for the injuries she sustained.

OPINION BY HILL, J. . . .

At the time the accident occurred, the plaintiff and her daughter were about a foot or two back of the line indicating the boundary of the playing field and were standing at a place where they were supposed to be as far as the defendant and its supervisors were concerned; that being off the field and back of the line. The plaintiff and Mrs. McLeod were conversing and none of them seemed to have been paying close attention to the progress of the game. Just before the accident the offensive team was starting a play from about the 30-yard line when the ball carrier . . . made a wide end run around the east side of the playing field, running close to the sidelines. As he arrived opposite where the plaintiff was standing, he was hit by two Garfield players, knocked out of bounds, and into the plaintiff, who was thrown violently to the ground and was severely and permanently injured. She was standing with all the other persons in the crowd which was watching the game; she did not watch the player carry the ball on the play in question and did not see him until just before she was struck when the player was tackled. . . .

"There was danger and hazard to spectators standing where the plaintiff stood when the play came her way unless such persons stepped away." . . .

The court finds that the plaintiff was invited by the defendant to attend the game in question and complied with the rules and requests of the defendant that she stand back of the line marking the playing field at all times. No other instructions were given to plaintiff. . . .

Reasonable minds might conclude that the school district was negligent in not having placed ropes five yards back from the side lines and in failing to keep spectators that distance from the playing field, or in failing to have had bleachers for spectators on both sides of the playing field (on the same theory that professional baseball parks are required to have certain areas in the grandstands, protected by netting, available to those who desire such protection). . . .

Other equally reasonable minds might conclude that the chances were minimal that the friends and relatives of the participants, together with the students and fans attending a third-team football game, would not be fully aware of the hazards involved in side-line spectatorship and that the chances of a spectator being seriously injured were remote. They would then reach the ultimate conclusion that the school district was under no duty to go to the expense of roping off the field and providing the necessary policing to try to keep spectators back of the ropes, or to provide bleachers for those, if any, who desired them.

Whether or not the plaintiff was as completely ignorant of the game of football as her testimony indicates, is not controlling on the issue of negligence. The question of the ordinary care required of the defendant must, to some extent, be predicated upon the knowledge of the ordinary person of the risk involved. As Prosser suggests, the owner of a hockey rink is not required to ask each entering patron whether he has ever witnessed a hockey game before, but can reasonably assume that the danger of being hit by the puck is understood and accepted.

There was substantial evidence to sustain the trial court's finding that the school district was not negligent.

We now turn our attention to the evidence supporting the trial court's finding that the plaintiff wife [Tom's grandmother] was contributorily negligent. . . .

Had she been watching it for the fifteen seconds prior to the time she was hit, she would have seen an end run developing and coming in her direction, and she could doubtless have gotten out of the way as everyone else did. However, she was not watching the game, but was engaging in a conversation with a friend; and she did not see the approaching ball carrier until he was too close for her to avoid him. Even, conceding the ignorance of the game of football claimed by the plaintiff wife, some objective standard of negligence must be applied. She cannot be heard to say that she did not comprehend a risk which would be apparent to a reasonably prudent and cautious person. . . .

The plaintiff wife had a duty to protect herself not only against dangers of which she had actual knowledge, but such dangers incident to the game as would be apparent to a reasonable person in the exercise of due care. . . .

The trier of the facts could certainly find, as the trial court did here, that the defendant School District was not negligent and that the plaintiff wife was contributorily negligent. . . .

It is argued that there could be no assumption of risk, as the plaintiff wife had no knowledge of the game of football and could not assume a risk of which she had no knowledge.

While it is clear that a plaintiff must know the risk before it can be assumed, it is equally clear that he cannot deny knowledge of the obvious. ". . . By entering freely and voluntarily into any relation or situation which presents obvious danger, the plaintiff may be taken to accept it, and to undertake to look out for himself and relieve the defendant of responsibility. Thus those who participate or sit as spectators at sports and amusements may be taken to assume all the known risks of being hurt by roller coasters, flying baseballs, golf balls, or wrestlers, or such things as fireworks explosions. . . ."

There is here a factual issue on assumption of risk both as to the actual knowledge of the plaintiff wife, and as to whether, if there was not actual knowledge, the danger was so obvious that knowledge could be implied.

The plaintiff knew that there was such a game as football. She had previously seen a game, albeit in the protection of the stands at the Seattle High School Memorial Stadium. The trier of the facts might well have inferred that anybody who had ever seen an entire football game must know that some plays do go out of bounds.

The trier of the facts might also have inferred that in the game at which the plaintiff wife was injured, it was obvious to any person of ordinary intelligence that plays might go out of bounds.

The trier of the facts, in this case, concluded that there was an assumption of risk, and it is our view that he was entitled so to do.

We, therefore, affirm on all three grounds relied upon by the trial court, i.e., no negligence on the part of the defendant; contributory negligence on the part of the plaintiff wife; and assumption of risk by the plaintiff wife.

It is to be noted that any one of these grounds is decisive of the case. . . .

DISSENTING OPINION BY HALE, J. . . .

I dissent from the majority opinion because, when analyzed in minute detail, it seems to exonerate the school district of every conceivable duty toward spectators except the obligation to refrain from inflicting willful injuries. The majority's ruling will make no distinction between the idly curious, informed football fan and the specially invited but uninitiated guest. . . .

Having found as a fact that players "frequently run or are knocked out of bounds," and that the defendant was aware of this, how can it be concluded that it "was not reasonably foreseeable to defendant that a risk of injury existed to a spectator in these circumstances?" . . . It would seem that this is the only type of injury that is clearly foreseeable—the one thing that, in the natural course of events, will likely occur. . . .

Having already found that plaintiff knew virtually nothing about football and that she had been especially invited by defendant to watch the game, how can the court logically conclude that she assumed the risk of or contributed to her injury in doing the very thing expected of her by defendant—stand along the sidelines among the spectators? The conclusions that plaintiff was both contributorially negligent and voluntarily assumed the risk by standing close to the sidelines relate to no facts showing appreciation of the hazards inhering in the situation, nor to acts or omissions showing want of ordinary care on the part of an uninformed, invited spectator. She stood where the district invited her to stand because it ignored its duty to instruct her otherwise. . . .

Moreover, if she had no . . . knowledge [of the danger of players running off the field] before arriving at the game, she could not be said to have acquired it at the game, for the trial court, in finding that players in the game of football may run violently out of bounds, also found in this game that "No players had been run off the field before the accident." Accordingly, it would seem the statement . . . that a spectator may be taken to assume all *known* risks from roller coasters, flying baseballs, golf balls, wrestlers, and such things as fireworks explosions, has little application to plaintiff's predicament here because she neither knew of the danger nor had anything occurred earlier to charge her, in the exercise of reasonable prudence, with such knowledge.

Therefore, since plaintiff had no knowledge of the likelihood that the players might come charging into her if she stood within a few feet of the sidelines, she cannot be held either contributorially negligent, or to have assumed the risk of injury or consented to it by standing there . . . unless she, in the exercise of ordinary care for her own safety, may be charged with such knowledge as a matter of law. I would be loathe to declare it the rule of law in this country that a 67-year-old woman, having seen only one game of football in her lifetime, and that one from the distant security of a grand-stand seat, and having no interest whatever in the game or the method of playing it, is held to understand that, without warning, the players may come running into her with great force at a place well outside the clearly marked playing field. Nor would I hold that same 67-year-old grandmother to possess as a matter of law the requisite peripheral vision, timing and agility to side-step or otherwise avoid the onrushing players. The facts, therefore, leave no basis for a conclusion of either contributory negligence or assumption of risk. . . .

On the question of defendant's negligence, we have already seen that it owed a duty of ordinary and reasonable care to the plaintiff under the circum-stances. Granted this duty, the facts show that defendant district took not a single step, significant or minor, to discharge its duty. It did nothing what-ever to warn this plaintiff that she should stand a safe distance from the sidelines. Its agents—the coaches and officials—said nothing; they uttered no cautionary words nor did they direct the bystanders to sit in the bleach-ers; no ropes, lines, signs or other devices cautioned her to stand back, although any one of these devices could have been readily provided. . . . The total absence of such precaution, the complete failure to do anything what-ever to protect the plaintiff from a hazard well known to the defendant, I think, leads to the conclusion of negligence from the facts found. . . .

§ 28:5.   Interstate Expansion of Liability

Interstate activity is a characteristic of modern life; and the question arises as to how liability of an actor is to be determined when he acts in one state, but the consequence of the act occurs in another state. What determines what he has caused? Here the general rule is that the liability of the actor is determined by the law of the state in which he acted. This conclusion is predicated to a large degree upon practical expediency, since a person is required only to conform to the standards of the local law rather than act in such a way as to satisfy the law not only of that state but also of the law of every state which might become thereafter involved in some way. To hold the converse would open the door to the oppression of the actor who might find that he was liable for failing to comply with standards of which he had no knowledge or even standards which conflicted with the standards that he was required to observe by the law of the state in which he acted.

MYERS v. GAITHER

232 A.2d 577 (C.A. Dist. Col., 1967)

Gaither owned an automobile. He left the ignition keys in the car while parked in front of his house in the District of Columbia. The car was stolen by a thief who, while speeding, collided in Maryland with the auto-mobile driven by Myers. Myers sued Gaither claiming that by the law of the District of Columbia, Gaither was liable for the harm done by the thief. Gaither raised the defense that the law of Maryland applied under which the theft of the car broke the causal chain so that he was not liable for the harm caused by the thief.

OPINION BY MYERS, A.J. . . .

Does the law of Maryland or that of the District of Columbia apply to this case?

Appellee urges the traditional application of *lex loci delictus,* the law of Maryland where the injury occurred. We have previously acquiesced in this application. . . .

In recent years various jurisdictions have applied a "contact" or "grouping of contacts" theory when faced with a conflict between the law of the forum and the law of the place of injury. . . . The Supreme Court has recognized that a strict rule of *lex loci* is not infrequently inadequate. In *Richards* v. *United States,* 369 U.S.: 1, 11-13, 82 S.Ct. 585, 592-593, 7 L.Ed.2d 492 (1962), an action under the Federal Tort Claims Act, where the negligence occurred in one state and resulted in death in another state, the Court held: "The general conflict-of-laws rule, followed by a vast majority of the States, is to apply the law of the place of injury to the substantive rights of the parties. . . . Recently there has been a tendency on the part of some States to depart from the general conflicts rule in order to take into account the interests of the State having significant contact with the parties to the litigation. We can see no compelling reason to saddle the Act with an interpretation that would prevent the federal courts from implementing this policy in choice-of-law rules where the State in which the negligence occurred has adopted it. Should the States continue this rejection of the older rule in those situations where its application might appear inappropriate or inequitable, the flexibility inherent in our interpretation will also be more in step with that judicial approach . . . ."

The Restatement (Second), Conflict of Laws § 379 (Tent. Draft No. 9, 1964) considers as important contacts, *inter alia,* the place of the injury, the place where the conduct occurred, the domicile of the parties, the place where the relationship between the parties is centered. In determining relative importance of the contacts, the forum will consider the issues, the character of the tort, and the relevant purposes of the tort rules of the interested states. See also *Vanston Bondholders Protective Comm.* v. *Green,* 329 U.S. 156, 162, 67 S.Ct. 237, 239, 91 L.Ed. 162 (1946), where it was stated: "Determination requires the exercise of an informed judgment in the balancing of all the interests of the states with the most significant contacts in order best to accommodate the equities among the parties to the policies of those states."

There has been some recent case treatment of the contacts theory in this jurisdiction. The United States Court of Appeals for the District of Columbia in *Tramontana* v. *S. A. Empresa de Viacao Aerea Rio Grandense,* 121 U.S. App.D.C. 338, 350 F.2d 468 (1965), cert denied sub nom., *Tramontana* v. *Varig Airlines,* 383 U.S. 943, 86 S.Ct. 1195, 16 L.Ed.2d 206 (1966), limited an airline's liability to survivor of decedent to the amount stated in a Brazilian statute on the ground that Brazil had contacts (domicile of corporate defendant, place of injury, wrongful death act creating the right of recovery relied upon, valid Brazilian interest in limiting recovery) superior to those of the District of Columbia (choice of forum, secondary place of business for corporate defendant—plaintiff was a Maryland resident). In *Williams* v. *Rawlings Truck Line, Inc.,* 123 U.S.App.D.C. 121, 357 F.2d 581 (1965), the same appellate court adopted a New York rule of estoppel fixing liability upon an automobile owner of record when he failed to register a change in title, although the District of Columbia, where the injury took place, follows a contrary rule. The opinion characterized the case as a "classic false conflicts situation," observing that New York policies would be thwarted by refusal to apply the New York estoppel rule but that no District policies would be weakened by its application. Recently that court in *Roscoe* v. *Roscoe,* D.C.Cir. 379 F.2d 94 (decided April 14, 1967), refused to apply the District interspousal immunity rule, applying instead the law of North Carolina, the situs of the accident. It observed that the Supreme Court in *Richards* v. *United States,* 369 U.S. 1, 82 S.Ct. 585 (1962), deemed it desirable to preserve flexibility in the choice of law "since there may be situations where the application of the older rule 'might appear inappropriate or inequitable.' "

The high incidence of auto thefts in the District of Columbia, the constant warnings to the public to remove keys to prevent such thefts, the frequency of high speed chases involving stolen motor vehicles, all persuade us that the District has an overriding interest in preventing such occurrences and in encouraging owners to exercise greater caution in parking their automobiles. The only contacts this case discloses which are purely Maryland are the domicile of the appellant and the location of the accident— . . . while the District's contacts are domicile of the appellee, the situs of the original or primary negligence, the chosen forum, and the overriding public interest in proscribing the conduct here alleged—which contacts are indeed superior to those of any other jurisdiction. We hold that the District of Columbia law on questions of negligence and proximate cause should be applied in this case.

DISSENTING OPINION BY HOOD, C.J. . . .

With respect to the second theory of liability, the majority opinion concedes that even if appellee were negligent in not removing the car keys, there could be no recovery under Maryland law. It seeks to apply District of Columbia law because, it says, the case has more important contacts with the District. The accident occurred in Maryland and a resident of Maryland was the injured party. I know of no more important contacts. . . .

Questions for Review

1. Analyze each opinion in this chapter in terms of the social forces involved in the decision. See § 5:5 for a list of the social forces. With respect to each opinion, explain why the prevailing social forces prevailed and why those rejected did not. In each case in which there is a dissenting opinion, also make this analysis for the dissenting opinion.

2-6. On the basis of the social forces involved, what decision should be made in each of the following cases?

2. Immunity. Judges. Is a judge subject to tort liability for his official actions? *Pierson* v. *Ray,* 386 U.S. 547. (Civil Rights Act)

3. Proximate cause. Overtime parking. When a plaintiff collides with a parked truck that has parked beyond the time allowed per vehicle, does the fact of such overtime parking impose liability in favor of the plaintiff? *Rhodes* v. *Baker,* 116 Ga.App. 157, 156 S.E.2d 545.

4. Proximate cause. Illegal sale to minor. When a tavern illegally sells liquor to a minor and the minor engages in a fight in which he fires a gun and injures a spectator, is the tavern liable to the victim? *Prevatt* v. *McClennan,* [Fla.] 201 So.2d 780.

5. Proximate cause. Key in ignition. When a policeman stops a motor vehicle, is his failure to remove the key from the ignition the proximate cause of the death of a third person killed when the driver seeks to drive away from the officer and the third person is killed in the resulting chase? *Stanton* v. *New York,* 29 App.Div.2d 612, 285 N.Y.S.2d 964.

6. Minor. Tort. When a boy of 13 voluntarily sets fire to boxes and the fire spreads to a grocery store, is his minority a defense to liability for damage to the store? *Allstate Fire Insurance Co.* v. *Singler,* 9 Ohio App.2d 102, 223 N.E.2d 65.

7-11. What were the social forces involved, which prevailed, and which were defeated in the following decisions?

7. Hospitals. Premature release of patient. The fact that a hospital prematurely released a person who suffered from amnesia did not make the hospital liable for an accident thereafter sustained by patient in absence of proof of a causal relationship between the condition of the patient and the accident thereafter occurring. *Sadler* v. *Sisters of Charity,* Ore., 426 P.2d 747.

8. Negligence. Proximate cause. The act of the truck driver in passing a horse ridden on the shoulder of the highway was the proximate cause of the injury sustained by the rider when the horse jumped onto the road and was hit by the truck, as against the contention that the conduct of the horse was an intervening cause, as such conduct was a foreseeable reaction. *Murchison* v. *Powell,* 269 N.C. 656, 153 S.E.2d 352.

9. Proximate cause. Worry over property damage. The fact that a homeowner was so distressed by damage to his property caused by construction work on adjoining tract that the nervous strain caused his death, does not impose liability on the contractor for such death where the contractor was not warned that his acts were causing emotional distress and contractor had no reason to foresee harm to person or death of owner. *Zeigler* v. *F. Street Corp.,* 248 Md. 223, 235 A.2d 703.

10. *Premises liability. Warm-up baseball.* It is a question for the jury whether a baseball club and the warming-up pitcher were liable for injuries sustained where a warming-up pitch struck the plaintiff, aged 13, who at his request was given a seat in the front row near the players' dugout, where there was no protective screening—plaintiff having been at the same ball park 6 to 12 times in the preceding several years and knowing of the absence of a protective screen at that point—and the warming-up pitches were thrown to the left of the plaintiff while the ball in the actual game was thrown to his right. *Maytnier v. Rush,* 80 Ill.App.2d 336, 225 N.E.2d 83.

11. *Negligence. Contributory negligence.* Driver is not guilty of contributory negligence when dust cloud created by preceding automobile partially impairs his vision and he merely slows down instead of stopping, where collision occurs when oncoming automobile approaches partially in both lanes; for in such case, the driver's negligence, if any, in merely slowing down rather than stopping, cannot be regarded as contributory negligence since had he stopped, he would still have been struck by the approaching vehicle in the wrong lane. *Brown v. New York Fire & Marine Underwriters,* [La.] 198 So.2d 550.

Chapter 29

MUST YOU PAY FOR THE ACT OF ANOTHER?

§ 29:1.   Generally

When someone else does an act, are you liable for what he does? In many instances you are, and this liability for an act "once removed" is known as "vicarious liability." If you directly cause the act of the other person, as by telling him to do the very thing that he did, we accept such liability without any question. Yet observe that on a strict basis of logic, it could just as well be said that when the harm is caused by the intentional act of another person, such action is an intervening event which breaks any chain of causal relationship. You are tempted to answer that where the instigator desires the event which actually occurs, the fact that he is able to get someone else to perform the "labor" involved does not make such other person an intervening agent.

Apply this test, however, to the case where X writes a book urging that all kings be assassinated. Z, who is unknown to X, buys a copy of the book in a general bookstore and is so impressed by its conclusions that he forthwith assassinates the king of a neighboring country. Is X guilty of murder? Had X made a direct contact with Z and persuaded him to assassinate the king, there would be no difficulty in holding that Z did not break the chain of causal relationship because X not only merely foresaw but also sought the action of Z; and, in effect, X set in motion the force which ended in the death of the king.

If you are tempted to say in the original case of the book that X is not liable because he did not know Z and did not know that Z would act, how will you distinguish this assassination case from the case in which the chief gangster tells the assistant gangster to see that anyone getting in the way of their activities is killed and to hire a professional gunman to do the killing? Later the assistant gangster hires G, a gunman, who in the performance of his undertaking kills a designated police officer; the chief gangster being unaware of any of the arrangements made by the assistant gangster. You are, of course, tempted to conclude at once that the two cases are different.

You will no doubt attempt to distinguish the assassination case from the gangster murder on the ground that the writer of the book was merely discussing abstract principles. If that be so, let us have him write a new edition of the book in which he does not mince words, but proclaims to his country that the hour of action has arrived and appeals to any man worth being called a man to rise and kill the neighboring country's tyrant king, T. The message is no less direct in this case than in the gangster case. It is true that a distinction might be made in terms of one is a killing for monetary gain, and the other is a killing for principle, which we might describe as for psychic income. But before you say that that is a valid distinction, think of the mercy killing case in which there is no question that the slayer receives no benefit by the death of the victim and kills the victim only to relieve him of useless suffering.

The question, "How far should you be liable for the act of another?" thus presents greater complexity than at first appears. While the question could be discussed in terms of contract, criminal, or tort law, this chapter will be devoted primarily to the field of tort law because it is this field that is most important to management generally; and it is the field in which the social forces that make the law are currently changing traditional principles of law.

§ 29:2. Liability for Act of Employee

(a) Generally. When an employee commits a wrong in the course of his employment, the employer, as well as the employee, is liable to a third person who is injured thereby. We are so accustomed to this vicarious liability, described by the term respondeat superior, that it is difficult to perceive that it is not the inevitable conclusion. The law could just as well have held that a person is liable only for his own fault and that if an employee is at fault, the third person should sue the employee; and he cannot sue the employer where the employer had been careful in the hiring of the employee and had given the employee instructions and the proper equipment. What more could the employer do? Why oppress the employer by making him pay for that which he did not commit and which he had done everything possible to prevent? This argument has long gone unheeded; and society has adopted the view that as between the innocent injured third person and the innocent employer, the loss should fall upon the latter, who after all was the one who stood to gain money by the enterprise which caused the harm.

It is thus seen that the very basis for respondeat superior is the concept of "enterprise liability," which many persons are now discovering in analyzing the modern concept of product liability of a manufacturer.

(b) Violation of instructions. The enterprise liability rationale for the rule of respondeat superior is further seen when the employee who causes harm does so in violation of instructions. Here the employer is still liable. For example, the employer is liable even though the harm is caused the third person by the employee's disregarding explicit instructions given by the employer, as when the employer tells the employee not to drive over 40 miles per hour; or when the employee in order to speed up his work removes safety devices that the employer furnished and directed him to use, which use would have prevented the harm that is sustained.

(c) Willful misconduct of agent. A departure from the strict concept of respondeat superior and a trend in the direction of supervisory (discussed in § 29:3) or of absolute liability (discussed in § 27:2), is found in the growing number of decisions that impose liability on the employer for the willful act or crime of his employee. At common law, if a watchman would injure boys playing near the premises in the effort to scare them away, the employer was not liable since the watchman was not hired to injure boys playing near the premises. Today, most courts would hold that since the watchman was motivated by the desire of performing his duties and benefitting his employer, the latter should be liable to the third persons injured by the watchman's conduct. Similarly, the growing trend of today's law is to hold that where the employee sent to collect a bill or to repossess an automobile gets into a fight with the debtor, the debtor may sue the em-

ployer for his injuries, as against the contention that the employee was not hired to fight with customers.

To turn for the moment to the criminal law side of the picture, a similar result is reached where the employer is made criminally liable for the act of his employees. Assume that the owner of a bar gives explicit and sincere instructions that no minors be served drinks. Assume further that, unknown to the owner and contrary to his instructions, drinks are sold to a minor. In most states, the owner is liable for the crime of illegally selling liquor to minors. In vain does he claim that a person cannot be held liable for the crime of another. In vain does he claim that there cannot be criminal liability without an intent to commit a crime. It is sufficient that the "enterprise" has furnished drinks to a minor, and therefore the owner is liable for the crime because society values more highly the protection of the public welfare and morals than it does the protection of the owner of the bar. It would be practically inexpedient to enforce the law if the bar owner could always raise as a defense that he had given instructions against the prohibited sale and had no knowledge thereof.

THROWER v. COBLE DAIRY PRODUCTS CO-OPERATIVE

249 N.C. 109, 105 S.E.2d 428 (1958)

Raymond Queen was the agent in charge of distribution and collections for his employer, Coble Dairy Products. Thrower, a customer of the employer, ran a grocery store and purchased dairy products. The agent made false invoice sheets showing delivery to the customer of greater quantities than the customer had actually ordered or received, collected from the customer on the basis of these increased amounts, and then kept for himself the difference between the increased amounts and the amounts that should have been charged. When the customer learned of this, he sued the employer for the loss he sustained through such excess payments. The employer denied that the agent was its employee in making the excess collections.

OPINION BY HIGGINS, J. . . .

(1) Is the defendant responsible to the plaintiff for the loss caused by Queen's falsification of the invoices? (2) Is the plaintiff barred from recovery by his negligent failure to discover and prevent Queen's fraud? . . .

The evidence is amply sufficient to support the court's findings that Queen was "an employee, agent, and servant of the defendant corporation . . . was acting in the course and scope of his employment in dealing with the plaintiff, and the controversy herein involved arises out of the acts of said Queen as agent, servant, and employee." The general rule is that a principal is responsible to third parties for the fraud of its agent while acting within his authority. "It is elementary that the principal is liable for the acts of his agent, whether malicious or negligent, and the master for similar acts of his servant, which result in injury to third persons, when the agent or servant is acting within the line of his duty and exercising the functions of his employment." . . . "There is no reason that occurs to us why a different rule should be applicable to cases of deceit from what applies to other torts. A corporation can only act through its agents, and must be responsible for their acts. It is of the greatest public importance that it should be so. If a manufacturing and trading corporation is not responsible for the false and fraudulent representations of its agents, those who deal with it will be practically without redress and the corporation can commit fraud with impunity." . . . The master is liable for the unlawful or negligent acts of his servant if about the master's business, and if doing or attempting to do that which he was employed to do. . . .

The evidence in this case shows the court found the fraud was committed in the sale of defendant's products and in the padding of accounts its agent was authorized to collect. The defendant is liable for plaintiff's loss.

The defendant here contends the plaintiff is barred from recovery by his own negligence in permitting Queen to deposit the invoices in a receptacle in plaintiff's office. This from his brief: "In permitting the practice to continue for that period (2½ years) the plaintiff chose to put his faith and trust in Queen. Such was not a faith and trust solicited by the defendant." The argument is not persuasive. It ignores the fact that Queen was selected and sent out by the defendant as its agent to sell and deliver, and collect for its products. "Where a loss is to be suffered through the misconduct of an agent, it should be borne by those who put it in his power to do the wrong, rather than by a stranger." . . . There must be reliance on the integrity of men, or else trade or commerce could not prosper. . . . The plaintiff's conduct in trusting Queen does not preclude the recovery. . . .

§ 29:3. Supervisory Liability

(a) Generally. Historically an employer was liable for the wrongful act of an employee only when the latter was acting in the course of his employment. Conversely, if the harm were done by the employee after working hours or for his own personal benefit, there was no liability of the employer.

This concept has been eroded by the application of a concept of supervisory liability that, in effect, makes the employer liable because it was his employee who did the wrong. Sometimes the conclusion is explained in the terms that the employer was in the better position to have avoided the harm through a more careful screening of his employees. This is ordinarily mere lip service to the concept that there must be fault as the basis for liability because ordinarily it would be impossible for the employer to have screened so carefully and so prophetically as to have avoided the harm that had resulted. The doctrine of supervisory liability has at present rather limited application, primarily because it is virtually a form of absolute liability; that is, imposing liability because harm has happened without regard to whether any fault was involved.

(b) Commercial law. The concept of supervisory liability is found as the basis for § 3-405(c) of the Uniform Commercial Code. That section

contemplates the situation in which an employee prepares checks for his employer to sign, but intentionally prepares checks drawn to dummy payees with the intent of using the checks for his own benefit; that is, the employee draws checks to the order of former customers, former employees, or non-existent persons. He then has his employer sign the checks, the employer believing that there is nothing wrong with the checks and relying upon the employee's having prepared them. After the checks are signed, the employee forges the payees' names on the backs of the checks, and then takes them to his own bank where he cashes them. Ultimately, the checks are returned by that bank to the employer's bank on which they were drawn and that bank deducts them from the employer's account.

By the classical law, the forgery by the employee of the name of the payee of a check was a forgery with the result that there was no negotiation of the check from the "payee" to the cashing bank; and, accordingly, it could not negotiate the check to the employer's bank and the latter, therefore, had no right to deduct the amount of the check from the employer's account. Under the Code, this rule was reversed so that in the deceiving employee case above described, the forgery by the employee is deemed effective as a negotiation, each bank has the right to deal with the paper, and the employer's bank therefore may deduct the amount of the check from the employer's account. Thus, the risk of loss for the misconduct of the employee is shifted from the bank to the employer. This conclusion is rationalized on the basis that the employer was in a better position to avoid the harm by better screening in the selection of employees and by maintaining a closer supervision over his employees. As a practical matter, it is impossible to detect such projected fraudulent conduct at the time of hiring an employee. Likewise, it would put an unreasonable burden upon the employer to verify the checks being written by his trusted employee.

(c) Tort law. In the field of tort law, the concept of supervisory liability is found primarily in the case of hotels. In one case it was held that the hotel was liable where a bellboy after his working hours stole the keys to a guest's automobile and removed the automobile from the private parking garage to which another hotel boy had taken it. Likewise, it has been held that a hotel is liable when conventioneers attending the hotel throw objects out of the window and a passing stranger is injured by one of such objects, as against a dissenting opinion which pointed out that as a practical matter the only way in which the hotel could have prevented the harm would be to assign an individual guard to each person on the premises. To a large extent, the rationale supporting supervisory liability is that the enterprise should pay.

CRAWFORD v. HOTEL ESSEX BOSTON CORP.

143 F.Supp. 172 (D.C.D.Mass., 1956)

The hotel detective told an unidentified person claiming to be a guest to **wait in the lobby** while the detective checked his registration. The detective checked and found that the person was a registered guest. Meanwhile, the guest had not waited for the detective but had taken the elevator up to his floor. The detective followed him to his floor, demanded why the guest had not waited as directed, and then hit him. The guest sued the hotel. The hotel defended on the ground that the act of the detective was outside the scope of his employment.

OPINION BY ALDRICH, D.J. . . .

It is admitted that the officer was employed to check on whether persons were registered, and to cause unruly and unauthorized persons to leave the hotel. A finding would be warranted that he could use force for such purpose. Under these circumstances the defendant would be liable for excessive force, provided he was engaged in an act within the scope of his employment, or perhaps, even if he only reasonably thought he was. . . . The defendant argues that a deliberate, unprovoked, and brutal assault, . . . was entirely "outside the scope of his duties, or in a spirit of vindictiveness or to gratify personal animosity." . . . I agree.

However, there is another principle to be taken into consideration. The plaintiff was a registered guest in the hotel. This gave him contractual rights, greater than those of the usual business invitee. He was entitled to "immunity from rudeness, personal abuse and unjustifiable interference, whether exerted by the defendant or his servants, or those under his control." . . .

"The guest is entitled to respectful and considerate treatment at the hands of the innkeeper and his employees and servants, and this right created an implied obligation that neither the innkeeper nor his servants will abuse or insult the guest, or engage in any conduct or speech which may unreasonably subject him to physical discomfort, or distress of mind, or imperil his safety." . . .

When such duty exists it may not make any difference that the defaulting servant was not, contrary to what might be argued here, one charged with protecting the plaintiff's safety. . . . The fact that the assault was not committed in the scope of the servant's employment is not a bar to recovery. Strictly the suit sounds in contract, rather than in tort. . . . The gravamen is the failure of the servants to protect the plaintiff from harm. . . .

I believe the Massachusetts law to be that if the guest of a hotel is assaulted by an employee, particularly by one whose duties include the preservation of order, he has at the least a contractual claim for consequential damages.

§ 29:4.   The Automobile and Vicarious Liability

(a) Generally. The growth of the automobile's use has made inroads into the concept of vicarious liability. Under strict principles of employment or agency law, the owner of an automobile is not liable for the misconduct of its driver unless the driver is driving the automobile in the scope or course of his employment for the owner. In the absence of such a relationship, there was no liability upon the owner of the car for harm caused by

the negligence of the driver. That is, the fact that the owner owned the car did not impose liability upon him. Likewise, the fact that there may have been a family relationship between the owner and the driver or even that the owner had supplied the automobile for use by the driver did not impose liability.

Inroads have been gradually made to this strict common-law rule, as will be discussed below. To some degree, these inroads on the common law may be regarded as replacing the concept of vicarious liability with the concept of supervisory liability. The extension is better analyzed as the imposition of an absolute liability (discussed in § 29:2) for the reason that it is, in fact, no defense to the owner that he exercised great care in the selection of the driver. The owner is liable because of the events that occurred, not because of any fault on his part. In effect, the owner is made the insurer against the negligence of the person driving the car.

(b) Bailor of automobile. An increasing number of states have adopted statutes by which a person granting permission to another to use his automobile thereby automatically becomes liable for any negligent harm caused by the person to whom he has entrusted the automobile. That is, permissive use imposes liability for the permittee's negligence. In some states, the operation of such a statute is limited to cases where the permittee is under a specified age, such as 16 years. Under some statutes, the owner is only liable with respect to harm sustained while the permittee is using the automobile for the purpose for which permission was granted.

(c) Family-purpose doctrine. In about half of the states, a person who owns or supplies an automobile that he permits to be used by members of his family for their own purposes is vicariously liable for harm caused by the negligent operation of the vehicle by any such member of the family. The family-purpose doctrine is repudiated in nearly half of the states as illogical and contrary to the general principles of agency law. Even when recognized, the doctrine is not applicable if the use of the vehicle is not with the permission of the owner or if the use is outside of the scope of that contemplated.

The family-purpose doctrine is not limited to cases involving minors nor to the children of the providing parent. That is, a person may be liable for providing an automobile to an adult; and the person so provided may be any family member, however related to the person providing the car. In some jurisdictions the person supplied the car may even be one who is not related to the provider, as long as he is a bona fide member of the household of the provider, such as a servant who is provided with or allowed to use the car for his own benefit.

Under the family-purpose doctrine, it is not essential that the provider of the car be the owner of it. The essential element is that he is the one who has control of it and has the power to grant or deny permission to use it, so that its use at any particular time is with his permission. Hence, the doctrine, when recognized, is applicable to impose liability upon the father who has control of the use of the car that the child has purchased but which is used by the family when and to the extent that the father permits.

(d) License sponsor. In a number of states, when a minor under a specified age applies for an automobile operator's license, his parent, or a person standing in the position of his parent, is required to sign his license application as a sponsor. Such a sponsor is by some statutes made jointly and severally liable with the minor for the latter's negligence in driving, although some statutes relieve the sponsor of liability if either he or the minor has filed proof of financial responsibility.

SMITH v. SIMPSON

260 N.C. 601, 133 S.E.2d 474 (1963)

Eddie Simpson, who was the head of the family, allowed his minor son, Wayne, to keep the money that he had earned raising a tobacco crop. The son purchased an automobile, but the seller would not accept the son as a credit buyer because he was a minor. The father, accordingly, signed the conditional sales contract and the automobile was registered in the father's name. The automobile was also insured in the name of the father under an assigned risk policy with the son as the principal driver. The registration card for the automobile was kept at all times by the father. The son paid the insurance premiums and drove and maintained the car in all respects as though he were the sole owner, for his own purposes, and without asking permission from his father. When he was involved in a collision, Smith, the other driver, sued Eddie, the father.

Opinion by Moore, J. . . .

At the time of the accident Wayne was 18 years of age, lived in his father's home, and went to school. He had always lived with his father. Mr. Simpson was a farmer and also operated a filling station. Wayne worked on the farm and was a member of his father's household. His father was head of the house. Wayne testified that he respected his father and was obedient to him. Until about a month before the accident, Wayne had owned a 1957 Chevrolet, the title to which was registered in his own name (source not disclosed). In 1960 Wayne made a profit from a tobacco crop on acreage he himself had rented from a pulpwood company—he did the work, bought the fertilizer, and paid all expenses of producing the crop. His father permitted him to keep these earnings. Wayne negotiated for the purchase of a new 1960 Chevrolet—his father had no part in the negotiations. The down payment was the 1957 Chevrolet and $400 in cash from his tobacco crop earnings; the balance was to be paid out of his tobacco crop the next fall. When the Motor Company refused to accept credit papers executed by Wayne, because he was a minor, Mr. Simpson, at Wayne's request, executed the note and conditional sales contract for the $1,754.09 balance, applied for and took the title certificate in his name, and obtained in his name liability insurance. The insurance was an assigned risk policy because Wayne, the principal driver, was a minor. Wayne paid the premium. The registration card was mailed to Mr. Simpson who retained it in his possession. After the credit papers were signed Wayne drove the car home— the keys were delivered to him, and he kept them continuously thereafter. Wayne bought the gas and oil for the car and stood for the repairs. He kept the car in his father's yard, drove it to school, and anywhere he wanted to go without obtaining specific permission from his father. Mr. Simpson testified that Wayne "has been going on his own since he was 16 without asking me when he could come or go." Neither Mr. Simpson nor any other member of the family, except Wayne, used the Chevrolet. Mr. Simpson owned a pickup truck and an Oldsmobile which anybody in the family could use. He listed the Chevrolet for taxes along with his other motor vehicles, but no taxes had been paid at the time of the accident. Wayne testified: "I was the only one who used the Chevrolet. It was mine."

The court submitted to the jury this . . . issue: "Was the defendant, Eddie Martin Simpson, the owner of the 1960 Chevrolet automobile for use as a family purpose automobile, and was Wayne Rosser Simpson using the 1960 Chevrolet automobile under such family purposes?" The jury after hearing the court's charge answered the issue "No." . . .

"It is said to be one of the indispensable requisites of the family-purpose doctrine that the person on whom it is sought to fasten liability under that principle *owns, maintains,* or *provides* an automobile for the general use, pleasure, and convenience of the family." . . . "An indispensable requisite of the family-purpose doctrine is that the person on whom it is sought to impose liability own, maintain, or furnish the automobile, and have or exercise some degree of control over its use. Thus, where the head of the family does not own, maintain, or control the family automobile, he is not liable under the family-purpose doctrine for negligence in its use by a member of his family; liability may not be imposed on the head of a family by reason of his knowledge and consent to its use for a family purpose where he does not have ownership, possession, or control of the vehicle, but where the head of the family controls and maintains the vehicle, he may be liable under the family-purpose doctrine even though he does not own it." . . .

It is the law . . . in North Carolina that one, not the owner, who *maintains* or *provides* an automobile for the use, pleasure, and convenience of his family, controls or has the right to control it in such use, and actually or impliedly authorizes members of his family to so use it, is liable under the family-purpose doctrine for the negligent operation of the car by a family member, causing injury. It has been held that the family purpose may extend to and be exercised by only one member of the family. . . .

We assume as the exception requires us to do and as the jury seems to have found, that the motor vehicle was not owned by Mr. Simpson but was owned by Wayne. There is no evidence that Mr. Simpson maintained it or that he, or any members of his family other than Wayne, used or directed the use of it or exercised any control of it. Wayne was a minor son of Mr. Simpson, and at the time of the accident was a member of his household. The inquiry then is whether Mr. Simpson *provided* the Chevrolet for Wayne and had the right thereby, or for some other reason, to *control* its use.

It may be that the use by us of the expression "control and right to control" without some explanation and restriction has led the bench and bar into uncertainty. The question here as to Mr. Simpson's liability does not relate to his right to control his minor son, but his legal right to control the use of the 1960 Chevrolet. We are too inclined to think of the family-purpose doctrine as a sort of antidote to juvenile delinquency or a palliative for traditional youthful recklessness. The doctrine is not confined to situations involving parent and minor child. It applies with equal force when the child is an adult. "It makes no substantial difference as regards the liability of a parent (under the family-purpose doctrine) whether the child is a minor or an adult. The question of liability does not depend upon the relation of parent and child, and the parent is under no more legal obligation to supply an automobile for the use and pleasure of a minor child than he is for the use and pleasure of an adult child." . . . A person may be liable under the doctrine for damage caused by the negligence of spouse, parent, brother, sister, nephew, niece, grandchild, or other of more remote kinship, or of one not of kin, provided he is a bona fide household member. . . .

"The mere fact of the relationship does not render a parent liable for the torts of his child. Liability of the parent must be predicated upon evidence that the child was in some way acting in a representative capacity, such as would make the master responsible for the servant's tort, or on the ground that the parent procured, commanded, advised, instigated, or encouraged the commission of the tort by his child, or that the parent was independently negligent, as in permitting the child to have access to some dangerous instrumentality." . . . The State of North Carolina passes upon the qualifications of and issues drivers licenses to children over 16 years of age, and as a matter of public policy places its stamp of approval on the operation by them of motor vehicles. The relationship does not alone make a parent answerable for the negligent conduct of his minor child. There must be something besides parenthood to connect him with the wrong before he may incur liability. . . . The question in a case such as the one at bar is whether the child, be he a minor or an adult, was acting for the parent, was using the automobile for the purpose for which the parent provided it. . . . The very genesis of the family-purpose doctrine is agency. The question of liability for negligent injury must be determined in that aspect. . . . The right and duty of a parent to control the activities of his minor child is not involved. It matters not whether Wayne was a minor or an adult. If Mr. Simpson had the right to control the 1960 Chevrolet, it must rest upon some ground other than the mere relationship of parent and child.

Ownership of personal property ordinarily carries with it the right of control and use. . . . For the purposes of this discussion, Wayne owned the car, not Mr. Simpson. A person having possession of an automobile by reason of a duty or license to preserve or use it, or by bailment, or acquiescence of the owner, or other special right, has the right to control its use. . . . Under the family-purpose doctrine, one who *provides* or *maintains* an automobile for the pleasure and convenience of his family is deemed to have the right, in the absence of circumstances requiring a different result, to control its use. In the instant case there is no evidence that Mr. Simpson maintained the car or had any special possessory right with respect thereto, so the question is whether he *provided* it. If he did not, there is no other status or relationship which bestows upon him the right of control.

The evidence is that Wayne personally negotiated with the Motor Company and agreed upon the terms of purchase of the automobile. He made the down payment by delivery of his 1957 Chevrolet, title to which was in his name, and payment of $400 in cash from his own earnings. When the purchase was consummated, the keys were delivered to him, he retained them continuously and exercised exclusive control and use of the car. He bought the gasoline and oil and took care of repairs. He paid the insurance premium. He was obligated to pay the balance of the purchase price from his tobacco crop, his own earnings. Because the Motor Company would not accept the credit instruments of a minor, Mr. Simpson, at Wayne's request, executed the note and conditional sale contract to secure the balance of the purchase price, applied for and obtained in his name the certificate of title, registration card, and liability insurance. He listed the car for taxes. So far as the record discloses Mr. Simpson did not pay one cent on the purchase and maintenance of the car. What he *provided* was credit. His position was the same as if he had become comaker on a note at the bank as an accommodation for Wayne. It was a service that a friend might have rendered as well. If Wayne defaulted Mr. Simpson had procedures for his protection. The question has been raised in some cases whether, by permitting a minor to use his earnings in purchasing a car, the parent was thereby providing the car. . . . A father is entitled to the earnings of an unemancipated child. But where a father permits his minor son to work for himself and receive the earnings of his own labor to do with as he wishes, there has been an emancipation with respect thereto. . . .

We are of the opinion that Mr. Simpson did not provide the automobile. His part in the transaction was only incidental and secondary. His acts amounted to an accommodation, an extension of credit. The decision to purchase and acquire the car was made by Wayne. The transaction was Wayne's idea, he managed it, and took responsibility for it. In order to qualify as a provider under the family-purpose doctrine, one must be a principal mover, one who intends to provide for another or others the particular thing, the automobile, and takes steps on his own responsibility to see to the consummation of the transaction, and contributes substantially of his own means toward that end without expectation of reimbursement or compensation. . . .

At best the family-purpose doctrine is an anomaly in the law. This Court was reluctant to adopt it initially. As the use of motor vehicles increased, the Court gradually expanded the application of the doctrine. We are not disposed to extend the doctrine in this State beyond the limits already reached. . . .

Dissenting Opinion by Sharp, J. . . .

The family purpose doctrine has been stated and restated many times by this Court and, collectively, the cases define it as follows: Where the head of a household owns, keeps, provides, or maintains an automobile for the convenience and pleasure of his family, he is liable for injuries caused by the negligent operation of the vehicle by any member of his family who is using the vehicle for the purpose for which it was provided. . . .

The necessity of affording greater protection to the ever increasing number of persons injured on our highways originated the family-purpose doctrine. The rationale is that a father, or other head of a household who has provided an automobile for the pleasure and convenience of his family, has made their transportation for this purpose his business, and the family-member operator is regarded as representing the family-member provider in such use. The result puts the financial responsibility of the *paterfamilias* behind the vehicle he has furnished for his family's use while it is being thus operated. Dependent members of a family are most often financially irresponsible and the minor members, like Wayne Simpson in this case, unable to obtain adequate insurance coverage. . . .

It is established that liability under the family-car doctrine does not depend upon ownership of the automobile if it is subject to the control of the head of the household. Therefore, the fact that Mr. Simpson never attempted to control either the car or the comings or goings of his son is not determinative of his legal liability for plaintiff's injuries. "The test is not who owns the vehicle but *control or the right to control*." . . . Therefore, the decisive question here is whether Mr. Simpson had the right to control the use of the Chevrolet which Wayne was driving on the occasion in question.

This right is in no wise dependent upon his right to control his minor son and, under this evidence, his liability for Wayne's negligent operation of the automobile would have been unchanged had Wayne been an adult. Of course, in the exercise of his parental authority, Mr. Simpson did have the right to control Wayne's use of the automobile. Whatever the actualities, the *legal* right of a parent to control his minor child is in no degree diminished or nullified when the child becomes the owner of an automobile. "A parent can, and often should, forbid his minor child to use an automobile . . . the entire ownership of which may rest in the minor." . . .

Here, Wayne kept the keys to the Chevrolet, but his father held the legal title to it. The registration card and the insurance were in Mr. Simpson's name. He listed it for taxes in his name. Although Wayne had made the down payment, Mr. Simpson had primarily obligated himself to pay $1,754.09, the balance of the purchase price due in the fall of 1961. The holder of the note and conditional sales contract securing that balance certainly looked to Mr. Simpson as the principal obligor and not as an accommodation indorser. Wayne's only hope of paying for the car was his expectation of a profitable tobacco crop in 1961. However, his 1960 crop had netted him only $400.

In the most practical sense, Mr. Simpson had *provided* this automobile for his son's pleasure and convenience and had made it possible for him to operate it upon the highways of the state. To hold otherwise is to be unrealistic. Without his father's credit and permission, Wayne could neither have acquired the automobile, maintained it, nor kept it at his father's home where he lived and was supported as an unemancipated child. Indisputably, Mr. Simpson wanted his son to enjoy the status and convenience which the unrestricted use of an automobile gives a teenager today. Therefore, Wayne's operation of the vehicle for that purpose became Mr. Simpson's business when he provided his son with the use of a Chevrolet registered in Mr. Simpson's name, insured in his name, and obtained with his credit. In my opinion, as long as Mr. Simpson allowed title to the automobile to remain in his name for that purpose, he had the right to control it, even though equitably he and Wayne were joint owners of the vehicle.

"The fact that a parent has title to a motor vehicle is, in and of itself, sufficient to justify the application of the family-purpose doctrine where the doctrine is otherwise applicable, even though the vehicle has been entirely paid for by the child in question, and the child has the beneficial ownership thereof." . . .

It does not take a vehicle out of the scope of the family-car doctrine that it was provided for one member of the family alone. . . . Surely, if a wealthy father with eight children living in his household provided an automobile for each child, it could not be successfully contended that each car did not come within the family-purpose doctrine. This doctrine is not restricted to a single car.

The evidence in this case illustrates graphically the factors which originally brought the family-purpose doctrine into being as an instrument of public policy. . . . It suggests that the abdication by parents of the right and duty to control their teenage children, whom they enable to acquire automobiles which they cannot afford and lack the discretion to operate safely, may be the explanation of the following statistics furnished by the North Carolina Department of Motor Vehicles:

In 1960, 32.11 percent of all drivers involved in motor vehicle accidents in this State were in the 16 through 24 age group. Nationwide, the percentage for this age group was 28.86 percent. In 1961, persons under 20 years old composed 6.64 percent of the drivers in this State but they had 14.29 percent of the accidents. More drivers in the 16 to 20 age bracket were killed than in any other. In the nation, traffic accidents are the leading cause of deaths among persons between the ages of 15 and 24.

Since this Court first recognized it . . . , it has said many times that the family-purpose doctrine is "firmly imbedded in the law of this jurisdiction." . . . However, the majority now declares that the doctrine is an anomaly in the law which the Court is not disposed to extend; that the Court was reluctant to adopt it initially. . . .

The majority opinion defines a provider as follows: "In order to qualify as a provider under the family-purpose doctrine one must be a principal mover, one who intends to provide for another or others the particular thing, the automobile, and takes steps on his own responsibility to see to the consummation of the transaction, and contributes substantially of his own means toward that end without expectation of reimbursement or compensation." . . .

It is assumed that by the descriptive phrases, "a principal mover" and one who "takes steps on his own responsibility," are not meant to suggest or require that the idea of purchasing the car must *originate* with the provider. No doubt many a father, who never thought to make such an expenditure, has succumbed to the importunities and blandishments of a son or daughter who thought the family needed another car.

Certainly, in a legal sense, Mr. Simpson became the principal mover and he took steps on his own responsibility when he consummated the purchase of the Chevrolet by signing the note and conditional sales contract to secure the balance due on the automobile, when he had the title issued in his name and applied for the license, and when he applied for the insurance—an assigned risk. Incidentally that insurance policy would cover Wayne, not as the owner of the car, but because he was operating it with the consent of the named insured, Mr. Simpson!

Under the majority's definition of a *provider,* in the absence of an admission, it will be extremely difficult for a plaintiff ever again to prove that an automobile registered in the father's name, but used by a son for his own pleasure and convenience, is a   family-purpose car. All that the solvent, inadequately insured father need do to avoid liability is to assert that he paid for the car, took title in his own name, and made it available for the use of his teenage son (an assigned risk!) upon the boy's promise to reimburse him some day. The law would not hold the son to such a contract. The father could no more recover the purchase price of the car from a minor son who chose to disaffirm the contract than could a dealer who had sold an automobile to a minor. Should this Court permit such an unenforceable contract to nullify the family-purpose doctrine which was created in the public's interest to protect it from financially irresponsible minors? I do not think so. . . .

§ 29:5.   Use of Independent Contractor

Historically, the use of an independent contractor shielded the owner from liability to a third person. Thus, if you had an independent contractor build a wall on your property, you were not liable if because of his negligence part of the wall fell on a passerby and caused injury. In the earlier days, when most work was done by employees, the fact that there was this independent contractor exception did not appear to work any social injustice. In the Twentieth Century with so many enterprises furnishing specialized services as independent contractors, thus doing the work which was formerly done by employees of the owner, the doctrine of immunity from liability for the actions of an independent contractor presents a social problem. For example, a hundred years ago, it would be your own employees who would do repair work on your premises, it would be your employees who would do the cleaning, and it would be your employees who would do the delivery and hauling of your finished products.

Under the law of master and servant, if any one of such employees were negligent and this negligence caused harm to third persons, you as the master of the wrongdoing employee would be liable. Assume that today you run the same enterprise as a hundred years ago but contract with independent contractors to do the repair work, the cleaning, and to make deliveries. Will this insulate you from liability? Legalistically, the answer is that it will. In many cases this conclusion may work no hardship since the independent contractor may be better financially able to pay a judgment against him or may be covered by public liability insurance. But apart from such considerations, notice that the continued application of the independent contractor immunity rule would permit your enterprise to insulate itself from liability to third persons. Theoretically, if you could run all your activities that came into contact with strangers by means of independent contractors, you could avoid all liability to third persons.

This has seemed unjust to society, and inroads have been made upon the concept of insulation from liability by the employment of an independent contractor. First, it was held that if the work for which you employed the independent contractor was inherently dangerous, you would remain liable for the misdeeds of the contractor. In effect, this was a form of supervisory liability imposed on the owner, even though as a practical matter he would not be able or would not have the knowledge to exercise any effective supervision. To that extent, the liability has the characteristics of absolute liability.

The limitation next developed that some functions of an enterprise were so "personal" that responsibility for their performance could not be shifted to another. That is, while the independent contractor could be hired to do the work, the owner-employer remained liable as though the contractor were merely an employee. On this basis, it has been held that when an employer hires a detective agency to act as a plant guard, the employer is liable for false imprisonment and false arrest resulting from the acts of employees of the detective agency, as against the contention that the employer could not be liable for the actions of the agency's employees because the agency was an independent contractor and the latter's employees were not the employer's employees.

VAN ARSDALE v. HOLLINGER

66 Cal.Rptr. 20, 437 P.2d 508 (Cal., 1968)

Van Arsdale was an employee of Savala Paving Co., a street improvement contractor, doing work under a contract with the City of Los Angeles. While at work removing traffic lane lines from a street, Van Arsdale was struck by an automobile driven by Hollinger. He sued Hollinger and the City of Los Angeles.

OPINION BY PETERS, J. . . .

In the contract between the city and Savala, the contractor was required to furnish fences, barriers, lights, and warning signs as necessary to warn the public of dangerous conditions resulting from the contractor's operations. The contractor was also required to provide flagmen wearing red coats and equipped with a red flag or sign. If the contractor failed to so provide, the city could do so at the contractor's expense. The contractor was also required to furnish safety devices and safeguards to protect the public and workmen from injury, and, in addition to those prescribed by the contract and by law, to provide such further safeguards as would be employed by a diligent and prudent contractor.

At the time of the accident, there was no flagman provided, and plaintiff was wearing a red and black shirt with grey pants and was not wearing a flaming red or orange jacket.

There was a city inspector on duty at all times to see that the work was being performed according to the plans and specifications and to call departures therefrom to the attention of the contractor's foreman. The inspectors understood that they could tell the contractor to correct any dangerous condition due to the lack of proper barricades and could see that such conditions were corrected. The senior inspector said that apart from such duties, he had no right to tell, and did not tell, the Savala employees how "to do things." . . .

Section 815.4 of the Government Code provides: "A public entity is liable for injury proximately caused by a tortious act or omission of an independent contractor of the public entity to the same extent that the public entity would be subject to such liability if it were a private person. . . ."

The language of section 815.4 of the Government Code is clear, and the conclusion is inescapable that it requires that we look to the city's undertaking and determine whether a private person engaged in such an undertaking would have been liable for the tortious acts and omissions of an independent contractor.

Section 815.4 of the Government Code was adopted as proposed by the California Law Revision Commission without change. . . . The commission's comment to the section . . . states: "The California courts have held that public entities—and private persons, too—may at times be liable for the acts of their independent contractors. . . . This section retains that liability. Under the terms of this section, though, a public entity cannot be held liable for an independent contractor's act if the entity would have been immune had the act been that of a public employee."

Reports of commissions which have proposed statutes that are subsequently adopted are entitled to substantial weight in construing the statutes. . . . This is particularly true where the statute proposed by the commission is adopted by the Legislature without any change whatsoever and where the commission's comment is brief, because in such a situation there is ordinarily strong reason to believe that the legislators' votes were based in large measure upon the explanation of the commission proposing the bill.

The commission has cited *Snyder* v. *Southern Cal. Edison Co.,* supra, 44 Cal.2d 793, 285 P.2d 912, as "discussing general rule," and we must look to the case as the point where we must commence our analysis of the liability of a public entity for torts of an independent contractor.

After setting forth the rule that a party is not liable for the torts of an independent contractor and a few of the exceptions, the court in Snyder discussed the status of the law in this area:

"The matter is discussed by Harper [Law of Torts (1933)], as follows: '. . . one who employs an independent contractor is, as a general rule, not liable for the misconduct of the latter or of his servants while acting within the scope of the contract. The idea responsible for this general rule of nonliability is the want of control and authority of the employer over the work, and the consequent apparent harshness of a rule which would hold one responsible for the manner of conducting an enterprise over which he wants the authority to direct the operations. Again, so far as the activity immediately causing the injury is concerned, it is the contractor rather than the contractee who is the entrepreneur and who should ordinarily carry the risk. . . .

" '[There are] certain exceptions and apparent exceptions which, with increasing tendency, seem likely to overshadow in importance and scope the rule itself. . . . A number of situations exist, however, which are actual cases of vicarious liability, that is, liability for the misconduct of the independent contractor and his servants although the contractee has himself been free from personal fault. A number of factors concur to constitute the grounds of policy for such allocation of risk from the immediate to the general entrepreneur. These considerations, in fact, constitute such a powerful argument for the liability of the employer of an independent contractor that it would seem highly desirable for the courts to adopt the rule of liability and confine nonliability to a few exceptional cases. This, the American courts, at least, have not yet done, but there is every reason to believe that sound social policy will induce the courts to make further inroads upon the rule of nonliability in this class of cases.

" 'The first genuine case of liability for misconduct of an independent contractor or his employees is the case of the so-called "nondelegable" duty. Where the law imposes a definite, affirmative duty upon one by reason of his relationship with others, whether as an owner or proprietor of land or chattels or in some other capacity, such persons cannot escape liability for a failure to perform the duty thus imposed by entrusting it to an independent contractor. . . . It is immaterial whether the duty thus regarded as "nondelegable" be imposed by statute, charter, or by common law. Thus where a railroad company was required by statute to construct fences along its right of way and it employed a contractor to construct the fences, the company was liable for the loss of a cow killed by reason of the contractor's failure to build the fences as required by the statute. The same rule applies to the duty imposed upon railroads to erect gates at crossings, to construct cattle guards, and to maintain crossings in good condition. So, too, the owner of land is liable for the failure of an independent contractor to perform affirmative duties toward invitees and others to whom the occupier is bound to keep his premises in a reasonably safe condition. . . .

" 'Another large group of cases predicate liability on the part of the employer of an independent contractor for the misconduct of the latter in the performance of certain "intrinsically dangerous" work. The policy of allocating to the general entrepreneur the risks incident to his activity is obvious when the activity carries with it extraordinary hazards to third persons. . . . [T]he principle may be generalized that one who employs an independent contractor to perform work which is either extra-hazardous unless special precautions are taken or which is inherently dangerous in any event is liable for negligence on the part of the independent contractor or his servants in the improper performance of the work or for their negligent failure to take the necessary precautions. This broad principle has been applied not only to excavations on private property, but on the public highway as well, to blasting operations, to the construction of a dam, to the use of fire in clearing land, to the demolition of walls and old buildings, and to several other types of intrinsically dangerous enterprises.

"'In both of the above types of situation in which the employer of an independent contractor is liable for the negligence of the contractor or his servants, there is the limitation that such liability extends only to negligence in the failing to take the necessary precautions, failing to adopt a reasonably safe method, or in failing to produce a result which it is the duty of the employer-contractee to have attained. Such liability does not ordinarily extend to so-called "collateral" or "casual" negligence on the part of the contractor or his servants in the performance of the operative detail of the work. The negligence for which the employer is liable, as general entrepreneur, must be such as is intimately connected with the work authorized and such as is reasonably likely from its nature. Negligence in the doing of ordinary acts, not necessarily incidental, but only accidentally connected with the work, do not fall within the policy of the law which imposes the extraordinary liability upon the employer.

"'The distinction between "collateral" or "casual" negligence and negligence of the contractor so intimately connected with the work to be done that the employer-contractee is liable therefor is a shadowy one at best.'" . . .

The prophesy of Professor Harper quoted in Snyder has come to pass; the exceptions to the general rule of nonliability have continued to be expanded. As pointed out in comment b of section 409 of the Restatement Second of Torts, the exceptions "are so numerous, and they have so far eroded the 'general rule,' that it can now be said to be 'general' only in the sense that it is applied where no good reason is found for departing from it. As was said in *Pacific Fire Insurance Co.* v. *Kenny Boiler & Mfg. Co.,* 201 Minn. 500, 277 N.W. 226 (1937), 'Indeed it would be proper to say that the rule is now primarily important as a preamble to the catalog of its exceptions.'" . . .

It is clear that the liability of an employer of an independent contractor for the latter's tortious conduct is broad, and it must be assumed that the Legislature was aware of the extent of the liability of employers when, by adopting section 815.4 of the Government Code, it chose with one exception not relevant here to waive the defense of sovereign immunity in cases involving tortious conduct of independent contractors. In these circumstances, a claim that application of the numerous and broad exceptions to the so-called general rule of nonliability will result in great liabilities of public entities for injuries caused by tortious conduct furnishes no basis to depart from those exceptions or to refuse to apply them in the instant case.

There are numerous considerations which have led courts to depart from the rule of nonliability of a private employer for the torts of an independent contractor. Some of the principal ones are that the enterprise, notwithstanding the employment of the independent contractor, remains the employer's because he is the party primarily to be benefited by it, that he selects the contractor, is free to insist upon one who is financially responsible, and to demand indemnity from him, that the insurance necessary to distribute the risk is properly a cost of the employer's business, and that the performance of the duty of care is of great importance to the public. . . .

These considerations are present here, and the instant case comes within at least one of the well-recognized exceptions to the rule of nonliability for the acts of an independent contractor. This exception to the rule of nonliability is for work dangerous in the absence of special precautions. In section 416 of the Restatement Second of Torts, the exception is stated as follows: "One who employs an independent contractor to do work which the employer should recognize as likely to create during its progress a peculiar risk of physical harm to others unless special precautions are taken, is subject to liability for physical harm caused to them by the failure of the contractor to exercise reasonable care to take such precautions, even though the employer has provided for such precautions in the contract or otherwise."

In *Courtell* v. *McEachen*, 51 Cal.2d 448, 456-457, 334 P.2d 870, it was held that section 416 of the original Restatement of Torts was applicable in California. Section 416 in the Restatement Second of Torts differs from the original in that the words "likely to create during its progress a peculiar risk of physical harm" were substituted for "necessarily requiring the creation during its progress of a condition involving a peculiar risk of bodily harm." The change is immaterial here because the undisputed facts meet either test.

This court has held that employees of an independent contractor come within the word "others" as used in sections 413, 414, and 428 of the Restatement of Torts, which like section 416, set forth rules relating to the liability of one hiring an independent contractor. . . . There is no reason to hold otherwise with respect to section 416. . . .

Under the undisputed facts, the conditions precedent to the nondelegable duty imposed by section 416 appear as a matter of law. The undertaking here was to eradicate the markings of the white lines on a busy street while one of the three lanes was kept open to traffic. Absent special precautions to keep the traffic proceeding on the open lane from going into the other lanes, the work was highly dangerous. The necessity for such precautions was inherent in the work and was obvious before the work commenced. The contract of the city provided for special precautions, but under the plain language of section 416 this does not satisfy its duty. The work here is analogous to that considered by the Restatement Second in two of its illustrations to section 416, showing that the section applies to the danger of personal injury due to use of a highway because of failure to barricade highways or to warn motorists of dangerous conditions on or adjoining highways. . . .

For the foregoing reasons it is clear that under the undisputed facts the city had a nondelegable duty to exercise due care, that an employee of the independent contractor could recover from the city for breach of that duty, and that the city could not avoid that duty by hiring an independent contractor.

In the instant case, the trial court, after advising the jury that if the contractor had taken control of the premises the city "would have no obligation toward persons in the position of plaintiff," stated that there was an exception to the rule. The court instructed the jury that one who employs an independent contractor to do work which the employer in the exercise of ordinary care should recognize as necessarily creating, during its progress, conditions containing an unreasonable risk of injury to others, unless special precautions are taken, is liable for injury proximately caused to them by the absence of such precautions, "if the employer either fails to provide in the contract that the contractor shall take such precautions, or fails to exercise ordinary care to provide in some other manner for the taking of such precautions." The court then pointed out that the city had provided in its contract with the independent contractor for the taking of certain precautions.

The instruction properly recognizes that liability of the city could be predicated on the ground that the work was dangerous in the absence of special precautions. The latter part of the instruction, when given without qualification in the circumstances of this case, is clearly erroneous, however, because when read with the introductory part of the instruction, it tells the jury that the city's duty in this respect may be satisfied by merely providing in its contract for the special precautions. Under section 416 of the Restatement Second of Torts, as we have seen, the city is liable for the failure of the independent contractor to take special precautions even though it has provided in its contract for the taking of the precautions. . . .

Upon retrial, if the evidence bearing on the issue of duty is unchanged, plaintiff will be entitled to an instruction stating that the city had a nondelegable duty of due care, and for this reason it is unnecessary to determine whether an employee of an independent contractor is among those who can recover for breach of the nondelegable duties set forth in section 417 of the Restatement Second of Torts dealing with work done in a public place and section 418 of the Restatement Second of Torts dealing with the nondelegable duty to maintain public highways or to determine whether section 428 of the Restatement Second of Torts dealing with the nondelegable duty relating to work carried on under public franchise is applicable. The Restatement recognizes that the exceptions stated therein to the rule of nonliability overlap so that in the ordinary case two or more of the exceptions will be applicable. . . . The applicability of the duty of care as a matter of law also makes it unnecessary to consider plaintiff's claim that the trial court erred in refusing to instruct the jury on the duty of an invitor and the conditions giving rise to such duty.

Plaintiff also urges that the court erred in refusing to instruct that the city was an employer as a matter of law and that certain sections of the Labor Code establishing safety rules were therefore applicable to it. The court instructed the jury that it was a question of fact whether the city was an employer as that term was defined in the Labor Code. The mere right to see that work is satisfactorily completed does not impose upon one hiring an independent contractor the duty to assure that the contractor's work is performed in conformity with all safety provisions. . . . There was evidence that the city did nothing more than exercise general supervision and control to bring about the satisfactory completion of the project and did not regulate the operative details of the work and, if the jury found that this was all that was done by the city, the Labor Code was not the measure of its responsibility. . . .

As to defendant Hollinger, plaintiff argues that the court improperly refused to instruct the jury in the language of section 21703 of the Vehicle

Code that a driver of a motor vehicle shall not follow another vehicle more closely than is "reasonable and prudent" under the circumstances. However, other instructions given by the court told the jury that a driver must exercise due care to avoid accidents, must be vigilant, and exercise such control that to avoid a collision he can stop as quickly as might be required by eventualities that would be anticipated by an ordinarily prudent driver. In view of the instructions given, it was unnecessary to instruct in the words of the statute. . . .

The judgment is reversed as to defendant City of Los Angeles and affirmed as to defendant Hollinger.

DISSENTING AND CONCURRING OPINION BY BURKE, J. . . .

I concur in the judgment of affirmance as to defendant Hollinger and of reversal as to defendant city. The evidence would support a jury finding that the city had retained some control over the premises where plaintiff's injury occurred. Accordingly, I believe the court erred to plaintiff's prejudice in refusing to give his requested instruction setting forth the liabilities of the city as an invitor in case the jury did so find, and that plaintiff is entitled to a reversal on that ground. . . .

However, issues relating to the theory of tort liability of one who engages an independent contractor found in section 416, Restatement Second of Torts, are not properly before this court. That section comes into play only if the work involves a peculiar risk of bodily harm. Plaintiff did not request an instruction based on section 416, and in his brief states that during trial he did not contend that the work in which he was engaged created an unreasonable risk of injury. He should not be permitted to raise the point for the first time on appeal.

Questions for Review

1. Analyze each opinion in this chapter in terms of the social forces involved in the decision. See § 5:5 for a list of the social forces. With respect to each opinion, explain why the prevailing social forces prevailed and why those rejected did not. In each case in which there is a dissenting opinion, also make this analysis for the dissenting opinion.

2-6. *On the basis of the social forces involved, what decision should be made in each of the following cases?*

2. *Automobiles. Family purpose.* Is the father liable for harm caused by his daughter using her father's car to purchase corn for family from roadside stand? *Grimes* v. *Labreck,* 108 N.H. 26, 226 A.2d 787.

3. *Automobiles. Family purpose.* Does the family-purpose doctrine impose liability where a member of family lends car to a nonfamily friend in order to obtain cigarettes for the family member? *Pritchett* v. *Williams,* 115 Ga. App. 8, 153 S.E.2d 639.

4. *Parental liability. Constitutional statute.* May a statute constitutionally impose liability upon parents for damages not exceeding $300 maliciously caused by their young minor child when no fault of the parent is shown? *Mahaney* v. *Hunter Enterprises,* Wyo., 426 P.2d 442.

5. *Employer's liability. Husband.* When a wife is driving her husband's automobile while shopping for items he is required to furnish her, is she his agent? *Talbott* v. *Gegenheimer,* 245 Md. 186, 225 A.2d 462.

6. *Proximate cause. Police chase.* Is the municipality or its police officer liable for harm caused the plaintiff by the automobile fleeing from the police officer when the fleeing car might have been apprehended by radioing alarm rather than pursuing it? *Roll* v. *Tiberman,* 94 N.J.S. 530, 229 A.2d 281.

7-11. What social forces were involved, which prevailed, and which were defeated in the following decisions?

7. *Negligence. Sponsoring grandparents.* Where grandparents assume custody of a teenage grandson who has committed criminal acts and has a known vicious character, they are liable to a third person assaulted by the grandson (whom they have permitted to live alone) on the theory that they were negligent in not exercising proper control over the grandson to prevent foreseeable harm to third persons. *Poncher* v. *Brackett,* Cal.App.2d, 55 Cal. Rptr. 59.

8. *Premises liability. Self-service store.* The fact that customers wait on themselves in a self-service store does not make them employees of the store so as to make the store responsible to another customer injured by falling on debris dropped on the floor by customers. *Cameron* v. *Bohack,* 27 App.Div.2d 362, 280 N.Y.S.2d 483.

9. *Negligence. Boomerang.* A merchant giving the father of a 10-year-old child a boomerang is not liable for the harm caused another child when the boomerang was thrown by the customer's child, even though the merchant knew that the customer's child was not skilled in throwing a boomerang, and could have reasonably foreseen that it would be used by the customer's child and knew that after being thrown, its flight could not be controlled. *Maramba* v. *Neuman,* 82 Ill.App.2d 95, 227 N.E.2d 80.

10. *Schools. Athletics.* The fact that wrestling matches were nominally conducted by a student body association will not shield the school from tort liability where the school had full veto power of association decisions, and consequently the school would be liable for failure to maintain proper supervision of extracurricular activity. *Carabba* v. *Anacortes School District,* Wash.2d, 435 P.2d 936.

11. *Premises liability. Concessionaire.* Where a nightclub leases a lot adjoining parking enterprise, it is estopped from asserting that the parking lot attendants were not its own employees where there was merely one obscure sign on the lot which would indicate its independent character and the lot appeared to be operated by the nightclub. *Eckerle* v. *Twenty Grand Corp.,* 8 Mich.App. 1, 153 N.W.2d 369.

Chapter 30

THE LAWSUIT

§ 30:1.   The Problem

(a) Generally. The object of a legal system is to ascertain the facts of a controversy and to apply the law thereto. This should be a very simple matter except that it is sometimes very difficult to tell what did happen and the exact rule of law to fit the case may not have been declared. This perhaps is an overgloomy statement of the situation for there are many cases in which the risk of being unable to prove the facts is relatively slight and

in which the law is relatively or definitely certain. Nevertheless, even at its best you will see from the following steps of a lawsuit that the best course is to avoid litigation by running your business in such a way that you minimize the possibility of being sued and to reduce the necessity of bringing a suit to enforce your rights. While you can leave the details of litigation to your attorney, you should appreciate what a lawsuit involves so that you do not lightly commit your business to the delays and hazards of litigation.

(b) *The typical lawsuit.* In the following sections a lawsuit will be analyzed step by step. Actually the procedure in one state may differ in many details, but the general plan will follow that set forth. Moreover, the following analysis will take the lawsuit from its beginning and run it through to its greatest length. In actual practice, many suits will not go that far.

For the purpose of simplicity, the procedure will be discussed in terms of the prepleading stage, the trial stage, post-trial proceedings, appeals, judgment and costs, and execution.

§ 30:2.   Prepleading Stage

(a) *Time for commencement of the action.* Actions are generally subject to time limitations called Statutes of Limitations. This means that if the action is not brought within a specified time, no action can ever be brought and the claim is barred. For example, in many states, an action to recover damages for personal injuries must be brought within two years after the injury is sustained. In the case of an action for product liability under the Uniform Commercial Code, the plaintiff has four years in which to bring the action.

(b) *Form of action.* The action will ordinarily be called a civil action or a civil action for damages. In some states, still retaining the common-law names, this will be called an action of assumpsit, if the claim is a contract claim, and action of trespass if a tort claim, as when the plaintiff is injured by the condition of the premises or the operation of an automobile.

An individual or an enterprise is, of course, legally capable of committing other civil wrongs and may therefore be sued in the form of action appropriate to such other types of claims. For example, if a business builds onto the neighboring land, the neighboring landowner may obtain an injunction to prevent such construction; or, in certain cases, he may sue in ejectment to cause the ouster of the encroaching business from such part of the plaintiff's land as had been encroached upon.

(c) *The court.* The plaintiff cannot bring his case wherever he chooses. To the contrary, he must bring it in a court which by statute or constitution has been given the power to hear the particular type of case involved. For example, the plaintiff claiming for damages for harm done because of the condition of premises cannot bring suit in a court that is only authorized to hear divorce actions.

Furthermore, a defendant may only be sued in a particular county or district. Thus, a business can be sued only in the county or district in which it is "located." This follows from the fact that the right to sue in a given district or county is generally dependent upon being able to effect service on the defendant in that district or county, and this, in turn, is limited by requiring that the defendant be "found" in that district or county. This rule is designed to further the convenience of the defendant for he does not have to go traveling away from home in order to defend the claim asserted against him.

As an exception to the rule above stated, it is generally provided that suit may be brought in the county or in the foreign state in which the harm is sustained where the claim is one for damage arising from the operation of a motor vehicle. Thus, if a business is run in County *A* but its automobile is being driven in the course of the business in County *B,* a suit may commonly be brought in County *B* when the automobile is involved in a collision which harms the plaintiff in County *B.* Likewise, if the enterprise's automobile is driven out of the state, nonresident motorist statutes will ordinarily be applicable. Under such statutes, the use of an automobile in another state automatically appoints the secretary of state or some other official of that state as agent to receive service of process directed against the operator or driver of the vehicle.

If the business is a corporation, and particularly if it is a corporation formed under the laws of another state, it is likely that the plaintiff will be permitted to serve a particular local government official who is designated as the statutory agent of the corporation for the purpose of being served with process.

(d) The parties. The action against the business may be brought against it alone. In many cases, the plaintiff will be allowed to join both the business and some employee involved. For example, a plaintiff harmed by the negligence of the business employee may, in most states, sue in one action both the employee and the business employing him.

In some cases, the plaintiff may join the business and an independent contractor. Thus, the plaintiff who is injured because of the maintenance contractor's failure to maintain the business elevators in good condition, may join both such contractor and the business, the latter not being released from liability because of the employment of an independent contractor. In product liability cases, the plaintiff, in many states, will be permitted to join the business that served or sold him the harmful product and the dealers or manufacturer who had supplied such goods or product to such business.

(e) Commencement of action. There are a variety of ways in which the action may be commenced. In the old common-law courts, an action was

commenced by filing an order with the keeper of the court records to issue a writ to the sheriff. This writ of summons ordered the sheriff to inform the defendant to appear before the court on a particular date. This method of commencing an action is still followed in some states.

By way of contrast, an action in a court of equity was begun when the plaintiff filed with the court a complaint in which he set forth the facts about which he complained. That is, the action was itself started by the beginning of the pleading stage by the filing of the first pleading, namely, the plaintiff's complaint. No writ was issued, and a copy of the complaint was itself served on the defendant. In many states, and in the federal courts, the procedural reforms of the last several decades have extended this practice to all legal actions. They are accordingly commenced today by the filing of the plaintiff's complaint.

Some states still preserve the former distinction between law and equity and their distinct methods of commencement, while others give the plaintiff the option of commencing the action by either method. This latter plan has the advantage of enabling the plaintiff to start the action quickly without taking the time to prepare his complaint where quick action is needed because (1) the Statute of Limitations period is about to expire or (2) the defendant is about to leave the jurisdiction and if service is not made within 24 hours or so, it may be impossible to ever effect service.

(f) Service of process. The defendant must be served with some paper for the purpose of making him subject to the jurisdiction of the court and to notify him that the action has been begun. This paper may take a variety of forms. It may be a writ, a notice, or a summons, or, the complaint itself.

Ordinarily, there is no difficulty in serving a business because of its fixed location where its building is located. As a minimum, the plaintiff will ordinarily be able to have service made upon the business by making service at the business building upon the owner, proprietor, corporate executive officer, or an agent or employee in charge of the business.

As soon as the business is served, it should communicate at once with its attorney and with its insurance company. The attorney will want to investigate before the facts have changed; witnesses have moved away; and, if possible, talk to witnesses before they have been discovered and talked to by the plaintiff's attorney.

By the terms of your insurance policy, it is generally necessary that you give your insurer prompt or immediate notice in order that it can also make an early investigation of the facts. When notice to the insurer is required, it is likewise generally provided that the failure to give notice as required shall bar your right against the insurer. In the absence of a contrary statute or some special circumstance, such a forfeiture provision is given effect and means that it is just the same as though you did not have any insurance policy.

§ 30:3.   The Pleading Stage

(a) Generally. After the action has been commenced, the next stage of the proceedings is to get before the court a statement of the facts as viewed by each party so that it can be seen to what extent the parties really disagree over the facts.

Apart from variations as to the names of pleadings, the time for filing them, and so on, there are two basic systems of pleading in the United States. The older or common-law system requires that a party be very specific and set forth all facts material to his case. The modern system, frequently described as the federal or notice-giving system, only requires the setting forth of such facts as give notice to the other party of the substance of the claim being asserted. For example, the plaintiff's complaint by the latter system might be nothing more than the statement that the plaintiff fell on a certain day in the defendant's business because of the defendant's fault. In contrast, the common-law system of fact pleading would require a pleading of just where the fall took place, what caused the fall, and in what respects the defendant was negligent or at fault, and so on.

(b) The plaintiff's complaint. The first pleading filed in the action is the complaint of the plaintiff. In some states this may have already been filed as a means of commencing the action. If the action was not commenced in this manner, the plaintiff must file the complaint.

After the complaint is filed, a copy is served on or sent to the defendant, who must then make some reply thereto, ordinarily within 15 or 20 days. If he does not, the plaintiff ordinarily wins the case by default and a judgment is entered in his favor against the defendant.

(i) *Necessity of prompt action on receiving the complaint.* Here is a danger spot in litigation. Namely, that you will let the 15 or 20 days for replying to the complaint slip by without doing anything about it. Remember, your attorney needs time to examine the facts before he will know just what type of paper or pleading he should file in reply to the plaintiff's complaint. You should therefore give him all the possible time you can by notifying him of the fact that you have been served with the complaint and forwarding it to him.

Your liability insurance policy will in most cases require that a copy of the complaint be forwarded to it promptly, immediately, or forthwith. Again, the failure to comply with the policy provision in this respect will ordinarily forfeit your rights under the insurance policy with respect to the neglected claim, although under special circumstances it may be held that the forfeiture provision is not effective.

(ii) *Relief from default judgment.* If through carelessness or for any other reason, the defendant fails to file anything in reply to the complaint and the plaintiff obtains a default judgment against it, is there anything that the defendant can do about it? In many states, the defendant, if it has a good excuse for the neglect and can show in addition that it probably has a good defense to the action if given the chance to formally prove such fact, will be allowed to proceed to do so. In many states, this is called petitioning to open the judgment for the purpose of making a defense.

While this remedy may frequently be invoked, it is not always certain that it will be allowed. The defendant should not, therefore, take it for granted that if its employees fail to act promptly in informing it that service has been made of the complaint, the defendant can thereafter be rescued by obtaining the opening of a judgment in this manner.

(c) Defendant's alternatives. After the complaint is filed, the defendant must take some step in court. Although he is required to file an answer, the defendant has the right to say, "Let's wait until later about my answer. There's something about your case or your claim that we should first discuss."

Specifically, the defendant before answering the plaintiff's complaint may point out errors relating to the case thus far. This the defendant does by filing what are sometimes called preliminary objections. For example, the defendant may claim that he was never served; or that the action has been brought in the wrong county, or in the wrong court; or that there is something wrong about the plaintiff's complaint. What happens at this point may end the case, depending upon the nature of the objection made. If the objection is upheld or sustained, the case may be ended, as when the objection is that the action is brought in the wrong court and it is held that that is true; or the plaintiff may be granted leave to correct his mistake, as when his complaint does not conform to the statutes or rules of court and he is then given leave to correct his mistakes by filing a new or amended complaint.

One of the objections which the defendant may raise is that the plaintiff's complaint, even if believed, does not set forth a claim or cause of action which the law recognizes and that the plaintiff is therefore not entitled to recover. This objection is often called a motion to dismiss or a demurrer. If this objection is sustained, the action of the court has the effect of saying that the plaintiff has nothing about which to complain, and the case is over in favor of the defendant, subject, of course, to the right of the plaintiff to file an amended complaint to state his case better, if he can, or take an appeal, or otherwise challenge the action of the court.

(i) Defendant's answer. If the defendant loses on his various preliminary objections or motions above described, he must then file an answer, which either admits or denies the facts averred by the plaintiff. Under the common-law system of pleading, the defendant must ordinarily deny the plaintiff's claim fact by fact, and, wherever possible, must aver just what did happen as opposed to what the plaintiff claims. Under the notice system

of pleading, it is generally sufficient that the defendant merely state that certain matters are denied, or he may even make a blanket denial of the entire plaintiff's claim as by saying that, "All facts averred by the plaintiff are denied."

For example, if the plaintiff averred that on a given date he fell in a given part of the defendant's building because the defendant negligently failed to take certain specified precautions and that in consequence the plaintiff suffered specified harm, the defendant might want to deny part or even all of these facts. To illustrate, if the claim is a false claim in that the plaintiff never was even hurt on the premises of the defendant, the defendant will deny the entire claim. On the other hand, the defendant may not dispute the fact that the plaintiff was harmed nor that the defendant's negligence was the cause thereof, but the defendant disputes that the plaintiff has suffered the damages claimed by him. For example, the plaintiff has claimed damages for permanent disability, whereas the defendant claims that there was not more than a few days of disability. Similarly, the defendant might admit all parts of the plaintiff's claim but dispute the amount that the plaintiff said he spent for doctor bills.

In these two situations, the defendant could admit the fact relating to the occurrence, the fact of the plaintiff's being harmed, and of the defendant's being negligent, but attack the damages claimed by denying that the plaintiff was injured or sustained damages to the extent claimed. Or the defendant may wish to admit that the facts occurred as claimed and that the plaintiff sustained the damages alleged, but wish to deny some or all of the facts on which the liability of the hotel is based. To illustrate, the defendant may wish to deny that part of the plaintiff's complaint which states that the automobile which ran over the plaintiff was being driven by an employee of the defendant while acting in the course of his employment. In the ordinary case, if the employee is outside the scope of his employment, there is no liability for the harm caused by him. The fact of his being in the course of his employment is therefore a pivotal fact in the determination of the lawsuit.

(ii) *Counterclaim or cross complaint.* It may be that the defendant has some claim against the plaintiff. For example, if the plaintiff sued because of the harm done by the defendant's automobile, the defendant may take the position that its automobile was properly driven, that it was the plaintiff's fault which caused the collision, and that the plaintiff should pay the defendant for the damage which had been sustained by the defendant's car.

This making of claims back against the plaintiff is called, depending upon the local procedure, either a counterclaim or a cross suit.

(iii) *New matter.* The position that the defendant takes may be that it admits all the facts as claimed by the plaintiff but asserts that because of some additional fact not set forth by the plaintiff, the latter had no right to sue the defendant. For example, the defendant may wish to claim that although the plaintiff had the right to recover as far as would appear from his complaint, there is the additional fact that the defendant had already given the defendant a release. That is, according to the defendant, the plaintiff gave up the claim against the defendant in return for the money received from the defendant.

Whenever there is some additional element which the defendant claims constitutes a bar to the plaintiff's claim, the defendant is allowed to put that additional matter in its answer. Frequently this additional information is called "new matter."

The pleading of new matter is not limited to cases in which the defendant admits the claim of the plaintiff as far as it goes and then raises the new matter as a defense. The defendant can also take the alternative position that the plaintiff's claim is not valid but that even if it were valid, it would be barred. By way of illustration, the defendant can take the position that the plaintiff who allegedly fell because of the condition of the premises cannot recover because the defendant was not negligent, but that even if the defendant was negligent, the plaintiff was barred by his contributory negligence.

(d) Plaintiff's alternatives. After the defendant files his answer, the plaintiff may generally file preliminary objections to the answer. Similar to the pattern of possible objections which the defendant could raise, the plaintiff may, in certain instances, take the position that a counterclaim cannot be asserted in the court in which the case is pending, that the answer is defective in form, or that the counterclaim is not legally sufficient as a claim or the new matter is not legally sufficient as a defense. These various objections are disposed of by the court and the case moves on.

In most instances, the pleadings will have come to an end by this time. The case may be such, however, that the plaintiff is allowed one more pleading. For example, if the defendant under new matter has raised the defense of a release given by the plaintiff, the plaintiff may wish to admit the release but then claim that the release is void because obtained from the plaintiff by fraud or when the plaintiff was in such a mental or physical state that the plaintiff had no capacity or ability to agree to anything.

If the plaintiff is permitted to file a reply, it is generally provided that the defendant may make preliminary objections thereto, or file a motion to dismiss or a demurrer. Beyond this point, it is generally provided that pleadings may not go.

(e) Classification and determination of issues. Generally, all of the pleadings in an action will raise only a few or perhaps only one question of law, or one question of fact, or both questions of law and questions of fact. To illustrate, the whole case may turn on the question of fact whether the

defendant warned the plaintiff with a notice of the condition of the premises. The nature of the case may be such that if it is true that the defendant gave such warning, it was not negligent and the defendant is then not liable to the plaintiff. Conversely, if the warning was not given, the defendant was negligent and was accordingly liable to the plaintiff.

By way of contrast, it may be admitted that notice of the danger was given but the plaintiff takes the position that more than notice was required. It is then a question of law of whether the defendant was legally required to do more than give notice, or whether it had gone as far as it was required to do when it gave the notice. Here the question is one of law. If the question is decided in favor of the defendant, judgment will be entered in its favor; if decided in favor of the plaintiff, he will recover against the defendant.

If the only questions involved are questions of law, the court will decide the case on the pleadings alone since there is no need for a trial to determine the facts. Conversely, if questions of fact are involved, then there must be a trial to determine what the facts really are. If there are both questions of law and fact, there must be a trial; and if the trial is before a jury, there will be a division of labor—the judge deciding the questions of law and the jury deciding the questions of fact, as will be described in § 30:5.

§ 30:4.   Pretrial Procedure

(a) Generally. In a strict sense, everything that has occurred up to this point is pretrial procedure for the reason that the trial has not yet been held. There are, however, a number of procedural steps which may take place before trial that are often classified as pretrial proceedings because they are modern innovations added on to the common-law or statutory form of procedure. The classification is arbitrary because some of the steps may be regarded as an extension of the pleading system and in many states are so classified, while other steps may be pursued while the pleadings are going on.

(b) Motions to end case without a trial. We have already considered as a part of the pleading stage the objection, motion to dismiss, or demurrer which is used by one party to show that the pleading of the other party does not state a cause of action or a defense which is valid. In many states there are two or more types of motions which can be made for the purpose of putting an end to the case without getting into a trial.

(i) *Motion for judgment on the pleadings.* After the pleadings are closed, many states permit either party to move for a judgment on the pleadings. When this motion is made, the court examines the entire case up to that point as shown by the pleadings and then enters judgment according to the merits of the case as shown by the record.

(ii) *Motion for summary judgment.* In some states, a party is allowed to bring into court sworn statements or affidavits which show that a claim or defense is false or a sham. This procedure can not be used when there is a substantial dispute of facts concerning the matters to be proved by the use of such affidavits.

(c) Pretrial conference. In many states a pretrial conference may be called by the court on its own initiative or upon the application of any party to the action. This conference was originally intended to be only a round table discussion by the judge of the court and the attorneys in the case with the object of eliminating matters that were not in dispute, agreeing on just what issues were to be determined at the trial, and cleaning up in advance procedural matters relating to the trial.

The pretrial conference is not intended as a procedure to compel the parties to settle their case. It not infrequently results, however, that when the attorneys discuss the matter with the court, they recognize that the differences between the conflicting points of view are not so great as originally believed or that one side has less merit than at first appeared; in consequence of which, the attorneys are able to come together and meet on a common ground and settle the case. With the development of a staggering overload of court dockets, the pressure to settle cases becomes increasingly greater.

The pretrial proceeding presents a danger area for the defendant. There is the danger that the plaintiff will make a false claim and then pressure will be brought to bear on the defendant's attorney to compromise the claim, rather than defend against it. This opens the door to fraud in that persons will make exaggerated and false claims, trusting that there will be just enough semblance of validity to their claims that the pretrial conference judge will seek to persuade the defendant to give the plaintiff something.

(d) Discovery. In the federal courts and in many state courts following the federal rules, parties to litigation have an almost free right to obtain discovery from the other parties and from third persons. The exact significance of this is more readily apparent if we first consider the common-law practice.

(i) *Common-law procedure.* Prior to the modern reforms, any party could before the trial, or before bringing an action, ask anyone any questions he chose; but whether the other person would answer was a matter which was up to him. That is, you could investigate a claim but you could not compel any answer nor compel the production of any information if the person questioned was hostile to you and did not wish to cooperate with you.

There was, accordingly, a race by parties to a lawsuit to reach the witnesses first; each party hoping that if he would examine a given witness first, he could thereby induce that witness to refuse to answer the investigator for the other party. The result of this technique was extreme secrecy without either party knowing for certain just what witnesses would be called by the adverse party nor what those witnesses would say when the trial actually took place. Those who criticized this system pointed out that it was a game of surprise in which no one knew what the trial would bring. Those who favored this system said that that was good because you would not be able to manufacture false testimony to overcome my truthful witnesses.

There was indeed an advantage in the old system of shaking a lying witness apart by producing evidence which showed that he was lying, without his having any opportunity other than the spur of the moment to think up some way out of his perjurious dilemma. Unfortunately, sometimes the one who was shaken by the surprise was the attorney whose client consciously or unconsciously had deceived him; and it was not until the moment of truth arrived at the trial that the attorney could see the entire picture and recognize that his client or his client's witnesses were not telling the truth.

(ii) *Modern procedure.* Under the modern procedure a wide range of examination may be conducted before trial by both parties not only of third persons but also of each other. The theory here is that everyone learns just what everyone else knows and the trial then becomes a matter of presenting the known facts in an orderly way rather than a battle of wits and of witnesses.

Under this modern procedure, one party can seek virtually as much information before the trial as he would be permitted to ask at the trial, and in certain respects his scope of pretrial examination is even wider than at the trial.

In terms of procedural forms, in many courts a party can (1) send a questionnaire to the other party asking him any questions about the facts of the case; (2) send a request to the other party to admit formal matters, such as the execution of a document; (3) require the adverse party and witnesses to appear before an examiner and answer under oath what they know about the case and state the names of other witnesses; (4) obtain a court order to allow the examining, inspecting, and photographing of books, records, buildings, and machines; and (5) obtain a court order to make a physical or mental examination of a party when his condition has a bearing on the case.

This system eliminates the evils of surprise, but it also eliminates the beneficial aspect of surprise since the perjurer is now forewarned of the evidence, which would otherwise trip him; and it becomes just a matter of a little more perjury for him to conjure up a rational excuse or explanation for the conflict within his testimony or between his testimony and the other evidence.

More important, the discovery procedure easily lends itself to being used as a means of harassing a party and of subjecting him to unnecessary and needless inconvenience and expense. In many instances, the criticism is heard that the net effect of the discovery procedure is to try the case twice, once by the discovery procedure and once by trial. When the adverse party is a corporation with scattered officers and employees, it becomes particularly annoying if discovery repeatedly involves different officers and employees or if the examination includes its many records. The acuteness of the problem increases where the defendant conducts a multistate operation, and the witnesses and employees who have been involved in the transaction giving rise to the lawsuit have been assigned to different jobs in different branches. As the witnesses are spread to the four points of the compass, the discovery procedure obviously spreads out over a larger geographic area.

The evils here depicted are not without remedy. It is generally provided that a court may be petitioned to enter a protective order against any excessive or abusive use of discovery, as well as for other grounds. But the very necessity of seeking a protective order in resisting proceedings is itself a burdensome thing. Moreover, the general inclination of the courts is to refuse to restrict the discovery proceeding. The net result is that the modern lawsuit brings with it the added threat of harassment by discovery procedures.

(e) Depositions. Ordinarily a witness testifies in court at the time of the trial. In some instances, it may be necessary or desirable to take his testimony out of the court before the time of the trial. This is the situation when he is aged or infirm and may die or be too ill to testify by the time of the trial. It is likewise true if he is about to leave the state or country so that he will not be available or within the reach of a subpoena at the time of the trial. In such cases, a party in interest, after giving proper notice to the adverse party and to the prospective missing witness, may require such witness to appear before someone authorized to administer oaths and to answer questions and to submit to cross-examination. All this testimony is recorded stenographically and then filed with the court as the testimony of the missing witness if, when the trial arrives, he is in fact then missing.

§ 30:5. The Trial

(a) Generally. The trial is the phase of litigation in which a trier of fact determines the facts of the case; the principles of law applicable to such facts are applied; and a conclusion as to liability or guilt is reached. As discussed earlier, it is possible that the parties may never reach a trial, as where the case is disposed of prior to trial for some reason, as when certain preliminary objections are sustained.

(b) The trier of fact. In most cases, the facts when disputed are determined by a jury, unless all parties to the action agree that the case be heard without a jury. If the parties agree to waive such jury, the case may be heard by the judge alone, or in some instances referred to a master or referee specially appointed by the court for such purpose.

(i) *Equity cases.* In an equity proceeding there is no right to trial by jury. This merely follows from the historical accident that in equity there is no constitutional right to a jury trial. Thus if an action is brought in equity to enjoin the defendant from doing certain acts, neither the plaintiff nor the defendant would be entitled to a jury trial.

The equity judge, if he desires, may submit questions to a jury in the same way that you might retain a body of experts to give you a report on a particular matter. That is, the verdict of the jury is only advisory and the equity judge who appointed the jury is not bound by their decision; whereas in the case of an action at law, the determination by the jury is binding in the absence of basic error. Although in most states there is no longer a separate court of equity, the above principles are still recognized when the modern court determines a case that historically would have been brought in an equity court.

(ii) *Administrative proceedings.* When new causes of action are created by statute and enforced by administrative boards or agencies, there is no constitutional right of trial by jury, the theory being that where the right was unknown to the common law, the right to trial by jury did not exist. Accordingly, the guarantee of the trial by jury does not extend to these hitherto unknown areas. For example, the discharge of an employee because of union membership never gave rise to any cause of action at common law; and being a new form of action it may, as is the case, be entrusted to an administrative agency to determine whether there is a breach of the duty imposed by that law.

(c) The basis for decision. The trier of fact, whether it is a jury, the judge, or an administrative body, can only decide questions of fact on the basis of the evidence presented before it. The evidence usually consists of the questions put to the witnesses in the court or trial and their answers to the questions. This is called the testimony. The evidence may also include real evidence consisting of tangible things, such as the piece of the broken chair involved in the accident, and other things to be seen, which are offered in evidence on the theory that seeing is better than hearing. In some cases, the trier of fact may be taken to view the premises; that is, go look at the actual place where the harm occurred, although here it is necessary that there be an explanation on the record as to whether the place is exactly the same as it was when the harm occurred, and, if not, in what respect it has changed.

(i) *The basis for testifying.* The witness who testifies in court or before an administrative agency is usually a person who had some direct contact with the facts in the case, such as a person who saw the events occur or who heard one of the parties say something. In certain cases, where the ordinary layman cannot appreciate or evaluate the significance of the facts, it is also proper to allow persons to testify on the basis of their expert knowledge in the particular field, stating their opinion as an answer to a hypothetical question put to them at the hearing or trial, or as a statement of the conclusion reached by them as the result of observation of the facts in the case or the making of tests and experiments.

(ii) *Inferences and presumptions.* As a general rule, each important fact of the case must be established by proof. Conversely, that which is not proven does not exist. In some instances, however, the law permits the trier of fact to conclude that if one fact is proven, another closely related fact may be deemed proven, without direct proof of its existence. For example, when the condition of the defendant's premises causes harm to the plaintiff and he sues the defendant, he must prove as a fact that the defendant was negligent. Under certain circumstances, however, the rule of res ipsa loquitur applies, which means that once the peculiar way in which the plaintiff was harmed is proven, the trier of fact may without further proof infer that the defendant was negligent.

Similarly, in many states, the fact that an employee is driving an automobile which bears the defendant's name may give rise to a presumption that at the time he was driving within the course of his employment. This is not a final determination or proof of the fact, for the presumption does not prevent the defendant from showing that such was not the case, that is, from rebutting the presumption.

There are definite limitations as to how far inferences and presumptions can go in taking the place of actual proof, and the law will not just "assume" that a fact exists or does not exist because you want it to do so.

(d) Conduct of the trial. Ordinarily a case is one of several listed or assigned for trial on a specified day or during a specified trial period. When the case is called, the attorneys seat themselves at tables before the judge and the jury is selected and sworn. The attorneys then usually make opening addresses to the jury. Details vary in different states, but the usual pattern is that each attorney states to the jury what he intends to prove at the trial. After this step, the presentation of the evidence begins.

The plaintiff's attorney calls his first witness and questions him. This is the direct examination of the witness since it is made by the attorney who called the witness. After direct examination, the opposing attorney questions the same witness in the effort to disprove his testimony. This is cross-examination. The opposing attorney may also call other witnesses to discredit or impeach the credibility of the witness.

After the cross-examination, the plaintiff's attorney may ask the same witness more questions in the effort to overcome the effect of the cross-examination. This is redirect examination. It may be followed by further examination by the defendant's attorney, called recross-examination.

After the examination of the plaintiff's first witness has been concluded, the plaintiff's second witness is then examined in the same way as the first.

This is repeated for each of the plaintiff's witnesses. Then the plaintiff rests his case, and the defendant's witnesses are examined. The pattern of examination is the same as above stated, except that the defendant's attorney conducts the direct and redirect examination, while the plaintiff's attorney now conducts the cross- and recross-examination.

When all witnesses have been examined and all the evidence has been presented, each attorney makes another address to the jury (a summation) in which he sums up what he has proved and argues to the jury that it should decide for his client.

(e) Charge to the jury and verdict.

(i) *Generally.* After the final address of the attorneys, the judge charges the jury. By this, he summarizes the evidence and explains the law which applies. He then tells the jury to retire and consider the case in the light of his charge and to return a verdict. The judge leaves the jury free to determine the facts but they must apply to such facts as they find the law stated by the judge. The jury deliberates in secret in the jury room.

(ii) *The determination of the truth.* The validity of the jury system, and of any system of trial, is based upon the premise that the jury or other trier of facts is able to determine the true facts. In many fields of the law, the sciences have greatly aided the trier of fact in determining what is the truth, as in the case of finger prints, ballistics, and blood tests. Unfortunately, in the ordinary type of lawsuit brought against a business, there is very little that is scientific and the trier of fact must fall back on which witnesses the trier believes. Even this may not be difficult in some cases for the skill of the attorneys may have made it clear to the trier of fact, ordinarily the jury, where the truth of the matter lies.

There is, nevertheless, a great area in which the jury's decision is nothing more than a guess or a hunch or is merely an averaging out of the different opinions of the jury, as by adding together what each juror would give the plaintiff, if anything, and then dividing by twelve. What is the difficulty?

Let's reduce the problem to the simplest terms. Have you ever taken care of two small children? Assume they are playing in the next room. Suddenly cries of combat rend the air and you go into the next room to find the two locked in battle. When you reprimand them and ask who started it, you are greeted with the unanimous reply, "He did." Can you tell in fact who began the fight? If you think you can, are you not really being guided by a prejudice against one of the children on the basis that he had started so many prior fights that he must have also started this one?

The jury is in much the same position. To illustrate with a fall-on-premises example, the jury was not present when the plaintiff fell on the premises of the defendant and possibly neither was anyone else. Now some time, even years later, the jury will attempt to reconstruct what happened and why. No employee may have been present and actually knows what happened. Not even the plaintiff who fell actually knows what happened. The plaintiff does not know exactly what happened for all the plaintiff knows is that he tripped and fell on an object. But does the plaintiff realize what the plaintiff was doing the moment before he fell so that he can give a truthful picture of the scene? It seems clear that what he knows of the scene is what he himself reconstructed in his mind immediately after falling. If he had had a clear picture of the scene before he fell, obviously he would have seen the object over which he fell and presumably would not have fallen. Now, having fallen and knowing very well that the offending object is there, he attempts to determine whether he could have seen the object before he fell.

The problem of determining what happened becomes the more complex when we have actual witnesses. For example, suppose that you are walking down the street and hear what you interpret as an automobile collision. Hearing the sound, you look toward its source and then see something. You do not see what happened because what happened occurred before you heard any sound. What you see is what existed x seconds or parts of a second after the event occurred. The less acute your hearing, the poorer your eyesight, the more you were concentrating on other matters, the longer will be the x-second interval of time between the actual event and your "perception" thereof, and the more difference will there be between what actually did occur and what you saw. That is why two equally honest witnesses can testify in flat contradiction to each other as to the color of a traffic light—one took just enough time longer than the other to "see" the light, and by that time it had changed.

On top of this is the matter of image memory and word equivalents. Remember now that we have our jury trial a long time, even years, after the event occurs. Do you have a clear image of some significant event which occurred three years ago? You probably think you do. You may even say most emphatically "I'll never forget the expression on his face . . . ," but actually if you were shown a perfect photograph of the event, you would be surprised to find that there were so many details which you have forgotten or so many things that you have "remembered" that were not so.

This takes place because our minds are not perfect filing cabinets. When we store away that past image, parts of it drop out like a jigsaw puzzle that is tilted, and parts of other images pour over into the particular image in question.

Then on top of all this, can you accurately describe the image which you do have in your mind? Try for example, to describe the degree of lighting in the area in which your customer fell. Was it brightly lit, well lit, semilit, dimly lit, partly dark, or dark? Can you pick just the right word to describe the degree of lighting, even if you had the area in front of you today, let alone remembering what it was several years ago? Obviously neither you nor I by our eyes alone or by our words can measure or describe scientifically and accurately the exact degree of lighting.

Yet, notice how innocently witnesses can change the whole complexion of a trial. This witness describes the area as dark, whereas someone else might say that the lighting was dim. Add also the problem of eyesight variation that might make the area seem dark to one and merely dim to another. Note also that these variations in eyesight can exist, although there is not a condition so serious as to be a "defect" that an attorney could show on cross-examination to discredit the witness.

If the whole problem is not yet sufficiently confused, consider where the witness was before he saw the area. One witness may have been in a darkened room before entering the significant area. His eyes are still accustomed to the dark room, and he does not notice that the area is particularly dark. Another witness has been working in front of a bright fluorescent light and is rushing out of his room and into the disputed area so that he will not be late for an appointment. The sudden contrast between the fluorescent lights and the area will undoubtedly make the area seem very dark to this witness.

And finally, we have the great problem of communication. If I say the area was dimly lit, will each of the twelve good men and true on the jury know how lit the hallway was, or will we have twelve different mental pictures in their respective minds as to what "dimly lit" means? Now observe how vital this is to the determination of the facts and the trial of our case. In one form of words or another, the judge is going to tell the jury at the end of the trial, "Now jury, you will return a verdict in favor of the plaintiff if you find that the defendant was negligent in that it did not adequately light the area in such a way as to avoid the harm which a reasonable man would foresee." Thus uncertainty progresses by geometric bounds, for now we have

[uncertainty as to how well lit the hall really was]

times

[uncertainty as to what a reasonable man would do]

as the evaluation which the jury must make in reaching its verdict. Even more uncertainties are generally introduced because the questions of whether the defendant had made reasonable inspections or had reason to know of the condition of the area, and whether the plaintiff had acted like a reasonable person or was guilty of contributory negligence, are also thrown into this kettle of jury deliberation.

Somehow, in spite of all these difficulties, the trier of facts decides what happened; or in substance, what it thinks happened and your liability is determined on this basis.

In the foregoing, the problem has been discussed in terms of the trial by jury. The basic difficulties of determining today what happened yesterday remains even though there is a trial without a jury, as by a judge or an administrative board. The only difference between the jury and the nonjury methods is that the complexities tend to be reduced as we move from twelve persons on the jury down to a smaller board and down to a single judge. Likewise, those who oppose a jury will take the position that the trial by judge or trial by administrative board will tend to be the more logical because of experience and training, and less subject to illogical or arbitrary influences.

(iii) *Function of the judge and jury.* The general rule is that the judge determines the law and the jury determines the facts. This tends to over-simplify the role played by the jury because it gives the impression that the judge and jury have equal importance in determining the outcome of the case. Actually, in the great run of cases, there is no question about the rule or rules of law to be applied. The big question in the case is what were the facts. In consequence, unless there is a new principle of law to be developed or an old principle of law to be reversed, your big question mark as you go into the court is what will the jury find as the facts?

Approaching the same conclusion from another direction, it has been repeatedly noted that the courts say that where it is debatable whether the defendant was negligent or whether the plaintiff was contributorily negligent, the case must go to the jury.

It is to be emphasized that this does not mean that when the evidence is fifty-fifty or an even toss either way that then the jury is called into action. Instead of being limited to the narrow, evenly-balanced case, the jury is required to determine every case when reasonable men believing one group of witnesses would reach one decision and other reasonable men believing another group of witnesses would reach a different decision. Otherwise stated, only in the very clear cases where there can be no doubt between reasonable men as to the conclusion to be made can the court decide negligence or other factual issues. The very fact that there is a lawsuit is a pretty fair indication that the two parties have different ideas about what happened and will present conflicting testimony on which the issues are debatable and which therefore takes the case to the jury.

From the practical point of view, this means that in the great majority of cases that might be brought against a business, the case will go to the jury with the freedom to find the facts as the defendant claims they were or as the plaintiff contends they were, and with the freedom to make judgments that certain conduct shall be deemed to impose liability or not to impose liability.

This becomes significant because in most instances the jury's verdict is final, not because the court believes that the jury was correct, but that even if the jury were wrong, it was not so far wrong as to be obviously wrong. Otherwise stated, as long as the matter is within a debatable area where there are two sides to the matter, the jury may take either side and the court will not reverse it merely because the court would have reached a different conclusion. Moreover, even when the jury is wrong, the court will not interfere unless the jury is so clearly wrong that there can be no question about it.

§ 30:6.   Taking the Case from the Jury

(a) Generally. At several points in the pleading stage, it is possible to bring before the court a question of law in the effort to have the case ended then and there by the decision of the court on the question of law. Similarly, during and after the trial, it is possible to take certain steps for the purpose of taking the case away from the jury and thereby bringing it to an end.

(b) Voluntary nonsuit. The plaintiff may be unhappy with the progress of the trial. He may stop the trial in most jurisdictions by taking a voluntary nonsuit and then begin another suit at a later date.

(c) Compulsory nonsuit. After the plaintiff has presented his case, the defendant may request the court to enter a nonsuit of the plaintiff on the theory that the plaintiff's evidence, even if believed, does not entitle him to recover.

(d) Directed verdict. At the end of the trial, either party may request the court to direct the jury to return a verdict in his favor. If the plaintiff could not recover even though all his evidence were believed, the court should direct the jury to return a verdict for the defendant. Similarly, the plaintiff is entitled to a verdict when the defendant's evidence, even if believed, does not establish a defense.

§ 30:7.   Attacks upon the Verdict

(a) Generally. After the verdict has been returned by the jury it is still possible to attack their action either on the ground that they have acted improperly or that they should never have been allowed to act at all.

(b) New trial. After the verdict has been returned, any party dissatisfied therewith may move for a new trial. If it is clear that the jury has made a mistake or if newly discovered, material evidence that could not have been discovered sooner is available, the court orders a new trial before a new jury.

The mere fact that you disagree with the jury or even that the judge disagrees with the jury does not mean that there is a "mistake" because of which the law will set aside the jury's verdict. If the jury's verdict could have been reached by reasonable men believing one set of the witnesses, the jury has not made a mistake. You will notice that this is the same test which was already applied in determining whether the case should be decided by the jury. If it is debatable on the facts, the case goes to the jury: if they decide either way in the debatable case, no one can say that the decision is wrong.

Now we can see the full significance of the jury's function for not only does it decide the heart of all the vital disputes but in the great bulk of cases the circumstances will be such that the jury's decision will be final.

Notice the element of hazard this introduces in litigation. But do not think that you can escape completely from this risk for when a case is tried without a jury, by a judge or by an administrator, the basic elements of uncertainty remain unchanged although there is some simplification in the sense that there is only one judge or a smaller number of administrators than there are jurors.

(c) Judgment n.o.v. If the verdict returned by the jury is clearly wrong as a matter of law, the court may set aside the verdict and enter a judgment contrary to the verdict. This, in some states, is called a judgment non obstante veredicto, or as it is abbreviated, a judgment n.o.v.

§ 30:8.   Damages

(a) Generally. In most lawsuits, the plaintiff seeks to recover money damages from the defendant. Other forms of relief may be obtained by legal proceedings, such as an order or injunction to require the defendant to perform some act or to prevent him from performing a specified act.

When damages are sought, questions arise as to how the damages are to be measured and whether punitive or exemplary damages may be imposed in addition to compensatory damages.

(b) Compensatory damages. The object of a lawsuit is to require the defendant to pay the plaintiff such amount of money as compensates or makes up for the harm caused by the defendant. This is not as simple a matter as it sounds because it is often a difficult matter to determine the value of what the plaintiff has lost.

If he has lost or been deprived of property, it is necessary to determine the value of the property at the time of the loss—not the cost of the property to the plaintiff, nor the cost of purchasing a replacement, but instead the secondhand value of the property at the time of the loss. That is to say, if the defendant is responsible for the theft or disappearance of a customer's coat, the plaintiff is entitled to compensatory damages equal to the second-hand value of the cost at the time of the loss, but not what the guest had paid for the coat nor what it would cost him today to buy the same coat.

The defendant may be liable under certain circumstances for damages caused the plaintiff when the latter is physically injured by the act of the defendant's employee or of another person. This injury may also include mental harm as when the plaintiff has experienced pain and suffering in consequence of the physical injury, or has been put in fear or humiliated. In such cases, in order to determine what damages will compensate, the question of valuation is made increasingly difficult because there is no mercantile standard or market value for determining the "price" of pain, suffering, or mental distress.

(c) Punitive or exemplary damages. In addition to the compensatory damages, which seek to compensate for the harm, the plaintiff may in some cases recover additional damages that are imposed to punish or make an example of the defendant for the outrageous way in which it has acted. That is, if the conduct of the defendant shows personal malice or a willful disregard of the rights of the plaintiff, such additional damages are properly allowed.

§ 30:9. Judgment and Costs

(a) Generally. If a new trial is not granted or a judgment n.o.v. is not entered, the court enters a judgment on the verdict. Generally whoever is the winning party is awarded costs. In equity actions and in some statutory proceedings, the court has discretion to allocate costs, as by awarding them to the winner, to dividing them between the parties, or having each party bear his own.

(b) What are costs? Costs ordinarily consist of the fees charged for filing papers with the court, for having the sheriff make service or other officers take official action, the statutory fees paid to the witnesses, the jury fee, if any, and the cost of printing the record, when required on appeal. Costs do not include compensation for the time spent by the party in preparing his case or in being at the trial, the expense of going to his attorney's office or to the court, the time lost from work because of the case, or the fee paid to his attorney. In some statutory actions, the recovery of a small attorney's fee is authorized. Thus, a mechanics' lien statute may authorize the recovery of an attorney's fee of 10 percent of the amount recovered, or a "reasonable attorney's fee." "Costs" thus represent only a small part of the total expenses actually sustained in litigation.

§ 30:10. Appeals

(a) Generally. A party aggrieved by a judgment may appeal, either because he did not win or did not win enough.

The appellate court does not hear evidence. It only examines the printed or typewritten record of the proceedings before the lower court to see if there was an error of law so bad as to require a reversal or modification. The parties' attorneys file arguments or briefs and generally make an argument orally before the appellate court.

(b) Action of appellate court. If the appellate court does not agree with the law as applied in the case, it generally sets aside or modifies the action of the lower court and enters such judgment as it decides the lower court should have entered. It may also set aside the judgment of the lower court and send the case back to hold a new trial or to enter a new judgment in accordance with the opinion of the appellate court.

§ 30:11.   Execution

(a) Generally. If a losing defendant does not comply with the final judgment in the suit, the plaintiff may execute on the judgment.

If the judgment is for the payment of money, the plaintiff may direct the sheriff or other judicial officer to sell as much of the property of the defendant as is necessary to pay the plaintiff's judgment, and costs. In most states the defendant is allowed an exemption of several hundred dollars and certain items of property, such as personal clothing and tools of his trade.

(b) Garnishment. In most states, a plaintiff may direct execution on a debt owed by a third person to his defendant or upon property of the defendant in the possession of a third person. Thus, the plaintiff suing a defendant may garnish the defendant's bank account, the account being technically a debt owed by the bank to the defendant. In some states, or under some liability insurance policies which do not permit a direct action by the injured claimant against the insurer, the claimant may obtain a judgment against the defendant and then garnish the obligation of the insurance company to the defendant. This procedure is commonly called "attachment" and the third person is called a "garnishee."

When garnishment is allowed prior to judgment, it is generally restricted to cases in which the original debtor is guilty of fraud or of concealing himself, or is not a resident of the state. When employed after judgment obtained by the original creditor against the original debtor, the fact that the judgment has been obtained in itself entitles the original creditor to garnish without proof of fraud or any other particular circumstances.

In some states, the procedure of garnishment does not exist as a distinct procedure but is made part of a judgment execution procedure.

Questions for Review

1. In what ways may a case be taken from a jury?

2. What are the advantages and disadvantages of discovery?

3. How is an action commenced?

4. What are the pleadings in an action?

5. How can a jury's verdict be set aside?

6. To what extent are damages recoverable?

7. How is a judgment collected if the defendant does not voluntarily pay it?

8. What is the nature and function of the pretrial conference?

9. What is the nature and function of the charge to the jury?

10. Why is service of process required in a lawsuit?

11. What determines which matters are decided by the judge and which by the jury?

Chapter 31

ADMINISTRATIVE AGENCY ACTION

§ 31:1. Who Shall Regulate?

In the early days of the rise of the various forms of government regulation, it was natural for society to seek to carry out its plans through the
governmental institutions it had on hand. Thus Congress and state legislators
made regulatory laws, the executive branch of national and state govern-

ments policed society to see that such laws were obeyed, and courts punished the violators for infractions of the regulatory laws. Gradually this system proved inadequate. The governmental structure, which had been devised to carry out a "do nothing" philosophy, was not adequate for giving effect to a "do something" philosophy. This is not surprising. If your main thought is to prevent an automobile from being driven away by a thief, a simple solution is to remove essential parts of the engine. If, however, you are thinking of using the automobile for transportation, this solution is not practical and some better compromise must be found between immobility and utility.

Gradually the existing three-branch division of government showed itself unable to coordinate activities with sufficient speed. For one reason or another, it takes a long time to get a law passed by Congress or a state legislature; delay in litigation virtually nullifies enforcement by the courts; and the executive branch of the government is typically confronted with other more pressing problems, or prevented by insufficient funds or personnel from carrying out a plan of regulating business with promptness and firmness. Add to this the increasing need for more technological knowledge on the part of government and it becomes apparent that neither the executive, the lawmaker, nor the judge possesses, nor reasonably could be expected to possess, the necessary training, experience, and knowledge to regulate business intelligently and effectively.

Faced with this dilemma, society did the reverse of what it had done back in 1790 when our Constitution was adopted. The fragments of power that had been carefully divided—legislative, executive, and judicial—were now put back together again; and society created special governing agencies or commissions which possessed the power to make the "law" within their authorized spheres, the power to police society to see that such laws were properly executed, and the power to sit as a court to determine whether there had been any violation thereof. When this stage is reached, we have the modern administrative agency which, at the national level of government, is typified by the Interstate Commerce Commission, the National Labor Relations Board, and the Securities Exchange Commission.

In the interest of historical accuracy, it may be noted that there was not an immediate transition from no government regulation to the modern type of administrative agency. Early administrators may have been a public official whose duty it was to remove obstructions or encroachments from the King's highways or, in the New England states, removal of obstructions from streams used for water power. When modern medicine began to appear, the health inspector or quarantine officer soon appeared. In cattle-raising areas, inspectors of cattle likewise became established. For practical purposes, these simple forms of administrators will be ignored. In the case of the health or the quarantine officer, we still have this administrator with us. It is his more complex relation—the administrator who exercises legislative, executive, and judicial power—who is more significant; and it is to such more complex administrator that we shall devote our attention. For purposes of brevity, the word "administrator" will be used to refer to a single individual, such as a state insurance commissioner, and a board or commission consisting of a number of men, such as the Interstate Commerce Commission. It is not the internal structure of the "administrator" that concerns us, but rather the fact that there is a branch of government which exercises the powers of all three traditional branches of government, although within a limited sphere, such as the sphere of insurance, transportation, and investment securities.

§ 31:2.   The Administrator's Powers

(a) Legislative. As already noted under § 2:2, the modern administrator has the power to make the laws that regulate the segment of life or industry entrusted to his care. There was for a time great reluctance to accept the fact that the administrator made the law because by our Constitutional doctrine only the lawmaker (the Congress or the state legislature) could make laws. It therefore seemed an improper transfer or delegation of power for the lawmaker to set up a body and give to it the power to make the laws.

The same forces that led society to create the administrator initially caused society to clothe the administrator with the power to make the laws. They also created the need for fast regulation by an expert through a flexible system that can be readily modified to meet changing conditions. This need argued against taking a bill to the lawmaker and trying to get it passed in competition with other often politically inspired measures. These factors gradually prevailed in favor of the conclusion tacitly accepted that if we want the administrator to do a job, we must give him the power sufficiently extensive to do so; and we must take the practical approach and ignore the theoretical objection that when we authorize him to do the job, we are in fact telling him to make the law which governs the area that he regulates.

In the early days of administrative regulation, the legislative character of the administrative rule was not clearly perceived, largely because the administrator's sphere of power was narrowed so that he was, in effect, merely a thermostat. That is, the lawmaker told him when to do what, and all that the administrator did was to act in the manner in which he had been programmed. For example, the cattle inspector was told to take certain steps when he determined that the cattle had hoof and mouth disease. Here it was clear that the lawmaker had set the standard and the administrator merely "swung into action" when the specified fact situation existed. Apart from the health inspectors, we have this same pattern of thermostat regulation in the case of tariff legislation, which has authorized the President of the United States to make certain changes to the tariff when he found that certain facts existed, such as a foreign country discriminating against United States goods, or a certain disparity as to labor costs between the foreign and American goods.

The next step in the growth of the administrative power was to authorize the cattle inspector to act when he found that cattle had a "contagious" disease, leaving it to him to formulate a rule or guide as to what diseases were "contagious." Here again, the discretionary and legislative aspect of the administrator's conduct was obscured by the belief that the field of science would define "contagious," leaving no area of discretionary decision to the administrator.

Today, a modern health inspector would be authorized to make such rules and regulations for the protection or improvement of the common health as he should deem desirable. In this phase, it would be clear that he was making the "health law" by his rules. While most health inspectors are not authorized to go this far, note that in regulating the various economic aspects of national life, the administrator is truly the lawmaker and has such wide power.

For a time, the courts were reluctant to admit this fact and found refuge in the consideration that the lawmaker has set standards within the scope of which the administrator was required to act. According to the courts, the administrator was not given a free hand nor the power to make laws. Gradually, the courts have come to recognize, or at least to tolerate, the entrusting of the duty of a certain job to an agency without doing more than stating to the agency the policy that the administrator should seek to advance, or the goal or objective that he should seek to attain. Thus, it has been sufficient to authorize an administrator to grant licenses "as public interest, convenience, or necessity requires;" "to prohibit unfair methods of competition;" to regulate prices so that they "in [the administrator's] judgment will be generally fair and equitable;" to prevent "profiteering;" "to prevent the existence of intercorporate holdings, which unduly or unnecessarily complicate the structure [or] unfairly or inequitably distribute voting power among security holders;" and to renegotiate government contracts to prevent "excessive profits."

AMERICAN TRUCKING ASSOCIATIONS v. UNITED STATES

344 U.S. 298 (1953)

The practice developed for owners of trucks who drove their loaded trucks from one point to another to hire themselves and their trucks out to a common carrier so that the return trip would not be made with empty trucks. The Interstate Commerce Commission concluded that these one-trip rentals made it possible for the carriers to operate in part without satisfying the requirements otherwise applicable to them. In order to stop this, the Commission adopted a set of rules which provided that trucks could not be rented by a carrier for less than thirty days. A number of suits were brought to prevent the enforcement of these rules on the ground that they were not authorized by the Interstate Commerce Act, and their enforcement would cause financial loss and hardship.

OPINION BY REED, J. . . .

All agree that the rules . . . abolish trip-leasing. Unfortunate consequences are predicted for the public interest because the exempt owner-operator will no longer be able to hire himself out at will—in sum, that the industry's ability to serve a fluctuating demand will suffer and transportation costs accordingly go up. It is the Commission's position that the industry and the public will benefit directly because of the stabilization of conditions of competition and rate schedules, and that in fact the continued effectiveness of the Commission's functions under the Motor Carrier Act is dependent on regulation of leasing and interchange. Needless to say, we are ill equipped to weigh such predictions of the economic future. Nor is it our function to act as a supercommission. So we turn to the legal considerations so strongly urged on us.

Here, appellants have framed their position as a broadside attack on the Commission's asserted power. All urge upon us the fact that nowhere in the Act is there an express delegation of power to control, regulate or affect leasing practices, and it is further insisted that in each separate provision of the Act granting regulatory authority there is no direct implication of such power. Our function, however, does not stop with a section-by-section search for the phrase "regulation of leasing practices" among the literal words of the statutory provisions. As a matter of principle, we might agree with appellants' contentions if we thought it a reasonable canon of interpretation that the draftsmen of acts delegating agency powers, as a practical and realistic matter, can or do include specific consideration of every evil sought to be corrected. But no great acquaintance with practical affairs is required to know that such prescience, either in fact or in the minds of Congress, does not exist. . . . Its very absence, moreover, is precisely one of the reasons why regulatory agencies such as the Commission are created, for it is the fond hope of their authors that they bring to their work the expert's familiarity with industry conditions which members of the delegating legislatures cannot be expected to possess. . . .

Moreover we must reject at the outset any conclusion that the rules as a whole represent an attempt by the Commission to expand its power arbitrarily; there is clear and adequate evidence of evils attendant on trip-leasing. . . .

So the rules in question are aimed at conditions which may directly frustrate the success of the regulation undertaken by Congress. . . .

We hold then that the promulgation of these rules for authorized carriers falls within the Commission's power, despite the absence of specific reference to leasing practices in this Act. . . .

From the foregoing, it may be deduced that our constitutional law theory has reached the point that it will sustain the creation of an administrator "to do a job," will sustain giving him general power to do what he deems necessary, and require obedience to his rules. In private enterprise, we might draw the analogy of a board of directors hiring a plant superintendent and telling him to do what a plant superintendent should do, leaving it to him to determine just what that is, and enforcing his decisions by firing or punishing any employee who does not follow his regulations.

It may seem that this is too extreme a statement since it is deeply rooted in our culture that government is subject to limitations and that the courts will protect us from improper regulation. As will be seen in § 35:4, however, the extent to which the courts will interfere with the administrative discretion is very slight, just as it would be rather rare that the board of directors having selected a qualified plant superintendent would interfere with his decisions.

(b) Executive.

(i) *Generally*. The modern administrator has executive power to investigate, to require persons to appear as witnesses, and to produce papers for any reason coming within his sphere of operation. Thus, the administrator may investigate merely to police the area subject to his control to see if there is any violation of the law or of its rules generally, to determine whether there is a need for the adoption of additional rules, to ascertain the facts with respect to a particular suspected or alleged violation, and to determine whether its decisions will be obeyed. The Federal Antitrust Civil Process Act of 1962 is an outstanding example of the extent to which administrative investigation is authorized. The Act provides that upon written demand to a corporation, association, or partnership, the production of documents can be compelled to provide the Department of Justice with information to determine whether there is sufficient ground to bring a civil antitrust suit against the enterprise so directed. Similar powers are possessed by the Federal Trade Commission, the Federal Maritime Commission, the National Science Foundation, the Treasury Department, the Department of Agriculture, the Department of the Army, the Department of Labor, and the Veterans Administration.

ENDICOTT JOHNSON CORP. v. PERKINS
317 U.S. 501 (1943)

The Walsh-Healey Act requires that contracts to supply the United States with materials at a cost greater than $10,000, specify that the contractor shall pay his employees in the manufacture of the materials not less than the minimum wages set by the Secretary of Labor nor employ them for more than 40 hours a week, except with the permission of the Secretary, in which case wages of no less than 1½ times the basic hourly rate must be paid. Endicott Johnson Corporation had several contracts in excess of $10,000 to supply shoes to the United States. The contracts conformed to the Act and specified the plants in which the shoes were to be made. The Secretary of Labor made an investigation that showed minor wage violations in the plants named in the contract. The Secretray of Labor then ordered the Corporation to produce records as to wages and hours in other plants, which were physically separate from the plants in which the contracts were being performed, because the Secretary "had reason to believe" that the employees in those plants were also covered by the contracts. The Corporation refused to produce the records on the ground that the subpoena power extended only to the plants specified in the contracts.

OPINION BY JACKSON, J. . . .

The Secretary is directed "to administer the provisions of this Act" and empowered "to make investigations and findings as herein provided, and prosecute any inquiry necessary to his functions." . . .

The matter which the Secretary was investigating and was authorized to investigate was an alleged violation of this Act and these contracts. Her scope [the Secretary's] would include determining what employees these contracts and the Act covered. . . . But because she sought evidence of underpayment before she made a decision on the question of coverage and alleged that she "had reason to believe" the employees in question were covered, the District Court refused to order its production, tried the issue of coverage itself, and decided it against the Secretary. This ruling would require the Secretary, in order to get evidence of violation, either to allege she had decided the issue of coverage before the hearing or to sever the issues for separate hearings and decision. The former would be of dubious propriety, and the latter of doubtful practicality. The Secretary is given no power to investigate mere coverage, as such, or to make findings thereon, except as incident to trial of the issue of violation. No doubt she would have discretion to take up the issues of coverage for separate and earlier trial if she saw fit. Or, in a case such as the one revealed by the pleadings in this one, she might find it advisable to begin by examining the payroll, for if there were no underpayments found, the issue of coverage would be academic. On the admitted facts of the case, the District Court had no authority to control her procedure or to condition enforcement of her sub-poenas upon her first reaching and announcing a decision on some of the issues in her administrative proceeding.

DISSENTING OPINION BY MURPHY, J., in which ROBERTS, J., concurs. . . .

Because of the varied and important responsibilities of a quasi-judicial nature that have been entrusted to administrative agencies in the regulation of our political and economic life their activities should not be subjected to unwarranted and ill-advised intrusions by the judicial branch of the government. Yet, if they are freed of all restraint upon inquisitorial activities and are allowed uncontrolled discretion in the exercise of the sovereign power of government to invade private affairs through the use of the subpoena, to the extent required or sought in situations like the one before us and other inquiries of much broader scope, under the direction of well-meaning but over-zealous officials, they may at times become instruments of intolerable oppression and injustice. This is not to say that the power to enforce their subpoenas should never be entrusted to administrative agencies, but thus far Congress, for unstated reasons, has not seen fit to confer such authority upon any agency which it has created. So here, while the Secretary of Labor is empowered to administer the Walsh-Healey Act, to "prosecute any inquiry necessary to his functions," and "to issue orders requiring the attendance and the testimony of witnesses and the production of evidence under oath," he alone cannot compel obedience of those orders. "Jurisdiction" so to do is conferred upon the district courts of the United States, and it is our immediate task to delineate the proper function of those courts in the exercise of this jurisdiction. Specifically, the question is: What is the duty of the courts when the witness or party claims the proceeding is without authority of law? . . .

The Government concedes that the district courts are more than mere rubber stamps of the agencies in enforcing administrative subpoenas. . . . But the Government insists that the issue of "coverage," i.e., whether the Act extends to plants of petitioner's establishment which manufactured materials used in making complete shoes but not named in the contracts, is not a proper ground for attack in this case. I think it is.

If petitioner is not subject to the Act as to the plants in question, the Secretary has no right to start proceedings or to require the production of records with regard to those plants. In other words, there would be no lawful subject of inquiry, and under present statutes giving the courts jurisdiction to enforce administrative subpoenas, petitioner is entitled to a judicial determination of this issue before its privacy is invaded. . . .

It is within the competence and authority of the court to inquire and satisfy itself whether there is probable legal justification for the proceeding, before it exercises its judicial authority to require a witness or a party to reveal his private affairs or be held in contempt. . . .

Petitioner has willingly complied with all demands of the Secretary relating to the plants of its establishment, named in the contracts, in which the shoes were manufactured. It resists the application for enforcement of the subpoenas directing the production of records of other plants, not named in the contracts. . . . The mere fact that petitioner voluntarily contracted with reference to some plants does not necessarily mean that the Secretary is free to investigate petitioner's entire business without let or hindrance. That depends upon whether or not the Act extends to those other plants. Petitioner was entitled to have this question determined by the district court before the subpoena was enforced over its objection. . . . Under the facts of this case the district court should not be compelled mechanically to enforce the Secretary's subpoena, in the exercise of its statutory jurisdiction. It should first satisfy itself that probable cause exists for the Secretary's contention that the Act covers the plants in question.

(ii) *Continuing investigation.* The power to investigate is a continuing power with the result that the administrative agency can, in effect, put the party on probation and require periodic reports to establish compliance with the law.

UNITED STATES v. MORTON SALT CO.

338 U.S. 632 (1950)

As the result of proceedings originating before the Federal Trade Commission, the Morton Salt Company and others were ordered by the Supreme Court to cease certain practices with respect to the pricing, producing, and marketing of salt and to file with the Commission a report showing compliance with this order. The Federal Trade Commission thereafter ordered the Morton Salt Company to furnish additional reports on its method of operation in order to determine whether the company was continuing to comply with the order. The company challenged the authority of the Federal Trade Commission to require the additional reports.

OPINION BY JACKSON, J. . . .

[Subsequent to the filing of an initial report directed by the original decree] the Commission ordered additional and highly particularized reports to show continuing compliance with the decree. This was done without application to the court, was not authorized by any provision of its decree, and is not provided for in § 5 of the statute under which the Commission's original cease and desist order had issued. . . .

The Trade Commission Act is one of several in which Congress, to make its policy effective, has relied upon the initiative of administrative officials and the flexibility of the administrative process. Its agencies are provided with staffs to institute proceedings and to follow up decrees and police their obedience. While that process at times is adversary, it also at times is inquisitorial. These agencies are expected to ascertain when and against whom proceedings should be set in motion and to take the lead in following through to effective results. It is expected that this combination of duty and power always will result in earnest and eager action, but it is feared that it may sometimes result in harsh and overzealous action. . . .

This case illustrates the difference between the judicial function and the function the Commission is attempting to perform. The respondents argue that since the Commission made no charge of violation either of the decree or the statute, it is engaged in a mere "fishing expedition" to see if it can turn up evidence of guilt. We will assume for the argument that this is so. Courts have often disapproved the employment of the judicial process in such an enterprise. Federal judicial power itself extends only to adjudication of cases and controversies, and it is natural that its investigative powers should be jealously confined to these ends. The judicial subpoena power not only is subject to specific constitutional limitations, which also apply to administrative orders, such as those against self-incrimination, unreasonable search and seizure, and due process of law, but also is subject to those limitations inherent in the body that issues them because of the provisions of the Judiciary Article of the Constitution.

We must not disguise the fact that sometimes, specifically in the early history of the federal administrative tribunal, the courts were persuaded to engraft judicial limitations upon the administrative process. The courts could not go fishing, and so it followed neither could anyone else. . . . It must not be forgotten that the administrative process and its agencies are relative newcomers in the field of law and that it has taken and will continue to take experience and trial and error to fit this process into our system of judicature. More recent views have been more tolerant of it than those which underlay many older decisions. . . .

The only power that is involved here is the power to get information from those who best can give it and who are most interested in not doing so. Because judicial power is reluctant, if not unable, to summon evidence until it is shown to be relevant to issues in litigation, it does not follow that an administrative agency charged with seeing that the laws are enforced may not have and exercise powers of original inquiry. It has a power of inquisition, if one chooses to call it that, which is not derived from the judicial function. It is more analogous to the Grand Jury, which does not depend on a case or controversy for power to get evidence but can investigate merely on suspicion that the law is being violated, or even just because it wants assurance that it is not. When investigative accusatory duties are delegated by statute to an administrative body, it, too, may take steps to inform itself as to whether there is probable violation of the law. . . .

Even if one were to regard the request for information in this case as caused by nothing more than official curiosity, nevertheless law-enforcing agencies have a legitimate right to satisfy themselves that corporate behavior is consistent with the law and the public interest. . . .

(iii) *Absence of constitutional limitations.* For practical purposes, there is no constitutional limitation on the extent to which the administrator may make investigations. The most common limitation that comes to mind is the protection against self-incrimination. At the outset, it must be recognized that this protection does not apply to corporate parties. Likewise, it does not apply to the officers keeping the corporate records even as against the contention that if they produce the records, they may incriminate themselves as well as the corporation.

But apart from whether there is any privilege of withholding records or information from an administrator, the lawmaker can easily circumvent such a privilege by requiring particular records be kept or authorizing the administrator to prescribe what records should be kept. It is then proper to give the administrator the power to demand the production of the required records so that he can assure himself that the records are in fact being kept as required by law. This means that if the lawmaker or the administrator takes the trouble to specify in advance what information should appear on the records of the regulated business or enterprise, that business or enterprise will not have any constitutional ground for refusing to produce those records when demanded by the administrator, even though such information be incriminating.

SHAPIRO v. UNITED STATES

335 U.S. 1 (1948)

Shapiro was a wholesaler of fruit and produce. The Price Administrator acting under the Federal Emergency Price Control Act subpoenaed him to produce his business records. Under protest of constitutional privilege, he furnished the records. He was later prosecuted for making illegal tie-in sales contrary to the Emergency Price Control Regulations. The evidence on which the prosecution was based was obtained from information found in the records that he had been required to produce before the administrator. He claimed that he was entitled to immunity from prosecution for any matter arising out of those records. His claim of privilege was overruled and he was convicted. He appealed from the conviction.

OPINION BY VINSON, C.J. . . .

The Circuit Court of Appeals ruled that the records which petitioner was compelled to produce were records required to be kept by a valid regulation under the Price Control Act; that thereby they became public documents, as to which no constitutional privilege against self-incrimination attaches. . . .

The language of the statute and its legislative history, viewed against the background of settled judicial construction of the immunity provision, indicate that Congress required records to be kept as a means of enforcing the statute and did not intend to frustrate the use of those records for enforcement action by granting an immunity bonus to individuals compelled to disclose their required records to the Administrator. . . .

"The physical custody of incriminating documents does not of itself protect the custodian against their compulsory production. The question still remains with respect to the nature of the documents and the capacity in which they are held. It may yet appear that they are of a character which subjects them to the scrutiny demanded and that the custodian has voluntarily assumed a duty which overrides his claim of privilege. . . . The principle applies not only to public documents in public offices, but also to records required by law to be kept in order that there may be suitable information of transactions which are the appropriate subjects of governmental regulations and the enforcement of restrictions validly established. There the privilege, which exists as to private papers, cannot be maintained." . . .

There is a sufficient relation between the activity sought to be regulated and the public concern so that the Government can constitutionally require the keeping of particular records, subject to inspection by the Administrator. . . . [Shapiro was therefore not deprived of any right by the use of his records.]

(c) Judicial.

(i) *Generally.* The modern administrator may be given power to sit as a court and determine whether there have been any violations of the law or of his regulations. Thus, the National Labor Relations Board sits to determine whether there has been a prohibited unfair labor practice, the Fair Trade Commission will act as a court to determine whether there is unfair competition, and so on. Here there is the theoretical objection that a non-judicial body is making decisions that should only be made by a court. Where the administrator sits as a judge as to the violation of a regulation that he has made, there is also the element that the "judge" is not impartial because he is trying the accused for violating "his" law rather than "the" law. There is also the objection that the administrator is determining important rights but does so without a jury, which seems inconsistent with the long-established emphasis of our history upon the sanctity of trial by jury.

In spite of these theoretical and psychological objections to the administrator's exercise of judicial power, such exercise is now firmly established. Generally, this result is achieved by considering that a speedier, more expert determination is afforded than could be made by a court of law. Also, a party can appeal to a court of law so that the administrator is in effect a preliminary screening device and the ultimate court of law determines the case. To a large degree this rationalization is now fallacious and will be considered under § 31:4 relating to the finality of administrative decisions.

Accepting as a fact that the administrator can make judicial determinations, the question arises as to whether he must proceed exactly as a court, following all of the procedure of a court.

(ii) *Pattern of administrative procedure.* At the beginning of the era of modern regulation of business, the administrator was, to a large extent, a minor executive or police officer charged with the responsibility of enforcing the laws applicable to limited fact situations. The health officer empowered to condemn and destroy diseased cattle was typical. In view of the need for prompt action and because of the relative simplicity of the fact determination to be made, it was customary for him to exercise summary powers; that is, upon finding cattle which he believed diseased, he could have them killed immediately without delaying to find their true owner or without holding a formal hearing to determine whether they were in fact diseased.

As we come down to the present day, the exercise of summary powers becomes the exceptional case. Today it is permitted mainly in connection with the fraudulent use of the mails or the sending of improper matter such as lottery tickets or obscene matter through the mails, the enforcement of navigation regulations and tax laws, and the exercise of the police power in order to protect the public health and safety. As the regulation of business assumes the aspect of economic rather than health or safety regulation, the need for immediate action by the administrator diminishes, if not disappears, when the administrator acts to determine whether particular conduct comes within the scope of a regulation or whether there has been a violation thereof, and accordingly, concepts of due process generally require that some notice be given those who will be adversely affected and that some form of hearing be held at which they may present their case. As a practical matter, also, the more complicated the nature of the determinations to be made, the longer the period of investigation and deliberation required.

In the more modern type of regulation, the proceedings before the administrator tend to follow the general pattern of an action in the law court. It is commonly provided that either a private individual aggrieved by the conduct of another or the administrator on his own motion may present a complaint. This complaint is served on the alleged wrongdoer, and he is given opportunity to file an answer. There may be other phases of pleading between the parties and the administrator, but eventually the matter comes before the administrator to be heard. After a hearing, the administrator makes a decision and enters an order either dismissing the complaint or directing the adverse party to do or not to do certain acts. This order is generally not self-executing and, in order to enforce it, provision is generally made for an application by the administrator to a court. Sometimes the converse is provided so that the order of the administrator becomes binding upon the adverse party unless he appeals to a court within a stated period for a review of the order.

The complaint filing and prehearing stage of the procedure may be more detailed than just stated. In many of the modern administrative statutes, provision is made for an examination of the informal complaint by some branch of the administrator to determine whether it presents a case coming within the scope of the administrator's authority. It is also commonly provided that an investigation be made by the administrator to determine whether the facts are such as warrant a hearing of the complaint. If it is decided that the complaint is within the jurisdiction of the administrator and that the facts appear to justify it, a formal complaint is issued and served on the adverse party, and an answer is filed by him as above stated.

With the rising complexity of the subjects regulated by administrative procedure, the trend is increasingly in the direction of greater preliminary examination upon the basis of an informal complaint.

Cutting across these procedures are the practical devices of informal settlement and consent decrees. In many instances, the alleged wrongdoer will be willing to change his practices or his conduct upon being informally notified that a complaint has been made against him. It is therefore sound public relations, as well as expeditious handling of the matter, for the administrator to inform the alleged wrongdoer of the charge made against him prior to the filing of any formal complaint in order to give him the opportunity to settle the matter voluntarily. A matter that has already gone into the formal hearing stage may also be terminated by agreement, and a stipulation or consent decree may be entered or filed setting forth the terms of the agreement.

A further modification of this general pattern is made in the case of the Interstate Commerce Commission. Complaints received by the Commission are referred to the Bureau of Informal Cases, which endeavors to secure an amicable adjustment with the carrier. If this cannot be done, the complainant is notified that it will be necessary to file a formal complaint. At this stage of the proceedings, the parties can expedite the matter by agreeing that the case may be heard on the pleadings alone. If this is done, the complainant files a pleading or memorandum to which the defendant files an answering memorandum, the plaintiff then filing a reply or rebuttal memorandum. If the parties do not agree to this procedure, a hearing is held after the pleadings have been filed.

(iii) *The administrative hearing.* In order to satisfy the requirements of due process, it is generally necessary for the administrator to give notice and hold a hearing. A significant difference between the administrator's hearing and a court is that there is no right of trial by jury before an administrator. The absence of a jury does not constitute a denial of due process. For example, a workmen's compensation board may and does pass on a claim without any jury, the theory being that a new right has been created that was unknown to the common law, and the right to a jury trial exists only where it was recognized at the common law. The law could have taken the position that whenever a person is brought before any tribunal, he is entitled to have the facts determined by a jury. But the law "froze" the right to trial by jury as it existed in pre-Revolutionary days so that if there was no right of jury trial in 1775, there is no right of trial by jury today. As the wide array of government regulation of business today was unknown in 1775, we have the consequence that a great area of Twentieth Century economic life is determined without a jury. If I wish to sue you for $100, you would be entitled to a trial by jury; but if I am complaining before an administrator, you are not entitled to a jury trial, even though his determination or regulation may cost you a million dollars. The inconsistency in the net result in these two situations is not regarded as having any legal importance.

Another significant difference between an administrative hearing and a judicial hearing is that the administrator may be authorized to make a determination first and then hold a hearing afterwards to verify his result, as contrasted with a court which must have the trial before it makes a judgment. This has important practical consequences in that when the objecting party seeks a hearing after the administrator has acted, he has the burden of proof and the cost of going forward. In consequence of this, the result is that fewer persons go to the trouble of seeking such a hearing. This, in turn, reduces the amount of hearing and litigation in which the administrator becomes involved with the resultant economy of money and personnel from the government's standpoint.

BOWLES v. WILLINGHAM
321 U.S. 503 (1944)

The Emergency Price Control Act of 1942 authorized the Price Control Administrator to fix maximum rentals for areas in which such control was, in his opinion, needed. A property owner sought to enjoin the enforcement of a rent order issued under the Act. It was claimed that the Act was unconstitutional because there was no hearing provided prior to the entry of a rent order.

OPINION BY DOUGLAS, J. . . .

It is finally [argued] that the Act violates the Fifth Amendment because it makes no provision for a hearing to landlords before the order or regulation fixing rents becomes effective. Obviously, Congress would have been under no necessity to give notice and provide a hearing before it acted, had it decided to fix rents on a national basis the same as it did for the District of Columbia. . . . We agree with the Emergency Court of Appeals . . . that Congress need not make that requirement when it delegates the task to an administrative agency. In *Bi-Metallic Investment Co.* v. *State Board*, 239 U.S. 441, a suit was brought by a taxpayer and landowner to enjoin a Colorado Board from putting in effect an order which increased the valuation of all taxable property in Denver 40 percent. Such action, it was alleged, violated the Fourteenth Amendment, as the plaintiff was given no opportunity to be heard. Mr. Justice Holmes, speaking for the court, stated . . . "Where a rule of conduct applies to more than a few people, it is impracticable that everyone should have a direct voice in its adoption. The Constitution does not require all public acts to be done in town meeting or an assembly of the whole. General statutes within the state power are passed that affect the person or property of individuals, sometimes to the point of ruin, without giving them a chance to be heard. Their rights are protected in the only way that they can be in a complex society, by their power, immediate or remote, over those who make the rule." . . . Where only property rights are involved, mere postponement of the judicial enquiry is not a denial of due process, if the opportunity given for the ultimate judicial determination of the liability is adequate. . . . Delay in the judicial determination of property rights is not uncommon where it is essential that government needs be immediately satisfied." . . .

Congress was dealing here with the exigencies of wartime conditions and the insistent demands of inflation control . . . Congress chose not to fix rents in specified areas or on a national scale by legislative fiat. It chose a method designed to meet the needs for rent control as they might arise and to accord some leeway for adjustment within the formula which it prescribed. At the same time, the procedure which Congress adopted was selected with the view of eliminating the necessity for "lengthy and costly trials with concomitant dissipation of the time and energies of all concerned in litigation rather than in common war effort." . . . To require hearings for thousands of landlords before any rent control order could be made effective might have defeated the program of price control. Or Congress might well have thought so. National security might not be able to afford the luxuries of litigation and the long delays which preliminary hearings traditionally have entailed. . . .

Congress has provided for judicial review after the regulations or orders have been made effective. It has done all that due process requires. . . .

In some instances, the administrator may even go to the extent of establishing standards that have the effect of barring a hearing unless there is compliance with such standards. This is an illustration both of the "lawmaking" power, that is, determining who shall be entitled to a hearing, as well as the extent to which a person is entitled to a "court form hearing."

As a general rule, an administrator is not bound by the rules of evidence but may hear any information, leaving it to his experience and judgment to evaluate properly what he hears. This is a sensible variation with respect to such rules as the hearsay evidence rule that was formed by the courts largely for the purpose of preventing juries from being misled by the kind of evidence that is excluded by this rule. As the administrator does not act with a jury, the reason for excluding the jury-prejudicing evidence ceases to exist and therefore the exclusionary rule is abandoned. A notable exception to this is the Federal National Labor Relations Act of 1947, which limits the National Labor Relations Board to hearing only that which would be admissible as evidence in the federal district courts. Originally, the Labor Relations Act of 1935 permitted the Board to hear any evidence, not bound by the rules of evidence, but it was felt by the critics of the Board that it was being influenced by hearsay evidence that did not have probative value, and that the way to remedy the situation was to return to the old rule of excluding hearsay evidence.

§ 31:3. Finality of Administrative Determination

(a) Limiting factors. Basic to the Anglo-American legal theory is that no one, not even a branch of the government, is above the law. Thus, the growth of powers of the administrative agency was frequently accepted or tolerated on the theory that the administrative agency could not go too far because the law courts would review the administrative action. This belief was encouraged by the fact that the typical modern statute provides that an appeal may be taken from the administrative action by any person in interest or any person aggrieved.

In actual practice, the appeal has little significance in the vast number of cases because of restraints which are imposed or which the court imposes upon itself, with the net result that the determination by the administrative agency will, in most cases, be final.

At the outset, notice may be taken of two procedural reasons why administrative appeals are frequently lost: (1) absence of standing to appeal, and (2) failure to exhaust the administrative remedy.

Illustrative of the former, the party appellant (the party that appeals) may lose because the regulatory statute does not show any intent that he may sue. Illustrative of the latter, if the appellant has not allowed the proceeding to take its full course before the administrator, it is generally held that he cannot take an appeal. Thus, it has been held that any employer contending that the National Labor Relations Board had no jurisdiction over him could not enjoin it from proceeding with an unfair labor practice hearing as a means of appealing from the board's decision that it had jurisdiction to proceed with the matter. The rule requiring the exhaustion of the administrative remedy is based in part on fairness to the administrator; namely, that he should be given full opportunity to dispose of the case before an appeal is taken, and in part upon the concept of practical expediency that it would impose an unreasonable burden upon the courts by increasing the number of cases which they would be required to hear if any disgruntled party before an administrator could at any point of the proceeding take an appeal.

(b) Discretion of the administrator.

(i) *Generally.* The greatest limitation upon the review of the administrative action is the rule that a matter involving discretion will not be reversed. Here the courts reason that since the administrator was created because of his superior expert ability, it would be absurd for the court that is manifestly unqualified to make a decision in the matter to step in and determine whether the administrator made the proper choice. As has been said by the Supreme Court with reference to the Securities Exchange Commission: ". . . The very breadth of the statutory language precludes a reversal of the Commission's judgment save where it has plainly abused its discretion in these matters . . . such an abuse is not present in this case.

". . . The Commission's conclusion here rests squarely in that area where administrative judgments are entitled to the greatest amount of weight by appellate courts. It is the product of administrative experiences, appreciation of the complexities of the problem, realization of the statutory policy, and responsible treatment of the uncontested facts. It is the type of judgment which administrative agencies are best equipped to make and which justifies the use of the administrative process. . . . Whether we agree or disagree with the result reached, it is an allowable judgment which we cannot disturb." [1]

And with reference to the Federal Communications Commission, the court has declared that ". . . it is the Commission, not the courts, which must be satisfied that the public interest will be served by renewing the license. And the fact that we might not have made the same determination on the same facts does not warrant a substitution of judicial for administrative discretion since Congress has confided the problem to the latter. . . ." [2]

---

[1] *Securities and Exchange Commission* v. *Chenery Corporation,* 332 U.S. 194 (1947).

[2] *Federal Communications Commission* v. *WOKO,* 329 U.S. 223 (1946).

MOOG INDUSTRIES v. FEDERAL TRADE COMMISSION

355 U.S. 411 (1958)

Moog Industries was ordered to stop certain pricing practices by the Federal Trade Commission. It raised the objection that its competitors were also guilty of such practices and that Moog would be ruined if it were required to stop the practices without also requiring its competitors to stop such practices. The Commission rejected this argument. Moog appealed.

OPINION BY THE COURT. . . .

The general question presented . . . is whether it is within the scope of the reviewing authority of a Court of Appeals to postpone the operation of a valid cease and desist order of the Federal Trade Commission against a single firm until similar orders have been entered against that firm's competitors. . . .

In view of the scope of administrative discretion that Congress has given the Federal Trade Commission, it is ordinarily not for courts to modify ancillary features of a valid Commission order. This is but recognition of the fact that in the shaping of its remedies within the framework of regulatory legislation, an agency is called upon to exercise its specialized, experienced judgment. Thus, the decision as to whether or not an order against one firm to cease and desist from engaging in illegal price discrimination should go into effect before others are similarly prohibited depends upon a variety of factors peculiarly within the expert understanding of the Commission. Only the Commission, for example, is competent to make an initial determination as to whether and to what extent there is a relevant "industry" within which the particular respondent competes and whether or not the nature of that competition is such as to indicate identical treatment of the entire industry by an enforcement agency. Moreover, although an allegedly illegal practice may appear to be operative throughout an industry, whether such appearances reflect fact and whether all firms in the industry should be dealt with in a single proceeding or should receive individualized treatment are questions that call for discretionary determination by the administrative agency. It is clearly within the special competence of the Commission to appraise the adverse effect on competition that might result from postponing a particular order prohibiting continued violations of the law. Futhermore, the Commission alone is empowered to develop that enforcement policy best calculated to achieve the ends contemplated by Congress and to allocate its available funds and personnel in such a way as to execute its policy efficiently and economically.

The question, then, of whether orders such as those before us should be held in abeyance until the respondents' competitors are proceeded against is for the Commission to decide. . . . If the Commission has decided the question, its discretionary determination should not be overturned in the absence of a patent abuse of discretion. . . .

(ii) *Nature of remedy.* The importance of the limiting effect of the "discretion" test is further seen in the case that follows.

AMERICAN POWER AND LIGHT CO. v. SECURITIES & EXCHANGE COMMISSION

329 U.S. 95 (1946)

Under the authority of the Securities and Exchange Act, the Securities and Exchange Commission directed the dissolution of a holding company that it found to serve no useful economic purpose. The objection was made that the policy of the Act could be carried out without going to the extreme of ordering the dissolution of the holding company.

OPINION BY MURPHY, J. . . .

Where Congress has intrusted an administrative agency with the responsibility of selecting the means of achieving the statutory policy, "the relation of remedy to policy is peculiarly a matter for administrative competence." . . . In dealing with the complex problem of adjusting holding company systems in accordance with legislative standards, the Commission here has accumulated experience and knowledge which no court can hope to attain. Its judgment is entitled to the greatest weight. While recognizing that the Commissioner's discretion must square with this responsibility, only if the remedy chosen is unwarranted in law or is without justification in fact should a court attempt to intervene in the matter. Neither ground of intervention is present in this instance.

Dissolution of a holding company or a subholding company plainly is contemplated by [the Act] . . . as a possible remedy. . . .

Nor can we say that the Commission's choice of dissolution with respect to American and Electric is so lacking in reasonableness as to constitute an abuse of its discretion. The Commission chose dissolution because it felt such action is calculated to correct the situation most effectively and quickly. . . .

The Commission is the body which has the statutory duty of considering the possible solutions and choosing that which it considers most appropriate to the effectuation of the policies of the act. Our review is limited solely to testing the propriety of the remedy so chosen from the standpoint of the Constitution and the statute. We would be impinging upon the Commission's rightful discretion were we to consider the various alternatives in the hope of finding one that we consider more appropriate. Since the remedy chosen by the Commission in this instance is legally and factually sustainable, it matters not that the American and Electric believe that alternative orders should have been entered. It is likewise irrelevant that they feel that Bond and Share is the principal offender against the statutory standards and that the Commission should merely have required Bond and Share to divest itself of its interests in American and Electric. . . .

(iii) *Absence of limitation.* The frequent reference of the courts to what would be done if action of the administrator was found to be "arbitrary or capricious" is somewhat misleading because it suggests that there is a wide area in which the court does actively review the administrative action.

As a practical matter, the action of the administrator is rarely found to be arbitrary or capricious. As long as the administrator has apparently conducted himself properly, the fact that the court disagrees with his conclusion does not make that conclusion arbitrary or capricious. The fact that the administrative decision will cause a person to lose money is not proof that the action of the administrator was arbitrary for the judicial attitude is that for protection from laws and regulations which are unwise, improvident, or out of harmony with a particular school of thought, the people must resort to the ballot box and not to the court.

(c) Nature of question as affecting scope or review.

(i) *Questions of fact.* The matter before the administrator may turn on a question of fact, such as whether the employee was fired because he belonged to a union or because he was a bad worker. When this is the case, the courts apply the same rule as has been applied for centuries to determine whether the verdict of a jury will be set aside. That is, the appellate court will not reverse if the jury or the administrator was presented with substantial evidence that if believed would have justified the conclusion which was reached. The circumstance that the court would have reached a different conclusion is immaterial. For example, where there is testimony for and against the employer in the above illustration with respect to cause of firing, it is apparent that the ultimate decision depends upon whether the evidence on behalf of the employer is believed, or the evidence against the employer is believed. Whichever decision the administrator makes, the appellate court will not reverse the administrative action. This is so, even though the court would have believed otherwise had it been in the administrator's position.

Thus, if the administrator decided against the employer, the court will not reverse the administrator when there is conflicting evidence, even though the court would have believed the evidence for the employer had it been the administrator. The result of this rule means that where there is conflicting evidence, some of which is sufficient to sustain the administrative action, it will be impossible to obtain a reversal of the administrative action merely because the court does not believe the witness that the administrator chose to believe.

In accordance with the general principles governing appeals from jury verdicts, it is likewise immaterial how many witnesses had testified on each side. Thus the fact that there was only one witness for and many witnesses against does not require a decision in favor of the view of the greater number of witnesses.

NATIONAL LABOR RELATIONS BOARD v. PITTSBURGH STEAMSHIP CO.

337 U.S. 656 (1949)

The National Labor Relations Board ordered an employee to cease and desist from specified unfair labor practices. The Court of Appeals refused to enforce this order on the ground that it was invalidated by the prejudice of the board's trial examiner as shown by the fact that he believed the witnesses of the board and disbelieved the employer's witnesses.

OPINION BY RUTLEDGE, J. . . .

We are constrained to reject the court's conclusion that an objective finder of fact would not resolve all factual conflicts arising in a legal proceeding in favor of one litigant. The ordinary lawsuit . . . normally depends for its resolution on which version of the facts in dispute is accepted by the trier of fact. . . . In the determination of litigated facts, the testimony of one who has been found unreliable as to one issue may properly be accorded little weight as to the next. Accordingly, total rejection of an opposed view cannot of itself impugn the integrity or competence of a trier of fact. . . . "The fact . . . that Examiner and Board uniformly credited the Board's witnesses and as uniformly discredited those of the respondent, though the Board's witnesses were few and the respondent's witnesses were many, would not furnish a basis for a finding by us that such a bias or partiality existed and therefore the hearings were unfair. . . ."

While there are not, and from the nature of things there could not be, any reliable statistics as to how many administrative agency cases turn on disputed questions of fact, any one familiar with administrative agencies can attest to the great number of cases before the administrator that depend upon which witness is believed or which set of data is accepted as reliable. In such cases, the administrative choice is final and as that choice decides the result of the administrative action, it follows as a practical matter that an appeal will not upset the determination by the administrator with the result that the court merely upholds the administrative action. Furthermore, for practical purposes, it can thus be said that in the great majority of fact-based disputes, the action of the administrator is ordinarily final and that the right of appeal is for practical purposes nonexistent or of no value.

(ii) *Questions of law.* This is the widest area of review of administrative action as the appellate court will reverse the administrator if he has applied what the court deems a wrong rule of law. When the question is one of law, the court will not consider whether the administrator's action was reasonable, as opposed to capricious and arbitrary, or whether there was any basis for the view applied by the administrator. With the minor qualification of tending to follow an administrative practice of long standing when the case is doubtful, the appellate court will ignore what the administrator did and apply its own version of what the law should be. Thus the Supreme Court has reversed the administrative determination as to what employees were covered by the Fair Labor Standards Act, whether "back pay" awarded a reinstated employee by the National Labor Relations Board was to be deemed "wages" for the purpose of social security computations, whether conduct of a carrier in the Alaskan waters prior to the admission of Alaska as a state was subject to the Interstate Commerce Commission, and whether hotels were engaged in "interstate commerce" so as to be subject to the National Labor Management Relations Act.

The prospect of winning an appeal on a question of law is not great, however, for the reason that only a small percentage of appeals involve questions of law. For example, consider the many murder trials in which the only issue is the fact question of "who done it?" without involving any real question of the "law" of murder. Moreover, the probability is that the "legal questions" tend to be raised and disposed of once and for all in the first years of the existence of the new administrative agency. As in the case of any enterprise, after the first few years, most problems are solved or settled in one way or another. From then on, the questions are primarily questions of fact with respect to which there is the narrow and virtually nonexistent review already noted.

(iii) *Mixed questions of law and fact.* Many questions that must be determined are a composite of both questions of law and fact. For example, whether a driver was "negligent" is both a statement of facts as to the conduct that he pursued as well as the classification of that conduct in terms of legal standards. That is to say, in order to determine whether a person was negligent, it is necessary to determine a myriad of underlying or subsidiary facts and to sum them up in some manner and apply thereto the concept of the standard of the law, reaching the ultimate conclusion that the person "was" or "was not" negligent.

How should a determination in this zone of mixed questions be reviewed? If it is treated as a question of fact, the court will not set aside the administrative or jury action if there is a conflict of evidence or an appraisal to be made of the significance of the various details. If it is treated as a question of law, the court will step in and reverse the decision whenever it disagrees with the conclusion that has been reached. The problem becomes all the more confusing when it is recognized that the sphere or extent of these mixed questions of law or fact becomes increasingly larger as we move into the more complex forms of regulation and the regulatory statutes become less specific, entrusting more and more to the judgment of the administrator. For example, if the statute does not define an "adequate reserve," the question of what kind of assets are acceptable as "reserve" and how much total assets are needed to be "adequate" become hybrid questions that have both the elements of questions of fact and those of questions of law.

FEDERAL TRADE COMMISSION v. MOTION PICTURE ADVERTISING SERVICE COMPANY

344 U.S. 392 (1953)

The Motion Picture Advertising Service Company produced and distributed interstate advertising motion pictures to theatre owners. These were distributed under exclusive dealing contracts. The Federal Trade Commission concluded that the exclusive dealing provision was an unfair method of competition unless the contracts were limited to a period of a year. It ordered the Company to so limit the contracts. The Company appealed.

Opinion by Douglas, J. . . .

An attack is made on that part of the order which restricts the exclusive contracts to one-year terms. It is argued that one-year contracts will not be practicable. It is said that the expenses of securing these screening contracts do not warrant one-year agreements, that investment of capital in the business would not be justified without assurance of a market for more than one year, that theatres frequently demand guarantees for more than one year, or otherwise refuse to exhibit advertising films. These and other business requirements are the basis of the argument that exclusive contracts of a duration in excess of a year are necessary for the conduct of the business of the distributors. The Commission considered this argument and concluded that, although the exclusive contracts were beneficial to the distributor and preferred by the theatre owners, their use should be restricted in the public interest. The Commission found that the term of one year had become a standard practice and that the continuance of exclusive contracts so limited would not be an undue restraint upon competition, in view of the compelling business reasons for some exclusive arrangement. The precise impact of a particular practice on the trade is for the Commission, not the courts, to determine. The point where a method of competition becomes "unfair" within the meaning of the Act will often turn on the exigencies of a particular situation, trade practices, or the practical requirements of the business in question. Certainly we cannot say that exclusive contracts in this field should have been banned in their entirety or not at all, that the Commission exceeded the limits of its allowable judgment . . . in limiting their term to one year.

The years ahead will undoubtedly show a collapse of the guidelines stated in terms of questions of law, questions of fact, and mixed questions of law and fact. In their place, the appellate courts will be content if the administrator has given indications of attempting to make a thorough appraisal of the problem and a reasonable analysis. Whether the court agrees with him in his final result will be unimportant. This future development has been foreshadowed by decisions of the United States Supreme Court in dealing with the Federal Power Commission and in the growing recognition that the division of questions into those of law and fact is merely a historical carryover when it was necessary to determine which phases of a case were to be determined by a judge, which by a jury, or the extent to which an appellate court could substitute its own conclusions for those of the lower court or the jury.

When this day is reached, judicial review of the administrative agency will, in effect, be limited to determining strict questions of law. In that area, the appellate court will substitute its own opinion for the administrative determination. With respect to all other matters, appellate review will be limited to merely checking to see that proper procedure was followed and that reasonable steps were taken, limiting reversals to the rare case in which the administrative action was so peculiar that the court feels justified in setting it aside as arbitrary and capricious. Conversely, in the great majority of instances, the administrative action to make decisions that in most cases cannot be reviewed by the courts will, for practical purposes, be final—this in a country which claims itself dedicated to the supremacy of the law.

§ 31:4. Significance of the Administrative Process

From the foregoing one realizes that the subject of government regulation of business is more than a simple matter of economics, more than a simple matter of should *A* or *B* act as the director. There is also a fundamental change in the relationship of the citizen and the enterprise to the government, and the responsibility of those in control to those regulated.

Generally, both management and the citizen are unaware of the change that is taking place or of the immense power that has been acquired by administrative agencies. A segment of an industry which is within an administrator's jurisdiction is virtually under his supreme and unlimited command. In many cases, by virtue of his rule-making authority he makes the law; through his investigative and prosecutory powers, he administers the law; and through his judicial powers, he decides and applies the law. Thus, in one man or agency we find combined the powers of the executive, legislative, and the judiciary. Yet this is a country which is proud of the division of the powers of government made by its Constitution into three branches—the executive, the legislative, and the judiciary—a division which, of course, was made to prevent tyranny.

We see that what government does to business depends upon what each voter does or fails to do. No longer is there a guardian constitution, a protective court, or a political party to remedy his negligence or to cure his mistakes or those of the lawmakers whom he has elected. This is a grave responsibility upon each one of us because just as the Congress has handed the problems to the commissions because the latter were experts, and just as the Courts have accepted the commissions' decisions because they were experts, we as voters are tempted to hand over control to others because everything is so technical and we are not experts.

Many wars have been fought to earn and to preserve our freedom and the right to determine our destiny. Let us not lose by default the right to be politically and economically free.

Questions for Review

1. What legal and practical objections are there to delegating rule-making power to administrators?

2. Is there any difference between the scope of judicial inquiry and of administrative inquiry?

3. When a hearing is required before an administrator, must there be a jury?

4. What practical difference is there between placing the administrative hearing before or after the administrator makes his determination?

5. Does it make any difference with respect to the administrator's power of investigation whether the person to be investigated is a natural person or a corporation?

6. In hearing an appeal from an administrator's action, does a court expressly recognize the economic consequences of the administrator's action as affecting the propriety of his conclusion?

7. Does the extent of judicial review of the administrator's action vary directly or inversely with the amount of discretion given the administrator?

8. Does the nature of the question before the administrator affect the extent to which the administrator's decision will be reexamined by the courts?

9. Will a court substitute its opinion for the action that it feels the administrator should have taken, where a claim is made that the administrator could have carried out the purpose of the statute without imposing as extreme a penalty or remedy as it did?

10. What are the arguments for and against (a) finality of administrative determination, and (b) complete judicial review of administrative determinations?

11. Is it inevitable that government by bureaucracy replace the ballot? Do you agree with this conclusion? If you do, is there any remedy or alternative plan to prevent this?

Chapter 32

HOW TO BE A GOOD CLIENT

§ 32:1. How You Can Help

(a) Generally. I suppose we all agree that a person could go see his doctor before he is so sick that it becomes difficult, if not impossible, for the doctor to make him well. I suppose we also agree that the person should make a mental or written note of his significant symptoms so that he can give his doctor a more accurate basis on which to diagnose the case. There should likewise be hardly any dispute that after having seen the doctor, the sick person should follow his instructions.

The general aspects of the matter are much the same when, instead of patient and doctor we have client and attorney. When management is the client, there is much that it can do to increase or decrease the amount of litigation in which it will be involved. Likewise, there is much that management can do to make the case against it more difficult to defend.

(b) Scope and purpose of this chapter. It is the purpose of this chapter to gather together some of the practical aspects of being a client or a potential client which should reduce the amount of litigation that you

have and also assist your attorney in defending you better when you are sued. As in the case of all general rules of human conduct, the suggestions made herein are generalities and are hence subject to exceptions and qualifications. Nevertheless, they could prove helpful as a point of beginning, to be contracted or expanded in the light of what is practical for your particular business and by what your personal experience and your attorney suggest.

As this chapter is, in effect, the synthesis of many man years of practicing law by both the author and other attorneys, cases are not incorporated into the text. The points emphasized in this chapter are practical rather than legal requirements, for the reason that except in a few instances, such as the case of the filing of statutory reports, there is no law involved. As stated by the title, the purpose of the chapter is not to teach you how to be your own lawyer, but rather how to be a good client for your lawyer.

§ 32:2. Inspection of Witnesses

(a) Generally. Many situations can arise in which a lawsuit will depend upon the word of your employee or officer against the word of the claimant or plaintiff. There may not have been any witnesses, or if there were, at the later date when you need them, such witnesses cannot be located.

It is thus a sound precaution for your employee or officer to handle trouble situations in pairs or as a team. Thus, it becomes the word of two employees against the one claimant. Of course the law does not weigh the testimony of witnesses by bulk and say that two witnesses weigh greater than one witness and therefore the employees are telling the truth. Nevertheless, there is the greater chance that with your two employees present, you will be the better able to find out just what did happen because you have the statements of two people on which to base your conclusion. Moreover, there is an undoubted factor operating that the jury will tend to believe the side with the greater number of witnesses, in spite of the fact that the judge tells them that they should not do so.

(b) Selecting the best witness. When management selects a person to be an additional observer, it is obviously desirable to select the highest ranking employee on the premises at that time who is the best qualified to speak in the area involved, assuming that the matter is one that could give rise to serious litigation. For example, if the question is observing the physical injury of a customer, it is clear that the company doctor or any physician should be selected when possible; whereas if an inspection of the physical condition of the premises is involved, a high employee in the maintenance or repair department would ordinarily be the better choice.

No simple rule can be laid down in advance because of the wide variation between the size and nature of different business operations, and the differences between the duties and backgrounds of different employees in different businesses, although each may have the same job classification or official title. The thing to remember is that a jury (1) is going to be more impressed by the testimony of a witness with particular training in the field involved than an ordinary witness; and (2) the higher the rank of the employee within the business, the more they are likely to believe his testimony. Like all generalities, it must be recognized that this is not always so; but since all we can do at this point is to make the best guess possible as a guide for the future, it is preferable to think in terms of the above suggestions.

In many instances, you will not have anyone in your employment who is particularly qualified to speak as an expert with respect to the matter involved. In such case, the answer is to call in the outsider, such as a neighboring physician, who is qualified to make the examination of the matter that is called for. When the matter comes within the scope of your insurance coverage, the problem may often be solved by notifying the insurer immediately and having the insurer send an adjuster. Even when you are not covered with respect to the claim by insurance, it may still be advantageous to call in at your own expense a professional claim adjuster.

The calling in of an outsider also has the advantage of creating a neutral or impartial witness. There is always the danger that the jury will not be convinced or will doubt witnesses who are your own employees because the jury may feel that your own employees will testify in your favor merely to save their jobs. This suspicion of bias is generally eliminated or, at least, reduced when outsiders testify on your behalf.

There is the danger, however, of delay when outsiders are called in. It may be that the conditions to be observed cannot be preserved in their exact present condition for a sufficiently long time to enable an outsider to come to the business premises and observe. If the circumstances appear to warrant it, a desirable combination would be to have both your employee make his observation "at once" and then have an outsider make his observation as soon as possible. Your employee should make a reexamination at the time when the outsider conducts his in order to tell the outsider whether there has been any change of the condition being examined; and if so, its extent and nature.

(c) *High-ranking employees.* Whenever possible, management should have as one of its witnesses a high-ranking employee. He will ordinarily be more intelligent and more perceptive, and he will create a greater impression of integrity upon the jury. There is, of course, the danger the jury may feel that however honest he may be, the high-ranking employee is not the man who has actual daily contact with the subject matter and therefore does not really know what this particular matter is about. It is for this reason that where the matter is outside of the daily experience of the high-ranking employee, management should also make use of such an employee who does have daily contact or dealing with the matter in question.

There is another psychological advantage in having a high-ranking employee as a witness. The case may be a borderline case in which the claimant is not going to sue if he feels that management has been reasonable about the matter. If you send a lower classification employee to the claimant, the claimant may feel slighted that you have sent just the "office boy." Moreover, there is the very real hazard that the lower-classification employee does not have the experience and the understanding to handle the situation as adroitly as the higher-ranking employee, and in many cases does not have any real interest in so doing. Hence, the sending of the lower-ranking employee may get everything off on the wrong foot and in itself tip the scales and make the claimant feel so hurt or insulted that he brings suit.

(d) Nonlitigation object of inspection. Because this chapter is directed to the problem of being a better client, inspection has been here discussed only in terms of preparing for a lawsuit. It is, of course, to the advantage of management to have a "good" inspection made of any matter in order for management to know just what is going on and in order to determine whether any corrective measures should be taken, either with respect to the past conduct of employees or to prevent future repetitions of the difficulty.

(e) Inspection of premises. If any claim is made that injury has been sustained because of the condition of the premises, immediate investigation should be made of both the injured persons and the part of the premises in question. With respect to the premises, the highest employees of the department that has charge of the area involved should make the inspection when reasonably possible. If this employee does not have actual daily contact with the area involved, the inspection should be made jointly with the employee who does.

The strategy underlying this suggestion is to have either one or two employees who will be able to testify that from personal experience he knew the area, such as the stairway on which the claimant fell; that he had seen this area every day or other reasonably short period of time; that it was or was not in the same condition in which it was when he had seen it the last time before the injury; the condition in which it was at the time of the injury; and if either of these witnesses is called to speak as an expert witness, whether such practice as was followed by management was a proper practice in the industry.

(f) Inspection of property damage. When the claim is made that property of the claimant has been damaged, management should have someone examine the damage who has familiarity with the nature of the property, if such is possible. For example, if damage is done to fabrics or clothing, it is probable that a woman employee will be a better witness than the

ordinary male employee who would not know what the materials were and could not very well describe what he saw. Of course, even the woman employee may not be a fit witness where the property is so valuable or unusual as to require an expert opinion.

In contrast, if the claimant's automobile is damaged, management's auto mechanic should be the witness. If management does not have such a person of sufficient experience, an outside mechanic or an insurance adjuster should be called. In many cases, the amounts involved will not be so great. You will be content to leave the matter up to the insurance adjuster, although this should not be done unless the conditions to be inspected are of such a nature that the delay in bringing in the adjuster will not cause any change, and the premises will be in exactly the same condition when the adjuster sees them as when you examined them.

(g) Inspection of injury of claimant. Here the inspection witness should, of course, be a physician whenever possible. If none is available on the premises, a physician from the neighborhood or a nearby hospital should be sought. If no better witness is available, a traffic policeman or a state trooper may be a good witness, although his experience is limited to particular kinds of injury.

In any case, where outsiders are called in, do not rely on them alone but have your own employee or employees observe the claimant's condition as soon as possible, and also at the time when the outsider arrives in order to inform the latter what changes have taken place.

It must be remembered that these statements are very general suggestions and that, in the given case, they may have no practical value because the injury of the claimant is internal and therefore not observable to the un-trained witness; or observation may require a personal examination of the claimant, which would not be proper or allowable in the absence of consent by the claimant or except by a physician. Nevertheless, there may be some-thing to observe in any case, and every bit of information helps defend the case against you.

§ 32:3. Reports

(a) Generally. At various stages or phases of operations, examinations or investigations will be made, either as a matter of routine, or because some unusual event has occurred. For example, there will be the regular, periodic examination of the condition of the premises, the more or less irregular and intermittent examination of applicants for jobs, and the very irregular inspections made in connection with someone being hurt on the premises.

Whatever the nature of the occasion or its frequency, management should require the making of a written report that it should preserve in its files, and depending upon the nature of the matter involved, should send a copy to its attorney and to its insurer.

(b) Utility of reports and records. The making of a record or a report means just so much more paper work, just so much more filing, and so on. Nevertheless this added labor is well worth the effort and is indeed essential when litigation or controversy arises thereafter.

(i) *A written memory.* If a report is not made, management will be trusting to the mere memory of man to recall at a later date just what had happened. The risk involved here is apparent, since few persons, if any, have a perfect, photographic memory that will retain all details accurately and indefinitely.

It is, of course, true that many times some occurrence will stamp itself in your memory because of its dramatic or terrifying nature so that it is likely that you will remember much of the transaction for a long time. But details will be forgotten and your half-recollection may be very misleading. Moreover, many controversies arise out of transactions which at the time appeared routine so that there was no reason for you to remember what happened. For example, you rejected an applicant because the applicant just did not seem right for the job, and it is not until some time later that the claim is made that you were guilty of improper discrimination in refusing to employ that applicant. Can you remember now just why you had rejected the applicant? Can you remember in a way which will convince the law that you acted on the basis of a sound judgment and not a prejudice? Or by way of further illustration, a person bites on a piece of glass while eating at your restaurant. No harm is apparently done and you have forgotten all about the matter until some time later when you find a large damage claim being asserted against you for harm and mental distress sustained by the patron. Do you know today what happened back then?

The making of the report substitutes a permanent writing for a fleeting memory. Moreover, it eliminates the task of trying to guess what is an important transaction which should be remembered. If you keep a report on every transaction, there is no question of selecting those which will give rise to litigation, because regardless of what transaction does give rise to litigation, you have your report.

The report can serve a double function as an aid to memory. When your attorney is preparing the case for you, the report will enable him to check the memory of your witnesses and the witnesses will be able to check against the report as to just what happened. Likewise, at the trial itself, if your witness has forgotten what happened, he will be permitted in most cases to look at the report, in order to refresh his memory.

(ii) *Missing witness.* In many instances, by the time the lawsuit against you comes to trial, the transient persons who were your witnesses have long since gone, and even employees may no longer be with you. It is possible that you might not have any witnesses to produce at the trial. Your attorney already will have safeguarded against this as far as he was able to do so by the taking of the testimony of witnesses by deposition as soon as he learned that there was a transaction which might give rise to a claim against you.

You can strengthen your position at the trial by maintaining regular reports. For if you have a regular system of making reports, the very fact that the reports were made in a regular systematic way vouches for the accuracy of any one report. Hence, in many states, such reports will be admissible in evidence as business records, even though the person who prepared the report is not available and even though it cannot be determined who such person actually was.

(c) Danger of report making. Great care must be exercised in making a report, because you can harm your position greatly by a report which does not accurately set forth the facts as they actually existed.

(i) *Wrong basis for defense.* The written report tends to be the basis around which management's case will be built. When you discuss the matter with your attorney or he discusses the matter with your witnesses, it is easy to understand that in case of any misunderstanding or ambiguity in the statements of witnesses, reference will be made to the report to get the facts straight. If the facts in the report are actually "not straight," it is apparent that the entire case of management may be built on a wrong premise and management, in effect, walks into a trap that it has created. If management did not prepare its case for the facts as they actually existed but instead prepared for the facts that is assumed to exist on the basis of the erroneous report, it may find itself unable to meet the actual facts shown by the plaintiff upon such short notice.

This danger may be lessened or avoided by the taking of depositions of the plaintiff and his witnesses in advance of the trial, since any conflict between the plaintiff's version of the facts and the report would at once become apparent.

(ii) *Impeaching the testimony of witnesses.* Under one theory or another, the adverse party can require the production of routine inspection reports. If at the trial the witness for management who prepared the reports says anything that is inconsistent with the statements in his report, the plaintiff may use the report to contradict the witness on the theory that he cannot be telling the truth today because the report made for management shortly after the occurrence said something else. This can, at least, cast doubt on the merits of management's case. Unless the discrepancy can be reasonably explained, it may in fact cause so much doubt that the jury concludes that the witness for management is not telling the truth, and consequently may decide the case against management.

In the situation above considered, the report was used to show that the witness who made the report was not telling the truth at the trial and was therefore a person who was a liar who should not be believed at the trial. In contrast with this use of the report, which is confined to the person who made it, the report once admitted in evidence can contradict the testimony of any witness or witnesses by providing a different version of the facts which the jury may choose to believe in preference to the version narrated by such other witness or witnesses at the trial.

(d) Supervision of report making. In view of the importance of reports, they should be made correctly or not made at all. To make them accurate, a comparatively high-ranking employee of management should examine carefully each report filed and, if necessary, discuss with the employee just what he meant to say in order to verify that the report as submitted states what the employee intended. This will, of course, mean much more office work for someone in management when they should be busy running the business. But again, the answer is that there are so many potential frauds facing management that defensive measures must be taken in all directions.

(i) *Integrity.* The employee in charge of reviewing reports must be particularly careful to detect any conscious or unconscious whitewashing of the situation in order to make it appear that the person making the report was not at fault. Thus, the reviewing employee must check carefully to see that the reporting employee is really telling the truth and the whole truth. This is not an easy task for the reporting employee may be subconsciously distorting the facts to show that he is not at fault, without realizing that he is doing so. It is human nature for us to seek the loophole and to reach the conclusion that really we were not at fault. For example, there is a natural reluctance on the part of the maintenance employee to admit that he improperly left a scum of soap on the marble floor. If he admits it, there will be a tendency to reduce the size of the spot so that it would not constitute a menace to navigation, and the report will make it appear that the claimant was guilty of contributory negligence for not walking around it. And this employee who is thoroughly familiar with the area and the lighting will probably not see why the claimant, who was a stranger in the place, did not perceive that the floor was wet. Inevitably, his reporting is colored by the fact that he thinks the whole matter was the plaintiff's fault.

The employee reviewing the reports must get to the truth as it will appear to jurors who are also strangers to the premises, and he must take great care in eliminating personal opinions of the reporting employee or the distortions that he makes—even in the best of good faith.

The reviewing employee has an unpleasant task in this respect because he must at the same time be careful to avoid making the employee feel that he thinks the latter is a liar. Management must continue in business and the reporting employee and the reviewing employee must still work together. The latter's effort to get to the truth must, therefore, not destroy such harmony as existed between these two employees prior to the reviewing of the report.

In most instances, this difficult situation can be handled by the reviewing employee by saying to the reporting employee, "That is a good report which you have made, but we should go into a few of the details a little more fully. Now you have seen trials in the movies and on television, and you know how the opposing attorney does his best to batter and tear down the witnesses. Let's just go all through this report and see if an opposing attorney could tear it down in any way. Remember I believe you because I know you. But a jury never saw you before and will not know you. Therefore, we must be sure that what you say cannot be twisted to mean something else and that the jury will also believe you." After this type of introduction, the reporting employee will ordinarily feel that he and the reviewing employee are fighting on the same team and will not develop any antagonism when the reviewing employee turns the report inside out to find its errors and flaws.

(ii) *Communication.* Having established in his mind what the facts of the case really are, the next problem of the reviewing employee is to determine that the report as filed actually says what happened. This is merely a matter of words, of the proper vocabulary, of communication. But here both the reporting employee and the reviewing employee may unconsciously fail to say in words exactly what they have in their minds. The fact that they are thoroughly familiar with the business and its plant may tend to lead them into this trap. The reviewing employee must therefore read slowly and think carefully to see that the words and events check with each other.

(e) Time of making report. A report should be made at the time the reported events occur or as soon thereafter as possible. If too much time intervenes, the making of the report may fail of its purpose because the persons making the report have already forgotten or have begun to forget some of the details. Moreover, if not made at the same time or very close after the time of the transaction, the report may not be admissible as evidence at the trial nor used by a witness to refresh his memory as to the past.

In many cases, it is obvious that events will occur so fast that there is not time for making reports until everything is all over. In other cases, notes may be made as the events take place on the basis of which the report itself is thereafter made.

(f) What a good report should contain. The standard is easy to state—a good report should set forth every important fact in the case and every important fact relating to proving the case and locating witnesses. The application of this standard to a given case may cause some difficulty.

As the starting point, it is necessarily recognized that a report cannot set forth every word that was said and everything that was seen. Necessarily the report is a boiling down or condensation of all this. It also requires the weeding out of some matters which will not be important. This opens the way to error as discussed in subsection (d) above. It is highly desirable that you discuss these matters with your attorney in advance of any trouble so that you have a pattern of questions or report forms ready when the trouble comes.

With respect to the physical form of the report, management should devise such forms of report that best suit its needs. A few mechanical details should be observed. The report should be dated, in order to show that its execution was at the same time or contemporaneous with the events in question. The report should also be initialed or signed by any party taking part in the making of the report and should indicate the capacity in which a person acted. Somewhere on the report should appear the typed or printed names of all persons signing the report and their addresses and phone numbers. This is for the convenience of identifying the signer and in making contact with him.

(g) Areas for reporting. It is desirable to discuss with your attorney what areas should be covered by reports in your business, for what may be beneficial, or even essential, to one type of business operation might be merely an unnecessary burden to another. For example, if the business has only a small employee staff, the reports suggested below may not be worth the keeping. Whereas, if the business has a substantially large or a large employee staff, such reporting systems are highly desirable.

(i) *Employment.* Reports should be carefully kept as to employees and applicants for employment with respect to such matters as showing that the decision of management was based upon the merits of the given case rather than upon prejudice against union membership or the absence of such membership, or prejudice against race, color, creed, sex, or national origin.

As the management may be liable to a third person harmed by its employees, it is important that the report on the hiring or job assignments show that the management acted with the prudence of a reasonable man in employing the given employee. Furthermore, there should be reports to show a continuing supervision of employees after they had been hired initially.

(ii) *Routine examination of premises.* As every business is under the duty to make its premises, furniture, fixtures, and so on, reasonably safe, or to warn others of danger, management must necessarily make periodic inspection of its premises.

In order to make sure that all things are checked each time and to make sure that there is an adequate check, a checklist of the entire plant should be made showing just what is to be inspected, and, if necessary, how the inspection is to be done. Separate checklists may be made for items on different time schedules. For example, a lobby floor must be inspected daily, whereas the sign on the roof, depending upon its construction, probably needs only to be inspected every six months.

The making of such checklists greatly simplifies the making of inspection reports because the inspecting employee can merely check off on the list each item as he covers it. Such lists also save management some training worries in that a new employee can be easily informed of what checking must be done by handing him the checklist report form.

The foregoing suggestions must, of course, be read in the light of your experience, the nature of the operations of your business, and the advice of your attorney. There is no necessity for you to spend all day making reports, and the extent of your inspections and their nature will obviously vary with the nature of the plant, its size, and the nature of your operations, and even the time of the year and the weather conditions. The important thing is that you maintain such inspection of your premises as satisfies your legal obligation to make reasonable inspection to keep the premises in a reasonably safe condition. All that is here suggested is that you make such reporting as shows that you have done just this and what it is that you have done.

(iii) *Liability claim inspection.* Apart from the regular inspection that management will make of its premises are the inspections and reports that should be made when some claim is asserted against it because of harm caused by a condition of the premises, the operation of an automobile, and so on.

Here the report should set forth all the facts that contributed to the occurrence of the harm, as well as these can be determined.

§ 32:4.   Names, Addresses, and Telephone Numbers

(a) Generally. At various times, it is important to know the names, addresses, and phone numbers of persons who were directly involved in transactions that have since gone into litigation. This becomes an acute problem where the persons in question were transients or licensees only temporarily in the building. Even in the case of employees who are more or less permanent, you cannot be sure that they will still be available at the future date when you need them.

Consequently, it is advisable whenever the name of any person is obtained to also print or type his name so that there is no question as to the spelling of the name thereafter; to obtain his address, and any proposed forwarding address; and to obtain any phone number which he may have.

(b) Change of address. Persons who are potential witnesses on your behalf might move away or employees leave or go to another city. In order

to protect yourself, keep a record of the addresses of your witnesses as up-to-date as possible. In many instances, the witnesses will not be difficult to locate because they have merely moved to another place in the same city; and by the time you need them, the new telephone book is available showing their new addresses. In many cases, however, you can imagine that the witness has departed; and since you do not know to what city he has gone, it is impossible to look for him if you do not have the necessary information already.

To some extent, your attorney will have guarded against this difficulty, assuming that you have given him timely notice, by taking the testimony of the potential witnesses before they have gone away. But even if this has been done, you should still assist your attorney by keeping a record of new addresses and phone numbers of the potential witnesses, whenever such information comes into your possession.

(c) Telephone numbers. Whenever possible, make a note of the telephone numbers of any potential witnesses and of any change of number that comes to your attention. In some instances, it will be easier to contact a witness by a phone than it will be seeking to find the new address to which he has moved. Often the phone number or the changed phone number that the telephone operator will give provides the means of finding out the whereabouts of the witness.

§ 32:5.   Notice and Forwarding Papers

(a) Notice to your attorney. Give your attorney notice of every event which may give rise to any claim against you. You should not attempt to judge whether it is a good claim or a bad claim. Nor should you try to prophesy whether a claim will grow out of an incident that has occurred. In many cases, the prompt notice to your attorney becomes doubly important because it may be that the only witnesses that you have in your favor are transients who may be leaving the city and the state within a very short time. If you delay before notifying your attorney, or never notify him at all, it becomes difficult, and sometimes impossible, for him to locate these witnesses, even for the purpose of taking their depositions to use at the trial.

The requirement of giving notice to your attorney is not based on any legal obligation in the sense that you are breaking a contract or law if you fail to notify him. It is merely a matter of common sense that since you are retaining the attorney, you should do your best to help him bring about the result which you desire.

When any papers are received, such as letters and notices sent to you, or legal process and pleadings served on you or sent to you in connection with a lawsuit, you should promptly forward such papers to your attorney.

(b) Notice to your insurer. Under your liability policy, notice, together with the subsequent furnishing of proofs of loss, is generally mandatory in the sense that you cannot recover on the policy if notice of loss is not given to the insurer within a time specified and proofs of loss are not furnished to the insurer thereafter within the period of time likewise specified by the policy.

The typical liability policy will also require the insured business to forward all process and papers served upon it, and to cooperate in the defense of any action. Management must perform according to these terms and if it fails to do so, the insurer is not bound by the terms of the policy.

(c) Form of notice. In addition to its attorney and insurer, management may be required to give notice to other persons, such as the supplier from whom it has purchased goods and food, notifying them that there has been a breach of warranty; to tenants in the company building who are being notified that the lease is being terminated; and to other persons with whom management has business dealings. In order to preserve a permanent record of the notice given, as well as that of satisfying statutory or policy requirements in others, management should always give a written notice which expressly states just what the notice is about and why it is being given. In some instances, it will be necessary to proceed more quickly than by mail. In such case a telephone notice is proper, but in order to provide a record of having given the notice and to satisfy any requirements which may make a writing necessary, management should promptly send a confirming letter, stating that it is confirming the notice that has been given over the telephone and repeat just what had been stated.

(d) Identity of person receiving telephone notice. Whenever notice is given to a person by telephone, management should ask for that person's name and title. This information should then be placed in the report or file on the matter so that at a later date if the giving of notice is disputed, management can pinpoint the person receiving the notice by telephone. In addition, management will have sent a confirming letter, and will be able to produce the carbon copy to support the testimony of the giving of oral notice by phone.

§ 32:6.　Unemotional Evaluation of Claims

(a) Generally. It is only human nature for a defendant to be prejudiced in his attitude against a person making a claim against him, and against the claim so made. Thus, it is a natural reaction to believe that a given claim is false because the thing alleged just could not happen in your plant. The difficulty is that such things often can and do happen, for the simple reason that the frailties of man and the mathematical probabilities are almost always

in favor of the breakdown of the most elaborate set of precautions at some time or other.

A blind and stubborn attitude that "it can't happen here" can lead into needless and expensive litigation, which could have been avoided by a recognition that it could happen and did happen—someone was tired, someone forgot, someone goofed; and the harm was done. It is, therefore, of prime importance that management act unemotionally and scientifically in seeking to learn the truth when inquiring of its employees with respect to the incident and in dealing with its attorney.

(b) Reasons for distorted claims. Out of a given number of claims made against you a substantial number will be distorted in some respect.

(i) *False claims.* Sometimes the distortion is intentional and the claim is fraudulent either in whole or in part. For example, the plaintiff seeing an "accident background" in your plant makes a false claim of having sustained harm. To illustrate, the claimant upon becoming aware that there is some slippery substance on the marble or tile flooring and seeing no one around, sits carefully down on the ground and then sets up loud cries of anguish and pain. When your employees or other persons come upon the poor, unfortunate claimant, a sad tale of woe and fault on the part of management is related. Of course all of this is false and if the claimant continues his false story in court, his statements constitute perjury. But the great difficulty is how can you tell when the claim of harm sustained without witnesses is perjurious or true? Even with witnesses, how can you be sure that the witnesses are telling the truth when their testimony supports the claimant, or whether they were merely fellow conspirators who have joined forces with the claimant to make the perjured statements in court on behalf of the claimant?

(ii) *False cause of harm.* More frequently the distorted claim is one in which it is true that the claimant sustained harm, but there is distortion as to the manner in which the harm was sustained or the extent to which the claimant has been harmed. For example, it may be true that the plaintiff fell in your plant, but he may not realize why he fell. To illustrate, the claimant fell on the dimly-lit stairs when he did not see the first step because he was carrying so many bundles in his arms that he could not see where he was stepping down. Under these circumstances, the fact that the hall was dimly-lit had nothing to do with the harm since it was the bundles that obstructed his view, and they would have done so regardless of how bright the hallway was lighted. The chances are great, however, that after the claimant has fallen, the claimant will not realize just how much the bundles in his arms obscured the stairs. If the claimant, seated on the ground with his bundles strewn about him surveys the scene of his disaster, he is likely to ignore the fact that he had bundles or that they obstructed his view and will perceive only that the stairs were dimly-lit and blame his misfortune upon that fact.

Or again, the plaintiff may realize just what was the cause of harm but falsely testifies that it was management's fault in not lighting the area properly.

(iii) *False extent of harm.* In other cases, it is true that the claimant sustains harm on the premises for a condition or cause for which management is liable. Nevertheless distortion enters into the picture because the claimant has made an exaggerated claim of the extent of the damages that he has sustained. Consider, for example, the low-cost, nearly wornout suit, that the plaintiff was wearing when he slipped and fell on a grease spot on the floor. Not infrequently, it thereby is transformed into a brand new, highly expensive, imported suit. The grease, instead of having come right out with a few cents worth of cleaner, was to the contrary as enduring and permanent as the Rock of Gibraltar and utterly ruined the plaintiff's clothing. Similarly, it is claimed that slight bruises or sprains actually sustained by the claimant have caused great pain and suffering, requiring large outlays of cash and the incurring of future liability for medical, hospital, and nursing care, and of course, have caused permanent disabilities. In many of these cases, the plaintiff is making a perjured statement as to the consequences of his "truthful" injury—the distortion entering the picture in terms of the consequences of the harm sustained.

In many cases, the claim as to the harm sustained is distorted, although not intentionally or consciously so. For example, the injury actually sustained by the claimant on your premises may make the claimant become aware of some prior or latent condition, but, and with all honesty, the claimant now blames the whole matter on management.

Distortion almost invariably enters into the area of stating a money value for nonmoney losses. For example, the claimant, because of the fault of management, has sustained pain and suffering or sustained a temporary disability or a permanent disability. For such loss, the plaintiff is entitled to claim money damages from management. But how much money? What is the money value of one day's pain and suffering? It is clear that there is no precise nor even a reasonably accurate method or technique of determining the loss in such situation. Consequently, the plaintiff claims whatever he thinks the pain and suffering are worth. Here is where the distortion enters into the picture. Even when the claimant is acting in all honesty, it is obvious that he will have an exaggerated idea of what his pain and suffering are worth. To illustrate, the claimant who has been hospitalized for one month may say that he would not go through that again for a million dollars. Does that mean that the pain and suffering were worth a million dollars? You and I as members of a jury might well conclude that this plaintiff in his entire life will not earn a million dollars and, therefore, it is a little difficult for us to believe that one month of his life, even when attended by pain and suffering, could have a value of a million dollars.

Also you and I might very well say that we would not take a million dollars in return for our health, our eyesight, or our ability to walk. Yet, if we are to be jurors, it is doubtful whether we would feel that a million dollars or more should be paid to the claimant just because his health has been impaired, even though permanently; or he has lost his sight; or he has been made a permanent invalid as the result of the harm sustained in your plant.

Furthermore, practically every injured person suffers in varying degrees from his friendly misadvisors. For example, the claimant's friends in order to make him feel better or because they want to sound important and know-it-all, may assure the claimant that he should not worry because the defendant is a big and rich business and carries large insurance, and the claimant will have no trouble in collecting a nice, fat sum, say a million dollars. Not infrequently, either or both the friendly advisors and the injured claimant are misled by something they had read in the paper or a magazine about someone who had a similar injury and who received a million dollars in damages for his claim. In many instances, the recollection of what was recovered in the other proceeding is wrong to begin with or the prior account was merely the entry of the verdict for the huge amount, and the newspaper never published what the claimant in the other action actually received after the verdict was set aside or reduced, or if it did, our injured claimant and his friends missed that edition. Or even if the verdict was not changed, there were significant factors differentiating the other case from the claimant's case, such as a difference between the earning power of the other plaintiff and of the present injured claimant, or of the inclusion of punitive damages in the former proceeding.

(c) Management's open mind. In view of the fact that the claimant's claim may be totally true, totally false, or true in part and false in part, it is obvious that management must keep an open mind in investigating the facts and in conferring with its attorney. Management, as is true of every other litigant, should not automatically make a compensating distortion by jumping to the conclusion that the plaintiff is a willful liar and that there is no basis whatsoever for his claim. An open mind, which is free from automatic prejudice, will enable management to think more clearly about the case, make it easier to find the truth, easier to know when to defend against the claim, and to know when and in what amount to compromise the claim.

§ 32:7. Do Not Expect an Easy Answer All the Time

(a) Generally. By now you have seen that the law is not a fixed, rigid set of rules. At first thought it would be much simpler to run your business

or to live your life if you had, or if your attorney could give you, a set of exact rules that you could always follow.

Society, however, does not wish to be bound by fixed and rigid rules, but wants its law to be able to change and grow with the times and to respond to the social values discussed in Part II.

(b) The jury question as the unknown answer. In many instances, the law does not lay down any exact rule but refers the matter to the jury to determine the facts, to apply the competing rules of law, and then to return a verdict in harmony with their conclusions. As you have already seen, the statement that a question is a question for the jury means that the jury can decide the case either way on the facts, and no judge or higher court will reverse or set aside the jury for what it has done.

In terms of guidance for you, it means that no guide can be given to you. All that your attorney can say is that if there is a dispute as to any significant or substantial question of fact, you cannot tell in advance of the trial whether the law requires a judgment for you or against you. All that you know is that there is no answer until the jury has returned its verdict, and that once it has done so, that verdict is, under the circumstances described, final and cannot be upset. This means that your attorney can merely answer you, "It depends."

Your attorney, however, can guide you; and with experience, you can recognize that there are certain steps which you can take either before or after a given situation has arisen; namely, those which you would expect of a reasonable man. Having taken such precautions or done such subsequent acts in good faith and in a reasonable manner, you might not be liable for the harm sustained by the plaintiff, assuming of course that the jury believes what you have done and how you have done it. The best protection you can have is a carefully selected staff, a good attorney, and a good insurance company.

And good luck!

Questions for Review

1. What should a client bear in mind about reports of occurrences?

2. What should a client bear in mind about sending notices and forwarding papers?

3. What factors cause emotional distortion of claims?

4. Is the law an exact science that results in a precise predictable answer?

5. Draft a set of accident and complaint report forms for the type of business in which you are most interested.

6. Draft a set of rules for inspection techniques to be used in the type of business in which you are most interested.

7. Draft a set of rules for the channeling of complaints and claims in the type of business in which you are most interested.

8. Draft a set of rules for the preservation of records of complaints and claims in the type of business in which you are most interested.

9. In what way can photographs assist you in being a good client?

INDEX